MUIRHEAD LIBRARY OF PHILOSOPHY

An admirable statement of the aims of the Library of Philosophy was provided by the first editor, the late Professor J. H. Muirhead, in his description of the original programme printed in Erdmann's *History of Philosophy* under the date 1890. This was slightly modified in subsequent volumes to take the form of the following statement.

'The Muirhead Library of Philosophy was designed as a contribution to the History of Modern Philosophy under the heads: first of Different Schools of Thought – Sensationalist, Realist, Idealist, Intuitivist; secondly of different Subjects – Psychology, Ethics, Aesthetics, Political Philosophy, Theology. While much had been done in England in tracing the course of evolution in nature, history, economics, morals and religion, little had been done in tracing the development of thought on these subjects. Yet the "evolution of opinion is part of the whole evolution".

'By the co-operation of different writers in carrying out this plan it was hoped that a thoroughness and completeness of treatment, otherwise unattainable, might be secured. It was believed also that from writers mainly British and American fuller consideration of English Philosophy than it had hitherto received might be looked for. In the earlier series of books containing, among others, Bosanquet's *History of Aesthetic*, Pfleiderer's *Rational Theology since Kant*, Albee's *History of English Utilitarianism*, Bonar's *Philosophy and Political Economy*, Brett's *History of Psychology*, Ritchie's *Natural Rights*, these objects were to a large extent effected.

'In the meantime original work of a high order was being produced both in England and America by such writers as Bradley, Stout, Bertrand Russell, Baldwin, Urban, Montague and others, and a new interest in foreign works, German, French and Italian, which had either become classical or were attracting public attention, had developed. The scope of the Library thus became extended into something more international, and it is entering on the fifth decade of its existence in the hope that it may contribute to that mutual understanding between countries which is so pressing a need of the present time.'

The need which Professor Muirhead stressed is no less pressing today, and few will deny that philosophy has much to do with enabling us to meet it, although no one, least of all Muirhead himself, would regard that as the sole, or even the main, object of philosophy. As Professor Muirhead continues to lend the distinction of his name to the Library of Philosophy it seemed not inappropriate to allow him to recall us to these aims in his own words. The emphasis on the history of thought also seemed to me very timely: and the number of important works promised for the Library in the very near future augurs well for the continued fulfilment, in this and other ways, of the expectations of the original editor.

H. D. LEWIS

MUIRHEAD LIBRARY OF PHILOSOPHY

General Editor: H. D. Lewis

Professor of History and Philosophy of Religion at the University of London

MUIRHEAD LIBRARY OF PHILOSOPHY

EDITED BY H.D. LEWIS

BERTRAND RUSSELL MEMORIAL VOLUME

BERTRAND RUSSELL MEMORIAL VOLUME

EDITED BY
GEORGE W. ROBERTS

London GEORGE ALLEN & UNWIN
New York HUMANITIES PRESS INC.

First published in 1979

© George Allen & Unwin (Publishers) Ltd, 1979

ISBN 0 04 192034 1

British Library Cataloguing in Publication
Data

Bertrand Russell memorial volume – (Muirhead
library of philosophy).
1. Russell, Bertrand, *Earl Russell* – Addresses,
essays, lectures
I. Roberts, George W.   II. Series
192   B1649.R9   77-30739

ISBN 0-04-192034-1

Printed in Great Britain
in 10 on 11 point Baskerville
by The Garden City Press Limited,
Letchworth, Hertfordshire SG6 1JS

PREFACE

This volume attempts to assess some of the achievements of Bertrand Russell in philosophy, logic and mathematics, ethics and politics. The contributions range from those more closely concerned with his work and writings to those concerned with Russell's background, his relations to his contemporaries and successors, and his subjects in a way that sheds light on Russell's efforts and accomplishments, his attempts and failures and on the matters with which he was concerned. To say that these studies are independent-minded and critical of Russell, or that they range freely over the topics with which Russell's work and influence has engaged their authors, is to say nothing of them that could not have been said of Russell's own work. Here at any rate are some efforts to describe and come to terms with the transformations of the intellectual and practical scene effected, or affected, by one of the best philosophers and best human beings of our time.

I have imposed no thoroughgoing uniformity in terminology or notation on the contributors. Each has been left free to deal with his subject as he thought best. Some of the work commissioned for this volume has appeared elsewhere in the meantime with my permission. Acknowledgment of permission to reprint materials not written on commission for this volume is due to the appropriate editors and publishers for Gilbert Ryle's 'Bertrand Russell: 1872–1970', from *Proceedings of the Aristotelian Society,* vol. LXXI (1970–1; 77–84), for William C. Kneale's 'Russell's Paradox and Some Others', from *British Journal for the Philosophy of Science*, vol. XXII (1971; 321–38) and for Renford Bambrough's 'Foundations', from *Analysis,* vol. XXX (1970; 190–7). Copyright in G. N. A. Vesey's 'Self-acquaintance and the Meaning of 'I' ' is reserved to him. Finally, special thanks are due to Joel I. Friedman for his assistance with this volume.

GEORGE W. ROBERTS

CONTENTS

1

BERTRAND RUSSELL: 1872–1970

Gilbert Ryle

We members of the Aristotelian Society are here tonight to say 'Goodbye and thank you' to that grand philosophical thinker, Bertrand Russell, who gave his first paper to this Society in 1896.[1] This is not an occasion for an exegetic commentary on the almost infinite variety of his thought, but rather one for concentrating our gratitudes on those three or four determining impulses by which his thinking has given to the philosophical thinking of all of us, quite irrespective of our particular opinions and specialities, much of its whole trajectory.

For what concerns us today and, I maintain, for what should chiefly concern the future historians of twentieth-century thought, it matters comparatively little whether a few or many of us accept, or whether a few or many of us reject, this or that Russellian doctrine. The fact that he did not found a school or capture disciples was due partly to the accidents of his career, but especially to certain admirable features of his thinking. Among these was his immunity from reverence in general and especially from reverence for himself. He would have found Russell-acolytes comical and Russell-echoes tedious. On the other hand, what matters immensely is that, not what we think but, so to speak, the very style of our philosophical thinking perpetuates, where we are ordinarily least conscious of it, a style of thinking that had not existed in philosophy before, say, 1900.

(1) In speaking, metaphorically, of the Russellian style of thinking, though I am not alluding primarily, I am alluding secondarily to one particular intellectual temper for which the credit – the great credit as I think – needs to be divided between William James and Russell. For in one respect James and Russell were quite unlike Mill, Sidgwick and Bradley, quite unlike Brentano, Meinong and Husserl, and quite unlike even Moore, namely in their combination of seriousness with humour. Hume and Bradley had wit, and Hume could play. But James and Russell found out for themselves and so taught us at our best how to pop doctrinal bubbles without drawing blood; how to be illuminatingly and unmaliciously naughty; and how, without being frivolous, to laugh off grave conceptual bosh. Stuffiness in diction and stuffiness in thought were not, of course, annihilated, but they were put on the defensive from the moment when James and Russell discovered that a joke can be the

beginning, though only the beginning, of a blessed release from a strangling theoretical millstone.

(2) Much more important was a new style of philosophical work that Russell, I think virtually single-handed, brought into the very tactics of philosophical thinking. Anticipated, I suggest, only by the unremembered Aristotle, Russell occasionally prescribed and often deliberately practised what can be called 'aporetic experimentation'. In his *Mind* article of 1905 'On Denoting', he says:

> A logical theory may be tested by its capacity for dealing with puzzles, and it is a wholesome plan, in thinking about logic, to stock the mind with as many puzzles as possible, since these serve much the same purpose as is served by experiments in physical science. I shall therefore state three puzzles which a theory as to denoting ought to be able to solve; and I shall show later that my theory solves them.

In 1904, near the beginning of his first *Mind* article on 'Meinong's Theory of Complexes and Assumptions', he had praised Meinong for the excellence of his quasi-empirical method of psychological research. His 1908 article 'Mathematical Logic as based on the Theory of Types' opens with a list of seven selected contradictions demanding some common solution. Now of course other philosophers, indeed all other philosophers worthy of the name, always had resolutely and conscientiously tried to overcome theoretical difficulties. They knew that their theories were in jeopardy so long as hurdles remained uncleared or uncircumvented. Nearly all of them, too, had from time to time opposed error by putting up obstacles in the way of the erroneous views or the bad arguments of others. It is not criticism or self-criticism that Russell invented. What was, I think, new was Russell's heuristic policy of deliberately mobilising, stiffening and constructing his own hurdles against which to pit his own nascent speculations. Difficulties in the way of a theory are no longer obstacles to thought; they can be and should be constructed or collected as aids to thought. They can be the self-applied tests by which philosophical thinking may become a self-correcting undertaking. As in the laboratory a well-designed crucial experiment tests a physical or chemical hypothesis, so in logic and philosophy a well-designed conceptual puzzle may be the *experimentum crucis* of a speculation.

To us, in 1970, this heuristic policy is obviously right. The most modest discussion note in one of our philosophical journals presupposes that philosophical progress requires positive and planned operations of sifting the tares from the wheat of doctrines and of arguments. Criticism is now not hostility; self-criticism is now not surrender. But we should, I suggest, search eighteenth- and nineteenth-century philosophy in vain, and even search contemporary continental philosophy nearly in vain for cases of a philosopher actively hunting for and designing conceptual hurdles to advance his own future progress.

In his *Principles of Mathematics,* chapter X, entitled 'The Contradiction', and in its second Appendix, Russell had launched himself on what was to prove to be that most arduous of his theoretical undertakings which culminated many years later in his history-making Theory of Types. Already, in 1903, he was marshalling a battery of heterogeneous paradoxes against which he would test the desiderated solution of the special paradox of self-membered classes. Each of these auxiliary paradoxes, whether superficial or fundamental, was to serve as a testing device, with its own special edges, of the theory-to-be of self-reference.

Two precautionary words. By 'aporetic experimentation' I do not mean tentativeness, diffidence or even undogmatism. Russell meant some of his conceptual experiments to yield not 'perhapses' but definite results. Next, in using the notion of *experimentation,* I am not, of course, referring to physical tests; and I am not supposing that it is the mission of conceptual experiments – if anything has this mission – to engender inductive generalisations.

Unlike Wittgenstein, Russell was not focally, but only peripherally concerned to fix the places in human knowledge of logic and philosophy. When, as in *Our Knowledge of the External World as a Field for Scientific Method in Philosophy,* he did try to do this, he adopted too easily the idea that philosophy could and should be disciplined into a science among sciences. It was not, however, by this sort of promised assimilation of philosophy to science that he taught us a new kind of dialectical craftsmanship, but by the examples that he set of planned puzzle-utilisation. Like Moore, Russell constantly preached Analysis; but what, when pioneering, he practised included this far more penetrating, because self-testing, method of inquiry.

(3) At the end of the ninth chapter of *The Problems of Philosophy* (1912) Russell wrote:

> The world of universals, therefore, may also be described as the world of being. The world of being is unchangeable, rigid, exact, delightful to the mathematician, the logician, the builder of metaphysical systems, and all who love perfection more than life. The world of existence is fleeting, vague, without sharp boundaries, without any clear plan of arrangement, but it contains all thoughts and feelings, all the data of sense, and all physical objects, everything that can do either good or harm, everything that makes any difference to the value of life and the world. According to our temperaments, we shall prefer the contemplation of the one or the other. The one we do not prefer will probably seem to us a pale shadow of the one we prefer, and hardly worthy to be regarded as in any sense real. But the truth is that both have the same claim on our impartial attention, both are real, and

both are important to the metaphysician. Indeed no sooner have we distinguished the two worlds than it becomes necessary to consider their relations.

Here Russell declares, what his writings show, that he himself knew and loved the views from the Alpine heights where there dwelled Plato, Leibniz and Frege, but also knew and loved the valleys that were tilled by Hume, Mill and James. Russell was that rare being, a philosopher whose heart was divided between transcendentalism and naturalism. His mind had been formed in his youth both by John Stuart Mill and by pure mathematics.

Indeed Russell got much of the impetus and nearly all of the turbulence of his thinking from his being homesick for the peaks while he was in the plains, and homesick for the plains when he was on the heights. However drastic, his reductionisms had some reluctances in them; however uncompromising, his Platonisms were a little undevout. Neither transcendent being nor mundane occurring felt to him either quite real, or gravely unreal. When in the mood he could think flippantly of either.

His ice-breaking and Ockhamising article 'On Denoting' came out only two years later than his ice-breaking, Platonising *Principles of Mathematics*; and in his *Our Knowledge of the External World* (1914) the second chapter 'Logic as the Essence of Philosophy', which is Fregean in inspiration, is immediately succeeded by two chapters entirely in the vein of the phenomenalism of John Stuart Mill. His paper of 1919 'On Propositions', which is very largely in the idioms of Watson, James and Hume, succeeds by only a year his lectures on Logical Atomism, where he is talking as if in the hearing of Meinong, Whitehead and the youthful Wittgenstein.

In his very early Platonising days he submitted in the *Principles of Mathematics,* section 427, a list of terms or objects that possess being, though they lack existence, namely, 'Numbers, the Homeric gods, relations, chimeras and four-dimensional spaces . . . if they were not entities of a kind, we could make no propositions about them'. Though he wrote this with complete seriousness, yet we can surely detect in his list an accent of sly shockingness, as if he could already guess what it would be like to season this overhospitable platter of being with a pinch of salt; and even what it would be like one day, though not yet, to investigate the credentials of the argument 'if they were not entities of a kind, we could make no propositions about them'.

Conversely, however far he moved away from the Platonism of his youth, he never conceded to Mill's reductionism about the truths of mathematics anything more than the recognition that it really is one business of pure mathematics to be capable of being applied to what there is in the everyday world. In the Introduction to the 2nd edition (1937) of his *Principles of Mathematics* he rejects the formalism of Hilbert for, apparently, excluding applications of mathematics to the real world; he allows, with regrets, that mathematical truths, with those of formal logic, being 'formal' truths, cannot, as he had once thought, be construed as describing transcendent entities. He allows too, again with regrets, that there is something in some way 'linguistic' about these formal truths. But not for a moment does he concede to Mill that these truths are merely high-grade inductive generalisations about things that exist and happen down here. None the less he would quite soon be developing a theory of perception and, therewith, a theory of physical objects which does not do very much more than bring up to date the phenomenalism of Mill's *System of Logic*.

It is sometimes said that Russell merely oscillated, pendulum-like, between transcendentalism and naturalism, or between Platonism and empiricism. The truth, I suggest, is that, anyhow in his formative and creative years, we find him neither at rest in the valley nor at rest among the peaks, but mountaineering – trying to find a way from the valley back to the peaks, or a way from the peaks back to the valley. He had two homes. But where he toiled, and where he was alone, and where he was happy was on the mountainside.

(4) The last of the four determining impulses by which Russell directed the course of subsequent philosophy is this. Russell was not only a pioneer formal logician, but, like Aristotle and Frege, he was a logician-philosopher. He saw every advance in formal logic as, among other things, a potential source of new rigours in philosophy; and he saw every philosophical puzzle or tangle as a lock for which formal logic might already or might some day provide the key. It was due to him, as well as, in lesser degree, to Frege and Whitehead that some training in post-Aristotelian formal logic came fairly soon to be regarded as a *sine qua non* for the philosopher-to-be; and debates between philosophers on philosophical matters quickly began often merely to ape but sometimes to apply or employ the blackboard operations of the formal logician.

Naturally it was, at the start, the more dramatic innovations in Russellian logic that were adopted by philosophers. The new term–relation–term pattern of simple propositions was for a time expected to accomplish nearly all the philosophical tasks at which the sub-ject–predicate pattern baulked. But even if not into this new pattern, still formalisation into some newly sponsored pattern or other was for a time expected to make short work of any surviving philosophical problems. But to say this is only to say that Russell, Whitehead and Frege made many philosophers enthusiasts for their new so-called Symbolic Logic – and enthusiasts are always impetuous. The remarkable thing is that these three – and Russell more than the other two – did fire this enthusiasm. Even outside the English-speaking world they fired it, partly through the mediation of Wittgenstein, as far away as Vienna; and without this mediation as far away as Poland.

Doubtless some of these zeals were ephemeral or factitious; doubtless, too, some of the Frege–Russell hopes for a monolithic Euclideanisation of mathematics were doomed to disappointment; and certainly we have long since forgotten the promise, if it was ever made, that philosophical problems would now receive their solutions by instant formalisation. None the less, philosophy in the English-speaking world has inherited from the *Principles of Mathematics* and *Principia Mathematica*, as well as from Frege's logical writings, not only a respect for rigour, but a discipline in rigour, the absence of which from what, with reservations, I label 'continental' philosophy still makes cross-Channel discussion unrewarding.

However, I do not wish merely to acknowledge the huge effects of, especially, Russell's logicising of philosophy. There was another massive legacy left by Russell, the logician-philosopher, which we can call the Theory of Types.

By 1903 Russell had found, and imparted to Frege, a contradiction in that notion of *class* which had been a central concept in the work of Cantor, as well as in Frege's and Russell's own definitions of *number*. With this contradiction the young Russell had associated a whole battery of partly similar antinomies, for all of which, it seemed, some general diagnosis and, hopefully, some general cure could be found. Either answer, 'Yes' or 'No', to the question 'Is "I am now lying," true?' seems to establish the other; 'Yes, if no; but no, if yes'. To the question 'Is the class of classes that are not members of themselves a member of itself?' the only answer again seems to be 'Yes, if no; but no, if yes'. Russell came, in the long-postponed end, to the conclusion that for a specifiable reason these questions are unanswerable by 'Yes' or by 'No'; they are improper questions. Epimenides's assertion was a pseudo-assertion; an assertion cannot be a comment upon itself; and a given class C can only be nonsensically spoken of as one of the items that belongs, or even does *not* belong as a member to C.

Besides the sentences that convey standard propositions that are true or else false, there are grammatically passable sentences which are neither true nor false, but nonsense. It was some, but only a very few, nonsense-excluding rules that Russell, in his Theory of Types, tried to formulate and justify.

It is of some historical interest that the Vienna Circle misappropriated Russell's notion of nonsense for its own special Augean purposes. But it is of huge historical importance that the whole *Tractatus Logico-Philosophicus* can be construed as a Procrustean essay in the theory of sense/nonsense. The *Philosophical Investigations* also is, in large measure, an inquiry into the rules of 'grammar' or 'logical syntax' of which patent or latent absurdities are in breach. In his lectures on Logical Atomism Russell showed how he had already been glad and proud to learn from the young Wittgenstein of 1912–3 some of the expansions, extensions and new applications of which his former Theory of Types had now become capable.

In these different, though doubtless internally connected ways, Russell taught us not to think his thoughts but how to move in our own philosophical thinking. In one way no one is now or will ever again be a Russellian; but in another way every one of us is now something of a Russellian. Perhaps we do not even read Russell very much; but in at least four radical ways what we say to philosophers and write for philosophers differs in intellectual method and intellectual temper from what we would have said and written in pre-Russell days and from what we would say and write today if we were – shall I say? – Ruritanians.

Magdalen College
University of Oxford

NOTE

1   This chapter was read at a meeting of the Aristotelian Society at 5–7 Tavistock Place, London WC1, on Monday, 7 December 1970, at 7.30 p.m.

2

PROPOSITIONS AND SENTENCES

Alan R. White

Russell's views both about the nature of analysis and about the analysis of belief were coloured – and, I think, vitiated – by his confusions about the notion of a proposition. He provides an interesting case history for the student of propositions since he was a prey to just those puzzles about their nature which have beset most investigators of the notion. Like them, he was torn between the reasons for identifying propositions and sentences and the reasons for distinguishing them. It is these reasons that I wish to discuss in the present chapter. Any attempt, however, to delineate his views is doubly difficult because he was, admirably, a changeable and, less admirably, a careless writer; careless both in that he neither took much care to be nor, apparently, cared much about being consistent even within the same piece of writing. The dating of the references shows his explicit changes of view; but they also show, I feel, that no consistent pattern of change can be found.

Russell, like other philosophers, introduced propositions to fill a variety of roles: (a) to be that which is asserted when it is asserted that p as contrasted with that which is questioned, commanded, etc. (e.g. 1918: 185; 1927: 271);[1] (b) more particularly to be that which is believed, doubted, desired, considered or in some other way regarded when it is believed, doubted, etc. that p (e.g. 1919: 285); (c) to be that which is true or false (e.g. 1903: xix; 1940: 76); (d) to be the meaning or significance of a sentence (e.g. 1940: 180); (e) to be what is related in some way to the facts (e.g. 1918: 182).

Having, for these reasons, introduced the notion of a proposition, he had to explain it. This he rightly tried to do, in the manner of most philosophers, by relating it to that form of words, e.g. the indicative sentence p, by which we assert something, express what we believe or doubt, or state what we take to be the facts. Sometimes Russell explicitly identified the proposition and the sentence which expressed it, sometimes he explicitly distinguished them and often, in one and the same passage, his implicit view on the question whether propositions and sentences are or are not to be distinguished is contrary to what by carelessness he explicitly states. When he did distinguish proposition and sentence he had various different views as to how they were related, for instance, that the proposition is a complex of constituents corresponding to the parts of the sentence which express it, that the proposition is the meaning or significance of the sentence, that it is what is asserted by the sentence or that it is a class of sentences with the same meaning.

As early as 1903 (e.g. p. 42), as late as 1959 (e.g. p. 182), and often in the intervening period (e.g. 1904: 209; 1937: ix; 1940: 180) Russell clearly distinguished the proposition from its linguistic expression, the sentence. He spoke (1905: 43–5; 1918: 250–1) of 'propositions in whose verbal expression denoting phrases occur', of 'the words in the statement of a proposition', of propositions as what may be expressed in any language (e.g. 1940: 10) or asserted by a sentence (1940: 42) or of what is common between sentences in different languages which say the same thing (e.g. 1959: 182). In 1940, he suggested, perhaps *en passant*, a definition of a proposition as, 'all the sentences (or "the class of all the sentences") having the same significance as a given sentence' (1940: 10, 158). But, although a proposition might be either expressed by or even equivalent to each and every member of a collection, it is difficult to see how it could be the collection itself. Collections or classes of sentences are not what we express by a sentence, nor what we believe, nor what is true or false, nor what occurs on the top line of a page. Here, and elsewhere (e.g. 1919: 290; 1921: 188; 1924: 332; 1940: 22–3; 1944: 692; 1959: 153, 172; contrast 1940: 76; 1959: 145) Russell seems to have confused a class and its members with something and its instances. But to say that there are ten instances of the word 'the' on this page, is not to say that 'the' is a class of which these are members. 'Dog' does not signify a set of dogs in the way that 'litter' signifies a set of dogs (contrast 1919: 290; 1940: 22).

Sometimes Russell's position became more ambiguous, for example, as signified by such a phrase as 'a proposition in which symbolically a class occurs' (e.g. 1918: 265). Sometimes he seems to have felt that it doesn't really matter whether one speaks of propositions or sentences (1918: 186).

None of this, however, prevented him from speaking in the same way, even in the same writings, both of propositions and of sentences (e.g. 1905: 45, 'propositions in which denoting phrases occur' and 'propositions in whose verbal expression denoting phrases occur'; 1918: 184–5, 'the words in a statement of a proposition' and 'a proposition is a sentence in the indicative', cf. 1903: 42–3). His first explicit equation of propositions and sentences seems to occur in 1918 when he stated that 'a proposition is a sentence in the indicative' (p. 185; cf. 1921: 240; 1924: 334; 1927: 271), and as such does not exist over and above such a sentence: a view which he sometimes expressed by saying that propositions are not real (1918: 214), not to be included in any inventory of the world; at other times in the extreme view that the word 'proposition' is 'meaningless' (1918: 263) because it does not stand for anything (1918: 289). In the following year he seemed to regard the identification of a proposition and a sentence, less dogmatically, as a plausible hypothesis rather than a definite conclusion (e.g. 1919: 289–90); though from 1918 to 1940 his usual manner of referring to propositions is as something composed of words or other symbols.[2] By 1940 he had moved back either to talking indifferently of propositions and sentences (e.g. p. 54) or to the admission of propositions as a class of sentences (e.g. p. 158) or as the significance of a sentence (p. 158), though he is still worried by the feeling that to admit that a sentence expresses a proposition is to admit the existence of an extra, mysterious thing called 'proposition' or 'the significance of a sentence'.

Russell's various views about the relation of a sentence and a proposition were naturally reflected in his views about the relation of a numeral and a number and of a symbol for a class and a class itself. But here, though he began his career with a firm belief in the independence of numbers from numerals and of classes from class symbols (e.g. 1903: 66–80), he soon reached the equally firm and lasting belief that numbers and classes did not exist over and above their numerals and class symbols (1918: 262–7; 1937: x–xi). This Ockhamite view was sometimes expressed as 'There are no such things as numbers', just as the parallel view about propositions was sometimes expressed as 'There are no such things as propositions'. It was, of course, also expressed in the view that 'numbers and classes are logical fictions' (e.g. 1918: 191, 270) or that numbers, like propositions, 'are not part of the ultimate constituents of our world' (1918: 270; 1937: ix). Russell's 'no-class' theory was probably not intended to mean that in ostensibly talking about classes we are really talking about class symbols, but that in using class symbols we are not talking about a constituent of the world called a 'class'. He possibly thought of a class symbol as, in this respect, analogous to the phrase 'the average man'. He would not have wanted to hold the absurd view that in ostensibly talking about the average man we are really talking about the phrase 'the average man'; but rather that in using the phrase 'the average man' we are not talking about a denizen of the world called 'the average man'. This plausible view, however, became assimilated to the view that numbers *are* the numerals that express them and that classes *are* the class symbols that express them (e.g. 1918: 253; 1937: ix–x). This would be like saying that 'the average man' is a phrase. In other words, the view that X is not something additional to Y was sometimes interpreted as X does not exist and sometimes as X is equivalent to Y.

A particular way in which Russell's ambivalence about the identity of propositions and sentences is reflected is in his corresponding ambivalence about what it is that plays certain roles, particularly that of being the bearer of truth or falsity, that of being the object of belief, that of being either molecular or atomic and that of having certain kinds of constituents. Let us consider each of these.

Truth and falsity were sometimes explicitly reserved for propositions (e.g. 1903: xix; 1918: 184; 1940: 76, 164), sometimes for sentences (1927: 245, 269, 272–3; 1940: 28, 60; 1948: 110), but were often explicitly or implicitly allowed to either propositions (1906: 48; 1918: 182, 208, 214;

1921: 273; 1927: 271; 1940: 9, 16; 1944: 14; 1948: 79, 133; 1959: 66, 111, 167) or sentences (1927: 270; 1940: 17; 1948: 75, 88, 100, 112, 115, 130; 1959: 186, 220) or both (1940: *passim*; 1948: 109). In his 1940 *An Inquiry into Meaning and Truth* especially, there are dozens of references for truth applied to propositions and dozens for its application to sentences. Even when Russell explicitly denies that propositions are real, he sometimes continues to wonder whether they can be true or false (e.g. 1918: 214); while, at others, insisting that 'really a proposition cannot be true or false because a proposition is nothing' (1918: 227).

Truth and falsity were also frequently attributed to beliefs (1906: 46; 1927: 182, 222, 227; 1919: 285; 1921: 232, 234; 1940: 304; 1948: 95, 119, 148). Indeed, it was said on occasion that beliefs are the primary bearers of truth or falsity (1910: 158; 1940: 203, 215, 223; 1948: 112, 148; 1959: 183; cf. 1927: 265; 1904: 204). But this is less of a difference than it sounds, since beliefs were at various times equated with propositions (1918: 182, 308) or sentences (1919: 308; 1927: 270) or both. Furthermore, on the one hand, a true belief is defined as 'a belief in a true proposition' (1918: 320), whereas, on the other, 'the relation of a sentence to the fact that makes it true or false' is said to be 'indirect through the belief expressed by the sentence' (1940: 199).

Part of Russell's reason – as we have just seen – for holding that truth and falsity apply to both sentences and propositions was the equation of both with beliefs. But he also frequently, though inconsistently, equated both sentences and propositions not merely with beliefs in a sense of what on occasion he called 'believings' (1918: 217; 1959: 118), but also with what is believed. Russell always held, for reasons I have given elsewhere,[3] that when A believes that p *what* is believed is the proposition that p (e.g. 1904: 204, 218, 339–50, 509, 522–3; 1905: 52; 1906: 48; 1918: 187, 218; 1919: 285, 307; 1921: 233, 241, 272; 1927: 272; 1940: 18, 79, 119, 142, etc.); even when he held that belief is not a relation between the believer and a proposition (1918: 217, 224, 226–7) and even when the believer is an animal (e.g. 1940: 79, 179). Indeed, one definition of a 'proposition' is 'what is believed' or 'the content of a belief' (e.g. 1919: 308–9; 1921: 240). Naturally, therefore, his ambivalent view about propositions and sentences sometimes led him to say that what is believed when one believes that p is the sentence 'p' (1921: 236, 245; 1927: 270; 1940: 179, 189, 199, 214; 1948: 98, 99, 101, 120, 125), since if there are no propositions, it cannot be the proposition that p. When, on the other hand, he distinguished propositions from sentences he asserted that 'what is believed is not the words "p" but what "p" signifies' (1940: 168, 255; 1948: 98–111, 146). Even when he held that 'what is believed' or 'the content of a belief' is a set of images (1921: 236, 241, 245), this could be reconciled with his view, since he also sometimes held that a proposition could be a set of images – what he called 'image-propositions' (1921: 275; 1940: 180).

Similarly Russell's distinction of molecular and atomic was expressed as a distinction sometimes between propositions (e.g. 1918: 199, 209, 211, 216; 1940: 29, 42; 1948: 120), sometimes between sentences (e.g. 1940: 29, 32, 42, 90, etc.; 1948: 120) and sometimes between propositions containing different kinds of words (e.g. 1918: 207, 208).

Another major clue to Russell's view about the relation of a proposition and a sentence lies in his views about the kinds of constituent each has. Identity of kinds of constituent would, in the usual sense of 'constituent', allow identity of kinds of things which had the constituents, while difference in the former would imply difference in the latter.

Unfortunately, Russell seems to have held, at various times, two quite different views as to what it is for something to be a constituent of a proposition. On one view 'constituent' is used in the ordinary sense of that which is contained in or occurs in something, that of which the something is composed or in which it consists. That Russell often, perhaps most usually, used 'constituent' in this sense is clear not only from his explicit assertions, as when he says that a proposition 'contains the class as a constituent' (1903: 67, 49, 83–5; 1918: 230; 1905: 55; cf. 'fact' 1959: 152), or that a proposition contains or is composed of its constituents (1906: 48; 1912: 91), but also from the context in which 'constituent' is used (e.g. of words in 1918: 192, 196–7, 239; 1959: 182; of things other than words in 1903: 49, 67; 1904: 204, 345; 1905: 42, 56; 1912: 85, 91, 198; 1918: 238; 1919: 316, 345) and from the context in which some such words as 'occurs in', 'contains', 'consists in', 'is composed of', 'component' is used (e.g. for words in 1903: 43; 1905: 45, 47, 50; 1918: 192–7, 204, 207–8, 241, 247; 1919: 308–9; 1924: 334; 1940: 49, 56, 74, 327; 1944: 15, 694; 1959: 67, 84; for things other than words in 1903: 43, 46, 47, 53, 73, 85, 89; 1904: 209; 1912: 92; 1919: 315). Furthermore, it is in this sense that he uses 'constituent' when he speaks of a constituent of a sentence (e.g. 1940: 28), of the world (1918: 270), of a fact (1918: 217, 270; 1919: 286–7; 1948: 126; 1959: 152; cf. 'component' 1918: 182), of a belief (1918: 196) or of the content of a belief (1921: 235), or of time (1904: 213).

On the other view, to be a constituent of a proposition is to be what the proposition is about, 1903: 45, 56 (a term); 1903: 54; 1912: 85 (a person); 1918: 250–2, 262 (a thing); 1903: 43 (a name); 1903: 90; 1918: 246; 1940: 253 (a thing, not a name) – as likewise to be a constituent of a fact is to be what the fact is about (1919: 286) – *or* what the proposition mentions (1918: 262), *or* what is the subject of the proposition (e.g. 1903: 44; 1918: 252; 1924: 328), *or* what is signified, expressed or denoted by the words which express the proposition (1905: 45, 55; 1918: 250), *or* what corresponds to the words which express the proposition (1906: 48; 1918: 247–8; 1924: 328; 1937: ix–x). Such a view of 'constituent' is, perhaps, analogous to the sense in which a person can be said to be in or to appear in a book, newspaper or list in which he is mentioned.

It is quite clear from the references I have given that Russell at various times throughout his life held both these views. Though he himself explicitly made some such distinction in 1919, it would be a mistake to suppose that such a date marks a clear line between an earlier and a later view.[4] Russell is, unfortunately, a prime example of someone to whom the difference between what a man says he thinks and what he actually does think is pre-eminently applicable. The 'container' view, namely, that the constituents of a proposition are what the proposition is composed of, is clearly stated both before and after this date and for both verbal and non-verbal constituents. Similarly, the 'reference' or 'mention' view, namely, that the constituents of a proposition are what the proposition is about, is also clearly stated both before and after this date, usually for non-verbal items, but, on occasion, for verbal items.

It is also quite clear how these very different views restrict the sorts of things that could be constituents of something. Thus, if a proposition were a sentence, then a verbal item could either be contained in and not mentioned in it or mentioned in and not contained in it or both contained in and mentioned in it. A non-verbal item, however, could be mentioned in it, but it could not be contained in it. On the other hand, if a proposition were not a sentence, then non-verbal items could either be contained in and not mentioned in it (e.g. 1903: 53) or mentioned in and not contained in it (e.g. 1903: 53) or both mentioned in and contained in it. A verbal item, on the other hand, could be mentioned in but not contained in it. Hence, if verbal items are constituents of a proposition in the container sense, then a proposition must be a sentence, and if non-verbal items are constituents in this sense a proposition cannot be a sentence. In the reference sense, on the other hand, both the verbal and the non-verbal items could be constituents of a proposition, whether or not it were a sentence. Unfortunately, at various times – including times both before and after 1919 – Russell allowed both verbal and non-verbal items to be constituents of propositions in the 'container' sense and, therefore, allowed propositions both to be and not to be sentences. He also, quite properly, allowed both verbal and non-verbal items to be constituents of a proposition in the 'reference' sense, since the type of constituent, in this sense, does not determine the type of thing of which it is a constituent and does not, therefore, allow one to differentiate between propositions as sentences and propositions as other than sentences. Even here, however, he frequently quite inconsistently spoke in successive breaths both of a verbal item and of its corresponding non-verbal item being, in this sense, a constituent of the same proposition, despite other occasions on which he explicitly insisted that it was, for instance, Socrates and not the word 'Socrates' which was, in this sense, a constituent of the proposition 'Socrates loves Plato' (e.g. 1918: 238–9).

Finally, to make confusion worse confounded, Russell frequently wrote, even in the same few pages, in such a way as to assimilate the 'container' view and the 'reference' view of constituents; thus allowing that what is mentioned in a proposition not merely could also be contained in it, but is necessarily contained in it. Thus, in 1903 (e.g. ch. 4) 'term' was invented as a technical word for the 'constituent' of a proposition, for whatever 'occurs in' a proposition, or whatever is the 'subject' of a proposition, for whatever the proposition is 'about' and for whatever the proposition 'contains'. In the same chapter words are both asserted and denied to be what occur in, are contained in, or are the subject of, a proposition, or are what the proposition is about. Nor is the assimilation of the container view and the reference view prevented by Russell's explicit insistence on the difference between the two, *either* in the 1905 form when he explained his allusion to 'denoting phrases occurring in propositions' but not 'standing for constituents of propositions' by treating the occurrence as occurrence in the verbal expression of the proposition (cf. 1918: 250; 1924: 328), *or* in the 1919 form when he insisted that the constituents of a proposition are the phrases which occur in the proposition and not anything referred to by such phrases, for the assimilation of the container and the reference view occurs in a random way at other dates (e.g. 1903: 43; 1918: 185).

The same ambiguities infect Russell's typical denial that a particular non-verbal item, such as a class, a number, Romulus or *or* could be a constituent of a proposition on the ground that such items do not exist and 'you cannot have a constituent of a proposition which is nothing at all' (1918: 242, 250, 253, 270; 1937: ix; cf. 1912: 139, 153). The relevance of such an argument is clear on the view (a) that a proposition is not a sentence and its constituents are what it contains, or (b) that a proposition is not a sentence and its constituents are what it mentions or (c) that a proposition is a sentence and its constituents are what it mentions; for on all three of these views non-verbal items are possible constituents of a proposition. The only view to which the argument seems irrelevant is (d) that a proposition is a sentence and its constituents are what it contains, for on such a view neither existent nor non-existent non-verbal items can be constituents of any proposition. Russell, however, might have overlooked this because he sometimes assimilated the view that numbers and classes do not exist to the view that they are the numerals or class symbols which express them. On the other hand, it is unlikely that in this context Russell was thinking either of view (d) or of view (c), for he usually stressed here the distinction between the proposition which wrongly appeared to have a number or a class as a constituent and the sentence which did have, for example, such a phrase as 'the number 2' or 'the class of all men' as a constituent. Nor is it likely that he was thinking of view (a), since he usually paraphrased his conclusion by saying that in such a case the proposition is not *about* a number or class and that neither of these is the *subject* of such-and-such a proposition. Furthermore, Russell subscribed to the very commonly held – but I think mistaken – opinion that what does not exist cannot be the subject of a proposition, or be what it is about or be mentioned or referred to by it. In such contexts it seems plausible, therefore, that Russell was thinking of view (b), namely, that a proposition is something other than a sentence and its constituents are what are mentioned in it. Unfortunately, however, since, as we saw, he often assimilates the 'container' and the 'reference' view, it may be that he held both (b) and (a).

Though there are lots of problems about what it is for a proposition to mention or be about something, such problems do not make it difficult to understand what a proposition is. A sentence, too, can quite understandably mention or be about so-and-so. When, however, a proposition is said to contain non-verbal items, puzzles do arise about the nature of a proposition. Nor are they solved by supposing these non-verbal items to be psychological, e.g. images. For Russell did not attach importance to the difference between propositions as composed of words – what he sometimes called 'word-propositions' – and propositions as composed of images – 'image-propositions'. The important difference is between the view of propositions as composed of, having as constituents in the 'container' sense, words or images, and the view of propositions as composed of non-verbal items. What sort of a thing is a proposition if its constituents are, as Russell often said they were, entities such as material objects and people? An important, but not a very satisfactory, part of the answer to this question hinges on the relation of propositions to facts.

Russell, rightly distinguishing between words and the meanings of words, was undecided whether propositions were composed of words or of the meanings of words. He was further undecided what it was to be composed of the meaning of words, because he thought of a meaning of a word as something meant by, that is, referred to by, the word and he thought, at various times, that this might be a psychological item such as an image, a non-psychological item such as a person or a thing or a hybrid item called a 'concept'. Hence, in juggling with the three notions, *sentence*, *proposition* and *fact*, Russell, even within the same paper, sometimes identified the proposition with a sentence as something whose components are words and sometimes identified it with something whose components are meanings, either in the sense of concepts (e.g. 1903: 53, 73; 1948: 107) or of images (e.g. 1919: 308, 319; 1940: 180–2) or in the sense of things, for instance, material objects and people which are what is 'meant by' the words (1904: 204; 1905: 56; 1912: 91; 1918: 194, 224; 1919: 290 ff.) or the images (1919: 316; 1921: 207). Since he sometimes called what is composed of the things meant by words a 'fact', he therefore sometimes distinguished propositions from facts and the constituents of propositions from the constituents of facts (1918: 182 ff., 196–8; 1924: 335), and sometimes identified them (1904: 523; 1905: 45–8; 1918: 191, 248; 1919: 309). His denial in 1918 of the separate existence of propositions led him to give to facts many of the jobs which propositions, or at least true propositions, had hitherto done, especially that of containing the constituents corresponding to the words of the appropriate sentence (e.g. 1918: 191 ff., 248) and that of being the subject matter of analysis (e.g. 1918: 191, 198). On one occasion he allowed that facts could be true or false (1918: 227). In 1919 he argued, supposedly under the influence of Wittgenstein, that a proposition, because it is something consisting of words or images, is one instance of a fact (1919: 309, 315–17; cf. 1921: 250; 1924: 332).

The difficulty about the identification of propositions is that, on the one hand, they seem inseparably linked to some means of (verbal) expression – hence, the temptation to identify them with sentences – while, on the other hand, they both lack the linguistic characteristics of sentences (e.g. being English, ungrammatical or misspelt) and possess non-linguistic characteristics inapplicable to sentences (being true, contradictory, unproved) – hence, the temptation to give them a separate existence of their own. Russell provides a salutary example of the difficulties inherent in either suggestion.

My own suggestion is that a proposition is the *logical role* which a sentence can, but need not, play. Meaningful sentences are capable of playing it, but meaningless ones are not. The same role can be played by various sentences, in the same or different languages – or even by things other than sentences – while the same sentence can play various roles or no role, just as Hamlet can be played by both Guinness and Gielgud, while both can also play Macbeth and Lear or can take a rest from acting. Furthermore, in uttering a sentence a man may play the role of making a statement just as in raising his arm he may be acting as a signal giver. Similarly the arabic numeral '9' and the roman numeral 'ix' both play the role of the number nine; a piece of paper can play the role of a legal contract; a physical movement that of an action.

Although role players can exist without playing a role, roles do not exist independently of being played. The temporal and spatial location of a role is that of what plays the role. Hamlet is on that part of the stage where Gielgud is standing. A contract is in the filing cabinet in which is the piece of paper on which it is drawn up, a number is on that part of the gate where its numeral is, a proposition occurs on the line where its sentence is written, a signal comes from the spot where an arm is raised. More importantly, role players can be said to *be* the role they are playing and roles said to *be* what is playing the role. In the context of the role, Gielgud *is* Hamlet and Hamlet *is* Gielgud, the piece of paper in the filing cabinet *is* the contract and a contract *is* that piece of paper, raising my arm *is* signalling and signalling *is* raising my arm. Similarly that numeral on the gate *is* my number and my number *is* that numeral, the sentence in the footnote *is* the proposition that *p* and the proposition that *q is* the sentence underlined.

But though role players can be said to be what they play and vice versa, roles have characteristics which role players in themselves lack, while role players have characteristics which their roles lack. Hence, Hamlet, but not Gielgud, is a Shakespearian character; while Gielgud, but not Hamlet, is an Englishman. Similarly contracts, but not pieces of paper, are legal, binding and harsh, while pieces of paper, but not contracts, are quarto, vellum and lined; numbers, but not numerals, are odd or even, while numerals, but not numbers, are arabic or roman; propositions, but not sentences, are true or false, while sentences, but not propositions, are English or French.

The impossibility of attributing all the characteristics of a role to its role player or of a role player to its role shows that the notion of a role is different from that of a role player, and hence the notion of a proposition different from that of a sentence, that of a number different from that of a numeral, that of a contract different from that of a piece of paper. But this difference between a notion of a role and that of a role player does not prevent the role player from *being* the role it plays. The notions of proposition and sentence, number and numeral, contract and piece of paper, signal and arm movement are different; yet sentences can *be* propositions, numerals numbers, pieces of paper contracts and arm movements signals. It is, I think, a misapplication of Leibniz's law to say that because we cannot attribute truth and falsity to the sentence '*p*' as we can to the proposition *p* and cannot argue from '*S* believes the proposition *p*' to '*S* believes the sentence "*p*" ', therefore a sentence cannot be a proposition or vice versa.[5] It is, on the other hand, a converse misapplication[6] of the law to argue that because a proposition can be a sentence, therefore a sentence can be true or false and people can believe sentences.

The insistence that, though the role is logically different from that which plays the role, it does not exist without it, does not imply that it makes no sense to speak of roles that have never been played any more than of threats that have never been uttered or of generations yet unborn.

To discover what, if any, proposition a given sentence expresses is, therefore, to discover the logical – as contrasted with the linguistic – role of that sentence. Two sentences express the same proposition if they play the same logical role. In addition to its purely logical role, a sentence – and also the proposition expressed by it – can play a wide variety of what might, perhaps, be called 'illocutionary roles.' Thus, a sentence might play the role of, and hence be said to *be*, a premiss, conclusion, hypothesis, claim, assumption or objection. This is why, like sentences, objections can be deleted, assumptions put in the footnotes and claims sent through the post; though, unlike the sentences used to express them, they can also be unjustified, invalid and inconsistent, but not ungrammatical, inelegant or English.

There are, I think, traces in Russell of my suggested analysis of *proposition* – e.g. 1921: 241, 'A proposition is a series of words expressing the kind of thing that can be asserted or denied' – but his usual picture of a proposition caused him to mistake an inquiry into the logical role of a sentence for an inquiry into the structure of a supposed complex of constituents corresponding to the sentence. It led him, and other analysts of the time, to look for 'the form of the proposition' or even 'the form of the fact' instead of for the logical behaviour of a sentence. Thus, the view that a sentence containing as grammatical subject the words 'The so-and-so' does not necessarily attribute a characteristic to anything became the view that the proposition expressed by these words does not contain a constituent named by the words 'The so-and-so' (e.g. 1905; 1924; cf. 1944: 14). When, on the other hand, Russell's sense of reality and his adherence to Ockham's razor led him to deny that there are any such things as propositions, he fell into the error of attributing the characteristics of propositions, e.g. the possibility of being true or false or believed, to the sentences which express them.

The realisation that it is certain characteristics of the behaviour of the verbal and not the structure of something non-verbal which analysts should seek, marks, I think, the transition from the thinking of Russell, Moore and the early Wittgenstein to the thinking of Ryle and the later Wittgenstein.[7]

Department of Philosophy
University of Hull

NOTES

1 The references, by date and page, are given at the end of this chapter.
2 Contrast A. J. Ayer, *Russell and Moore: The Analytical Heritage* (London, Macmillan, 1971: 81).
3 In Chapter 14, 'Belief as a Propositional Attitude', in this book.
4 For example, D. F. Pears, *Bertrand Russell and the British Tradition in Philosophy* (London, Collins, 1967: ch. 13).
5 For example, G. E. Moore, *Lectures on Philosophy* (London, George Allen & Unwin, 1966:132–49).
6 For example, Russell, *passim*; or W. V. Quine, *Word and Object* (Cambridge, Mass., MIT Press, 1960: *passim*).
7 I am indebted to D. R. Cousin and P. T. Geach for comments on an earlier draft of this chapter.

REFERENCES

1903 *The Principles of Mathematics*, 1st edn (Cambridge University Press, 1903); references here are to the paperback edition, undated.
1904 'Meinong's Theory of Complexes and Assumptions', *Mind*, vol. XIII, 1904: pt I, pp. 204–19; pt II, pp. 336–54; pt III, pp. 509–24.
1905 'On Denoting', *Mind*, vol. XIV (1905: 479–93); references here to the reprint in *Logic and Knowledge*, R. C. Marsh, ed. (London, George Allen & Unwin; New York, Macmillan, 1956).
1906 'On the Nature of Truth', *Proceedings of the Aristotelian Society*, vol. VII (1906–7: 28–49).
1910 'On the Nature of Truth', in *Philosophical Essays* (London, Longmans, Green, 1910); references here are to the revised edition (London, George Allen & Unwin, 1966).
1912 *The Problems of Philosophy* (London, Home University Library, 1912); references here are to the 1936 reprint.
1918 'The Philosophy of Logical Atomism' (1918–19), in *Logic and Knowledge*, R. C. Marsh, ed., op. cit.

1919   'On Propositions: What They Are and How They Mean' (1919), in *Logic and Knowledge*, R. C. Marsh, ed., op. cit.

1921   *The Analysis of Mind* (London, George Allen & Unwin, 1921: ch. XII); references here are to the 1924 reprint.

1924   'Logical Atomism' (1924), in *Logic and Knowledge*, R. C. Marsh, ed., op. cit.

1927   'Truth and Falsehood', in *An Outline of Philosophy* (London, George Allen & Unwin, 1927).

1937   *The Principles of Mathematics*, 2nd edn (Cambridge University Press, 1937); references here are to the paperback edition, undated.

1940   *An Inquiry into Meaning and Truth* (London, George Allen & Unwin, 1940); references here to the Penguin edn (Harmondsworth, 1962).

1944   *The Philosophy of Bertrand Russell*, P. A. Schilpp, ed. (Evanston, Northwestern University Press, 1944); references here are to the 3rd edn (1951).

1948   *Human Knowledge: Its Scope and Limits* (London, George Allen & Unwin, 1948); references here are to the second paperback reprint (New York, Simon & Schuster, 1964).

1959   *My Philosophical Development* (London, George Allen & Unwin, 1959).

3

RUSSELL'S PARADOX AND SOME OTHERS

William C. Kneale

(1) In a recent paper (1972[1]) I argue (i) that a language which makes possible the characteristically human form of social life must allow for talk not only about its own sounds, but also about communication by means of those sounds, (ii) that failure to recognise this had led many philosophers into a dangerous confusion between sentences and propositions, (iii) that attempts to formulate logic as a theory of grammatically well-formed sentences involve neglect of the token-reflexive device and misunderstanding of the role of definite descriptions and (iv) that the paradox of the Liar holds no terrors for those who realise how the notion of truth is related to that of a proposition. My reason for concluding with an attempt to solve the old problem by means acceptable to a student of natural languages was, of course, a wish to counter Tarski's thesis that natural languages are all inconsistent through failure of their users to observe the distinction between language and metalanguage which he considers essential for solution of the Liar paradox. But it may be of interest to show that similar methods are sufficient for solution of Russell's paradox and some others that were formulated in the early years of this century during debates on the theories of Cantor and Frege.

In the Introduction to the first edition of *Principia Mathematica* Russell listed seven paradoxes, or apparent contradictions, for which he undertook to find solutions, namely:

(a) The Liar paradox.
(b) His own paradox of *the class of all classes that are not members of themselves*.
(c) The corresponding paradox of *the relation between two relations when one does not have itself to the other*.
(d) Burali–Forti's paradox of *the ordinal number of all ordinals*.
(e) Berry's paradox of *the least integer not nameable in fewer than nineteen syllables*.
(f) König's paradox of *the least indefinable ordinal*.
(g) Richard's paradox of *the class of all decimals definable by a finite number of words*.

In each of these, he maintained, something is said about everything of a certain kind, and then from what is said there seems to be generated a new case which both is and is not of the same kind as the case or cases covered by the original remark (Russell and Whitehead, 1910). By the time of the second edition of *Principia Mathematica* a new paradox of the same general character had become popular, namely:

(h) The paradox of Nelson and Grelling about the adjective *'heterological'*. But Russell had always held that there was no limit to the possibility of creating vicious-circle paradoxes by talk of illegitimate totalities, and he continued to maintain that all alike were to be solved by his theory of logical types.

In his essay of 1925 on 'The Foundations of Mathematics' Ramsey argued that of all the paradoxes listed above only those listed as (b), (c) and (d) could properly be classified with Cantor's worries as mathematical, or logical in that sense in which the mathematical had been identified with the logical (Ramsey, 1931: 20). All the others, he said, involved linguistic or epistemological notions, and it was significant that in Russell's treatment they alone required his distinction of orders within types. My own view is that all alike originate in misuses of language (how else could we fall into such contradictions?) and that none of them requires for its solution a restrictive theory of types, either simple or ramified. But I believe that (d), (f), and (g) are to be distinguished from the rest as involving essential use of terminology peculiar to the theory of sets, and I intend to consider here only the other five. Of these Berry's is the only one involving reference to numbers, but I think it is in some ways the simplest of all, since it requires for its solution no more than a recognition of the power of indefinite self-enrichment which belongs to all natural languages, and I shall therefore deal with it first.

(2) When we first read the phrase 'the least integer not nameable in fewer than nineteen syllables', we think that it must refer to some rather large number whose name in the common notation of 'hundred', 'thousand', 'million', etc. contains at least nineteen syllables. But then we realise that, if the phrase does indeed refer to such a number, it is itself a name of that number (in a large sense of the word 'name'), although it contains only eighteen syllables, and so we are bewildered for a moment. When, however, we recover from our shock, we naturally say 'The trick depends on using "nameable" in different ways', and we are right, though our explanation requires a little development to make it entirely satisfactory.

Just because natural languages contain words like 'name' and 'designation' they allow for talk about communication by use of language and so indirectly for a new style of talk about other things. Let us say for clarity that phrases like 'fifty-four' and 'one hundred and seventy-three' are primary designations of numbers. Then clearly with the vocabulary at our disposal we can make up secondary designations such as 'the least integer with a primary designation containing ninety syllables', and if the spirit moves we can go on to produce number designations of the third and even higher levels. There is indeed no highest level of designation beyond which we may not progress, and no danger of paradox to be anticipated from addition of new levels, provided always we make clear in every utterance the level or levels with which we are concerned. In Berry's paradox, however, it is essential that the word 'nameable' is used without restriction to the first or any other level, and so his phrase 'the least integer not nameable in fewer than nineteen syllables' must be understood as though it were an abbreviation for 'the least integer not nameable *by a designation of any level* in fewer than nineteen syllables'. When, however, this has been conceded, it becomes clear that the phrase cannot designate any number at all not because of a fault in the supplementary words I have italicised, but simply because there is no limit to the developments of notation we may introduce, and so no limit to the magnitude of the integers that we may designate somehow or other in fewer than nineteen syllables. Thus if anyone maintains that among numbers which can be designated in fewer than nineteen syllables there must be a largest, we can easily refute him by stipulating first that the single letter 'l' is to be taken in the context as a short sign for his supposed upper bound and then, with this convention, writing '$l+1$' as a sign which he should admit to stand for something larger.

According to Russell's ramified theory of types the simple solution I have just indicated is not acceptable because there is a vicious circle involved in the use of the phrase 'the least integer not nameable in fewer than nineteen syllables'. In the Introduction to *Principia Mathematica* he writes:

The word 'nameable' refers to the totality of names, and yet is allowed to occur in what professes to be one among names. Hence there can be no such thing as a totality of names, in the sense in which the paradox speaks of 'names'. It is easy to see that, in virtue of the hierarchy of functions, the theory of types renders a totality of 'names' impossible. We may, in fact, distinguish names of different orders as follows: (a) Elementary names will be such as are true 'proper names', i.e. conventional appellations not involving any description. (b) First-order names will be such as involve description by means of a first-order function; that is to say, if $\phi!\hat{x}$ is a first-order function, 'the term which satisfies $\phi!\hat{x}$' will be a first-order name, though there will not always be an object named by this name. (c) Second-order names will be such as involve a description by means of a second-order function; among such names will be those involving a reference to the totality of first-order names. And so we can proceed through a whole hierarchy. But at no stage can we give a meaning to the word 'nameable' unless we specify the order of names to be employed: and any name in which the phrase 'nameable by names of order n' occurs is necessarily of a higher order than the nth. Thus, the paradox disappears (Russell and Whitehead, 1910: 63–4).

Essentially the same treatment of the paradox can be presented more simply by means of Tarski's distinction between a language and its metalanguage. According to this doctrine no language can provide for talk about the work of designation done by its own constituent symbols, nor yet for talk of the truth of its own propositional formulae. Any such word as 'designates' must be understood in relation to a particular language, i.e. as short for 'designates in L', where L is the name of a language under consideration and not itself part of that language. Thus, in order to avoid confusion or contradiction, we must recognise a hierarchy of languages. At the bottom there will be a language L_0 in which we can talk of various things but not of anything linguistic except perhaps spoken sounds and written or printed shapes. Above this there will be a language L_1 in which we can talk of the work of L_0, and in general above any language L_n another language L_{n+1} in which we can talk of the work of L_n. In an ideally simple scheme it may be assumed that each language L_n is contained in its metalanguage L_{n+1}, but it is essential that the symbols 'designates in L_n' and 'designates in L_{n+1}' should be distinguished and that no attempt be made to talk of designation without reference to a particular language, since the penalty for doing so is the kind of contradiction we find in Berry's paradox.

It cannot be denied that some signs presuppose others in the way indicated by Russell. No one, for example, can understand the mathematical notion of a limit unless he already understands the notion of series, and he may fall into absurdity if he assumes that the limit of a series is also a term in it. It is also beyond doubt that words like 'designate' involve at least implicit reference to a language, and that any one who ignores this fact does so at his logical peril. But there is a paradox already in Russell's insistence on the need for avoiding confusion of types, and again in Tarski's insistence on a strict distinction of every language from its metalanguage, namely that each philosopher violates his own rule when formulating it and cannot do otherwise. If Tarski wishes to tell us something of general importance about designation or truth, he must talk about all languages at once, including that which he is using, though he holds that any language which contains provision for talk about its own work is inconsistent. The objection is so obvious that it cannot be overlooked. That Tarski has nevertheless made a declaration against general talk about languages of all levels must be due, I think, to a belief that what he says in ordinary language is only an informal, unofficial introduction to the serious work of building a well-regulated hierarchy of languages fit for the work of science.

It is certainly necessary for scientists to formulate systems that may be called artificial languages, and it may perhaps be useful for certain purposes to construct a hierarchy of artificial languages in which each higher language is the metalanguage of that below it. But whatever is done in this way must be done by use of a natural language. No formalised language of the sort that interests Tarski has been established, or could be established, in the direct way in which carters used to teach their horses to behave at the orders 'Gee-up' and 'Whoa'. And the reason is that life presents no situations with which even a mathematical genius might conceivably learn to correlate formulae of abstract geometry or axiomatic set theory before he had learnt his mother tongue. There are indeed contexts especially appropriate for the production of scientific generalities; but they are linguistic contexts such as argument, and they are recognisable only by persons who have already acquired a full natural language, i.e. a system for communication that includes not only signs like 'Gee-up', 'Whoa', 'All gone', 'Nice pussy', and 'Stop kicking', but provision for talk about talk. In short, any distinctions of level that we may ever need to draw between artificial languages made for the purposes of science will be drawn with and within a natural language, since artificial languages of this kind are not, like Esperanto, capable of maintaining an independent existence.

The point may be illustrated most clearly by consideration of the various kinds of definition from which signs may acquire sense in scientific writings. When a new sign is introduced with an explicit definition for economy and perspicuity in the exposition of a formal system, the rule of substitutability by which it is introduced is not a formula of the artificial language to which the sign is added, but a formula of the metalanguage which has been used already in enunciation of rules of inference. Similarly when a set of axioms are said to furnish an implicit definition for a sign that has been used in them without explicit definition, what delimits the range of permissible interpretations for the sign is not the set of axioms, considered merely as a sequence of formulae in the basic language, but rather a declaration in a metalanguage of the way in which the formulae are to be received. And more important still, when a new mathematical sign is defined by abstraction, the linguistic level of the discourse by which it is introduced must be higher than that of the discourse in which it is to be used. When, for example, we use the Greek letter ω for the order type exhibited by the series of natural numbers, we talk at a higher level of language than that in which we do elementary arithmetic. But in explaining at the beginning of this development of mathematics how and why we propose to use ω we must already, it seems, be using language of a level still higher; and this is possibly only because such distinctions of levels are drawn inside one omnicompetent language with a power of indefinite self-enrichment. As soon as we have full mastery of a natural language we have an instrument adequate in essentials for the whole work of science; and when later we find it necessary to make a distinction of levels, we can do so without attempting the impossible feat of constructing a series of new linguistic instruments from the beginning. For the distinctions of importance in science and philosophy are not absolute distinctions of level in a single hierarchy such as that between 'Snow is white' and 'Tom said that Dick said that

Harry said that snow is white', where the second sentence (if admissible at all) belongs to the meta-meta-metalanguage, but relative distinctions, such as that between real numbers and rational numbers, which may be required in many different kinds of discourse.

If I am right, there is no good reason for banning talk about all number designations, and I do not think that anyone would have supposed for long that there was if the only problem he had in mind was that posed by Berry's paradox. But Poincaré, who was anxious to find arguments against Cantorism, had declared that Richard's paradox (itself a parody of Cantor's diagonal procedure) arose from trying to think of decimals as forming an actually complete totality instead of a potentially infinite supply, and Russell was anxious to show, in the interests of the doctrines he had inherited from Cantor and Frege, that none of the paradoxes recently formulated in arithmetical or set-theoretical terms depended solely on illegitimate use of the ideas of number and quantity. It was for this reason he wrote:

> We shall begin by an enumeration of some of the more important and illustrative of the contradictions which have beset mathematical logic, and shall then show how they all embody vicious-circle fallacies, and are therefore all avoided by the theory of types (Russell and White-head, 1910: 60).

Clearly his ramified theory of types is sufficient for the purpose of eliminating all the paradoxes he had in mind, since they all involve a kind of reflexiveness banned by his theory. But that is not to say that the theory is necessary for the purpose and plainly true. On the contrary, it involves the sacrifice of a great deal that we should like to retain, as he himself came to realise; and I have argued that it commits him to an untenable theory of language. For a satisfactory solution of Berry's paradox, we have had to show that the trouble arises from a very special sort of mistake made possible by reflexive use of language but not essential to it. Similarly for an understanding of the other four paradoxes with which this chapter is concerned we must notice how reflexive talk may lead to nonsense in certain special circumstances, and it will be convenient to begin this task by examining once more the Liar paradox which has been supposed to prove the inconsistency of any language with pretensions to omnicompetence.

(3) In any fully human language it is possible for men to talk about talk and about what is said in talk. As might be expected, the most primitive way of indicating what a man has said is by direct quotation, that is to say, by production of another specimen of a pattern of which his utterance was a specimen. Sometimes when we speak in this way of what a man has *said* we are interested in the sounds of his utterance for their own sake; and when this is so, we are careful to indicate the pattern by means

of a new specimen, even though what we say about it is couched in another language. Thus if one Englishman asks another 'What did the Chinaman say?' and the second thinks the first is interested for some reason in the sounds made by the Chinaman, he will reply 'He said . . .' and then do his best to imitate those sounds. But very often when we talk about what has been said we are not interested in the sounds of an utterance for their own sake, but rather in the role of the utterance in communication; and when this is so, we do not hesitate to indicate what was said by producing a specimen of some other sound or sounds which can be used for making the same communication. Thus if one Englishman asks another 'What did the Chinaman say?' and the second, who is familiar with the Chinese language, thinks the first wants to know what the Chinaman communicated (or purported to communicate), he may reply in English, 'He said "Long live Chairman Mao!"' '

Obviously there is an ambiguity in the verb 'say' (and similar verbs of other languages) which can only be removed by other elements in a context of use; and it is therefore not surprising that nouns by means of which we refer to what men say sometimes have similar ambiguities. In modern English the word 'sentence' is normally reserved for a form of words with the kind of completeness needed for making a successful communication. It was in this sense, for example, that our teachers used the word when they told us to translate into French the sentence 'My uncle has the pen of the gardener's wife'. But it is clear that the word once had a wider range of use, since it is just an English modification of a Latin word that covered the range of our words 'opinion', 'judgment', 'sentiment'. Similarly the word 'proposition', which is now used most commonly for talking of what utterances exemplify when they do the same work, apart from manifesting states of mind such as belief or curiosity, was sometimes defined in the past by the phrase 'verbal expression of a judgment' and has been used by some philosophers, in particular by Russell in his later writings, to cover a range of meanings almost as wide as that of the German *Satz*.

Unfortunately philosophers who are aware of a difference between the modern usages of 'sentence' and 'proposition' sometimes suppose that a proposition may be identified with the meaning of a sentence. But this is plainly unsatisfactory as an account of the relationship between the two notions. For just as utterances which are specimens of the same proposition may be specimens (or, as philosophers often say, tokens) of different sentences because they belong to different languages or involve different words from the same language, so utterances which are specimens of the same sentence (e.g. 'It is raining here') may be specimens of different propositions because they occur at different times and places or are spoken by different people. There are, it is true, some sentences so constructed that each corresponds to a single proposition in accordance with the customs of the language in which it is made. But these are the purely general sentences of science; and our ability to construct them depends on our already having a language in which we can refer to individuals by means of the token-reflexive device. Without that device there could be no learning of language, and no use of language at any level of development. Those who suppose it possible in principle to communicate all thoughts by means of 'eternal' context-free sentences overlook the important fact that it is useless to know that you have an appointment for 1 January 1972 if you can never answer a question of the form 'What is the date *today*?'

For a proper understanding of the relation between sentences and propositions, it is necessary to start with the notion of communication. When once we have mastered the essentials of language, we can do many new things with words, including lying, getting married, conducting examinations and passing on orders that we dislike. But the basis of all these strange achievements is our understanding of the various ways of self-expression through sound which have become customary in our society. In particular, if we are to use words consciously for fulfilment of our purposes, we must be familiar with patterns of speech which normally manifest belief, curiosity and desire. These, however, all involve or presuppose presentation of possible states of affairs whose actuality the speaker assumes, questions or desires, as the case may be; and to say that an utterance is a specimen of a proposition is just to say that it presents a possible state of affairs for consideration. Sometimes philosophers (including myself) have confused propositions with possible states of affairs, perhaps because they have assumed too readily that sentences are the only kinds in which to classify utterances for the purposes of a theory of language. But it seems obvious on reflection that what a man desires when he makes a sincere request is not a proposition, but a state of affairs presentable by the specimens of a proposition; and the fact that we talk of believing propositions, rather than of believing states of affairs, can be explained satisfactorily by the consideration that 'belief' is primarily a word for trust in persons and their utterances. In order to remove any danger of confusion which there may be in writing of the proposition that Brutus murdered Caesar, we may, if we choose, follow the practice of G. E. Moore and write of *the proposition 'Brutus murdered Caesar'*. Inverted commas are not, as some philosophers suppose, a device for making a name of the symbol type of which they enclose a token, but simply a device for introduction of a specimen, and an utterance, as we have seen, can be a specimen of a proposition as well as of a sentence. If what we offer is not in fact a specimen of a proposition but something like a token of 'My uncle has the pen of the gardener's wife', said without reference to any uncle or any gardener, then, of course, we shall not succeed in referring to a proposition merely by introducing it with the words 'the proposition'. By contrast the notion of a sentence is a good deal more complicated.

In the first place, we do not call a phrase a sentence unless we think of it as containing all that is needed for manifestation of an attitude such as belief, curiosity or desire. But provided it has this, it may be accounted a sentence even though it contains no separate provision for presentation of a possible state of affairs. Thus the one word 'Yes' is a sentence suitable for use in reply to an interrogative utterance which is itself a specimen of a proposition. It is possible, however, in many languages for a form of words to have some tokens which are specimens of sentences and others which are not. Thus an utterance of the English words 'it is raining' is a specimen of a sentence if it occurs in relative isolation, but not so if it occurs inside an utterance of the larger group 'if it is raining you had better take your umbrella'. In modern writing and printing the necessary isolation is produced by the capital letter with which a sentence begins and the full stop with which it ends, but in speech the distinction depends on distribution of pauses and contrasts of intonation. In those languages which have special subjunctive and conditional forms of the verb the possibility of using a form of words sometimes as a sentence and sometimes as a mere clause is less than in modern English; and so far as I can see, there might very well be an ordinary spoken language which resembled Frege's ideography in making no provision at all for such doubling of roles. It is a pity, therefore, that in quite recent times some English-speaking logicians have blurred an important distinction by using the word 'sentence' as though it were equivalent to the German *Satz* and therefore applicable to clauses.

Second, those sentences and clauses which may be called propositional phrases, because they contain grammatical provision for presentation of possible states of affairs, may nevertheless have tokens which are specimens of different propositions. This arises, as we have seen, from our dependence on the token-reflexive device and cannot be eliminated from natural human languages.

Third, sentences and other phrases which are propositional in the sense just explained may nevertheless have tokens which are not specimens of any propositions at all. This possibility arises from the fact that some of our partial utterances may have the syntactical forms of designations without in fact designating anything. When this happens the larger utterances in which they occur cannot be specimens of propositions even though they are tokens of grammatically well-formed sentences. An obvious example of such failure would be a present token of the sentence 'The king of France is bald'. Frege, Russell and Hilbert have made different attempts to eliminate such possibilities from the symbolic systems they have devised for mathematics, but in a language suitable for all purposes the risk is inevitable, because there can be no signs of the sort Russell called logically proper names.

With these distinctions in mind, let us examine the sentence 'What I am now saying is false'. Obviously it is well formed according to the rules of ordinary grammar, and it is a propositional phrase in the sense I have explained, but the solution of the Liar paradox consists in showing that no ordinary token of it can be a specimen of a proposition. Anyone who finds an antinomy in an utterance of the sentence begins by assuming that the phrase 'what I am now saying' is used to refer to something which must of its nature be either true or false: that is essential to development of the argument. For reasons which I have tried to explain it is clear, however, that the Law of Bivalence holds neither of sentences nor of sentence tokens as such, but primarily of propositions and secondarily of their specimens. So in order to get properly started in the production of a paradox, we must assume that the phrase 'what I am now saying' is to be taken as short for 'the proposition of which my present utterance is a specimen'. But if we take it in this sense and draw the natural consequences, we find a very curious situation. The utterance as a whole cannot be a specimen of a proposition unless the opening part designates something; and the opening part cannot designate anything unless the utterance as a whole is a specimen of a proposition. That is to say, there is a vicious circle of preconditions, and so the utterance as a whole cannot be a specimen of any proposition. If anyone doubts that the circle is indeed vicious, he may perhaps be convinced by the reflection that the opening part cannot designate a proposition unless it is possible in principle to make another designation of the same proposition by putting the nominaliser 'that' in front of a specimen of the proposition. For from this it follows that, if the original utterance was a specimen of a proposition, another specimen can be produced by pronouncing a sentence of the form 'It is false that . . .', with the blank filled by a specimen of the proposition. But any such attempt leads only to the fatuous infinite progress, 'It is false that it is false that it is false that . . .'.

The puzzle depends on construction of a sentence in which the subject phrase purports to designate a proposition expressed by utterance of the sentence as a whole. In order to get the appearance of an antinomy, we must arrange for the sentence to be completed with the predicative phrase 'is false' or something equivalent. But the vicious circle of preconditions to which I have drawn attention is not due to choice of that or any other special phrase from among those suitable for talk of propositions. It could be found, for example, in an utterance of the sentence 'What I am now saying was asserted by Aristotle', if that was taken to refer to a proposition which it also expressed. And so we are entitled to conclude that there can be no completion which expresses a proposition already designated by utterance of the opening phrase. It might indeed be perfectly proper for a speaker to pronounce the sentence 'What I am now saying is false', if he did so in a parenthetical way, that is to say, for the purpose of warning his hearers against accepting some suggestion that he had been engaged in expounding at the moment he interrupted himself. But it seems clear beyond all doubt that expression of a proposition can never depend essentially on designation of the same proposition and this principle is sufficient for solution of the Liar paradox.

(4) At first consideration Russell's paradox of the class of all classes that

are not members of themselves seems far removed from the Liar paradox, and we have seen that writers who try to distinguish between
mathematical and semantic antinomies count it as mathematical, while
grouping the Liar with the inventions of Berry, Richard and Nelson.
Russell himself did not hold this view, and it is interesting to notice that
his first version of his paradox is concerned with predicates rather than
with classes. In *The Principles of Mathematics* he introduces it as follows:

> Among predicates, most of the ordinary instances cannot be pre-
> dicated of themselves, though, by introducing negative predicates, it
> will be found that there are just as many instances of predicates which
> are predicable of themselves. One at least of these, namely pre-
> dicability, or the property of being a predicate, is not negative; pre-
> dicability, as is evident, is predicable, i.e. it is a predicate of itself. But
> the most common instances are negative; thus non-humanity is non-
> human, and so on. The predicates which are not predicable of them-
> selves are, therefore, only a selection from among predicates, and it is
> natural to suppose that they form a class having a defining predicate.
> But if so, let us examine whether this defining predicate belongs to the
> class or not. If it belongs to the class, it is not predicable of itself, for
> that is the characteristic property of the class. But if it is not predicable
> of itself, then it does not belong to the class whose defining predicate it
> is, which is contrary to the hypothesis. On the other hand, if it does not
> belong to the class whose defining predicate it is, then it is not
> predicable of itself, i.e. it *is* one of those predicates that are not
> predicable of themselves, and therefore it does belong to the class
> whose defining predicate it is – again contrary to the hypothesis.
> Hence from either hypothesis we can deduce its contradictory
> (Russell, 1903: 79–80).

And a little later, when he tries to solve the paradox, he writes:

> Let us assume that 'not predicable of oneself' is a predicate. Then to
> suppose that this predicate is, or that it is not, predicable of itself, is
> self-contradictory. The conclusion, in this case, seems obvious: 'not
> predicable of oneself' is not a predicate (ibid.: 102).

I believe that when he wrote the last of the sentences quoted above he
was very near the truth, and that he failed to give a wholly satisfactory
solution of the problem only because he did not consider carefully
enough what was involved in his own use of the word 'predicate', though
he had said earlier 'No subtlety in distinguishing is likely to be excessive'
(ibid.: 80).

'Predicate' is a technical term of logic and grammar, but it has been
used differently in the two sciences. For although both logicians and
grammarians agree that a predicate is what is said of a subject, the

former think of what is said as something ascribed in a proposition, while the latter think of it as something pronounced in a sentence or clause. Since the Latin word *praedicatum* was introduced as a rendering of Aristotle's *kategoroumenon*, there can be no doubt that the logician's use is the older; and its primacy is confirmed by the fact that the correlative word 'subject' still seems more at home in its logical than in its grammatical role. If the name 'London' can be described as grammatical subject of the sentence 'London is a large city,' that is only because London, the town, is the subject of discourse to which we ascribe the predicate of being a large city when we pronounce the sentence. In the first of the passages I have quoted above Russell undoubtedly used the word 'predicate' in the traditional logical way, which accords well with his use of the word 'proposition' for what is essentially true or false (ibid.: ix). In what follows I shall maintain the same practice strictly; and when I have occasion to talk of what grammarians call a predicate, I shall therefore describe it as a predicative phrase, meaning by this not a phrase whose tokens are all specimens of a predicate, but one of a grammatical style appropriate for use in the expression of predicates.

Just as a token of a propositional phrase is a specimen of a proposition when it presents a state of affairs for consideration, so a token of a predicative phrase is a specimen of a predicate when it presents a property (in a large, non-Aristotelian sense of the word) for consideration in connection with a subject of discourse. At one point in the first of the passages quoted above Russell identifies a predicate with a property. This mistake is like the identification of a proposition with a possible state of affairs, but it has been even commoner among philosophers – indeed almost universal, probably because we can speak of *the predicate being-a-large-city* just as we speak of *the property being-a-large-city*. I recognise that by trying to distinguish them I lay myself open to a charge of multiplying entities beyond necessity, but I think it important to maintain that predicates, like propositions, are kinds to which utterances can belong and yet not phrases such as grammarians study. That we often indicate them by using words like those we use for talking of properties is perhaps no odder than the fact that a phrase such as 'the murder of Caesar' may be used in different contexts for a proposal, an event, and a fact. In order to avoid any danger of confusion we may, if we choose, talk of *the predicate 'is a large city'* just as we talk of *the proposition 'London is a large city'*. But it is important to realise that we may not always succeed in designating a predicate merely because we pronounce the words 'the predicate' before a predicative phrase. For whether or not a token of a predicative phrase is also a specimen of a predicate may depend on non-linguistic facts. Thus no use of the predicative phrase 'saw Merlin the magician' can ever serve to express a predicate, because there was no such person as Merlin; and no use of the predicative phrase 'saw his own wife' can express a predicate unless it is an application of the phrase to a married man. On the other hand, when we succeed in designating a predicate by pronouncing the words 'the predicate' before a predicative phrase, *every* token of that phrase occurring in a predicative position in a token of a propositional phrase must also be a specimen of a predicate.

Obviously we cannot doubt that the sequence of words 'is not predicable of itself' is a well-formed predicative phrase according to ordinary rules of English grammar. And it seems good sense to say that a token of this phrase may be a specimen of a genuine predicate, as in the statement 'The predicate "is human" is not predicable of itself'. But Russell was right in thinking that the phrase is not used to express a predicate by anyone who produces the sentence 'The predicate "is not predicable of itself" is not predicable of itself', and also right in thinking that there is a similarity between this new paradox and that of the Liar, though he did not locate the source of the trouble correctly in either case. According to the theory of types, in which he systematised his views some years after the publication of *The Principles of Mathematics*, the sentence which I have just quoted does not express a proposition because no predicate can be affirmed or denied significantly of itself. I believe, on the contrary, that every genuine predicate must divide the whole universe of which it is a member and so be either true or false of itself. This thesis is more radical than that of Frege, who thinks that a concept, or predicate, cannot belong to the universe of objects it divides. But his exclusion of *concepts* in general from the realm of *objects* seems to be solely due to the fact that he allows no place in his symbolism for a distinction between the expression of concepts and the designation of them. If I am right, the fault of the paradoxical sentence cannot be its reflexiveness (since there is nothing wrong in the statement that being a predicate is a predicate) but must lie in some peculiarity of the phrase 'is predicable of itself'. In order to produce the appearance of an antinomy, we have to add the negative particle; but if, as Russell maintains, the paradoxical sentence does not express a proposition, the same must be true also of the sentence 'The predicate "is predicable of itself" is predicable of itself', and conversely. It will be sufficient therefore to examine the simpler positive sentence.

Whereas Russell thinks his paradox can be solved only by denying the significance of all reflexive predication, I wish to suggest that it is enough for his purpose to deny the significance of asking whether such reflexiveness is reflexive, and that, since this denial, unlike the general theory of types, is necessary for independent reasons, it is no real limitation of the possibilities of language. According to this view, Russell's paradox results, as Gödel once conjectured (Gödel, 1944: 150), from ignoring a very special rule something like that in arithmetic against dividing by zero. In order to test the thesis let us consider carefully what is involved in saying that anything is predicable of itself.

We have seen that the expression 'is true' goes properly with talk of propositions. In the same way the expression 'is predicable of' goes properly with talk of predicates, and the correspondence is very close indeed when the second expression is used, as Russell uses it, with the special sense that Aristotle sometimes gave to *kategoreitai*[2], namely, 'is predicable *with truth* of' or more shortly 'is true of', 'is satisfied by'. For just as it is only of a proposition (as distinct from a propositional phrase) that we can say it must be either true or false, so it is only of a predicate (as distinct from a predicative phrase) that we can say it must divide the universe exhaustively by being either true or false of any given subject. And similarly, just as 'is true' undoes the nominalising work done by the prefix 'the proposition' when this appears before a specimen of a proposition, so 'is predicable of' undoes the nominalising work of the prefix 'the predicate', with the result that from 'The predicate "is a large city" is predicable of London' we can proceed immediatley to 'London is a large city'. In Greek and the symbolism of formal logic, where predicate phrases often come before their grammatical subjects, this principle is even more obvious than in English, but we can easily see that it must hold for any language in which it is possible to designate predicates. Writing 'κ' as an abbreviation for Aristotle's *kategoreitai* and '$\S x[F(x)]$' as an abbreviation for 'the predicate which is satisfied by x if and only if $F(x)$', we may put the rule of reduction shortly by saying that, except in contexts where designation of a predicate is required for faithful reporting, any proposition expressed in the form '$\S x[F(x)]\kappa A$' can be expressed equally well in the form '$F(A)$' without either '$\S$' or 'κ'. To reject this would be to suggest that there might conceivably be a predicate which was expressible only by use of '$\S$' and 'κ' or their equivalents in other symbolism; and that is plainly absurd, since it goes against the fundamental principle of semantics that for propositions and predicates alike expression is logically prior to designation.

In our problem sentence the subject phrase, namely 'the predicate "is predicable of itself" ', cannot designate anything unless there is one and the same predicate expressed by the predicative phrase 'is predicable of itself' whenever this occurs in predicative position in a token of a propositional phrase. In other words, 'itself' must be understood here as it is in 'The locomotive moves itself and so does the bus' rather than as it is in 'The locomotive moves itself and the carriages as well'. In a passage which I have quoted Russell slips into writing 'oneself' instead of 'itself', and I think that when he makes this curious change he probably intends us to take the grammatical subject with the sense which '$\S x(x\kappa x)$' has in my symbolism and the whole sentence therefore with the sense of

$$\S x(x\kappa x) \; \kappa \; \S x(x\kappa x).$$

For unless we are prepared to render the English phraseology into logical symbolism by the device which logicians call identification of variables, we must immediately give up the claim that we are using the words 'is predicable of itself' to express a single predicate. But when we consider our new formula in detail, we find that it has a very curious property. Although it contains 'κ' as its central sign, it can never be reduced to anything simpler in accordance with the rule of reduction set out above. For if we try to apply the rule, putting '$x\kappa x$' for '$F(x)$' and '$\S x(x\kappa x)$' for 'A', we merely get again what we had at the beginning. It is true that when we first constructed the formula we intended it to be read with the articulation

$$[\S x(x\kappa x)] \; \kappa \; [\S x(x\kappa x)],$$

which corresponds best to the suggestion that reflexiveness is reflexive. But the sense of 'κ' requires us to consider it also with the articulation

$$\S x(x\kappa x) \; \kappa \; [\S x(x\kappa x)],$$

and once this reading has been admitted there can be no end to the process of reduction. In short, 'κ' can never be eliminated from its central position, and so the phrase which precedes it cannot designate anything of the appropriate kind, namely, a predicate, just as the subject phrase of 'What I am now saying is true' cannot designate anything of the appropriate kind for its place, namely, a proposition, because there is no way of paraphrasing it without 'is true'.

Clearly there is nothing in all this to make us adopt Russell's theory of types and abandon such theses as

$$\S x(x \text{ is a predicate}) \; \kappa \; \S x(x \text{ is a predicate}).$$

For the peculiarity of the situation we have just discovered is to be explained by the peculiarity of the sign 'κ' and its equivalents in natural languages. When we say with Aristotle '$A\kappa B$', we think of 'κ' primarily as a copula introduced for application of predicates after these have been designated. Admittedly it has the grammatical form of an ordinary relational sign and can be used with some sort of sense between genuine designations of any kind. If, for example, it occurs in a sentence such as 'London κ Washington', we can read it explicitly as 'is *a predicate* true of' and say that the whole sentence expresses a false proposition. But in the use for which it is intended 'κ' always follows a sign which purports to designate a predicate, that is a sign of the form '$\S x[F(x)]$' or one which could in principle be replaced by something of that form, and this, as we have seen, implies that it can always be eliminated if the sign which it follows genuinely designates a predicate. Thus the thesis cited at the beginning of this paragraph can be restated more simply in the form

$$\S x(x \text{ is a predicate}) \text{ is a predicate,}$$

and in general every reflexive thesis expressible by use of 'κ' can be expressed also in a fashion in which its predicate can be seen clearly to be the same as its subject and, therefore, different from the predicate of any reflexive thesis with a different subject. From this, however, it follows that '$x\kappa x$' cannot properly be taken as the expression of a single predicate. Obviously it is a predicative phrase from which we can obtain an expression of a proposition by putting a genuine designation in each of the places marked by an occurrence of the variable 'x'. But this is not enough to justify saying that it expresses a predicate.

When Russell sent his famous letter to Frege, he formulated his paradox in terms of classes. The change was easy because

$$\hat{x}(x\epsilon x) \; \epsilon \; \hat{x}(x\epsilon x)$$

has the same sort of oddity as

$$\S x(x\kappa x) \; \kappa \; \S x(x\kappa x),$$

and Russell probably chose to dwell on the class version of his paradox because it was the only one he could present in Frege's symbolism as well as being that most likely to attract the attention of mathematicians working on the theory of sets. On receipt of the letter Frege jumped to the conclusion that there was no way of saving the system of his *Grundgesetze* from contradiction except by weakening Axiom V, in which he had assumed that for every propositional function, or predicate, there must be a corresponding class. From the beginning Russell had seen that the trouble could be found already in a theory of predicates if, unlike Frege's, it allowed for a distinction between the expression and the designation of them. But it seems that in his early discussion of the problem he did not take seriously enough the implications of his own suggestion that an apparently well-formed propositional phrase might fail to express a proposition through failure of its subject phrase to designate anything; and when he adopted his theory of descriptions, he finally blocked the way to a solution such as I have proposed. Perhaps, however, the fact that neither of them looked in the right place for a solution is to be explained primarily by their common belief that in a symbolism such as they had adopted every well-formed predicative phrase must express a predicate. Though Frege had no doubt of the need for a distinction between phrases and what they express, he thought that in drawing up the rules of his ideography he had excluded all those features of ordinary language which allow for construction of predicative phrases without corresponding predicates. The special interest of Russell's paradox is that it shows the falsity of this belief.

(5) Russell's adaptation of his paradox to talk of relations seems to raise no new issues. But the Nelson–Grelling paradox requires separate notice, because it can be presented with an explicit distinction between predicative phrases and what they are supposed to express. First, the phrase 'is heterological' is introduced with an explanation which makes it equivalent to 'does not satisfy the predicate it expresses' or, more explicitly, to 'does not satisfy the predicate of which all its tokens occurring in predicative position are specimens'. And then it is asked, with surprising results, whether or not the phrase 'is heterological' is heterological. If it is heterological, then apparently it is not; and if it is not, then apparently it is. But in the presentation of the paradox it has to

be assumed, without justification, that there is a predicate of which all the tokens of the phrase occurring in predicative position must be specimens; and this is not so. For whether or not a token of the phrase is a specimen of a predicate depends on the nature of the grammatical subject with which it is associated. Thus if I say 'London is heterological', the token of 'is heterological' which I then produce is not a specimen of any predicate, because my grammatical subject does not designate a phrase expressive of a predicate which it might or might not satisfy. And in our problem sentence, 'The phrase "is heterological" is heterological', although the grammatical subject does indeed designate a predicative phrase which can be used to express a predicate, the phrase is not one whose tokens occurring in predicative position are all specimens of the same predicate. Those who think that it always expresses a single predicate must assume this to be §x (x does not satisfy the predicate x expresses), for designation of which it is proper to use the device called identification of variables. But there is no such predicate. In order to see clearly why this is so, let us for a moment drop 'is heterological' and consider instead its positive contrary 'is autological', which has been introduced as an abbreviation for 'satisfies the predicate it expresses'.

Using '$\bar{x}$' as short for 'the predicate x expresses' and 'κ' with the sense of 'is satisfied by', which we gave to it in the last section, we can write '$\bar{x}\kappa x$' as an abbreviation for 'x is autological'. Then if we introduce 'A' as a designation for that same phrase, we can write '$A\kappa A$' as a simple rendering of 'The phrase "is autological" is autological'. And finally '$A\kappa A$' can be expanded when necessary to

$$\S x(\bar{x}\kappa x)\kappa A,$$

since 'A' and '$\S x(\bar{x}\kappa x)$' are just different designations for what A is supposed to express. When '§' and 'κ' occur, as here, in a combination covered by the reduction rule of the last section, it should be possible to eliminate them both. But application of that rule to the formula set out above yields only '$A\kappa A$'. It is clear therefore that 'κ' cannot be eliminated, and that there is no single predicate designated by '$\S x(\bar{x}\kappa x)$', that is to say, no predicate which has for specimens all the tokens of '$\bar{x}\kappa x$' or 'x is autological'. From this, however, it follows immediately that there is no predicate which has for specimens all the tokens of '$\sim(\bar{x}\kappa x)$' or 'x is heterological'. And with that conclusion the paradox of Nelson and Grelling is solved.

Corpus Christi College
University of Oxford

NOTES

1 See Kneale (1972).
2 For example, *Analytica Priora*, s. i, 4 (26^b7).

REFERENCES

Gödel, K., 'Russell's Mathematical Logic', in P. A. Schilpp, ed., *The Philosophy of Bertrand Russell* (Evanston, Northwestern University Press, 1944).
Kneale, W., 'Propositions and Truth in Natural Languages', *Mind*, n.s., vol. LXXXI (1972).
Ramsey, F. P., *The Foundations of Mathematics and Other Essays* (London, Routledge & Kegan Paul, 1931).
Russell, B., *The Principles of Mathematics* (Cambridge University Press, 1903).
Russell, B. and Whitehead, A. N., *Principia Mathematica*, vol. 1 (Cambridge University Press, 1910).

4

A DIAGNOSIS OF THE LIAR AND OTHER SEMANTICAL VICIOUS-CIRCLE PARADOXES[1]

Charles S. Chihara

> *The appearance of an antinomy is for me a symptom of disease.*
>
> Alfred Tarski

Bertrand Russell studied the vicious-circle paradoxes in order to gain insights into the nature of logic, mathematics and language. In this respect, his judgment was sound. His pioneering work has proved to be extremely fruitful, and his logical writings have stimulated an enormous amount of research. In this chapter I develop an idea put forward by Russell and Henri Poincaré that the paradoxes are due to viciously circular definitions.[2]

On page 65 of the June 1969 issue of *Scientific American*, one will find only one sentence printed in red, and this sentence says: 'The sentence printed in red on page 65 of the June 1969 issue of *Scientific American* is false.' Let us use the Greek letter 'α' as a name of this unusual sentence that appeared in *Scientific American*. By one form of the Law of Excluded Middle, either α is true or it is false. Assume that it is true. Then, since α, itself, is the very sentence said to be false, we can conclude that α is false. Thus, we have established by *reductio ad absurdum* that α is false. But if α is false, it follows that the sentence in red on page 65 of the June 1969 issue of *Scientific American* is not false; so we can infer that this sentence, namely, α itself, is true. Here, we have just one version of the Liar or the Epimenides paradox, which has perplexed philosophers and logicians alike for over 2,000 years.[3]

Since the above chain of reasoning is so simple, it may come as a surprise to some to learn that there is as yet no generally accepted solution to the paradox, despite the fact that some of the best minds in philosophy and logic have attempted to untangle the puzzle. Of course, there is not a tremendous pressure to find a solution: as in the case of most philosophical problems, the lack of a solution does not, in general, cause a tremendous amount of pain and anxiety. I say 'in general', since, according to Alfred Tarski, the Liar paradox 'tormented many ancient logicians and caused the premature death of at least one of them, Philetas of Cos'.[4] But for most people, the lack of a solution does not bring any sleepless nights, and many are convinced that such paradoxes are little more than illusions created by some logical sleight of hand. Indeed, some philosophers do not even find them puzzling.[5] However, a quite different attitude is expressed by Tarski when he writes:[6]

> I am not the least inclined to treat antinomies lightly. The appearance of an antinomy is for me a symptom of disease . . . an antinomy leads us to nonsense, a contradiction. Whenever this happens, we have to submit our ways of thinking to a thorough revision, to reject some premises in which we believed or to improve some forms of argument which we used.

Interest in the paradox was renewed in the late nineteenth and early twentieth century by the discovery of the famous set-theoretical antinomies of Cantor, Burali-Forti, and Russell, which shook the foundations of mathematics and stimulated so much research in logic. It was Bertrand Russell, more than anyone else, who focused the attention of the philosophical world on a whole cluster of paradoxes, which he called 'vicious-circle paradoxes'. These include, in addition to those already mentioned above, such paradoxes as the Richard, the Berry and the Grelling or Heterological. Russell, himself, spent a good many years attempting to solve these paradoxes, and he set forth the results of his researches on the subject in that classic work, which he wrote with Alfred North Whitehead, *Principia Mathematica*. However, few philosophers today accept Russell's solution, and the search continues.[7]

One explanation of the fact that the solutions to the paradoxes have been so elusive is that we are muddled about what we are looking for. It has been suggested by James Thomson, for example, that it is not clear what a solution is supposed to be.[8] I believe there is something to such charges. Part of the difficulty is due to the fact that there are two distinct, but related, problems to which the paradoxes give rise. Reverting to Tarski's medical analogy, we should distinguish the *diagnostic* from the *preventative* problem. We have an argument that begins with premises that appear to be self-evident, that proceeds according to rules of inference that appear to be valid, but ends in a contradiction. Evidently, something appears to be the case that isn't. And the diagnostic problem is to seek out that which is deceiving us and, if possible, explain why we have been deceived. The preventative problem, briefly put, is the problem of how to set up, with the least loss of expressive and deductive power, logical systems or, perhaps, languages, within which such paradoxes cannot arise. One reason talk about solutions gets confused is because there is a tendency to feel that what is in fact a solution to the preventative problem is also, in effect, a solution to the diagnostic problem.[9] For example, to one convinced that none of the paradoxes can be formulated in the language of *Principia Mathematica*, it is natural to think that the paradoxes are due to violations of the particular formation rules of *Principia Mathematica*, such as the ones restricting the types of variables that may appear in combinations, that determine what a sentence of the system is. The trouble with such a diagnosis is that there are many logical systems within which the paradoxes cannot arise, just as there are many ways of ensuring that the paradoxes cannot be stated. Tarski points out that one can prevent the Liar paradox from arising by eliminating the words 'true' and 'false', with all their synonyms, from the English vocabulary.[10] Of course, this would not be a very satisfactory solution to the preventative problem since the resulting loss of expressive power would be too high a price to pay. But in any case, it is easy to see that one ought not to assume that a unique solution to the preventative problem exists.

In this chapter, I shall not concern myself with the preventative problem at all; and I shall further restrict my investigations here to only one of the two main types of vicious-circle paradoxes, namely, the *semantical*, as opposed to the set-theoretical or mathematical paradoxes mentioned earlier.

The first paradox I shall take up is, strictly speaking, not a paradox at all; but it does have certain features that are to be found – at least under my analysis – in all the semantical paradoxes, and for this reason it is a useful pseudo-paradox to study. Imagine that we are given the following definition of the expression 'glub':

For every animal x,
(a1) x is a glub if, and only if, x is not a mouse,

and

(a2) x is a glub if, and only if, x is a mouse.

It does not take much perspicacity to see that this definition is defective.[11] Such definitions are meant to specify how a term is to be used; but what this definition tells us is inconsistent. Since Lassie is not a mouse but a dog, clause (a1) tells us that the term 'glub' is to be applied to her, whereas clause (a2) tells us that the term is not to be applied to her. Suppose, however, that for some strange reason we were blind to the defects of the above definition. The following argument might then be puzzling: Assume that Lassie is a glub. By (a1), it follows that Lassie is not a mouse. But if Lassie is not a mouse, we can conclude by (a2) that Lassie is not a glub. Thus, by *reductio ad absurdum,* we have shown that Lassie is not a glub. But by similar chain of reasoning, we can show that Lassie is a glub.

That one can engender a contradiction using the above definition is not at all surprising. Students of logic are well aware of the dangers of introducing contradictions by means of so-called 'creative definitions'.[12] What I wish to consider now is the possibility that the various semantical paradoxes involve the use of something like the above defective definition.

The first genuine paradox I wish to discuss requires that we imagine a situation in which many clubs and social organisations have hired secretaries but have established rigid rules excluding such secretaries from membership. One day these secretaries band together and form their own club, *Secretary Liberation* (or 'Sec Lib' for short), whose rules of eligibility state: 'A person is eligible to join Secretary Liberation if, and only if, he or she is a secretary of exactly one club or organisation and is not eligible to join that club or organisation.' The club flourishes, and soon many of them are meeting every day for lunch. A new club is formed, the Lunch Club, and the only condition that must be met to be eligible is that one be eligible to join the parent organisation, Sec Lib. All goes well until the Lunch Club hires itself a secretary, a certain Miss Fineline, who has the misfortune of being secretary of just one club. Naturally, she too wishes to join the Lunch Club, and at a general meeting she is able to put forward a strong case: 'I must be eligible to join,' she says, 'for if I were not, I would be a secretary of just one club and I would not be eligible to join that club, so by Sec Lib's rules I would be eligible to join Sec Lib, and hence by the Lunch Club's rules, I would be eligible to join the Lunch Club.' Unfortunately, Miss Fineline's hopes are immediately dashed by the president of the club who retorts: 'But if you are eligible to join our club, then you are eligible to join the club of which you are a secretary. It surely follows that you are not eligible to join Sec Lib; and no one is allowed to join our club who is not eligible to join Sec Lib.' Then, the whole meeting is thrown into disarray by the sergeant-at-arms who argues that since no person could be both eligible to join and not eligible to join at the same time, it follows that Miss Fineline cannot be a person. 'She must be an impostor!' he shouts, reducing poor Miss Fineline to tears.[13]

The logical nature of the Sec Lib paradox should be distinguished from that of the paradox of the barber who lives in a village, each inhabitant of which is shaved by this barber if, and only if, the inhabitant does not shave himself. The Barber paradox is not very paradoxical since it is evident that all the derivation of the contradiction shows is that there is no such barber.[14] In the case of the Sec Lib, one cannot argue that the contradiction shows that there is no such pair of clubs or that there is no such person as Miss Fineline, for it is obvious that there could very well be such clubs and people.

To facilitate analysing the Sec Lib puzzle, I suggest that we strip away some of the literary embellishments and try to get down to essentials. We have two clubs A and B with rules of eligibility that interlock. Imagine that A's rules say: 'Any person is eligible to join if he or she is not eligible to join B.' And imagine that B's rules say: 'Any person is eligible to join if he or she is eligible to join A.' Obviously, one can go through the usual *reductio* reasoning to arrive at a contradiction in this case also. So we get another paradox which, for obvious reasons, I shall call the 'simplified Sec Lib'.

The first point I should like to make concerning this paradox is that the above statements of rules of eligibility function very like definitions: they tell us what conditions must be met in order that someone be eligible to join club A, and hence they are thought to give us, indirectly, necessary and sufficient conditions for the truth of such sentences as 'Miss Fineline is eligible to join club A', and, like definitions, they are supposed to express what has been laid down by fiat. (I shall use the letter 'F' to refer to the sentence about Miss Fineline mentioned in the previous sentence.) If we follow Frege in speaking of sentences as having *sense*, where a sentence's sense is given by specifying its truth conditions, then it is clear that the above statements of eligibility conditions must be consulted in determining the sense of a sentence such as F. That these statements of eligibility rules are essential factors in determining the sense of such sentences, is evidenced by the fact that in generating the paradox, we must appeal to these eligibility rules to support the claim that, say, 'Miss Fineline is eligible to join club B' is a consequence of F. We consult the statements of eligibility conditions in determining whether one of these sorts of sentences is or is not a consequence of some other, just as we consult the statements of truth conditions of a formal language in determining whether one formal sentence is a consequence of another. To say that the eligibility rules function like definitions in specifying the sense of such sentences as F is not to deny that F has a certain significance regardless of what, if any, eligibility conditions have been laid down and hence regardless of whether or not it has any definite sense: even without a definite sense, F would still be a grammatical sentence possessing certain semantical properties.

Some readers may prefer to develop the above points in terms of the distinction between statements (or assertions) and sentences. For example, one might say that the eligibility rules must be consulted in determining what conditions, if any, have been laid down which are necessary and sufficient for the truth of a statement or assertion made in uttering the sentence F. Essentially everything I say in this chapter, my whole diagnosis of the paradoxes, can be expressed in terms of the statement–sentence distinction, if one prefers to do so. However, I shall continue to develop my diagnosis in terms of sentences rather than statements or assertions, primarily for the sake of brevity and simplicity, but also to avoid murky ontological problems.

The next point to notice is that the above statements of rules give us an inconsistent pair of definitions. This can easily be seen by comparing the above with the definition of 'glub': both are of the form:

x is K if, and only if, x is not G

and

x is K if, and only if, x is G.

The point can be made another way. Notice that A's eligibility conditions could have been stated in the terminology of set theory as follows:

The set of those eligible to join A is the complement of the set of those eligible to join B

(the universe of discourse being the set of all human beings). When B's eligibility conditions are also stated in terms of sets, we get:

The set of those eligible to join B is identical to the set of those eligible to join A.

Clearly, these 'definitions' contradict one another.

What then should we say about the *reductio* reasoning used in deriving the contradiction? Well, what should we say about the analogous piece of reasoning in the Glub paradox? The reasoning begins with the 'assumption' that Lassie is a glub. But what precisely is one assuming? One is assuming, it might be said, that Lassie satisfies the conditions for being a glub laid down by the definition. But that definition is inconsistent. So we have not yet said, in any consistent fashion, what it is to be a glub. Thus, the *reductio ad absurdum* is suspect from the start. We have a similar situation in the case of the simplified Sec Lib. Once it is seen that the two statements of eligibility conditions contradict one another, the argument becomes questionable. We are asked to assume that Miss Fineline is eligible to join A. But given the rules of eligibility of the two clubs, it is not clear what sense we can attach to such an 'assumption'.

To supplement these informal comments, let us analyse the reasoning of the paradox by expressing it in a first-order formal language, such as Mates's language £. We can interpret the language as follows:

A: ① is eligible to join club A
B: ① is eligible to join club B
f: Miss Fineline.

The argument seems to begin with the simple assumption 'Af', from which '$\sim Af$' is inferred. But upon reflection, we can see that 'Af' does not really do justice to the assumption of the informal argument. 'Af' is interpreted as 'saying': f belongs to the set of things that are A. But what set is the set of things that are A? And what set is the set of things that are B? Whatever sets they may be, they must satisfy the 'definitions' laid down by the eligibility rules, which in the formal language we would express:

$$(x) \; (Ax \leftrightarrow \sim Bx)$$

and

$$(x) \; (Bx \leftrightarrow Ax).$$

But this pair of formal sentences is unsatisfiable: there is no pair of sets that can be assigned as extensions of the predicate 'A' and 'B' so as to satisfy the above pair. So if we wish to capture in the formal argument the incoherence of the 'assumption' of the informal argument, it would be well to incorporate the inconsistent definition into the assumption. We would then have:

$$Af \; \& \; (x) \; (Ax \leftrightarrow \sim Bx) \; \& \; (x) \; (Bx \leftrightarrow Ax).$$

From this, we can indeed infer a contradiction, as we do in the informal argument. However, what we can legitimately infer from this contradiction by *reductio ad absurdum* is not '$\sim Af$' as we seem to do in the case of the informal argument, but rather the negation of the complex sentence displayed above. Actually, in the informal argument, we infer by *reductio* 'Miss Fineline is not eligible to join Club A'; but the conditions of eligibility are still regarded as determined by the two rules, as can be seen by the fact that we go on to infer from this conclusion that Miss Fineline is not eligible to join the club. So the conclusion we draw in the informal argument corresponds to

$$\sim Af \; \& \; (x) \; (Ax \leftrightarrow \sim Bx) \; \& \; (x) \; (Bx \leftrightarrow Ax).$$

Analysed in the above way, the informal argument can be regarded as invalid. One can also see that in the informal argument, the 'defining rules' are never questioned: they are taken to be 'true by fiat'. But the definitions are just the things that ought to be questioned. For the defining statements, being inconsistent with one another, could not both be true and, *a fortiori*, could not both be true by fiat. Thus, once it is seen that the two rules of eligibility form an inconsistent pair, the reasoning of the paradox breaks down – or, as I said before, never gets off the ground.

The paradox can be analysed in a slightly different way as involving two steps, the first of which purports to show that a contradiction is deducible from the 'definitions' and the second of which claims that since the definitions are true by fiat, we can conclude by *modus ponens* that p and $\sim p$ are both true. If the argument does proceed in this way, it is easy to see that the second step should be rejected. Whichever way we may analyse the paradox, it can be seen that the puzzle is partially due to our tendency not to question the truth (and hence the consistency) of definitions or stipulated rules.

But if the simplified Sec Lib paradox is essentially the same as the Glub, why does it seem more puzzling? The answer is because the essential factors are concealed in the one and not in the other. For example, it is obvious that the conditions that must be satisfied by Lassie to be a glub are to be determined by reference to the definition of 'glub', and the inconsistency of that definition strikes one immediately since one's attention is drawn to the conflicting clauses, (a1) and (a2). In the case of the Sec Lib, one can be misled by a number of confusing elements. For example, there is a tendency to regard each statement of eligibility conditions as only specifying the conditions that must be met to be able to join that one club. It is easy to overlook the fact that there is an undetermined factor in A's statement, namely, B's eligibility conditions, which requires that both A's and B's statements be taken into account in determining the conditions under which Miss Fineline is eligible to join A.

Another factor that tends to conceal from us the source of the paradox can be discerned by comparing the sentence 'Lassie is a glub' with F. No one is apt to assume that the former sentence is even meaningful; whereas it is quite natural to think that the latter has a definite sense, even if one has not seen any statement of A's eligibility conditions, for the phrase 'eligible to join' has a certain significance apart from any eligibility conditions that may be specified.

In the original version of the Sec Lib paradox, the essential elements are even more heavily disguised. For Sec Lib gives its eligibility conditions not in terms of those of a single club, but rather in terms of those of an indefinite totality of organisations, and this raises complications. Let us give a general analysis of the paradoxical situations to see more clearly what gives rise to these complications. Reviewing the simple case first, notice that we have a predicate P ('is eligible to join A') and a set of rules that supposedly specify the conditions under which a thing is P. Regarding these rules as straightforward statements, we can conclude that the set of rules is inconsistent. But the set of rules of the original Sec Lib requires a more complicated analysis since, in most situations, Sec Lib's rules function without difficulty, leaving no doubt as to whether or not a candidate is eligible. Hence, one may not think of raising questions of consistency at all. The idea that a general rule might be perfectly adequate in most situations and yet unintelligible or even inconsistent when applied to special cases may not be a familiar one to most people. Yet it is easy to construct such rules once the possibility enters one's mind. For example, suppose a country levies a special disaster tax one year because of an earthquake. The computation of this tax is to be done by a simple formula: take the number of dollars of taxable income, subtract the number of one's dependants, and compute the square root of that difference to the second place to the right of the decimal. Supposedly, this rule determines the amount each person is to pay. And for most citizens, there are no problems: this rule is perfectly sensible so long as one is dealing with a certain range of possibilities. Now suppose Mr

Jones had no taxable income that year but had one dependant. The rule says he is to pay $\sqrt{-1}$ dollars, which is nonsense. Sec Lib's rules are a bit like the above: it is only in special cases that what the rule says is inconsistent. We can analyse the rules by breaking up the 'argument range' of the predicate P into sub-ranges and determining what the rules say about the objects in each of the sub-ranges. We can then represent the rules according to the following schema:

For every object x that is G_1, Px if, and only if, ---
For every object x that is G_2, Px if, and only if, . . . etc.

Now it turns out that, in the case of the Sec Lib, the inconsistency appears only for those objects with a particular property, that is, not all the statements of eligibility conditions represented in the schema are inconsistent. Hence, in such cases, I shall say that the set of rules or definitions is *inconsistent over a subset of the argument range of P* (as opposed to being *everywhere inconsistent* as are the eligibility rules of the simplified Sec Lib).

We have seen that in each of the paradoxes examined thus far, certain key sentences of the form 'n is P' or 'n is not P' have been found to be semantically defective in a very special way: the set of rules (or definitions) specifying the conditions that must be satisfied for a thing to be P was analysed to be either everywhere inconsistent or inconsistent over a subset (to which n belongs) of the argument range of P. To mark this special sort of defectiveness, such sentences will be said to have *inconsistent senses*.

Some may feel that when the eligibility rules of a club X are inconsistent over a subset of its argument range, as are Sec Lib's, every sentence of the form 'a is eligible to join X' should be regarded as, in some sense, senseless. One might argue that if the rules are inconsistent over a subset, they are inconsistent and as a result should be rejected completely. This feeling should be counterbalanced by the conviction that the rules may enable one to decide the eligibility of all but a small number of possible cases, as the Sec Lib example brings out. A contradiction might never have emerged in that case, had not the Lunch Club hired itself a secretary who was not a secretary of any other organisation. It is only for those with 'very special properties' that the rules get entangled. As Wittgenstein once wrote: 'A signpost is in order – if, under normal circumstances, it fulfils its purpose'.

The unsimplified Sec Lib paradox raises one problem for me, however, that the simplified version did not. In the simple situation, it is obvious that the statements of eligibility conditions are inconsistent with one another: one can see the inconsistency straight off. In the more complicated situation, the inconsistency of the statements of eligibility conditions was inferred. This inference was based primarily on the following considerations. From a logical point of view, when we are given the fact that Miss Fineline is secretary of the Lunch Club and of no other organisation, the statements of eligibility in the unsimplified case function in essentially the same way as the corresponding statements of eligibility conditions in the simple case, as can be easily seen by analysing Sec Lib's rule according to the above schema, making sure that one of the sub-ranges is the set of those who are secretaries to just the Lunch Club. It is hard to see how the one set of eligibility statements could be consistent if the set of simpler statements is inconsistent. Indeed, once the strong similarities in the paradoxes are noted, the hypothesis that they should be diagnosed in completely different ways is highly implausible. Furthermore, if it is claimed that the contradiction was not derived from the rules using *valid* rules of inference, it would be reasonable to ask 'Which rule of inference used is not valid?' I cannot find any plausible answer to this question.

However, since these grounds may not appear to be sufficiently strong to warrant much confidence in my diagnosis of the unsimplified paradox, additional grounds will be given to support the position. I need to make it highly improbable that I am making an incorrect diagnosis. In particular, I wish to avoid the error of attributing to some definition the defects of something else, such as a rule of inference. Imagine, for example, that some people have, for some strange reason, accepted the following rule of inference (affirming the consequent):

(AC)   From $\ulcorner$ If p, then q $\urcorner$
        and q, infer p.

Suppose also that the following definition is given:

For every object x, x is a *flub* if, and only if, x is a two-headed dog.

It is established that Lassie is a dog with only one head, so we can regard the following as axioms:

(A1) Lassie is a dog.
(A2) Lassie is not two-headed.

Within this system, a contradiction can be derived:

(1) If Lassie is a flub, then Lassie is a dog.
                                    (Definition and simplification)
(2) Lassie is a dog.   ((A1))
(3) Lassie is a flub.   (From (1) and (2) using (AC))
(4) Lassie is not two-headed.   ((A2))
(5) Lassie is not a flub.   (From (4) and the definition)

The question is: What is producing this absurdity? Now if a definition is inconsistent, one can derive a contradiction using this definition and *correct* (or *valid*) rules of inference. And if a definition is inconsistent with (or contradicts) certain axioms, then one can derive a contradiction from the axioms using this definition and correct rules of inference. But suppose one does derive a contradiction using some definition. Can one conclude that it is the definition that is responsible? When dealing with paradoxes, one must consider the possibility that the rules of inference one uses are not valid. Thus, if I argued that the definition of 'flub' is the source of the above contradiction by deriving an absurdity both from the assumption that Lassie is a flub and also from the assumption that Lassie is not a flub (using, of course, the axioms and rule (AC)), I would be committing a serious blunder. How can this sort of mistake be precluded or at least made highly improbable? In the case of each paradox, I propose to apply two new tests which will serve to check my diagnosis. The first of these tests, the 'first-order test', will consist in 'translating' the relevant definitions and axioms (if any) into some standard first-order quantificational language, and then testing the set of formal sentences for satisfiability, using some well-studied and provenly acceptable methods, such as truth tables and trees. For example, applying this test to the example discussed above, we find that the definition of 'flub' translates into '(x) $(Fx \leftrightarrow (Gx \ \& \ Hx))$' and the axioms into '$Ga$' and '$\sim Ha$'. Since this trio of sentences can easily be shown to be satisfiable, there is a strong implication that the definition is not responsible for the contradiction derived. Applying the test to the definition of 'glub', however, yields a quite different result, for the formal sentence '(x) $(Fx \leftrightarrow \sim Gx) \ \& \ (Fx \leftrightarrow Gx))$' is clearly unsatisfiable and can be shown to be so by any number of methods. The first-order test also brings out clearly an important logical difference between the inconsistent definition of 'glub' and the following definition with which it has been confused. For every animal x, x is a *glup* if, and only if, x is a mouse and x is not a mouse. One might say with Frege that the concept *glup* is an inconsistent concept, but the definition of 'glup' is perfectly consistent, as the first-order test clearly shows. For the formal sentence '(x) $(Fx \leftrightarrow Gx \ \& \ \sim Gx)$' is satisfiable, unlike the one above.[15]

Any particular application of this test might be challenged. It might be argued, for example, that the definition under question was not adequately translated into the formal language, that is, it might be said that the formal sentence selected does not adequately express the definition. In such a case, the challenger would be expected to give grounds for his claim and indicate the respects in which the proposed translation is defective. A more drastic challenge would be to question the methods of first-order logic used to establish the unsatisfiability of the formal sentence. One can imagine some philosopher questioning even the truth-table method of determining unsatisfiability. I think it is safe to say, however, that such a radical challenge would not be taken very seriously by most philosophers and logicians unless some very good grounds were adduced in its support. For these methods have been extensively and intensively studied, and no good reasons have as yet been put forward for questioning them.

My second test, which I call the 'elimination test', requires us to determine whether the relevant definitions allow us to eliminate the defined terms from all the sentences occurring in the derivation of the paradox. If the terms can be so eliminated, then we would have strong evidence that the definitions are not at fault. If the terms cannot be eliminated, this would suggest that the definitions are playing some essential role.[16] Thus, applying this test to the 'flub' example, it can be seen that 'is a flub' can be replaced throughout the argument by the phrase 'is a two-headed dog', so we get the intuitively acceptable result that it is not the definition of 'flub' that is responsible for the paradox.

Neither of these new tests is absolutely decisive; but in many cases in which both tests confirm the primary diagnosis, we will have extremely strong reasons for accepting the analysis. Since the results of applying the tests to the unsimplified Sec Lib paradox agree with the diagnosis I gave above (the details of applying the tests will be left as an exercise for the reader), I conclude that the analysis is correct.[17]

The Heterological or Grelling paradox does not introduce any radically new ideas and is in some respects even easier for me to diagnose than the Sec Lib, since it contains an explicit definition to test for consistency. However, it will be discussed here in order to clarify my general approach to these paradoxes. Some predicates apply to themselves and others do not. The predicate 'consists of fewer than twenty English words' applies to itself, since 'consists of fewer than twenty English words' consists of fewer than twenty English words, whereas 'consists of more than twenty English words' does not apply to itself. A predicate consists of more than twenty English words if, and only if, 'consists of more than twenty English words' *applies to it*. A predicate that applies to itself is said to be *autological*, and one that does not is said to be *heterological*. The question arises: is the predicate 'is heterological' heterological? By the familiar *reductio* route, we can derive a contradiction.

Here again, all the tests point to the conclusion that it is the definitions in accordance with which we determine the truth conditions of the paradoxical sentences that are at fault. By an almost direct application of the definitions, we obtain the following statement of truth conditions: ' "is heterological" is heterological' is true if, and only if, it is not the case that 'is heterological' is heterological. What this suggests is that the above paradoxical sentence and its negative counterpart have inconsistent senses. Applying the first-order test is straightforward. However the term 'applies' may be defined, it is clear from the derivation of the paradox that one consequence of the definition would have to be: A predicate is heterological if, and only if, 'is heterological' applies to it. This consequence we can express formally: '$(x)\ (Hx \leftrightarrow Ahx)$'. The definition of 'heterological' can be symbolised: '(x) $(Hx \leftrightarrow \sim Axx)$'. Clearly, this pair of sentences is unsatisfiable. Notice that this analysis of the situation also indicates that the sentences corresponding to 'Hh' and '$\sim Hh$' have inconsistent senses. Further confirmation of the diagnosis is provided by the elimination test.

It is useful, at this point, to compare my diagnosis of this paradox with other well-known 'solutions'. In his paper 'On Some Paradoxes', J. Thompson writes:[18]

> It may be worth pointing out that all the 'solutions' of this paradox which are usually discussed come to the same thing. . . . The essential thing in each case is that the word 'heterological' is so explained that for it itself to be heterological it is necessary and sufficient that it both be not heterological and also satisfy some other condition. Then we seek to avoid the paradox by denying, with or without argument, that this further condition is satisfied.

Thomson then goes on to point out that these 'solutions' are generally felt to be unsatisfactory, partly because such declarations of what 'heterological' must mean have an air of dogmatism. It is easy to see how one can construct a version of the Grelling in which 'heterological' is so defined that Gilbert Ryle's analysis holds: we can imagine that there is some totality of philological properties (not including heterologicality and autologicality) in terms of which 'heterological' and 'autological' are defined, a word being heterological just in case there is a member of this totality for which that word stands and which does not belong to that word. Given such a definition, one can indeed argue that 'heterological' is not heterological, without running into paradox. Obviously if one construes the crucial definitions of a paradox in such a way that no contradiction is derivable, one will avoid the puzzle. But we should consider versions of the paradox that do not yield to such treatment. And we should consider the possibility that by analysing the definitions so as to avoid the contradiction, we change the nature of the paradox, substituting a less paradoxical situation for the original. Suppose that the people laying down the definitions leave us no room for construing their definitions in a non-paradoxical way. We can imagine that they give us a formal counterpart of the definitions of 'heterological':

$$(x) \; (Hx \leftrightarrow \sim Axx),$$

specifying explicitly that the predicate 'is heterological' belongs to the range of the bound variable 'x'. And if we ask what it means to say of a predicate P that it applies to an object y, they reply that P applies to y if and only if placing a name of y immediately before P results in a true sentence.

Now it may be said that these definitions are defective. Richard,

Poincaré and Russell noticed many years ago that such definitions are, in a sense, circular. After all, 'is heterological' has been defined in terms of the predicates that fall within the range of the bound variable 'x', and to that extent it has been defined in terms of itself. However, a definition can be defective in more ways than one. And it is a significant fact about these definitions that they form an inconsistent set. Having seen this, the logical mechanism of the paradox is much easier to discern. One is no longer puzzled by the fact that a contradictory pair of sentences can be inferred from these definitions. And so long as one does not assume that these definitions must be true, there should be no temptation to conclude (by *modus ponens*) that the contradictory pair of sentences are both true.

Actually, Thomson himself gives an analysis of the Grelling which is similar in certain respects to Ryle's. After presenting an analysis under which a predicate is taken to be a special kind of function, he suggests that the simplest way out of the difficulty is to say that the 'function' 'x is heterological' is not defined for itself as an argument. He then claims that 'if "heterological" is not within its own domain of definition, there is no paradox'. Evidently, he believes that by this device he can justify his claim that 'we have given no sense to saying "heterological" is heterological'.[19]

Despite the obvious similarities between Thomson's analysis and mine, there are important differences. Imagine that the following have been put forward as definitions of number-theoretic functions:

$$f_1(n) = \begin{cases} n + 1 \text{ if, and only if, } n < 5 \\ n - 1 \text{ if, and only if, } n > 5 \end{cases}$$

$$f_2(n) = \begin{cases} n + 1 \text{ if, and only if, } n \leqslant 5 \\ n - 1 \text{ if, and only if, } n \geqslant 5 \end{cases}$$

The first simply defines a partial function: f_1 is undefined for the argument 5. The second does not define a partial function: for one argument, it gives us inconsistent directions; more specifically, for argument 5, the definition tells us that the value of f_2 is 6 (and no other number) and also that it is 4 (and no other number). Now one significant difference between Thomson's analysis and mine comes to this: Thomson regards the definition of 'heterological' as specifying a kind of partial function, i.e. about certain predicates the definition is supposed to say nothing; whereas I regard the key definitions as being closer to that of 'f_2'. Roughly speaking, on my view, those definitions are not silent regarding the truth conditions of the paradoxical sentences: on the contrary, they say too much, for what they say is simply inconsistent.[20] However, it must be admitted that the two analyses are in agreement on one point:

they both attribute a semantical defect to the crucial sentences. The differences in analysis may not seem important here, but they will become crucial later.

The disagreement between Thomson and me described above should not be judged by the criterion of correspondence with English usage. From the point of view of diagnosing the paradoxes, it does not matter which of the two gives a better analysis of the definition of 'heterological' regarded as an English sentence. Obviously, we could have defined 'heterological' using variables and quantifiers so as to leave no doubt that 'heterological' belongs to its own argument range. The important question is: which of the two analyses gives us a better insight into the paradoxes? It is relevant to mention in this regard that the Thomson analysis is not at all convincing when it is applied to some of the paradoxes discussed in this chapter. Furthermore, it has a kind of incompleteness that is unsatisfying. To see this, let us characterise it by means of a simple diagram. Draw a circle. This represents the argument range of the predicate 'is heterological'. Draw a line through the circle and shade one of the resulting areas. The shaded area represents that part of the range to which 'is heterological' applies. Thomson attempts to deal with the paradox by putting 'is heterological' completely outside the circle. But notice: since 'is heterological' lies outside the circle, it also lies outside the shaded area. Does it not follow that 'is heterological' does not apply to itself? And if so, can we not infer, using the definition, that 'is heterological' is heterological after all? Surely, something more needs to be explained.

Since the Grelling is so similar to the Sec Lib, I see no need to discuss in more detail my diagnosis of this paradox. So I shall turn instead to more troublesome ones. The Berry paradox is a simplified version of its more famous cousin, the Richard. The latter, I believe, has seemed more disturbing to many, especially mathematicians, because the form of argument used is so similar to standard proofs of Cantor's theorem that the set of real numbers is non-denumerable. But under analysis, it can be seen that the Richard is just a more complicated version of the Berry.[21]

The Berry begins with a rule which gives the conditions under which *phrase e definitely describes a natural number n* (to abbreviate what appears in italics, I shall write '*eDn*'). Form the sentence σ from the schema

$$(*)\ eDn\ \text{if, and only if, } N = E$$

by replacing 'N' with the Arabic numeral denoting n and 'E' with a token of the same type as e. Then σ gives necessary and sufficient conditions under which e definitely describes n. It follows that the phrase 'the successor of three' definitely describes four and 'the first prime number' definitely describes two. Now consider the phrase 'the least natural number not definitely described by any phrase consisting of fewer than twenty English words'. Let us use the Greek letter 'α' to denote this phrase. Since there are only finitely many phrases consisting of fewer than twenty English words, there must be infinitely many natural numbers not definitely described by a phrase consisting of fewer than twenty English words. Hence, the set S of natural numbers not definitely described by any phrase consisting of fewer than twenty English words must be non-empty. By a well-known law of number theory, it follows that S has a least element, say m. Thus, $m =$ the least natural number not definitely described by any phrase consisting of fewer than twenty English words. Using (*), we see that αDm. But α is a phrase consisting of fewer than twenty English words. So by the definition of 'm', it follows that $\sim \alpha Dm$.

What is wrong with this reasoning? Here again, it will be useful to examine a simplified version of the paradox. Let β be the (token) phrase of the same type as 'the least natural number not definitely described by the phrase on my blackboard right now', which happens to be the only phrase on my blackboard right now. Since there are infinitely many natural numbers not definitely described by β, it seems safe to conclude that the set of natural numbers not definitely described by the phrase on the blackboard is non-empty. Hence this set must have a least element, the name of which shall be the Greek letter 'γ'. It follows that β definitely describes γ. But clearly if β definitely describes γ, then γ cannot be a member of the set of natural numbers not definitely described by β. So, by essentially the same line of reasoning as was used in the Berry paradox, we arrive at a contradiction.

Keeping in mind the previously diagnosed paradoxes, it is natural to suspect that there may be something wrong with the definition of some key term. The definition of 'definitely describe' is an obvious one to investigate, since it has certain similarities to both the specification of Sec Lib's eligibility conditions and the definition of 'heterological'. Applying this definition, we obtain:

β definitely describes zero if, and only if, β does not definitely describe zero and zero is the least natural number not so described.

Is this statement consistent? Not within a system accepting a very elementary property of zero, namely that zero is the least natural number. For we can infer from the above statement of truth conditions both that the sentence is true and (assuming that we are given the elementary property of zero) that it is not true.

To confirm the tentative diagnosis arrived at above, we can apply the two diagnostic tests developed earlier. Making the first-order test should present no difficulties so long as it is noted that the rule in question gives us definite description conditions by means of a schema. Essentially, we have infinitely many 'axioms' only one of which is relevant here, namely, the one that we can express by means of the formal sentence

$$Dbo \leftrightarrow (\sim Dbo \ \& \ (x) \ (\sim Dbx \rightarrow Lox) \ ),$$

where 'b' and 'o' are the names in the formal language of β and zero respectively, and 'L' is interpreted as the *less than or equal to* relation. All that we need from number theory is the theorem that zero is less than or equal to every natural number, which we can express by means of '$(x)L0x$'. Since these formal sentences form an unsatisfiable pair, we get a confirmation of the diagnosis. It can also be seen without much difficulty that the elimination test yields a confirmation.

But now we can see clearly that the reasoning used in producing the above paradox has an unstated but highly questionable assumption: it is assumed that there is a set of natural numbers not definitely described by β. I would agree that if such a set existed, it would have to have a least element; but the above analysis suggests that there is no such set (some mathematicians might prefer to say that the set is not 'well-defined'). For if the sentence 'β definitely describes zero' has not been given a consistent sense, as my diagnosis implies, then clearly the negative sentence 'β does not definitely describe zero' has not been given a consistent sense either. So we should not expect there to be a set of natural numbers not definitely described by β.

Since my analyses of the (unsimplified) Berry and the Richard are so similar to the above, I see no need for further discussion of these paradoxes. I shall turn instead to the oldest and the most difficult of all these paradoxes: the Liar. Let us first take up the Jourdain version which concerns a card, one side of which has printed on it:

The sentence on the other side of this card is false,

and the other side of which has printed on it:

The sentence on the other side of this card is true.

Let ϕ and φ be the two sentences printed on the card, ϕ being the sentence mentioned first. As in the other paradoxes, one can produce *reductio* arguments which apparently show that ϕ is true and also that ϕ is false.[22]

It has been known for a long time, however, that the derivation of the contradiction makes use of an unstated assumption that is questionable: it is assumed that the Liar sentences are either true or false. Since a contradiction can be derived from this assumption, one can argue that the paradox provides us with a *reductio ad absurdum* of this assumption. It is not surprising, then, that a great many solutions to the Liar have been proposed that involve rejecting the assumption that the Liar sentences are either true or false.

Unfortunately, the paradox cannot be resolved so easily. For new 'strengthened' versions of the paradox have been devised which reintroduce the basic puzzle. Consider the following version. Suppose we print on side A of a card the sentence:

The sentence on side B of this card is not true,

and print on side B:

The sentence on side A of this card is true.

Let eta be the name of the sentence on side A and theta be the name of the sentence on side B. Now if it is said that θ is neither true nor false, as is suggested above, it would seem that we can conclude that θ is not true. But since η says that θ is not true, we can conclude that η is true. But if η is true, surely so is θ. So we are landed again in contradiction.

It has been suggested by William Kneale that the Liar paradox arises out of the mistaken belief that truth and falsity can be attributed to sentences, and hence can be solved when we notice that, strictly speaking, truth and falsity can only be ascribed to 'propositions considered under various special descriptions such as "statement", "premiss", "conclusion", ...'[23] This suggestion seems to be mistaken. I do not wish to deny that the derivation of the above contradiction can be blocked by maintaining that sentences are neither true nor false. But such a move can hardly be called a 'solution' to the paradox. The reason is: no matter what one takes to be the 'carriers of truth values', sentence tokens, sentence types, statements, assertions, speech acts or propositions, one can still formulate essentially the same paradox. For example, we can construct the Liar using Kneale's terminology as follows. Suppose I write on side A 'In writing the sentence on side B, Jones did not construct a specimen of a true proposition', while Jones writes on side B 'In writing the sentence on side A, Chihara constructed a specimen of a true proposition'. It is this version of the Liar that Kneale must 'solve' if he is to convince many philosophers that 'the paradox of the Liar holds no terrors for those who realise how the notion of truth is related to that of a proposition'.[24]

Notice that strengthened versions of paradoxes other than the Liar can also be constructed. Consider, for example, this version of the simplified Sec Lib, according to which club A alters its rules of eligibility to read:

A person x is eligible to join A if, and only if, the sentence consisting of the legal name of x followed by the sequence of words 'is eligible to join A' is not true.

For this case, too, we seem to find ourselves in a contradiction if we maintain that the sentence 'Mary Sue Fineline is eligible to join A' is without definite sense ('Mary Sue Fineline' being the legal name of Miss Fineline).

At this point let us review the diagnoses already given. In each of the previously analysed paradoxes, there was a predicate P and a rule or definition that supposedly gave the conditions under which P applies to some object. In the Sec Lib, there were rules stating *eligibility conditions*; in the Grelling, a definition provided *satisfaction conditions*; and in the Berry, a rule gave the *definite description conditions*. This suggests that, in the case of the Liar too, there is some set of rules or definitions that determine the *truth conditions* of sentences of the relevant sort. Furthermore, since in each of the previous cases, the key set of 'definitions' was found to be inconsistent over a subset of the argument range, we should expect the set of 'definitions' for which we are looking to have that feature too. It is possible, of course, that we can be led astray by projecting from the other paradoxes, but surely it is reasonable to proceed on the assumption that the Liar does not essentially differ from the others. Besides, such an assumption would give us an easy explanation of the plausibility of the derivation of the Liar contradiction – an advantage not to be relinquished without good reason.

The investigation has now led to a search for a 'very creative' definition or at least something that functions like such a definition. But unlike the previously analysed paradoxes, the Liar does not immediately present us with any obvious candidates.[25] There is a clue, however: the key sentences are of the form 'S is true' and 'S is not true', so what is needed is some sort of definition or semantical rule of the language that determines the truth conditions of sentences of these forms. Are there any obvious candidates? Let us consider a simple example to awaken our intuitions. Suppose John utters the sentence, 'The sentence on the board is true', pointing to the blackboard in my office. And suppose there is only one sentence on the board. Clearly, the sentence uttered by John is true if, and only if, the sentence on the board is true. This statement of truth conditions can be arrived at by a direct application of the following rule:

(R) If δ is a sentence of the form 'S is true', where S is a referring expression used to denote the sentence ζ, then ζ is true if, and only if, δ is true. If δ is of the form 'S is not true', where S is a referring expression used to denote the sentence ζ, then δ is true if, and only if, ζ is not true.

In applying this rule to a concrete situation, one would have to abstract from the situation the following relevant features: the syntactical type of the sentence uttered or produced in some way, the referring expression of the sentence and the reference of the referring expression. Others may wish to formulate the sort of rule I have in mind in terms of a sentence type, a speaker and a time, along the lines suggested by Donald Davidson,[26] or perhaps in even more complicated terms involving speaker intentions and rules about speech acts. It can be seen that the essential features of this rule do not depend on taking any specific sort of entity as the 'carriers of truth values' and that the central idea can be reformulated to accommodate any of the well-known candidates. The rule can be regarded as a sort of 'truth condition' rule analogous to the eligibility rules of the Sec Lib, the satisfaction rule of the Grelling, and the definite description rule of the Berry: it gives the conditions under which the predicate 'is true' applies to certain types of sentences. And like the previously discussed rules or definitions, rule (R) seems close to being either definitional or at least directly connected with the definition or meaning of the relevant predicate. In particular, given that δ 'says' that ζ is true and ζ 'says' that δ is not true, rule (R) does little more than draw out the consequences of the correspondence notion of truth discussed by Tarski in his celebrated papers on truth, namely, the idea that *a sentence is true if, and only if, what it says to be the case is in fact the case.*

Notice that it allows us, in many situations, to 'reduce' the truth conditions of 'atomic' sentences containing the word 'true' to those of a sentence not containing that word. For example, if the sentence on my board is 'It rained in Berkeley on 1 June 1972', then rule (R) tells us that the sentence uttered by John is true if, and only if, 'It rained in Berkeley on 1 June 1972' is true. Thus, rule (R) is in one respect like the rule of disjunction:

$$\ulcorner S \text{ or } T \urcorner \text{ is true if, and only if, } S \text{ is true or } T \text{ is true,}$$

which allows us to 'reduce' the truth conditions of sentences containing the word 'or' to those of sentences not containing that word. However, unlike the case of the rule of disjunction, we are not guaranteed that repeated applications of rule (R) will eventually give us truth conditions in terms of sentences not containing the word in question. It is clear, in the case of the Liar sentences, that (R) does not give us the sort of 'reduction' given above.

Now my analysis of the Liar parallels the analysis already given of the simplified Sec Lib. Recall that B's eligibility rules tell us that a person is eligible to join B just in case he (or she) is eligible to join A. B's eligibility conditions are thus defined to be essentially the same as A's and are, one might say, parasitic upon A's. So to determine, more specifically, just what those conditions are, we must turn to A's eligibility rules. However, when we do, we find that A's rules are parasitic upon B's and furthermore tell us that the conditions under which a person is eligible to join A are incompatible with those under which a person is eligible to join B. Hence, we get the inconsistency of sense of such sentences as 'Miss Fineline is eligible to join A'. Now we find a similar situation in the case of the Liar. Consider, first, the sentence θ. It 'says' that η is true. Hence, it will be true under just those conditions under which η is true, that is, the conditions under which θ is true should be essentially the same as, and parasitic upon, those under which η is true. (Notice that this is what rule (R) tells us.) So to determine, more specifically, just what those conditions are, we need to look at η. But since η 'says' that θ is not true, the conditions under which η is true are just those under which θ is not true (which is what rule (R) tells us also). So, from the intuitive point of view, it is natural to conclude that both θ and η lack definite sense.

Let us now supplement this intuitive analysis by proceeding more directly in terms of rule (R). Since (R) seems to be one of the semantical rules in accordance with which the truth conditions of the relevant sentences are determined, let us consider the possibility that it is the 'creative definition' we are looking for. Applying this postulated semantical rule to the sentences of the strengthened Liar paradox, we obtain the statements:

(b1) η is true if, and only if, θ is not true

and

(b2) η is true if, and only if, θ is true.

Since these statements are inconsistent with one another, we can conclude that a direct application of the rule gives us a contradiction. So it is tempting to adopt the sort of position taken in all the preceding cases. Just as we had, in the case of the Sec Lib paradox, eligibility rules which, when applied to a certain person, produced an inconsistent pair of statements of eligibility conditions, we have in this case a 'truth condition rule' which, when applied to certain sentences, produces an inconsistent pair of statements of truth conditions. What I am suggesting is that we do not respond to (b1) and (b2) by concluding that we must have misapplied the rules or made some sort of logical mistake in arriving at these statements of truth conditions, but rather take (b1) and (b2) to be accurate reflections of the senses given to η and θ by the language and conclude as a consequence that these sentences have inconsistent senses.

But now we must test this diagnosis in the two ways described earlier. To apply the first-order test, we must express the postulated semantical rule within some standard formal language, says Mates's £. This can be done as follows. Let the universe of discourse be the set of sentences occurring or mentioned in this chapter. Interpret the unary predicate 'T' to hold of all those sentences that are true. Let 'G' be interpreted to hold of ordered pairs of sentences $\langle x,y \rangle$ just in case x is a sentence of the form 'S is true' and its referring expression (corresponding to 'S') denotes y. And let 'H' be interpreted to hold of $\langle x,y \rangle$ just in case x is a sentence of the form 'S is not true' and its referring expression denotes y. We need to specify individual constants to function as names of the sentences η and θ, respectively. Let us use 'a' and 'b' for this purpose. Then 'Hab' and 'Gba' express the given relationships that hold between η and θ. Rule (R) corresponds to:

$$(x)(y)\,[Gxy \leftrightarrow (Tx \leftrightarrow Ty)] \;\&\; (x)(y)\,[Hxy \leftrightarrow (Tx \leftrightarrow \sim Ty)].$$

Since the set consisting of the above three formal sentences is unsatisfiable, the first-order test confirms the diagnosis given above.

This analysis by way of formal logic points to an interesting fact: the only semantical information, apart from mere reference, needed to generate a contradiction is rule (R). To establish the truth of '*Hab*' and '*Gba*', we needed only syntactical information and the fact that certain referring expressions were used to denote certain sentences. Hence, so long as the truth conditions of sentences of the form '*S* is true' and '*S* is not true' are determined in accordance with rule (R), the Liar sentences will end up with inconsistent senses.

The elimination test provides us with additional confirmation of the diagnosis. It hardly needs mentioning that (R) does not allow us to eliminate 'true' and 'not true' from the sentences used in deriving the contradiction. All in all, we have strong reasons for analysing the paradoxical Liar sentences in the way the other paradoxical sentences were analysed.

We can now see how closely the Liar parallels the other paradoxes. But there is one logical feature of the Liar that presents me with fresh difficulties. According to my diagnosis, the key sentences have inconsistent senses. Now I am strongly inclined to say that such sentences cannot be true. For how can a true sentence have an inconsistent sense? If this intuition is correct, we can infer from the analysis given above that η is not true. But this inference puts us right back into the puzzle. For if η is not true, does it now follow that θ is true after all (cf. *ante* the discussion of Thomson's solution)?

Let us reconsider the glub example. Notice that since Lassie is not a mouse, it seems to follow by (a1) that Lassie is a glub. But is it legitimate to conclude that the sentence 'Lassie is a glub' is true? Surely not: the definition of 'glub' gives 'Lassie is a glub' its inconsistent sense, and the inconsistency of this definition is not affected by the fact that one limb of the definition, namely (a1), gives conditions for being a glub that are satisfied. Similarly, turning to the strengthened version of the simplified Sec Lib, the fact that club A's rules give conditions for eligibility that are satisfied by Miss Fineline does not affect the fact that the sentence 'Mary Sue Fineline is eligible to join A' has an inconsistent sense. For this reason, we cannot infer that the sentence is true. By parity of reasoning, the inference to the truth of θ cannot be made either. In effect, we have a sort of over-ride rule that says: Regarding those elements in the subsets of the argument range over which the rules are inconsistent, pay no attention to what the rules say about them, since it cannot be true anyway.

The position at which I have now arrived has one consequence that, initially at least, is paradoxical. Evidently, when I wrote θ, what I wrote has inconsistent sense. But if I now write, say on another card, a sentence token, θ', of the very same type as θ, I succeed in saying something true. How can that be? There is, of course, nothing paradoxical about the claim that two sentence tokens of the same syntactical type can differ in truth values. We are all aware of the fact that the sentence token 'It is now raining' which I utter in Cambridge may differ in truth value from the token of the same type I utter later in Berkeley. And it is easy to see that the difference in time and place of utterance accounts for the difference in truth value. The case of θ and θ' seem to be quite different, since it is hard to find any difference of reference in the two sentences.

It should be stressed at this point that what must be understood is how the one sentence can be true when the other has an inconsistent sense. Now it is easy to see how the inconsistency of sense of θ comes about by means of a kind of (indirect) self-reference. Notice that θ enters into a peculiar referring relationship with η from which θ' stands aloof. This can be seen more easily by means of a simple diagram:

$$\theta \rightleftarrows \eta \qquad \theta' \rightarrow (\eta \rightleftarrows \theta).$$

So it is not hard to see how the one can have peculiar semantical properties that the other lacks.[27]

I cannot logically *prove*, of course, that all these diagnoses are correct, but this should not bother anyone since it is unreasonable to expect such a proof. However, I can provide some evidence for accepting them. It is important that supporting evidence be presented here because many so-called 'solutions' to these paradoxes have been advanced and one wants some reason for choosing one over its competitors. Actually, a real difficulty encountered by anyone working on these paradoxes is knowing when one has hit upon the right diagnosis.

I think it will be allowed by everyone that a good diagnosis should not merely provide us with a way of avoiding the contradictions. Obviously, one can block the derivation of a contradiction by rejecting some logical law or rule of inference, or by claiming that some sentence is not a well-formed sentence. But one wants some good reason for accepting one of these alternatives other than the fact that by doing so one can avoid the contradictions. Although this minimum condition of adequacy may seem obvious once it is stated, it is surprising how many proposed 'solutions' fail to meet it. For example, Frederic Fitch has advanced a 'solution' to the Liar which consists in maintaining that the Liar sentences are not well-formed sentences. But the only reason he gives for adopting such a remarkable position is the fact that by doing so one can then maintain that 'there is no resulting well-formed sentence to cause trouble'.[28] It is clear that one should not argue 'This must be what is going wrong in the paradoxes, since otherwise one could derive a contradiction'. Practically any diagnosis can be defended in that way. What one wants from a diagnosis is an insight into the logical mechanism of the paradoxes: one wants a theory, plausible on its own and not *ad hoc*, which shows us both what gives rise to the contradiction and what particular assumptions of the paradoxes should be rejected. My own analysis, I submit, does provide the sort of diagnosis we are looking for.

Consider, for example, my analysis of the Sec Lib which, like Fitch's 'solution', questions some specific premiss or presupposition of the derivation of the paradox. I reject the belief that the statements of the eligibility rules of Sec Lib and the Lunch Club express truths. However, unlike Fitch, I gave reasons for accepting the analysis in addition to showing how one can thus avoid being committed to the conclusion of the paradox. I gave independent reasons for thinking that the statement of the eligibility rules were inconsistent over a subset of the relevant argument range. Furthermore, my analysis provided us with a simple explanation of why the paradox is puzzling and why the solution to the diagnostic problem is so easily overlooked. As I pointed out earlier, the inconsistency is disguised in various ways. Besides, there is a tendency not to question the truth of a club's own statement of eligibility rules, since these are generally thought to be true by fiat.

Closely connected with the above criterion of adequacy is another that should be met. A diagnosis supposedly shows one, in a general way, what gives rise to the paradoxes. We should be able to test diagnoses, then, by seeing if paradoxes result when we reproduce the conditions that, according to the diagnosis, engender the paradoxes. To clarify this point, let us again turn to a medical analogy. One convincing way of testing the claim that a particular virus causes cancer is to isolate the virus, apply the virus to appropriate test organisms, and then see if the disease is produced. One should test proposed solutions to the paradoxes in a similar manner. Take, for example, the claim that the paradoxes arise from self-reference.[29] Now there are many sentences involving self-reference that have never been shown to generate contradictions (e.g. 'This sentence consists of more than one English word'); so this diagnosis does not pass the test under consideration.[30] I do not deny that self-reference and, as in the case of the Sec Lib and the Jourdain version of the Liar, mutual reference play significant roles in producing the paradoxes. As I see it, self-reference and mutual reference are part of the 'mechanism' by which sentences with inconsistent senses are produced, which is not to say that all self-reference and all mutual reference are nonsensical or illegitimate.

By the above two criteria, the diagnosis I have produced fares much better. It is easy to see both how and why contradictions can be derived using sentences with inconsistent senses. Indeed, once one sees how these semantical paradoxes are produced, it is quite easy to construct new ones. Permit me to do so as an illustration of how easy it is. To disguise the fact that definitions (or things that function as definitions) are giving inconsistent senses to some sentences, let us devise a situation in which we get the effect of a definition by the mere uttering of words. Thus, imagine a game that requires each player to choose an area of the globe to be 'his area', subsequent play depending on whether certain cities fall within a participant's chosen area. My choosing an area, then, in effect, determines the senses of sentences of the form 'City x is in my area'. To produce a paradoxical situation, we need only suppose that the choices produce a set of 'definitions' that is either logically inconsistent or inconsistent with certain facts of geography. Obviously, there are countless ways in which this can be done. One might frame the 'definitions' on the pattern of some inconsistent set of sentences of a formal language selected from an elementary logic text. And one might express the 'definitions' in the terminology of set theory. Thus, we can have Mr Smith say: 'My area is to be England if the intersection of England with Jones's area is empty; otherwise, my area is to be Canada.' When Mr Jones says 'My area is to be the union of Cuba with Smith's area', we get the usual paradoxical situation.

Another reason for preferring one diagnosis over others is its power to unify under a single explanation, with a minimum number of special assumptions, a whole range of data. Part of the strength of my diagnosis lies in the fact that all the versions of the paradoxes are handled in essentially the same way. The diagnosis makes clear what is common to all these paradoxes – in fact, what is essential to them all. One can see why there can be both referential and non-referential forms and why these different forms are not essentially different. Even the various strengthened versions of the paradoxes are handled in the way the others are.

We can also evaluate competing solutions by means of the criterion of *theoretical conservatism*, which Willard Quine has mentioned so often. In general, when faced with data that seem to conflict with established views, we look for a resolution that disrupts our basic theories as little as possible. The rationale behind this criterion is essentially this: if a solution to the diagnostic problem requires rejection of some well-established theory (or law), then the reasons we already have for accepting the theory (or law) are reasons for rejecting the solution. The criterion of theoretical conservatism reflects the fact that science is basically conservative: we prefer explanations that require the least amount of theoretical revision. Thus, L. E. J. Brouwer's diagnosis of the paradoxes, according to which the contradictions are due to the use of classical logic in mathematics, is not at all conservative.[31] For it implies that all our scientific theories that presuppose the validity of classical mathematics should be abandoned or at least drastically revised. Russell's analysis of the paradoxes is also not conservative: it requires a complete revision of logical theory and the development of a whole new system of mathematics. My own diagnosis, however, is on the whole quite conservative, as can be easily verified.[32]

I wish now to consider the widespread, commonsensical conviction that whatever may be the true diagnosis of the paradoxes, the contradictions derived do not undermine the theorising of scientists working on, say, the Apollo programme or the mode of operation of juvenile hormone in *Drosophila* imaginal discs. Now at first sight, it might appear that my diagnosis conflicts with this view, for if there are sentences of

English with inconsistent senses, this may suggest to some that all reasoning carried out in the language should be suspect – a suggestion that will not appear implausible to those influenced by Tarski into thinking that all scientific reasoning should be carried out in formal languages. Is this unpleasant state of affairs a genuine consequence of my diagnosis? I think not. On my view, only certain sentences have inconsistent senses, and so long as these paradoxical sentences do not enter into one's reasoning as meaningful steps, there is nothing in my analysis to suggest that they can lead to error. Neither θ nor any of the other paradoxical sentences we have discussed occur in the usual informal proofs of the binomial theorem. I see no reason to suppose that the paradoxes make such proofs suspect. So also the existence of these paradoxes does not cast doubt on the long chains of deductions carried out in the course of planning the flight of a moon rocket. If, as Tarski says, the appearance of a paradox is a symptom of disease, my diagnosis of the disease is encouraging: no radical surgery is required; and with care, no serious malfunctions should occur.

Department of Philosophy
University of California at Berkeley

NOTES

1   Research for this chapter was supported in part by a grant from the University of California Humanities Institute. An early version was read at the 7 February 1973 meeting of the Cambridge University Moral Science Club. Later versions were read at the University of Kent and the University of Warwick. I am grateful to those who participated in the discussions for useful criticisms (see n. 15). I am also grateful to Bob Ray, Jerry Fodor, Timothy Smiley and Robert Martin, for helpful discussions on the paradoxes.
2   The solutions to the paradoxes advanced by Russell and also by Poincaré are discussed in detail in my *Ontology and the Vicious-Circle Principle* (Ithaca and London, Cornell University Press, 1973: chs 1 and 4).
3   This particular version of the Liar is to be found in Alfred Tarski, 'Truth and Proof', *Scientific American*, vol. CCXX, no. 6 (June 1969) and is due to Jan Lukasiewicz. The reader can find an amusing account of this paradox in Alan Anderson, 'St Paul's Epistle to Titus', in Robert L. Martin, ed., *The Paradox of the Liar* (New Haven, Yale University Press, 1970); hereafter, Martin's book will be *PL*.
4   Tarski (op. cit.: 66).
5   J. F. Thomson claims, for example, that there is no reason why the paradoxes should be found puzzling. According to Thomson, it is easy to see that the relevant arguments are indeed valid and 'in each case it is easy to see what conclusions we should draw about the relevant subject matter'. (See 'On Some Paradoxes', in R. J. Butler, ed., *Analytic Philosophy* (Oxford, Basil Blackwell, 1962: 119). The claim that it is easy to see what conclusions we should draw about the relevant subject matter is implausible, as a glance at the enormous literature on the topic will show. Furthermore, as I shall argue in this paper, Thomson himself did not always draw the correct conclusions about the paradoxes. For a critical discussion of Thomson's paper, see J. L. Mackie, *Truth, Probability and Paradox* (Oxford University Press, 1973: ch 6, sect. 4).

6   Tarski (op. cit.: 66).
7   For a detailed exposition and criticism of Russell's proposed solution to the paradoxes, see my *Ontology and the Vicious-Circle Principle* (Ithaca and London, Cornell University Press, 1973: ch. 1).
8   Thomson in Mackie (op. cit.: 104, 118).
9   Irving Copi attempts to justify his claim that Russell's Ramified Theory of Types 'resolves' the paradoxes by arguing that the derivations of the contradictions cannot be carried out within the formal system developed in *Principia Mathematica*. See his *Theory of Logical Types* (London, Routledge & Kegan Paul, 1971: 88, 91).
10   Tarski (op. cit.: 66).
11   Obviously, the inconsistency of the definition of the Glub paradox can also be disguised in such a way that for every animal but Lassie there would be no problem in applying the definition.
12   Roughly speaking, a creative definition is one that generates new theorems within which the defined symbol does not occur. The reader can find more precise accounts of creative definitions in such standard logic texts as B. Mates, *Elementary Logic* (New York, Oxford University Press, 1972). If the vocabulary of a consistent theory T is increased to include a new symbol introduced by an inconsistent definition or a definition incompatible with the axioms of T, there will be a considerable increase in theorems within which the defined symbol does not occur – indeed, every sentence in the vocabulary of the original theory will be a theorem of the expanded theory. So I shall call such definitions 'very creative definitions'.
13   The above version of the Sec Lib paradox is based on a paradox set into circulation by Frank Cioffi, who has informed me that he got the idea from some science fiction story.
14   For the above reason, the Barber paradox is sometimes classified as a pseudo-paradox. See, for example, E. W. Beth, *Aspects of Modern Logic* (Dordrecht-Holland, D. Reidel, 1970: 77). (For a more detailed discussion of the Barber, see Thomson, op. cit.)
15   At the Moral Science Club Lecture, several Cambridge philosophers denied the existence of any significant difference between the inconsistent definition of 'glub' and such consistent definitions of 'inconsistent concepts' as that of 'glup'. It was even argued that these definitions were equivalent! Not surprisingly, several of these philosophers could see nothing inconsistent or defective about the definition of 'glub' or the various definitions and rules involved in the paradoxes. So it was argued (by one well-known Wittgensteinian philosopher among others) that my diagnoses were 'circular'. The reasoning behind this charge is still somewhat unclear to me, but evidently it came to this: supposedly, a crucial part of my diagnosis of the paradox is the claim that a certain set of definitions is inconsistent. But how does one tell whether a set of definitions is inconsistent? Surely, by deriving a contradiction from them. But the derivation of a contradiction just is the paradox. (One critic made the Russellian remark that my method of diagnosis has the benefits of theft over honest toil.) The suggestion here is that to attribute inconsistency to a set of definitions is to say no more than that the definitions are involved in a paradox (which is clearly mistaken). Perhaps this objection can be put into perspective by noting that Russell uncovered a difficulty in Frege's system by constructing what is now called 'Russell's paradox'. It is now generally accepted that Frege's system is inconsistent. But we can imagine these Cambridge philosophers arguing as follows: How do you tell that Frege's system is inconsistent? Surely by deriving a contradiction from the axioms. But that just is Russell's paradox. So to claim that Frege's system is inconsistent is circular!
16   The elimination test is clearly related to Heinrich Behman's proposed solution to the paradoxes which depends on showing that in each case the crucial definitions are non-*Pascalian* (where a definition is *Pascalian* if it allows us to replace the definiendum with the definiens). For details, see E. W. Beth (op. cit.: 81–2). As a solution, Behman's proposal is not satisfactory for a variety of reasons. For example, as J. van Heijenoort points out in 'Logical Paradox', in Paul Edwards, ed., *The Encyclopedia of Philosophy* (New York, Macmillan and Free Press, 1967), we want to know whether all non-Pascalian definitions lead to paradox and if so why they do: to be satisfactory, the

solution should tell us what it is about these definitions that creates the contradictions. Notice that what I claim for my test is much less than is claimed by Behman.

17 The above diagnosis applies equally to self-referential versions of the paradox. One can get a self-referential version by supposing that Sec Lib hires itself a secretary who is a secretary of no other organisation. Clearly, no significantly new problems are raised by this version.

It may be thought, especially by those who have been influenced by such papers by H. Herzberger as 'The Truth-Conditional Consistency of Natural Languages', *Journal of Philosophy*, vol. 64, no. 2 (2 February 1967), that no natural language could have an inconsistent set of definitions. Herzberger claims to have shown in this paper that 'no logical or semantical antinomy can be "present" or "derivable" within natural languages' (p. 35). The bases for this claim are to be found in his arguments that natural languages are (and indeed must be) *consistent*, in various senses of that word. For example, Herzberger argues that any natural language must be *consistent in its analytical sentence*, where a language L is inconsistent in its analytic sentences if L contains a non-empty set A of sentences such that every sentence in A is analytic and A is an inconsistent set. My diagnosis of the paradoxes does not contradict Herzberger's argument, for I would not maintain that every definition is an analytic sentence. Indeed, if an analytic sentence must be true, then no inconsistent definition can be analytic.

18 Thomson (op. cit.: 113).

19 Ibid. (p. 112).

20 I recently came across an article by Eric Stenius presenting an analysis of the Grelling which, in one important respect, is quite similar to mine. By a line of reasoning distinct from the one pursued here, Stenius came to the conclusion that the rule prescribing the use of the word 'heterological' is contradictory and that 'a contradiction arises if we assume that the rule can be adopted in the sense of being followed'. (See E. Stenius, 'Semantic Antinomies and the Theory of Well-Formed Rules,' *Critical Essays* (Amsterdam, North-Holland, 1972: 134).) Stenius's analysis is rather sketchy, however, and he makes no attempt to analyse any of the other paradoxes. Although he does suggest that his analysis can be extended to cover the other paradoxes, he makes no attempt to show, for example, how the Liar paradox involves a contradictory definition.

21 The Richard paradox is discussed in detail in Chilhara (op. cit.: 139–40). The König paradox should also be mentioned here: it is essentially the same as the Richard and can be dealt with in essentially the same way as the Berry. The reader can find a short discussion of the König in J. van Heijenoort, in Edwards, op. cit.

22 This version of the Liar, due to P. E. B. Jourdain, is discussed by Alonzo Church in 'Paradoxes, logical', ín Dagobert Runes, ed., *The Dictionary of Philosophy* (London, Peter Owen and Vision Press, 1942).

23 'Propositions and Truth in Natural Languages', in *Mind*, vol. LXXXI (1972: 238). He goes on to claim that since the sentence 'This very sentence is false' cannot be either true or false, it gives rise to no paradox: 'For what is then really false, namely the proposition of which he intends his utterance to be a specimen, is not the same as what he says is false, namely the sentence.'

24 The quotation is from Kneale's 'Russell's Paradox and Some Others', *British Journal for the Philosophy of Science*, vol. 22 (1971: 321–38). Kneale has suggested to me that what I have done above is formulate a new paradox (personal communication). He still maintains that he has solved 'the standard Liar'. At this point, I may be disagreeing with little more than his terminology, but it does seem wrong to me to claim that Kneale has solved the standard form of the Liar. First, it should be remarked that many formulations of the Liar do not require that sentences be 'carriers of truth-values'. For example, Russell stated the Liar in terms of propositions. And one frequently finds it expressed in terms of what is said (see Mackie, op. cit.: 296). Secondly, one can see that Kneale's solution does not really get at what is logically essential in the paradox. It is as if one claimed to solve Russell's version of the Liar by

pointing out that, since lying involves intention, a person might state a falsehood without lying. (For more details on this point, see Chihara, op. cit.: 8.) Can one imagine Quine claiming to have solved the Russellian version of the Liar by saying that there is no paradox since there are no propositions? Few would take such a solution seriously. What Quine does, of course, is much more reasonable: he simply ignores the propositional version and tries to deal with the sentence version.

25 Poincaré once argued – and Russell agreed with him – that the paradoxes were due to viciously circular definitions. This fundamental idea was very fruitful and gave birth to the vicious-circle principle and predicative set theory (see Chihara, op. cit.: chs 1 and 4). But the Liar paradox did not seem to fit this analysis, for the question arose: What definition is viciously circular?

26 See D. Davidson, 'Truth and Meaning', in J. W. Davis, D. J. Hockney and W. K. Wilson, eds, *Philosophical Logic* (Dordrecht-Holland, D. Reidel, 1969: 16–17).

27 There are many other strengthened versions of the Liar. One variation has me writing, instead of θ, 'The sentence on side B of this card is either false or without definite sense.' According to another variation, the sentence 'There is no sentence on card C that is true' is the only sentence written on card C. All of the variations I have seen can be diagnosed in the above way.

28 F. B. Fitch, 'Comments and a Suggestion' (*PL*: 77).

29 Solutions based on the rejection of self-reference have been inspired by Russell's theory of types which, in conjunction with the theory of descriptions, rules out self-reference. For details, see Chihara (op. cit.: ch. 1). There are several explicit attempts to solve the paradoxes by rejecting self-reference. An extreme view is expressed by Jørgen Jørgensen in 'Some Reflections on Reflexivity', *Danish Year-Book of Philosophy*, vol. VI (1969), where he argues not only that 'no sentences are self-referring' (p. 31), but even that there 'are no reflexive phenomena at all' (p. 32). The latter claim is based on the grounds that 'any relation presupposes at least two terms which may be more or less alike in various respects, but which can never coalesce into a single term' (p. 32). A more moderate (and somewhat more plausible) position is taken by Alf Ross in 'On Self-Reference and a Puzzle in Constitutional Law', *Mind*, vol. LXXVIII (1969: 309) where explicit reference is made to Russell's theory of types.

30 Jørgensen argues that the self-referential sentence mentioned above is simply meaningless (op. cit.: 30). Ross takes a different route, suggesting that the above sentence involves spurious self-reference (op. cit.: 11–12); but as Mackie remarks (op. cit.: 285), it is hard to see why the *self-reference* of the paradoxical sentences is any more genuine than that of the non-paradoxical ones.

31 See L. E. J. Brouwer, 'On the Significance of the Principle of Excluded Middle in Mathematics, Especially in Function Theory', in Jean van Heijenoort (ed), *From Frege to Göbel: A Source Book in Mathematical Logic, 1879-1931* (Cambridge, Harvard University Press, 1967: 336).

32 For example, many of the paradoxes involve the use of diagonal arguments. This has led some mathematicians and logicians to have doubts about the validity of diagonal arguments. My diagnosis clears this type of reasoning of the charge of producing the contradiction.

5

A REFUTATION OF AN UNJUSTIFIED ATTACK ON THE AXIOM OF REDUCIBILITY

John Myhill

The purpose of this chapter is to vindicate the axiom of reducibility not in the sense of adducing fresh grounds for believing it, but in the sense of demolishing once and for all an argument which has repeatedly been used against it (by Ramsey, Chwistek and Copi in particular). The argument runs as follows. To avoid the semantical paradoxes, Russell complicated simple type theory by introducing *orders*; this led to *ramified type theory*. However, it proved impossible to construct classical mathematics in this framework, in part because of a difficulty connected with mathematical induction; Russell therefore introduced the *axiom of reducibility*, according to which every propositional function was materially equivalent to a *predicative* propositional function, i.e. one whose order was greater by 1 than the order of its arguments. But (so runs the argument) this renders the ramified theory indistinguishable from the simple one, apart from a vacuous multiplication of subscripts; consequently, since the simple theory did not eliminate the semantical paradoxes, the ramification has failed of its purpose. This is as though a man had built a wall around himself to keep out his enemies and then, finding himself in need of a door, had knocked out part of the wall and let them all in again. Or so the critics claim. We shall show that they are wrong.

Since Russell's own formalisation of the ramified theory leaves much to be desired by modern standards of rigour, and since the problem is one of some delicacy, our first step must be to make a precise formalisation of the theory. We shall follow approximately Kurt Schütte's treatment in his book *Beweistheorie* (Berlin, Springer, 1960). 0 is a *signature* (that of the type of individuals), and its level is 0. If $\sigma_1, \ldots, \sigma_n$ are *signatures* and m is any number greater than the levels of all the σ_i, then $m(\sigma_1, \ldots, \sigma_n)$ is a *signature* and its level is m. This is the signature of the type of all those relations $R(x_1, \ldots, x_n)$ for which x_i is of type σ_i; and which do not involve quantification over any types of level $\geq m$. In particular, if $n = 0$ and $m \geq 0$, then $m()$, also written m, is the signature of the type of all propositions not involving quantification over any types of level $\geq m$. Variables are $x_\sigma, y_\sigma, z_\sigma$, etc. where σ is any signature. *Terms* of type σ

include (a) variables of type σ, (b) formulas of level m (defined below) if σ is m and (c) abstracts $\{x^1_{\tau_1}, \ldots, x^n_{\tau_n} \mid \mathfrak{A}\}_\sigma$ if σ is $m(\tau_1, \ldots, \tau_n)$ $(n > 0)$ and $\mathfrak{A}$ is a formula of level m. Atomic *formulas* are (a) variables of type m, (b) formulas t $(t, \ldots, t)$ $(n > 0$; written $t^1 \in t$ if $n = 1)$, where $t, t^1, \ldots, t^n$ are terms of types $m(\tau_1, \ldots, \tau_n), \tau_1, \ldots, \tau_n$, respectively, and (c) formulas $t^1 = t^2$, where t^1 and t^2 are of the same type. Other *formulas* are built up from these by connectives and quantifiers of all types (including propositional types) in the usual way. The *level* of a term (including a formula) is defined as follows: the level of a variable x_0 is 0, of a variable x_m is m, of a variable $x_{m_{\tau_1, \ldots, \tau_n}}$, is m, of an abstract $\{\ldots\}_{m(\tau_1, \ldots, \tau_n)}$ is m; of t $(t^1, \ldots, t^n)$ is the same as the level of t; of $t_1 = t_2$ is the same as the level of t^1 (or t^2); of $\sim \mathfrak{A}$ is the same as the level of $\mathfrak{A}$; $\vee \mathfrak{B}$ is the maximum of the levels of $\mathfrak{A}$ and of $\mathfrak{B}$; and of $(\forall x_\sigma) \mathfrak{A}$ is the least number which is greater than the level of σ and $\geq$ the level of $\mathfrak{A}$. The *axioms* are the axioms of the many-sorted predicate calculus with identity (and bound propositional variables in each type m) together with the predicative comprehension-schema:

$$\{x^1_{\tau_1}, \ldots, x^n_{\tau_n} \mid \mathfrak{A}\}_\tau \, (x^1_{\tau_1}, \ldots, x^n_{\tau_n}) \leftrightarrow \mathfrak{A}.$$

(For a reason that will be stated at the very end of the chapter we do not include extensionality.)

This system we call *RP* (for 'Ramified *Principia*'). It is not (even if we add extensionality in all types and any *finite* number of other axioms, or even any infinite number of axioms provided their levels are bounded above) adequate for elementary arithmetic, in the sense that there are no terms 0_σ, $[s(x_\sigma)]_\sigma$, $N_{m(\sigma)}$ for which we can prove the five Peano axioms:

$$0 \in N$$
$$x \in N \rightarrow s(x) \in N$$
$$sx \neq 0$$
$$sx = sy \rightarrow x = y$$

and

$$\mathfrak{A}\,(0) \wedge (\forall x)(\mathfrak{A}(x) \rightarrow \mathfrak{A}(s(x))) \rightarrow (\forall x)(x \in N \rightarrow \mathfrak{A}(x))$$

for all formulas of $\mathfrak{A}(x)$. (This is proved in my paper in the Indiana Russell centenary volume; actually the result stated there is a bit weaker, but the argument establishes the present one.)[1] Consequently (despite an abortive attempt in Appendix B of volume I of the 2nd edition of *Principia*; see my Indiana paper) Russell was obliged to add the *axiom of reducibility*, which we symbolise as:

$$(\exists y_{m\,(\tau_1, \ldots, \tau_n)})(\forall x^1_{\tau_1}) \ldots (\forall x^n_{\tau_n}) \, (y(x^1, \ldots, x^n) \leftrightarrow \mathfrak{A})$$

where $\mathfrak{A}$ is of arbitrary level and m exceeds by 1 the maximum of the levels of $\tau_1, \ldots, \tau_n$. The resulting system we call *PM*; the question is whether, as the critics claim, *PM* reinstates the semantic paradoxes.

Actually what are called semantic paradoxes are of two kinds, exemplified by the Epimenides and the heterological paradox, respectively. The first kind does not involve any mention of expressions, but only of propositions; it does not depend on syntax, but (at least in the case of the Epimenides) on the pragmatic relation of assertion. The other kind includes, besides the heterological paradox, the paradoxes of the least integer not nameable in fewer than nineteen syllables; of the least indefinable ordinal; and of Richard. It *also* includes 'This sentence is false' which can be rigorously presented using Gödel's diagonalisation technique, and which is concerned with falsehood of *sentences* not *propositions* (and therefore is distinct from the Epimenides with which it is frequently confused).

Because of its special nature we shall consider the Epimenides first, and then the heterological one by way of illustration of the ordinary semantical paradoxes. We shall in both cases first derive the paradox in the notation of the ordinary theory of types (*TT*), and then show how *PM* prevents its derivation. Thus we shall disprove the contention of the critics, that *PM* and *TT* are the same thing. Or rather (since presumably there is a translation of *PM* into *TT*) that *PM* + semantics is not the same as *TT* + semantics; this is perhaps the essence of the critics' error, that they infer from the supposed equivalence of *PM* and *TT* that those systems continue to be equivalent after the relevant semantical notions are added to both.

Let E be the set of all propositions asserted by Epimenides, and suppose, to avoid unnecessary complications, that E contains only one proposition, to the effect that all elements of E are false. Reasoning within *TT*, we have

$$(1) \qquad p \in E \leftrightarrow p = (\forall q)(q \in E \rightarrow \sim q).$$

Abbreviate $(\forall q)(q \in E \rightarrow \sim q)$ by $\mathfrak{E}$; then the two halves of the contradiction are derived (in *TT*) as follows. Assume $\mathfrak{E}$, then

(2)	$(\forall q)(q \in E \rightarrow \sim q)$	(by definition of $\mathfrak{E}$)
(3)	$p \in E \leftrightarrow p = \mathfrak{E}$	(from (1))
(4)	$\mathfrak{E} \in E$	(from (3))
(5)	$\mathfrak{E} \in E \rightarrow \sim \mathfrak{E}$	(from (2))
(6)	$\sim \mathfrak{E}.$	(from (4) and (5))

Conversely assume $\sim \mathfrak{E}$, then

(7)	$(\exists q)(q \in E \wedge q).$	(by definition of $\mathfrak{E}$)

Let q_0 be such a q, then

$$(8) \qquad q_0 \, \epsilon \, E$$

$$(9) \qquad q_0$$

$$(10) \qquad q_0 \, \epsilon \, E \leftrightarrow q_0 = \mathfrak{E} \qquad\qquad \text{(from (1))}$$

$$(11) \qquad q_0 = \mathfrak{E} \qquad\qquad \text{(from (8) and (10))}$$

$$(12) \qquad \mathfrak{E}. \qquad\qquad \text{(from (9) and (11))}$$

Thus, we see that *the assumption (1) leads to a contradiction within TT.* On the other hand, *the assumption (1) cannot even be stated within PM.* We have to indicate the types of p, E and q in (1). If the type of p is, say, m, then the type of E must be $n(m)$ for some $n > m$; then we have

$$(13) \qquad p_m \epsilon E_{n(m)} \leftrightarrow p = (\forall q) \, (q \epsilon E_{n(m)} \to \sim q).$$

For $q \, \epsilon \, E_{n(m)}$ to be well formed, q must have type m. But then the level of $(\forall q_m) \, (q \, \epsilon \, E_{n(m)} \to \sim q)$ is max $(n, m + 1) > m$ and so the right-hand side of (13) is not well formed. The most the axiom of reducibility can do for us is to replace the n on the left-hand side of (13) (and perhaps, after a little sleight-of-hand, the n on the right-hand side too) by $m + 1$; but this affects the argument not one whit.

In a fresh bid to reinstate the paradox, we might consider replacing identity by material equivalence in (13). (Thus, Epimenides's assertions would be all those and only those propositions (of a specified type m) which were materially equivalent to 'All Epimenides's assertions of type m are false'.) The resulting variant of (13), namely,

$$(14) \qquad p_m \, \epsilon \, E_{n(m)} \leftrightarrow [p_m \leftrightarrow (\forall q_m) \, (q_m \, \epsilon \, E_{n(m)} \to \sim q)]$$

is now at least well formed. Further it *does* lead to a contradiction. For first assume $(\forall q_m) \, (q_m \, \epsilon \, E_{n(m)} \to \sim q)$, which we abbreviate by $\mathfrak{E}'$. Then we get

$$(15) \qquad (\forall q_m) \, (q_m \, \epsilon \, E_{n(m)} \to \sim q) \qquad\qquad \text{(hyp.)}$$

$$(16) \qquad p_m \, \epsilon \, E_{n(m)} \leftrightarrow [p_m \leftrightarrow \mathfrak{E}']. \qquad\qquad \text{(from (14))}$$

Let $\mathfrak{T}_m$ be any provable formula of level m, then

$$(17) \qquad \mathfrak{T}_m \leftrightarrow \mathfrak{E}' \qquad\qquad \text{(by hyp.)}$$

$$(18) \qquad \mathfrak{T}_m \, \epsilon \, E_{n(m)} \qquad\qquad \text{(from (16) and (17))}$$

$$(19) \qquad \mathfrak{T}_m \, \epsilon \, E_{n(m)} \to \sim \mathfrak{T}_m \qquad\qquad \text{(from (15))}$$

$$(20) \qquad \sim \mathfrak{T}_m \qquad\qquad \text{(from (18) and (19))}$$

$$(21) \qquad \mathfrak{T}_m. \qquad\qquad \text{(by hyp.)}$$

The hypothesis $\mathfrak{E}'$ thus leads to a contradiction, and we get, independently of any assumption except (14),

$$(22) \qquad \sim \mathfrak{E}'$$

and

$$(23) \qquad (\exists q_m) \, (q_m \, \epsilon \, E_{n(m)} \wedge q). \qquad \text{(by def. of } \mathfrak{E}')$$

Let $q^0{}_m$ be such a q_m, then

$$(24) \qquad q^0 \, \epsilon \, E$$

$$(25) \qquad q^0$$

$$(26) \qquad q^0 \, \epsilon \, E \leftrightarrow [q^0 \leftrightarrow \mathfrak{E}'] \qquad \text{(from (14))}$$

$$(27) \qquad q^0 \leftrightarrow \mathfrak{E}' \qquad \text{(by (24) and (26))}$$

$$(28) \qquad \sim q^0 \qquad \text{(by (22) and (27))}$$

which contradicts (25). So (14) is indeed a 'paradox'; it does lead to a contradiction. Before we despair, however, observe that in the deduction of (25) and (28) from (14), *the axiom of reducibility is nowhere used; it is therefore a deduction in RP, and if (14) is indeed a paradox, it is one that the ramified Principia is powerless to avoid.* I do not believe, however, that it is one; the deduction of (25) and (28) from (14) merely shows that for each person x and each propositional type m, it is not the case that the propositions of type m asserted by x are all those and only those propositions of type m which are materially equivalent to 'all propositions of type m asserted by x are false'. We escape this by denying the existence of any such person, just as we escape the analogous pseudo-paradox of the 'Barber' by denying *his* existence.

Thus, one form of the Epimenides cannot even be stated in *PM* (a point made by Russell quite clearly in 1908 – see *Logic and Knowledge*, R. C. Marsh, ed. (London, George Allen & Unwin, 1956: 82–3), and the other form turns out to be only a pseudo-paradox like the 'Barber'.

We turn finally to the Heterological paradox. This is the one used by Copi to deliver the *coup de grâce* in his proof of 'the inconsistency or redundancy of *PM*', and it is therefore crucial that we deal with it in order to counter Copi's criticism.

Russell considers all expressions (as objects) to be of the same type (ibid., p. 332); actually this type is $4(3(2(1(0)), 0))$, but since it is the lowest type considered in what follows, we shall call it 0 for brevity. Thus in *TT* the word 'heterological' which we shall denote by the astrological symbol $\hbar$ is of type 0, and the set *Het* of heterological words is

$$\{x_0 \mid (\exists y_1)\, D\,(x_0, y_1) \wedge x_0 \notin y_1\},$$

where D is the relation between an expression and the type (1) class which it designates. We have

$$(29) \qquad D(\hbar, y_1) \leftrightarrow y = Het.$$

The derivation of the paradox in TT runs as follows. Assume $\hbar \in Het$, then

$$(\exists y_1)\, (D\,(\hbar, y_1) \wedge \hbar \notin y_1). \qquad \text{(by def. of } Het)$$

Let y^0_1 be such a y_1, then

$$(30) \qquad D(\hbar, y^0)$$

$$(31) \qquad \hbar \notin y^0$$

$$(32) \qquad y^0 = Het \qquad\qquad\qquad\qquad \text{(from (30) and (29))}$$

$$(33) \qquad \hbar \notin Het. \qquad\qquad\qquad\qquad \text{(from (31) and (32))}$$

Conversely assume $\hbar \notin Het$, then

$$(34) \qquad (\forall y_1)(D(\hbar, y) \rightarrow \hbar \in y) \qquad\qquad \text{(by def. of } Het)$$

$$(35) \qquad D(\hbar, Het) \qquad\qquad\qquad\qquad\qquad \text{(from (29))}$$

and

$$\hbar \in Het. \qquad\qquad\qquad\qquad \text{(from (34) and (35))}$$

Let us see how this looks in RP and PM. $\hbar$ is again of type 0; it is 'Het' which designates the property of being a word which designates a property (of some given type $m(0)$) which it does not have. Thus,

$$(36) \qquad Het = \{x_0 \mid (\exists y_{m(0)})\, (D_{n(0,\,m(0))}\,(x, y) \wedge x \notin y)\}\,_{r(0)},$$

where $r = \max (n, m + 1)$. If now we try to parallel in RP the deduction of $\hbar \,\mathfrak{B}\, Het$ and $\hbar \notin Het$ from (29), the ramification blocks us. Instead of (29), we have to write either

$$D_{n(0,\,m(0))}\,(\hbar, y_{m(0)}) \leftrightarrow y_{m(0)} = Het\,_{r(0)}$$

which is not well formed, or else

$$(37) \qquad D_{t(0,\,r(0))}\,(\hbar, y_{r(0)}) \leftrightarrow y_{r(0)} = Het_{r(0)},$$

where $D_{t(0,\ r(0))}$ is a higher-type designation relation.
Now assume $\hbar \in Het$; we get as before

$$(\exists y_{m(0)})\ (D\ (\hbar, y) \wedge \hbar \not\in y)$$

(38) $\qquad D_{n(0,\ m(0))}\ (\hbar, y^0{}_{m(0)})$

$\qquad \hbar \not\in y^0{}_{m(0)}$

but we cannot go on to infer $y^0{}_{m(0)} = Het_{r(0)}$ from (38) and (37) as we
inferred (32) from (30) and (29), since (among other things) it is not even
well formed. Thus, the proof of $\hbar \not\in Het$ is blocked. If conversely we
assume $\hbar \not\in Het$, a precisely parallel difficulty occurs; though as a matter
of fact $\hbar$ (i.e. '*Het*' as defined by (36) is *not* heterological simply; there is *no*
property of type $m(0)$ designated by $\hbar$, and *a fortiori* no such property
which $\hbar$ does not have).

So much for the *RP* solution of the paradox. We have to consider the
critics' contention that *PM*, i.e. *RP* + reducibility, reinstates it. Again $\hbar$
has type 0; let $D_{n(0, 1(\omega)}$ be the relation of a word to a property of type 1 (0)
which it designates (i.e. a predicative property of individuals). As above
define

(39) $\qquad Het = \{x_0\ |\ (\exists y_{1(0)})\ (D_{n(0,\ 1(0))}\ (x, y) \wedge x \not\in y)\ \}_{r\ (0)},$

where $r = \max(n, 2)$. This *Het* does not yield a paradox for the same
reason that the *Het* of (36) did not yield a paradox in RP; but the axiom of
reducibility tells us that there is a predicative property (i.e. of type 1(0))
coextensive with *Het*, and it is here that the troubles begin. Let $Het^*{}_{1(0)}$ be
this predicative property, and let $\hbar^*$ designate it. Corresponding to (29)
we have

(40) $\qquad D_{n(0,\ 1(0))}\ (\hbar^*, y_{1(0)}) \leftrightarrow y = Het^*{}_{1(0)}$

and this time a contradiction *does* follow. If $\hbar^* \in Het$, then

$$(\exists y_{1(0)})(D_{n(0,\ 1(0))}\ (\hbar^*, y) \wedge \hbar^* \not\in y). \qquad \text{(from (39))}$$

Let $y^0{}_{1(0)}$ be such a $y_{1(0)}$, then

(41) $\qquad D_{n(0,\ 1(0))}\ (\hbar^*, y^0{}_{1(0)})$

(42) $\qquad \hbar^* \not\in y^0$

(43) $\qquad y^0{}_{1(0)} = Het^*{}_{1(0)} \qquad\qquad\qquad$ (from (41) and (40))

$\qquad \hbar^* \not\in Het^* \qquad\qquad\qquad\qquad\qquad$ (from (42) and (43)) and finally

(44) $\quad\quad ħ^* \notin Het$

since Het and Het^* are coextensive. If, on the other hand, $ħ^* \notin Het$, then

(45) $\quad\quad (\forall y_{1(0)})(D_{n(0,\ 1(0))}\ (ħ^*, y) \rightarrow ħ^* \in y)$ $\quad\quad\quad\quad$ (from (39))

(46) $\quad\quad D_{n(0,\ 1(0))}\ (ħ^*, Het^*{}_{1(0)})$ $\quad\quad\quad\quad\quad\quad$ (from (40))

$\quad\quad\quad ħ^* \notin Het^*$ $\quad\quad\quad\quad\quad\quad\quad\quad$ (from (45) and (46))

and

(47) $\quad\quad ħ^* \notin Het.$

Thus, the assumption (40) has led within PM to a contradiction. Thus $ħ^*$ either does not designate Het^*, or designates something else besides. Since we assume that no word designates more than one entity, we have proved that $ħ^*$ doesn't designate Het^*, a result that seems flatly to contradict the construction. It is at this point that the critics claim that the paradox has been reinstated, and that PM is no more adequate to deal with it than is TT. This is the heart of their attack, and what follows is the heart of our defence.

First, observe that $ħ^*$ in (40) – (47) can be regarded as a *variable* and the argument is still valid. Thus, we have shown that *nothing* denotes Het^* – that Het^* simply has no name at all. Is this a paradox? We have just *given* it a name – that is, 'Het^*', otherwise known as $ħ^*$. But in what language is 'Het^*' a name? Certainly not in the language of PM! What the argument shows is only that nothing designates Het^* in the language whose designation relation is given by $D_{n(0,\ 1(0))}$. Or more generally: given any designation relation D (of type $n(0, 1(0))$), we can find a predicative property of individuals (words) which has no name in the sense of D. This is scarcely a paradox: it is simply a proof of the denial of (40) (a proof that there is no such $ħ^*$ – remember the 'Barber'), i.e. a proof of

$$(\forall\ D_{n(0,\ 1(0))})\ (\exists\ y_{\ 1(0)})\ (\forall ħ^*{}_0) \sim (\forall z_{1(0)})(D\ (ħ^*, z) \leftrightarrow z = y).$$

And this is an evident consequence of the fact that there are more (predicative) properties of words than there are words. In fact, apart from notation, all that the derivation of a contradiction from (40) does is to mimic Cantor's standard proof of this. This concludes our defence.

There remain a few points. First, is 'heterological' heterological or not? To answer this question we must specify what language L we are talking about – i.e. we must specify the relation D of (39). Once this is fixed, the meaning of 'heterological' is given precisely by (39); it is a certain predicative property of words of L. This property has no name in L; in particular 'heterological' is not its name in L. So 'heterological' or more precisely 'heterological-in-L' is *not* heterological-in-L, for the trivial reason that it is not an expression of L at all. Or to put it in another way: unless we specify the language L, the word 'designate' and the word 'heterological' have no meaning. As soon as we do, the paradox becomes merely a proof that a certain particular property of words of L has no name in L. Since 'heterological' is a name of that property, we conclude that it is not a name in L, but in another bigger language.

There is no difficulty at all in extending the same line of thought to the other properly semantical paradoxes (all of which involve designation). In each case the argument of the paradox shows only the non-existence of certain names in certain languages. And in each case the argument can be routinely carried out in PM, and the axiom of reducibility does not convert the pseudo-paradox into a paradox.

In fact, the error involved in the semantical paradoxes (other than the Epimenides) is nothing so sophisticated as a violation of the 'vicious-circle principle' – it is a simple fallacy of ambiguity. Thus, in the heterological paradox, we first define 'x is heterological' to mean 'x designates a property that x does not have' and then ask whether 'heterological' designates a property that 'heterological' does not have. For this to have any cogency, we ought first to define precisely what the first occurrence of the word 'designates' means; but if we do, it turns out that in *this* sense the word 'heterological' does not designate anything, and so the tacit assumption (corresponding to (29), (37) or (40) above) that it designates the property of heterologicality is correct only in another sense of 'designate'. We here simply changed the meaning of this word in the middle of the argument, and need no special 'vicious-circle principle' to avoid a contradiction.

This being so, it might be thought that there is no point in studying PM, even though it *is* vindicated against its critics. I think this would be wrong, on two counts. First, the above remarks about ambiguity do *not* apply to the Epimenides, which does not involve designation but only assertion and the apparently innocuous notion of a proposition. I really think this should be separated from the other 'semantical' paradoxes and perhaps be designated (like the 'Hangman') as a *pragmatic* paradox; it is as different from the ordinary semantic paradoxes as both are from the logical paradoxes. There is no *ambiguity* that I can find in the Epimenides. There is, I think, a *genuine* violation of a vicious-circle principle which receives its embodiment in RP and PM. At the risk of appearing harsh to Russell at the end of my defence of him, I would conjecture that his assimilation of the Epimenides to the properly semantic paradoxes stems from a confusion of use and mention: the totality of 'all propositions' in the non-linguistic sense is illegitimate because it involves a vicious circle, while the totality of 'all propositions' in the sense of *sentences* is simply ill-defined. Since at least on occasion he is prone to confuse a proposition with its verbal expression, he may have been misled into ascribing to the set of sentences the same kind of illegitimacy which he, in our opinion quite correctly, assigned to the set of propositions.

The second reason why I believe that *PM* is still worthy of study is more technical. It seems quite plausible that we can enrich it by a formally defined notion of designation (defined within the system, i.e. in terms of ϵ) such that every property is (or can consistently be assumed to be) *extensionally equivalent to* one which has a name in the system. This enrichment would certainly be mathematically curious, but it might, too, be of some philosophical interest in connection with the 'absoluteness' or otherwise of the notion of non-denumerability. It was with these future developments in mind that I abstained from introducing the axiom of extensionality into *RP* or *PM*; for we could probably not, on pain of contradiction, maintain in such a system that

$$D(x,y) \wedge (\forall z)\, (z \in y \leftrightarrow z \epsilon y') \rightarrow D(x,y').^{2}$$

Department of Mathematics
State University of New York at Buffalo

NOTES

1   'The Undefinability of the Set of Natural Numbers in the Ramified *Principia*', in *Bertrand Russell's Philosophy*, George Nakhnikian, ed. (London, Duckworth, 1974: 19–27).
2   Research on this chapter was in part supported by National Science Foundation grant GP 21189.

6

ON CONSTRAINED DENOTATION

Abraham Robinson

(1) Both by the choice of its subject and by its mode of discussion, Russell's essay 'On Denoting'[1] has remained one of the conspicuously influential philosophical papers of this century. Yet its main thesis has not found universal acceptance. The details of Russell's solution of the problem of descriptions are well known and need not be repeated. Here I wish to recall only that Russell rejected the notion that a description is a name. The following argument is given in *Principia Mathematica* in support of this view:[2]

> For if that were the meaning of 'Scott is the author of *Waverley*' [i.e. that 'Scott' and 'the author of *Waverley*' are two names for the same object], what would be required for its truth would be that Scott should have been *called* the author of *Waverley*: if he had been so called, the proposition would be true, even if someone else had written *Waverley*; while if no one called him so, the proposition would be false, even if he had written *Waverley*.

However, in spite of the apparent force of this line of reasoning, many writers, both before and since, have propounded theories which imply that a description is indeed a name or a sort of name. The fact that they could do so with impunity indicates that there is a flaw in Russell's argument. It seems to me that this flaw can be found in the tacit assumption that the name of a person or object can always be chosen arbitrarily; or, to put it the other way round, that the interpretation of a name is, initially, a matter of choice. I can see no compelling reason for this assumption. In the present chapter we shall be concerned with several formal frameworks which are based on a contrary point of view.

Once we grant that the interpretation of a name may be affected, or *constrained*, by circumstances, my own preference goes to a setting in which a description has a denotation only if there exists a unique object which satisfies its defining condition. This is, roughly, the point of view adopted by Hilbert and Bernays.[3] Their procedure has been criticised[4] because it implies that a formula involving a description can be regarded as well formed only if it has been proved that the description in question has a denotation. However, this objection is met if – as is natural in a model-theoretic approach – we distinguish clearly between well-formedness on the one hand and interpretability in a structure on the other hand. Some of the formal details of a programme based on this distinction are carried out below. However, it will be our main purpose to discuss possibilities rather than to work out all the consequences of a particular point of view.

(2) We may ask whether any particular solution of the problem of descriptions is the 'best possible'. However, I do not think that this question can be answered with finality. Indeed, given any particular feature of a formal language, we first have to make up our minds whether it is our aim (a) to make the language as effective a tool as possible for a particular purpose such as the investigation of the physical world or the formalisation of a mathematical theory, or (b) to give a precise explication of a corresponding feature found in a natural language. In the present instance, contemporary practice seems to show that as far as (a) is concerned, descriptions can be dispensed with altogether, or can be replaced by the successive introduction of new function symbols or individual constants. As for (b), a complete explication would have to take into account modal contexts and even the distinction between objective situations and subjective knowledge, and it seems unlikely that all these can be covered by a single formalisation. At any rate, we shall not consider these aspects of the matter in the present chapter.

(3) We proceed to specify the vocabulary of our formal language L. It is to consist of (i) individual constants $a, b, c, \ldots$; (ii) function symbols $f, g, h, \ldots$; (iii) relation symbols $R, S, T, \ldots$; (iv) the identity $=$; (v) connectives $\neg, \vee, \wedge, \supset$; (vi) quantifiers $(\exists), (\forall)$; (vii) the descriptor (ι); (viii) variables $x, y, z, \ldots$; and (ix) brackets $[,]$. In (ii) and (iii), the number of places may or may not be specified for each symbol, as we please.

On the basis of the above vocabulary, we may now compose well-formed formulae (*wff*). The laws of formation of *wff* are as usual in the lower predicate calculus, except that the rules for the formation of terms are extended by the stipulation that $[(\iota x)Q(x)]$ is a *term* if Q is any well-formed formula which contains x free – i.e. not under the sign of a quantifier or the descriptor. More generally, we choose to rule out empty quantifications or descriptions (e.g. $[(\iota x)Q]$, where Q does not contain x). Also, in principle, we introduce brackets in order to obtain a *wff* from an atomic formula and after each introduction of a connective or of the identify or of a quantifier or of the descriptor. For example, $[R(f(a), [(\iota x)[(\exists y)S(x,y)]])]$ and $[y = [(\iota x)T(x)]]$ are *wff*. We measure the *complexity* of a *wff* by the number of pairs of (square) brackets in it. However, in actual fact, we shall omit brackets if no misunderstanding is likely.

A *description* is a term of the form $t = [(\iota x)Q(x)]$. Q is called the *scope* of t. The description $t' = [(\iota x')Q'(x')]$ is said to be an *immediate component* of the description $t = [(\iota x)Q(x)]$ if t' is contained in $Q(x)$, and if no description which is contained in $Q(x)$ has t' in its scope. Let $t_1, \ldots, t_k, k \geq 0$ be the immediate components of t. Then t is a description *of order* 1 if $k = 0$, and t is of order $n \geq 2$ if all its immediate components are at most of order $n - 1$ and at least one of them is exactly of order $n - 1$.

(4) Now let M be a first-order structure and suppose that we are given a (many–one) map C from a set V of individual constants and of relation and function symbols in L onto individuals and functions and relations with the corresponding number of places in M. Let $W_0(V)$ be the set of *wff* formed from V without the use of the descriptor (but including the use of $=$) and let $S_0(V)$ be the set of sentences (*wff* without free variables) within $W_0(V)$. Assuming that we have enough individual constants in V to denote all individuals of M, we then proceed (using the so-called substitution approach to quantification) to determine for all $X \in S_0(V)$ whether or not X *holds in* M (*is true in* M, *is satisfied by* M), in symbols $M \vDash X$. The procedure is too well known to require repetition here. Let us recall only that $M \vDash \neg X$ by definition if, and only if, X is not satisfied by M *but is meaningful* for M, i.e. the extralogical constants (individual constants and relation and function symbols) which occur in it belong to the domain of the map C.

Thus, the (meta-) relation $\vDash$ depends not only on M and on X, but also on C although this is not apparent in our notation. In particular, C induces a correspondence or map also from the set of terms which occur in $S_0(V)$, $T_0(V)$, say, onto the set of individuals of M; in other words it defines a *denotation* in M for any $t \in T_0(V)$.

So far, the map C from the extralogical constants of V onto entities of M has been entirely arbitrary (except for the condition that individual constants are mapped on individuals, function symbols on functions with the same number of places, and relation symbols on relations with the same number of places). The map of the remaining terms of C into M is then determined uniquely, and without the intervention of the relation $\vDash$.

(5) We still have to clarify the role of the identity. One correct definition of the identity from the point of view of first-order model theory is undoubtedly to conceive of it as the set of diagonal elements of $M \times M$, i.e. as the set of ordered pairs from M whose first and second elements coincide. The symbol ('$=$') then denotes this relation and it is correct that $M \vDash a = b$ if 'a' and 'b' are individual constants which denote the same individual in M or, more generally, that $M \vDash s = t$ if 's' and 't' are terms which denote the same individual in M. But the identity may also be *introduced* by this condition so that $M \vDash s = t$, *by definition*, if 's' and 't' denote the same individual[5] under the correspondence C, which is again assumed implicitly, and this seems more apposite in connection with the discussion of sentences which involve both descriptions and identity. It

should be pointed out that this definition has the unusual and, at first sight, disturbing, feature that it involves a proposition *about symbols*. This is masked in the notation '$M \vDash s = t$' which seems to indicate that the formula after the double turnstile '$s = t$' is, like any other *wff*, a statement about M. However it appears that, once we have appreciated the situation, no harm will come of it. The purist who would write 'a' = 'b' will perceive his error by looking at the result. And if we interpret the 'is' in 'Scott is the author of *Waverley*' by the identity sign in the sense of our second definition, then we obtain just what we want, i.e. that 'Scott' and 'the author of *Waverley*' *denote* the same individual.

(6)   Let $[(\iota x)Q(x)]$ be a description of order 1 such that $Q(x) \in W_0(V)$. (We use x *typically*, i.e. we may have any other variable in place of x.) Suppose that $M \vDash (\exists x)Q(x)$ and $M \vDash (\forall x)(\forall y)[Q(x) \wedge Q(y) \supset x = y]$, where y is some variable not in Q. Then there exists an individual constant a such that $M \vDash Q(a)$, and *we extend C* by mapping $[(\iota x)Q(x)]$ on the individual of M which is the image of a under C. This definition is independent of the particular choice of a. Applying it to all descriptions of order 1 such that $Q \in W_0(V)$, we obtain an extension C_1 of C. Next, we extend $T_0(V)$ to the set $T_1(V)$ consisting of the terms which can be formed from V together with the descriptions of order 1 in the domain of C_1, but without further introductions of the descriptor. (For example, $f([(\iota x) S (x)])$ belongs to $T_1(V)$ if $[(\iota x)S(x)]$ is a description of order 1 such that $S \in W_0(V)$, but $(\iota y)R(f([(\iota x)S(x)]),y)$ does not.) Then C_1 induces a map from $T_1(V)$ into M. Without fear of confusion, we shall still denote this map by C_1. We extend $W_0(V)$ and $S_0(V)$ correspondingly to sets $W_1(V)$ and $S_1(V)$. Since we have now defined a denotation in M for all terms which occur is $S_1(V)$, we may extend our truth definition in M from $S_0(V)$ to $S_1(V)$, i.e. we may define the relation $M \vDash X$ for all $X \in S_1(V)$ in the usual way.

Suppose, next, that $Q(x)$ belongs to $W_1(V)$ but not to $W_0(V)$ so that $[(\iota x)Q(x)]$ is a description of order 2. Suppose that $M \vDash [(\exists x)Q(x)]$ and $M \vDash (\forall x)(\forall y)[Q(x) \wedge Q(y) \supset x = y]$. Then we extend C_1 to a map C_2 by mapping $[(\iota x)Q(x)]$ into an element of M which is denoted by some a for which $M \vDash Q(a)$. Proceeding as before, we then define sets $T_2(V)$, $W_2(V)$, $S_2(V)$ such that all terms of $T_2(V)$ have a denotation in M and there is a truth definition in M for all sentences of $S_2(V)$.

Continuing in this way through the natural numbers, we finally put $T(V) = U_n T_n(V)$, $W(V) = U_n W_n(V)$ and $S(V) = U_n S_n(V)$ so that every term that belongs to $T(V)$ has a denotation in M and there is a step-by-step (but not a constructive) procedure for determining for any $X \in S(V)$ whether or not $M \vDash X$.

Our definition of the denotation of a description is purely semantical; it does not affect the question of the well-formedness of a string of symbols and, on the other hand, it is not affected by questions of provability. Like the usual truth definition, it is effective (in the sense of being decidable for a finite structure M but not for a general infinite structure). Indeed, in order to determine whether a description t has a denotation in M, we may proceed as follows. We list t as well as its immediate components and their components, etc., yielding a finite set of descriptions $\{t_v\}$, $t_v = [(\iota x v) Q_v (x v)]$, which we arrange in rising order. We then check, one by one, whether or not the conditions $M \vDash [(\exists x v) Q_v(x v)]$ and $M \vDash (\forall x v) (\forall y) [Q_v (x v) \wedge Q_v (y) \supset x v = y]$ are satisfied. The procedure is effective if M is finite.

By analogy with the double turnstile $\vDash$, which denotes satisfaction, we introduce the *double wedge* $\lhd\lhd$, to indicate denotation. Thus, for given M and correspondence C (which is again ignored in the notation), we write $M \lhd\lhd t$ and $M \lhd\lhd Q$ if t and Q are contained in $T(V)$ and $W(V)$, respectively. Then $M \lhd\lhd X$ is a consequence of $M \vDash X$.

(7) The framework outlined above permits the *elimination of descriptions* in the following sense. Let X be any sentence in the language L. Then there exists a sentence X', containing the same extralogical constants but not involving any descriptions such that the following is true. For any structure M and for a specified map C from the extralogical constants of X into appropriate entities of M, M satisfies X' if, and only if, the descriptions which occur in X have a denotation in M and M satisfies X.

The proof is by induction on the highest order of the descriptions contained in X. If X contains no descriptions, put $X' = X$. If X contains descriptions of order 1 but of no higher order, let these be $t_j = [(\iota x_j) Q_j (x_j)]$, $j = 1, \ldots, m$, where the $Q_j(x_j)$ are then free of descriptions. We then put $X' = \dot{X}$ where

$$\dot{X} = (\exists x_1) \ldots (\exists x_m) [X(x_1, \ldots, x_m) \wedge Q_1(x_1) \wedge \ldots \wedge Q_m(x_m) \wedge (\forall y_1) \ldots (\forall y_m) [Q_1(y_1) \wedge \ldots \wedge Q_m(y_m) \supset x_1 = y_1 \wedge \ldots \wedge x_m = y_m]].$$

If X contains descriptions up to order $n + 1$, $n \geq 1$, we use the same definition for $\dot{X}$ with respect to the descriptions which are contained in X immediately. $\dot{X}$ then contains descriptions up to order n only. This proves the assertion.

(8) We shall now consider the deductive aspects of our approach. Disregarding individual variations, it is the purpose of an adequate set of axioms and rules of deduction to enumerate all elements of a certain subset T of the set of all sentences of the given language. In the case of the ordinary lower predicate calculus without extralogical axioms, where T is the set of all 'tautologies', this enumeration is effective. If extralogical axioms are present in finite numbers, the enumeration is still effective and the same applies if the set of extralogical axioms is countable and effectively given.

If descriptions are present, we have the additional task of enumerating all those descriptions t that have denotations in all structures in which the extralogical constants that occur in t have been interpreted by means of a mapping C. For this purpose we introduce a (meta-) relation $\lhd$ ('wedge') which is related to the double wedge in roughly the same way as the turnstile is related to the double turnstile. Thus, the intended meaning of $K \lhd t$ is 't possesses a denotation in, or is interpreted in, K'. (More precisely, 'in every model of K'.)

Thus, let K be a set of extralogical axioms (*wff*) of the lower predicate calculus, without descriptions and, for convenience, without free variables. Then, in the usual versions of the calculus we may have $K \vdash X$, even if X contains free variables, and the rules of deduction are then arranged in such a way that $K \vdash X$ (X is deducible from K) if, and only if, the sentence X' is deducible from K, where X' is obtained from X by applying universal quantification to the free variables of the latter. We shall retain this feature here. However, the usual calculus also permits the occurrence of extralogical symbols in X which do not occur in K, for example, when X is a tautology (theorem of the lower predicate calculus). Here it is appropriate to exclude this possibility since $K \lhd X$ is introduced precisely in order to deal with interpretability in K.

(9) After these preliminary remarks, we are going to describe the details of a suitable deductive calculus. We keep K listed and, for brevity, omit it in our notation. Thus, we write $\lhd X$ and $\vdash X$ in place of $K \lhd X$ and $K \vdash X$. We recall that a *term* is a variable or an individual constant or is obtained from variables and individual constants by one or more applications of function symbols or of the descriptor:

(i) $\lhd t$ where t is any individual constant which occurs in K or any variable.

(ii)
$$\frac{\lhd t_1, \ \lhd t_2, \ \ldots, \ \lhd t_n}{\lhd f(t_1, \ldots, t_n)}$$

for any n-place function symbol which occurs in K.

(iii)
$$\frac{\lhd t_1, \ \lhd t_2, \ \ldots, \ \lhd t_n}{\lhd R(t_1, \ldots, t_n)}$$

for any n-place relation symbol R which occurs in K.

Thus, (ii) is a first rule of deduction. The remaining rules of deduction involving only the wedge are

(iv)
$$\frac{\lhd X}{\lhd \neg X}, \ \frac{\lhd X, \ \lhd Y}{\lhd [X \vee Y]} \ \frac{\lhd X, \ \lhd Y}{\lhd [X \wedge Y]}, \ \frac{\lhd X, \ \lhd Y}{\lhd [X \supset Y]}$$

provided X and Y are *wff*, according to the rules laid down previously.

(v)
$$\frac{\lhd X}{\lhd (\exists y)X}, \frac{\lhd X}{\lhd (\forall y)X}, \frac{\lhd t_1, \lhd t_2}{\lhd [t_1 = t_2]}$$

provided $(\exists y)X$ and $(\forall y)X$ are *wff*.

These are all the axioms and rules of deduction which involve only the wedge.

(vi) $\vdash X$ for all $X \in K$

(vii)
$$\frac{\lhd X_1, \lhd X_2, \ldots, \lhd X_n}{\vdash \psi(X_1, \ldots, X_n)}$$

when $\psi(p_1, \ldots, p_n)$ is any tautology of the *propositional calculus* which involves only the connectives $\neg, \vee, \wedge, \supset$.

As usual, (vii) may be replaced by a finite set of axioms for the propositional calculus (anticipating the rule of *modus ponens*; (ix) below, first rule).

(viii)
$$\frac{\lhd (\forall y)Q(y), \lhd t}{\vdash [(\forall y)Q(y)] \supset Q(t)}, \frac{\lhd (\exists y)Q(y), \lhd t}{\vdash Q(t) \supset [(\exists y)Q(y)]}$$

where t is a term and where y is free in $Q(y)$, for an arbitrary variable. For a given $Q(y)$, $Q(t)$ means that we replace any occurrence of y by t.

(ix)
$$\frac{\vdash X, \vdash X \supset Y}{\vdash Y}, \frac{\vdash X \supset Q(y)}{\vdash X \supset [(\forall y)Q(y)]}, \frac{\vdash Q(y) \supset X}{\vdash [(\exists y)Q(y)] \supset X}$$

provided X does not contain y.

(x) In the formula following $\vdash$ we may replace any variable by a variable not present previously, provided we do so everywhere. However, for a bound variable which appears repeatedly under the sign of a quantifier, it is permissible to carry out the substitution in a single quantifier and in its scope.

Next, we have the following axiom schemes for the identity.

(xi)
$$\frac{\lhd t}{\vdash t = t}, \frac{\lhd s, \lhd t}{\vdash s = t \supset t = s}, \frac{\lhd s, \lhd t, \lhd v}{\vdash s = t \wedge t = v \supset s = v}$$

and
$$\frac{\lhd s, \lhd t}{\vdash s = t \wedge Q(s) \supset Q'}$$

where the last expression is supposed to be a *wff* and such that Q' is obtained from $Q(x)$ by replacing some or all of the occurrences of s by t.

Finally, we introduce the crucial rules of deduction which relate to descriptions.

(xii)
$$\frac{\vdash(\exists x)Q(x),\ \vdash(\forall x)\ (\forall y)\ [Q(x) \wedge Q(y) \supset_x = y]}{\lhd[(\iota z)Q(z)]}$$

(xiii)
$$\frac{\lhd[(\iota z)Q(z)]}{\vdash Q([(\iota z)Q(z)])}.$$

(10) Employing the axioms and rules of deduction detailed above, we may now derive *theorems* in the usual way, except that in the present circumstances the theorems may be of the form $\vdash X$, where X is a *wff*, or $\lhd X$, where X is a *wff* or a term.

We are going to show that our calculus is *adequate* in the following sense:

(a) Suppose that M is a model of K under a map C whose domain contains individual constants for all individuals of M, among them the individual constants which occur in K, if any. Then for any well-formed formula *or term* $Q(y_1, \ldots, y_n)$ in the vocabulary of K whose free variables are just $y_1, \ldots, y_n$, $n \geq 0$, and for any individual constants $a_1, \ldots, a_n$ in the domain of C, $\lhd Q(a_1, \ldots, a_n)$ entails $M \lhd\!\lhd Q(a_1, \ldots, a_n)$; and if in particular $Q(y_1, \ldots, y_n)$ is a *wff*, then $\vdash Q(y_1, \ldots, y_n)$ entails $M \vDash Q(a_1, \ldots, a_n)$.

By checking through the axioms and rules of deduction of section (9) it is, in fact, not difficult to verify that (a) is satisfied. The fact that $\vdash Q$ and $\lhd Q$ may hold even if Q contains free variables, while $M \vDash Q$, $M \lhd\!\lhd Q$ can apply only in the absence of free variables, does not interfere with this conclusion.

(b) Given K as before, i.e. such that it consists of *wff* without free variables or descriptions, let $Q(y_1, \ldots, y_n)$ be any *wff* or term in the vocabulary of K for which the following condition is satisfied. For any mapping C as considered previously, whose domain D includes the vocabulary of K, onto a structure M which is a model of K (under C) and for any $a_1, \ldots, a_n$ in D, $M \lhd\!\lhd Q(a_1, \ldots, a_n)$. Then $\lhd Q(y_1, \ldots, y_n)$. And if, moreover, Q is a *wff* and $M \vDash Q(a_1, \ldots, a_n)$ for all such M, then $\vdash Q(y_1, \ldots, y_n)$.

It will be seen that (b) expresses the completeness of our calculus for the circumstances considered here. To show that it holds, we refer to the definition of the order of a description (section (3) above) which applies equally if the description includes free variables. We introduce a corresponding notion of order for any *wff* or term X by defining that the order of X is that of the description of highest order contained in it. If X does not contain any description, then we say that it is of order 0. In order to establish (b), it is now sufficient to show that it is correct for all *wff* and terms of order up to $n + 1$, $n \geq 1$, provided it is correct for all *wff* and terms of order up to n. We may disregard the slight verbal modification which is necessary for $n = 0$ and we may rely on the extended completeness theorem of the lower predicate calculus to tell us that (b) is correct for terms and *wff* which are free of descriptions.

So let $t(y_1, \ldots, y_n)$ be any description of order $n + 1$ in the vocabulary of K, $t = [(\iota x)Q(x, y_1, \ldots, y_n)]$, where Q contains descriptions up to order n only. Whenever $M \vartriangleleft\vartriangleleft t(a_1, \ldots, a_n)$ we then have, by the definition of a description, that $M \vDash X_1$ and $M \vDash X_2$, where $X_1 = (\exists x)Q(x, a_1, \ldots, a_n)$ and $X_2 = (\forall x)(\forall y)[Q(x, a_1, \ldots, a_n) \wedge Q(y, a_1, \ldots, a_n) \supset x = y]$. Since this is true for arbitrary M, C and $a_1, \ldots, a_n$, subject to the stated conditions, we then have, by our inductive assumption, $\vdash Q_1(y_1, \ldots, y_n)$ and $\vdash Q_2(y_1, \ldots, y_n)$, where $Q_1 = (\exists x)Q(x, y_1, \ldots, y_n)$ and $Q_2 = (\forall x)(\forall y)[Q(x, y_1, \ldots, y_n) \wedge Q(y, y_1, \ldots, y_n) \supset x = y]$. Hence, by rule (xii), $\vartriangleleft t$. Rules (i)–(xiii) are now sufficient to establish $\vartriangleleft X$, also for any other term or *wff* of order $n + 1$ in the vocabulary of K.

Now let $X = Q(y_1, \ldots, y_k)$ be a *wff* of order $n + 1$ such that in all the stated circumstances $M \vDash Q(a_1, \ldots, a_k)$. This implies $M \vartriangleleft\vartriangleleft Q(a_1, \ldots, a_k)$ and hence $M \vartriangleleft\vartriangleleft t_j(a_1, \ldots, a_k)$ for all descriptions t_j which are contained in $Q(y_1, \ldots, y_k)$, although $y_1, \ldots, y_k$ need not appear effectively in all of them. By what has been proved already, we may conclude that $\vartriangleleft t_j(y_1, \ldots, y_k)$. Suppose in particular that $t_1, \ldots, t_r$ are the descriptions of order $n + 1$ which appear in X, $t_j(y_1, \ldots, y_k) = [(\iota x_j)Q_j(x_j, y_1, \ldots, y_k)]$. Since $\vartriangleleft t_j(y_1, \ldots, y_k)$ has been derived, this must have been done by means of rule (xii), implying that $\vdash(\exists x_j)Q_j(x_j, y_1, \ldots, y_k)$ and $\vdash(\forall x_j)(\forall z_j)[Q_j(x_j, y_1, \ldots, y_k) \wedge Q_j(z_j, y_1, \ldots, y_k) \supset x_j = z_j]$. Also, by (xiii), $\vdash Q_j(t_j(y_1, \ldots, y_k), y_1, \ldots, y_k)$, and so

$$\vdash(\forall x_j)[Q_j(x_j, y_1, \ldots, y_k) \supset x_j = t_j(y_1, \ldots, y_k)]. \tag{10.1}$$

We may write Q in more detail as $Q(t_1, \ldots, t_m, y_1, \ldots, y_k)$, indicating the appearance of the descriptions $(t_1, \ldots, t_m)$ in Q. Then $Q'(y_1, \ldots, y_k) = (\exists x_1) \ldots (\exists x_m)[Q(x_1, \ldots, x_m, y_1, \ldots, y_k) \wedge Q_1(x_1, y_1, \ldots, y_k) \wedge \ldots \wedge Q_m(x_m, y_1, \ldots, y_k)]$ is a *wff* of order n, at most. Also $M \vDash Q'(a_1, \ldots, a_k)$ for all the M and $(a_1, \ldots, a_k)$ which have to be taken into account and so, by the inductive assumption,

$$\vdash(\exists x_1) \ldots (\exists x_m)[Q(x_1, \ldots, x_m, y_1, \ldots, y_k) \\ \wedge Q_1(x_1, y_1, \ldots, y_k) \wedge \ldots \wedge Q_m(x_m, y_1, \ldots, y_k)]. \tag{10.2}$$

Using familiar procedures of the lower predicate calculus, we obtain from (10.1)

$$\vdash(\forall x_1) \ldots (\forall x_m)[Q(x_1, \ldots, x_m) \wedge Q_1(x_1) \wedge \ldots \wedge Q_m(x_m) \supset x_1 \\ = t_1 \wedge \ldots \wedge x_m = t_m] \tag{10.3}$$

where, for the sake of brevity, we have not displayed $(y_1, \ldots, y_m)$. Also, from the last axiom scheme of (xi),

$$Q(x_1, \ldots, x_m) \wedge x_1 = t_1, \wedge \ldots \wedge x_m = t_m \supset Q(t_1, \ldots, t_m). \tag{10.4}$$

Combining (10.2) with (10.3) and (10.4), we deduce finally,

$$\vdash Q(t_1, \ldots, t_m). \tag{10.5}$$

But $Q(t_1, \ldots, t_m)$ is X in a different notation. This completes the proof of (b).

Observe that we were able to deduce $\vdash(\exists x)Q(x)$ and $\vdash(\forall x)(\forall y)$ $[Q(x) \wedge Q(y) \supset x = y]$ from $\lhd[(\iota x)Q(x)]$ because the latter assertion can be obtained only by way of the first and second. The situation would be different if we had admitted descriptions to K.

As Scott observes,[6] if a formula involving a description is regarded as well-formed only if the intended 'value' of the description exists, then the class of *wff* may be undecidable. In our approach, there is a corresponding phenomenon. Thus, for a suitable structure M there may be no decision procedure for establishing whether or not a term t has a denotation in M, i.e. whether or not $M \lhd t$. More particularly, we recall the fact that in arithmetic there is no decision procedure for $(\exists y)T_1(x, x, y)$, where T_1 is Kleene's predicate[7] and x ranges over the natural numbers. But if M is the standard model of arithmetic, then, for any numeral n, $M \lhd [(\iota y) T_1(n, n, y)]$ if, and only if, $M \vDash (\exists y)T_1(n, n, y)$. Accordingly, there is no decision procedure for settling whether a given description is meaningful in the domain of natural numbers. Similarly we may use the undecidability of Peano arithmetic in order to show that it does not have a decision procedure for establishing whether or not $\lhd t$ for a given term t.

Suppose that it is a sentence or consequence of K that, for a particular binary relation symbol R,

$$(\exists x)(\exists y)[R(x, y) \wedge (\forall z)[R(x, z) \supset y = z]].$$

This is equivalent to saying that in any model M of K there exists an element, to be denoted by a, such that $M \lhd [(\iota y)R(a, y)]$. Yet there is, in general, no theorem of our deductive calculus which would reflect this fact since $\lhd[(\iota y)R(x, y)]$ asserts that $[(\iota y)R(x, y)]$ is meaningful in M whatever the choice of a.

(11) I called this chapter 'On Constrained Denotation' in order to indicate that we are concerned with circumstances in which the denotation of a symbol, or complex of symbols, is *constrained*, or *restricted*, by the context. For the case of a description the constraint is maximal, in the sense that if a description is meaningful at all, its denotation is completely determined by the very sentences which establish that it *is* meaningful (see section (9), rule (xii)). There is a more trivial situation, for which the constraint is maximal, i.e. the case of a term composed of constants and function symbols only. Thus, let a, b denote individuals in a structure M, and let f be a function symbol denoting a specific function in M. Then the denotation of $f(a, b)$ is determined completely.

By contrast Hilbert's ϵ-*symbol* provides examples of terms whose denotation is constrained only partially. For orientation, $[(\epsilon x)Q(x)]$ is intended to denote some individual which satisfies Q provided such an individual exists.[8] We shall call (ϵ) the *selector* and we shall call any instance $[(\epsilon x)Q(x)]$ a *selection*, by analogy with our previous terminology. For simplicity, we shall consider a formal language with selector but without descriptor, although the reader should have no difficulty in combining the two.

Our formal language, L, will be as in section (3), except that in (vii) the descriptor (ι) is replaced by the selector (ϵ). With this modification, well-formed formulae are obtained exactly as before. Next we proceed, as in section (iv), to determine the satisfaction relation for a structure M with respect to a map C of extralogical constants of L onto appropriate entities of M, yielding truth-values for sentences which are free of selectors. We then define the order of a selection exactly as the order of a description was defined at the end of section (3).

Now let $t = [(\epsilon x)Q(x)]$ be a selection of order 1. If $M \vDash [(\exists x)Q(x)]$, then we extend C by *choosing* an element of M for which there exists an individual constant a such that $M \vDash Q(a)$, and we map t on the image of a in M. The simultaneous choice of such interpretations for all first-order selections yields an extension C_1 of C but, in contrast with the case of descriptions, the extension is not more unambiguous. We extend C_1 as before to all terms and *wff* in the vocabulary of M, and we define satisfaction in M for all sentences which can now be interpreted in M. We then repeat the procedure for selections of higher order and the terms, *wff*, and sentences which involve them.

The *elimination of selections* is analogous to the elimination of descriptions in section (7). Instead of the definition given there for $\bar{X}$, we now take

$$\bar{X} = (\exists x_1) \ldots (\exists x_m)[X(x_1, \ldots, x_m) \wedge Q_1(x_1) \wedge \ldots \wedge Q_m(x_m)].$$

The repeated application of this formula leads from a sentence with selections, X, to a sentence X' free of selections such that for a given structure M and map C, M satisfies X' if, and only if, the domain of C can be extended to the selections of X so that M satisfies X. Also, in order to obtain an adequate deductive calculus in the sense of (a) and (b) of section (9), we have to replace rules (xii) and (xiii) in that section by

$$\frac{\vdash (\exists x)Q(x)}{\lhd [(\epsilon z)Q(z)]} \quad \text{and} \quad \frac{\lhd [(\epsilon z)Q(z)]}{\vdash Q([(\epsilon z)Q(z)])},$$

respectively.

(12) We now return to the case of a language with descriptors in order to discuss certain alternatives to the formalism developed in sections (3)–(10).

Let us replace the deductive calculus of section (9) by some standard version of the deductive lower predicate calculus supplemented by the axiom scheme

$$\vdash [(\exists x)[Q(x, y_1, \ldots, y_k) \wedge (\forall y)[Q(y, y_1, \ldots, y_k)$$
$$\supset x = y]] \supset Q([(\iota z(Q(z, y_1, \ldots, y_k)], y_1, \ldots, y_k)] \quad (12.1)$$

for an arbitrary *wff* Q in which x, y_j and z are not quantified or bound by the descriptor. As long as we avoid clashes of bound variables, we may then deduce

$$\vdash (\forall y_1) (\exists y_2) \ldots (\forall y_k) [(\exists x) [Q(x, y_1, \ldots, y_k) \wedge (\forall y) [Q(y, y_1, \ldots, y_k)$$
$$\supset x = y]] \supset (\forall y_1) (\exists y_2) \ldots (\forall y_k) [Q([(\iota z) Q(z, y_1, \ldots, y_k)], y_1, \ldots y_k)]$$
$$(12.2)$$

and there are analogous formulae for any other sequence of quantifiers applied to $y_1, \ldots, y_k$. The sentences (12.1) and (12.2), etc. are satisfied in all models of K *in which they are meaningful*, i.e interpreted in the sense of the relation $\lhd\!\lhd$. However, it is entirely possible that the implicans of (12.2) is not satisfied by any model of K even though K is consistent. If so, the implicate of (12.2) is not meaningful in any model of K. Thus, we now have the possibility that a sentence X is a theorem of our deductive calculus, yet it is not meaningful in any model of K. Nevertheless, the calculus is adequate in the following sense:

(a) $\vdash Q(y_1, \ldots, y_n)$ entails $M \vDash Q(a_1, \ldots, a_n)$, where $a_1, \ldots, a_n$ denote individuals in a model M of K, *provided* $M \lhd\!\lhd Q(a_1, \ldots, a_n)$.

(b) Given a *wff* $Q(y_1, \ldots, y_n)$ in the vocabulary of K, suppose that the following condition is satisfied. Suppose that $M \lhd\!\lhd Q(a_1, \ldots, a_n)$ and $M \vDash Q(a_1, \ldots, a_n)$ for any map C from extralogical constants of L onto entities of a model M of K, as before. Then $\vdash Q(y_1, \ldots y_n)$.

In order to confirm (a), it suffices to check out the case that $Q(y_1, \ldots, y_n)$ is the *wff* of (12.1) (where Q has a different meaning). In order to verify (b), we refer to the proof of the corresponding assertion in section (10) and observe that the present system is at least as strong as that of section (9) as far as the derivation of assertions of the form $\vdash X$ is concerned. In particular, the rule (xii) in section (9) follows from (12.1) by means of *modus ponens*. However, we now have no deductive procedure for deciding whether a term or *wff* is meaningful for all models of K.

(13) A more radical departure from the formalism adopted so far is as follows. Instead of introducing $\lhd$ as a metalogical sign analogous to the symbol of assertion, $\vdash$, we adjoin to the formal language L a one-place relation $\mathfrak{q}(x)$, whose intended meaning is 'the term x denotes'. This may seem like a confusion of levels in the semantic hierarchy, since $\mathfrak{q}(x)$ really makes our assertion about the symbol x and not about the individual denoted by the symbols. However, this is entirely analogous to the phenomenon observed previously in the case of the definition of

the identity adopted in section (5), for there also $a = b$ was interpreted as a relation between symbols (i.e. that they denote the same individual).

We define terms and *wff* as in section (3), placing $ᗡ(x)$ among the one-place relations (just as the identity is counted among the two-place relations as far as the rules of formation are concerned, whatever its interpretation).

Now let C be a map from a set V of extralogical constants in L onto corresponding entities of a structure M as in section (4), so that all individuals of M are in the range of C. Let $T_0(V)$, $W_0(V)$, $S_0(V)$ be the terms, *wff*, sentences, respectively, formed from V together with $ᗡ$ and the identity. We determine for all $X \in S_0(V)$ whether or not $M \vDash X$ by the usual procedure, supplemented by the stipulation that $M \vDash ᗡ(t)$ for all $t \in T_0(V)$.

Let $t = [(\iota x)Q(x)]$ be a description of order 1 such that $Q(x) \in W_0(V)$. We then put $M \vDash ᗡ(t)$ if, and only if, $M \vDash (\exists x)Q(x)$ and $M \vDash (\forall x)(\forall y)$ $[Q(x) \wedge Q(y) \supset x = y]$. More generally, we put $M \vDash ᗡ$ *(t)* for any *term* of order 1 if $M \vDash ᗡ(t_j)$ for all *descriptions* of order 1 which are contained in t. Also, if R is an n-place relation symbol and $t_1, \ldots, t_n$ are terms of order 1, then we put $M \vDash R(t_1, \ldots, t_n)$ if $M \vDash ᗡ(t_j), j = 1, \ldots, n$, and $M \vDash R(a_1, \ldots, a_n)$ for some $a_1, \ldots, a_n$ which denote the same individuals of M as $t_1, \ldots, t_n$, respectively. Similarly $M \vDash t_1 = t_2$, if t_1 and t_2 denote, i.e. if $M \vDash ᗡ(t_1)$, and $M \vDash ᗡ(t_2)$ and, moreover, denote the same individual in M. Having now laid down the rules for the validity of the satisfaction relation $M \vDash X$ for all atomic sentences $X \in S_0(V)$, we may proceed to determine it for all other $X \in S_0(V)$ by the usual rules. We repeat this procedure for terms and sentences of higher order.

In this way, the satisfaction relation $M \vDash X$ is determined, ultimately, for all sentences X formulated from the vocabulary of V together with $ᗡ$ and, of course, the identity. This determination is 'ambiguous' only in the sense that an assertion such as $M \vDash \neg R(t)$ does not enable us to decide whether it is the case that t does not denote or that t denotes, but the corresponding instance of the relation does not hold in M. In order to decide this question, we need to know in addition whether or not $M \vDash ᗡ(t)$. But although the information provided by $M \vDash \neg R(t)$ thus is perhaps less complete than we might want it to be, it is, nevertheless, perfectly determinate. However, it is a consequence of our definitions that not all theorems of the lower predicate calculus remain valid here. For example, it is quite possible that $M \vDash \neg[(\forall x)Q(x) \supset Q(t)]$. This will be the case if $M \vDash (\forall x)Q(x)$ but t is a description of order 1 which has no denotation in M, $M \vDash \neg ᗡ(t)$. Even so, we still have $M \vDash ᗡ(t)$ $\supset [(\forall x)Q(x) \supset Q(t)]$, in any case.

Department of Mathematics
Yale University

NOTES

1 B. Russell, 'On Denoting', *Mind*, vol. XIV (1905: 479–93).
2 A. N. Whitehead and B. Russell, *Principia Mathematica*, 2nd edn, vol. 1 (Cambridge University Press, 1910; 1925).
3 D. Hilbert and P. Bernays, *Grundlagen der Mathematik* (Berlin, Springer, 1934; 1939).
4 D. Scott, 'Existence and Description in Formal Logic', in *Bertrand Russell: Philosopher of the Century*, R. Schoenman, ed. (Boston and Toronto, Little, Brown, 1967: 181–200).
5 cf., e.g., D. Kalish and R. Montague, *Logic, Techniques of Formal Reasoning* (New York and Burlingame, Harcourt, Brace & World, 1964); and P. Lorenzen, *Formale Logik* (Berlin, de Gruyter, 1962).
6 Scott, op. cit.
7 S. Kleene, *Introduction to Metamathematics* (Amsterdam, North-Holland, 1952; 1962).
8 Hilbert and Bernays, op. cit.

IS PHILOSOPHY
'AN IDLENESS IN MATHEMATICS'?

Alice Ambrose

The dispute between logicists and intuitionists concerning the applicability of the Law of Excluded Middle to propositions whose expression requires quantifiers ranging over an infinite domain is intimately connected with differing views about the nature of the entities in the domain. Intuitionists challenged the accepted use of the law in mathematics, and thereby raised the general question about what constitutes proof. Along with the question as to the validity of certain sorts of proof, questions have arisen concerning the legitimacy of certain mathematical operations (e.g. set formation in accordance with the axiom of inclusion), and the legitimacy of any use of impredicative definitions. At the core of disagreements over principles lay a number of ill-defined problems about the conception of the infinite. These problems arise in part over the conception of an infinite totality (the 'consummated infinite'), and in part over the mere fact that individuals in an ordered series having no last member cannot all be examined for possession of a property. It might be supposed that what look to be philosophical questions about the individuals of a domain could be eliminated by the minimal requirement that the individuals shall constitute a well-defined, non-empty class.[1] But it may be that the notion of being well-defined cannot be made clear – for example, when the individuals are real numbers. As is known, the work of Russell in logic, as well as that of Frege, is an attempt to deduce arithmetic from logic. On Bernays's account of Frege, logic is to be viewed as 'the general theory of the universe of mathematical objects'.[2] These objects are held to exist independently of our constructions, whether they be points, sets of points, numbers, sets of numbers, functions, etc. Gödel asserted that we have as good a ground for believing in the existence of sets, namely, our perception of them, as is given by our perceptions of physical bodies.[3]

These remarks make it appear that work in mathematics is governed by a philosophy of mathematics, in particular, that this is true of Russell's attempt in *Principia Mathematica* to give a foundation to mathematics. The same can be said of the mathematical work of the intuitionists. The cleavage between logicists and intuitionists over the amount of classical mathematics which is logically secure is sometimes thought to reflect a difference of opinion over the character of the entities the propositions of a given branch refer to. This difference would seem to be philosophical. Thus, according to intuitionists, a mathematical entity in the range of a variable is constructed, not discovered; and construction is taken to be a mental operation. An integer, for example, is the result of a mental process. A real number is a sequence of integers for which a method for constructing the nth member of the sequence can be given or a sequence resulting from arbitrary choices. A. Heyting characterises a mathematical theorem as 'a purely empirical fact' – to the effect that a construction has succeeded. An intuitionist mathematician who asserts $2 + 2 = 3 + 1$ is to be understood as saying, 'I have effected the two constructions, $2 + 2$ and $3 + 1$, and found that they lead to the same result'.[4] Both mathematical entities and the truth-values of mathematical propositions are mind-dependent. It is natural to suppose that the two opposing philosophical positions, conceptualism and Platonic realism, determine whether infinite totalities are to be counted among the values over which a variable ranges, and whether, for example, mathematics should contain the theorem that there are non-denumerably many sets of integers, which Cantor claimed to have proved by using the diagonal argument. If 'to exist' means the same as 'to be constructed', as it does according to intuitionism, then the existence theorems within a branch of mathematics will be restricted to what is created by a mind. Creation of numbers has been described as proceeding from 'the basal intuition of two-oneness . . . which creates the numbers one and two . . . and all finite ordinal numbers'.[5] The application of the Law of Excluded Middle will accordingly be restricted to the domain of entities which the mind can construct. 'Constructive' definitions are described quite differently by logicists and intuitionists. According to the former, such definitions merely give means for picking out an object from a totality which exists independently of and prior to being exhibited.[6] Each such object will either have the property under consideration, or lack it.

In extreme contrast to these two positions, both of which represent philosophical views as bearing on the development of mathematics, stands Wittgenstein's claim that philosophy 'leaves mathematics as it is', that 'A "leading problem of mathematical logic" is for us a problem of mathematics like any other',[7] '. . . labour in philosophy is as it were an idleness in mathematics'.[8] If this claim is correct, then the mathematician need not in the course of his work settle any question of ontology, and a philosophical mathematician who considers it his task to 'adjudicate among rival ontologies'[9] will not be doing something requisite for securing the foundations of mathematics. A philosophical problem, in whatever area, is according to Wittgenstein misconceived as a problem of deciding what is true; instead, it is to be seen as a puzzle engendered by language, to be dissolved rather than solved. In the present context one philosophical problem is the ancient one regarding the existence and nature of universals. The *meta*philosophical problem is to understand this problem and consequently the nature of the disagreement between the logicists and intuitionists. W. V. O. Quine says 'This opposition is no mere quibble; it makes an essential difference in the amount of classical mathematics to which one is willing to subscribe'.[10]

The purpose of this chapter is to try to arrive at an understanding of Wittgenstein's opposition to the consensus among mathematicians and logicians of the two schools regarding the bearing of a philosophy of mathematics on the actual practice of mathematics. In so doing, it may be possible to make some assessment of it. This is a difficult task if one is to attend to detail. What needs to be decided is whether a philosophical position connects up with the body of mathematics in the sense of having logical consequences for certain of its developments, or whether it is a mistake to suppose it does. I shall argue that some positions at issue are philosophical, and idle, that others which in important respects resemble philosophical positions but appear to be mathematical as well are not idle. In connection with the latter, I shall try to specify in what way the development of mathematics is made to depend on them. Before this can be done we shall need to make a distinction between a philosophical view and a statement belonging to mathematics. Because the nature of the opposing claims of intuitionists and logicists is unclear, disputes between the two schools, e.g. over the Law of Excluded Middle, over indirect proof and the extent of acceptable mathematics, over infinite totalities, look to be disputes *within* mathematics which *derive from* rival theories we all take to be philosophical. Once we become clear on the nature of a philosophical view in general and of the rival claims, and on the relation of philosophical views to the claims, what Wittgenstein meant by a philosophy of mathematics being idle in mathematics may then become clear.

Before coming to these central questions it will be useful to review the disagreements between members of the logicist school associated with Russell, and followers of Brouwer, Weyl and the French 'semi-intuitionists'. One well-known area of dispute concerned the relation of logic to arithmetic, number theory, analysis and set theory. Russell's thesis was that logic and mathematics are continuous, in the sense that the concepts of mathematics could be defined in terms of concepts of logic, and that the propositions of mathematics were deductive con-sequences of the primitives of a formalised logical system. Logic was primary, being the foundation, and laws of logic such as the Law of Excluded Middle were taken to be universally applicable. The opposite point of view was that mathematics is primary, that the formal logical principles it exemplified could not exist prior to its exemplification of them. As N. Bourbaki put it, 'logic, so far as we mathematicians are concerned, is no more and no less than the grammar of the language we use, a language which had to exist before the grammar could be con-structed'.[11] In so far, then, as the body of intuitionist mathematics differs from that of classical mathematics, the logical systems which conform to the character of each will differ. As is known, certain proofs occur within classical mathematics which are excluded from intuitionist mathematics, sometimes because the proof is indirect, i.e. has embedded in its structure the principle $p \vee \sim p$. Various systems of intuitionist logic have been set out,[12] and since they codify the logical inferences in intuitionist mathematics, $p \vee \neg p$ (the intuitionist analogue of $p \vee \sim p$) and $(x)A \vee (\exists x)\neg A$ will not appear in them as an axiom or theorem.

Another area of dispute between classical mathematicians and intuitionists concerns the existence of infinitely membered classes – classes whose number is $\aleph_0$ or greater. Neither side denies that there is an infinity of natural numbers, but intuitionists will mean by this, not a set of entities which has $2\aleph_0$ subsets, but an indefinitely proceeding sequence, one which, as Wittgenstein said, does not have the institution of an end. Terms which can be generated indefinitely in accordance, say, with some rule, will not form a *whole*, that is, a set which can itself be treated as an individual thing. Hence the dispute over the legitimacy of the operation 'set of x's', where x ranges, for instance, not only over integers, but over sets of integers, sets of sets of integers, etc.

This dispute has an intimate connection with the dispute over whether every instance of the formula $p \vee \sim p$ is valid. In the case where x ranges over an unending sequence of individuals, intuitionists claim that some predicates f are such that the formula $(x)fx \vee (\exists x)\neg fx$ does not hold. For example, for the disjunction, 'There either is a greatest pair of primes of the form p and $p + 2$, or every pair of this form is such that it is not the greatest', i.e. the number of twin primes is either finite or infinite. In consequence, to use an example from Heyting,[13] the following will not serve to define an integer l: l = the greatest prime such that $l - 2$ is also prime, or $l = 1$ if such a prime does not exist. Since this disjunction does not define an integer, it cannot be said that $l = 1$, or that $l \neq 1$. This situation obtains because it is not known whether the sequence of pairs of primes $p, p + 2$ is finite or not.

Another instructive example for purposes of contrasting the two schools of thought is the decimal expansion of π. Consider P, 'There either are or are not ten consecutive 7's in π', and Q, 'There either are or are not ten 7's in the first million places'.[14] Finding ten 7's in the first million places will establish the first alternative of both disjunctions, whereas not finding ten 7's in the first million places will establish the second alternative of disjunction Q but not of disjunction P. There is a boundary to the number of steps which must be taken to establish the negative alternative in Q, so that not finding ten 7's has the force of finding there are not ten 7's. In the case of the negative alternative in P, for which we have no *reductio ad absurdum* proof, not finding ten 7's leaves it open, no matter how far we have developed the expansion, whether there is no such sequence or whether we have not persisted long enough to establish the first alternative.

Both logicists and intuitionists would assent to this account of the proof-status of the two alternatives with regard to π, but they differ in what they then go on to say. According to logicians like Russell, the fact that neither alternative is *known* to be true does not in the least militate against asserting that one of them nevertheless is true. 'There are ten 7's in the infinite development of π' only differs from 'There are ten 7's in the first million places' with regard to its proof-status, not with regard to its having a truth-value. If there is one day a proof of one of the alternatives, this proof will show which truth-value it in fact possesses. Similarly for the disjunction 'Either there are or are not a finite number of twin primes'. Because one of these disjuncts must be true, the disjunction 'l is the greatest prime such that $l - 2$ is also prime, or $l = 1$ if such a prime does not exist' will define an integer; and the integer is either equal to 1 or it is not equal to 1. Presumably any well-formed declarative expression will serve as a value of p in $p \vee \sim p$.

According to the intuitionist, the existence of propositions of which we can neither assert that they are true nor that they are false precludes our asserting that they are either true or false. The fact that there is no proof either of $l = 1$ or of $l \neq 1$ precludes our saying that $l = 1 \vee l \neq 1$. Accordingly, in the logic which Heyting formulates to conform to intuitionist practice in mathematics, $p \vee \neg p$ will not be a theorem. Neither '$l = 1 \vee l \neq 1$' nor 'There are or there are not ten 7's in π' is an instance of a logical law; that is, $p \vee \neg p$ does not hold universally. This is not to say that $\neg(p \vee \neg p)$ is a theorem of the Heyting system, for some propositions, namely, Q, 'There either are or not ten 7's in the first million places', are instances of $p \vee \neg p$, and are valid. The classical law applies to this proposition because it meets the intuitionist condition for an assertable disjunction $P \vee Q$, namely, that P is assertable or that Q is assertable. Using the usual concepts of the propositional calculus and the concept 'p is provable' (symbolised by Bp) and assuming for the latter an axiom system S, Gödel gave an interpretation[15] of Heyting's propositional calculus in which '$p \vee q$' means $Bp \vee Bq$, and from its axioms no formula of the form $Bp \vee Bq$ is provable unless Bp or Bq is provable.[16] This condition precludes $p \vee \neg p$ from being a theorem, and correspondingly, within the intuitionist predicate calculus, $(x)fx \vee (\exists x)\neg fx$ will not be a theorem.

This fact about intuitionist logic reflects an important restriction on proof within mathematics. Given that $(x)fx \vee (\exists x)\neg fx$ is not a theorem, neither is $\neg(x)fx \rightarrow (\exists x)\neg fx$ (and in general $\neg\neg p \rightarrow p$). This means the exclusion of indirect proofs of existence. In accordance with principles of classical logic, a proof of the self-contradictoriness of $(x)fx$ or of $\neg(\exists x)fx$ allows the inference of an existential statement. Indirect proofs are a common means of establishing existence. But it is obvious that the self-contradictoriness of $(x)fx$ might be proved without this being a means for exhibiting something which lacks property f. The same thing obtains for a proof of the contradictoriness of $\neg(\exists x)fx$. Within intuitionist mathematics there exist only 'constructive' proofs. 'I am unable,' says

Heyting, 'to give an intelligible sense to the assertion that a mathematical object which has not been constructed exists.'[17] ' "To exist" must be synonymous with "to be constructed".'[18] In consequence it will not be the case that there is a class of mathematical objects of which constructed objects are a proper subclass. Nor will a mathematical object be definable unless it is constructible (or nameable).[19]

The limitations imposed by rejection of indirect proofs and of definitions other than constructive ones, as might be expected, do not gain the assent of classical mathematicians. Gödel objected to the fact that in the definition of constructible sets 'not all logical means of definition are admitted . . .; quantification is admitted only with respect to constructible sets and not with respect to sets in general'.[20] According to him, sets which cannot be proved to be constructible can be defined, and there will be non-denumerably many sets definable in his sense (by expressions containing names of ordinals – an infinity of them – and of logical constants, including quantification over sets). He conceded that '. . . it has some plausibility that all things conceivable by us are denumerable even if you disregard the question of expressibility in some language'.[21] He goes on to remark that he thinks 'the concept of definability satisfying the postulate of denumerability is not impossible but . . . that it would involve some extramathematical element concerning the psychology of the being which deals with mathematics', such as 'comprehensibility by our mind'.[22]

In order to assess the claim that mathematical developments are sometimes determined by extramathematical, i.e. philosophical considerations, we need a general characterisation of a philosophical statement. For this purpose it is useful to examine some views which would be taken by everyone to be philosophical. Here it is especially useful to focus on views of the two schools about the nature of natural numbers – the 'objects' in virtue of which statements of arithmetic and number theory are true. One of the obvious features of both Platonism and conceptualism is their failure to have been either established or refuted, and their total lack of promise of being so in the future. The prospect of their continuing irresolvability may reflect an *intrinsic* irresolvability, which is to say that they may be *in principle* not decidable by any new fact and, therefore, not decidable by recourse to fact. This possibility implies that they may not be truth-value statements. It is a perplexing feature of philosophical views, as contrasted with factual statements of science and everyday life, that a doubt about their truth-value status can arise, since they appear so convincingly to make factual claims. The same doubt arises about claims which figure in what appears to be a strictly mathematical controversy between schools of mathematics. An explanation is called for. I shall try to show that the explanation of both is similar. Let us consider now the two rival views, the one formulated by Plato and the other by Locke, on universals – in the present context, on natural numbers.

Russell put the Platonist position in the following way: '. . . the statement "two and two are four" deals exclusively with universals, and therefore can be known by anybody who is acquainted with the universals concerned and can perceive the relation between them which the statement asserts'.[23] Numbers, if anything, said Theaetetus,[24] 'have real existence'. They and their relations, an infinite totality of them, constitute a world of abstract objects independent of us – 'uncreated and indestructible'[25] – and open to our observation as surely as are the objects of sense. The task of the mathematician, as G. H. Hardy said, is to look into the special network of abstract entities that constitute the world of mathematics and note down his observations.[26] The theorems he proves are truths (about a non-empirical reality) which force themselves on the trained mind and so produce the remarkable agreement characteristic in so many areas of mathematics. Gödel's proof that there are undecidable propositions is taken merely to show that within *that* theory they are undecidable, that is, the axioms of the theory do not contain a *complete* description of the reality in question, but the reality described makes the undecidable propositions either true or false.

In opposition to this view Brouwer maintained that the natural numbers are mind-created. The numbers 1 and 2 are said to result from a 'basal intuition of two-oneness' which consists in abstracting from the special character of successive mental states, and each number thereafter results from repetitions of the process of using one of the elements of the original two-oneness to form a new two-oneness. Unclear as this account is, its intent is unmistakable: that the natural numbers be understood as mental products. It is clear also that the result of constructing natural numbers by the process of iteration can never be a *totality*.

There is one assumption common to both schools, which is, as Dummett put it, that 'if a statement is true there must be something in virtue of which it is true'.[27] The difference between them is over the kind of objects which make it true. Intuitionists hold that in the absence of a mental activity of construction, an existential proposition referring to numbers cannot be true, or false; and if true, it will be so at the date on which an entity exhibiting the property in question is constructed. All truths will be known truths, since proof will not consist in uncovering a prior existent fact about prior existing objects. But it will nevertheless be true in virtue of the objects it refers to. Brouwer expressed his divergences from other schools in terms of the entities each 'recognises'.[28] He objected to such expressions as 'the set of all real numbers between 0 and 1', 'the set whose elements are the points of space', 'the set whose elements are the continuous functions of a variable', on the ground that they fail to denote anything.

About natural numbers, then, there is no dispute over whether there are such objects. What appears to be in dispute is the *truth* of the claim, 'Numbers exist even though no minds exist'. The classification of both this view and the counterclaim, 'Numbers cannot exist apart from a mind', as *philosophical* is hardly in question. They, therefore, provide paradigm examples for the investigation of the character of philosophical views in general. One fact is immediately evident about these two special examples: that when each of the disputants who understands a number word, say, 'two', has before his mind a certain object, he cannot hope to settle its character by appealing to a more careful introspective scrutiny. 'Being mind-dependent' and 'being mind-independent' are not features exhibited on the face of the object, the way redness is exhibited on the face of a red image. The disputants are, therefore, forced to support their positions by argument.

In philosophical literature more argumentation is to be found for the Platonic view than for Lockeian conceptualism, and very little support is provided by philosophical mathematicians. I shall try to detail here a few arguments that may be, or may have been, in the minds of the proponents of the two views. First of all, taking intuitionists at their word, that to be is to be constructed, it follows that there are but a finite number of natural numbers unless an infinite mind exists which has constructed *all* of them. This latter alternative is not open to them if an infinite totality is impossible. Kronecker's remark that God made the integers cannot be true if such a creation is impossible in principle. Allowing, however, that the intuitionist acceptance of 'the potential infinite' implies that 'to exist' means 'to be construc*tible*,' there are again difficulties. If 'possibility of constructing' denotes a psychological capability, then it would be 'medically impossible',[29] to use Russell's language, for numbers to be constructed indefinitely unless the race does not die out or unless an eternal God with this capacity exists. Supposing that God does not exist or that the race does not die out, but that rocks, trees, gravestones remain, there could not be two, three or any number of them. To maintain that these have a number is to give up the mind-dependency of numbers. Numbers would be independently existing abstract entities. And in as much as every number has a successor, there would be infinitely many of them.

Against this argumentation the intuitionist can say that the Platonist is in no position to go beyond argument – to verify by experience that the objects before both their minds when they grasp a proposition of arithmetic can exist independently of their apprehension. The Platonist is in an egocentric predicament[30] with regard to what is before his mind – he cannot, by experience, establish the existence of numbers when not before his mind. As for the statement, 'There are an infinity of natural numbers', the intuitionist can maintain that all that is required is a proper interpretation of it to see that it expresses a truth: it asserts that for every natural number constructed another can be constructed. What is denied is that it asserts the existence of an infinite totality.

One striking feature of this dispute, and of philosophical disputes in general, is that advocates of rival views need not give way to each other. No matter how conclusive the argument against a view appears, it need convince no one but its proponent. Nor will an appeal to facts compel acceptance of one view or the other – and not because philosophical opponents are obtuse or hold their views in irrational disregard of the facts. There are no facts which decide, for example, between Leibniz's, Berkeley's and Locke's views on the nature of physical objects. Similarly there are no facts available, or theoretically possible, which decide whether or not the domain of individual variables, say, in number theory, consists of entities which exist in the absence of minds. Quine asserts that the acceptance of an ontology is like the acceptance of a scientific theory.[31] But if this were the case it should make a difference to the truth-value of some mathematical statements whether their subject matter were mind-dependent or not. Quine is explicit that there is something in virtue of which a theorem is true. He writes: 'a theory is committed to . . . those entities to which the bound variables of the theory must be capable of referring in order for the affirmations made in the theory to be true'.[32] Gödel says of set theory that it 'describes some determinate reality'.[33] It is an odd situation that mathematicians are unable to come to an agreement on what it is that makes their statements true. And this would indicate that very little, or nothing whatever, hangs upon an agreed on subject matter. It is, therefore, questionable whether an ontology in mathematics is comparable to a scientific theory. What, then, is the peculiar character of the view that natural numbers are independent existents, and of the contrary view that natural numbers are mind-dependent? If we can assess Wittgenstein's general view with respect to these paradigm philosophical positions, namely, that they are idle in mathematics, we shall be better able to assess conflicting positions regarding the Law of Excluded Mean, indirect proof, and set theory.

The two contrary views are expressed in what might be called the 'fact-stating idiom': they are assertions ascribing a feature to natural numbers. But this is not to say they are matter-of-fact propositions, for it can scarcely be doubted that intuitionists and Platonists wish to be understood as asserting the 'essential' features of natural numbers, i.e. as asserting something necessary. They express themselves with the assurance one has in asserting that a yard is three feet, or that lions are felines, and are not shaken by arguments against their positions. To see, then, what these philosophical views come to, we should note some important features of necessary propositions. One is that they are not *made* true by some fact and another is that they are not about words. To illustrate with a proposition free from questions surrounding the philosophical propositions under discussion, consider 'Lions are felines'. Its truth can be known without observing lions. No empirical fact about lions has any bearing on its truth – something that cannot be said of 'Lions are carnivores', which is also expressed in the fact-stating idiom. All that is required to know that it is true is the verbal fact about the words used to express it, in the English language the use of the words 'lion' and 'feline'.

To know that the sentence 'Lions are felines' expresses a necessarily true proposition, is to know that ' "Feline" applies to what "lion" applies to' expresses a factually true verbal proposition. It is an empirical fact of the English language that the first sentence expresses a necessity. Its equivalence to the fact that the second sentence expresses a truth about the use of 'feline' and 'lion', shows that it does not assert anything about what the words apply to – no knowledge of lions is required. The same verbal fact verifies that it expresses a necessity and that the second sentence expresses a factually true verbal proposition.[34] It should be noted that the sentence 'Lions are felines' does not state a verbal fact; it does not mention, and is therefore not 'about', the words 'lion' and 'feline', as is the sentence 'The word "feline" applies to whatever "lion" applies to'. It does not *state* the verbal fact required for knowing that what it expresses is true. What it states is a (non-verbal) necessary proposition, which is not to be confused with the verbal and factual proposition that 'feline' applies to what 'lion' applies to. Nevertheless, though the necessary proposition is not about lions nor about the word 'lion', the fact that the *sentence* expresses a necessity is equivalent to the fact that a related sentence about the use of words expresses something true. In an oblique way its import is verbal, but it is not itself a verbal proposition.

If this account of necessary propositions is correct, then even though the sentence 'Natural numbers are mind-dependent' expresses a necessary truth, it cannot be construed as expressing a fact about numbers. It is ontologically idle – giving no information about the nature of what there is – since were it true that it expresses a necessity, this truth would rest on a verbal fact about the use of the words 'number' and 'mind-dependent'. Here it is instructive to compare it with the sentence 'Lions are felines', or 'A yard is three feet'. Unlike these, it is not a fact of English that it expresses a necessity, for it is not a fact that there is an established convention for the use of words to the effect that 'mind-dependent', as English is used, applies to everything 'natural number' applies to. Nor is it the case that 'independent abstract entity' applies to what 'natural number' applies to. Sentences for neither view express anything necessarily true.

How then are we to understand the claims of intuitionists and Platonists that they are stating the essential features of natural numbers? Both know the linguistic conventions, and know that their sentences do not express necessary propositions. Yet they argue as if in support of the truth of a view. The verbal aspect of what they are doing is concealed by the fact-stating idiom in which they announce them. When the philosophical mathematician says 'Numbers are to reckoned among the things that are',[35] he is *inventing* a subject matter – in name if not in fact, to correspond to substantive terms which do not have a use to refer to things one can point to. As Wittgenstein put it, 'When we perceive that a substantive is not used as what in general we should call the name of an object . . . we can't help saying to ourselves that it is the name of an aethereal object'[36] (whether or not the object exists only if a mind exists). 'What you want is . . . a new notation, [but] by a new notation no facts of geography are changed'.[37] It appears to me that what here looks to be argumentation for a position is to be interpreted as a means of persuading one to accept a convention where none exists. Actual usage is mute on the connection between 'natural number' and 'mind dependency', and also on whether 'number' and 'independent entity' are connected. This being the case, there is leeway for argument that will incline one to accept a new convention. In what follows I take argumentation by each school which on the surface purports to establish a necessary truth about numbers as showing not that a necessary truth *is* being expressed by the sentence uttered, but that it *should* be. Proceeding in accordance with the analysis of 'Sentence *S* expresses a necessary proposition', I shall treat the assertion that a sentence should express a necessity as having a verbal point, to introduce a new way of speaking. The point is concealed by the declarative form of 'Numbers are mind-dependent', 'Numbers are independent existents'. But since these are not in fact correlated with any accepted convention, I shall take them to present in a concealed way a preference for a notation.

In various ways the preferences are idle. The fact that there is no resolution of the dispute between intuitionists and Platonists is reflected in the verbal fact that no new convention has been generally accepted. So the philosophical labour of trying to resolve it has had no fruits within mathematics. But supposing the dispute were resolved, the labour required would seemingly still be 'an idleness'. For it is hard to suppose that anything in mathematics would change. The notation would remain unaffected. The historical dispute over '$\sqrt{-1}$' was resolved in favour of its introduction, and the course of mathematics changed. But such terms as 'mind-dependent entity', 'independent existent' and their equivalents seem to have no place in mathematics.

The views at issue are idle in another way. Whether the arithmetical symbols in the sentence '$2 + 1 = 3$' denote entities of any kind, and whether the bound variables in 'All primes greater than 2 are odd' do so, the propositions expressed by them are not made valid or invalid by their failure to be 'true of something'. As for the mind-dependency of numbers, $2 + 1 = 3$ is such that its opposite is logically impossible whether one takes the Platonic view about numbers or the Berkeleian view that any general term stands for a particular (dependent) idea. Both views 'leave mathematics as it is'.

The idea that there is a logical dependency between these views and the mathematical developments with which they are associated is dispelled on closer scrutiny. Although it is natural to associate a philosophical view about the essential nature of numbers with the mathematical development its proponents engaged in – the view that natural numbers are mental constructions with taking the natural numbers to be primitive, and the view that they are independent entities with defining natural numbers as predicates taken in extension, i.e. as sets – the two are logically independent. For the notion of a natural number could be primitive without numbers being either the mind's creation or the mind's discovery. Also, a subjectivist philosophical view about predicate terms is compatible with defining numbers as sets. The relation between the fundamental ideas of a branch of mathematics and their philosophical analysis seems to be no closer logically than that between 'Numbers are sets' and 'Jupiter is the largest planet'. Furthermore, although on the philosophical view held by intuitionists construction is a mental process and its result a mind-dependent entity, a constructivist requirement can be framed independently of this view. Heyting says, 'it must be clear what it means that a given operation is the construction of a certain object',[38] and asserts that construction is a mental operation. But the requirement that a construction be effective can be met without subscribing to the view that it is mental. E. W. Beth asserts that 'axiomatic set theory is the final result of the development of Cantor's strongly platonist conceptions',[39] but at the same time admits that it is compatible with radically opposed conceptions.[40]

Nevertheless there are parts of mathematics which are done differently according as one philosophical view or the other is subscribed to, and some parts of intuitionist mathematics have no counterpart in classical mathematics. Intuitionist mathematics is not merely what remains of classical mathematics as a result of eliminating objectionable concepts, operations and methods of proof.[41] These facts suggest that philosophy does not 'leave mathematics as it is'. The question is: in what way are these differences determined by a philosophical view? S. C. Kleene speaks of a development of mathematics being 'based on a philosophy of mathematics',[42] and of a position apparently within intuitionist mathematics being taken 'on philosophical grounds'. I wish to hold that the relation of the rival philosophical views we have discussed is a causal or associational one, not a logical one, that these views are no more integral to a mathematical development than Newton's theological views to his physical theories. There are other points of divergence between classical and intuitionist mathematicians whose status – whether philosophical or mathematical – is not clear, and which are not logically neutral. These must be considered separately. Whether the divergent positions eventually connect through some causal link with Platonism and conceptualism need not be investigated here. That there is a merely contingent relationship between the philosophical views and certain statements expressed in wholly mathematical terms in one development or the other can be made relatively convincing.

To illustrate, consider the Platonist view that numbers are abstract entities existing independently of a mind with respect to the statement that numbers are classes of classes. It is plain that these are not logically related. However, misconceiving the philosophical statement as asserting a fact about numbers and misconceiving similarly the statement that classes are independent existents made it natural for Platonists to couple the expressions 'number' and 'class'. The definition of a natural number as a class of similar classes is only expressible in a logical language quantifying over classes. (In a lower order language numbers will be primitive.) In consequence of it, it was possible to incorporate arithmetic in a system of logic. Since Frege's class logic was found to involve antinomies, Russell's system, in avoiding them through a types theory, had to add a postulate asserting the existence of an infinite set in order to make sure that there is no greatest cardinal number. Thus, in the sense that the philosophical view that numbers are independently existing entities has been a motive force behind an analysis of numbers as classes, which itself was embodied in the fabric of mathematics, it has indeed not been idle. It had the effect of encouraging the axiomatisation of foundations supposedly required to make mathematics logically secure, which in turn gave impetus to the metamathematical study of the properties of formal systems, and to the addition of a new branch, proof theory. Hilbert's programme of proving the consistency of arithmetic was given urgency by the class paradoxes. However, I think this is hardly the sense in which mathematicians of the two schools suppose their respective work is based on a philosophy of mathematics. If they suppose their work to be logically connected with the rival philosophical views I have considered here, then I believe them to be in error.

Nevertheless, there exist disagreements between logicists and intuitionists which are framed in the current language of mathematics – something which cannot be said of the disputes over the mind-dependency of numbers. These concern claims which have a logical relation to a mathematical development, yet resemble in important respects philosophical views. To these I now turn. If the claims at issue are classified as philosophical, then we must say that philosophy does not leave mathematics as it is. How they are to be classified, and therefore whether or not Wittgenstein is right, is unimportant if we can get clear on what their points of similarity to philosophical theories are. I shall try to show that, like philosophical theories, their import is misconceived. It will be recalled that the sentence expressing a 'view' about numbers was taken to express a necessary proposition, and that since there is no accepted linguistic convention establishing that it in fact expresses a necessity, it was interpreted as introducing in a concealed way a linguistic innovation. In my opinion, the same description holds for claims at issue between mathematicians which are apparently *within* mathematics since they can be expressed in mathematical terms. Although they make no mention of language, and appear to state essential features of 'mathematical structures', as in the case of opposing philosophical theories what is at issue is a terminological decision (like the decision on '$\sqrt{-1}$'). The difference is that once a decision is come to, this makes a difference to the course of mathematics.

Sometimes it is open to a person to throw a pair of semantical dice, with quite different consequences dependent on the outcome. To carry the analogy to the context of the logicist-intuitionist controversy, the throwers here weight the dice – decide how the dice are to fall. But this is done without awareness that the course of mathematics is being changed by a linguistic decision rather than by a perception of a fact of ontology.

In the remainder of this chapter I shall try to apply this thesis, which it is needless to say is not Russell's or Brouwer's, to various sources of controversy: the nature of real numbers, the existence of certain sorts of sets, the legitimacy of certain operations and of indirect proofs. It is instructive to begin with the Russell–Frege account of a natural number as a class of similar classes. On first meeting this account, my own reaction was that Russell and Frege had assigned a new meaning to the term 'number' (inasmuch as the dictionary was silent on this matter), rather than that they had explicated its conventional meaning. Doubtless they were governed by a condition for proper explication of a familiar concept which Carnap much later made explicit: that the analysis supply a corresponding exact concept by means of 'explicit rules for its use, for example, by a definition which incorporates it into a well-constructed system of . . . scientific concepts'.[43] It is clear that this procedure replaces the familiar concept by another. R. L. Goodstein remarks that Russell and Frege 'found . . . a new concept',[44] which is to say they offered a new definition of a word (although under the guise of analysing a familiar idea). The definition, which represents a *decision*, is not an idle one. It sets the future course of language.

I wish, now, to examine some of the propositions which occur within mathematics but have the earmarks of philosophical statements. They are at the centre of a controversy which is carried on as though one of two contrary propositions is mistaken. Their affinity with the two philosophical statements we have considered is clear: the question as to their *truth* cannot be settled by mathematics itself, any more than the same question about a philosophical statement can be settled by appeal to fact. So long as they are not shown to issue in a contradiction, there is no deciding between them. The fact that attempts to justify a decision on their truth have been fruitless suggests the possibility that no mistake has been made, and that disputation over their truth is idle. If I am right in supposing that this possibility obtains, then we have an explanation of the intractability of the disputation: the nature of what is in dispute has been misconceived. It would also be a possible explanation of Wittgenstein's claim that a philosophy of mathematics is idle. But the propositions in dispute do not leave mathematics as it is, inasmuch as they entail differing consequences. In this sense they differ markedly from the philosophical propositions discussed here, which are not logically connected with a mathematical development. My thesis is that propositions of the following list present concealed decisions governing the use of language (or derive logically from others which do) and that with the acceptance or rejection of the decisions different bodies of mathematics result.

The number of the set of real numbers between 0 and 1 is greater than $\aleph_0$.

$2^{\aleph_0} > \aleph_0$

There is no set of real numbers greater than the set of integers but smaller than the set of all real numbers.

Given any class of mutually exclusive classes (non-null) there is at least one class having exactly one element in common with each of the classes.

There are functions which cannot be effectively computed.

A real number. $a_1 a_2 a_3 \ldots$ can be generated by a succession of free choices of 0 and 1.

In describing the controversy over these propositions I shall use the language of the protagonists, that is, the idiom natural to it, in which 'entities recognised' or 'concepts admissible' by one side or the other are supposedly at issue. Central to the controversy are questions which are framed as questions about sets and set formation. Putting them in this way is, I think, misleading, and I shall try to indicate how 'acceptance' of a truth disguises making a linguistic decision. According to Cantor a set G exists which has as members all objects x for which $S(x)$ holds. The existence of the Burali-Forti paradox forced a modification of this axiom of set formation[45] (the axiom of inclusion), so that sets could be introduced only if they are subsets of pre-existing sets: given a set H, there exists a set G having as members all objects x which $x \epsilon H$ and $S(x)$ holds. Brouwer says that since the existence of a collection of sets has to be postulated to begin with and since the only objection classical mathematicians can bring to the introduction of a new set is the discovery of a contradiction, in practice the result has been to avoid formation of such sets while continuing to operate with other sets introduced on the basis of the old axiom of inclusion.[46] The linguistic consequence is that such expressions as 'the set of all real numbers between 0 and 1', are acceptable, the new language of the theory of powers was created, and with it the wherewithal for expressing Cantor's continuum problem: whether there is a set of real numbers greater than the set of integers (with number χ_0) but smaller than the set of all real numbers, that is, whether the power of the continuum is the second smallest infinite power.[47]

By unrestricted iteration of the operation *set of*, classical mathematicians are able to obtain Cantor's ascending orders of infinity. The totality of sets obtained is itself treated as a set, and a number is assigned to it. If, for example, the totality of subsets of a set is not finite and not one-to-one correlatable with the natural numbers, classical mathematicians say its number must be some $\aleph$ greater than $\aleph_0$. Galileo said that infinite sets are not comparable as to size, that, for example, one could not say of the cardinals 1, 2, 3, 4, . . . , that their number is either greater than or equal to that of the cardinals 1, 4, 9, 16, . . . ; he said this while recognising that 1 could be paired with 1^2, 2 with 2^2, etc. 'The cardinals are one-to-one correlatable with their squares' is now a generally accepted description, which is to say that the phrase 'one-to-one correlation' has been extended to cover $\aleph_0$ correlations. The intuitionists' proviso is that '$\aleph_0$ correlations' denotes merely an unending process, and they do not go on to compare the sizes of infinite sets which cannot be one-to-one correlated. Their constructibility requirement compels them to stop with the lowest order of infinity $\aleph_0$. And this is the number, not of a totality of things existing all at once, [48] but of an unending sequence ('the potential infinite') whose elements can be computed separately.

It is clear that this requirement entails a different account of real numbers. Cantor's definition of a real number, say, between 0 and 1, as a convergent sequence of rationals, and Dedekind's definition of it as a section of rationals, are replaced by a 'law of constructing a series of digits after the decimal point, using a finite number of operations'.[49] A real number is also definable according to intuitionists as a 'free-choice sequence', a sequence resulting from a wholly irregular way of picking out an indefinite number of elements. On this account, a real number can be generated by a random device such as the throwing of a coin, each digit being 0 or 1 according as the coin falls heads or tails. Digit by digit development of a decimal by free choices is very different from development in accordance with a law, and it has been objected that the operation yields only 'a daily changing collection of terminating decimals',[50] and no more *results* in a real number than does, for a different reason, *throwing endlessly*. Goodstein says 'it seems to me that only [where a law exists] can we speak of a real number, the . . . law itself'. As Wittgenstein put it:[51]

> A real number *yields* extensions but is no extension. A real number is an arithmetical law which endlessly yields the places of a decimal fraction.

In this discussion we have a good example of the concealment, by the fact-stating idiom, of a recommendation on how the expression 'real number' should be used. 'Real number' is to be applied to what is calculable (according to Kronecker and the French semi-intuitionists, to what is nameable). The disagreement over its use remains unsettled, but opting for one decision or the other results in a different theory of real numbers. The same remark applies to the term 'function'. The question, 'Are there non-computable functions?', although so framed as to make no mention of words, is according to Goodstein not over the existence of a function but about how the term 'function' is to be used.[52] Is a term to be called a function, if it admits no computation procedure?

That conditions which intuitionists impose on the application of the terms 'real number', 'set' and 'function' have consequences for real number theory can now be usefully illustrated. The different conclusions drawn by Cantor and non-Cantorians from the diagonal process may appear to reflect a difference of opinion over their validity. But I think it will be evident that something arbitrary is involved, that the conclusion represents a decision. Mathematicians of each school will agree that denumerably infinite sets of real numbers can be constructed, and that for every such set a real number between 0 and 1 can be constructed which is not in the set. That is, the diagonal process can be used to generate, for every array of decimal sequences, a decimal different from any decimal occurring in the array. The difference lies in what each school then goes on to say. Cantor claimed to have proved by it the existence of a non-denumerable set, namely, the set of all decimal sequences. For his proof proceeds by *reductio ad absurdum* from the hypothesis that one has an enumeration of all decimal sequences. The diagonal process generates a sequence not in the enumeration, and in doing so shows the hypothesis to be contradictory. The question is whether in showing that there cannot be an enumeration of the totality of real numbers one has shown that there is a non-denumerable totality of them. In some axiom systems there is a 'powerset axiom' which post-ulates the existence of all subsets of a set, in the present case that all the sequences of decimal fractions form a set. This set can then be proved to be non-denumerable. The question is whether the diagonal process, without the axiom, provides the set.[53] Limitations intuitionists impose on the operation *set of* preclude such sets. The diagonal process is taken merely to show that an enumeration of all real numbers is impossible. In consequence 'function which enumerates the real numbers' has no use.[54] But intuitionists stop short of allowing a use to 'set of all real numbers'. In claiming to have proved the set of real numbers to be non-denumerable, Cantor takes the sentence 'The real numbers are non-denumerable' to assert something necessarily true. In conformity with my earlier account of sentences of this sort, this is to say that 'non-denumerable' applies to the class 'real numbers' applies to. And this, in my view, is to opt for a convention, for which the diagonal argument is the justification. I say Cantor opted for a convention rather than proved a truth because there is another possible explanation of what the diagonal process does, and does not, justify saying, namely: (a) that from any sequence of decimal fractions another can be constructed which is not in the array, (b) in consequence 'enumeration of the real numbers' has no use in the language of set theory, (c) that it does not require giving 'non-denumerable set of real numbers' a use.

The exposition given thus far of views of classical mathematicians serves also as an exposition of Russell's views. In his Preface to *Our Knowledge of the External World* he says of the theories he puts forward in that book that '*except in regard to such matters as Cantor's theory of infinity*, no finality is claimed for them'.[55] This claim to finality has been brought in question by the still extant division between classical and intuitionist mathematicians on precisely this matter. At any rate the usual description of the division is that it is basically a difference over the existence of infinite totalities. If we look to the language of classical mathematicians, we can, I think, find the linguistic analogy which their language accentuates. The language is that used to describe empirical reality, the language by which we assert truths about things and classes of things perceptible to the senses. Wittgenstein pointed out that the question 'How many?' could be answered by '3' or by 'infinitely many'.[56] The answers suggest that 'infinitely many' equally with '3' is a number designation. Talk of transfinite cardinals is modelled directly on that of natural numbers. Cantor defines equality between finite cardinals and extends it to infinite cardinals. The existence of a cardinal number with property P is defined to mean that a set having that cardinal exists. Gödel says:[57]

> On the basis of these definitions it becomes possible to prove that there exist infinitely many different cardinal numbers or 'powers', and that, in particular, the number of subsets of a set is always greater than the number of its elements. . . . Owing to the theorem that for each cardinal number and each set of cardinal numbers there exists one cardinal number immediately succeeding in magnitude and that the cardinal number of every set occurs in the series thus obtained, it is possible to denote the cardinal number immediately succeeding the set of finite numbers[58] by $\aleph_0$ (which is the power of the 'denumerably infinite' sets), the next one by $\aleph_1$, etc.

Proof of this theorem requires the axiom of choice, a proposition which presents no puzzlement in regard to classes of objects we meet with in sense-experience. The source of the language of sets is to be found in the language of every day. Stressing its features – such features as its subject–predicate structure – bolsters the Platonic philosophical view and encourages decisions which introduce linguistic innovations into mathematics, such as the similar use of '3' '$\aleph_0$,' and '$2^{\aleph_0}$' as names of numbers. Platonists take the proposition 'There are sets with $2^{\aleph_0}$ elements' to be true of a non-empirical reality. But their implied claim that the sentence expressing it, as well as the sentence expressing their philosophical view, stands for a necessary truth, is not backed by an established convention. Instead, it introduces a convention which stresses a similarity between 'set of all real numbers' and 'class of lepidoptera', between '3' and '$2^{\aleph_0}$'. The difference is muted – such a difference, for example, as that one cannot sensibly say a larger number is nearer to $\aleph_0$ than a smaller one. The view that a mathematical development is based on a philosophy of mathematics arises from a misconception: a philosophical position and disputed mathematical statements alike are of the same nature, the concealed linguistic decisions in each being prompted by analogies with ordinary language. That there is a misconception is most strongly suggested by the following questions: how is Russell to show the intuitionist that 'series of natural numbers' means something more than 'unending sequence' – that it denotes a totality with the smallest infinite power $\aleph_0$? How is he to convince the intuitionist that one of the two sentences, 'There are ten 7's in the expansion of π', 'There are not ten 7's in the expansion of π' expresses a truth? And how is the intuitionist to show Russell that in an indirect proof it is illegitimate to come to an existence-conclusion in the absence of a means of exhibiting what is said to exist? To none of these questions is it relevant to turn to mathematics for an answer. I hold that reasons given do not logically entail one answer as against another. They are means of persuading the acceptance of a language decision.

This thesis may appear especially unconvincing as applied to the controversy over indirect proof and the Law of Excluded Middle which figures in it. About a question of logical validity it would seem that one of the two opposing positions must be mistaken. A perception of a difference from usual questions of validity is evident in the following:[59]

> Brouwer demands of the mathematicians a profound change of their habits of thought on grounds which for them are not wholly convincing. . . . So long as they apply the methods stigmatized by Brouwer carefully and consistently, they do not have to come to contradictory results. Therefore, the position of Brouwer and his followers is much more difficult than that of the founders of modern analysis who also have pointed out the necessity of jettisoning various customary methods of reasoning [e.g. arguing as though every continuous function could be differentiated]. In such cases, one could conclusively convince his opponents of their errors through counter-examples. Brouwer's counter-examples, however, are not so convincing.

And, in fact, the prospect of resolving the dispute is as unpromising as is the Platonist-conceptualist controversy over universals. Why this should be true is suggested by the kind of support the two schools marshal for their positions on what they both conceive to be the universal validity of the Law of Excluded Mean and of a standard form of proof employing it. In what follows, I shall try to show that the controversy in a concealed way concerns a matter of terminology.

It is interesting that intuitionist objection to the 'admissibility' of certain 'concepts' is often framed as an explicit objection to terminology. For example, it is asserted that 'set of real numbers between 0 and 1', 'totality of integers', 'numbers greater than $\aleph_0$ are *meaningless*, and that there will be an answer to Cantor's question about the power of the continuum as soon as it can be interpreted so as to have meaning.[60] Likewise they give as a ground for rejecting indirect proof as generally valid that sentences of the form $(\exists x)fx$ which appear at the end of a proof sequence are meaningless if there is no method of exhibiting the thing whose existence they purport to assert. Heyting says: 'I am unable to give an intelligible sense to the assertion that a mathematical object which has not been constructed exists.'[61]

What is curious about this assertion is that as language is used within mathematics these expressions are not meaningless. Further, the practice of intuitionists belies that they are. For despite saying that the final sentence '$(\exists x)fx$' occurring in a classical proof sequence of sentences is meaningless, intuitionists attempt proving the truth of $(\exists x)fx$ constructively. They also attempt to 'reconstruct' classical mathematics in intuitionist terms. Have they by a constructive proof demonstrated the *same* thing as was proved non-constructively? If so, how could they know this if '$(\exists x)fx$' in the classical context was meaningless?

To apply the term 'meaningless' to many phrases and sentences now in use might be thought to be a mere mistake. But this is not plausible. Intuitionists' use of this term is motivated: its point is to exclude certain forms of expression in classical mathematics, and in addition, to curtain off from view the innovations in terminology which they themselves have introduced and incorporated into their mathematical practice. What is not evident to them is that they have put into operation a notational preference rather than discovered a fact about what exists or a fact about a class of propositions (that the Law of Excluded Mean does not apply to them). In support of this thesis, I cite their assertion that 'to exist' means 'to be constructed'. Just as Hume could defy anyone to find a simple idea without a correspondent impression, because by 'ideas' he 'mean[t] the faint images of [impressions]',[62] so the intuitionist can be sure there will be no non-constructive existence proofs. It has already been decided that an existence proof will contain a construction of what is said to exist. On this Wittgenstein remarks:[63]

> One can merely say, 'I call an existence proof only one which contains such a construction'. . . . Intuitionists [who] say '. . . existence can only be proved so and not so', . . . have only defined what *they* call existence.

Note that it is a definition, not a truth, which alters the course of mathematics.

Russell's position can now be viewed as supporting the linguistic *status quo* (though certainly not conceived in this way by Russell). He maintains that as soon as he knows the meanings of sentences of the form '$(x)fx$' and '$(\exists x) \sim fx$', he knows that one of them states something true though he may not know which.[64] That is, both sentences express *propositions*. Although the term 'proposition' is not part of the apparatus of mathematical terms and has a minimal use in ordinary speech, whatever use it has is I think correctly characterised by Wittgenstein: 'The word "proposition" is equivalent to a calculus . . . in which $p \vee \sim p$ is a tautology (the Law of Excluded Middle holds)'. That is, according to current conventions 'proposition' means what is either true or false. 'If the Law of Excluded Middle does not hold, then we have changed the concept of a proposition.'[65] Intuitionists claim to have discovered propositions to which this logical law does not apply. Accordingly, their calculus of propositions does not include $p \vee \neg p$. At the same time they say that existence sentences which conclude proof sequences expressing indirect proofs are meaningless. The first claim denies that $p \vee \neg p$ is a defining characteristic of propositions, the second appears to retain this criterion for being a proposition and to deny that these sentences express propositions. About the first claim Wittgenstein's remark seems to me to be correct: that no discovery has been made of something to which the Law of Excluded Mean does not apply but that 'a new stipulation has been made'.[66] As for the second claim, whether a sentence of the form '$(\exists x) fx$' expresses a truth or a falsity, like the question whether there are propositions to which $p \vee \sim p$ does not apply, is not to be settled mathematically. Both are matters of semantic decision. If the decision is in favour of its expressing something true or false, then indirect proof is admissible.

Arguments in favour of a position on these matters, I take to be means of gaining acceptance of a linguistic decision. To illustrate, consider the logicist claim that ten 7's either occur or do not occur in the expansion of π. Suppose one gives as justification, as Russell would, that 'all members of the series from the 1st up to the 1000th . . . and so on, are determined; so surely *all* the members are determined'.[67] This comes to saying that the law for expanding π makes it necessary that they occur or necessary that they do not occur. It should be noted that 'It is necessary that p' and 'It is necessary that $\sim p$' are not contradictories, that their relation is not that of P to $\sim P$.[68] In number theory if the assumption of p's truth leads to a contradiction there is no hesitation about inferring that p is logically impossible, i.e. $\sim \Diamond \sim (\sim p)$ – not merely that it is not necessary, $\sim (\sim \Diamond \sim p)$. We proceed as though $\sim \Diamond \sim p \vee \sim \Diamond \sim (\sim p)$ is an instance of $P \vee \sim P$. The decision has been made to treat them analogously to empirical propositions. The alternatives in 'There either are or are not ten 7's in the infinite expansion of π' seems to 'put two pictures before us to choose from . . . one [of which] must correspond to the fact'.[69] The Platonist view that they are assertions about abstract entities reinforces the idea that these entities, like empirical objects, make one of them true – even though it is recognised that a necessary proposition has no truth conditions. Russell argued for treating 'the expansion of π' as standing for a sequence whose members are given in extension by arguing for the logical possibility of completing infinitely many operations in a finite time.[70] Such an argument, of course, lies outside any mathematical proof. It is truly idle in mathematics. But the decision made on the validity of $\sim \Diamond \sim p \vee \sim \Diamond \sim (\sim p)$, which may be *prompted* by it, is not idle – even though, like a philosophical claim, it cannot be shown to be true because a decision had no truth-value.

Department of Philosophy
Smith College

NOTES

1   Alonzo Church, *Introduction to Mathematical Logic* (Princeton University Press, 1944: 33).
2   P. Bernays, 'On Platonism in Mathematics' (trans., C. D. Parsons), in *Philosophy of Mathematics*, Paul Benacerraf and Hilary Putnam, eds (Englewood Cliffs, N.J., Prentice-Hall, 1964: 282).
3   'What is Cantor's Continuum Problem?', in Benacerraf and Putnam (op. cit.: 271).
4   *Intuitionism: an Introduction* (Amsterdam, North-Holland, 1956: 8).
5   L. E. J. Brouwer, 'Intuitionism and Formalism' (trans., Arnold Dresden), in *The Bulletin of the American Mathematical Society* (1913); reprinted in Benacerraf and Putnam (op. cit.: 69).
6   P. Bernays (op. cit.: 276).
7   *Philosophical Investigations* (trans., G. E. M. Anscombe) (Oxford, Basil Blackwell, 1953: 49).
8   *Remarks on the Foundations of Mathematics* (trans., G. E. M. Anscombe), G. H. von Wright, R. Rhees and G. E. M. Anscombe, eds (Oxford, Basil Blackwell, 1956: 157).
9   W. V. O. Quine, 'On What There Is', in *From a Logical Point of View* (Cambridge, Mass., Harvard University Press, 1953: 15).
10 ibid., p. 14.
11 'Foundations of Mathematics for the Working Mathematician', *Journal of Symbolic Logic*, vol. 14 (1949: 14).
12 See A. Heyting, *Intuitionism: an Introduction*, ch. 7; and S. C. Kleene, *Introduction to Metamathematics* (Amsterdam, North-Holland, 1952).
13 Heyting, *Intuitionism: an Introduction*, p. 2.
14 Or some number of places not yet computed. By 1967 computation has been carried to 500,000 places. See P. Beckmann, *A History of π (Pi)*, 2nd edn (Boulder, Colorado, Golem Press, 1971: 181).
15 *Ergebnisse Eines Mathematischen Kolloquiums (An Interpretation of the Intuitionistic Sentential Logic)*, vol. 4 (1933: 39–40); trans., J. Hintikka and L. Rossi, in *The Philosophy of Mathematics*, J. Hintikka, ed. (London, Oxford University Press: 1969).
16 It is of interest that this system is equivalent to Lewis's system of strict implication if Bp is replaced by Np, and if to Lewis's system Becker's axiom $\square$ $(Np \supset NNp)$ is adjoined.
17 Heyting, ed., *Constructivity in Mathematics* (Amsterdam, North-Holland, 1959: 69).
18 Heyting, *Intuitionism: an Introduction*, p. 2.
19 The requirement made by the French semi-intuitionists.
20 'Remarks before the Princeton Bicentennial Conference on Problems of Mathematics', in *The Undecidable*, Martin Davis, ed. (Hewlett, New York, Raven Press, 1965: 86).
21 ibid., p. 86.
22 ibid., p. 87.
23 *The Problems of Philosophy* (New York, Henry Holt, 1912: 164).
24 *The Sophist*, s. 238, Jowett translation.
25 *The Timaeus*, s. 52, Jowett translation.
26 'Mathematical Proof', *Mind*, vol. XXXVIII (1929: 18).
27 M. Dummett, 'Wittgenstein's Philosophy of Mathematics', in Benacerraf and Putnam (op. cit.: 499).
28 'Consciousness, Philosophy, and Mathematics', *Proceeding of 10th International Congress of Philosophy*, vol. I, fascicule 2; reprinted in Benacerraf and Putnam (op. cit.: 79).
29 Russell held it to be only medically impossible, not logically impossible, to run through the series of integers. See 'The Limits of Empiricism', *Proceedings of the Aristotelian Society*, vol. XXXVI (1934–5: 143).
30 R. B. Perry's term.
31 Quine (op. cit.: 16).
32 ibid., pp. 13–14.
33 'What is Cantor's Continuum Problem?', in Benacerraf and Putnam (op. cit.: 263).
34 This account of the relation between a necessary proposition and a verbal fact is given in various places by M. Lazerowitz. See especially *The Structure of Metaphysics* (London,

Routledge & Kegan Paul, 1955: 266–71; *Studies in Metaphilosophy* (London: Routledge & Kegan Paul, 1964: 46–66).

35   Plato, *The Sophist*, s. 238, Jowett translation.

36   *Preliminary Studies for the 'Philosophical Investigations' Generally Known as the Blue and Brown Books* (Oxford, Basil Blackwell, 1958: 47).

37   ibid., p. 57.

38   *Constructivity in Mathematics*, p. 70.

39   Evert Willem Beth, *Mathematical Thought* (Dordrecht, Holland, D. Reidel, 1965: 161).

40   ibid., pp. 161–3.

41   Beth's comparison of the two developments: ibid., p. 89.

42   'Foundations of Mathematics', *Encyclopedia Britannica* (London, 1973: vol. 14).

43   *Logical Foundations of Probability* (University of Chicago Press, 1950: 3).

44   *Essays in the Philosophy of Mathematics* (Leicester University Press, 1965: 113).

45   See 'Intuitionism and Formalism', in Benacerraf and Putnam (op. cit.: 71).

46   ibid., p. 73.

47   Attendant questions can also be formulated, e.g. the question whether from current systems of axioms for set theory it is demonstrable, disprovable or undecidable which infinite cardinal is the number of the set of all real numbers; also its partial answers: that the hypothesis that its number is $\aleph_1$ (the next cardinal after $\aleph_0$ in magnitude) is consistent with the axioms, proved by Gödel, and that its negative is consistent with them, proved by Paul Cohen.

48   Hilbert's words.

49   L. E. J. Brouwer (op. cit.: 74).

50   *Essays in the Philosophy of Mathematics*, p. 104.

51   *Philosophische Bemerkungen*, Rush Rhees, ed. (Oxford, Basil Blackwell, 1964: 228); translation mine.

52   *Essays in the Philosophy of Mathematics*, p. 100.

53   For this point see R. L. Goodstein, 'Wittgenstein's Philosophy of Mathematics', *Ludwig Wittgenstein: Philosophy and Language*, A. Ambrose and M. Lazerowitz, eds (London, George Allen & Unwin, 1972: 275–6).

54   As Wittgenstein put it, 'a combination of words is withdrawn from circulation'. (See *Philosophical Investigations*, p. 139).

55   Pt. 7; italics mine.

56   *Philosophische Bemerkungen*, pp. 162, 209; *Philosophische Grammatik*, Rush Rhees, ed. (Oxford, Basil Blackwell, 1969: 463).

57   'What is Cantor's Continuum Problem?', in Benacerraf and Putnam (op. cit.: 259).

58   As Russell put it, 'the first infinite number . . . beyond the whole unending series of finite numbers'. See *Our Knowledge of the External World* (Chicago, Open Court, 1914: 181).

59   Beth, *Mathematical Thought* (op. cit.: 84–5).

60   L. E. J. Brouwer, 'Intuitionism and Formalism', in Benacerraf and Putnam (op. cit.: 74). Gödel remarks that 'The power of the continuum is the second smallest infinite cardinal' has been given several different meanings by intuitionists, all quite different from the original hypothesis (see 'What is Cantor's Continuum Problem', op. cit.: 261).

61   *Constructivity in Mathematics*, p. 69.

62   *A Treatise of Human Nature*, bk 1., pt 1., s. 1.

63   *Philosophische Grammatik*, p. 374; translation mine.

64   'The Limits of Empiricism', p. 145.

65   *Philosophische Grammatik*, p. 368.

66   ibid., p. 368; 'Eine neue Festsetzung getroffen'.

67   *Remarks on the Foundations of Mathematics*, pp. 139–40. Wittgenstein comments: 'That is correct if it is supposed to mean that it is not the case e.g. so-and-so many'th is *not* determined'.

68   ibid., p. 141.

69   ibid., p. 139.

70   'The Limits of Empiricism', p. 144.

8

POST *PRINCIPIA*[1]

R. L. Goodstein

At the beginning of the seventh chapter of his authoritative survey of mathematical logic, G. T. Kneebone makes this striking observation on Russell's *Principia*: 'For all the inspiration that *Principia Mathematica* has communicated to the logicians and philosophers of mathematics of the twentieth century, and for all its rich fecundity as a source of concepts and symbolic devices, this great work remains, in the literature of the foundations of mathematics, a lone classic without progeny.'[2] In this chapter I propose to examine some of the ideas which have dominated thinking about the foundations of mathematics during the sixty years which have elapsed since the publication of the first edition of *Principia* to see what, if anything, they owe to Russell and what they tell us of the reasons for the abandonment of Russell's programme of logicism to which Kneebone alludes.

In certain respects the *Principia* represents a peak of intellectual attainment; in particular the theory of ramified types with the axiom of reducibility is as subtle and ingenious a concept as is to be found anywhere in the whole literature of logic and mathematics. The sheer difficulty inherent in the theory of types, though clearly a significant barrier to progress, cannot, however, be the whole explanation for the *Principia*'s failure to influence the subsequent course of development of mathematical logic, for difficulty alone has never discouraged mathematicians.

Russell sought for an absolute, universal logic and saw no value in any piecemeal development of logic of intentionally limited application, but the greatest achievement of the past half-century has been the gradual acceptance of the *relativity* of logic. It is ironic that Russell, who was among the first to understand and popularise Einstein's great work on the relativity of simultaneity, should be constitutionally incapable of accepting the relativity of logic. L. E. J. Brouwer's paper which initiated his attack on classical logic and which led eventually to the overthrow of the concept of an absolute logic, was published a year before the first volume of the *Principia*. Brouwer's critique was intended to replace one logic by another, not to undermine the very standing of logic, and Brouwer scarcely deserves more credit for the development of relativism in logic than Russell. What happened was that Heyting's formalisation of Brouwer's logic inspired the study of a continuum of logics lying between classical and intuitionist logic, and slowly eroded away th nineteenth-century notion that logic was, not the product of thought, but the essence of thought, conditioned by the very structure of our brains and reflecting that structure in a unique form. Another development which led to the same end was that of logic-free formalisations of arithmetic, formalisations in which the axioms of logic played no role and within which not only classical logic, but also many-valued logic and even intuitionistic logic, could be introduced as interpretations of classes of formulae. From this point of view a logic serves not as a foundation of arithmetic, but as a means of organising arithmetic. In one particular study which I made[3] I found a deduction theorem corresponding to the implication of each logic under consideration; these deduction theorems were of differing strengths, with that corresponding to the implication of classical logic having the greatest strength. Of course, the development of logic-free formalisations negatived Russell's programme of reducing arithmetic to logic, by reducing logic to arithmetic.

Logic-free formalisations of arithmetic are based on the concept of a primitive recursive function. This concept was first introduced by Dedekind in 1888 but played no role in the *Principia*. It was the great Norwegian Th. Skolem who first exploited the fundamental role of recursion in his famous paper 'Begründung der elementaren Arithmetik durch die rekurriende Denkweise ohne Anwendung scheinbarer Veränderlichen mit unendlichen Ausdehnungsbereich',[4] published ten years after the *Principia*. Skolem was not concerned in this paper to free arithmetic from logic but to make it independent of set theory and to exclude the use of unbounded quantifiers, as a means of protecting arithmetic from the Russell paradox. However, the axioms of classical propositional logic and the rule of induction which Skolem postulated proved to be dispensable, as I showed in my construction of arithmetic as an axiom-free equation calculus in 1945.[5] In this calculus all sentences are equations between recursive terms (a recursive term is either a primitive recursive function or a numeral), there are no axioms except the defining equations of primitive recursive functions, and the rules of inference secure the transitivity and reflexiveness of equality, the substitution of a recursive term for a variable, the passage from $A = B$ to $F(A) = F(B)$ with recursive terms A, B and recursive function F, and the uniqueness of a function defined by recursion (so that two functions which satisfy the same defining equations are equal). The system admitted various technical simplifications during the past thirty years which I have described elsewhere.[6]

The discovery of the relativity of logic has been paralleled in recent years by the discoveries of the relativity of set theory and of the very concept of the non-denumerable. Contemporary with Russell's development of the theory of types, designed to protect mathematics from the contradiction which Russell had discovered in Cantor's theory of sets, Zermelo presented an account of set theory in axiomatic form which sought to protect set theory from the Russell paradox by imposing restrictions on the means of forming new sets. Zermelo's theory, as modified by Fraenkel (by the introduction of a formalisation of the concept of property), has become the central tool for research in set theory, displacing type-theoretic formulations. It is not entirely clear why the Zermelo–Fraenkel theory has enjoyed this success; no formulation of set theory is demonstrably free from contradiction, but there is a widespread feeling among logicians that the Zermelo–Fraenkel system, because of the difficulty it imposes on the formation of 'very large' sets, is less likely to be found inconsistent than such modern versions of type theory as Quine's *Mathematical Logic*. (In fact, the first version of Quine's system was found to be inconsistent, though the second version was shown by Hao Wang to be consistent if Quine's earlier, more restrictive system known as *New Foundations*, is consistent.) Another disadvantage of type theory is the multiplication of a concept at different levels which it engenders so that there is not a single concept of natural number, for instance, but natural numbers of all type levels.

Interest in set theory in this century has centred on the axiom of choice, what Russell called the multiplicative axiom, and Cantor's continuum hypothesis. The axiom of choice was discovered by Zermelo in his attempt to prove that every set can be well ordered (although there is a reference to the idea in an earlier paper of Peano's on an existence theorem for differential equations). The axiom of choice (in one of numerous equivalent forms) affirms the existence of a set which has one member in common with each set of any family of non-empty, non-overlapping sets. Fraenkel[7] observes that despite its late appearance the axiom of choice is one of the most discussed axioms of mathematics, second only to Euclid's axiom of parallels. Some of the suspicion in which the axiom was held was dispelled in 1938 when K. Gödel showed[8] that, if set theory was consistent without the axiom of choice, then it remained consistent if the axiom was included. However, the question whether or not it could be derived from the remaining axioms was not settled for another quarter of a century when Paul Cohen proved[9] that the axiom of choice was indeed independent of the other axioms. The continuum hypothesis, which Cantor sought in vain to prove for many years, states that the cardinal of the continuum (the set of all one-variable functions) is the smallest cardinal after the cardinal of the set of natural numbers, i.e. the continuum is the smallest non-denumerable set. In the paper to which we have already referred, Paul Cohen established in 1963 that even the axiom of choice is not strong enough to prove the continuum hypothesis, so that more than one set theory is possible, a set theory which affirms the continuum hypothesis and a set theory which denies it (and even finer graduations are possible if one considers generalisations of the continuum hypothesis).

Russell's belief in an absolute logic which (although he did not use this language) was rooted in reality loses all credence in the light of this multiplicity of set theories. For if, as Russell supposed, sets are real objects in the real world, the continuum hypothesis must necessarily be either true or false, and not, as Cohen showed, undecidable by means of the resources of set theory. Of course, Russell might have argued (as indeed some neo-realists argue today) that Cohen's result only shows that the way in which set theory is currently formulated fails to decide the truth of the continuum hypothesis, and that what is lacking is the discovery of some new, deep, fundamental property of sets which will settle the continuum question and obviate the need for the axiom of choice. However, although the future may admit the discovery of a property of sets which settles the continuum problem, set theory is necessarily incomplete and no enrichment of it can suffice to settle all questions. This is a consequence of a remarkable discovery which in part goes back to L. Löwenheim in 1915[10] and which was completed much later by Abraham Robinson[11] and Leon Henkin,[12] that any consistent set of sentences of predicate logic (or set theory) has a denumerable model, i.e. an interpretation in which the set of individuals is denumerable, in particular is the set of natural numbers. Skolem used this result to establish the incompleteness of set theory and the relativity of the concept of non-denumerability in the following way. Assuming that set theory without the axiom of choice or the continuum hypothesis is consistent, consider an extension of set theory by some new axiom strong enough to prove the axiom of choice and settle the continuum hypothesis one way or the other, without introducing an inconsistency. Then there is an interpretation of this extended theory in which all sets are natural numbers and so the totality of sets is denumerable; but it is a well-known theorum of set theory, discovered by Cantor, that the totality of subsets (of a denumerable set) is non-denumerable (proved by the famous Cantor diagonal process). This is not, as at first appears, the discovery of a contradiction in set theory. For the proof within a system, for instance in Zermelo–Fraenkel set theory, that a certain set is non-denumerable, is a proof that there is no enumeration of that set in the system, i.e. no function in the system which enumerates the set. Thus what has been established is that the system (and, in fact, any system of set theory) is necessarily *incomplete*, by lack of some function, and furthermore that the concept of the non-denumerable is relative to a formal system, and a set which is non-denumerable within a certain system because the system necessarily is without the means of enumerating the set, may nevertheless be enumerable outside the system.

The concept of completeness enters foundation studies at an even more elementary stage than that of set theory, for the notion is relevant and important in propositional logic. Russell must have been aware of this notion since he stated in the Preface (written in 1910) to the *Principia* that the axioms (of *Principia*) are sufficient, but he gives no demonstration of this, and his reluctance to identify sentences with truth functions denies him the use of the method which was introduced by

Emil Post ten years later of showing that every tautology is provable from the axioms. This remarkable identification of two classes of sentences, those provable from a set of axioms by rules of inference and those which only take the value true under the truth tables was a milestone in the development of mathematical logic which has not perhaps been fully appreciated. Russell did not apparently concern himself with proving the independence of his axioms, and as is well known Paul Bernays later showed that Russell's postulation of associativity was superfluous. The method which Bernays used to establish the independence of the remaining axioms (and other related results) involved the introduction of three- and four-valued truth tables, and this method has proved to be highly significant and fruitful, finding numerous subsequent applications. Surprisingly, Russell does not appear to have made an attempt to prove the consistency of his propositional axioms under the rules of inference, despite the fact that the paradox of set theory was his own discovery. Of course, the simple observation that all provable propositions are tautologies, and a contradiction is not, was not admissible to him since, as we noted above, the identification of propositions with truth functions was blocked by his analysis of such propositions as 'I think that p'.

Another notion which has dominated foundation studies during the past half-century has been that of a decision method, and there is no hint of this idea in the *Principia*. Of course, a full analysis of the concept had to wait for a whole series of discoveries in the 1930s, but in the case of propositional logic the notion of a decision method is a very simple one, granted of course the identification of proposition with truth function.

It is no criticism of the *Principia* to say that the possibility that formalisations of arithmetic are essentially incomplete did not occur to Russell, since it did not occur to anyone for another twenty years. So surprising was the discovery when Gödel first made it, and so difficult the technical details underlying the proof of incompleteness, that even a shadowy guess of the very possibility made twenty years earlier would have been truly remarkable. The incompleteness theorem, in Gödel's paper 'Über formal unentscheidbare Sätze der *Principia Mathematica* und verwandter Systeme', rests essentially upon the notion of a primitive recursive function.[13] Gödel showed that in any adequate formalisation of arithmetic there is a primitive recursive function $g(x)$ such that for any numeral $\mathbf{n}$, $g(\mathbf{n}) = 0$ is provable in the formalisation, but the universal sentence $(\forall x)\,[g(x) = 0]$ is not provable. The essential ingredients of the proof are a procedure for assigning a unique number to each sign, sentence and proof in the system, a demonstration that for any primitive recursive function $f(x, a)$ the relation $y = f(x, a)$ is representable within the system, and verifications that the property of being the number of a provable sentence, and that the function which gives the number of a sentence which results from substituting a term for a variable in a given sentence, are primitive recursive. Without Skolem's prior work on recursive arithmetic the proof would scarcely have been conceivable. A little later, and quite independently of Gödel's result, Skolem found the explanation of the incompleteness by showing that any formalisation of arithmetic admits an unintended interpretation (what is now called a non-standard model) in which the set of admissible values for the number variables is ordinally richer than the natural numbers. Skolem's demonstration of this fact, with the simplicity characteristic of genius, involves little more than setting up an order relation on a class of one-variable functions, which preserves all the theorems of arithmetic. Within the past decade Skolem's non-standard model of arithmetic has been the source of the development of a non-standard analysis which re-establishes the infinitesimal of the early discoverers of the calculus in its original role, and rescues it from its nineteenth-century banishment.

Gödel's account of the incompleteness of arithmetic did not stop short at the discovery of a recursive function $g(x)$ such that $(\forall x)[g(x) = 0]$ is unprovable, but went on to show that a fundamental relation of the system has the same property, namely, the relation affirming the consistency of the system (the relation in question saying that for any numbers $a,b,c,$ it is not the case that a is the number of a proof of sentence number c, and b is the number of the proof of the denial of this sentence). In his original paper Gödel remarks that, by formalising his proof of the unprovability of this relation, it follows that it is impossible to prove the consistency of a formalisation of arithmetic by methods which do not transcend the resources of the system, but it is only in the second volume of the Hilbert–Bernays *Grundlagen der Mathematik* which appeared in 1939 that a detailed proof of this claim is given. The result is, of course, a refutation of the hope Hilbert expressed in the 1920s that it would be possible to give a proof of consistency 'by finite means', but seen out of context the result appears to be pointless, for of what use is a proof of consistency of a system carried out within the system itself? Subsequent proofs of the consistency of formalised arithmetic were given by G. Gentzen, whose early death in Prague during the Russian defeat of the German army of occupation in the Second World War was such a tragic loss to foundation studies. Gentzen's proof utilises transfinite induction, but the apparent absurdity of introducing transfinite induction to prove the consistency of arithmetic with ordinary induction is not a valid criticism of Gentzen's result, for what in fact he shows is that a proof of consistency of a system with quantifiers and ordinary induction may be carried out within a free variable system postulating transfinite induction. If one believes that the use of quantifiers is the source of the major known contradiction in set theory, the Russell paradox, then of course a free variable system – even one postulating transfinite induction – is less suspect than one like the *Principia* which admits quantifiers.

The chief value of Gödel's result does not lie, however, in its denial of the possibility of a 'finitist' proof of consistency, but rather in the role which it has been found to play in independence proofs, for instance in proofs that valuation functions which suffice to establish the consistency of a system are not definable in the system.

Above all others the idea which has dominated research in the foundations of mathematics during the past sixty years has been the idea of constructive function and constructive proof. This concept of *constructive* is rather different from that which Russell employed, for example, when he discussed the notion of a Dedekind section in his *Introduction to Mathematical Philosophy*,[14] Dedekind postulated the existence of a real number separating every non-empty lower and upper section, but by *defining* real numbers in terms of sections of rationals Russell was able to prove the existence of the real number in question. He comments that postulation 'has the advantage of theft over honest toil' in making Dedekind's theory of real numbers seem simpler than his. Certainly a *constructive* theory of real number which proceeds from sets to natural numbers, and then to integers, rationals and sections of rationals, appears to offer greater security from contradiction than an axiomatic theory which postulates the existence of objects, the real numbers, with certain properties; the axiomatic theory seeks freedom from contradiction by appeal to 'real models', or to the constructive theory itself, but in both theories we are really laying down the use of the term real numbers, and both theories are at risk from the underlying theory of sets. Despite the language we are accustomed to use, an axiomatic theory does not postulate the existence of anything in the real world, but delimits a concept.

The constructivist tendency, in the modern usage of the term, goes back to L. E. J. Brouwer and his requirement that a valid proof of existence provide a means of finding the entity whose existence is being proved. Brouwer was not able to make this requirement precise but subsequent analysis showed that what was often involved in the distinction between a constructive and a non-constructive existence proof was the notion of a constructive function. For example, the classical proof that in a non-decreasing infinite sequence of 0's and 1's there exists a number which occurs infinitely often, argues that if both digits occur only finitely often then the sequence is finite, yet from this proof it is impossible to say which digit in fact occurs infinitely often. No finite initial segment of the sequence, however long, if it consists only of 0's can tell us whether the 0's will continue indefinitely or if a 1 will subsequently appear. Within the framework of *Principia* it is easy to show that there exists a term in the sequence, let us say the kth, such that every term from the kth onwards has the same value. In outline the proofs proceed as follows: let s_n be the nth term of the sequence; *either* there is a k such that for all $n > k$, $s_n \leqslant s_k$ and so $s_n = s_k$ since the sequence is non-decreasing) *or* to any k corresponds an $n > k$ such that $s_n > s_k$. In the latter case we must reject $s_0 = 1$ since there is no n for which $s_n > 1$, and we must reject also $s_0 = 0$ since there is first an n_0 such that $s_{n_0} > s_0$ and so $s_{n_0} = 1$, and then there is an n_1 such that $s_{n_1} > s_{n_0} = 1$ which again is impossible. But what is known about this number k? Is it zero, or is it different from zero? The proof provides no answer to this question. If instead of a single sequence (s_n) we consider a succession of sequences, say (s_n^1), (s_n^2), (s_n^3), . . . , then the *Principia* proof asserts the existence of a *function* $i(m)$ such that, for each m, the sequence $s^m_1, s^m_2, s^m_3, . . .$, is constant from the term $s^m_{i(m)}$ onwards, i.e. in the mth sequence the digit $s^m_{i(m)}$ occurs infinitely often. Even in the most favourable case when s^m_n is a primitive recursive function, the function $i(m)$ cannot be computed, so that, for instance, we cannot determine the value of $i(m)$ even for the first argument value 0. The constructivist in modern foundation studies considers that it is a primary requirement of the function concept that for any assigned argument in the range of definition of the function the value shall be determined. Of course, the critical question is how the value is determined.

In the case of a function defined by primitive recursion the value is determined by repeated substitution in the defining equations of the function, the number of substitutions required to determine the value for an assigned argument being known in advance. However, the class of primitive recursive functions, extensive though it is known to be through the work of Rosza Peter, does not exhaust the class of functions for which there is a procedure for calculating the values. For instance, the class of multiply recursive functions is known to transcend the class of primitive recursive functions and yet a multiply recursive function is effectively calculable in the most stringent sense of the term effective. Beyond the multiply recursive functions are the transfinite recursive functions, also effectively calculable. What, then, is the limit to the series of effective operations? In the mid-1920s a number of different approaches to the problem of determining such a limit led to a common class of functions. On the one hand, this class was arrived at by isolating a property which primitive and multiply recursive functions have in common, namely, that the values of the function are obtained by substitution from a given finite set of equations; however, no limit is imposed in advance on the number of substitutions required to determine a particular value, except that the number is finite. The class of functions determined in this way was called the class of general (originally quasi-) recursive functions. Another entirely different approach was found by A. M. Turing. Turing discovered the specification of a very general kind of theoretical computing 'machine' which was in certain respects the ancestor of the modern computer, and the class of functions which could be specified by a Turing 'machine' proved to be identical with the class of general recursive functions. A third approach was that found by Alonzo Church in his calculus of λ-conversion, and this too led to the same class of functions. Yet another route to the same class of functions is the Markov algorithm. No one has since discovered a function which deserves to be called effectively calculable and which does not belong to this common class. However, it must be recognised that the general recursive function (or any of its equivalents) is not itself necessarily effectively calculable, although the general recursive functions provide an upper bound to the class of effectively calculable functions. This is most readily seen from the following example. Suppose the natural number separated into two classes C_1, C_2 which are effectively enumerable. Let a function $f(n)$ be defined so that $f(n) = 1$ if n belongs to C_1, and $f(n) = 2$ if n belongs to C_2. Then it is known that $f(n)$ is general recursive; to determine the value of f for an assigned argument n, we look in turn at the first terms of the classes C_1, C_2, then at the second terms, then at the third terms, and so on. Since between them C_1, C_2 comprise *all* natural numbers, the chosen argument n must eventually occur in either C_1 or in C_2, but we have no means of knowing how long the search must be continued. A search without limit, even if ultimate success is assured, is not an effective operation.

The determination of an upper bound to the class of effectively calculable functions has been one of the most outstanding successes in foundations research in the past half-century. Parallel to the development of a theory of effectively calculable functions, there has grown up a variety of systems of constructive analysis, some richer, some more exiguous than the classical analysis of the *Principia*. At one extreme are systems like my *Recursive Analysis*,[15] a free variable theory of functions based on primitive recursive arithmetic, which formulates analogues in the rational field of classical theorems by means of a relativisation of concepts. At the other extreme are systems which study constructive objects (recursive real numbers and functions) by entirely classical methods. The most extensive and successful system of constructive analysis is, however, that which has been developed by the Leningrad school under A. A. Markov,[16] N. A. Shanin,[17] G. E. Minc, A. O. Slisenko, G. S. Tseytin[18] and others; this system is based on Markov algorithms and adopts a form of intuitionist logic weakened by the inclusion of Markov's principal of choice

$$\{[(\forall x)P(x) \vee (\exists x) \neg P(x)] \,\&\, [\neg (\forall x)P(x)]\} \rightarrow [(\exists x) \neg P(x)]$$

which permits a form of the classical non-constructive existence proof subject to the intuitionist provability of the disjunction

$$(\forall x)P(x) \vee (\exists x) \neg P(x).$$

The discovery of an upper bound to the class of effectively calculable functions clarified the concept of a *decidable* system to which we have already referred. The intuitive notion of a decision method is that of a purely automatic process by which it can be determined whether or not a sentence is provable in some system, a process like the truth tables to determine which propositions are derivable from the *Principia* axioms. A decidable system is one in which every problem is solvable, and so the existence of such famous unsolved problems in arithmetic as Fermat's last theorem, or the Goldbach hypothesis that every even number after four is a sum of two odd primes, makes it intrinsically unlikely that arithmetic is decidable. However, belief is one thing, and proof another. By means of Gödel's process of arithmetisation which assigns each sentence a unique number and provides arithmetical equivalents of syntactical concepts like provability, the question of the decidability of a system reduces to the existence of a decision function $D(n)$ which vanishes if and only if n is the number of a provable sentence. Of course, the decision function must be effectively calculable and so a proof of *undecidability* becomes a proof that the decision function is not effectively calculable, and since every effectively calculable function is general recursive, to prove undecidability it suffices to show that the decision function is not general recursive. The first proof of the undecidability of predicate logic and arithmetic was obtained by Alonzo Church in 1936.[19] Since then many classes of problem have been shown to be undecidable. Conceptually the simplest of these is the word problem for semigroups. A semigroup consists of an alphabet and certain stated equivalences of words written in this alphabet, and the word problem is that of deciding whether two arbitrary words are or are not equivalent. In 1946 and 1947 A. A. Markov and E. Post found examples of undecidable semigroups, examples which were later greatly simplified by the Leningrad mathematicians G. S. Tseytin and Yu. V. Matijasevič. The much more difficult word problem for groups was solved some years later by P. S. Novikov and William Boone.

The most recent success in the field of decision problems has been Matijasevič's solution of Hilbert's tenth problem. At the Congress of Mathematicians in Paris in 1900 David Hilbert proposed twenty-three problems, the tenth of which was to find if there is a procedure for deciding of any polynomial with integral coefficients whether it has an integral root or not. Matijasevič showed in 1970 that no recursive decision procedure exists; in the opposite direction it had been shown in 1966 that there is a procedure for deciding whether or not any equation $f(x_1, \ldots, x_n) = c$ has a solution or not, when f is composed from natural numbers and variables by addition, multiplication and the functions $a \div x$, $x \div a$ (where $\div$ is the recursive difference function); if it had been possible to replace the differences $a \div x$, $x \div a$, with a constant a, by the full difference function $x \div y$, this would have led to a decision procedure for determining the existence of roots of polynomials. Thus, the border between the decidable and the undecidable may be reduced to that between the difference $x \div y$ when one of x, y is constant, and when both are free to vary.

Department of Mathematics
University of Leicester

NOTES

1   B. A. W. Russell and A. N. Whitehead, *Principia Mathematica* (Cambridge University Press: vol. I, 1910; vol. II, 1912; vol. III, 1913).

2   G. T. Kneebone, *Mathematical Logic and the Foundations of Mathematics* (London and New York, Van Nostrand, 1963).

3   R. L. Goodstein, 'Models of Propositional Calculi in Recursive Arithmetic', *Math. Scand.*, vol. 6 (1958: 293–6).

4   T. Skolem, 'Begründung der elementaren Arithmetik durch die rekurriende Denkweise ohne Anwendung scheinbarer Veränderlichen mit unendlichen Ausdehnungsbereich', *Videnskapsselskapels Schrifter*, vol. I (Math.-Nat. Klasse, 1923: 38).

5   R. L. Goodstein, 'Function Theory in an Axiom-free Equation Calculus', *Proc. London Math. Soc.* (2), vol. 48 (1945: 401–34).

6   *Development of Mathematical Logic* (London, Logos, 1971).

7   A. A. Fraenkel, *Abstract Set Theory* (Amsterdam, North-Holland, 1961).

8   K. Gödel, 'The Consistency of the Axiom of Choice and of the Generalised Continuum Hypothesis with the Axioms of Set Theory', *Proc. Nat. Acad. Sci.*, vol. 24 (1939: 556–7); *Annals Math. Studies*, vol. 3 (1940).

9   P. J. Cohen, 'The Independence of the Continuum Hypothesis', pt I, *Proc. Nat. Acad. Sci.*, vol. 50 (1963: 1143–8); pt II, vol. 51 (1964: 105–10).

10   L. Löwenheim, 'Über Möglichkeiten im Relativkalkül', *Math. Annalen*, vol. 76 (1915: 447–70).

11   A. Robinson, *On the Metamathematics of Algebra* (Amsterdam, North-Holland, 1951).

12   L. Henkin, 'The Completeness of the First Order Functional Calculus', *J. Symbolic Logic*, vol. 14 (1949: 159–66).

13   *Monatshefte für Mathematik und Physik*, vol. 38 (1931).

14   B. A. W. Russell, *Introduction to Mathematical Philosophy* (London, George Allen & Unwin, 1919).

15   R. L. Goodstein, *Recursive Analysis* (Amsterdam, North-Holland, 1961).

16   A. A. Markov, 'On Constructive Mathematics', *Proc. Steklov Math. Inst.*, vol. 67 (1962: 8–15).

17   N. A. Shanin, 'A Constructive Interpretation of Mathematical Judgements', *Proc. Steklov Math. Inst.*, vol. 52 (1958: 226–311); 'On Constructive Real Numbers and Constructive Function Spaces', *Proc. Steklov Math. Inst.*, vol. 67 (1962:15–294).

18   G. S. Tseytin, I. D. Zaslavsky and N. A. Shanin, 'Peculiarities of Constructive Mathematical Analysis', *Proc. Int. Congress Math., Moscow* (1966: 253–61).

19   Alonzo Church, 'A Note on the Entscheidungsproblem', *J. Symbolic Logic*, vol. 1 (1936: 40–1); 'An Unsolvable Problem of Elementary Number Theory', *Am. J. Math.*, vol. 58 (1936: 345–63).

9

RUSSELL AND MODAL LOGIC

Nicholas Rescher

(1) *Introduction*

Russell's repute as one of the founding fathers of modern symbolic logic is secure for all time, and his claims to greatness as a logician are established to an extent beyond my meagre capacity to alter for better or for worse. Accordingly, it is no real unkindness to Russell's memory to observe in the interests of historical justice that he, too, once more illustrates the rather trite precept that even scholars of deservedly great stature can exhibit a bias of intellect that produces unfortunate side effects. At any rate, the aim of this present discussion is to note the substantially negative import of Russell's work for the evolution of modal logic, whose rapid growth since the late 1940s is unquestionably one of the most exciting developments in contemporary logical research.

(2) *Philosophical background*

From the very first, Russell was on philosophical grounds reluctant, nay unwilling, to recognise the merely possible (i.e. the *contingently* possible) as a distinct category. His *Critical Exposition of the Philosophy of Leibniz* (Cambridge University Press, 1900) exemplifies this attitude. It was, Russell held, improper for Leibniz, given his own commitments, to espouse the category of mere possibility, and to maintain the contingency of factual truth: he should have held that all truths about the world are necessary. Thus, Russell reproached Leibniz with not reaching more Spinozistic conclusions: had Leibniz traced out his own lines of thought more rigorously he would have arrived at the position of Spinoza.

Russell's criticism of Kant in the *Principles of Mathematics* (Cambridge University Press, 1903) gives another revealing insight into his position. According to Russell, the Kantian analysis of the foundations of necessity is drastically insufficient. In tracing the source of necessity to the categories and forms of the human understanding, Kant – so Russell holds – merely provides a contingently factual basis that cannot provide an appropriate foothold for necessity proper:

> [On the Kantian theory of necessity] we only push one stage farther back the region of 'mere fact,' for the constitution of our minds remains still a mere fact. The theory of necessity urged by Kant,

and adopted . . . by Lotze, appears radically vicious. Everything is in a sense a mere fact. (section 430)

The philosopher, Russell seems to imply, is engaged on a quest for the necessity of things that does not permit him to rest content, at any stage, with anything that is a matter of mere fact. Just this attitude lay behind Russell's rejection at this stage of the empiricist philosophy of mathematics of John Stuart Mill, which would not provide a suitable account of the necessity of mathematical truth.

The philosophical roots of the early Russell's discontent with merely factual truth are to be found in his prolonged flirtation with the philosophy of Spinoza, a marked feature of *Mysticism and Logic* and vividly at work in the splendid essay on 'A Free Man's Worship'. Drawn to Spinozistic necessitarianism on powerful ideological grounds, Russell shied away from all traces of Leibnizian possibilism.

Himself a determinist of more or less classical proportions, Russell was committed to a necessitarianism that left him disinclined on philosophical grounds to allocate a logically useful role to the modal distinctions between the possible, the actual and the necessary. Like his hero, Spinoza, he was prepared to maintain that there will, in the final analysis, be a *collapse* of modality: that the actual itself is more or less necessary, so that the possible vanishes as a distinct category. This philosophical stance was, I believe, significantly operative in Russell's negative view *as a logician* regarding the utility and prospects of modal logic.

(3) *Mathematical background*

Russell's philosophical perspectives were, of course, substantially influenced by his preoccupation with mathematics. The early Russell pioneered the tendency, destined to become predominant in his later years, of approaching logico-philosophical problems from the mathematical point of view. Now mathematics has, of course, no place for modal distinctions: in mathematics it is altogether otiose to differentiate between the actual and the necessary, and there is no room at all for the contingently possible. Throughout the mathematical domain the drawing of modal distinctions is effectively beside the point.

Moreover, it seems particularly pointless to apply the concept of necessity to the theses of a mathematical system like Riemannian geometry; what is necessary – and also what is mathematically interesting – are the relationships of deductive consequence by which theorems follow from axioms. Accordingly, we find Russell maintaining in *The Principles of Mathematics* (1903) that:

> Thus any ultimate premiss is, in a certain sense, a mere fact. . . . The only logical meaning of necessity seems to be derived from implication. A proposition is more or less necessary according as the class of propositions for which it is a premiss is greater or smaller. In this sense

the propositions of logic have the greatest necessity, and those of geometry have a high degree of necessity. (section 430)

The *relative* necessity of mathematical propositions is to be defined in terms of implicative relationships, according as the body of the propositions that are needed as premisses for it is the less or as that of propositions for which it can serve as premiss is the greater. And the necessity of deductive consequence is the basic mode of necessity as well as the only ultimately genuine form thereof. But now – once one follows Russell in defining pure mathematics as 'the theory of propositions of the if–then form' – one arrives at a view of pure mathematics that sees all its propositions as having this necessity of consequence. This strictly relativised necessity of deductive consequence is all one needs in the philosophy of mathematics, and so there is – for example – little point of speaking of the theorems of a mathematical system as necessary in ways other than as shorthand for 'necessary relative to the axioms'. Absolute and unrelativised necessity is not only otiose, but obscurantist as well: the 'necessity of consequence' is the ultimately basic form of necessity.

At this point Russell's logicism intervenes decisively in the dialectic of thought. If the basis of our concern with logic is its role in the rational articulation of mathematics; nay, if there is at bottom a fundamental *identity* of logic with mathematics, then the handwriting is on the wall. For if mathematics has no real need for modal distinctions and no room for contingent possibilities, a modal *logic* becomes almost a contradiction in terms. This standpoint blocks any concern on the logician's part with mere possibilities and alternative possible worlds. Such concerns of traditional philosophy come to be seen as metaphysical sophistries upon which the logician must simply turn his back.

Thus, both from the point of departure of his philosophical determinism and from that of his mathematical logicism, Russell was powerfully predisposed against the maintenance of modal distinctions which could only secure their validation in a rationale that recognises the prospect of contingent possibilities. These considerations provide the background for understanding Russell's relationship to those logicians – pre-eminently Hugh MacColl, C. I. Lewis and Jan Lukasiewicz – who pressed for the recognition of modal distinctions during the period (roughly 1895–1925) when Russell was actively preoccupied with logic. Let us examine this phenomenon in some detail.

(4) Interactions: (A) Russell and MacColl
In a series of articles published over a period of some thirty years beginning *c*. 1880,[1] Hugh MacColl argued a number of points which any modern modal logician will recognise as foundational for his entire subject:

a that there is a crucial difference between propositions that obtain merely *de facto* and those that obtain of necessity; between those which *must* hold and those which *may or may not* hold (even if they actually do so). (The former type of truths MacColl characterised as *certain*, the latter as *variable*.)

b that there is a crucial difference between a *material* implication and genuine implication. 'For nearly thirty years', he complained in 1908, 'I have been vainly trying to convince them [i.e. logicians] that this supposed invariable equivalence between a conditional (or implication) and a disjunction is an error'.[2]

c that a satisfactory logic of modality must distinguish between actually existing individuals and merely possible ones; and that, accordingly, in constructing quantificational logic we should *not* simply and automatically presuppose that we are dealing with actually existing individuals.

Russell, of course, would have none of this. As far as he was concerned, all of MacColl's doctrines were the results of rather elementary errors. His distinction between certain and variable statements, for example, results from not distinguishing between propositions and propositional functions, and is simply a misguided and misleading way of dealing with the difference between them. There is no need to go beyond the twofold categorisation of propositions proper as true and false.[3]

In sum, Russell's philosophical positions and allegiances led him to dismiss all of MacColl's doctrines as so much old-fashioned fairytale nonsense.[4]

(5) *Interactions: (B) Russell and Meinong*

One idea operative in MacColl – and even more prominently in the work of Alexius Meinong – came to arouse Russell's particular ire: the idea of unrealised or non-actual particulars. The conception that there are non-existent individuals – i.e. particulars which don't exist in this, the actual world but could exist in some alternative dispensation – represents an idea of longstanding credentials in philosophy, figuring in the Presocratics, in medieval scholasticism, and in Leibniz, in addition to its prominent role in the philosophy of Brentano.[5]

According to Russell, MacColl's distinction between actual and merely possible individuals is the result of an incorrect theory of naming according to which any combination of letters which functions grammatically as a name must actually name something in virtue of this function. When in fact the name names nothing (e.g. 'Pegasus') – and is thereby in Russell's opinion not properly speaking a name at all – Mac-Coll, under the spell of linguistic usage, provides a referent for the name in the guise of a merely possible individual. For Russell those theoreticians who, like MacColl and Meinong, accept an ontology of 'merely possible objects' have fallen victim to the logically deceptive distortions inherent in our ordinary use of language.[6]

This conception of merely possible individuals is altogether anathema to Russell, who indeed flatly dismisses the very meaningfulness of ascribing existence to individuals. He writes:[7]

> For the present let us merely note the fact that, though it is correct to say 'men exist', it is incorrect, or rather meaningless, to ascribe existence to a given particular x who happens to be a man. Generally, 'terms satisfying ϕx exist' means ϕx is sometimes true'; but 'a exists' (where a is a term satisfying ϕx) is a mere noise or shape – devoid of significance.

Rather than run the risk of having to put up with non-existent possible individuals, Russell is willing to dispense altogether with the whole process of attributing existence to things.

(6) *Interactions: (C) Russell and C. I. Lewis and J. Lukasiewicz*
It is also illuminating to consider Russell's reactions to the work of two other pioneers of modal logic in its contemporary guise as a branch of symbolic logic. I think here primarily of C. I. Lewis whose important *Survey of Symbolic Logic* appeared in 1918 and Jan Lukasiewicz whose important historical and systematic inquiries came into increasing prominence after the early 1920s. It is a perhaps surprising, but, I think, interesting and not insignificant fact that one can search Russell's pages in vain for any recognition of the work of these men. (Both in the second edition of the *Principia* (1925–7) and in the second edition of the *Principles* (1937) Russell preserves total silence with respect to all these developments.) And this seems especially inexplicable in view of the fact that the issues that provided these writers with their entry-point into the realm of modal ideas were topics of very special interest to Russell. (In Lewis's case the motivating issue was the philosophy of Leibniz, in Lukasiewicz's it was that of determinism and problems of prediction and future contingency in the context of the philosophy of Aristotle.) Again, it is also startling that Russell also ignores totally the development of mathematical intuitionism, especially the writings of L. E. J. Brouwer, whose work provides a possible bridge to the modal realm from points of departure in the philosophy of mathematics.
    A clear picture emerges: in pre-*Principia* days Russell sharply opposed philosophers like MacColl and Meinong who sought to promote concern with the logic of modalities; in post-*Principia* days, secure on his own logico-mathematical ground, Russell simply ignored writers like Lewis and Lukasiewicz and the intuitionists whose work could provide a basis for the introduction of modalities into the framework of symbolic logic. Where modal logic was concerned, Russell adopted Lord Nelson's precedent, and stolidly put his telescope to the blind eye.

(7) *The fascination with truth-functionality: logical atomism and logical positivism*
The line of thought operative here is, of course, intimately linked to

Russell's theory of logical constructions, and to the methodological precept of logical constructionism, which he articulates as follows:[8]

> The supreme maxim in scientific philosophising is this: Whenever possible, logical constructions are to be substituted for inferred entities.

Clearly the dismissal of all inferred entities and processes points towards a demise of potentialities, powers and causal efficacy that pulls the rug out from the main motivation for recognising possibility and contingency. The logical construction of something real will, quite evidently, be a construction from elements that are themselves altogether actual (real). This facet of Russell's philosophy provides yet another facet of his rejection of modality.

The generally reductivist penchant of the theory of logical constructions found its clearest expression in various aspects of Russell's reductivistic programme in logic and the extraction of all logical operations from atomic elements by truth-functional modes of combination.

It is important to recognise that Russell was himself deeply caught up in the ideology of two-valued truth-functionality that was part of the heritage of Frege and received its canonical formulation in Ludwig Wittgenstein's *Tractatus Logico-Philosophicus*. The Russellian programme of 'The Philosophy of Logical Atomism' – as well as Wittgenstein's Tractarian theory correlated with it – envisaged the definitional reduction of all concepts of interest and utility in the precise sector of philosophy to truth-functional conjoinings or combinations of basic propositions which (since meaningfully definite) will themselves be either true or false.[9] Being truth-functional, these modes of combination have the feature that the truth-status of a compound can always be determined in terms of the respective status of its several constitutive components.[10]

Thus significant weight came to be borne by not strictly logical, but essentially methodological (perhaps even metaphysical) considerations, as built into the philosophy of logical atomism. We do not have a rationally adequate grasp of theses that have not been analysed into their components. Such analysis calls for indicating the component elements and composing structures through which the logical character of complexes is determined (*truth-functionally* determined) in terms of the status of the component elements. If a thesis that is internally complex in its conceptual structure does not submit to truth-functional analysis, this is a mark of an internal imprecision whose toleration is a concession to obscurantism.

The stress upon logical reducibility was, of course, vastly congenial to the ethos of logical positivism. This took increasingly definite form during the first decade after the First World War, whose programmatic menu offered a Hobson's choice between the *reduction* and the *abandonment* of philosophically problematic concepts. We are brought back to the influence of that 'paradigm of philosophy' (according to F. P. Ramsey and G. E. Moore), the Theory of Descriptions, according to which some conception that is standardly operative in our ordinary scheme of thought about things is reductively annihilated as the mere product of linguistic illusion.

Now the critical fact which all concerned recognised as a feature of modal concepts is that none of them – be they absolute (like possibility or necessity) or relative (like entailment or strict implication) – will be truth-functional. It was throughout recognised by all concerned as a vain enterprise to analyse modal concepts in two-valuedly truth-functional terms. And for Russell and the bulk of the positivistically-inclined logical tradition that followed him down to the days of Goodman and Quine, this very fact provided the basis for a rejection of modality.

But from the first there were dissentients. The logical structure of the basic conceptual situation was created by an inconsistent triad:

a the insistence upon propositional two-valuedness;
b the insistence upon the truth-functionality of all proper propositional operators and connectives;[11]
c the legitimacy of modal distinctions.

As indicated, Russell and his positivist congeners abandoned (c), but others took a different route. In his single-minded pursuit of a concept of relative necessity and a really viable analysis of if–then, C. I. Lewis gave up the truth functionality of (b) and developed the theory of strict implication. Jan Lukasiewicz in his pursuit of an Aristotelian theory of future contingency gave up (a), and developed many-valued logic. (Brouwer and his Intuitionist followers gave up the entire concept of mathematico-logical analysis upon which the concept of propriety operative in (b) is based.)

The ideological penchants and predilections of logical positivism involved: (i) a commitment to a sharp-edged criterion of truth that was unwilling to tolerate the pluralism of a theory of degrees of truth or to acknowledge – as apart from the altogether meaningless – any shades and gradations as between the true and the false, and (ii) a commitment to a criterion of meaning unwilling to recognise as meaningful conceptions not definitionally reducible to the clear conceptions of a canonical basis. Accordingly, while the appropriateness of efforts at a corresponding reduction of conceptions like absolute and relative modalities (or of counterfactual conditionals, to take another example) might be recognised, the failure of such a quest for two-valued reduction was taken as to be construed to spell not the inadequacy of the reductive programme, but the illegitimacy of the putatively irreducible concepts. In this positivistic atmosphere, the Russellian distaste for modal concepts hardened into an attitude of virtually dogmatic rejection of modal logic.[12]

(8) *Effects*

Orthodox two-valued and truth-functional logic – 'classical' logic as it is now frequently called – in the form given it by Russell, his associates, and their followers, enjoyed enormous successes. The mainstream of development in the tradition of logicians like Hilbert, Gödel, Tarski, Church, Rosser, *et al.* developed logic into a powerful instrument for exploring the foundations of mathematics and more than justified Russell and Whitehead's selection of that proud title of their monumental work.

Modal logic remained in the shadows for a long time. It did not really begin to come into its own until the development of modern modal semantics, largely under the impetus of Rudolf Carnap[13] (erecting a structure of his own on foundations laid by Wittgenstein and Tarski). It was Carnap who first successfully elaborated the possible-world semantics which those who followed in his wake were to build up into the grandiose structure we know today. Until the late 1940s it remained to all intents and purposes the concern of a few eccentric philosophical guerrillas concerned to snipe from the sidelines as the main column of modern mathematical logic marched by *en route* from victory to victory in directions appointed for it by the orientation of Russell's work. Thus, during the period from the early 1920s to the late 1940s, the great bulk of logicians and logically-concerned philosophers – indeed virtually everyone outside the range of the personal influence of Lewis and Lukasiewicz[14] – adhered to Russell's negative stance towards modal concepts. The great successes of the Russellian vision of logic in the mathematical sphere gave a massive impetus to his negative view of modality. The upshot was, I think it not unfair to say, that the development of modal logic was set back by a full generation.

There is no fundamental historical reason why modern symbolic modal logic could not have developed substantially sooner. The basic tools forged by MacColl and Lewis lay to hand by 1920, as did those hints of Wittgenstein's *Tractatus* (relating to probability) from which Carnap first systematised the possible-worlds interpretation of modal logic. There is no reason of historical principle why the logic of modality which surged up shortly after Carnap's *Meaning and Necessity* (University of Chicago Press, 1947) could not have begun soon after 1920. This development was certainly delayed by a full generation during the period between the two world wars. This delay can be attributed in no small part to views and attitudes held by Russell and promulgated under the influence of his massive authority.

It would be just plain wrong to say that the time was not ripe for the development of modal logic in the period between the two world wars. The ideas were there, the pioneering work was being done, the relevant publications were part of the public domain. But this work simply did not have the reception it deserved – far too little attention was paid to it. And this was due not to any lack of intrinsic interest or importance or to any *logical* disqualifications, but principally to *ideological* factors. Put bluntly, the development of modal logic was retarded primarily because Russell and his positivist followers found modal conceptions *philosophically* uncongenial. And the influence of Russell was a crucially operative factor here. There is no question in my mind that if Russell had possessed a more urbane, tolerant and receptive interest in logical work that did not resonate to his own immediate philosophical predilections, it would have done a great deal of good.

(9) *Assessment*

Russell's work and the stimulus it exerted upon others was responsible for a massive forward step in the development of modern symbolic logic in its 'classical' articulation, in a form eminently suited to mathematical developments and applications. The massive proportions of his contribution cannot be questioned. Nevertheless, in so far as the line of thought presented here is at all correct, it appears that baneful consequences ensued from Russell's work and its influence for the development of modal logic. But the question remains: Was this just an unfortunate historical accident or was it something for which Russell himself deserves a certain measure of responsibility?

This question is certainly not otiose or irrelevant. We know full well that the blame for abuse by later followers of the contributions of a master must not inevitably be laid on his own doorstep. We cannot reproach the humane Dr Guillotin – concerned only to minimise the agonies of criminals condemned to execution – with the excesses of the abuse of his favoured implement during the Terror phase of the French Revolution. Nor can we reproach that devoted and conscientious scholar Darwin for the callous application of his ideas by some among the Social Darwinists. A master innovator can fall blameless victim to the rationally unbridled zeal and unrestrained excesses with which his followers exploit his ideas. He can certainly fall the unhappy hostage of an unforeseen and to him almost certainly unwelcome abuse of his ideas.

But is this defensive line available in Russell's case to blunt the charge of responsibility for impeding the development of modal logic? I think not, because in this case the central factor is a question not of the unforeseen and presumably undesired consequences of certain innovations, but of Russell's own views and positions. His own deliberately held negative views towards modal conceptions – opinions espoused on conscious and philosophically reasoned grounds – were themselves operative forces behind the impact of Russell's position in this sphere.

The distaste for modal logic in Anglo-American philosophy during the period between the two world wars was virtually initiated by Russell and largely propagated by his great influence. The development of modal logic was impeded neither by accidental factors nor because this branch of logic is itself lacking in substantive interest from a logical point of view, but because many logicians were led under Russell's influence to regard it as philosophically distasteful. It seems to me by no means unjust to place squarely at Russell's door a substantial part of the responsibility for the stunted development of modal logic during the two generations succeeding the pioneering days of Hugh MacColl. Russell's philosophically inspired attitudes propagated a negative view of modal logic and helped to produce that disinclination to take modality seriously which can still be seen at work among our own contemporaries of the older generation (e.g. W. V. Quine and N. Goodman). The very success of Russell's work in the more mathematically oriented sectors of logic gave authority and impact to his antagonistic stance towards the logic of modality. For the development of *this* area of logic, at any rate, Russell's work represented a distinctly baneful influence.

Please do not misunderstand my intentions. It is not really my aim to accuse Russell of any moral dereliction in regard to modal logic. After all, every philosopher is entitled to his full share of human failing, myopia and even prejudice. My concern is not so much with moral as with causal responsibility. It is my prime aim to establish the *causal* fact that Russell's disinclination towards modal conceptions substantially retarded the development of modal logic. As regards issue of praise or blame I leave it to the reader to draw his own conclusions.

Certainly nothing could be more wise and urbane than the pious sentiments of the concluding paragraph of Russell's review in *Mind* of MacColl's *Symbolic Logic and Its Applications*:[15]

> The present work . . . serves in any case to prevent the subject from getting into a groove. And since one never knows what will be the line of advance, it is always most rash to condemn what is not quite in the fashion of the moment.

Anyone concerned for the health and welfare of modal logic as an intellectual discipline cannot but wish that Russell himself – and especially that majority among his followers who were perhaps even more royalist than their king – had seen fit to heed this eminently sound advice.

Department of Philosophy
University of Pittsburgh

NOTES

1   MacColl published some forty books and papers during the years 1877–1910. For details see the bibliography by A. Church in *Journal of Symbolic Logic*, vol. 1 (1936: 132–3).

2   *Mind*, vol. XVII (1908: 151–2); see p. 152.

3   ' "If" and "Imply": a reply to Mr. MacColl', *Mind*, vol. XVIII (1908: 300–1; cf. *Introduction to Mathematical Philosophy* (London, George Allen & Unwin, 1919: 165).

4   For Russell the uncongeniality of MacColl's ideas was compounded by that of his

somewhat idiosyncratic logical symbolism. The Russell Archives at McMaster University contain some twenty-five letters and postcards sent by MacColl to Russell over the years 1901–9. In one of these MacColl complains that he and Russell have as much difficulty understanding one another as would an Englishman who knows little or no French and a Frenchman who knows little or no English. In a later handwritten annotation of a typed transcription of a letter of MacColl's, dated 28 May 1905, Russell writes: 'MacColl was a symbolic logician of some eminence. I have a very large number of letters from him, but I have not included them in this [typed] selection because they are in his difficult symbolism.'

5 For the history see the chapter on 'The Conception of Nonexistent Possibles' in N. Rescher, *Essays in Philosophical Analysis* (University of Pittsburgh Press, 1969).

6 These considerations in the backwash of Russell's classic paper: 'On Denoting', *Mind*, vol. XIV (1905): 479–93) – that 'paradigm of philosophy' as F. P. Ramsey and G. E. Moore called it, and as indeed it was for much of English philosophy during the interwar era – are doubtless too familiar to need detailed documentation.

7 *Introduction to Mathematical Philosophy*, op. cit.

8 Quoted in Rudolf Carnap, *Der logische aufbau der Welt: Scheinproblem in der Philosophie* (Berlin-Schlachtensee, Weltkreis-verlag, 1928: 1).

9 But note that Wittgenstein gave hints from which Carnap developed his rationalisation of modal logic.

10 The strengths and limitations of this programme were brought into clearest relief in A. Tarski's classic essay on the concept of truth in formalised languages, 'Der Wahrheitsbegriff in den formalizierten Sprachen', *Studia Philosophica, Warsaw*, vol. 1 (1935–6: 261–405); German trans., original in Polish (1930). It is of interest in illustrating the pervasiveness of the truth-functional tenor of thought that Tarski in the early 1930s rejected the proposal (of Z. Zawirski and H. Reichenbach) to consider the probability calculus as a form of many-valued logic on the grounds that probabilities do not behave in a truth-functional manner; cf. the discussion in N. Rescher, *Many-valued Logic* (New York, McGraw-Hill, 1969: 184–8).

11 There is no essential link between two-valuedness and truth-functionality. Connectives in a many-valued logic can, of course, be truth-functional.

12 The reluctance or inability of logical positivism to come to serious and effective grips with the logic of modality proved a serious stumbling-block to the success of the movement. See Hans Poser, 'Das Scheitern des logischen Positivismus an modaltheoretischen Problemen', *Studium Generale*, vol. 24 (1971: 1522–35).

13 *Introduction to Semantics* (Cambridge, Mass.: Harvard University Press, 1942); and especially *Meaning and Necessity* (University of Chicago Press, 1947).

14 Brouwer and the non-classicists in the foundations of mathematics, of course, had no interest in modal logic, since modal concepts play no role in mathematics.

15 *Mind*, vol. XV (1906: 255–60; see p. 260).

10

RUSSELL AND BRADLEY ON RELATIONS

Timothy Sprigge

(1) Not least among the many philosophical achievements of Bertrand Russell was his highly successful critique of the kind of idealist philosophy which dominated Great Britain in his youth. This was not merely a matter of detailed argument, for it was a matter largely of establishing a different tone in philosophising, something which was in many respects desirable. Not only was the British Idealism (unlike the German Idealism from which it derived) of such as Bradley and McTaggart increasingly distancing itself from any involvement in the ferments of contemporary science, but it purveyed a kind of metaphysical, almost Panglossian, optimism which Russell was right to find offensive and perhaps detrimental to social progress. (Compare in this connection Oxford as viewed by Bradley and as viewed by Jude the Obscure.)[1] Over all hung the feeling that the higher intellectual and emotional states of dons were the heart of, perhaps the one real thing in, the universe, and a stuffy unawareness of the mass of human suffering and of the non-human immensities surrounding it. In spite of the fact that in a strangely transmuted form some of these features have been present in more recent Oxford philosophy, Russell's achievement was considerable, more so in the respects I have mentioned than that of Moore with whom one naturally pairs him as an opponent of Bradleyism.

We should remember, however, that Bradley was admired in his day as a brilliant master of argument. Both Bradley and Russell were great philosophers, and it is unlikely that all the wisdom lay on one side. It seems not inappropriate, therefore, that this memorial volume should contain some discussion and assessment of their respective positions on a subject which loomed large in both their philosophies, namely, the status of relations. I shall be considering some arguments Russell used against Bradley in this connection, and seeking to show that there are problems which arise from this controversy which have never as yet been cleared up.

According to Russell, incorrect theories about relations had, until his time, impeded the development both of logic and philosophy. The refusal to accept propositions which assert a relation between two or more particulars as having their own distinctive form, no less basic than and not reducible to the form of those propositions which ascribe a predicate to a subject, prevented logic from advancing much beyond the

Aristotelian stage, and formed the basis of far-fetched monadistic and monistic metaphysical systems.

In *The Principles of Mathematics* and elsewhere Russell clears the ground for his own treatment of relations by a quite detailed attack upon two theories of relations which had tended to hold the field, what he calls the monadistic view, which he attributes to Leibniz and with qualifications to Lotze, and what he calls the monistic view which he associates with Bradley and Spinoza. In this chapter I want to evaluate his critique of the latter, as contained in certain sections of *The Principles of Mathematics* (1903) and in the 1906 essay 'On the Nature of Truth' (*Proceedings of the Aristotelian Society*, 1906–7). Since Bradley is probably the most important philosopher in respect of his treatment of relations, of those whom Russell can be taken as attacking, I shall be concerned not simply with the way in which Russell deals with the monistic theory as specified by himself, but with the extent to which his discussion undermines the actual position held by Bradley. I shall endeavour to show that though some of Bradley's positions are undermined, there is an important aspect of his thought to which Russell does not do justice, and that there may be more in the monistic theory than Russell was prepared to allow.[2]

In chapter XXVI of *The Principles of Mathematics* Russell tells us that both the monadistic and the monistic view of relations try to reduce relational propositions to ones of subject–predicate form (meaning such as ascribe a predicate to a *single* subject).

> Given, say, the proposition aRb, where R is some relation, the monadistic view will analyse this into two propositions, which we may call ar_1 and br_2, which give to a and b respectively adjectives supposed to be together equivalent to R. The monistic view, on the contrary, regards the relation as a property of the whole composed of a and b, and as thus equivalent to a proposition which we may denote by $(ab.)r$ (p. 221).

This passage comes in a chapter on 'Asymmetrical Relations' and introduces an attempt to demonstrate that neither theory can deal with the logic of these. Leaving aside the discussion of the monadistic theory (in which, I think, Russell is decidedly in the right), let us turn to the case as it concerns the monistic theory. Should there be an error here, that is a matter of some importance, since, I believe, Russell's first argument has been considered decisive by almost all subsequent writers on the subject.

(2) Russell's first argument rests upon the supposed incapacity of the monistic view to deal with the difference between 'aRb' and 'bRa', where R is an asymmetrical (or, one may add, a non-symmetrical) relation. If 'aRb' ascribes to the whole (ab) a certain predicate which takes the place of R, then 'bRa' will do so likewise, for evidently the whole (ab) is not to be distinguished from the whole (ba), since we are simply speaking of that

total object they jointly compose. Thus there will be no difference between '*a* is greater than *b*' and '*b* is greater than *a*', for both will mean simply something like '(*ab*) contains diversity of magnitude'.

That there is a fairly obvious line of reply on the part of the monist has, I think, not struck people (though it is, indeed, suggested by many a passage in Bradley), because they have tended to think in terms of a proposition '*aRb*', where '*a*' and '*b*' function roughly as what Russell was later to call logically proper names. It is then overlooked that what the monist will transform into a predicate applicable to the whole is not simply the relation, but also the meaning or connotation of the expressions denoting the terms of the relation.

The monist will, for example, interpret the proposition, 'This cup is above that saucer' as a characterisation of a certain total situation comprising the cup and the saucer. If he took it as the predication of something like *aboveness* of that situation, then indeed he would not distinguish its significance from that of 'That saucer is above that cup'. It is evident, however, that he will take it as the application to a sensibly presented totality of the predicate being (the totality of) a cup on top of a saucer, which is a very different *gestalt* quality from that of being (the totality of) a saucer on top of a cup.

The view we are attributing to the monist is close to that advanced in chapter 1 of Bradley's *The Principles of Logic*. Consider for instance: 'We saw that all judgement is the attribution of an ideal content to a reality, and so this reality is the subject of which the content is predicated. Thus in "A precedes B". the whole relation A–B is the predicate and, in saying this is true, we treat it as an adjective of the real world' (*The Principles of Logic*, 2nd edn, Oxford, vol. I, p. 28). We should perhaps note that by 'the relation *AB*' Bradley means the whole relational situation of *A* preceding *B*, not the mere relation of precedence, which happens to hold between *A* and *B*.

There are two objections to this reply on behalf of the monist which might be raised from a Russellian point of view. It might be urged, first, that 'This cup is on top of that saucer' is equivalent to the conjunction of three independent propositions, 'This is a cup', 'That is a saucer', and 'This is on top of that'. If this were so, the monist would then have a difficulty in distinguishing the third proposition from the different one 'That is on top of this'. Evidently he could no longer employ a predicate including the notions of cup and saucer, since this third proposition does not imply that it is a cup and saucer which is in question. If he made use of any other concepts supposed to be connoted, in this context, by 'This' and 'that', a similar reduction to that applied to 'This cup is on that saucer' could produce three independent propositions of which the third, which we may represent as '*a* is above *b*', would imply nothing whatever as to any difference in character between what is above and what is below.

However, the monist can repel this line of attack by simply denying that there can be a proposition of the form '*aRb*' which implies nothing regarding any difference in character between the terms other than that the sense of the relation runs from the one and to the other. Whatever the truth of the matter, one can hardly say that the *onus probandi* lies with the monist here. It is hard to see what observable difference there could be between the situations described, for example, by '*a* is above *b*' and '*b* is above *a*', if we suppose no observable difference between *a* and *b* other than that the one is above and the other below. Moreover, it is of the essence of monism to deny that there can be logically proper names or what, at the time of *The Principles of Mathematics*, Russell spoke of as names 'which indicate without meaning' (p. 502).

A Russellian might concede some of this but still argue somewhat subtly along the following lines. Granted, he might say, that if we treat 'This cup is above that saucer' as ascribing to the presented reality the *gestalt* quality of being a cup on top of a saucer, we do indeed distinguish it from 'That saucer is above this cup', we still do not do justice to the original proposition, for we leave unexpressed the fact that it is this object here which is the cup on top and that object there which is the saucer below.

The point insisted on here is that there are two distinct particulars which we attend to and note as playing their distinctive role in the total relational situation, and that any suggestion that we only attend to the whole and characterise that misses this point. If one were impressed by this point, but also felt the force of the monistic contention that to observe that certain terms are in a certain relation is to perceive them as constituting a certain sort of totality with its own *gestalt* quality, one might seek to develop a compromise position for which the relational proposition does indeed ascribe a special sort of predicate to the whole, but also indicates the role which each term plays in producing a whole of this character. I have myself sought to develop such a position elsewhere.[3] Yet even this supposition may concede too much to the Russellian. Having noticed that there is a cup and a saucer before me, is there really anything additional to be noted which can be described as its being *this* particular which is the cup on top, and *that* which is the saucer below? If there is not, we cannot object on this ground to the equation of 'This cup is on that saucer' with 'This totality is a cup on a saucer'.

A Russellian might, however, develop his objection to this equation by pointing out that the former contains distinctive references to the two particulars which can be taken up by further questioning, as the latter does not. Thus, the former may lead me on to the question 'Is it, the cup I mean, chipped?' as the latter evidently could not.

But this is not really true. Whenever a predicate is applied to a subject, one may go on to ask that the description be made more precise in certain respects by the provision of further, more determinate predicates. Just as 'scarlet' is more determinate than 'red', so is 'being a chipped cup on a saucer' more determinate than 'being a cup on a saucer', and one could press the line of inquiry supposed to be difficult on the monistic analysis by asking whether the latter predicate also applied to the totality in question.

So far as I can see, then, Russell's claim that the monistic view cannot deal with asymmetrical relations is ill-founded, or, at least, begs the question. I suppose an objector might say that I have defended the monistic view by reducing it to vacuousness. Of course, he may say, if you introduce not only the relation into the predicate, but also the terms related, you can make the relational proposition ascribe a single, if complex, predicate to a certain totality (perhaps ending up with Reality as a whole as the sole subject), but one can hardly maintain that the possibility of such a minor verbal reshuffling shows anything about the logical structure of the proposition.

If there were anything in this it would follow, not that Russell is right and that the monist is wrong, but that the point at issue between them is an essentially empty one. This I do not think it is, for reasons which will emerge. We must admit in any case that the monistic analysis only needs to be carried out with due thoroughness in order to meet this famous objection of Russell's. It was, after all, always an essential part of Bradley's view that all ordinary terms of discourse belong logically to the predicate of the judgments in which they occur (a view not without its influence on Russell's theory of descriptions).

My example has concerned a type of relational proposition or judgment which could only be made when the terms of the relation are sensibly present. One might well argue that this has brought us to fundamentals, since the real question at issue is as to what one becomes aware of, when one perceives that terms stand in a certain relation. However, the same essential points would arise if one considered 'Brutus killed Caesar' (to take the usual heroes of these philosophical debates). For the monist this asserts that a certain total historical event had a certain characteristic, that of being Caesar's death at the hands of Brutus. Provided we do not seek to deny connotation to 'Brutus' and 'Caesar', Russell's present objection fails in this case too, because there is no reason to identify this characteristic with that of being Brutus's death at the hand of Caesar.

(3) In *The Principles of Mathematics* Russell follows up the argument we have considered with another to do with the relation of whole and part. He asks how the monist is to deal with '*a* is a part of *b*' which, if the monistic theory is correct, asserts 'something of the whole composed of *a* and *b*, which is not to be confounded with *b*'. This leads to difficulties. Either the proposition about the new whole is not a proposition concerning whole and part, or it is. If the former, we have eliminated the class of propositions about whole and part, and have thereby eliminated the very category of wholes, yet if there are no wholes the monistic theory breaks down. If the latter, we start on an infinite regress of a vicious kind because each whole and part proposition presupposes another. Russell

then considers the possibility that the monist might hold, after all, that the whole which becomes the subject of the *analysans* in the monistic analysis of '*a* is a part of *b*' is *b* itself. But this he regards as incompatible with the monistic denial that the whole is the sum of its parts, and urges that in any case the problem of asymmetry remains. The last point (unless I misunderstand it) seems a rather weak reversion to the argument we were considering previously.

It is hardly possible to discuss this alleged incompatibility without going more deeply into rival theories as to the relation of whole and part than space permits. In fact, I believe that some quite various sorts of proposition or judgment might be expressed by sentences which say that one thing is part of another. (The distinctions I have in mind are not those made by Russell in chapter XVI of *The Principles of Mathematics*. It is, indeed, only in his account of his first sense of 'whole' in section 135 that he comes anywhere near talking of whole and part, and this very unsatisfactorily, in the quite simple sense in which my arm is part of my body. This is the sense we should initially have in mind when considering the monistic analysis. Of course, that chapter represents a very early stage of Russell's thought on these topics.)

The monist might propose two types of analysis for judgments concerning whole and part where these concern things which are perceptible or sensible, and perhaps in some other cases too. In one set of cases one might take the judgment as really asserting that *a* and *X* (where *X* is the 'rest' of *a*) are related so as to constitute a whole of a certain sort. This can then be reinterpreted by the monist as the judgment that *b* has the property of being a certain combination of *X* and *a*. In another set of cases one might not need to introduce the element *X* at all, but could read the judgment straight off as ascribing the property of *containing a* to *b*.

Dr Frankenstein, about to pick up a hand in his laboratory, might notice just in time that the one in question was, in fact, part of his servant standing there. I suggest he might be noticing that, together with certain other bodily parts, it made up his servant; in short, that his servant was the combination of it and various other parts. The other type of case might be illustrated by my noticing for the first time that a painting contains an angel's face in one corner. My judgment here may be regarded as ascribing a certain character to the totality which is the painting.

Essentially I am taking it that the whole which becomes the subject is the same whole as that which was originally one term of the relation. I do not believe that this entails that the whole is the sum of its parts in any sense which the monist would wish to reject. One may add, surely, that part–whole judgments are peculiar from the point of view of the monist, in that they are expressed in language which already approximates to the form to which he wishes to reduce all relational judgments, and therefore are not in need of the like type of reduction. For, in a way, the monist assimilates all relational judgments to part–whole judgments, or holds at least that they all consist in recognising that something is a complex whole of a certain kind. If he regards the category of whole and part as ultimately misleading, it is because he thinks the so-called parts are better regarded as aspects of the total character of what, for lack of a better word, he may still call the whole.

So far I have not seriously queried the correctness of Russell's description of the monist position. It is now time to point out that the view taken at least by Bradley of relations is in an important respect different from the one which Russell describes.

(4) Russell's monist regards the proposition 'aRb' as equivalent to one in which something is predicated of the whole (ab). Bradley's actual view is more complex and obscure, and I cannot pretend to give a full account of it here. What I can do, however, is pick out one aspect of what he seems to be saying, which I believe to be of special interest.

For Bradley relational thinking arises when we try to explain to ourselves how it is that items which we attend to as though they are distinct items in their own right belong together in the same world. In reality they belong together because they are not distinct items in their own right, but mere aspects of a greater totality (ultimately of the world as a whole, but on the way to this of totalities themselves really abstractions from the whole world) or of the character of a greater totality – for Bradley there is really no distinction between these two – but to recognise this is to give up thinking of them as distinct items in their own right, and this, for deep reasons to do with the status in reality of the human mind, we cannot do. Thus we fabricate the notion of relations which bind distinct items together, a notion which cannot be thought through with consistency but which serves as a device to allow us to oscillate between thinking of them as items in their own right, and recognising something of the character of the totality from which they are really mere abstractions.

Where Bradley differs most essentially from an atomist such as Russell is in this. For Russell one could identify an individual of some kind A and learn all one could about it as a thing in its own right, then go on to do the same thing with an individual B, and then as a third enterprise study the relations between A and B. This third study would add to one's stock of truths, so that one could formulate lots of truths of the form 'A is R to B', but this would not require abandonment or modification of what one learnt about A and B in one's original two inquiries.

Bradley would allow that there could be two distinct inquiries centring on each of A and B, respectively, such as aimed to characterise them in a fair degree of detachment from any larger context (though doubtless he would hardly take seriously the idea that they could be studied in complete isolation). What he would add, however, is that when one studied them in relation, as we must put it, to one another, one would really be studying a whole in which they were both included, and that the concept of them which one would then acquire would be incompatible with the concepts of them one acquired in the original separate investigations of each. That is, the study of them together would not merely add new ideas to the old ones, but would require radical modification of the old ones.

If we represent the results of the first two inquiries as FA and GB, respectively, then the results of the third inquiry, HW, will for Bradley be incompatible with FA and GB, as ARB was not for Russell. However, Bradley acknowledges that we will still frequently need to think of A and B as though FA and GB were true, and this is where relations come in. Propositions of the form ARB represent an attempt to combine the ideas expressed by FA and GB with the incompatible idea expressed by HW, or at least express our readiness to oscillate between the two views according to convenience. In general there is more truth at the level of HW, but much of the time such truth is too rich and total for practical purposes.

Suppose one made a separate study of each member of the Brontë family, and tried in each case to sum up the very essence of each personality. One might write essays on each one ending '. . . Such was Charlotte Brontë', '. . . Such was Emily Brontë', and so on. Subsequently one might study the family as a whole and conclude '. . . Such was the family Brontë'. Of course, the studies could not really be independent of one another (a point which supports Bradley) but the total impression of Charlotte given in the one study and in the other would be different. The final study might lead to a vision which (grammar apart) is non-relational, for which the family is a unity from which Charlotte considered as an individual in her own right is a mere abstraction, so that all characterisations of her which do not present her behaviour as an aspect of the family's development are distortions. Talking of the relations between Emily and Charlotte is keeping oneself ready to oscillate between these two viewpoints, which are not really compatible.

This example may help to bring out a point we have ignored. For Bradley, we said, thinking of things in relation to one another represents a wish to combine, or oscillate between, the view of them as individuals in their own right and the incompatible view of them as mere aspects in the character of a greater whole. Both views were practically necessary, but (we suggested) the latter was, for Bradley, the truer. Now we point out that if the whole characterised in the latter view were the universe, then indeed that would be truer still, indeed it would be the ultimately true view. (I shall ignore the fact that for Bradley even absolute truth is not quite true.) But since the wholes we can deal in are at a lower level, then even granted that we are to treat an individual such as Charlotte Brontë as an abstraction from a larger whole, there are various alternative such wholes, all giving different and incompatible visions of her. The relational mode of thought, then, serves not only to reconcile the vision of Charlotte as individual in her own right with that of her as abstraction from the family, but also to reconcile the latter with the vision of her as abstraction from various other wholes, say, the literary scene of the time.

Bradley often thus speaks of the particular thing as an abstraction from a larger whole, ultimately from the universe. By this he means essentially that any conception we form of it in relative isolation is falsified, rather than merely supplemented, by correct conceptions we form of wholes to which it belongs. The term 'abstraction', however, suggests what he often seems to think the case, that it is *we* who have produced the abstraction by somehow ourselves treating it in isolation from a totality within which it was originally presented to us. He should have made it clearer that this is only one case, and that often the relevant wholes to which it belongs are quite beyond our initial experience of it. (This distinction is only deviously connected with that he makes between pre-relational and post-relational unities.)

Our other example concerns rather the immediacies of sense experience and is very basic. Bradley holds, I take it, that to see (for example) an object as an element in a larger perceived totality is to see it as having a character incompatible with that which it has when seen rather as an item on its own, or at least against an only vaguely presented background. The seen character of the cup as element in the unity cup and saucer is different from that which it has as this cup. The relational judgment 'The cup is on the saucer' allows us to retain both visions of the cup as valid, though in fact they annul each other.

It is, of course, no objection to Bradley's claim, as illustrated in these two examples, that the incompatibility in question cannot be brought out in any ordinary formal logic, since this logic is simply the instrument of that discursive relational thinking (what Hegel would call *Verstand* as opposed to *Vernunft*) the whole point of which is to disguise it. If one were to pursue this matter further, it would be useful to consider what Bradley and those like him have said about 'and'.[4] For formal logic it is basic that 'A is F and G' is compatible with, indeed entails, 'A is F'. Any hint of a denial of this will seem a merely whimsical confusion of 'A is F' with 'A is merely F'. But for Bradley, if you think about A as being F and characterise it in no other way to yourself, you cannot help thinking of it as having a kind of F-ness, different from the F-ness which is merely an element in a richer characteristic which includes G as well. Nor can 'F and G' really be regarded as an adequate characterisation of such a richer characteristic. Properties cannot be merely conjoined; they must belong together in some distinctive kind of way, and nothing is really conveyed by 'A is F and G' unless some particular mode of being together is implicitly taken as intended.

The relation of Bradley's position on relations to that of Russell's monist may now be illustrated as follows. Suppose we have straight lines A, B and C bound by the three-term relation, call it R, which makes them constitute a triangle.[5] Then Russell's monist identifies the meaning of 'R

(ABC)' with 'X is a triangle' (or, perhaps, more strictly, the boundary of a triangle), where X is the relevant totality. Such an example puts the monistic view in a not unfavourable light, but it is not quite the view I find in Bradley. For Bradley $R(ABC)$ would represent a compromise between the state of mind in which what there is really is the triangle X, an individual which certainly is complex but which is not made up of distinct bits such as could be characterised other than as just the elements which they are in that whole, and that in which we concentrate attention successively on each of A, B and C and note that they are straight lines. They really only belong visually together so long as they are seen as mere aspects of the triangle, but if we regard them as three straight lines in relation to one another we reserve our right to annul the *gestalt* form from our consciousness as convenient and see each of them successively as a merely isolated straight line, without the admission that this line has a quality incompatible with that of the line which belonged to the triangle.

Many, of course, will see obscurity or confusion in the notion of incompatibility here in question. For myself I am persuaded that the qualities which things exhibit when seen in isolation are incompatible with the qualities they seem to have as elements in larger totalities. There is, of course, sufficient affinity between certain of the qualities exhibited in each case to justify using the same term for them, but there is no genuinely determinate feature which is one and the same in each case.[6]

It may be replied that the metaphysical implications of something which at most concerns the qualities immediately exhibited to our senses are limited, that, for instance, the distinctively visual qualities and forms of which we have been speaking are in any case not reasonably taken as belonging to the natures of physical things as they really are, and that, say (as Russell sometimes urged), we only know the structure, not the quality of the physical world. But I do not think this really affects the issue in any very essential way, for the general point I have illustrated by reference to these visual qualities and forms must be true, it would seem, of whatever characteristics there are which qualify the ultimate constituents of reality as they are in themselves. (For Bradley, though he does not put it in quite this way, these ultimate constituents are finite centres of experience, and the problem is as to the relation between the character which these have considered each in its own right and the character they have as abstractions from the total experience of the universe or absolute. We need not accept this, in order to see the force of the points we have been discussing.)

(5) Let us now turn to another place where Russell criticises a theory of relations associated with philosophical monism, namely to his 1906 article 'On the Nature of Truth' (*Proceedings of the Aristotelian Society*, 1906–7).[7] The first two parts of this are intended as an attack upon the

monistic view of truth, as presented in H. H. Joachim's *The Nature of Truth* (1906), and the second part isolates what Russell calls the axiom of internal relations as the central logical doctrine from which that view is deduced. Our concern is with the bearings of Russell's critique of this axiom on Bradley's theory of relations. Since Joachim's point of view is closely related to that of Bradley, and Bradley is in any case referred to and quoted by Russell as a supporter of this axiom, this is a quite appropriate point of view from which to approach this part of Russell's essay.

By the *axiom of internal relations* Russell means the doctrine that 'Every relation is grounded in the natures of the related terms':

> It follows at once from this axiom that the whole of reality or of truth must be a significant whole in Mr Joachim's sense. For each part will have a nature which exhibits its relations to every other part and to the whole; hence, if the nature of any one part were completely known, the nature of the whole and of every other part would also be completely known; while conversely, if the nature of the whole were completely known, that would involve knowledge of its relations to each part, and therefore the relations of each part to each other part, and therefore of the nature of each part. (Russell, op. cit.: 37)

Russell also points out that the converse holds, and that the monistic theory of truth implies the axiom.

There is no doubt that some philosophers have inclined to hold such an axiom. That is, they have thought that from propositions describing the nature of two terms one could deduce every true proposition regarding their relations to one another. We should note, however, that though what is deducible in the relevant sense would follow with a necessity of an essentially logical sort, it would not necessarily be displayable as an implication of a kind valid in any standard formal logic. How Bradley stands towards the axiom, we shall consider shortly.

Clearly, the interpretation of the axiom turns in great part on the interpretation of 'nature'. If absolutely every truth about a thing counts as a part of its nature, then the axiom holds in an absurdly trivial sense. We get a more significant proposition if we suppose that a thing's nature comprises all those of its characteristics which do not consist in its relation to something outside its own boundaries.

There certainly are relations which are internal in the sense that they conform to the axiom thus taken. If one patch is brighter in colour than another, that follows from two true propositions each asserting of one of the patches that it is of a certain shade, and each of these two propositions, taken singly, says nothing of the patch's relation to anything outside its boundaries. The same is true of the geometrical relations between figures of two different sorts. Although this is one of the things which have been meant by calling a relation internal, it is by no means the only thing, and so I shall use the less ambiguous term 'ideal relation' to specify relations of this sort henceforth and let the axiom of internal relations become the axiom of ideal relations when interpreted in this way. It is of interest to note that the universe Leibniz described in which officially there were no relations between different monads would really be one in which there were only ideal relations between them. Maybe the forms of proposition he recognised did not allow for assertion of the fact, but the universe he was envisaging was one in which the monads had very complex and interesting ideal relations one to another, such as constituted them highly systematic perspectival variants, as it were, of one another.

Such an interpretation of the axiom seems the only one which makes it both clear and interesting. However, neither Russell nor his opponents confine it to this sense. As a result they get bogged down in essentially useless wrangles as to the nature of natures. Let us, in any case, follow Russell's argumentation against the axiom awhile.

(6) Both Russell and Bradley see a close connection between the axiom of internal relations and a monistic metaphysic according to which there is only one genuine individual of whom all genuine truths predicate some character. Bradley's actual position is that all relational thinking represents a distortion of reality which is, however, practically and indeed intellectually necessary, for finite beings, but that relations conceived as internal distort it less than relations conceived as internal.[8] He added, however, and it is a point that is too often forgotten, that the greater distortion may often be the more necessary, and that, for many purposes, many relations are better conceived as external than as internal. Russell, likewise, sees the axiom of internal relations as a step towards a monism which will turn round and deny the reality of relations altogether. I shall be suggesting that there was a confusion in both their minds, the more serious in the case of Bradley, their proponent, between the axiom interpreted as the axiom of ideal relations, and the axiom taken as a way, certainly a bad way, of formulating the monistic theory of relations or that aspect of Bradley's position which approximates to this. That the axiom, taken in the former sense, is far from implying monism, should be suggested by the point I made above about Leibniz, a point indeed at which Russell himself hints ('On the Nature of Truth', p. 38).

One argument Russell uses to link the axiom with monism concerns the relation of diversity. If (argues Russell) the diversity of A and B is grounded in their adjectives (such as constitute their nature) this must be in virtue of their adjectives being different. But if difference must be grounded in a difference between the adjectives of the different, then the difference between the adjectives of A and B must be grounded in a difference of *their* adjectives. This leads to a regress of a vicious kind, for every difference will have to be grounded in a more basic difference. It follows that if there is to be a diversity of things, there must be some diversity not grounded in the natures (adjectives) of the diverse terms, and the axiom of internal relations falls. *Per contra*, if the axiom is upheld, there cannot be a diversity of things.

The trouble about this argument of Russell's is that it interprets the axiom of internal relations as applying in the same way to particulars and to universals. The more intelligent way of taking it, however, would distinguish here and say that with regard to particulars, A and B, ARB must follow from the conjunction of two such facts as that A has a certain quality F and B has a certain quality G, but that with regard to the qualities F and G (and similarly in the case of all universals) any relation in which they stand will follow the conjunction of $F = F$ and $G = G$. Although the nature of a thing consists in qualities it possesses, the nature of a quality or nature can only reasonably be thought of as consisting in its being itself. This exhibits itself clearly in the example of two coloured patches; the one is brighter than the other in virtue of the shade of each, but the one shade is brighter than the other in virtue of each being just itself.

These relations are clearly of the type to which I have applied the expression 'ideal'. Since relations between particulars and between universals are on different logical levels it might be better not to use the same expression in each case, but I shall simply urge the reader to bear the distinction in mind. Of course, in ontologies where a particular is identified with its total quality (an identification often found in Bradley) our distinction falls, but then so does Russell's point, since to speak of a relation as grounded in the nature of the terms will be simply to say that it is grounded in each being itself.

(7) Russell now goes on to consider the grounds on which the axiom is asserted, and says: 'There is first the law of sufficient reason, according to which nothing can be a brute fact, but must have some reason for being thus and not otherwise'. He quotes Bradley here: 'If the terms from their own inner nature do not enter into the relation, then, so far as they are concerned, they seem related for no reason at all, and, so far as they are concerned, the relation seems arbitrarily made' (*Appearance and Reality*, 2nd edn, George Allen & Unwin, p. 575).

Actually Russell does not consider this grounding of the axiom at much length, since he thinks that 'the law of sufficient reason should mean that every proposition can be deduced from simpler propositions', which consorts ill with the monist's contempt for simplicity. Russell is surely right that the law of sufficient reason does loom somewhat vaguely behind those of Bradley's and Joachim's assertions which sound most like the axiom, as in the passage he quotes from Bradley, and that when this is so they are inclining to uphold the axiom in what seems its clearest (not most acceptable) sense. I believe, however, that Bradley was quite wrong in supposing that this altogether unacceptable axiom follows from those insights which, at least for me, represent the real challenge of his monism. Let me explain.

His real point is this. One cannot really imagine certain things standing in a certain relation to one another without imagining a certain sort of totality within which those things figure as elements. Now either there is or there is not such a totality in reality. If there is such a totality, then, whenever we imagine those things other than as elements in such a totality, we imagine them as really they are not. Thus, any account of them which suggests we can imagine them as they really are without imagining them in this context sets them up as having an individuality of a kind they do not really have. In short, if they really belong to such a totality, all thinking about them as having any other status than as just the elements they are in that totality misrepresents them. On the other hand, if there is not such a totality, we can only imagine them as in relation to one another by imagining something which really there is not.

The point, it should be noted, is that when we imagine things which really do belong to such a totality without imagining that totality, we do not merely fail to bring into our picture of the situation a feature which could be added without modifying anything we have imagined, but we imagine them as having a positive character which is incompatible with their belonging to such a totality. The characteristic of being a certain element in a certain kind of totality is incompatible with being a complete entity in one's own right in the same kind of way as one shade of colour is incompatible with another. A sense of this incompatibility is best evoked by an appeal to imagine the situations in question. If people are resistant to recognising the point with regard to the characteristics of being an element in a totality and being a complete item in one's own right, or being an element in another sort of totality, that is because the whole logic of our language is designed to divert attention from it. This is the kind of point Bradley is making.

The most basic illustration concerns the relations between the distinguishable components within a single state of mind, i.e. within the totality of someone's experience at a certain moment. Whether we are thinking merely of them as related by what Russell has called 'compresence', or as related in some more specific way, we can only really imagine this state of affairs by imagining a single state of mind which has these two aspects to it. Such a totality actually exists, and any conception of the elements within the totality which suggests that we can be imagining the components as they really are, when we imagine them in isolation, seems evidently mistaken. The varied contents of a single experience are not bound together somehow so as to constitute it; rather, the only genuine individual is the whole, and these elements are mere abstractions therefrom.

Suppose now that I believe that certain relations hold between certain experiences of yours and certain experiences of mine, and let us for the moment ignore relations of mere contrast or affinity in quality and form. I may believe, for example, that they are simultaneous. If, however, I try to imagine the state of affairs in which this simultaneity consists, I can only do so by imagining a certain sort of totality, in which both experiences figure as elements. This totality may be thought of as a certain portion of space–time, or it may be thought of as a sort of more comprehensive experience or state of mind in which they both figure. In either case there is a totality of a kind there is good reason to doubt the actual existence of, the first because states of mind are not in space, the second because we are unready to believe in the required supermind or superexperience. Yet if there is not such a totality, there seems no imaginable way in which the two experiences can be related.

Now imagine two physical things in a certain spatial relation. You can do this only by imagining a certain spatial totality in which each is a component. If there is such a totality, this seems to be incompatible with there being such other totalities as you imagine when you imagine one of these things on its own (or with the vaguest of backgrounds) or as that you imagine when you imagine the relation of your first spatial totality to other parts of space. That is, if X and Y are related spatially because they are essentially components in a portion of space Z, then X cannot be a totality in its own right, nor can some space larger then X be, for then it would be that, not Z, which you should imagine when imagining how X and Y belong together spatially. Of course, one may think, on general grounds, that a real portion of space is not like anything one can imagine, but this does not affect the general point which these thought experiments are designed to suggest, namely, that it is hard to imagine or in any way clearly to conceive (where this amounts to something more than the mere ability to use language as a tool for dealing with things) what it is for things to stand in relations of any kind to each other (leaving aside, perhaps, relations which are merely ideal) where this is not a matter of their being mere aspects of more comprehensive totalities and therefore not genuine totalities in their own right.

These considerations suggest a quite different interpretation of the expression 'internal relation' than that which equates it with 'ideal relation' in the sense explained above. In this sense, the relation between two items is internal if their being in this relation is a matter of their being mere abstractions from a more genuine individual which embraces them both. I shall call such relations 'holistic'.

One would not be very far from Bradley's position, I believe, if one held the view that the only genuine relations between things are holistic, so that their being in a certain relation is always really a matter of there being a totality of which each is merely a certain aspect, as the so-called individuals known as my visual and auditory sensations are merely aspects of my total state of mind. Bradley seems to differ from this only in as much as he thinks the expression 'relation' misleading in this connection, since it is essentially involved with the idea that the terms in the relation are items which can be considered as individuals in their own right. To hold that all genuine relations are holistic, is to hold that all true relational propositions can be given the monistic analysis. For Bradley, on the other hand, the monistic analysis ignores certain false ideas implicit in the relational proposition, such as that the terms are individuals in their own right and are not necessarily misconceived when conceived apart from their position in the whole. Thus the claim that all genuine relations are holistic would, for Bradley, come very near to the truth of the matter, but it would not adequately convey the downgrading of the status of all finite individuals required in any ultimate grasp of how things are. For present purposes I do not think we need make too much of this difference, and we will not go far wrong, and will be able to discuss some things more succinctly, if we interpret Bradley as holding that all genuine relations between things must be holistic.

Whether it is true or not that all genuine relations between things must be holistic, Bradley does, I think, make a case for this claim the force of which was not appreciated by Russell, nor has it been by subsequent philosophers. Bradley is himself in large part to blame for this, for he confuses this claim with the quite other claim that all genuine relations are ideal, a confusion implicit in the expression 'internal relation', which seems sometimes to mean 'holistic', sometimes 'ideal'.

One cannot say that Bradley showed no recognition of this distinction. It is, indeed, present, though expressed in quite different terms, in his discussions of comparison.[8] Quite apart from Bradley, there is a real problem as to how they stand to one another. It would be possible for someone who held that all other genuine relations were holistic to regard ideal relations as in a different case. He might hold that things could contrast in quality, or have forms geometrically related to each other in a certain way, without being components in any more comprehensive totality, but that these were the only relations of which this was true. On the other hand, he might hold that such relations can only hold when the possibility of comparison exists, and maintain that only components in such a totality can be compared. If he took this view (as, in effect, do all philosophers who have tried to reduce the question whether you and I see the same colours to meaninglessness), I believe he might find himself eventually committed to demanding something more than a mere possibility of comparison (i.e. some actual form of togetherness), since the significance of comparing what was previously uncompared presupposes the holding of an ideal relation between the terms when being compared and the terms previous to comparison, which cannot itself be reduced to the fact that comparison will have a certain upshot. In short, the difficulties found in ideal relations between items not jointly experienced cannot be eliminated by talking of a possibility of their being experienced together, and, if real ones, imply that only terms which are actually experienced together, perhaps at the level of the divine, can be in ideal relations one to another.

Monadism depends, in effect, upon the view that there can be ideal relations between items which stand in no other sort of relation to one another, for the fact that they are all perspectival variants of one another is a matter of their ideal relations. The monist has usually regarded such a universe, or rather state of things, as strictly impossible. He could, however, take a more modest line and claim simply that it is incredible that there should be no more connection between things than lies in the contrasts and affinities between their characters. If he could, then, show that the only other sorts of relation, beside the ideal, which are really possible, are holistic ones, he would have gone a long way to establishing his position, even if without quite the absolute demonstration he craved. Actually, monists have usually also claimed that terms could not even exist in isolation from one another, without at a deeper level belonging to a whole of which their diversity is ultimately predicated. Here again they have weakened their case by the craving for an absolute demonstration. It would be much better not to treat absence of a relation as itself a relation, and to urge simply that if we once grant, as we can hardly help doing, that things are in any genuine positive relation to one another (and not merely an ideal one), we should grant that this is because they are all abstractions from a greater whole.

To scotch this kind of monism, one would have to show that fully external relations are conceivable, and that means relations which are neither ideal nor holistic. The holding of such a relation between two terms would not be equatable with their being merely elements in a more comprehensive totality. I must confess that Bradley has exhibited to me the difficulties of such a notion, difficulties which Russell does little to meet.

Let us turn back now to the alleged dependence of the axiom of internal relations upon the principle of sufficient reason. If by an internal relation is meant an ideal one, I think Russell is right. The geometrical relations between two figures have a sufficient reason in certain independent facts about the two of them. The belief that all relations must be grounded in the nature of their terms, as the holding of these ideal relations does, probably does rest in part upon some acceptance of this principle. But in this form the axiom consorts rather with monadism than with monism.

Monism rests rather upon an axiom of holistic relations. This has nothing to do with a principle of sufficient reason. It is not that the relations follow from the nature of their terms, but that the holding of the relations is identical with the terms being mere aspects in a certain totality. No notion of necessitation needs even to be raised.

Bradley certainly speaks at times as though he accepted the axiom in a form in which it is derivable from the principle. This arises partly through his own confusion between the two different sorts of internal relation, partly for other reasons into which we cannot enter, for they can be explained only by charting his relation to Hegelianism. At times he seems to recognise the distinction quite clearly, but only in order to make dubious moves from the one position to the other. The upshot of all this is that there is a strand of compelling thought in Bradley's treatment of relations which is impervious to this particular line of attack.

(8) I have represented Bradley as concerned about the imaginability of the state of affairs described in relational propositions, suggesting that for him this required the imagination of a whole including both terms in which the terms have a character incompatible with that which one imagines them as having, if one imagines them as existing as entities in their own right. The reference here to imaginability may be impugned both as a distortion of Bradley's approach and as an unhappy or irrelevant concern in itself.

With regard to the second point, I do indeed believe that it is approximately true that a proposition describing a state of affairs of a kind which is neither directly nor indirectly imaginable cannot be accepted as giving that real insight into how things are for which a philosopher should strive, however useful it may be pragmatically in view of its conventional entailment relations with other more basic propositions. (In calling a situation indirectly imaginable, I mean that it can be described in terms of its imaginable relations to directly imaginable situations, where an imaginable relation is one which can be exemplified in directly imaginable situations. A four-dimensional space is an example, since it relates to three-dimensionality by such imaginable relations as relate that to a four-dimensional surface.) This is too large a claim to be defended or indeed adequately explained here, but it is as well to point out that it does not rest on an imagist theory for which imagination must constantly accompany understanding, nor on any restrictive Berkeleyan theory as to what it is to imagine that something is the case.

As to whether Bradley was using such a principle, I admit that he does not formulate it, and that his uneasy feeling that Hegel knew best seems to make him feel guilty at his own hankering for the fleshpots of imagery. None the less in his actual style of thought, as well as in some of his writings on psychology, there is ample confirmation of my interpretation, though this is hardly the place to urge it. One might cite his attempt to show that we can form an adequate idea of the absolute, for what he does in effect is try to show that the absolute is indirectly imaginable. Or one might consider his Berkeleyan approach to a world of mere primary qualities; like Berkeley he really insists that we cannot imagine, say, extension without quality. Actually the present point is very much of the same order. We are invited really to bring home to ourselves the character of a situation in which things belong together as they must do to be in a relation, and to recognise that such belonging together seems to presuppose a whole from which, if they really belong to it, they are in a manner mere abstractions.

Russell suggests that the axiom of internal relations is also supported on a second ground, namely, that 'if two terms have a certain relation, they cannot but have it, and if they do not have it they would be different, which seems to show that there is something in the terms themselves which leads to their being related as they are'. ('On the Nature of Truth', p. 40).

He replies that if there are terms not in that relation, they cannot indeed be numerically the same terms as those which are, but they may none the less each be identical in quality with one of them; hence the relations cannot thus be proved to depend on the qualities of the relata. Although Russell utilises his infamous identification of material and logical implication in his precise statement of this point, we may grant that the argument he attacks is unsound for reasons approximating to those he gives. As Russell emphasises, this in no argument against the axiom, and, we may add, the reasoning Russell has attacked has no bearing on the Bradleyan thesis with which we have expressed sympathy.

It would take us too far afield to discuss the three positive reasons against the axiom which Russell produces, especially as the first two are applicable rather to monadism that to monism (and could be met, indeed, as we met the argument about *diversity*). As for the third argument, it certainly bears on Bradley, but not so much on his treatment of relations as on his general view of predication, and raises issues we cannot possibly discuss here.

Whatever the force of Russell's particular arguments, I think we may agree that there is little force in the axiom of internal relations, taken in the most natural way, namely, as stating that all relations are ideal in the sense explained above, that is, are such that their holding always follows from the natures of the terms they relate, where these natures are each accessible independently of the relational truths grounded by their conjunction. There are relations of this sort, but one cannot possibly maintain that all relations are such. The alternative ways of taking the axiom seem to be two. One can make it true in an entirely trivial way by simply identifying a thing's nature with all that is true of it, but the only interest this possesses is as an impetus to some more useful account of a nature. Finally, one can take it as a rather unhappy way of insisting that all relations are holistic (with the exception perhaps of ideal ones), that is, that things can only be in a relation of any (at least non-ideal) kind when what essentially they are is components within a more comprehensive whole, and components of such a kind that any conception we form of them as though they were individuals in their own right contains an element of distortion. It is much better, however, to discuss this last contention under another title, say, as the doctrine that all relations are holistic (with or without an exception in the case of ideal ones).

We may sum up as follows. Bradley tended both to hold that all relations are ideal, and that all relations are holistic. The reasons he and others had for the first view were not good ones, and Russell helped to show this. Bradley had some good reasons for the latter view, and Russell did not grasp these, as is shown by the way in which he attacked the closely related monistic theory of relations.

Further investigation of this topic should distinguish three sorts of putative relation: (1) ideal relations; (2) holistic relations; (3) external relations (i.e. such as are neither ideal nor holistic). There are great difficulties in conceiving relations of class (3), yet if there are not such relations either monadism or monism is true. Both theories are fantastic, but the latter somewhat less so. Russell might have disagreed, however, for in spite of everything there are hints of monadism, from time to time, in his treatment of private spaces.

Department of Philosophy
University of Sussex

NOTES

1 Of the life lived in this world by men of good will, Bradley is evidently prepared to say: 'If this is not Heaven, it at least comes nearer to the reality of the Blessed Vision than does any stupid Utopia or flaring New Jerusalem adored by the visionary' (*Essays on Truth and Reality*, London, Oxford University Press, 1914: 469). Bosanquet seems to have thought this of the deserving London poor. As for Bradley's vision of Oxford, it is reported that in 1919, speaking against a proposal to place captured German field guns in the college garden at Merton, he said that wars 'and the feelings they aroused were transitory things, but Merton Garden was a symbol of peace and had in it something of the eternal' (*Postmaster*, a Merton College magazine, vol. ii, no. 3 (December 1959: 13). The war, and, in general, the life of those excluded from such peace, like Jude, was doubtless among those 'discords' for which the life of the absolute is 'richer', and includes the pain which, it is possible though far from certain 'serves as a kind of stimulus to heighten the pleasure' in the absolute and which, in any case, 'will have ceased to be pain when considered on the whole' (*Appearance and Reality*, London, George Allen and Unwin, 1897: ch. XVII).

2 Relevant passages from Russell are indicated in the text. I shall not give many precise references to Bradley as his position is often so obscurely put that it can only be understood by a grasp of his writings as a whole. Most important is Appendix B, 'Relation and Quality', to the 2nd edition of *Appearance and Reality* (London, Oxford University Press, 1914) and Essay XXII of *Collected Essays*, vol. II (London, Oxford University Press, 1935). In my whole discussion, I am greatly indebted to John Watling, *Bertrand Russell* (London, Oliver and Boyd, 1970: ch. IV).

3 T. L. S. Sprigge, *Facts, Words and Beliefs*. (London, Routledge & Kegan Paul, 1968: ch. II, s. 5). See also my 'The Common Sense View of Physical Objects' (*Inquiry*, 1965).

4 See especially *Essays on Truth and Reality*, op. cit.: 226–33 (including footnotes, esp. on p. 231); cf. William James, *A Pluralistic Universe* (London, Longmans, Green, 1909: 60). James had more sense of the force of this aspect of monism than did Russell, but it is doubtful whether he was right in thinking he had found the right way round it.

5 I should point out that, somewhat disconcertingly, Bradley seems to hold that relations are essentially two-term. (See *Essays on Truth and Reality*, op. cit.: 306; and *Collected Essays*, vol. II, op. cit.: 674.) I do not find, however, that he is very clear on the issue and it seems evident that his insights, as even these very passages bear out, can be illustrated particularly well by relations with more than two terms.

6 For a version of this thesis which is said not to entail monism, see George Santayana,

The Realm of Essence (London, Constable, 1928: ch. V). See also my *Santayana: An Examination of his Philosophy* (London and Boston, Routledge & Kegan Paul, 1974: ch. IV, s. 4; chs. VII and VIII).

7 *Appearance and Reality*, 2nd edn, (op. cit.: Appendix B, esp. 576); *Collected Essays*, vol. 11 (op. cit.: 641–7).

8 See, for example, *Appearance and Reality*, 2nd edn (op. cit.: 578–82).

11

ON RUSSELL'S CRITIQUE OF LEIBNIZ'S PHILOSOPHY

Stephan Körner

In a well-known passage of his Preface to the 2nd edition of *The Philosophy of Leibniz* Russell accuses Leibniz of having two philosophies, 'a good philosophy which (after Arnauld's criticisms) he kept to himself' and 'a bad philosophy which he published with a view to fame and money'. The accusation is elaborated throughout the book as well as in the chapter on Leibniz in the *History of Western Philosophy* and in the third part of *The Philosophy of Bertrand Russell.*[1] It seems to me wholly unjust and, in so far as it is based on Russell's exegesis and criticisms of Leibniz's philosophical writings, to rest on certain preconceptions about logic, metaphysics and their interconnection which are mistaken or, at least, controversial and capable of rejection by perfectly competent and honest philosophers. It is the purpose of this chapter to uncover some of these preconceptions in Russell's interpretation of Leibniz's philosophy and by critically examining them to make room for their replacement by altogether different theses. If the critical examination is sound, then it destroys or greatly weakens the force of Russell's philosophical testimony in support of the dishonesty charge. The temptation to show this in detail as well as the temptation to rebut some of Russell's non-philosophical evidence will, however, be resisted.

This chapter is divided into two parts. The first part briefly expounds Russell's views on the systematic character of Leibniz's philosophy and some alleged inconsistencies in it (sect. 1), in particular an alleged inconsistency between a 'good' and a 'bad' logic (sect. 2), and a 'good' and a 'bad' ontology (sect. 3). The second part argues for a revision of Russell's theses on the relation between Leibniz's 'good' and 'bad' logic (sect. 4), his 'good' and his 'bad' ontology (sect. 5), and on the relation between Leibniz's logic and his ontology (sect. 6).

I

(1) *Russell on the systematic character of Leibniz's philosophy*
According to the *Monadology* (sects. 31–33), the whole of Leibniz's philosophy follows from two fundamental principles, a principle of logic,

namely, the principle of contradiction, and a principle of factual truth, namely, the principle of sufficient reason. Since, whatever the precise nature of Leibniz's version of the Aristotelian logic, the whole of it cannot be deduced from the principle of contradiction alone, I shall assume that Leibniz's principle of logic is a conjunction of postulates from which the Leibnizian version of Aristotle's logic is deducible. As regards the principle of factual truth, Leibniz sometimes asserts it to be included in the *praedicatum-inest-subjecto* principle according to which every subject contains all its predicates. It is, moreover, controversial whether on Leibniz's view his *principe de meilleur*, i.e. that the actual world *is* the best of all possible ones, follows from the principle of sufficient reason. To avoid unnecessary controversy, I shall regard as Leibniz's principle of factual truth the conjunction of the principle of sufficient reason, the *praedicatum-inest-subjecto* principle and the *principe de meilleur*, and leave the question of their logical independence open.[2]

According to Russell L 3 ff.), the fundamental premisses from which 'Leibniz's philosophy follows almost entirely' are: (i) Every proposition has a subject and a predicate. (ii) A subject may have predicates which are qualities existing at various times. (Such a subject is called a substance). (iii) True propositions not asserting existence at particular times are necessary and analytic, but such as assert existence at particular times are contingent and synthetic. The latter depend on final causes. (iv) The ego is a substance. (v) Perception yields knowledge of an external world, i.e. of existents other than myself and my states. For our present purpose it is not important to decide whether the entire or almost entire philosophy of Leibniz follows from either the Leibnizian or the Russellian postulates. But it could easily be shown that – subject to possible disagreements about the definition of certain terms – Russell's postulates are among the theses of Leibniz's philosophy.

In asserting that almost the whole of Leibniz's philosophy follows from five fundamental premisses, Russell seems to assert the unity of Leibniz's thought rather than its alleged duplicity. He makes, however, some curious comments which, though confused and confusing, remind one of his exegetic *Leitmotiv*. On the one hand, he says that Leibniz's system 'does follow, correctly and necessarily, from these premisses' and that this is 'the evidence of Leibniz's philosophical excellence, and the permanent contribution which he made to philosophy'. On the other hand, he also says that the five fundamental premisses 'though at first sight compatible, will be found, in the course of argument, to lead to contradictory results (loc. cit.). Since, at least according to Russell's logic, a set of premisses which leads to contradictory results logically implies any proposition whatsoever, it should be neither surprising nor praiseworthy that it also logically implies Leibniz's system.

The first three of the fundamental premisses can be taken as a fair interpretation of Leibniz's *praedicatum-inest-subjecto* principle – provided one properly understands Leibniz's distinction between necessary and contingent propositions: in both, a necessary and a contingent proposition, the predicate is 'contained in' the subject. Yet while in the case of a necessary proposition, such as '*Being a man* implies *being mortal*', the implication is deducible from the 'general' concept *man* in a finite number of steps, in the case of a contingent proposition, such as '*Being Adam* implies *being at a certain time expelled from Paradise*', the implication is deducible from the individual concept *Adam* only in an infinite number of steps, which can be taken only by God. The number of steps is infinite because establishing the implication involves comparing an infinite number of possible worlds – including the actual world – with each other in the light of Leibniz's principle of factual truth.[3]

(2) *Russell on the alleged inconsistency between Leibniz's 'bad' and his 'good' logic*
What Russell regards as Leibniz's 'bad' logic is not simply Leibniz's version of the Aristotelian logic, but this logic together with the thesis that all atomic propositions are reducible to propositions of subject–predicate form – a thesis which Russell considers mistaken because he holds that some relational propositions cannot be so reduced and that the concept of a relation is more fundamental than the concept of a property. Leibniz's reducibility thesis, as it may be called, has to be understood as a thesis of intensional logic according to which two *different* attributes (properties or relations) may have the same extension. It implies the weaker or extensional reducibility thesis to the effect that if one considers two attributes with the same extension as one and the same attribute (or as 'extensionally the same attribute'), then all atomic propositions are of element–class form or can be reduced to this form. Thus the extensional version of 'Adam is a man' is 'Adam is an element of the class of men' (which is extensionally the same as, for example, the class of rational bipeds). Leibniz accepts, and Russell rejects, both the intensional and the extensional reducibility principle.

In order to be brief, specific and fair, it seems best to examine only the extensional principle and, more generally, to deal only with extensional logic. This procedure has two additional advantages. It will allow us to avoid certain controversial, and for our purpose peripheral, issues about the relation between extensional and intensional logic. And it will allow us to use the standard elementary logic – propositional calculus, quantification theory and theory of identity – together with its extension by the theory of types of *Principia Mathematica*, as a logical system in which the extensional notions of an element–class proposition and of a relational proposition are clearly defined and in which Leibniz's extensional reducibility thesis can be clearly stated.

Let $x_1, \ldots, x_m$ be variables ranging over individuals, classes of individuals, classes of classes of individuals, etc.; let $\langle x_1 \rangle$, $\langle x_1, x_2 \rangle$, $\ldots$, $\langle x_1, \ldots, x_m \rangle$ be variables ranging over sequences (ordered n-tuples) of one, two, $\ldots$, m members taken from the domain of individuals, classes of individuals, classes of classes of individuals, etc.; and let $R^1, R^2, \ldots$,

R^m be variables ranging over sets of sequences of one, two, . . . , m members such that these sets and the statements involving them conform to the theory of types (of the second edition of *Principia Mathematica*).[4] An element–class proposition can then be extensionally characterised as having form: $x_1 \in R^1$ and a relational proposition as having form: $\langle x_1, \ldots, x_m \rangle \in R^m$, where $m \geq 2$ and 'ϵ' stands for the relation 'is an element of'. And Leibniz's extensional reducibility principle can be formulated as stating that every set of relational propositions, i.e. proposition of form: $\langle x_1, \ldots, x_m \rangle \in R^m$, can be reduced to a set of element–class propositions, i.e. propositions of form: $x_1 \in R^1$. It should be noted that 'ϵ' is itself a relation, namely, the extensional counterpart of the copula 'is' occurring in intensional propositions of the form '*S* is *P*', and that this is acknowledged by both Leibniz and Russell.

If Leibniz's extensional reducibility principle and the stronger intensional principle represents Leibniz's 'bad' logic, then their denial must according to Russell represent his 'good' logic. Russell exemplifies the apparent conflict between Leibniz's two logics by a passage in which Leibniz not only shows awareness of the 'good' logic, but 'thrusts aside the awkward discovery' (*R*: 12 ff.). In this passage[5] Leibniz considers three *prima facie* possible ways of conceiving the proportion between two lines *L* and *M*, namely, 'as a ratio of the greater *L* to the lesser *M*; as a ratio of the lesser *M* to the greater *L*; and lastly, as something abstracted from both, that is, as the ratio between *L* and *M* without considering which is the antecedent, or which the consequent; which the subject, which the object . . .'. According to Russell, Leibniz's intellectual and, it would seem, moral mistake consists in asserting that a relation, conceived in the third manner as having two subjects, is a 'purely ideal thing, the consideration of which is nevertheless useful [*une chose purement idéal, dont la considération ne laisse pas d'être utile*]'.

(3) *Russell on the alleged inconsistency between Leibniz's 'bad' and his 'good' ontology*

Russell distinguishes between two mutually inconsistent ontologies within Leibniz's philosophy, namely, his official pluralistic monadology and an unofficial Spinozism into which 'Leibniz fell . . . whenever he allowed himself to be logical' (*L*: ch. VII). Russell's attitude to these two ontologies is, for example, described in his *History of Western Philosophy*. He points out that both Spinoza and Leibniz use 'logic as a key to metaphysics' and do so by 'drawing inferences from syntax to the real world'. While he does 'not care to dogmatize' whether 'any valid inferences are possible from language to non-linguistic facts', he does hold that 'the inferences found in Leibniz and other *a priori* philosophers are not valid, since all are due to a defective logic'. This is 'the subject–predicate logic which all such philosophers in the past assumed' and which 'either ignores relations altogether or produces arguments to prove that relations are unreal'. So far Leibniz and Spinoza are equally to blame. Yet Leibniz is 'guilty of a special inconsistency in combining the subject–predicate logic with pluralism' for 'the proposition "there are many monads" is not of the subject–predicate form'. (*W*: 618).

It is a little difficult to disentangle the reasons for Russell's dissatisfaction. According to Russell, Leibniz, it seems, had the following options: to avoid an additional mistake by deriving monism from the official subject–predicate logic; to avoid an additional mistake by deriving pluralism from the unofficial relational logic; to make an additional mistake by deriving monism from the unofficial relational logic; and to make an additional mistake by deriving pluralism from the official subject–predicate logic. Russell blames Leibniz for having taken the last of these options. It seems that on Russell's view honesty would have required of Leibniz to have stuck to his official subject–predicate logic, which because of 'the awkward discovery' of relational logic he did not really trust, and to derive from it a monistic ontology, which he also rejected, 'largely owing to his interest in dynamics, and to his argument that extension involves repetition, and therefore cannot be an attribute of a single substance' (*W*: loc. cit.). Thus in so far as Leibniz, as interpreted by Russell, would have been less mistaken in arguing for monism rather than pluralism, monism is his 'good' and pluralism his 'bad' ontology.

As Russell clearly explains, the Leibnizian notion of substance is conceived as an ultimate logical subject, i.e. a subject 'to which several predicates can be attributed' while it 'in turn cannot be attributed to any other subject' (*R*: 43, quoting *G*, vol. II: 457–8). This logical feature the Leibnizian notion shares not only with the Spinozist and Cartesian, but also with the Aristotelian. The various notions differ in their non-logical features. Thus whereas substance, as understood by the three great rationalist thinkers, persists through change or, to use a later scientific locution, is subject to a conservation law, Aristotelian substances are capable of straightforward transubstantiation. Leibniz's doctrine of substance is explained throughout his writings, although for our present purpose the *Monadology* is sufficient: there exists an infinity of persisting mental atoms or monads whose inner nature as active, perceiving and desiring (having perception and appetition) is to some extent revealed to us in our awareness of our own *ego*. The concept of a monad logically implies its general characteristics, which it shares with other monads, as well as its concrete characteristics, which are unshared. The doctrine of physical atomism is rejected as entailing a contradiction between the assumption that a physical atom is indivisible and the assumption that it has a shape and is, therefore, divisible. It is worth noting that the correctness of the argument is, for example, acknowledged by Dirac,[6] but made harmless by postulating that independently of mathematical divisibility there is as a matter of fact a smallest absolute size in nature.

II

(4) *On the connection between the subject–predicate and the relational logic*
A person who accepts the subject–predicate logic as correct or fundamental commits, according to Russell, an intellectual mistake, unless he is aware of the logic of relations. If he is aware of this logic, then he is guilty of a moral mistake, the gravity of which depends on the degree of awareness. Russell, as his writings on Leibniz make abundantly clear, held that Leibniz was always more or less aware of the correctness or fundamental nature of relational logic and, hence, always more or less dishonest. The curiously mixed charge of a partly intellectual and partly moral defect in Leibniz's logical pronouncements can be explained and refuted by showing that in logical matters Russell tended to be dogmatic and that he misunderstood the relation between the two logics or, at least, Leibniz's way of viewing it.

Just as a dogmatic believer in the truth of the papal bull *Unam sanctam habemus ecclesiam* will consider any dissenter, who believes in the sanctity of another church or the equal sanctity of two or more churches as intellectually or morally wrong, so a dogmatic believer in the principle *unam sanctam habemus logicam* will similarly consider any dissenter, who believes in the correctness of another logic or the equal correctness of more than one logic, as also either intellectually or morally wrong. Although Leibniz is the logical dissenter whom Russell attacks most violently for alleged dishonesty, he is not the only logical dissenter whose dissent is, according to Russell, at least tainted with insincerity. Thus Russell defends the principle of excluded middle against the proponents of intuitionist and many-valued logics on the ground that it is needed 'for the interpretation of beliefs which none of us, if we are sincere, are prepared to abandon' (*R*: 682).

Because Russell considered both the intensional and the extensional reducibility of relational to subject–predicate or element–class propositions as mere philosophical propaganda, he never seriously considered Leibniz's attempt to analyse all relational propositions, such as 'the line *L* is greater than the line *M*', as 'abstractions' from subject–predicate propositions with the predicates conceived as ultimately relational properties, such as 'being greater than *M*' and 'being smaller than *L*'. From an extensional point of view the reduction would consist in replacing any relation between two or more terms by a coextensive class. And one might regard Leibniz's attempted reduction of relations to relational properties as stating a programme rather than its execution.

Indeed, it would have been natural if Russell, without casting doubts on Leibniz's honesty, had made this point. Up to the time of the publication of *Principia Mathematica* he might have argued, for example, that Leibniz's metaphysical *praedicatum-inest-subjecto* principle required the possibility of reducing relations to classes; that Leibniz's arguments in favour of this possibility are not very strong; that accepting the logical framework of *Principia Mathematica* would seem to give little hope that the argument might eventually be strengthened; and that if one has to reject the possibility of reducing relations to classes, one has to give up one of the pillars of the Leibnizian metaphysics. But it is more difficult to understand why Russell did not change his mind about the possibility of reducing relations to classes, or why he did not give reasons for not changing his mind about it when, shortly after the publication of *Principia Mathematica*, Wiener produced, and showed him, a proof to the effect that any binary relation (and hence any extensional relation) can be defined as a class of elements within the framework of *Principia Mathematica*. The main idea of the reduction has also been put forward by Hausdorff and Kuratowski and is well-known in mathematical logic and set theory.[7] Thus, for example, the extension of the relation 'x is greater than y' is uniquely determined by the class of all ordered couples, whose first member is greater than the second; and the ordered couple $\langle x, y \rangle$ can, for instance, be defined as the unordered couple, or class, of two classes $((x),$ $(x, y))$, one of which contains the first, the other the first and the second member of the ordered couple. It is easily seen, or shown, how this method of reducing ordered couples to unordered classes of classes can be extended to all finite sequences and, hence, to extensional relations between any finite number of terms.

It is important to distinguish clearly between those philosophical and exegetic theses of Russell's which do, and those which do not, stand refuted by the Wiener–Hausdorff–Kuratowski method of reducing extensional relations to classes. The applicability of the method refutes Russell's thesis of the extensional irreducibility of relations to classes or of relational propositions to element–class propositions. It *eo ipso* refutes the logical thesis that extensional relations are *logically* fundamental to classes. It does *not* refute the metaphysical thesis that extensional relations are *ontologically* fundamental to classes. Yet since Russell derives the ontologically fundamental nature of relations from their alleged logically fundamental nature, the metaphysical statement is, though not refuted, left without supporting arguments. (As mentioned earlier, we are concerned only with extensional logic. It is, however, possible – if somewhat tedious – to suspend the principle of extensionality by introducing a suitable modal operator, and thus to prove the reducibility of intensional relations to intensional one-place attributes.)

(5) *On the relation between the monadology and competing ontologies*
Leibniz was very seriously interested in Spinoza's philosophy. But there is little evidence that he felt committed to it either by his logical convictions or by some secret atheism, which would be wholly incompatible with the role played by the conception of God in his philosophical system. He did, as is obvious from his correspondence and his essays, at times feel that other ontologies made claims which, though insufficent to overthrow those of the monadology, must be accommodated by it. The

ontological claims which, because of their relevance to physics, he took most seriously, are those of a Democritean atomism according to which the world consists of infinitely small particles whose motions are governed by efficient causes, and not by final causes, as would follow from the principle of sufficient reason. Leibniz's accommodation of Democritean atomism to his own monadology allows one to conjecture how he might have accommodated Spinoza's monism, which as a fundamental ontology he regarded as even more mistaken than Democritus's pluralism.

In Leibniz's discussion of the relation between the Democritean physical and his own mental atomism, it is possible to distinguish between, at least, two positions which are not sharply opposed to each other. One is to regard Democritean atomism as a *superficial* ontology which, as can be shown by a deeper inquiry, is based on, and analysable into, the fundamental ontology of monads.[8] The other is to regard it as a *fictitious* ontology which, though false, can for certain purposes and in certain contexts be treated as if it were true, e.g. because it fulfils the heuristic function of leading to the truth. The first position is explained in a letter to Bierling written in 1711 (*G*, vol. VII: 500), in which Leibniz distinguishes between different levels of inquiry (*in inquirendo gradus*) – that of the architect, who in the soil discerns merely sand, clay, stones, and the like; that of the chemist, who discerns salts, sulphurs and similar elements; that of the physicist, who inquires still further into the constitution of the salts and sulphurs and investigates the mechanical reasons of the phenomena; and lastly that of the metaphysician, who shows that the efficient causality of the laws of motion governing physical particles on the Democritean level flows 'from the perception of that which is best' (*ex eo quod est convenientissimum*). Or, as he put it in the *Monadology* (para. 73), the 'minds or monads' which are the ultimate simple existents 'act in accordance with the laws of final causes', whereas the bodies which exist on a more superficial level 'act in accordance with the laws of efficient causes'.

The second position according to which Democritean atomism is regarded not as a relatively superficial, but as a fictitious ontology is explained by Leibniz *inter alia* in a number of passages in which he justifies his employment of infinitesimals as useful fictions. He points out, for example, that 'the rules of the finite succeed in the infinite just as if there were atoms even though there does not exist any matter which is actually subdivided without end [*quoiqu'il n'y en ait point la matière étant actuellement sousdividée sans fin*]'.[9]

To return to the relationship between Leibniz's monadology and Spinoza's monism, it is clear that this particular ontology – to which, according to Russell, Leibniz was committed by his 'bad' logic – cannot be construed as a superficial ontology, the underlying foundation of which is the universe of monads. It could, however, in principle be construed as a fictitious ontology which for certain purposes and in certain contexts could be usefully treated as if it were true. One might, for example, even if one held with Leibniz that human beings are complexes of monads whose dominant monad is a self-conscious soul, nevertheless find it useful to treat human beings as modes of Spinoza's *deus sive natura*.

It would, admittedly, be difficult to think of a theoretical inquiry in which the assumption of Spinozistic modes would play the kind of heuristic role which is played by Democritean atoms in physics or by Leibnizian infinitesimals in mathematics. But one could easily think of a practical reason for so accommodating a Spinozistic or other competing ontology, namely, the need for peaceful coexistence and co-operation between people of different ontological convictions in fields where ontological differences can be ignored or ought to be ignored on moral grounds. Leibniz had worked throughout his life for such an accommodation between the various Christian sects and even all the monotheistic religions of his time.[10] However, this ecumenism, which from a purely methodological point of view could have embraced even Spinoza's philosophy of substance, did as a matter of fact quite clearly exclude the ontology of that wholly admirable saint of pantheism. Yet, there is nothing in Russell's exegesis of Leibniz's philosophy that might count as reasonable evidence that the motives for excluding Spinoza from the reconciliation of competing ontologies were those of a secret pantheist afraid of being found out.

(6) *On the relation between Leibniz's logic and his ontology*
If, as Leibniz holds, the principles of logic are true in all possible worlds, then they do not imply any metaphysical proposition which is true only in the actual world. Russell agrees with this general thesis, but holds that Leibniz's logic – as a subject–predicate logic – has been conceived too narrowly so that it is not even true in the actual world, in which relations are fundamental. In other words, good logic implies nothing about the actual world, bad logic implies something about it, namely, falsehoods; and Leibniz's logic is, according to Russell, a bad logic. Against this it has been argued, especially by appealing to the Wiener–Hausdorff–Kuratowski method of reducing relations to classes, that if the logic of *Principia Mathematica* is a good logic, so is Leibniz's logic. It must, of course, be admitted that even if Leibniz's and Russell's logic stand or fall together, they may have to fall together. Thus, an intuitionist logician might argue that the Law of Excluded Middle is not a principle of logic, not true in all possible worlds and false in the actual world.

Having agreed that if Leibniz's logic is true, it cannot imply his metaphysics, we may naturally ask whether his logic is implied by his metaphysics. The answer to this question is that it is so implied – but only trivially so. More precisely, according to the extensional version of the Leibnizian logic, all its principles are materially implied in virtue of the principle *verum ex quo libet*; and according to its intensional version all its principles are logically implied in virtue of the principle that a logically valid proposition is logically implied by any proposition.

What, then, is the place of the principle *praedicatum inest subjecto* in Leibniz's philosophy? It is, as Leibniz clearly stated, a metaphysical principle about the nature of substances and does not belong to logic at all. To see this, one may consider the effect of replacing the principle by its negation. Such a replacement – whether made as the result of a philosophical conversion or in the spirit of a logical exercise – necessitates no change in the framework of Leibniz's logic or of *Principia Mathematica*, but merely a different philosophical assessment of Wiener's (or Leibniz's) method of reducing relations to classes. While the method is of great importance to a Leibnizian who needs it for the refutation of spurious arguments to the effect that Leibnizian 'windowless' monads are logically impossible, it will be of only mild interest to those who hold with Russell that relations are ontologically 'more fundamental' than classes. Yet, be this as it may, Leibniz's logic and his ontology are logically independent. More particularly, his subject–predicate and his relational logic form a consistent system with which both the *praedicatum-inest-subjecto* principle and its negation are logically compatible.

Russell's misinterpretation of Leibniz's philosophy is based on mistaking the resolution of real or apparent conflicts between logical or ontological systems for inconsistency, duplicity or a mixture of the two. It, therefore, seems worthwhile to conclude with some general, partly retrospective remarks on Leibniz's method of reconciliation and the use he makes of it – especially as both the method and its application are not limited to the logical and ontological problems which were Leibniz's special concern. The main instrument for the mutual accommodation of different logics and ontologies is the distinction between ultimate entities or substances, entities which though not ultimate are well-founded phenomena (*phaenomena bene fundata*), and entities which, though neither ultimate nor well-founded phenomena, are well-founded fictions (*fictiones bene fundatae*). In Leibniz's philosophy the first kind of entities consists only of monads, the second includes bodies, the third infinitesimals.

To the three kinds of entities there correspond three kinds of propositions which might be called 'ultimate', 'phenomenal' and 'fictitious'. Leibniz tries to show that all contingent phenomenal propositions are analysable into logically equivalent ultimate propositions and that all fictitious propositions are transformable into phenomenal propositions (from which they differ in precisely determinable respects). Thus no inconsistency arises so long as one does not confuse ultimate, phenomenal and fictitious propositions with each other. In the case of logically necessary propositions, which are true in all possible worlds, the analysis or transformation of their phenomenal or fictitious components may, but need not be, undertaken.

As to the application of Leibniz's distinction between substances, well-founded phenomena and well-founded fictions, it may be used after his fashion in explaining the relationship between different levels of theoretical inquiry, for example, physics and metaphysics; in theoretical heuristics, for example, the infinitesimal calculus; and in the reconciliation of similar ontologies, as in the endeavour to unite the Christian sects. It may also be used in the effort to gain access to a wholly alien ontology or logic by imagining what it would be like to grant its entities the status of well-founded phenomena or fictions in one's own categorial framework. But a discussion of this use of the Leibnizian distinction transcends the scope of this chapter.[11]

Departments of Philosophy
University of Bristol
and Yale University

NOTES

1 The 1st edition of *The Philosophy of Leibniz* appeared in 1900, the 2nd edition in 1937. It will be referred to as *L*. *The History of Western Philosophy*, briefly *W*, was published in 1946, and *The Philosophy of Bertrand Russell*, briefly *R*, was published in 1944 in the Library of Living Philosophers, edited by P. A. Schilpp. References to Leibniz's works will, as far as possible, be independent of any specific edition, otherwise they are to Gerhardt's edition, briefly *G*.

2 My own view is that the principle of sufficient reason, as understood by Leibniz, is deducible from the other two conjuncts and that these are independent. In a letter to Arnauld (*Correspondence with Arnauld*, IX, *G*, vol. II: 56) Leibniz explicitly declares the principle of sufficient reason as one of the corollaries of the *praedicatum-inest-subjecto* principle.

3 *Correspondence with Arnauld*, VIII (*G*, vol. II: 38 ff.). See also *Theodicy*, para. 415 ff.

4 The theory of types of the 2nd edition (Cambridge University Press, 1925–7) is less complex than the original theory, but the difference is irrelevant to Wiener's proof.

5 Fifth letter to Clarke, para. 47 (*G*, vol. VII: 401).

6 Dirac, *The Principles of Quantum Mechanics* (London, Oxford University Press, 1930: ch. I, para. 1, 'The Need for a Quantum Theory').

7 N. Wiener, 'A simplification of the logic of relations' (*Proc. Camb. Phil. Soc.*, 1914), reprinted with useful bibliographical notes in J. van Heijenoort's *From Frege to Gödel* (Cambridge, Mass., Harvard University Press, 1967).

8 It could be argued that on this view physical atoms are 'logical constructions' out of monads. See Russell's 'The Relation of Sense-data to Physics', *Scientia* (1910), republished in *Mysticism and Logic* (London, Longmans, Green, 1918).

9 *Mathematische Schriften*, vol. V, C. I. Gerhardt ed. (p. 350). The passage is quoted in A. Robinson's *Non-Standard Analysis* (Amsterdam, North Holland, 1966) where the Leibnizian account and use of infinitesimals as mathematical fictions is explained, refined and justified.

10 For Leibniz's ecumenism see, for example, his correspondence with M. Remond de Montmort (*G*, vol. III: 603).

11 Among the expositions of Leibniz's logic, I have found the following particularly useful: R. Kauppi, 'Über die Leibniz'sche Logic', in *Acta Philosophica Fennica* (Helsinki, 1960); G. H. R. Parkinson, *Leibniz, Logical Papers* (London, Oxford University Press, 1966). My own views about the structure and function of ontological and logical presuppositions are found in *Categorial Frameworks* (Oxford, Basil Blackwell & Mott Ltd, 1970) and in pt. IV of *Fundamental Questions of Philosophy* (Harmondsworth, Penguin Books, 1971).

12

ON SOME RELATIONS BETWEEN LEIBNIZ'S MONADOLOGY AND TRANSFINITE SET THEORY: A COMPLEMENT TO RUSSELL'S THESIS ON LEIBNIZ

Joel I. Friedman

Introduction

It is generally agreed that Leibniz was one of the greatest theoretical minds of all time. Leibniz, the mathematician, invented the differential and integral calculus; Leibniz, the logician, invented mathematical logic; Leibniz, the physicist, developed the relational notions of space and time, and was thus a precursor to Einstein's Theory of Relativity; and finally, Leibniz, the metaphysician, invented the monadology. (Besides all this, Leibniz was a practical inventor, a geologist, an historian, a diplomat, a librarian, a lawyer and a few other things).[1] It is clear that Leibniz was not only one of the greatest technical minds, but also one of the greatest intuitive minds (he must have been, otherwise he couldn't have done all the things he did).

It should not be too surprising, then, if Leibniz should also turn out to be a philosophical precursor to transfinite set theory, even though it is questionable whether he was even dimly aware of this connection. Recall it was a thesis of Couturat and Russell that Leibniz's logic is the key to Leibniz's metaphysics, a view seconded recently in a paper by Hintikka.[2] No double there is much truth in this thesis. However, in this chapter we shall argue for a complementary thesis, namely, that Leibniz's metaphysical system is an intuitive key to transfinite set theory, both at its beginnings and even up to the present set-theoretical frontiers. This becomes more plausible when one considers the set-theoretical character of the monadology.

For historical support of our thesis, we shall consider, to some extent, the metaphysical-historical background to set theory. In particular, we shall be concerned with Leibniz's views on the infinite, as well as those of Georg Cantor, the inventor of set theory. Also, we shall consider the influence of certain metaphysical ideas of the Leibnizian variety on Cantor. But the main support for our thesis are certain objective analogies between the monadology and set theory. Thus, in general, one of the main concerns of this chapter is an investigation of various analogies and relations between (i) certain metaphysical concepts, distinctions and principles of Leibniz's metaphysical system, and (ii) corresponding set-theoretical concepts, distinctions and principles. One of the main aims is to discover new axioms or principles of set theory; another is to shed new light on Leibniz's metaphysical system.

In particular, we will show that certain maximising principles in Leibniz's monadology are analogous to certain maximising principles in set theory. Moreover, it has been shown in previous publications that these set-theoretical maximising principles are equivalent to, and therefore decide, the two most celebrated undecidable statements of set theory, namely, the (global) Axiom of Choice (AC) and the Generalised Continuum Hypothesis (GCH) (see von Neumann (1929) and Friedman (1971)).[3] (A set-theoretical maximising principle is roughly any statement which maximises the number of sets of a certain kind, or the number of sets in a set of a certain kind.) Also it should be emphasised that in this chapter we are dealing with *pure* sets only, that is, sets built up from the empty set as the only individual. Thus, from this pure point of view, no other individuals but the empty set enter into consideration in transfinite set theory.

Analogously, the corresponding Leibnizian maximising principles decide important metaphysical statements. These maximising principles are derivatives of Leibniz's Principle of Perfection, and, according to him, God follows this principle in order to decide which possible monads (simple substances) and which possible world to create.

Here, then, is our deepest analogy: just as in Leibniz's monadology, certain maximising principles decide important metaphysical statements, so in set theory, corresponding maximising principles decide important set-theoretical statements. It is this analogy which gives the primary justification for our first thesis that Leibniz's metaphysical system is an intuitive key to transfinite set theory. Moreover, we hope to show that not only does Leibniz's system shed light on set theory, but also, conversely, set theory sheds light on Leibniz's system.

Given Leibniz's doctrine that all contingent statements, upon infinite analysis, are reducible to God's choices, and given Leibniz's doctrine that the Principle of Perfection always 'inclines' God's choices, it follows that the Principle of Perfection, together with its derivative maximising principles, decides all statements about the actual world of monads. From this, together with our previous analogy, arises the main thesis (conjecture) of this chapter: that maximisation implies decidability in transfinite set theory, just as in Leibniz's monadology. Thus, our conjectured thesis is to be understood in a strong sense, namely, that maximisation implies decidability *in all cases*.

This thesis, however, has alternative formulations. Moreover, we regard the strongest of these formulations as a replacement for Hilbert's Decidability Thesis (every mathematical problem is solvable, that is, every mathematical statement is provable or disprovable from a consistent set of recursively given mathematical axioms).

Given the above, we claim that Leibniz's metaphysical system may be utilised as an intuitive preliminary at the very set-theoretical frontiers, just as Cantor utilised metaphysical ideas of the Leibnizian variety at the very creation of set theory. Thus, in the search for new set-theoretical maximising principles, it is reasonable to consider Leibniz's metaphysical system, or any other system (even a magical system), so long as justification is treated independently. (Later we will briefly consider some other philosophers' metaphysical ideas in relation to set theory.) And indeed, in this chapter, we shall consider additional maximising principles suggested by Leibniz's metaphysical system. However, we do not assert that one must consult Leibniz's system (or any other system) in order to discover new set-theoretical principles. But we do claim that there are important relations between metaphysics and set theory, and these might very well be effectively utilised. Moreover, since we are still in a set-theoretical crisis, more radical methods of investigation are in order. Thus we offer this history of ideas approach to set theory.

(1) *The metaphysical-historical background: Leibniz and Cantor on the infinite*
(a) We, first, consider some of Leibniz's views on the infinite. In the realm of mathematics, Leibniz quite definitely rejects the existence of actually infinite mathematical entities, such as infinite numbers, infinite space and even infinitesimals. At most, he accepts potentially infinite mathematical entities. However, in the realm of metaphysics, as we shall see, he does accept the existence of actually infinite totalities of metaphysical entities.

Let us consider his views regarding infinite mathematical entities. Consider, for example, what he states in a letter to Bernouilli (1698):[4]

In fact many years ago I proved that the number or sum of all numbers involves a contradiction (the whole would equal the part). The same is true of an absolutely greatest number and of an absolutely smallest number (or absolutely smallest fraction).

One might interpret this passage as a denial of the existence of transfinite numbers. But we will say more about this later on. In another passage Leibniz also rejects the actual existence of infinite space and the actual existence of infinitesimals. Consider his statement in the *New Essays*:[5]

The idea of the absolute in relation to space is no other than that of the immensity of God, and so of the others. But we deceive ourselves in wishing to imagine an absolute space, which would be an infinite whole, composed of parts. There is no such thing. It is a notion which involves a contradiction, and these infinite wholes, and their opposites, the infinitesimals, are only admissible in the calculations of geometers, just like the imaginary roots of algebra.

Thus, it is clear that Leibniz rejects the existence of such actually infinite mathematical entities. However, in the above passage we see that Leibniz will allow that these may be used for purposes of calculation by geometers (though they had better be careful about those contradictions).

With regard to Leibniz's views on the infinitesimals (those mathematical entities infinitely small yet different from 0), the author would like to note an important point made by Professor Abraham Robinson, who has done truly excellent work in reconstructing Leibniz's infinitesimal calculus (using the methods of non-standard models of analysis).[6] According to Robinson, Leibniz regarded the infinitesimals of his calculus as merely ideal elements (useful fictions) which *obey the same laws as the real numbers*. But they have no reality themselves. As regards infinite totalities in mathematics, Robinson also points out that Leibniz accepts only potentially infinite totalities, that is, totalities which grow in number indefinitely, but are nevertheless still finite at any stage. Thus, it seems that Leibniz might very well have disapproved of the actually infinite totalities in Cantor's set theory. On the other hand, given the above passage in the *New Essays*, it is likely that Leibniz would have regarded such entities as merely ideal and thus admissible in the calculations of set-theoreticians. (But they had better be careful about those contradictions). Transfinite sets would thus be on a par with infinite space, infinitesimals, imaginary numbers, etc. All such mathematical entities have for Leibniz no metaphysical reality.

We next consider Leibniz's views on the infinite outside the context of mathematics. Here we find quite a different and even opposite view. Consider first what Leibniz states in a reply to Foucher (1693):[7]

> I am so much for the actual infinite that instead of admitting that nature abhors it, as is commonly said, I hold that it affects nature everywhere in order to indicate the perfections of its Author. So I believe that every part of matter is, I do not say divisible, but actually divided, and consequently, the smallest particle should be considered as a world full of an infinity of creatures.

Thus, Leibniz here emphatically affirms the existence of the actual infinite in nature. And again, in the *Monadology*, it is clear that he holds that there exists an actually infinite totality of monads. Consider, for example, section 57:[8]

> And as the same city regarded from different sides appears entirely different, and is, as it were multiplied respectively, so, because of the infinite number of simple substances [monads], there are a similar

infinite number of universes which are, nevertheless, only the aspects of a single one as seen from the special point of view of each monad.

Thus, though Leibniz rejects the actual infinite in mathematics, he affirms it in nature and in his metaphysical system. Moreover, he even invented maximising principles for these actually infinite totalities of metaphysical entities; he had no qualms about maximising those entities he regarded as metaphysically real. We will treat this later in the chapter.

(b) We next deal with some historical considerations regarding transfinite set theory and also the metaphysical background. First, we point out, especially for those who have qualms about our attempt to relate Leibniz's metaphysics and set theory, that the founder of set theory himself, Georg Cantor, was very much influenced by metaphysical ideas, including those of the Leibnizian variety, and moreover, he utilised these ideas in the creation of set theory. This can be seen from the historical evidence of Cantor's writings.[9] Here we are much indebted to Professor Friedrich Kambartel for his paper, 'Mathematics and the Concept of Theory', in which he discusses the rationalist influence on Cantor and translates some of Cantor's statements. From these it is clear that Cantor was utilising arguments of the Leibnizian variety to 'prove' the existence of transfinite sets. Indeed, Cantor was so concerned to establish the existence and respectability of transfinite sets that he actually wrote a letter to a cardinal, not in the sense of cardinal number, but to Cardinal Franzeln in 1886, as pointed out in Kambartel's paper and translated in part as follows:[10]

> One proof proceeds from the concept of God and concludes first from the divine perfection that God has the possibility of creating a Transfinitum ordinatum. It then goes on to conclude from the divine all-goodness and glory that a Transfinitum has actually been created.

This is an argument of the Leibnizian variety. For it was Leibniz who argued, in effect, that God has the power (and thus the possibility) to create an infinite world of monads, and thus from God's all-goodness it follows that he actually did create such an infinite world. Indeed, according to Leibniz, God actually created the best of all possible worlds, which must contain an infinity of monads, since for Leibniz, quantity (as well as quality) of existence is a measure of perfection. Thus, a key premiss in the argument (often implicit) is that existence is good, more existence is better, and the most existence is best. So to reiterate, just as Leibniz thought that God had the power to create an infinite world of monads, so Cantor thought that God had the power to create a transfinite set. And just as Leibniz thought that God in his divine goodness (in accordance with the Principle of Perfection (or of the Best)) did utilise this power and did create such an infinite world, so Cantor thought that God did utilise this power and did create a transfinite set. An analogous form of this argument goes back to Leibniz's version of the ontological argument for God's existence. Leibniz argued, first, that the existence of God, the most perfect Being, is possible, and second, that from this possibility His actual existence follows, since existence is a perfection and thus part of God's essence.

Cantor, however, differed with Leibniz on certain crucial matters regarding the actual infinite. To see this, consider the following passage:[11]

First, one can reject the actual infinite *in concreto*, as well as *in abstracto*, as occurs for example in von Gerdil, Cauchy, Moigno, in the writings cited by Ch. Renouvier . . . and in all the so-called positivists and their adherents.

Second, one can affirm the actual infinite *in concreto*, while rejecting it *in abstracto*; this point of view is to be found in Descartes, Spinoza, Leibniz, Locke and many others, as I have pointed out in my *Grundlagen*. . . .

Third, the actual infinite can be affirmed *in abstracto*, while being rejected *in concreto*; some of the Neo-Scholastics are in accord with this point of view, while perhaps a greater number of them, mightily influenced by Leo XIII's Encyclical of August 4, 1879 . . . still seek to defend the first of these four points of view.

Fourth and finally, the actual infinite can be affirmed *in concreto*, as well as *in abstracto*; on this ground, which I take to be the only correct one, I am perhaps the first in time, who represents this point of view with complete determination and in all its consequences; still I know for certain that I will not be the last to defend it!

Thus we see that Cantor affirmed the actual infinite *in abstracto*, as well as *in concreto*. Recall that Leibniz regarded the infinite in mathematics (abstract infinite) as merely ideal (as opposed to actual) and often contradictory though useful. Thus Cantor is closer here to the views of some neo-scholastics of his time (with some of whom he was in communication, as pointed out by Kambartel). But Cantor also affirmed the concrete infinite, and here he is closer to the views of Leibniz than to those of the above-mentioned neo-scholastics. Indeed, consider the following passage:[12]

Correspondingly I distinguish between an 'Infinitum aeternum increatum sive Absolutum', which refers to God and his attributes, and an 'Infinitum creatum sive Transfinitum', which is predicated whenever an actual infinite must be acknowledged *in natura creata*, as for example, according to my firm conviction, in relation to the actual infinity of created individuals in the universe as well as on our earth, and, in all probability, even in each ever so small extended part of space, in which I agree completely with Leibniz. (*Epistola ad Foucher*, t. 2 *operum*, Dutens, ed., p. 1, para. 243)

(Note that Cantor refers to Leibniz's letter to Foucher. This is the very same letter (reply) quoted above in this chapter, as we have verified.) From the above passage we see that Cantor, in agreement with Leibniz (and perhaps other philosophers), makes another important metaphysical distinction between two kinds of infinity: absolute infinity and the merely transfinite.[13] But, as we shall see, Cantor, as opposed to Leibniz, applies this distinction to the abstract infinite as well as to the concrete infinite. For Cantor, knowledge about absolute infinity is impossible, but knowledge about the transfinite is possible. Thus, according to Cantor, God is absolutely infinite and cannot be an object of our knowledge. However, not only the concrete world (and its parts), but also abstract transfinite sets of various kinds and cardinality may be objects of our knowledge. It is mainly here that he goes beyond the mainstream of Western philosophical tradition.

In particular, it is apparent from Cantor's writings that he was very concerned to refute Kant's view that actually infinite totalities do not exist, or at least, are beyond the power of human reason to deal with. Thus, referring to Kant's 'transcendental dialectic', Cantor writes (as translated by Kambartel): 'Even taking into consideration the Pyrrhonic and Academic scepticism . . . hardly anyone discredited human reason and its abilities more than Kant by this part of the critical transcendental philosophy.'[14] In fact, so bitter was Cantor against Kant's view that in a letter to Bertrand Russell (1911) he refers to Kant as 'yonder *sophistical philistine*, who was *so bad a mathematician*', and then on the cover of a book which he sent to Russell he wrote, 'I see your motto is "Kant or Cantor" '.[15] We can well understand such antagonism, given the fact that Cantor suffered lack of recognition by the general mathematical community for most of his life. Some of his contemporaries even regarded transfinite set theory as pathological mathematics. So it seems that, in desperation, Cantor was driven to pre-Kantian arguments of the rationalist tradition; some of the Leibnizian variety, some of the neo-scholastic variety, and some of a different variety. He synthesised all of these views and arrived at an original position.

It is interesting to note, and important in supporting the claims of this chapter besides, that analogous to Cantor's metaphysical distinction between the absolutely infinite and the transfinite, is Cantor's historically important set-theoretical distinction between inconsistent multiplicities and consistent multiplicities. Consistent multiplicities he called 'sets'. Now this distinction is the forerunner to the von Neumann–Bernays–Gödel distinction between proper classes (which are non-elements) and sets (which are elements). Cantor communicated his distinction clearly in a letter to Dedekind (1899).[16] He defines an inconsistent multiplicity (such as the multiplicity of all sets) as any multiplicity which cannot be regarded, without contradiction, as 'one finished thing' or as something whose elements are 'all together' (these are Cantor's expressions). Thus, also, Russell's multiplicity of all those sets which are not members of themselves is an inconsistent multiplicity. Hence, it is clear that inconsistent multiplicities, though they exist in some sense, cannot be regarded as ordinary objects of set-theoretical knowledge, according to Cantor. They cannot be operated on as with other objects of knowledge.

This important Cantorian distinction is, in our view, a naïve kind of type distinction. And thus we claim that Cantor's naïve set theory is by no means inconsistent, as is usually asserted by commentators on the philosophy of mathematics. For, it is our view that with this naïve type distinction, Cantor had a perfectly adequate though naïve method for avoiding the set-theoretical antinomies. He simply excluded inconsistent multiplicities from the universe of sets, as they arose, but he did not exclude them from the universe of discourse. They still have existence of some sort. However, it must be pointed out that Cantor gave no formal definition of 'inconsistent multiplicity'. Still, the primary evidence for the adequacy of his naïve method is simply the present adequacy of the method of the von Neumann–Bernays–Gödel set theory for avoiding the antinomies. However, further treatment of this particular topic is beyond the scope of this chapter.

In any case, given the above, we see that there is an important analogy between Cantor's metaphysical distinction and Cantor's set-theoretical distinction. Moreover, having shown that the founder of transfinite set theory utilised metaphysical ideas, including those of the Leibnizian variety, to support the existence of transfinite sets, we should be more prepared to pursue further analogies and relations between metaphysics and set theory.

(2) *Analogous maximising principles*

(a) In this section we will consider some of the more profound analogies between Leibniz's monadology and transfinite set theory, in particular, analogies between corresponding maximising principles.

But let us, first, consider in more detail Leibniz's theory of monads. According to him, the universe consists ultimately of monads, or simple substances, each of which has perceptions according to a unique law of development, falling under the complete concept of the monad. Thus, monads are the basic 'atoms' with which he reconstructs the physical world. But unlike the modern notion of atom (or even the Greek atomists' notion), a monad is not a physical body or physical entity of any kind. It has no physical dimensions. Nor is a monad in physical space or time. Indeed, for Leibniz, space and time are a system of relations among monads.[17] Thus, all physical bodies, including present-day atoms, as well as space and time, are ultimately reducible to monads and their properties.

Now, according to Leibniz, a physical body could not be a true substance, because a substance by its very nature is simple, that is, without parts, whereas a physical body could not be simple. The reason for this is that a physical body by its very nature is extended, and extension involves plurality or composition. Thus there could be no extended simple substance, and thus a physical body has no metaphysical reality, since only a substance has such reality. Consequently, a physical body is merely an ideal entity (a useful fiction).[18] Only monads have ultimate reality.

For Leibniz, a monad is a sort of mental substance or soul, characterised by its perceptions (in the widest sense of 'perception'). Each monad has perceptions of varying degrees of clarity and distinctness. Moreover, no two monads (at least in the actual world) have the same equally clear and distinct perceptions. This follows from Leibniz's law of the Identity of Indiscernibles (if no difference in properties is discernible in two given things, then they are identical).[19] This law should be distinguished from Leibniz's law of the Indiscernibility of Identicals (if two given things are identical, then no difference in properties is discernible in them). It is also important to note that each monad has a primitive active force, which is the cause of its perceptions. Moreover, each monad has within its nature a law of development in accordance with which the active force of the monad produces the perceptions sequentially. This sequential development is called *appetition*.

There are various kinds of monads. A person, or rather, the soul of a person, is a monad. Such a monad is called *dominant* because it dominates over the monads composing that person's body. Body monads are thus subordinate to their soul monad. Moreover, according to Leibniz, animals and possibly even plants have souls or what he called *substantial forms*. Such forms are also dominant monads, dominating over the objects with a structure imposed on the set. Every physical body may be God, the most perfect monad, who dominates over all the other monads, although he doesn't have a body. With the exception of God, all such domination, however, is merely ideal, since each (finite) monad has no effect on any other, but rather, all such monads develop according to their own internal laws, in conformity with the pre-established harmony orginally created by God. All this according to Leibniz.[20]

Given the above picture, we claim that Leibniz's monadology has a set-theoretical character. The universe may be regarded as a set of monads with a structure imposed on the set. Every physical body may be regarded as a set of monads with a structure imposed on the set. And, finally, every monad itself may be regarded as (or at least correlated with) a set or sequence of perceptions with a structure imposed on the sequence. Moreover, vertically and horizontally throughout, there are properties of and relations among the perceptions, the sequences of perceptions, the structured sets of these sequences, and the whole system of these structured sets. Thus, the monadology presents a very complicated set-theoretical character, indeed, a transfinite set-theoretical character.

Recall the previous section in which we stated that, according to Leibniz, it is possible for God to create an infinite world of monads, and since God follows the Principle of Perfection (or of the Best), He does in fact create such an infinite world, indeed, the best possible world. Recall also that this infinity of monads was asserted in section 57 of the *Monadology*. But now consider the following passage:[21]

> From the conflict of all the possibles demanding existence, this at once follows, that there exists that series of things by which as many of them as possible exists; in other words, the maximal series of possibilities.

Again consider:[22]

> For a thing to be rightly estimated I state as a principle, the Harmony of things, that is, the greatest amount of essence exists that is possible. It follows that there is more reason in the existence of a thing than in its non-existence. And everything would exist if that were possible.

It is clear from these passages that Leibniz intends to assert more than a bare infinity of monads. He intends to assert the existence of as many monads as possible. Indeed, there is a subtle distinction here worth noting. One must distinguish the maximum number of monads from the maximal series of monads. In set-theoretical terms, the maximum number would be a cardinal number, whereas the maximal series would be an ordering, possibly associated with an ordinal number. Thus, even if the maximum number of monads existed, it doesn't follow that there would be a maximal series of monads, or as many monads as possible.

Next, we consider Leibniz's view that there is a conflict among possibles. Here one must distinguish logical incompatibility from disharmony. It seems that Leibniz held to both these kinds of conflict among monads. Thus, two possible monads may not be logically compatible ('compossible') and hence their joint existence would be logically impossible. On the other hand, two monads may be compossible but still very disharmonious. As Leibniz says, 'Everything would exist if that were possible', but alas it is impossible, logically, morally and even aesthetically. So what does God do in the face of these harsh possibilities? Well, naturally, He does the best He can. He always acts in accordance with the Principle of Perfection in deciding what to do.

Before going on, let us first consider more relevant passages. Consider, for example, article V of the *Discourse on Metaphysics*: 'In what the principles of the divine perfection consist, and that the simplicity of the means counterbalances the richness of the effects.'[23] And within article V consider:

When the simplicity of God's way is spoken of, reference is specially made to the means which he employs, and on the other hand when the variety, richness and abundance are referred to, the ends or effects are had in mind. Thus one ought to be proportioned to the other, just as the cost of a building should balance the beauty and grandeur which is expected.

Finally, consider what he says in section 58 of the *Monadology*: 'Through this means has been obtained the greatest possible variety, together with the greatest order that may be; that is to say, through this means has been obtained the greatest possible perfection.'

From these passages of Leibniz we may infer that simplicity of laws, harmony and order, on the one hand, must balance out richness of effects, quantity and variety, on the other hand. Thus, for example, there are conflicts involved between simplicity of laws and richness of effects or between variety and order, but these must be balanced out. Thus God must create the most for the least, so to speak. This is what is most perfect. In other words, logically-economically speaking, the universe must be cost-effective. (We shall talk about the means of obtaining this end later.)

All talk about existence reduces to talk about existence of monads, since this universe (or any possible universe) is ultimately a universe of monads. Thus, in the beginning before the dawn of creation, there were many possible combinations of monads which God could have created. But, as implied above, God, in accordance with the Principle of Perfection, chose to create the most perfect or best of all possible combinations of monads. Thus, condensing the above passages and applying them to monads, we may state for Leibniz that the most perfect combination of monads is the greatest combination of compossible monads, with the greatest possible variety and the greatest possible order (thus simplest in its laws). And thus we may state the following maximising principle, which is a derivative of the Principle of Perfection.[24]

L_1 – The universe contains the greatest combination of compossible monads, with the greatest possible variety and the greatest possible order (thus simplest in its laws).

It is important to note that, for Leibniz, the notion of 'most perfect' or 'best' reduces to a maximising (or optimising) notion. And so God decides what should exist by maximising existence (subject to constraints). We certainly agree with Rescher's statement, 'Thus the Principle of Perfection is a maximum principle, and it furnishes the mechanism of God's decision among the infinite mutually exclusive systems of compossibles'.

(b) We are about to consider a principle in set theory analogous to L_1, but first some preliminaries. Recall Cantor's distinction between inconsistent *versus* consistent multiplicities. This led to the present-day distinction between proper classes and sets. A proper class is defined as a class which is not an element of any class. A set is defined as a class which is an element of some class. 'Class' is the primitive term, and thus every class is either a set or a proper class, but not both. Since a proper class is not an element, it cannot be operated on in the same way as with sets. For example, V, the universal class of all sets, is a proper class. So is Russell's class of all sets which are not elements of themselves. Hence we must not treat V and Russell's class as ordinary set-theoretical objects to be operated on in the ordinary way. For example, we cannot apply the powerclass operation to V, otherwise the antinomies are lying in wait. Thus, in our view, the class–set distinction is a type distinction of sorts.

As examples of sets, consider the empty class, the class containing the empty class (which is called the unit class of the empty class), and also the class of all unit classes finitely built up from the empty class. All these classes are sets, the latter being infinite. Indeed, all sets may be generated from the empty set by iterating the various set-theoretical operations arbitrarily often (and even transfinitely often), but the generation is not constructive.

It was von Neumann who first formalised the distinction between proper classes and sets.[25] Moreover, he was bold enough to conjecture that the universal class V is maximised, in the precise sense that V contains as an element every class which is not in one–one correspondence with V. Thus, we have the following Maximisation Principle, which we call *MP*:

$$V \text{ is maximised } ((\forall X)(X \not\approx V \rightarrow X \in V)).$$

Note that the converse of *MP* can be proved easily, using Cantor's theorem $(x \prec Px)$. In 1929 von Neumann actually proved *MP* using the (global) Axiom of Choice $((\exists F)(\forall x)(x \neq \phi \rightarrow F(x) \in x))$.[26] Now, *MP* is a maximising principle because, intuitively speaking, *MP* implies that V contains just about as many sets as possible, for any class which V does not contain is in one–one correspondence with V and thus 'too big' to be an element of V. Indeed, *MP* is equivalent to the statement that every proper class is in one–one correspondence with V. Antinomies arise when such big classes are treated as sets, and thus they must not be so treated, by *reductio ad absurdum*: 'But every class would be a set, if that were possible.'

It should be clear that von Neumann's principle *MP* is analogous to Leibniz's principle L_1. Indeed, there are at least three analogies worth noting.

First analogy: Just as L_1 asserts that the universe contains the greatest combination of compossible monads, so *MP* implies that the set-theoretical universe has the maximum number of sets (consistent multiplicities). This may be seen as follows. Let On be the class of all ordinal numbers. Then On is itself an ordinal number and, therefore, must be a proper class (Burali–Forti paradox). Consequently, On is the maximum ordinal number, and according to current conceptions, the maximum cardinal number also. Now, MP implies that V is equinumerous with (that is, in one–one correspondence with) On, since On is a proper class. Therefore, V has the maximum number of sets. Note again our previously mentioned distinction between 'V has the maximum number of sets' and 'There are as many sets as possible in V'. We can express the one statement formally: $(V \approx On)$, but we don't know how to express the other formally. Also, it should be noted that compossible monads correlate well with consistent multiplicities.

Second analogy: Just as L_1 asserts that the universe has the greatest possible variety, so MP implies the axioms of Choice and Replacement, both of which allow for a great variety of sets not otherwise provable (or known to be provable). Now Choice is a consequence of MP, since MP implies that V is equinumerous with On, as mentioned above, and thus that V can be well-ordered. From the well-ordering of V, Choice follows, as is well known. As regards Replacement, we will first state this axiom as Cantor stated it in a letter to Dedekind (1899), since Cantor's version is the most intuitively simple: 'two equivalent multiplicities either are both "sets" or are both inconsistent multiplicities',[27] or to use more modern terms, 'two equinumerous classes are either both sets or both proper classes' $((\forall X)\,(\forall Y)\,(X \approx Y \rightarrow (X, Y \in V \text{ or } X, Y \notin V)))$. Now consider the following intuitive proof that MP implies Replacement. Assume MP and suppose we have two equinumerous classes such that one is a proper class, whereas the other is a set. Then the proper class is equinumerous with the universal class; and by the transitivity of equinumerosity, so is the set equinumerous with the universal class. But no set can have this property, by Cantor's theorem that the powerclass of any set always has greater cardinality. Thus we have reached a contradiction, and so our original supposition is false. Therefore, Replacement follows from MP.

We now deal with the great variety of sets which follow from the axioms of Choice and of Replacement. It is well known that Choice yields various kinds of sets in other branches of mathematics, as well as in set theory. For example, in algebra, Choice yields the existence of maximal ideals; in analysis, the existence of unmeasurable sets of reals; in topology, the existence of strange partitions (Tarski–Banach paradox); and in metamathematics, the existence of models of consistent sets of statements in uncountable languages (general completeness theorem). Thus, the Axiom of Choice yields the existence of various kinds of sets not otherwise obtainable, or at least not known to be obtainable. In some cases, however, it can actually be shown that Choice is essential (using P. J. Cohen's methods of forcing and generic models).[28] As regards Replacement, it is well known that this axiom yields a great variety of sets and cardinal numbers not otherwise obtainable. Thus, without this axiom, for example, $V_{\omega+\omega}$ (that set resulting from iterating the powerclass operation $(\omega + \omega)$ times, starting with the empty set) could not be shown to have the appropriate cardinality (since $V_{\omega+\omega} \epsilon\ V_{\omega+\omega+1}$, $\aleph_0$ is the largest cardinal in $V_{\omega+\omega+1}$, and $V_{\omega+\omega+1}$ is a standard model of set theory minus Replacement).[29] Even for a given set, Replacement yields the existence of all the various sets equinumerous with the given set.

Thus, we see that a great variety of sets follows from MP via Choice and Replacement. But, of course, we do not claim the greatest possible variety of sets follows from MP (whatever that means).

Third analogy: Just as L_1 asserts that the universe has the greatest possible order, so MP implies the Well-Ordering Principle in its strongest form, namely that V is equinumerous with On, and thus V can be well ordered. This implies that any two sets can be compared in the ordering and that any class of sets has a 'least' element relative to the ordering. Also, one can show the validity of set-theoretical induction on the ordering relation, $<$. Thus, we see that MP implies that V has a great amount of order, though of course we do not claim the greatest possible order (whatever that means).

To summarise these three analogies: just as L_1 asserts that the universe contains the greatest combination of compossible monads, with the greatest possible variety and with the greatest possible order, so MP implies that the set-theoretical universe has the maximum number of sets, with a great amount of variety and with a great amount of order. And, thus, we see that MP is very analogous to L_1.

(c) We now return to Leibniz's monadology. Recall that monads are simple substances which have perceptions. Some perceptions are clear and distinct, while others are confused, dim or just totally unconscious. Thus, a monad may have unconscious perceptions – a very pregnant idea of Leibniz – full of Freudian implications. Moreover, God's perceptions have the greatest degree of clarity and distinctness, and none are confused, dim or unconscious; not so with all other monads. Nevertheless, according to Leibniz, every monad, however confusedly, represents the entire universe from its point of view as best it can. Moreover, it represents it more clearly and distinctly from anear than from afar.

Again, let us consider various passages. Consider for example what Leibniz says in section 56 of the *Monadology*:

Now this interconnection, relationship, or this adaptation of all things to each particular one, and of each one to all the rest, brings it about that every simple substance has relations which express all the others and that it is consequently a perpetual living mirror of the universe.

Also consider article IX of the *Discourse on Metaphysics*:

> That every individual substance expresses the whole universe in its own manner and that in its full concept is included all its experiences together with all the attendant circumstances and the whole sequence of exterior events.

And within article IX consider:

> Furthermore, every substance is like an entire world and like a mirror of God, or indeed of the whole world which it portrays, each one in its own fashion; . . . It can indeed be said that every substance bears in some sort the character of God's infinite wisdom and omnipotence, and imitates him as much as it is able to; for it expresses, although confusedly, all that happens in the universe, past, present, and future, deriving thus a certain resemblance to an infinite perception or power of knowing.

From these passages it should be clear that each monad has as many perceptions as possible from its point of view. Moreover, although a person monad or a plant monad represents the universe so much less perfectly than God, each has the maximum series of perceptions it can have from its point of view. God, the ultimate monad, has the greatest amount of perceptions possible. And just as God has all those perceptions which perfectly represent all other monads, so every other monad has all those perceptions which, from its point of view, represent all other monads. Hence, each monad is a world unto itself, with no need of windows. Thus, generally we agree with Mates's statement:[30]

> possible worlds are maximal sets of mutually compossible complete individual concepts [monads] and a complete individual concept [monad] is a maximal set of (or a 'maximal' attribute composed of) compatible simple attributes [perceptions].

Given the above remarks, we may condense the above passages and thus arrive at the following maximising principle:

L_2 – Every monad represents the entire universe from its point of view, with the greatest possible series of perceptions it may have.

Now we claim that not only is L_2 a maximising principle, but also it is a derivative of the Principle of Perfection. To support this contention, we cite section 58 of the *Monadology* in which Leibniz refers to the *means* by which the greatest possible perfection of the universe has been obtained. From the context (following sections 56 and 57) it is clear that Leibniz means by the 'means' just the sum total of monadic representations of the universe. Thus, on this interpretation, the greatest possible perfection of the universe is obtained (at least to a great extent) by means of the most perfect representations of the universe possible for each of the monads. Thus, L_2, as well as L_1, is a maximising principle derivative from the Principle of Perfection, and God acts in accordance with these maximising principles to decide which possible world and which possible monads to create. Moreover, He acts in accordance with L_2 as a means of acting in accordance with L_1. Furthermore, L_1 and L_2 may be interpreted so that God, as the ultimate monad, falls under these principles.

(d) We next consider a set-theoretical principle analogous to L_2. This is the Generalised Maximisation Principle:

GMP – Every local universe is maximised.

Recall von Neumann's Maximisation Principle, MP, which states that V is maximised. GMP is a generalisation of MP, for whereas MP maximises the universal class, GMP maximises every local universe. (Note that the universal class also is regarded as a local universe.) A local universe is like V except that it doesn't have to satisfy the Powerclass Axiom (V_ω being the only exception and indeed the only countable local universe). A local universe may also be defined as any non-empty class closed under the union, pairing and replacement operations. Thus, intuitively speaking, every local universe may be regarded as representing the universal class from its point of view. In a sense our definition is quite arbitrary, but originally we were looking for a maximising principle to decide GCH, and as mentioned in note 3, GMP was shown to be equivalent to GCH, within the von Neumann–Bernays–Gödel set theory (NBG).

We next consider the notion of a maximised class. To say that V is maximised is to say that V contains as an element every class which is not equinumerous with V. This notion, as it is given, applies only to V and not to classes in general. However, it is not difficult to define the more general notion of a maximised class. Consider, therefore, the following: a class is maximised if, and only if, it contains as an element every subclass (of that class) which is not equinumerous with that class. Thus, a maximised class contains just about as many of its subclasses as possible, for any subclass which it does not contain as an element is equinumerous with it and thus 'too big' to be in it.

It should be clear that L_2 is analogous to GMP. There are at least four analogies worth noting:

First analogy: Just as L_2 maximises every monad, so GMP maximises every local universe. From L_2 it follows that every monad can be regarded as (or correlated with) a maximal series of perceptions, that is to say, maximal relative to its point of view. Analogously, GMP implies that every local universe has the maximum number of sets, relative to its point of view; which may be given the precise meaning that the statement (V is equinumerous with On) holds in every local universe, given GMP. This can be seen as follows: local universes have a canonical form, as shown in Friedman (1971). Thus, a local universe is roughly the region below a given regular cardinal (formally, it is the set of sets hereditarily cardinally less than the given regular cardinal).[31] Now, by GMP, such a local universe is maximised, and this implies that the region below the given regular cardinal is equinumerous with that cardinal. Since V gets interpreted as this region and since On gets interpreted as this regular cardinal, it follows that the statement (V is equinumerous with On) holds in this local universe.

Second analogy: Just as L_2 implies a hierarchy of monads, depending on the degree to which each monad represents the universe, so GMP implies a hierarchy of maximised local universes. To see this we note that the local universes form an inclusion chain, since the regions below the given regular cardinals clearly form an inclusion chain; moreover, by GMP, these local universes are maximised.

Furthermore, just as the hierarchy of monads has a maximal element, namely, God, so the hierarchy of maximised local universes has a maximal element, namely, the universal class. Note that there is nothing contradictory in talking about the universal class as an element, so long as it is not taken to be an element of another class, or even of itself (see Friedman, 1969).

Third analogy: Just as GMP implies MP, so L_2 implies L_1. This needs some proof. First, consider GMP. Now V is a local universe as mentioned above. Hence, by GMP, we have that V is a maximised class. From this, MP quickly follows. Therefore, GMP implies MP. Now consider L_2. This principle applies also to God, the ultimate monad. Thus God also represents the universe, from His point of view, with the greatest possible series of perceptions. But since God is perfect, He must represent the universe perfectly. His point of view is in no way limited or distorted, and He in fact has the greatest possible series of perceptions, absolutely. Therefore, the universe, which He perfectly represents, must have the greatest possible combination of compossible monads so perceived. Moreover, since God is perfect, He must have the greatest possible variety and the greatest possible order in his perceptions. Therefore, the universe, which He perfectly represents, must also have the greatest possible variety and the greatest possible order so perceived. Thus L_1 follows, and thus L_2 implies L_1.

Fourth analogy: Just as L_2 does not imply L_1, if we except God from falling under L_2, so GMP does not imply MP, if we except V from falling under GMP. (Note that by 'imply' we mean 'imply in NBG^*', where NBG^* is the result of replacing Global Choice by Local Choice in NBG. Otherwise, MP is implied by NBG alone.) To show this, first suppose that we exclude God from L_2. Then since every monad (except God) is both imperfect and represents the universe imperfectly, no inference from any such monad to the greatest possible perfection of the universe is valid. For although the representation of the universe by a monad is as perfect as it can be, from its point of view, still, it is not perfect enough to imply the greatest possible perfection in the universe itself. Thus, L_2 (with God excepted) does not imply L_1. Now consider GMP (with V excepted). As shown in Friedman (1971), V is the only proper class which is a local universe and the only proper class which is maximised. Any other local universe or maximised class is a set. Hence, GMP (with V excepted) is equivalent to a statement of ZFC. Call it GMP_s. Thus, $(GMP_s \leftrightarrow GCH)$ is a theorem of NBG^* (indeed, of ZFC). Easton has shown that Global Choice is independent of NBG^* (assuming consistency),[32] and from this it should not be too difficult to show that Global Choice is also independent of $(NBG^* + GCH)$ (assuming consistency). Hence, MP is independent of $(NBG^* + GCH)$ (assuming consistency), since MP is equivalent to Global Choice in NBG^*. Thus, MP is independent of $(NBG^* + GMP_s)$ (assuming consistency). This shows that GMP (excepting V) does not imply MP in NBG^*.

To summarise these four analogies: just as L_2 asserts (or implies) that every monad may be regarded as a maximal series of perceptions, which is in a hierarchy with other such maximal series, so GMP implies that every local universe has the maximum number of sets, from its point of view (this can be technically defined), and is in a hierarchy (actually an inclusion chain) with other such local universes (this is a non-trivial technical result). And just as L_2 implies L_1, but L_2 (excepting God) does not imply L_1, so GMP implies MP, but GMP (excepting V) does not imply MP. Thus, we see that GMP is very analogous to L_2.

Taken together, L_1 and L_2 maximise the whole and each of its parts. Analogously, MP and GMP maximise the whole and arbitrarily many of its parts (and thus arbitrarily large parts). We admit that this analogy is uneven, but we know of no way at present to make it more even. However, our main analogy is the following:

Main analogy: Just as L_1 and L_2 decide important metaphysical issues, so MP and GMP decide important set-theoretical issues. For, as mentioned above, L_1 and L_2 are derivatives of the Principle of Perfection, and God acts in accordance with this principle, together with its derivative maximising principles, in deciding which possible world and which possible monads to create. Thus, L_1 and L_2 decide important metaphysical issues. Also, as mentioned above, MP is set-theoretically equivalent to, and therefore decides, the Global Axiom of Choice; and GMP is set-theoretically equivalent to, and therefore decides, GCH. Therefore, MP and GMP decide important set-theoretical issues (see note 3).

(3) *The main thesis*

From the main analogy arises the main thesis (conjecture) of this chapter, namely, that maximisation implies decidability (in all cases) in transfinite set theory, just as in Leibniz's monadology. Thus, our conjectured thesis is to be understood in a strong sense. However, as mentioned in the Introduction, there are alternative formulations of the thesis. Consider, then, the following formulation.

First decidability thesis (DT_1): Given any undecidable statement of set theory, there exists a relatively consistent conjunction of intuitively plausible maximising principles which decide it (within set theory). First, it should be noted that DT_1 is a generalisation of the previously mentioned results regarding AC and GCH. Second, it should be repeated that a set-theoretical maximising principle is roughly any statement which maximises the number of sets of a certain kind, or the numbers of sets in a set of a certain kind. Third, it should be noted that an intuitively plausible statement has a certain likelihood or appearance of being true. However, as we are using the notion, intuitive plausibility is stronger than comprehensibility but weaker than self-evidence. Clearly, every intuitively plausible statement is comprehensible but not conversely. Also, every self-evident statement is intuitively plausible but not conversely. A crucial difference is that whereas it is necessary that every self-evident statement is true, it is not even the case that every intuitively plausible statement is true. Thus, it is logically impossible for two incompatible statements both to be self-evident, whereas, as mentioned above, it is logically possible for both to be intuitively plausible. It should be clear that no knowledge claims are intended by asserting intuitive plausibility. Thus, a statement may be intuitively plausible, yet may in no sense be known to be true. However, in our view, intuition may give us lines into knowledge, even when it does not give us knowledge. The relation between intuition and knowledge is a very difficult topic and beyond the scope of this chapter. Finally, we note that a conjunction of intuitively plausible statements might not itself be intuitively plausible, even if relatively consistent. This suggests the following stronger formulation.

Second decidability thesis (DT_2): Given any undecidable statement of set theory, there exists a relatively consistent, intuitively plausible maximising principle which decides it (within set theory). First, we note that DT_2 clearly implies DT_1, but not conversely. Second, we note that a maximising principle might very well be a conjunction of maximising principles. Indeed, it seems that any relatively consistent conjunction of maximising principles is itself a maximising principle, though it might not be intuitively plausible. Finally, we note that DT_2 implies the possibility of an intuitive breakthrough in any given set-theoretical problem, no matter how complex. Thus, in our view, DT_2 is itself intuitively plausible, and so is DT_1, derivatively.

A word should be said about incompatible maximising principles. As pointed out above, such principles may be incompatible, even when each is relatively consistent and intuitively plausible. In our view, whenever such maximising principles are found to be incompatible, one should search for a more general maximising principle, relatively consistent and intuitively plausible, which will decide between the first two. This presupposes some sort of partial ordering of such maximising principles, although we are quite unclear as to how to define such an ordering. In any case, given any undecidable non-maximising principle, DT_2 implies that it can be decided by a maximising principle. But given incompatible maximising principles, new considerations must be brought to bear.

As an example of incompatible maximising principles, consider GMP and some of Takeuti's hypotheses on the powerset (see Takeuti, 1971). These hypotheses, which are no doubt intuitively plausible, maximise the effect of the powerset operation in various ways, and thereby imply the negation of GCH, and hence the negation of GMP (since GCH is equivalent to GMP). On the other hand, GMP maximises the effect of the union, pairing and replacement operations, and thereby implies GCH, and hence the negation of some of Takeuti's maximising principles. Now GMP can be shown to be relatively consistent, via the relative consistency of GCH, as shown in Gödel (1940). On the other hand, some of Takeuti's hypotheses can probably be shown to be relatively consistent, via the relative consistency of the negation of GCH, as shown in Cohen (1966) (although we are not really sure about this).[33] Thus, GMP and some of Takeuti's hypotheses are each (most likely) relatively consistent, intuitively plausible maximising principles, yet incompatible with each other. In our view, this situation may be remedied by finding an even more general maximising principle, relatively consistent and intuitively plausible, which decides among GMP and Takeuti's hypotheses. But all this is open. However, by the above considerations, we are led to the following alternative formulation of our main thesis.

Third decidability thesis (DT_3): There exists a relatively consistent set of intuitively plausible maximising principles which decides (within set theory) *all* undecidable statements of set theory. First, we note that DT_3 implies DT_1, since whenever a set of statements implies a given statement, then there is a finite conjunction of statements in that set, which implies the given statement. However, DT_1 clearly does not imply DT_3, for reasons dealt with above. Second, we note that DT_3 does not imply DT_2, and conversely, for reasons dealt with above. Third, we note that DT_3 implies that there is a relatively consistent conjunction of intuitively plausible maximising principles which decides among GMP and some of Takeuti's hypotheses on the powerset. However, the conjunction may not itself be intuitively plausible, for reasons dealt with above. Thus we are led to our strongest formulation of the main thesis of this chapter.

Main decidability thesis (DT_s): There exists a relatively consistent set of intuitively plausible maximising principles which decides (within set theory) *all* undecidable statements of set theory; and moreover, for any finite conjunction of statements in the set, there exists a statement in the set which implies this conjunction.[34] First, we note that DT_s clearly implies DT_3 and hence DT_1. Second, we note that DT_s implies DT_2. This is not difficult to see. For, given any undecidable statement of set theory, the relatively consistent set mentioned in DT_s decides the given statement; thus, there is a finite conjunction of statements from this set which decides the given statement; and therefore, by DT_s, there is a single statement in this set which implies the finite conjunction and thus decides the given undecidable statement. Consequently, DT_2 follows. Thus we see that DT_s implies DT_1, DT_2 and DT_3, but not conversely, for reasons dealt with above. Clearly, then, DT_s is our strongest formulation. Finally, we note that DT_s implies that there exists a single, relatively consistent, intuitively plausible maximising principle which decides among GMP and some of Takeuti's hypotheses on powerset. Indeed, DT_s implies the possibility of infinitely many compatible intuitive breakthroughs in correspondingly many set-theoretical problems, taken together. In our view, DT_s is barely intuitively plausible.

We regard DT_s as a replacement for Hilbert's Decidability thesis. Recall that Hilbert held in the pre-Gödelian age that every mathematical statement is decidable, or equivalently, that every mathematical problem is solvable. More precisely, this meant that there exists a consistent set of recursively given axioms (perhaps infinitely many) which decides all mathematical statements.[35] Gödel destroyed this thesis by showing that in every consistent (recursively) axiomatisable theory sufficiently strong to develop number theory, there exist undecidable statements (Gödel's Incompleteness Theorem). Fortunately, our decidability thesis, DT_s, survives Gödel's theorem. For, assuming set theory to be consistent and given DT_s, it follows by Gödel's theorem that the set of intuitively plausible maximising principles asserted to exist in DT_s is not (recursively) axiomatisable. Here, however, some real difficulties arise. For, it also follows that this set is infinite and thus contains maximising principles of arbitrary length (note that every finite set of statements is (recursively) axiomatisable, trivially).

One may wonder, first of all, how there can be infinitely many maximising principles which are not generated by any recursively given rule, yet are still intuitively plausible (and also simultaneously consistent). Second, one may wonder how there can be arbitrarily long maximising principles which are still intuitively plausible, yet not generated by any recursively given rule. Third, one may wonder how there can be a single relatively consistent, intuitively plausible maximising principle which implies (within set theory) a given relatively consistent conjunction of intuitively plausible maximising principles, no matter how long this conjunction might be.

We shall take each of these difficulties in turn. In answer to the first, we reply that intuitive breakthroughs do not necessarily involve recursively given rules, but on the contrary often involve breaking such rules. Intuition, as opposed to reason, often utilises what is random rather than what falls under a rule. Thus, there may be infinitely many different intuitive breakthroughs possible, though no possible rule for such breakthroughs.

In answer to the second difficulty, we reply that the intuitive plausibility of an arbitrarily long maximising principle depends on the possibility of intuitively plausible definitions, which would considerably simplify such a lengthy principle. Such definitions are essential. Note, for example, that GMP, GCH and $(V \approx On)$ are all intuitively plausible, yet their plausibility depends to a large extent on the intuitively plausible definitions which considerably simplify their expression. (By hand count, $(V \approx On)$ contains, in primitive notation, about 550 symbols; GMP contains, in primitive notation, about 980 symbols; and GCH, in one of its simplest formulations, contains, in primitive notation, about 1500 symbols. Thus, without definitions, these statements would be incomprehensible.) Again, in general, there could be no recursive rule for generating such definitions or the defined symbols used. Their existence would be part of the intuitive breakthroughs. Moreover, the defined symbols introduced would have to be of bounded length. They could not grow arbitrarily in length. Otherwise, the definitions involved would not be comprehensible, and thus not intuitively plausible. From this we may conclude that the defined symbols introduced could not always be obtained by combining letters of an alphabet, for example.[36] Eventually, there would have to be radically new symbols, each reasonably short. This suggests that the notion of intuitive plausibility is a time-dependent notion, and thus, a given definition or maximising principle may be intuitively plausible at one stage in time but not at another. Indeed, intuitive plausibility is relative to the state of knowledge at a given period of time. Thus, one might have to know which symbols had previously been picked for use in definitions so that one could then pick a new simple symbol. Also, one might have to know which maximising principles were intuitively plausible relative to the previous states of knowledge in order to find a new maximising principle, intuitively plausible at the present state of knowledge.

Finally, in answer to the third difficulty, we reply that this difficulty would be overcome if the following thesis were accepted: given any relatively consistent conjunction of *two* intuitively plausible maximising principles, there is a relatively consistent, intuitively plausible maximising principle which implies this conjunction. This thesis implies that a single intuitive breakthrough can always be synthesised from two separate intuitive breakthroughs. Since intuition always strives to synthesise or integrate separate components within its range, the above thesis seems to us intuitively plausible. And this is our answer to the third difficulty. No doubt these difficulties deserve more thorough consideration, but we must end our discussion of them here.

Though we have no proof of DT_s, still it seems to us barely intuitively plausible, and also relatively consistent. Thus, DT_s is a good candidate for replacing Hilbert's Decidability Thesis, which Gödel showed to be inconsistent. In spite of the difficulties with DT_s, it seems reasonable to salvage something of Hilbert's original idea, and thus we propose DT_s (which in a way maximises, in Leibnizian fashion, the power of Intuition). And so, with this inspiration from Leibniz, we have thereby supplemented the weakened power of Reason in this post-Gödelian age with the growing power of Intuition in this dawning Aquarian age.

(4) *Further analogies*

In this section, we present analogies of a different kind from those previously presented. In particular, we shall consider some analogies between certain of Leibniz's logico-metaphysical ideas and corresponding ideas in metamathematics.

(a) Let us start with Leibniz's notion of (logical) necessity. According to him, all true statements are either (logically) necessary or contingent (but not both). He gives at least two characterisations of (logical) necessity.[37]

I: A statement is necessary if, and only if, it is resolvable, upon finite analysis, into identical statements.

(Note that an identical statement is defined as one whose opposite involves an express contradiction.)

II: A statement is necessary if, and only if, it is true in every possible world.

It should be noted that the notion of necessity in I is syntactical. To see this, we first note that the notion of an identical statement is clearly syntactical. Secondly, we note that the notion of resolvability is syntactical, because it itself resolves into deducibility, that is to say, if one reverses the finite analysis, one can start from the identical statements and then deduce the given necessary statement. Clearly, then, the notion of necessity in I is syntactical. Also, we see from the above that the opposite of a necessary statement implies the opposite of an identical statement (or a truth-functional expression of identical statements), which in turn involves an express contradiction. Thus, we get another of Leibniz's characterisations of a necessary statement as one whose opposite implies a contradiction. However, this equivalent characterisation is also syntactical, and so we need not consider it separately.

Regarding the notion of necessity in II, it is clearly semantical, because the notion of *true in a possible world* is clearly semantical. Now we claim that Leibniz's syntactical and semantical characterisations of logical necessity are analogous to the modern syntactical and semantical characterisations of logical validity, respectively (for statements and arguments expressible in first-order logic). Consider:

> Def. 1: A statement S (in a first-order formal system F) is syntactically valid if, and only if, S is derivable in the first-order predicate logic underlying F (or, a contradiction is logically implied by the negation of S).

Also consider:

> Def. 2: A statement S (in a first-order formal system F) is semantically valid if, and only if, S is true in every model or interpretation (associated with F).

It should be clear that I is analogous to definition 1. Also, II is analogous to definition 2, especially since Leibniz's notion of possible world is analogous to the present-day notion of model. To see this, consider that a possible world is, for Leibniz, a possible aggregate of monads (or an aggregate of possible monads) with various relations among them. Similarly, a model is a set of actual objects with various relations among them. However, the following important difference should be noted. A model is a set-theoretical entity, whereas a possible world is a metaphysical entity, which, for Leibniz, resides in the understanding of God. (For a discussion of the relationship between these two notions, see Mates, 1968.)

It is important to note that, for Leibniz, there is an equivalence between his two notions of (logical) necessity. And in the modern age, Gödel proved the equivalence between the two notions of logical validity (actually, he needed to prove only the implication between the semantical notion and the syntactical notion, the reverse implication being relatively trivial). Thus, we have Gödel's Completeness theorem,[38] and given the above, we may regard Leibniz as the precursor of this theorem. Going further, Gödel proved an even stronger form of the Completeness theorem, namely, that if a set of first-order statements is (syntactically) consistent, then it has a model (even a model in the natural numbers). Also, the converse clearly holds. Now from Leibniz's equivalence between I and II above, together with the fact that a statement is consistent (non-self-contradictory) if, and only if, its negation is not necessary, we obtain by simple logical transformations the following analogue to Gödel's theorem:

> III: A statement is consistent (non-self-contradictory) if, and only if, it is true in some possible world.

Here we make two digressions.

Digression 1: let us reconsider Leibniz's version of the ontological argument for God's existence. It is generally agreed that Leibniz considerably improved previous versions of this argument. According to him, if one can prove the possibility of God's existence, then one can prove God's existence. He has more than one version of this argument, but we shall consider only one of them. In good scholastic tradition, Leibniz proceeds as follows.[39] He defines God as the most perfect being, that is, the subject of all perfections. Moreover, he defines a perfection as a 'simple quality which is positive and absolute, and expresses without any limits whatever it does express'. Leibniz then argues that all perfections are compatible, and hence he concludes that God's existence is possible. (Note that there is an analogous result in logic, namely, that any set of negationless formulas in the first-order predicate logic is consistent.) From the possibility of God's existence Leibniz then goes on to argue for the existence of God, in the manner of the classical ontological argument. He argues that existence is a perfection and therefore part of the essence of God, and since God is possible, then God exists. This at least is one version of the argument.

The ontological argument appears highly questionable to modern minds, and indeed, both Frege and Russell found formal fallacies in it.[40] Nevertheless, we will attempt to reconstruct Leibniz's argument, perhaps in a manner he would not have approved, but still instructive, in our view. We apply III, above, as follows: if God's existence is possible (consistent, i.e. non-self-contradictory), then God exists in a possible world. Thus, Leibniz's proof of the possibility of God, together with III, yields that God exists in a possible world. Hence, this possible world must have the greatest quantity of essence or perfection. At this point we consider some relevant passages from Leibniz:[41]

> . . . To say that some essences have an inclination to exist and others do not, is to say something without reason, since existence seems to be universally related to every essence in the same manner.

> . . . If there were not some inclination inherent in the nature of essence to exist, nothing would exist.

From these passages, applied to the present context, we may infer that any possible world has an inclination to exist, that any possible world with a greater quantity of essence than another possible world has a greater inclination to exist, and that the possible world with the greatest quantity of essence has the greatest inclination to exist, and therefore does in fact exist. Thus, the possible world in which God exists does actually exist, and therefore God exists.

This reconstruction of Leibniz's argument at least has the merit of showing how much is packed into his notion of possibility. And from this we arrive at the following analogy: just as the strong version of Gödel's

Completeness Theorem shows us how much is packed into the notion of (syntactical) consistency (since consistency implies existence in a model), so Leibniz's ontological argument shows us how much is packed into his notion of possibility (since possibility implies existence in a possible world, as well as a striving or inclination toward existence).

In our view, the above reconstruction of Leibniz's ontological argument also sheds some light on the following historical puzzle: how could Leibniz, the inventor of mathematical logic, have accepted the validity of the ontological argument, even his own improved version? Certainly, he was not logically naïve, yet to our modern logical sense, his argument appears clearly fallacious. However, as indicated above, much more is involved in Leibniz's notion of possibility than meets our logical sense, just as, to reiterate, much more is involved in the modern notion of (syntactical) consistency than meets our untrained logical sense. Thus, in Leibniz's ontological argument there may be involved sufficiently strong presuppositions, perhaps implicitly held, which would allow him in good logical conscience to derive the existence of God from the possibility of God. Such presuppositions would be about possible worlds, possible objects and the inclinations of these possibles. However, it must be confessed that his notion of inclination is quite unclear, to say the least. But it must be more than a mere metaphor if Leibniz is to be absolved of apparently bad reasoning.

Digression 2: it may be worth considering some of Hilbert's views regarding mathematical consistency and existence. According to Hilbert, all non-finitely constructed mathematical objects (as opposed to the finitely constructed natural numbers, for example) are merely ideal elements which are added to the universe of discourse for purposes of utility and also aesthetic considerations of simplicity and elegance.[42] For Hilbert, it is sufficient to show consistency in order to justify the mathematical existence of these ideal elements. Thus, according to Hilbert, consistency implies (ideal) existence for infinite mathematical objects. Hilbert regarded this primarily as a methodological principle. Now Hilbert's view is loosely analogous to Leibniz's view regarding God's existence, since both require a proof of consistency. However, their views differ in that Leibniz regarded God as having real existence, as opposed to merely ideal (possible) existence. Hilbert's view, however, is also analogous to Leibniz's view about infinite mathematical objects, since, for Leibniz, such objects also have merely an ideal existence (he called them useful fictions). Nevertheless, their views differ in that Leibniz did not require a proof of consistency for these ideal elements. They could be used for purposes of calculation, even if they produced contradictions (see passages in section 1). Given these considerations, it seems that Hilbert's views about infinite mathematical objects, though more rigorous, owe much to Leibniz's views.

Actually, Hilbert's methodological principle regarding infinite mathematical objects is more clearly analogous to a principle of Kant, as pointed out by Professor Stephan Körner.[43] Consider the following Kantian principle: whenever certain Ideas of Reason, such as immortality or God (analogous to Hilbert's ideal elements), can be shown to be consistent with any given concrete theory whose truth is already established, then the extension of this theory, which now includes these Ideas of Reason, may also be accepted as true. Thus, Kant made room for immortality and God. And to reiterate, Hilbert had as part of his programme an analogous methodological principle, namely, that whenever certain ideal elements such as transfinite set-theoretical elements, can be shown to be consistent with a given finitary theory (such as finitary set theory), then the extension of the finitary theory, which now includes these ideal elements, may be accepted as true. And thus Hilbert made room for Cantor's Paradise of transfinite sets, or at least he tried to, until Gödel showed that one must already be in Cantor's Paradise before one can show its consistency with finitary set theory. In any case, Kant's Principle of Ideas of Reason is clearly analogous to Hilbert's Principle of Methodological Finitism, and thus Hilbert owes much to Kant also.

(b) Returning to Leibniz, we next consider his notions of contingency and truth. According to him, a contingent statement is one which is not logically necessary (nor logically impossible). Now as mentioned above, a logically necessary statement is one which is resolvable, upon finite analysis, into identical statements. For Leibniz, at least in the esoteric writings,[44] a true contingent statement is also resolvable, but only upon infinite analysis, into identical statements. One has to look more closely at this. Let us approach from another direction and consider Leibniz's notion of truth.[45] According to him, a true statement (of subject–predicate form) is one in which the predicate does in fact belong to the subject. According to Leibniz, this implies always that the concept of the predicate is in some sense involved in the concept of the subject. Note that, for Leibniz, a monad contains within its concept all its properties and all its relations to all the other monads compossible with it, that is to say, it contains within its concept the one unique possible world to which it can belong. Therefore, since truth divides into necessary truth and contingent truth, we may conclude the following: for a necessary truth, we finite minds can make the finite analysis which shows that the concept of the predicate is involved in the concept of the subject; but for a contingent truth, only God can make the infinite analysis required to show that the concept of the predicate is involved in the concept of the subject. We can never do this. Even a true contingent statement asserting existence (for example, 'there is (or was) a man fulfilling Napoleon's description') is resolvable, upon infinite analysis, into identical statements. To see this, we shall attempt a reconstruction of Leibniz's view. We first note that such an existence statement is resolvable, upon infinite analysis, into God's decrees. But these decrees are, according to Leibniz, moral necessities as opposed to logical necessities.[46] Thus, these decrees are just as contingent as any other contingent truths. So again, such decrees are resolvable, upon infinite analysis, to identical statements, via statements about God's non-moral attributes. Hence, the infinite analysis must involve, among other things, a consideration of all the possible worlds which God surveys, and all the various properties of each such possible world. Thus, for example, the contingent, though morally necessary, statement that God decreed the most perfect possible world is resolvable, upon infinite analysis, into identical statements, via statements about God's survey of all the possible worlds and about each possible world. It should be clear from the above that, for Leibniz, 'ought' is derivable from 'is', but only upon infinite analysis. Hence, we see that even true contingent statements of existence are infinitely analytic. Thus we see that, according to Leibniz, all truths are analytic, but whereas necessary truths are finitely analytic, contingent truths are infinitely analytic.

We next consider a result in metalogic which has some analogy to Leibniz's esoteric view about contingent statements. First, consider that Leibniz's notion of a contingent statement is analogous to the notion of an undecidable statement. For, a statement which is undecidable in a given theory cannot be proved (or disproved) in that theory (and so cannot be 'resolved' in a finite number of steps). However, it is known that certain (though by no means all) undecidable statements can be proved by infinitary means. Thus, for example, certain statements which are undecidable in number theory, using only finitary rules of inference, become decidable in number theory, if certain infinitary rules of inference are allowed. Similarly for set theory.

We shall consider one important case. As is well known, in 1931 Gödel showed that there are undecidable (contingent) statements of number theory (assuming number theory is consistent). In fact, Gödel showed how to construct such statements. Now though these statements are number-theoretical (that is, about numbers), they still express certain metamathematical conditions. Gödel achieved this feat by the process of 'arithmetisation', correlating Gödel numbers with symbols, terms, statements and even proofs, and correlating number-theoretical relations with metalogical (or metamathematical) relations. Thus, one such undecidable statement, which Gödel showed how to construct, actually expresses (within number theory) the consistency of number theory itself. Let us call this statement, *Consis (Peano)*. Thus, Gödel showed that if number theory (Peano's postulates) is consistent, then the number-theoretical statement, Consis (Peano), is undecidable in number theory. It is this result which destroyed Hilbert's programme in its original form, that of finding a proof for the consistency of number theory (and of all mathematics) using only finitary rules of inference.

However, in 1936 Gerhard Gentzen proved that Consis (Peano) is provable in number theory, augmented by the infinitary rule of ω-induction, as well as certain transfinite induction principles.[47] The rule of ω-induction allows a conclusion about all numbers to follow from infinitely many premisses about particular numbers. More formally speaking, the infinitary argument $(P_0, P_1, P_2, \ldots, P_n, \ldots / (\forall n) P_n)$ is regarded as valid, according to the infinitary rule of ω-induction. Thus, Consis (Peano) follows from infinitely many premisses by the application of such infinitary rules. Moreover, many of the premisses must themselves be established by infinitary rules, and similarly for the premisses of these premisses, and so on. That is why transfinite induction up to a certain infinite ordinal (namely, the first ϵ-number) is required.[48] Thus, we may regard these rules as providing an 'infinite analysis' of Consis (Peano).

From the above, we have the following analogy: just as for Leibniz, contingent truths are not resolvable, upon finite analysis, but are resolvable, upon infinite analysis, into identical statements, so in number theory (or set theory) certain undecidable statements, for example, Consis (Peano), are not provable by finitary rules of inference, but are provable by infinitary rules of inference.[49]

Thus, we see that Leibniz was not only a precursor to Gödel's Completeness theorem, but also to Gentzen's Infinitary Consistency Proof for Number theory, which is a response to Gödel's Incompleteness theorem. This should not be too surprising if we recall that, for Leibniz, no statement is undecidable, given the Principle of Perfection (since maximisation implies decidability).

(5) *Is Leibniz unique?*

Now that we have shown that there are various non-trivial analogies between Leibniz's metaphysical system and set theory (and also metamathematics), we may wonder to what extent these analogies are characteristic of Leibniz's system. He may very well have the greatest monopoly of such analogies. However, he does not have all of them. We have already considered Körner's analogy between Kant's Principle of Ideas of Reason and Hilbert's Principle of Methodological Finitism. Moreover, in this section we shall consider some analogies between certain metaphysical ideas of Descartes and Spinoza and corresponding set-theoretical ideas.

(a) Descartes, an inventor of analytic geometry and the founder of modern philosophy, naturally concerned himself with the infinite. Unlike Leibniz, however, he was unwilling to commit himself to the actual infinite in nature or in created metaphysical entities. He committed himself to the actual infinite only with respect to God. Thus, whether there exists an infinite quantity of matter in the universe or an infinite number of souls, is quite unknown to our finite minds. So also, Descartes is unwilling to commit himself to finitism, regarding the world. For him, the quantity of matter in the world is *indefinite*, and indeed, the number of created substances is likewise indefinite.[50] God alone, according to Descartes, is infinite, and can be known to be infinite.

In the Third Meditation[51] Descartes attempts to prove God's existence. He argues from the very idea of God to God himself. How does he manage such an argument? Well, he argues that he, Descartes, is a very finite being. But he has an idea of God, a very infinite being, a perfect being in fact. Next, Descartes claims that the very idea of such an infinite being has more reality in it than Descartes himself. Crucial to supporting this claim is the further premiss that the notion of infinite is prior to the notion of finite and, indeed, that 'finite' means 'non-infinite', rather than vice versa. Descartes then goes on to cite the scholastic maxim that whatever has less reality cannot be a cause of what has more reality. It follows from all this, according to Descartes, that he cannot be the cause of his idea of God, and with a bit more argument, it follows that only God can be the cause of Descartes's idea of God.

All this may sound strange to our modern ears. However, there is a very crucial premiss here which is worth noting. That is the premiss which asserts that the notion of infinite is prior to the notion of finite. This is the premiss we will focus on, leaving all the rest to our own meditations. Without this key premiss, Descartes would have to acknowledge the collapse of his entire argument. For he admits that he is capable of producing the idea of a finite being and the idea of negation, and he also admits that he can produce that idea which is merely a combination of these two ideas, namely, the idea of a non-finite being. Thus, for Descartes, there is no more reality in the idea of a non-finite being than there is in Descartes himself. But, to reiterate, there is more reality in the idea of an infinite being, since this idea is prior to the idea of a finite being. The notion of infinite is positive, whereas the notions of finite and non-finite are negative, since 'finite' means 'non-infinite'. Thus, we see that Descartes distinguishes the infinite from the non-finite.

We next consider an analogous distinction in set theory, namely, the distinction between infinite set and non-finite set. It was Dedekind who defined the notion of a (reflexively) infinite set as any set which can be put into one–one correspondence with one of its proper subsets.[52] Clearly, this notion of infinite set is positive. Thus, for example, the set of natural numbers is infinite because it can be put into one–one correspondence with the set of even numbers, which is one of its proper subsets. Now consider the notion of non-finite set, which is simply defined as any set which is *not* in one–one correspondence with a finite number. Here the notion of finite number is presupposed as understood (or previously defined). Clearly, then, this notion of non-finite set is negative.

Now the question arises whether there is more 'set-theoretical reality' in the notion of (reflexively) infinite set than in the notion of non-finite set. This question can be reduced to the precise set-theoretical question: is it provable in set theory that every non-finite set is an infinite set? The answer to this question is not simple. It turns out that in set theory, with the Axiom of Choice, there is an affirmative answer to the question. But in set theory, without the Axiom of Choice, the answer is negative. For, using Cohen's methods of forcing and generic models,[53] one can find a model of set theory in which the Axiom of Choice fails but in which there is a non-finite set which is, however, not infinite, from the point of view of the model. That is to say, in the model there is no one–one correspondence between the non-finite set and any of its proper subsets. However, even though this non-finite set is not infinite, from the point of view of the model, it may actually be infinite. Given the above, we see that without the Axiom of Choice, the notion of (reflexively) infinite set is independent of the notion of non-finite set (and therefore the one notion has more 'set-theoretical reality' than the other notion).

So to summarise our analogy: just as, for Descartes, a finite being cannot produce the idea of an infinite being without some outside help from God, so in set theory, a non-finite set cannot always be shown to be (reflexively) infinite, without some outside help from the Axiom of Choice.

Thus we see that beside Leibniz, some ideas can be found in Descartes (as well as in Kant) which are analogous to certain set-theoretical and metamathematical ideas. Finally, we shall make a few inquiries about Spinoza.

(b) Since Spinoza is the middle man in the traditional rationalist team, it is natural to inquire whether Spinoza's metaphysical ideas have any non-trivial analogies with set-theoretical and metamathematical ideas. Spinoza has been called 'that God-intoxicated man', because in his metaphysical system there is only one substance, namely God (or Nature). All other so-called 'things' he regarded as mere modifications of the one substance. Note that there is not only one kind of substance, for Spinoza, but actually only one instance of this kind.

Now a set-theoretician inspired by Spinoza might very well be intoxicated with the universal class V. He might even try to show that sets in V are really only modifications of V, and he might try to define what this might mean. Also such a set-theoretician would search for special theorems or maximising principles involving V, especially those which involve V essentially. (This has a precise set-theoretical meaning. For let ψ be any one-place formula of NBG. Then consider the following definition: 'V' occurs in $\psi(V)$ *essentially* if, and only if, there is no statement χ of ZF (χ has only set variables occurring in it) such that $(\chi \leftrightarrow \psi(V))$ is provable in NBG.)

In the light of one of Professor Robert Solovay's results,[54] it is especially important to search for maximising principles which not only contain 'V' essentially, but also are sufficiently powerful to imply new consequences for sets. For Solovay has shown that every theorem of NBG, which is a statement of ZFC, is also a theorem of ZFC. In other words, though NBG is stronger than ZFC and implies new statements about V and other proper classes, it implies no new statements about sets. And thus we should search for new maximising principles which do have new consequences for sets, as well as for V and other proper classes.

Thus, it might be of good consequence for set theory, after all, if set-theoreticians became more intoxicated with the universal class and found out more about its 'modifications'.

It should be stated that in so far as Spinoza asserted the existence of infinitely many attributes of God and of infinitely many modes under each attribute, he, too, in a way, 'maximised' the 'whole' and each of its 'parts'. Also, for Spinoza, maximisation implies necessity (and thus decidability, but in a trivial sense). Therefore, given the above, Spinoza also deserves a share of credit as a precursor to transfinite set theory.[55]

Since Descartes, Spinoza and Leibniz all had metaphysical ideas fruitful (or potentially fruitful) for set theory, we conclude that modern continental rationalism as a whole was a fruitful precursor to transfinite set theory.

(6) The search for new maximising principles

In this section we shall consider whether Leibniz's metaphysical system might be utilised in the search for new maximising principles of set theory. Realistically speaking, one does not expect to obtain set-theoretical results, but rather intuitive, schematic set-theoretical ideas. Certain disanalogies with Leibniz's metaphysical system are good sources of such ideas.

Let us start off, for example, with an important difference or disanalogy between L_2 and GMP. Thus, whereas L_2 applies to every monad, GMP does not apply to every set, but only to arbitrarily large sets. Hence, it would be an improvement if we could replace GMP by the following (possible) principle:

GMP' – Every set is maximised-from-its-point-of-view.

Now the problem with GMP' is that we don't know how to naturally define the predicate, 'maximised-from-its-point-of-view'. And even if we did, GMP' might be too strong, that is, inconsistent with set theory. So by considering the above disanalogy we have come upon the following problem: find a natural definition of the above-mentioned predicate such that GMP' implies GMP and such that GMP' is relatively consistent with set theory (and perhaps such that GMP does not imply GMP').

Since a metaphysical principle is always less precise than a set-theoretical principle, and since an analogy is only an analogy, we should expect that a given metaphysical principle will have many set-theoretical principles analogous to it. So let us consider L_2 again. Given any property of the universe, and given any monad, we may wonder whether that monad represents that property from its point of view. It seems likely that Leibniz held this view, but not necessarily. In any case, our answer to the question is definitely negative. And the proof is roughly as follows: any given monad, considered as a sequence of perceptions, has properties applying to the whole sequence rather than to any particular perception in the sequence. Now by Cantor's theorem $(x \lessdot Px)$, we may conclude that the whole sequence has more properties (because it has more subsets) than there are perceptions in the sequence. Thus, not all these properties can be represented by perceptions in the sequence, unless of course, whole groups of them were represented by single perceptions. Thus, we should never expect that any given monad would be able to represent every property of the universe, since it cannot even represent every property of itself.

We may also wonder whether in set theory the following analogous intuitive schema holds:

M_1 – Given that the universal class has a certain definable property, every set represents that property from its point of view ($\psi(V) \rightarrow$ ($\forall x$) $\psi_x(x)$).

Note that M_1 is a generalisation of GMP' (since V is maximised). M_1 seems to be a very strong schematic principle. And if there are difficulties in defining the predicate, 'maximised-from-its-point-of-view', then there should be even greater difficulties in defining the schematic predicate, $\ulcorner$ represents the property ψ from its point of view $\urcorner$.

A weaker schematic principle than M_1 is the following:

M_2 – Given that the universal class has a certain property, there are arbitrarily large sets representing that property from their points of view ($\psi(V) \rightarrow \{x/\psi_x(x)\} \approx V$).

We point out that M_2 has a loose connection with a powerful maximising principle given in Bernays (1961) and explained in Quine (1963: 328). It seems to us qualitatively easier to define $\psi_x(x)$ for arbitrarily large x than it would be to define it for every set x. Also, we note that M_2 has a loose connection with other reflection principles of set theory. Thus, M_2 may be worth investigating further.

In this way, we see that L_2 is suggestive of possible maximising principles in set theory. No doubt there are other principles of Leibniz which are similarly suggestive, but we shall let the matter rest here.

(7) *Conclusion (notes of caution)*
With this we conclude our discussion of the various analogies and relations between metaphysics and set theory. It might be wise to end this chapter on several notes of caution:

(a) No method of discovery is presented in this chapter. There is only the suggestion to consider, and perhaps utilise, various metaphysical concepts, distinctions and principles. But this is not a method of discovery, only at best a heuristic. Also there is nothing systematic in the presentation of the analogies considered in this chapter, and they are perceived to be either trivial, far-fetched or important, depending on one's point of view. But there is no way to decide this.

(b) It is never claimed in this chapter that Leibniz's metaphysical system exerted a direct influence on discoveries in set theory. Only an indirect influence is suggested.

(c) The truth or falsity of metaphysical principles is never in question in this chapter. For that matter, neither is the truth or falsity of set-theoretical principles. Metaphysical principles are intended only to serve as stimulation, or to give us enlightenment about general structure or form. And set-theoretical principles are regarded as at most intuitively plausible.

(d) There may be diminishing returns in investigating further analogies between Leibniz's metaphysical system (or any other system) and transfinite set theory. Thus, it is conceivable that we have found the best analogies around.

(e) Perhaps the actual study of metaphysical systems by set-theoreticians would be less effective than rest and relaxation in between hard work in set theory. Or to put the matter another way, as Professor Körner did put it (in conversation): how can we be sure that drinking wine is not just as effective for stimulating set-theoretical ideas as studying metaphysical systems? Again, one should distinguish these psychological considerations from the objective relations that do hold between metaphysical ideas and ideas in set theory. Knowledge of these objective relations may not be the primary source of new set-theoretical ideas, but it may be of some use, and, in our view, is of value in and of itself.

(f) The context of discovery must be distinguished from the context of justification. Thus, in whatever context we discover a set-theoretical principle, whether it be in the context of being guided by an analogous metaphysical principle or whether it be in the context of relaxation, there is always the problem of afterwards providing independent justification. Thus, for example, to independently justify a particular maximising principle, say *GMP*, it is necessary to show, at least, that such a principle is relatively consistent and moreover, that it has other desirable metamathematical and model-theoretic properties. Also it might be shown to have far-reaching consequences for other mathematical theories. Such has been the case for the Axiom of Choice, and such may become the case for *GCH*. We do not make any predictions at this stage.

(g) Finally, we wish to note those positivists who have a definite aversion for anything metaphysical. For them, any metaphysical thinking, because of its inherent ambiguity, as well as lack of precision, is anathema. Such positivists wish to leave aside all pre-scientific forms of thought and to stick closely to the formalism of their discipline. While we quite understand this position, nevertheless, we still assert that the consideration of, and possible utilisation of, pre-scientific forms of thought, in particular, metaphysical systems, can be of great value for set theory and logic, and even for science in general. Thus, in our view, further investigation is warranted.

One never ceases to be amazed at Leibniz's universality not only in theoretical but also in practical matters. Thus, the man who (independently of Newton) discovered the infinitesimal calculus was also an expert on jurisprudence and 'On Perplexing Cases in Law' (Leibniz's doctoral dissertation, completed at the age of 20); the man who developed the notion of kinetic energy (which he called derivative force, proportional to mv^2) was also an expert on mining and rock formations; and finally, the man who discovered the binary number system (0, 1, 10, 11, 100, etc.), which was published years later in *Mémoires de l'académie des sciences* (Paris, 1703: 85–9), also invented the first calculating machine which could add, subtract, multiply and divide (the author saw this machine in Hanover and was quite impressed with its design). Also, it should be noted that the binary system serves as the basic number system (machine language) for modern digital computers, all data and instructions being expressed in this system.

Finally, à propos of Leibniz's universality, we would like to mention that Leibniz was also interested in Chinese philosophy, especially the *I Ching* (Book of Changes). He learned about the *I Ching* through his contacts with Jesuit missionaries. Indeed, thanks to Father Bouvet, Leibniz rediscovered the binary system in the trigrams and hexagrams of the *I Ching*. So impressed was Leibniz with this parallelism of discovery that he published his own system (which he had discovered years earlier), as well as an account of this parallelism, in the above-mentioned article in the *Mémoires de l'académie des sciences*. Moreover, Leibniz believed that the binary system and much of the *I Ching* was a key to science (see H. Wilhelm's article, 'Leibniz and the *I Ching*' in *Collectanea Commissiones Synodalis* (Peking, vol. 16 (1943: 205–19); also D. Lach's more easily accessible article, 'Leibniz and China' in *Journal of the History of Ideas*, vol. VI (1945). Finally, the author acknowledges his debt to Mr Peter Hartman for first pointing out Leibniz's connection with the *I Ching*, as well as for some of the references dealing with this topic.

Department of Philosophy
University of California
at Davis

NOTES

1 For a short biography of Leibniz see Vennebusch (1966). Also see Parkinson (1966) for Leibniz's logical papers and see the *Leibniz–Clarke Correspondence* for his views on space and time.

2 See Russell (1900; 1937), especially the Preface to the 1937 edition, as well as Couturat (1902: 19). Also, see Hintikka (1972: esp. 189).

3 The Continuum Hypothesis (*CH*) was conjectured by Georg Cantor, about 100 years ago, and later generalised to the *GCH*. In 1900, at the International Congress of Mathematicians, Hilbert listed *CH* as the number one mathematical problem on his famous list of outstanding unsolved problems. In 1938, Gödel showed the relative consistency of *GCH* (see also Gödel (1940)), and in 1963, P. J. Cohen showed the relative consistency of the negation of *GCH*, that is, the independence of *GCH* from the

axioms of set theory (see also Cohen (1966)). The two results combined thus showed that GCH is undecidable in set theory, as we know it (assuming that set theory is consistent).

The author showed in Friedman (1971) that GCH is equivalent to the Generalised Maximisation Principle (GMP). Now GMP is a generalisation of von Neumann's Maximisation Principle (MP), which asserts that every class not equinumerous with the universe of sets is itself a member of this universe; or, in brief, that the universe of sets is maximised (which implies that this universe has the maximum cardinal number). Moreover, it was shown in von Neumann (1929) that the (global) Axiom of Choice (AC) is equivalent to MP. More generally, GMP asserts that every local universe is maximised. This statement in turn was shown in Friedman (1971) to be equivalent to the following model-theoretic statement: every super-complete model of set theory, minus the Powerset axiom, is also a model of MP. Thus GCH, via GMP, is equivalent to an external model-theoretic statement, a clue, perhaps, as to why GCH is undecidable in set theory. Also there is at least one other such model-theoretic statement, as pointed out in correspondence by Professor H. J. Kiesler:

'The following model-theoretic fact is equivalent to the GCH: for every regular cardinal $\kappa > \omega$, every complete theory for a countable language which has an infinite model has a saturated model of power κ. This fact is of central importance to the subject and seems plausible to me. However, my own philosophical views are such that the question 'Is the GCH true?' is meaningless, while '$V = L$' and '$2^{\aleph_0}$ is weakly inaccessible' are both plausible. (A model $\mathfrak{A}$ is *saturated* if, and only if, for every $X \subset A$ of power $|X| < |A|$, every set of formulas $\varphi(\nu)$ finitely satisfiable in $(\mathfrak{A},a)_{a\epsilon x}$ is satisfiable in $(\mathfrak{A},a)_{a\epsilon x}$.' (2 November 1971).

4   Wiener (1951: 99).
5   ibid., p. 424.
6   See Robinson (1966), especially the chapter, 'Concerning the History of the Calculus', pp. 261–4.
7   Wiener (1951: 99). Also see the passage by Cantor referenced by n. 12.
8   Leibniz (1962).
9   See especially Cantor's papers, 'Über die verschiedenen Standpunkte in bezug auf das aktuelle Unendliche' and 'Mitteilungen zur Lehre vom Transfiniten', in Cantor (1932).
10 See Kambartel (1965: 216); trans. from 'Mitteilungen' in Cantor (1932: 400), which contains the letter to Cardinal Franzeln.
11 I am grateful to Professor William Bossart for translating this passage from Cantor's paper, 'Verschiedenen Standpunkte', in Cantor (1932: 372–3), and also the immediately following passage (see n. 12).
12 This is translated from Cantor's paper, 'Mitteilungen' (Cantor: 399).
13 See also 'Verschiedenen Standpunkte', Cantor (1932: 372).
14 ibid., p. 216, trans. from Cantor (1932: 375).
15 Russell (1967: 357–8).
16 This letter is translated in van Heijenoort (1967: 114). Also, van Heijenoort points out that Schröder in 1890 had also introduced this distinction, defining a consistent multiplicity as one whose elements are compatible with each other. For a formal definition of this distinction, see Gödel (1940: 3).
17 See the Leibniz-Clarke correspondence (Leibniz, 1956) for Leibniz's views about space and time, and then apply these views to the Monadology.
18 See the correspondence with Arnauld, Leibniz (1962: e.g. 154–5).
19 For various statements of this principle, see sec. 9 of the *Monadology*, as well as secs 5 and 6 of Leibniz's fourth letter in Leibniz (1956); also Russell (1900; 1937: 219–22).
20 See Russell (1900; 1937: 141).
21 This is translated in Lovejoy (1936; 1960: 178).
22 Wiener (1951: 93).
23 Leibniz (1962: 8–9).
24 L_1 is associated with the Principle of Plenitude, expounded in Lovejoy (1936; 1960:

esp. ch. V); in Rescher (1967: 50–1); and in Hintikka (1972). However, we wish to sidetrack the issue of just what the Principle of Plenitude states, since it is so enmeshed in controversial formulations. On the other hand, L_1, as distilled from the various passages quoted above, is relatively clear. We will make one crucial point, namely, that L_1 maximises the quantity of monads, subject to the constraints of variety and order.

25   See von Neumann (1925), trans. in van Heijenoort (1967). It is important to note that von Neumann used 'function' instead of 'class' as a primitive notion. However, the present-day class-set distinction, whose formalisation derives from von Neumann, uses 'class' as a primitive.

26   See von Neumann (1929). Note that besides Global Choice, von Neumann also used the axioms of Replacement and of Foundation. On the other hand, Choice and Replacement are implied by MP. Now let NBG be the von Neumann–Bernays–Gödel set theory. Then it is clear from the above that Global Choice is equivalent to MP in (NBG–Global Choice).

27   This is the same letter mentioned in n. 16. In 1922, A. Fraenkel, as well at T. Skolem, introduced the Axiom of Replacement as a first-order axiom schema, thereby considerably augmenting Zermelo's set theory.

28   See Cohen (1966: ch. IV), for an exposition of his methods. We will consider one important case: the Boolean Prime Ideal theorem (every ideal of a Boolean Algebra can be extended to a (maximal) prime ideal (ultrafilter)). In Feferman (1965) it was shown, using Cohen's methods, that the Boolean Prime Ideal theorem is independent of Zermelo–Fraenkel set theory without the (local) Axiom of Choice (assuming consistency). On the other hand, it is well known that with Choice, one can prove the Boolean Prime Ideal theorem. Thus, we see that Choice can be shown to be essential for proving this theorem, and thus for proving the existence of various prime ideals. Also, it should be noted that in Halpern and Levy (1967) it is shown that Choice is independent of the Boolean Prime Ideal theorem.

29   To see this, suppose that it is provable (in NBG-Replacement) that $V_{\omega + \omega}$ has the appropriate cardinality; then it is provable (in NBG-Replacement) that $\aleph_0 \neq$ card $(V_{\omega + \omega})$. Therefore, $V_{\omega + \omega + 1}$ is a model of '$\aleph_0 \neq$ card $(V_{\omega + \omega})$'. Now in $V_{\omega + \omega + 1}$, '$\aleph_0$' gets interpreted as $\aleph_0$, and 'card $(V_{\omega + \omega})$' gets interpreted as $\aleph_0$, since $\aleph_0$ is the largest cardinal in $V_{\omega + \omega + 1}$. Therefore, $\aleph_0 \neq \aleph_0$. This is impossible, assuming that NBG is consistent. This shows that (in NBG-Replacement), it cannot be shown that $V_{\omega + \omega}$ has the appropriate cardinality.

30   See Mates (1968: 354).

31   A regular cardinal is defined as a cardinal which is not the union of fewer smaller cardinals. A set x is hereditarily cardinally less than a cardinal number κ if, and only if, x is cardinally less than κ, every member of x is cardinally less than κ, every member of every member of x is cardinally less than κ, etc.

32   See Easton's doctoral dissertation (1964). This result requires complicated variations of Cohen's methods.

33   This is more of a conjecture on our part. However, we note that Cohen showed that '$P\omega$' can be made to have arbitrarily large cardinality in the various Cohen extensions, and this fits in well with Takeuti's hypotheses. The following historical points should also be noted. In his book, *Set Theory and the Continuum Hypothesis* (1966), Cohen argued that GCH is a restrictive principle, since it restricts the powerset operation. However, in a private communication to the author in 1969, Cohen admitted, regarding my GMP, that, 'I think that you have succeeded well in "turning the tables on Cohen" in that you have axiomatised precisely the idea that replacement and union are "all-powerful". Whether or not your new formulation is totally convincing is of course more difficult to say.' Thus, Cohen seems to agree here that GMP is a maximising principle of a sort, and if so, then GCH is also and thus cannot be regarded as a restrictive principle in any absolute sense. In my view, it would be best to regard GCH as a maximising principle in conflict with other maximising principles, for example, those which assert the 'all-powerfulness' of the powerset operation. See Friedman (1971).

34 The author is indebted to Professor Jack Silver for suggesting the clause that for any finite conjunction of statements in the set there exists a statement in the set which implies this conjunction.

35 It is not clear that Hilbert actually meant this, but that is the way his thesis came to be interpreted. As can be seen from Hilbert (1926) (trans. in van Heijenoort, 1967), Hilbert admitted that one could not prove this thesis and that there was no general method of solving every mathematical problem, but he did claim that the thesis is consistent and that one could prove its consistency (see p. 384). Gödel showed that this thesis is inconsistent, at least as it was usually interpreted.

However, it should be mentioned that in his 'Remarks before the Princeton Bicentennial Conference on Problems in Mathematics' in 1946 (reprinted in *The Undecidable*, Martin Davis ed., 1965), Gödel stated a decidability thesis (or 'completeness theorem' as he called it) to which our DT_2 is very much akin. Here is what Gödel said: 'It is not impossible that for such a concept of demonstrability, some completeness theorem would hold which would say that every proposition expressible in set theory is decidable from the present axioms plus some true assertion about the largeness of the universe of all sets.'

It should be noted that our DT_8 is stronger than Gödel's decidability thesis. Also, the author arrived at DT_1–DT_8 independently of Gödel's remarks. Nevertheless, Gödel has first priority for stating a decidability thesis which might serve as a replacement for Hilbert's inconsistent thesis.

36 This was, in effect, pointed out by Professor W. Craig, in conversation. He noted that eventually the sequence of letters in the defined expressions would themselves grow arbitrarily long, and thus would not be comprehensible. He also pointed out that the notion of intuitive plausibility is time-dependent.

37 For characterisation I, see Leibniz's esoteric piece, 'Necessary and Contingent Truths' in Smith and Grene (1940), trans. from *Opuscules et fragments inédits de Leibniz*, L. Couturat, ed. (1903). The relevant pages are 306-7. For characterisation II, see *New Essays*, trans. Langley, p. 714, as pointed out in Mates (1968).

38 See Gödel's (1930) paper, trans. in van Heijenoort (1967). This is Gödel's revised version of his doctoral thesis.

39 See Russell for passages of Leibniz on the ontological argument (1900; 1937: 286–8).

40 Russell utilised his theory of descriptions to show that any proposition containing a primary occurrence of the description, 'the most perfect being', necessarily implies that there is exactly one most perfect being, and hence the ontological argument begs the question. See Russell's article 'On Denoting' in Copi and Gould (1967).

Frege utilised his theory of concepts to show that existence is not a first-level concept (predicate) but rather, a second-level concept and, therefore, cannot be regarded as a perfection (predicate) of God. See Frege's papers in Geach and Black (1952).

41 Wiener (1951: 92).

42 See Hilbert (1926: esp. 379).

43 See Körner (1960: 73). Here I wish to acknowledge a real debt to Professor Körner, whose book containing the above analogy first stimulated me to look for further analogies between philosophical ideas and logico-mathematical ideas.

44 See Leibniz's esoteric piece previously referred to (Smith and Grene, 1940: 307-8) (see n. 37).

45 ibid., p. 306.

46 See paras 7 and 8 of Leibniz's fifth letter in the Leibniz-Clarke correspondence (Leibniz, 1956). Also, the *Theodicy* (Leibniz, 1966).

47 See Gentzen's article, 'The Consistency of Elementary Number Theory' in the collected papers, Gentzen (1969), translated from the original 1936 article.

48 ϵ_0 is the first ϵ-number. It is the limit of all ordinals in the sequence $(\omega, \omega^\omega, \omega^{\omega^\omega}, \ldots)$. Note that ϵ_0 is countable and that the exponentiation in question is defined, not for cardinal numbers, but for ordinal numbers.

49 I wish to express my gratitude to Dr John Bell, who first brought this analogy to my attention (in conversation).

50   I am grateful to Professor Neal Gilbert for pointing out the relevant passages in Descartes's *Principles of Philosophy* (in Latin).

51   Eaton (1927).

52   This definition appeared in Dedekind's 1888 article, 'Was sind und was sollen die Zahlen', as pointed out in Fraenkel and Bar-Hillel (1958: 2–3).

53   I am indebted to Professor Robert Solovay, as well as to Professor Jack Silver, for pointing out that this result was obtained (probably by A. Levy) not long after Cohen's results were obtained. They also pointed out that it is a relatively easy result compared with other independence results.

54   I wish to note that Professor Solovay, in conversation, has pointed out that this result was discovered independently by others and that he was one among them. This result is alluded to in Cohen (1966: 77) (see the last theorem on the page, which however, is weaker than this result). Also note that ZFC is simply the Zermelo–Fraenkel set theory with Local Choice, which may be formulated as follows:

$$(\forall x)(\exists f)(f \text{ is a function \& Domain } (f) = x \text{ \& } (\forall y)(y \neq \phi \text{ \& } y \in x \rightarrow f(y) \in y).$$

55   See Cantor's reference to Spinoza in the longest quoted passage in section 1. Also it should be stated that in a more recent paper by the author it has been shown that V has a Spinozistic partitioning, that is, a partitioning with an absolutely infinite number of partition classes, each one of which is ϵ-isomorphic to V. See Friedman (1974; 1976); the proof is contained in the latter.

REFERENCES

Bernays, P., 'Zur Frage der Unendlichkeitsschemata in der Axiomatischen Mengenlehre', in *Essays on the Foundations of Mathematics Dedicated to A. A. Fraenkel on his Seventieth Anniversary* (Jerusalem, Magnes Press, 1961).

Cantor, Georg, *Gesammelte Abhandlungen*, E. Zermelo, ed. (Berlin, Springer, 1932).

Cohen, P. J., *Set Theory and the Continuum Hypothesis* (New York, W. A. Benjamin, 1966).

Copi, I. M. and Gould, J. A. (eds), *Contemporary Readings in Logical Theory* (New York, Macmillan, 1967).

Couturat, L., 'On Leibniz's Metaphysics', trans. in Frankfurt (1972) (see below); originally in *Revue de Metaphysique et de Morale*, vol. 10 (1902).

Davis, M. (ed.), *The Undecidable* (Hewlett, NY, Raven Press, 1965).

Easton, W. B., 'Powers of Regular Cardinals', Ph.D. dissertation (Princeton University, 1964).

Eaton, R. M. (ed.), *Descartes Selections* (New York, Charles Scribner's, 1927).

Feferman, S., 'Some Applications of the Notions of Forcing and Generic Sets', *Fundamenta Mathematica*, vol. LVI (1965: 325–45).

Fraenkel, A. A. and Bar-Hillel, Y., *Foundations of Set Theory* (Amsterdam, North-Holland, 1958).

Fraenkel, A. A., Bar-Hillel, Y., and Levy, A., *Foundations of Set Theory* (Amsterdam, North-Holland, 1973).

Frankfurt, H. (ed.), *Leibniz: a Collection of Critical Essays* (Garden City, New York, Doubleday, 1972).

Friedman, J. I., 'Proper Classes as Members of Extended Sets', *Math. Ann.*, vol. 183 (1969: 232–40).

Friedman, J. I., 'The Generalized Continuum Hypothesis is Equivalent to the Generalized Maximization Principle', *Journal of Symbolic Logic*, vol. 36 (1971: 39–54).

Friedman, J. I., 'Some Set-theoretical Partition Theorems Suggested by the Structure of Spinoza's God', *Synthese*, vol. 27 (1974: 199–209).

Friedman, J. I., 'The Universal Class Has a Spinozistic Partioning', *Synthese*, vol. 32 (1976: 403–418).

Geach, P. T. and Black, M. (eds), *Translations from the Philosophical Writings of Gottlob Frege* (Oxford, Blackwell, 1952).

Gentzen, G., *The Collected Papers of Gerhard Gentzen*, M. E. Szabo, ed. (Amsterdam, North-Holland, 1969).

Gödel, K., 'The Completeness of the Axioms of the Functional Calculus of Logic', trans. in van Heijenoort (1967); originally in *Monatshefte für Mathematik und Physik*, vol. 37 (1930).

Gödel, K., 'On Formally Undecidable Propositions of *Principia Mathematica* and Related Systems I', trans. in van Heijenoort (1967); originally in *Monatshefte für Mathematik und Physik*, vol. 38 (1931).

Gödel, K., *The Consistency of the Continuum Hypothesis* (Princeton University Press, 1940).

van Heijenoort, J., *From Frege to Gödel* (Cambridge, Mass, Harvard University Press, 1967).

Hilbert, D., 'On the Infinite', trans. in van Heijenoort (1967); originally in *Math. Ann.*, vol. 95 (1926), and originally given as an address in 1925.

Hintikka, J., 'Leibniz on Plenitude, Relations, and the "Reign of Law"', in Frankfurt (1972).

Kambartel, F., 'Mathematics and the Concept of Theory', in *Proceedings of the 1964 International Congress for Logic, Methodology, and Philosophy of Science* (Amsterdam, North-Holland, 1965).

Körner, S., *The Philosophy of Mathematics* (New York, Harper & Row, 1962); originally published in 1960.

Leibniz, G. W., *New Essays Concerning Human Understanding*, trans. A. G. Langley (Chicago, Open Court, 1916).

Leibniz, G. W., *The Leibniz–Clarke Correspondence*, H. G. Alexander, ed. (New York, Philosophical Library, 1956).

Leibniz, G. W., *Basic Writings*, McCormack, ed. (contains the *Discourse on Metaphysics, Correspondence with Arnauld* and the *Monadology*) (LaSalle Ill, Open Court, 1962).

Leibniz, G. W., *Theodicy*, trans. E. M. Huggard (New York, Bobbs-Merrill, 1966).

Levy, A. and Halpern, J. D., 'The Boolean Prime Ideal Theorem Does Not Imply the Axiom of Choice', given at the 1967 Set Theory Symposium in Los Angeles, published in *Proceedings of Symposia in Pure Mathematics: Axiomatic Set Theory*, vol. XIII, no. 1 (Providence, RI, American Mathematical Society, 1971).

Lovejoy, A. O., *The Great Chain of Being* (New York, Harper & Row, 1960); originally published in 1936.

Mates, B., 'Leibniz on Possible Worlds', in Frankfurt (1972); originally published in 1968.

von Neumann, J., 'An Axiomatization of Set Theory', in van Heijenoort (1967) (translated); originally published in *Journal fur die reine und angewandte Mathematik*, vol. 154 (1925).

von Neumann, J., 'Über eine Widerspruchsfreiheitsfrage in der axiomatischen Mengenlehre', *Journal für die reine und angewandte Mathematik*, vol. 160 (1929).

Parkinson, G. H. R., *Leibniz: Logical Papers* (London, Oxford University Press, 1966).

Quine, W. V. O., *Set Theory and its Logic* (Cambridge, Mass, Harvard University Press, 1963).

Rescher, N., *The Philosophy of Leibniz* (Englewood Cliffs, NJ, Prentice-Hall, 1967).

Robinson, A., *Non-Standard Analysis* (Amsterdam, North-Holland, 1966).

Russell, B., *A Critical Exposition of the Philosophy of Leibniz* (London, George Allen & Unwin, 1937); first published in 1900.

Russell, B., *Autobiography of Bertrand Russell* (1872–1914) (Boston, Atlantic, Little, Brown, 1967).

Russell, B., 'On Denoting', in Copi and Gould (1967); first published in *Mind* (1905).

Smith, T. V. and Grene, M., *From Descartes to Locke* (University of Chicago Press, 1940).

Spinoza, B., *Ethics* (New York, Hafner, 1949).

Takeuti, G., 'Hypotheses on Powerset' (given in 1967), in *Proceedings of Symposia in Pure Mathematics: Axiomatic Set Theory*, vol. XIII, no. 1 (Providence, RI, American Mathematical Society, 1971).

Vennebusch, J., *Gottfried Wilhelm Leibniz* (Bad Godesberg, Inter Nationes, 1966).

Wiener, P. (ed.), *Leibniz Selections* (New York, Charles Scribner's, 1951).

13

THE INFINITE

Morris Lazerowitz

In their everyday, popular use the words 'finite' and 'infinite' are connected with the idea of quantity: the first with the idea of a limited quantity or amount, the second with the idea of the unlimited and the vast. Thus, in everyday talk something is said to be infinitely far from us, e.g. a remote galaxy, when it is a vast distance away, in contrast to something which is said to be far but not infinitely far; and infinite wealth, as against limited assets, is understood to be enormous wealth. If we were told that Jones had infinite credit at the bank, we should naturally infer that he had more credit than people who had only limited credit. The words 'finite' and 'infinite' are not used in their popular senses in mathematics, but the ideas of the huge and the less than huge seem, nevertheless, to be in the background of the thinking of at least some mathematicians. One mathematician inadvertently revealed this in the lapse shown in the following words: 'Representation of a complex variable on a plane is obviously more effective at a finite distance from the origin than it is at a very great distance'.[1] This brings to mind a description in a brochure about a marshland in Ohio, as 'almost endless'.

Wittgenstein is said to have remarked in lectures that 'The idea of the infinite as something huge does fascinate some people, and their interest is due solely to that association, though they probably would not admit it'. There is reason for thinking that this remark applies to many mathematicians who adopt Cantor's notion of the 'consummated infinite', the notion that, for example, the series of numbers, 1,2,3,4,5, . . . , forms a completed totality of elements, just as the first forty odd numbers form an entire set of numbers or just as the chimney-pots in Bloomsbury make up a whole class of objects in London. He is also reported as having said:

> When someone uses the expression 'plus 1' we get the picture of 1 being added to something. If I speak of 'the cardinal number of all the cardinal numbers' all sorts of expressions come to mind – such as the expression 'the number of chairs in this room'. The phrase conjures up a picture of an enormous, colossal number. And this picture has charm.

Wittgenstein declared, as did Gauss, that infinity has nothing to do with size, and there is reason to think that transfinite arithmetic is primarily a semantic creation for representing the mathematical infinite as the colossal. It may turn out that despite its containing solid mathematics, the discipline which Hilbert described as the paradise created by Cantor and which Poincaré characterised as a disease from which mathematics will eventually recover is at bottom a semantic contrivance for the production of an illusion.

Many people take the view that all numbers are *finite* numbers, and Russell gives one explanation as to why they do this. The phrase 'finite number' means, according to him,[2]

> 0 and 1 and 2 and 3 and so on, forever – in other words, any number that can be obtained by successively adding ones. This includes all the numbers that can be expressed by means of our ordinary numerals, and since such numbers can be made greater and greater, without ever reaching an unsurpassable maximum, it is easy to suppose that there are no other numbers. But this supposition, natural as it is, is mistaken.

Russell's idea is that it is natural to think the finite numbers are the only numbers, and Zeno gives an argument for this notion. One thesis of Fragment 3 goes as follows:

> If there is a multiplicity of things, they necessarily are as many as they are, and not more or fewer. If they are exactly as many as they are, then they will be finite in number.

The counterthesis is that they must also be infinite in number, but that is not to the point here. Zeno's argument amounts to the contention that a number of things must be a definite number (though we may not know what it is) and therefore finite, i.e. a number expressible by one of our 'ordinary' numerals.

In Russell's opinion the weak point in the thesis that 'if they are just as many as they are, they will be finite in number' is that it is based on the assumption that definite infinite numbers are impossible.[3] It is by no means clear what is meant by the phrase 'definite infinite number'. The idea of a *definite* infinite number would seem to be that of a number that is like one denoted by an 'ordinary' numeral but greater than any such number. This may well strike one as being a number that is finite or 'terminate' (Galileo's word), but too great to be finite, a *finite infinite* number. The phrase 'the consummated infinite' also suggests the notion of an infinity of elements whose number is made definite and thus finite. Be this as it may, Russell's objection brings to our attention an important point about the words 'All numbers are finite': this is that if the word 'finite' has a correct application to numbers, then its associated antithetical word 'infinite' must also have a correct application to numbers.

It *may* be that, in fact, the application of 'finite' to numbers does not represent a correct use of the word: it *may* be that the sentences '5 is a finite number' and 'A thousand billion is a finite number' do not represent a correct use of the word. But if they do, then 'infinite' must also have a correct application to *some* numbers, otherwise 'finite' would not have a use to distinguish between numbers, set off some from others, as do, for example, the terms 'prime number' and 'proper fraction'. Without its antithesis, 'infinite number', the expression 'finite number' would contain a word which serves no function, and 'finite number' would have no use different from that of the word 'number'. It is a curious feature of the view that all numbers are finite that it rests on a distinction which at the same time it obliterates. Without a distinction between finite and infinite numbers, Zeno's putative demonstration could not even have been formulated. But if his first thesis is in fact demonstrated, there could *in principle* be no infinite numbers, which would imply that there is *no distinction* between finite and infinite numbers.

Wittgenstein has pointed out that in philosophy words are often used without an antithesis, in what he described as a 'typically metaphysical way'.[4] He conceived his task as being 'to bring words back from their metaphysical to their everyday usage'.[5] If, allowing that 'finite' has a correct application to numbers, we preserve the distinction implied by its use, we have to 'bring back' into usage the application of 'infinite' to numbers. Doing this upsets the thesis that *all* numbers are finite and would seem to open the way to the claim that there are numbers which are not expressible by any of the 'ordinary' numerals. Russell has remarked: 'When infinite numbers are first introduced to people, they are apt to refuse the name of numbers to them, because their behaviour is so different from that of finite numbers that it seems a wilful misuse of terms to call them numbers at all'.[6] But if it is not a misuse of terminology to call '5' a finite number, it cannot be a misuse of terminology to call an infinite number a number, regardless of how it may differ from finite numbers. And, of course, it would be a wilful misuse of terminology to deny that the number of primes is infinite.

It is a curious and striking thing about the idea of the infinite that in some connections it would be considered unnatural to deny that 'infinite number' has a correct application, while in other and comparable connections it is natural to deny this. There would be no temptation to deny that there is an infinite number of numbers from 1 on. But it seems entirely natural to state (as the cosmological argument does) that it is in principle impossible for there to be an infinite series of causes. No one could take exception to the statement, that the geometric series, $1 + \frac{1}{2} + \frac{1}{4} + \ldots$, is an infinite series, as against one of its parts, e.g. $1 + \frac{1}{2} + \frac{1}{4} + \frac{1}{8}$; but many would take exception to the claim that an infinite series forms a whole. Again, no one would say that $\frac{1}{2}, \frac{3}{4}, \frac{7}{8}, \frac{15}{16}$ is the entire series generated by $(2^n - 1)/2^n$. But many people would, nevertheless, deny that there is such a thing as an entire unending series, and therefore would deny that '1 is *beyond*[7] the whole of the infinite series, $\frac{1}{2}, \frac{3}{4}, \frac{7}{8}$, $\frac{15}{16}, \ldots$'.[8] Russell asserted that the first infinite number is 'beyond the whole unending series of finite numbers',[9] and went on to remark that it will be objected that there cannot be anything beyond the whole of a series that is endless. What is the difference between speaking of an infinite series and speaking of the whole infinite series, which makes people accept the one and dispute over the other? No one would be tempted to reject the statement that there is an infinite number of natural numbers or that there is an infinite number of primes; and it is mystifying that people who are introduced to infinite numbers are likely to refuse to apply the word 'number' to them. What, we may ask, is the difference between allowing that there is an infinite number of natural numbers and allowing that there is a number which is infinite?

Russell offers the following explanation:[10]

the number of inductive numbers is a new number, different from all of them, not possessing all inductive properties. It may happen that 0 has a certain property, and that if n has it so has $n + 1$, and yet that this new number does not have it. The difficulties that so long delayed the theory of infinite numbers were largely due to the fact that some, at least, of the inductive properties were wrongly judged to be such as *must* belong to all numbers; indeed it was thought that they could not be denied without contradiction. The first step in understanding infinite numbers consists in realising the mistakenness of this view.

In philosophy we are not strangers to 'mistakes' which have the quality of elusiveness: they strongly impress some people as being mistakes, while making no such impression on others. The 'mistake' of thinking that certain of the inductive properties, such as that $n + 1$ is greater than n, are properties of all numbers, would not be accepted as a mistake by all who are competent to express an opinion. Russell has remarked that the 'astonishing difference' between any number occurring in the sequence $1,2,3,\ldots$, and the number of all the numbers in it, is that[11]

this new number is unchanged by adding 1 or subtracting 1 or doubling or halving or any of a number of other operations which we think of as necessarily making a number larger or smaller. The fact of being unchanged by the addition of 1 is used by Cantor for the definition of what he calls 'transfinite' cardinal numbers.

And one mathematician has spoken of the 'crude miracle' which 'stares us in the face that *a part of a set may have the same cardinal number as the entire set*'.[12]

As is known, Leibniz was not unaware of the miracle which Cantor later performed, except that he called it a contradiction. 'The number of all numbers', he declared, 'implies a contradiction, which I show thus: To any number there is a corresponding number equal to its double. Therefore, the number of all numbers is not greater than the number of even numbers, i.e., the whole is not greater than its part'.[13] What Russell calls a 'new' number with astonishing properties, Leibniz calls an impossible number because of these astonishing properties. And the fact of being unchanged by the addition of 1, or the fact of the whole not being greater than its parts, which Cantor used to define the term 'transfinite number', was used by Leibniz to deny that there could be such a number. If he had been shown Cantor's symbol for the first transfinite number, '$\aleph_0$', it is fair to suppose he would have said that it is not the name of a possible number, and thus that it is not actually the name of a number. It will be remembered that Gauss protested against the use of the actual or completed infinite as something which is 'never permissible in mathematics'. The important thing to notice about this disagreement is that it is not the result of incomplete knowledge of the facts on the part of anyone. If it is a fact that $n + 1$ is greater than n for *any* number, then all the parties to the disagreement know this; and if it is not a fact, then this too is known. There is no disagreement over whether every number n has a double, $2n$, and over whether every number n has a square, n^2, but there is disagreement over whether facts like these show that there is a contradiction in the idea of an infinite totality of numbers or whether it brings to light a characteristic of such a totality. And nothing new can be brought in to help us decide one way or the other.

Galileo gives a different answer to the question about infinite numbers. Leibniz and others think that infinite numbers are impossible, the implication being that there are none. Cantor and others think that there are such numbers and that, unlike finite numbers, an infinite number can be equal to a proper part of itself, and also that some infinite numbers are greater than other infinite numbers. Galileo's position is that such terms as 'greater than', 'equal to' and 'less than' are not applicable to infinite numbers. From the fact that there cannot be fewer squares than there are numbers of which they are the squares, i.e. than 'all the Numbers taken together', he does not conclude that there can be no infinite numbers or that infinite numbers have paradoxical properties which defeat our understanding. In the first of his *Dialogues on Motion*, Salviati asserts:

> These are some of those Difficulties which arise from Discourses which our finite understanding makes about Infinites, by ascribing to them Attributes which we give to Things finite and determinate, which I think most improper, because those Attributes of Majority, Minority, and Equality, agree not with Infinities, of which we cannot say that one is greater than, less than, or equal to another.

Against Galileo's solution Russell has the following to say: 'It is actually the case that the number of square (finite) numbers is the same as the number of (finite) numbers'.[14] What makes this 'actually the case', we are entitled to ask, as against Galileo's conclusion that 'equal to' is not applicable to the number of numbers and the number of squares?

According to some philosophical mathematicians, commonsense thinkers (as well as mathematicians who might side either with Leibniz or with Galileo) have been taken in by the maxim that if the elements of one set α are some only of all the elements of another set β, then α has fewer elements than β has and β more elements than α. Russell writes:[15]

> This maxim is true of finite numbers. For example, Englishmen are only some among Europeans, and there are fewer Englishmen than Europeans. But when we come to infinite numbers this is no longer true. This breakdown of the maxim gives us the precise definition of infinity. A collection of terms is infinite when it contains as parts other collections which have just as many terms as it has. If you can take away some of the terms of a collection, without diminishing the number of terms, then there are an infinite number of terms in the collection. For example, there are just as many even numbers as there are numbers altogether, since every number can be doubled. This may be seen by putting odd and even numbers in one row, and even numbers alone in a row below:
>
> 1,2,3,4,5, *ad infinitum*
> 2,4,6,8,10, *ad infinitum*.
>
> There are obviously just as many numbers in the row below as in the row above, because there is one below for each one above. This property which was formerly thought to be self-contradictory, is now transformed into a harmless definition of infinity, and shows, in the above case, that the number of finite numbers is infinite.

The idea this passage tends to produce in one's mind is that a popular belief is being exposed as nothing more than a superstition, that a plain fact is being stated, and that something is being shown. Thus, the phrases 'breakdown of a maxim', 'there are obviously just as many even numbers as both odd and even numbers', 'shows that the number of finite numbers is infinite' create the impression that a proposition is being upset and that a truth about infinite sets is being held up. Parenthetically, it is worth noticing that Galileo's claim that 'equal to' does not apply to infinities is pushed aside with the words 'there are obviously just as many . . .'. Galileo certainly was not unaware of the obvious fact that every number has a square, in the face of which he held his own view. If we can ward off the hypnotic effect of Russell's words, supported as they appear to be by the actual transfinite arithmetic developed by Cantor and others, what we see is not that a position is being shown true and rival positions false. What we see, at first glance at least, is that one position is being arbitrarily embraced and that rival positions, rather than being shown false, are simply dismissed. What is called the 'breakdown' of a commonly accepted maxim turns out to be merely a rejection. And we may wonder what the nature of the 'transformation' is which consists of changing a property that is thought by some to be self-contradictory into 'a harmless definition of infinity'.

Russell speaks of 'those who cling obstinately to the prejudices instilled by the arithmetic learnt in childhood'.[16] And R. L. Wilder tries to reassure those who may feel uneasy about the notion of actual infinite numbers that the symbol '$\aleph_0$' for the first transfinite number will with practice come to have 'the same significance for us as the number 15, for example'.[17] If we take into account the difference between numbers and the numerals which denote them, or between symbols and their meanings (to which Wilder himself calls attention),[18] then what we are being assured about is that with practice we will think of '$\aleph_0$' as the name of a number, or, better, that along with '15' we will come to think of '$\aleph_0$' as a numeral. The idea which cannot fail to cross one's mind is that Cantor christened the infinite and that followers of his are trying to assure us that there really is an infant. The question is whether '$\aleph_0$' *is* a cardinal number, one which gives the *size* of a collection, and whether the *actual use* of '$\aleph_0$' is to denote a number which in any way is comparable to the number 15.

As is known, not all mathematicians accept the notion of a consummated infinite. One mathematician has described an opposing position in the following way: 'Some intuitionists would say that arbitrarily large numbers can perhaps be constructed by pure intuition, but not the set of all natural numbers'.[19] A metaphysical haze surrounds talk of 'constructing numbers in pure intuition', but undoubtedly what it comes down to is talk about the ability to think of various numbers. Some people are able to think of greater numbers of objects than are others. Some arithmetical prodigies are able to do enormous multiplications in their heads, and probably can consciously and all at once entertain a large array of natural numbers. But no one, according to the intuitionist claim, has the capacity for presenting to himself the set of all natural numbers. Wilder writes:[20]

If we analyze the psychology of the 'intuitive meaning' of the number 2, we shall probably conclude that '2 apples' brings up to the mind of the hearer an image of a *pair*, here a pair of apples. A similar remark might hold for the phrase '20 apples'; but it would hardly hold for '200 apples'. From the psychological viewpoint, it seems probable that 200 is simply one of the numbers one ultimately gets at by starting with the numbers whose mental images are distinct – 1,2,3, – and applying consecutively the operation of adding 1, as taught in the elementary schools. (This is certainly the case with a number like 3,762,147; it is conceivable that, owing to some special circumstances of our occupation, our experience with 200 may induce a special intuitive knowledge of 200.) But numbers such as $\aleph_0$ and c are hardly to be attained in any such manner (by adding 1, that is).

The number for the consummated infinity of natural numbers cannot be attained by the successive operation of adding 1. However astronomically vast a number may be, and however out of the question physically it may be to reach it by the successive addition of 1, a natural number can, in principle, be reached by the operation of addition. Aleph-null, however, cannot in principle be arrived at by starting with *any* natural number and continuing to add 1 to it. Furthermore, the cardinal number supposedly named by the symbol '$\aleph_0$' cannot in principle be conceived, or be an 'object of thought'. It is psychologically impossible to imagine a trillion farthings spread out before us, although we have some idea of what this would be like. But we have no idea of what it would be like to have in view an infinite number of farthings. This is because it is logically, not psychologically, impossible to view or imagine an infinite array of objects. The expression 'sees an infinite number of farthings arrayed before him' does not have a descriptive use in the language, unless 'infinite' is used in its popular meaning.

The set of natural numbers, 1,2,3,4, . . ., is said to be countable, but it cannot be run through, as it forms a non-terminating series. It has been argued that it is only physically impossible, not logically impossible, to run through the terms of an infinite series, because it is in principle possible to count off each successive number in half the time it takes to count off its predecessor: supposing 1 takes a half-minute, 2 takes half of a half-minute, etc., then at the end of a minute *all* of the numbers of the infinite series will have been counted off, and the number of natural numbers, $\aleph_0$, will have been reached.[21] Without going into a detailed examination of this argument, it can be seen that since the natural numbers are endless, counting them off would be a task that could not come to an end – *after* which another task might be started. A curious consequence of this argument is that if a minute were composed of an infinite geometric series of time intervals, $\frac{1}{2} + \frac{1}{4} + \frac{1}{8} + \ldots$, then since the series has no end, a minute could come to no end. Furthermore, the entire array of natural numbers cannot be given all at once (as an extension), for if it could be, then in principle it would be possible to run through the entire set of numbers. It is just as impossible to think of all the numbers at once as it is to finish running through them. If the series, 1,2,3,4, . . ., were a 'consummated' series of numbers, then it would be possible to run through them – as it is in theory possible to run through the series of numbers up to 73,583,197,773. And if they could be viewed all at once, as a whole, they could be run through.

It has been maintained that a collection the elements of which can neither be run through nor displayed all at once may nevertheless exist as a complete totality, and in a sense be given. According to this thesis, the succession of natural numbers covered by the expression '. . . etc., *ad infinitum*' form a completed set just as do the numbers up to the expression, and are given along with them but in a different manner. Thus, Russell has written:[22]

> it is not essential to the existence of a collection, or even to knowledge and reasoning concerning it, that we should be able to pass its terms in review one by one. This may be seen in the case of finite collections; we can speak of 'mankind' or 'the human race', though many of the individuals in this collection are not personally known to us. We can do this because we know of characteristics which every individual has if he belongs to the collection, and not if he does not. And exactly the same happens in the case of infinite collections: they may be known by their characteristics although their terms cannot be enumerated. In this sense, an unending series may nevertheless form a whole, and there may be new terms beyond the whole of it.

And also:[23]

> Classes which are infinite are given all at once by the defining property of their members.

Aristotle held the theory of the concrete universal, according to which 'no universal exists apart from its individuals', the Parmenidean implication being that whatever we can think of exists.[24] But this is a philosophical view and has nothing to do with fact. It *is* an everyday fact, hardly worth mentioning, that we can and often do think of what does not exist: it is possible to entertain a concept to which nothing answers, e.g. the concept of a cat with five heads; and it is possible to entertain a defining property of a class which happens to be empty, e.g. the property of being a pterodactyl. A class that is determined by a given defining property ϕ may be null, and entertaining a concept is no guarantee that there is anything answering to it. To say that a class is *given* by its defining property is to say only that its defining property is given; and to say that an infinite set is 'given all at once' by the defining property of its members is to say only that the defining property is given. The impression created is that more than this is being said, but this impression is delusive. Furthermore, to argue that an infinite collection can be known by its characteristics and that 'in this sense' an unending series may form a whole is merely to assign a sense to the phrase 'unending series which forms a whole': the phrase is arbitrarily made to mean the same as 'series which is known by its characteristics'. For example, saying that the series, $1,4,9,16, \ldots$, forms a whole *in the sense* that its terms are characterised by being values of n^2 is to create by fiat a semantic identity: 'forms a consummated series' means the same as 'consists of successive values of n^2'.

There is a further consideration in support of the proposition that an infinity of elements can form an actual class. The idea that there cannot be a completed infinite series is connected with the idea that there cannot be anything beyond an infinite series. The idea behind this would seem to be that there can only be something after, or beyond, a series which forms a whole, and that since a series which comes to no end cannot form a whole series, nothing can come after it. Russell's answer to this is that 1 is beyond the infinite series, $\frac{1}{2}, \frac{3}{4}, \frac{7}{8}, \frac{15}{16}, \ldots$, the implication being that an unending series can be consummated and form a whole class.[25] About the series of natural numbers he wrote:[26]

> every number to which we are accustomed, except 0, has another immediately before it, from which it results by adding 1; but the first infinite number does not have this property. The numbers before it form an infinite series, containing ordinary finite numbers, having no maximum, no last finite number, after which one little step would plunge us into the infinite. If it is assumed that the first infinite number is reached by a succession of small steps, it is easy to show that it is self-contradictory. The first infinite number is, in fact, beyond the whole unending series of finite numbers.

As in the case of the infinite series, $\frac{1}{2}, \frac{3}{4}, \frac{7}{8}, \frac{15}{16}, \ldots$, with regard to which Russell states that 1 lies beyond the *whole* series, so in the case of the natural numbers he states that $\aleph_0$ lies beyond the *whole* series. Since the possibility of an unending series being a whole is at issue, Russell appears to be begging the question. Undoubtedly what he wished to say was that the fact that 1 lies beyond the series, $\frac{1}{2}, \frac{3}{4}, \frac{7}{8}, \frac{15}{16}, \ldots$, shows that the series is a whole; and the fact that $\aleph_0$ lies beyond the series of natural numbers shows that $1,2,3,4, \ldots$, is a whole, or a consummated series.

It is not clear what is meant by 'is beyond' or 'comes after' the whole of an infinite series. It is natural to say that 5 lies beyond $1,2,3,4$; but 1 is not beyond the series, $\frac{1}{2}, \frac{3}{4}, \frac{7}{8}, \frac{15}{16}, \ldots$, in this sense. The only sense in which 1 might be said to be beyond the series is that it is the *limit* of the series in the mathematical sense. We may be puzzled to know why the word 'beyond' rather than the more usual term is used, until we realise that 'beyond' suggests the idea of something finished which is followed by something else, i.e. the idea of one thing coming after another. The term 'limit' does not carry with it this suggestion, although there is a tendency sometimes to think of the limit of an infinite geometric series like $\frac{1}{2} + \frac{1}{4} + \frac{1}{8} + \frac{1}{16} + \ldots$ as being its arithmetical sum, which also suggests the idea of a completed series. But no series has an arithmetical sum whose terms cannot *in principle* be summed up; and this is not the case with regard to an unending series. Expressed somewhat differently, the series, $\frac{1}{2} + \frac{1}{4} + \frac{1}{8} + \frac{1}{16} + \ldots$, has no sum because the sequence, $\frac{1}{2}, \frac{3}{4}, \frac{7}{8}, \frac{15}{16}, \ldots$, has no last term; and this means that neither array of terms is a completed whole. Putting this aside, it can be seen that to contend against the view that 'there cannot be anything beyond the whole of an infinite series' by stating that '1 is beyond the whole of the infinite series $\frac{1}{2}, \frac{3}{4}, \frac{7}{8}, \frac{15}{16}, \ldots$', [27] is not to show that an infinite series is a whole, any more than to demonstrate that a given infinite series has a limit is to show that the series is a whole.

Similarly to say that $\aleph_0$ is 'beyond the whole unending series of finite numbers' is not to show that the series exists as a completed whole. The series, $1,2,3,4, \ldots$, is said to increase without limit, but Russell states that $\aleph_0$ is the limit of the series. He writes:[28]

> The cardinal number $\aleph_0$ is the limit (in the order of magnitude) of the cardinal numbers $1,2,3, \ldots n, \ldots$, although the numerical difference between $\aleph_0$ and a finite cardinal is constant and infinite; from a quantitative point of view, finite numbers get no nearer to $\aleph_0$ as they grow larger. What makes $\aleph_0$ the limit of the finite numbers is the fact that, in the series, it comes immediately after them, which is an *ordinal* fact, not a quantitative fact.

One impression a close reading of this passage is liable to create is that a fast-and-loose game is being played with terminology: a series which increases without limit is said to have a limit, but in an *ordinal* sense; and $\aleph_0$ is said to come *immediately* after the series, although the series has no last term. The number 5 comes immediately after the series of numbers 1,2,3,4. But if we stop to think about it, if we get behind the words, so to speak, we find that we have no idea of what it is for something to come *immediately* after a series which increases without limit. Light is thrown on the passage if we bring it into connection with the assertion that '1 is beyond the whole of the infinite series, $\frac{1}{2}, \frac{3}{4}, \frac{7}{8}, \frac{15}{16}, \ldots$', What comes through is that the series, $1,2,3,4,5, \ldots$, is represented as being like the geometric series:

$\aleph_0$ is the limit of (and is beyond)
$$1,2,3, \ldots n, \ldots ;$$
1 is the limit of (and is beyond)

$$\frac{1}{2}, \frac{3}{4}, \frac{7}{8}, \frac{15}{16}, \ldots \frac{2^n - 1}{2^n}, \ldots .$$

To say that the series, $1,2,3,4, \ldots$, has a limit which lies beyond the whole of it, and that $\aleph_0$ comes immediately after it, induces one to think of the series as consummated. But this is not the same as showing that it is. We might say that this way of talking about the series shows nothing about it, but it does produce a change in the atmosphere.

The symbol '1' denotes a number which is the limit of the series, $\frac{1}{2}, \frac{3}{4}, \frac{7}{8}, \frac{15}{16}, \ldots$; and the symbol '$\aleph_0$' is represented as denoting a cardinal number which is the limit of the series of natural numbers $1,2,3,4, \ldots .$ The question is whether '$\aleph_0$' has, in fact, a use to denote a number, or whether we become dupes when with practice we reach a state of mind in which we think of '$\aleph_0$' as a numeral, like '15'. It has been seen that there is no way in which an infinite number of objects can be given. It is impossible to finish passing in review an infinity of entities, or to arrive at an infinite totality by counting. It is also impossible to envisage an infinity of objects spread out as a whole before us. The impossibility of counting the elements of an infinite set and of arriving at their number by adding them up is theoretical, as is also the impossibility of viewing an infinite array and noting its number, rather than entertaining the defining property of its members. The impossibility is logical, not one which is due to a psychological or a 'medical'[29] shortcoming. Any shortcoming which makes it impossible for us to carry out a task could in theory, if not in fact, be made good and the task brought within our reach. We know what it would be like to do things that are immeasurably beyond our actual abilities, like snuffing out the sun or jumping to Neptune, but we have no idea of what it would be to finish running through an infinite series or to see it as a completed totality. This is because the expressions 'comes to the end of an endless task' and 'sees an infinite totality before him' describe nothing whatever: the terms 'consummated infinite series' and 'actual infinite collection' have been given no application. Their actual use, regardless of the talk surrounding them, is neither to describe a series nor to describe a collection. If the phrase 'the infinite series of natural numbers' described a consummated series, it would describe what in theory, if not in fact, we could run through. The phrase 'finished running through the series, 1,2,3,4, . . . n . . .', would then have descriptive sense, which it does not.

There is no number which is the number of the totality of natural numbers, because there is no such logically possible totality. Russell asserted that 'It cannot be said to be certain that there are any infinite collections in the world'.[30] This observation carries with it the suggestion that the question whether there are infinite collections in the world is factual, to be investigated by empirical procedures. It should now be clear that the question is not a request for empirical information, and the statement that the series of natural numbers is not a totality of numbers is not an empirical statement. It follows that the statement that there is no number which is the number of the totality of natural numbers is not empirical: the phrase 'the number of the totality of natural numbers' does not describe or refer to a number. And the symbol '$\aleph_0$', which supposedly denotes the number referred to by the descriptive phrase, is, unlike the numeral '15', not only not an 'ordinary' numeral, but not the name of a number at all.

It need hardly be pointed out that we do speak of the existence of an infinite number of natural numbers and of the existence of an infinite number of rational numbers; and it would be foolish to deny that sentences declaring the existence of an infinite number of terms and the existence of an infinite series, etc. are perfectly intelligible. How is this fact to be brought into line with what has just been said about '$\aleph_0$', which is represented as denoting the number of their terms? Consider the proposition that there exists an infinite number of prime numbers. Proving it is the same as proving that the hypothesis that there is a greatest prime number is self-contradictory: supposing P to be the greatest prime, then $P! + 1$ either is itself prime or contains a prime factor which is greater than P. That is, the proof of the proposition that there is an infinite number of primes consists of showing that the concept of a greatest prime implies a contradiction, and thus that no number answers to it – just as no number answers to the concept of an integer between 5 and 6. This means that any expression whose meaning is the concept (in the English language the expression 'greatest prime number') has no use to describe a number. Restated in terms of language, demonstrating the proposition expressed by the sentence 'There is an infinite number of primes' is nothing in addition to demonstrating that the proposition expressed by the sentence 'There is a greatest prime' is self-contradictory, and this in turn is the same as showing that the phrase 'greatest prime number' has no use to describe or to refer to a number. The important point to grasp is that a sentence which declares the existence of an *infinite number* of terms in a mathematical series means nothing different from a sentence which declares the *non-existence* of a term answering to a putative description, 'the last number' or 'the least number' or 'the greatest number', and the like. Undoubtedly it was a kind of recognition of this fact that was responsible for John Locke's observation that we have no *positive idea* of the infinite.[31] The sentence 'there exists an infinite number of natural numbers' says the same thing as does the sentence 'There is no greatest natural number'. And the sentence 'There is no greatest number' conveys, without *expressing* what it conveys, the verbal fact that the expression 'greatest natural number' has no use to refer to a number. In other words, the *implicit* import of the sentence 'There exists an infinite number of natural numbers' is wholly verbal and negative, to the effect that a certain expression has no application in the language of mathematics.

It can now be seen why it implies no contradiction to say that an infinite number is not a number, and we can understand why 'when infinite numbers are first introduced to people, they are apt to refuse them the name of numbers'. If we give a moment's thought to Locke's remark that '. . . there is nothing yet more evident than the absurdity of the actual idea of an infinite number'[32] and consult the workings of the language of the infinite, we will see that talk of the consummated infinite is bogus. Wittgenstein made the remark that what the bed maker says is all right, but what the philosopher says is all wrong, and we might now be inclined to think that what the mathematician shows about infinite series, denumerable, non-denumerable, etc. is all right, but that what the philosophical mathematician says about the actual infinite is all wrong. Instead of declaring that what the philosophical mathematician says is wrong, that he is making mistakes, it is more enlightening to think of him as making up a special language game, in which '$\aleph_0$' and other symbols, e.g. 'c', are treated *as if* they are the names of numbers, for the special aura doing this provides for a certain part of mathematics. It is a secure maxim that philosophers do not make mistakes, mistakes to which they are incorrigibly attached. Instead, they play games with language for whatever subterranean value they may have. A mathematician who surrounds his work with a dramatic language-game undoubtedly derives hidden satisfaction from it.[33]

The assertion that an unending series forms a whole, or a completed extension, 'in the sense' that the characteristic of the series is known is an imaginative way of speaking about a rule (whether explicitly formulated or not) for generating terms in serial order, no term being the last that is constructable by the rule. This is what is meant and all that is meant by saying that a series is infinite. The *substance* behind talk of the completed infinite, the actual mathematics behind it, is just the explication of the characteristics of formulas for constructing series. To revert to Russell's talk about finite and infinite numbers, the terms 'finite' and 'infinite' have actual applications only to series, not to numbers: the number 7 is not a 'finite' number, it is a number. A series is said to be finite when a number applies to the set of its terms, as in the case of an arithmetic series, and it is said to be infinite when it is linked with a rule which implies the logical (not physical or psychological) impossibility of any term being the last in the series constructable by it. In its actual use 'infinite number of terms' does not refer to a *number* of terms. And to say that a series contains an infinite number of terms is not to make a statement about the number of terms in the series: 'series which contains an infinite number of terms' means the same as 'infinite series', which in turn means the same as 'series that is generated by a formula with regard to which it is *senseless* to say that it generates a last term'. The likeness between such expressions as 'the number 37', 'huge number' and the term 'infinite number' lies in their 'grammar', to use a word made popular by Wittgenstein: like them it is, grammatically, a substantive expression, but unlike them it neither describes nor names a number.

The grammatical likeness between the term 'infinite number' and terms like 'large number' and 'small number', as well as the grammatical likeness between 'infinite series' and 'finite series', creates possibilities of playing exciting games with language. The idea that this is what mathematical philosophers of the infinite are doing helps us understand the import of the remark that with practice $\aleph_0$ will acquire 'the same significance for us as the number 15'. The underlying meaning plainly is that in time people will enter into the language game and will come to *feel* about '$\aleph_0$' much as they feel about numerals, especially numerals which denote prodigious numbers. The idea that philosophical mathematicians who are concerned to provide a 'theoretical' background for their actual mathematics, who, in other words, wish to have one or another philosophical 'centre piece'[34] for mathematics, gives us insight into the mysterious and continuing dispute between finitists and Cantorians. No mathematical statement or demonstration is actually in dispute. And it gives an improved understanding of the divergence of opinions represented by Galileo, Leibniz and Cantor.

To go to the matter directly, a philosophical mathematician like Leibniz (and a person to whom 'infinite numbers are first introduced') seems to be impressed by the semantic dissimilarity, i.e. the difference in use, between 'infinite number', 'huge number', and like expressions, and unimpressed by the similarity of their grammar. In his opinion, it would seem, the grammatical similarity tends to cover up an important difference in the actual use of terminology. And in play, if not in fact, he 'corrects' this shortcoming in language. He declares infinite numbers to be self-contradictory, which, like the greatest prime and a rational number whose square is equal to 2, do not exist. His argument is that no whole number can be equal to a fraction of itself, and since a whole infinite number would be equal to a fraction of itself, e.g. $\frac{1}{2}\aleph_0 = \aleph_0$, it is impossible for there to be an infinite number.

Galileo, it would seem, was intrigued by the grammar of the term 'infinite number' and came out in favour of treating the term *as if* its use was to refer to a number. Equally with Leibniz, he was aware of the fact that nothing is plainer than 'the absurdity of the actual idea of an infinite number', which is a non-verbal way of stating the verbal fact that 'infinite number', unlike the expressions, 'vast number' and 'the first prime number greater than 1,000,000', does not function in the language to refer to or to describe a number. Nevertheless he chose to group it, artificially, without changing its actual use, with what might be called substantive number expressions. Parenthetically, it is worth remarking that although Leibniz and Galileo give opposing answers to the question, 'Is an infinite number a number?', their answers are not the result of any difference in their knowledge of numbers, which would be inexplicable if the question were a request for information about them. To put it in John Wisdom's way, the question is not a request for mathematical information; it is a request for a redecision with regard to the term 'infinite number', as to whether to classify it with substantive number expressions. The answers represent opposing linguistic decisions, which make no difference to the doing of mathematics and thus can be argued interminably. Treating 'infinite number' as if it is a substantive number expression which gives the number of terms in the series, 1,2,3,4, . . ., generates the paradoxical property of an infinite set that some only out of all of its elements are no fewer than all of the elements. Leibniz claimed that the property was self-contradictory, and thus that the idea of an infinite number was self-contradictory. Galileo took a different view of what the paradoxical property showed about infinite numbers: its possession is *proof* that 'the Attributes or Terms of Equality, Majority, and

Minority, have no place in Infinities, but are confin'd to terminate quantities'. What, according to Leibniz, demonstrates the impossibility of infinite numbers according to Galileo demonstrates that, unlike 7 and 23, infinite numbers are not comparable: the number denoted by '$\frac{1}{2}\aleph_0$' cannot be said to be either less than or equal to the number denoted by '$\aleph_0$'. What can be seen here are not different opinions regarding what is *entailed* by the possession of a certain property, but different ways of marking the unlikeness between 'infinite number' and substantive number expressions. Galileo classifies the term with substantive number expressions, and marks the difference between them by stating that infinite numbers are mysterious, elusive numbers which cannot be compared with each other, numbers over which our 'finite understanding' creates difficulties. No actual entailment-claim is in question. Only a way of marking the difference between the actual use of terminology is being put forward.

Cantor, who according to Russell transformed a property formerly thought to be self-contradictory into a 'harmless definition' of infinity, goes against both Leibniz and Galileo. In his view, infinite numbers are not self-contradictory, nor are they mysteriously different from 7 and 23 and $3^3 - 2^2$ in not being comparable in terms of less than, equal to, and greater than. Two sets are said to have the same cardinal number (Cantor's term was '*Mächtigkeit*'), or to be equal, if there exists a correspondence between their elements. In the words of E. T. Bell:[35]

> Two sets are said to have the same *cardinal number* when all the things in the sets can be *paired off* one-to-one. After the pairing there are to be no unpaired things in either set.

He states that 'Cantor proved that the set of all rational numbers contains precisely as many members as the (infinitely more inclusive) set of *all* algebraic numbers'.[36] He might also have said that Galileo *proved* that the set of all rational numbers contains precisely as many members as the infinitely less inclusive set of all the squares of the rational numbers. There is no reason for thinking that Galileo would have agreed about what he had *proved*. Russell stated that the property of having no more terms than does a proper subset of itself shows a set to be infinite, and that it shows that the number of natural numbers is infinite. There is no reason for thinking that Russell's words would have made Leibniz admit to being mistaken. This is because there is no true opinion and no false opinion about whether infinite sets exist as wholes and about whether the conceptions of *equal to*, *less than* and *greater than* apply to them. What can be seen is that 'transforming' a supposedly self-contradictory property into a 'harmless definition' of the term 'infinite number' comes down to marking the difference between the use of 'infinite number' and that of substantive number expressions. Like Galileo, Cantor classifies 'infinite number' with substantive expressions like 'large number', but instead of marking the unlikeness between them as Galileo does, he marks it differently. Galileo's conclusion that infinities are not comparable (which is a hidden way of stating that 'infinite number' does not refer to a number) results in one kind of mystification. The Cantorian conclusion that a fraction of an infinite number can be equal to the whole number (which is also a hidden way of stating that 'infinite number' is not a substantive *number* expression) results in another kind of mystification. Nevertheless, the claim that the terms 'equal to', 'less than' and 'greater than' apply not only to the natural numbers, but also to infinite numbers, brings the term 'infinite number' into line with substantive number expressions – which makes it possible with practice to come to think of '$\aleph_0$' as having a use like that of '15'.

In the theory of infinite sets some sets are said to be equal to each other or to have the same cardinal number, namely, those whose elements are one-to-one correlatable, as are, for example, the terms of the sets of natural numbers, their squares, and the squares of their squares:

$$1, 2, 3, 4, \ldots$$

$$1^2, 2^2, 3^2, 4^2, \ldots$$

$$1^{2^2}, 2^{2^2}, 3^{2^2}, 4^{2^2} \ldots$$

Some infinite sets are said not to be equal to each other and, thus, to have different cardinal numbers. Cantor showed that the real numbers (roughly, numbers which can be represented by unending decimals) are not one-to-one correlatable with the natural numbers, the conclusion being that c, the number of the totality of the real numbers, is not equal to $\aleph_0$. Not to go into the actual demonstration, he showed that assuming the totality of real numbers to be in an array, it is possible to produce real numbers which are not in the array. Hence, there can be no one-to-one matching of the real numbers with the natural numbers. Imitating the language of E. T. Bell, *after* the pairings of the reals with the natural numbers there will be unpaired terms left in the set of cardinal number c. The fact that the natural numbers cannot be matched one-to-one with the real numbers is taken to imply that there are *more* real numbers than there are natural numbers and, thus, that c is a *greater* cardinal number than $\aleph_0$, just as 9 is greater than 7. The reason is that since c is not equal to $\aleph_0$, it must be greater: $c > \aleph_0$, in contrast to $\aleph_0{}^2 = \aleph_0$. The assimilation of transfinite cardinal arithmetic to the natural number arithmetic, which is characterised by the concepts *equal to, greater than* and *less than*, is impressive. The infinite and the superinfinite to all appearances are tamed to the harness of the 'finite' numbers.

The theory of the actual infinite creates the 'crude miracle' of a proper part of a set being no less than the whole set, and to this it adds the further miracle of an infinity that is greater than other infinities, an inexhaustible that is more inexhaustible than an infinitely inexhaustible. Bell writes:[37]

> try to imagine the set of *all* positive rational integers 1,2,3, . . ., and ask yourself whether, with Cantor, you can hold this totality – which is a 'class' – in your mind as a definite object of thought, as easily apprehended as the class x, y, z of three letters. Cantor requires us to do just this thing in order to reach the *transfinite* numbers which he created.

It will be plain that just as we cannot hold the set of all positive rational integers in our mind as an object of thought (not only not as easily as we can hold a set of three elements but because it is logically out of the question), so we cannot envisage the set of real numbers as a whole. Just as we have no idea of what it would be to apprehend *all* the terms of an unending set, so we have no idea of what it would be to entertain all the terms of a set that has more terms than an unending set. The transfinite numbers which Cantor 'created' are creations of a different kind from what it is natural to take them to be: '$\aleph_0$' and 'c' are *als ob* names of numbers.

There can be no doubt that '$\aleph_0$' and 'c' do have a use in mathematics, although their use, except in semantic appearance, is not to refer to numbers. What their actual use is, as against their apparent use, can now be seen: '$\aleph_0$' refers to rules or formulas for constructing series of terms, no term of which is the last constructible by the formula, and 'c' refers to rules for constructing from sets of terms new terms which are not in the original sets, however large those sets are made. There is no hint of a miracle or of paradox in the fact that for every term constructible by n^2 a uniquely related term is constructible by n^{2^2}, but an exciting paradox makes its appearance when we state that there are just as many natural numbers of the form n^{2^2} as there are natural numbers of the form n^2, or that only some out of all the members of a certain collection are no fewer in number than all of the members. It is interesting, but nothing strange, to be shown, by the so-called diagonal method, that from any array of real numbers a new real number can be constructed which is not in the array, and thus that terms constructed by n^2 cannot be exactly matched with those constructed by the diagonal rule. But there is excitement and strangeness in being told that there is an infinity which is greater than the infinity of natural numbers. The excitement and the appearance of the miraculous are produced not by what is said but by the way it is said. Stating that the real numbers are not one-to-one correlatable with the natural numbers stirs up no thoughts of the miraculous, but saying that the set of real numbers is more huge than the infinite set of natural numbers creates in some people awe and wonder, although what is being said is the same. One way of speaking opens the gate to paradise for some mathematicians, although to other mathematicians it looks like a disease-ridden land. The actual mathematics is the same for all. It is the surrounding philosophical talk, the mathematical theatre, which attracts some and repels others; but the philosophical talk has no effect on the actual mathematics in transfinite number theory.

Department of Philosophy
Smith College

NOTES

1   Cited by P. E. B. Jourdain, *The Philosophy of Mr. B*rtr*nd R*ss*ll* (London, George Allen & Unwin, 1918: 63).
2   B. Russell, *Our Knowledge of the External World* (Chicago, Open Court, 1914: 175).
3   ibid., p. 185.
4   *Preliminary Studies for the 'Philosophical Investigations' Generally Known as the Blue and Brown Books* (Oxford, Basil Blackwell, 1958). This passage is taken from the *Blue Book*.
5   *Philosophical Investigations*, trans. G. E. M. Anscombe (Oxford, Basil Blackwell, 1953: 48).
6   *Our Knowledge of the External World*, p. 216.
7   Italics my own.
8   Bertrand Russell, *Our Knowledge of the External World*, p. 188.
9   ibid., p. 196.
10 *Introduction to Mathematical Philosophy* (London, George Allen & Unwin, 1919: 78–9).
11 ibid., p. 79.
12 E. T. Bell, *Men of Mathematics* (New York, Simon & Schuster, 1937: 567).
13 *Die philosophischen schriften von Gottfried Wilhelm Leibniz*, vol. I, C. J. Gerhardt, ed. (Berlin, Weidmann, 1875–90: 338).
14 *Our Knowledge of the External World*, p. 211.
15 'Mathematics and the Metaphysicians', *Mysticism and Logic* (New York, Longmans, Green, 1918: 86).
16 *Our Knowledge of the External World*, p. 188.
17 Wilder, *Introduction to the Foundations of Mathematics*, 2nd edn (New York, John Wiley, 1965: 87); see also p. 101.
18 ibid., p. 81.
19 Hans Hahn, 'Infinity', in *The World of Mathematics*, James R. Newman, ed. (New York, Simon & Schuster, 1956: 1602).
20 Wilder (op. cit. 101).
21 Russell, 'The Limits of Empiricism', *Proceedings of the Aristotelian Society*, vol. XXXVI (1935–6: 131–50).
22 *Our Knowledge of the External World*, p. 197.
23 ibid., p. 170.
24 *Metaphysics*, W. D. Ross, ed. (Oxford, Clarendon Press, 1908), bk Z.
25 *Our Knowledge of the External World*, p. 189.
26 ibid., p. 196.
27 ibid., p. 188.
28 *Introduction to Mathematical Philosophy*, p. 97.
29 'The Limits of Empiricism', p. 143.
30 *Introduction to Mathematical Philosophy*, p. 77.
31 See *An Essay Concerning Human Understanding*, bk II, ch. 17, s. 13.
32 I may allow myself a conjecture as to one component of the hidden satisfaction. Maimonides said that to study nature is to study God, and this certainly is implied in Spinoza's philosophy. The idea that cannot fail to cross one's mind in connection with Cantor is that to study mathematics is also to study God. It should be remembered that Kronecker declared that God made the integers. It is hard to think

that the idea of the consummated infinite is not in some way unconsciously linked with the idea of God as the consummation of infinite greatness.

33 *An Essay Concerning Human Understanding*, s. 8.

34 Taken from Freud's well-known observation, 'Putnam's philosophy is like a beautiful centre piece; everyone admires it but nobody touches it'. Wittgenstein observed that the philosopher's labour 'is, as it were, an idleness in mathematics'. See *Remarks on the Foundations of Mathematics*, G. H. von Wright, R. Rhees and G. E. M. Anscombe, eds (trans. G. E. M. Anscombe) (Oxford, Basil Blackwell, 1956: 157).

35 *Men of Mathematics*, p. 566.

36 ibid., p. 565.

37 ibid., p. 567.

14

BELIEF AS A
PROPOSITIONAL ATTITUDE

Alan R. White

To believe is to believe somebody or something. Philosophers, inquiring into the nature of belief, have not bothered much about *who* is believed, partly because it seemed so obvious and partly because they quickly concluded that to believe *somebody* is to believe *something,* namely, what somebody says. What has interested them is *what* is believed. *Prima facie,* there are two obvious kinds of candidate for this role. On the one hand, there is what is said, e.g. in people's actual or possible statements, stories, hypotheses, theories, rumours, alibis, etc. – what can, for short, be called a *proposition.* So that to believe the hypothesis that the butler committed the crime is to believe the proposition that the butler committed the crime. These are undoubtedly things we commonly believe. On the other hand, we may believe, e.g. that the earth is round, that tomorrow will be fine, that we have been swindled in the sale of our car, whether or not anything to this effect has been or will be said.

Now Russell, like most other philosophers, usually held that what we believe when we believe any of these latter is the same sort of thing as what we believe when we believe any of the former, e.g. that to believe either that the butler committed the crime or the hypothesis that the butler committed the crime is to believe the proposition that the butler committed the crime. In short, that to believe that p is to believe the proposition that p. Hence, that whatever we believe when we believe is a proposition and any analysis of belief will involve an analysis of believing a proposition.

I have elsewhere[1] argued that this supposition is mistaken, and that it is mistaken because it assimilates two different kinds of answer to the question 'What is believed?'. Here, I want only to show that and how it led Russell into many of his difficulties in the analysis of belief; though lessons drawn from his mistakes can be applied to similar moves in philosophers from various ages.

At most periods throughout his life Russell undoubtedly held the view that *what* someone believes when he believes *that p,* e.g. that the world is round or that there is a life after death, is *the proposition that p* (1904: 204, 218; 1906: 45–8; 1918: 187, 217, 220–6; 1919: 285, 320; 1921: 233, 240–1; 1927: 272; 1940: 79, 119, 142, 160, 168, 179, 235–6; 1948: 98–101, 120,

125).[2] He held this view throughout the many changes in his views about the nature of propositions.[3] Hence, for him, the view that to believe that p is to believe the proposition that p sometimes entailed that believing that p is believing something non-mental, whether this non-mental item is a complex of the things mentioned in, that is, in one sense 'constituents of', the proposition that p (e.g. 1904:.205, 218), or is the sentence 'p' (e.g. 1940: 179, 199, 214; 1948: 98–101, 120, 125) or is the meaning of the sentence 'p' (e.g. 1940: 255). Sometimes it entailed that believing that p is believing something mental, such as a set of images (e.g. 1921: 233–4, 241).

What were his reasons for holding the view that to believe that p is to believe the proposition that p?

(a) One reason may have been a view which he took, especially in his earlier days, of a proposition, namely, as something whose constituents or terms are the people, relations, things, etc. *mentioned* in it rather than the words or images *contained* in the verbal or psychological medium of its expression. On this view, believing the proposition that Desdemona loves Cassio and believing that Desdemona loves Cassio could both be construed as having a relation to Desdemona, Cassio and loving, whether these were regarded in their own right or as the constituents of the proposition that Desdemona loves Cassio (e.g. 1910; 1912). When Russell adopted a more linguistic or psychological interpretation of a proposition, naturally the items to which belief was supposed to be a relation became words or images and not the things symbolised by these (e.g. 1921; 1940).

(b) Another reason for holding the view that believing that p is believing the proposition that p may be simply the mistaken opinion that this view follows from the facts that we do sometimes undoubtedly believe the proposition that p and that the proposition that p is expressed by the same words, 'p' or 'that p', which express what we believe when we believe that p. Indeed, it may have been because the same words are used to express both a proposition and what we believe that Russell sometimes *defined* a 'proposition' as 'what we believe when we believe' (1919: 285, 308).

(c) A kindred reason is certainly an assimilation of the correct point that commonly what we believe is *expressed* or *stated* by a proposition to the incorrect point that what we believe *is* a proposition.

Thus, Russell asserted (1940: 171, cf. 62, 155, 189; 1919: 307): 'If this sentence begins "I believe that", what follows the word "that" is a sentence signifying a proposition, and the proposition is said to be what I am believing.' He even seems to have thought that if a belief 'involves' a proposition, then this is *prima facie* evidence for supposing that what is believed is a proposition (e.g. 1918: 187, 220; 1919: 310). Similarly he argues that when several people *express* the same belief in different sentences, then 'they are all believing the same proposition, though they are believing quite different sentences' (1940: 179).

The fallacy of arguing that because what we *V* – where '*V*' is any verb – is *expressed* or *stated* by a proposition, therefore what we *V* *is* a proposition is clear. Though what is said or denied, stated or expressed may be both expressed (stated) by and equivalent to a proposition, it is obvious that what is, for instance, feared, suspected or remembered, though it may be expressed or stated by the proposition that *p*, is not itself that proposition. To fear, suspect or remember that I left my passport behind is not to fear, suspect or remember the proposition that I left my passport behind.

So convinced, however, was Russell that what is believed is a proposition that such a *reductio ad absurdum* would not, and did not, dissuade him. On one occasion he boldly said: 'It seems natural to say one believes a proposition and unnatural to say one desires a proposition, but as a matter of fact that is only a prejudice' (1918: 218). Nor would he, like some philosophers, have tried to avoid this *reductio* by putting 'believe' into the same class as 'say', 'deny' and 'assert', rather than into the same class as 'fear', 'suspect' and 'remember'. On the contrary, he explicitly added in the same passage: 'What you believe and what you desire are of exactly the same nature.' In short, the strength of his conviction that what is believed when one believes that *p* is the proposition that *p* led him to hold that very frequently what is *V*'d when one *V*'s that *p* is the proposition that *p*. He certainly subscribed to this view for 'desire' (1904: 352; 1918: 218; 1921: 243), 'assume' (1904: 339, 343, 348, 522), 'know' (1904: 217; 1905: 52), 'judge' (1904: 509), 'entertain' (1906: 45), 'expect' (1919: 309; 1921: 243; 1940: 235), 'remember' (1919: 311; 1921: 243, 251; 1940: 235), 'hope' (1921: 243), 'fear' (1921: 243) and even 'good', 'adventurous', 'unwise', etc. (1904: 520–1); though he once expressed some doubts whether it held for 'perceive' and 'will' (e.g. 1918: 218).

Furthermore, the conviction that because one expresses or states one's belief that *p* by means of the words '*p*' or the proposition that *p*, therefore what one believes is the proposition that *p*, led Russell not merely to suggest that when animals believe that *p* they do something analogous to believing the proposition that *p* (e.g. 1919: 183; 1940: 79) but, on occasion, to suggest (e.g. 1940: 179) that they actually believe the proposition that *p*. Nor is he alone in this absurdity. A similar line of argument and assumption has led W. V. Quine to suppose that, though mice don't speak English, it is not wrong, however unnatural, to 'treat a mouse's fear of a cat as his fearing true a certain English sentence'.[4]

It was not until 1948 (pp. 146–7) that Russell seems to have realised that to express or state one's belief in words does not imply that what one believes is those words or the proposition expressed by those words.

(d) Perhaps because 'believe' is a transitive verb, and certainly because 'What do you believe?' is a sensible question, Russell usually insisted that 'when we believe we believe something' (1906: 46; 1940: 167). Often he expressed this insistence by saying that, like knowledge or perception (e.g. 1904: 204, 217), 'every belief has an object' (1904: 204, 219: 1906: 46; 1940: 167). He, therefore, looked for a type of object which all beliefs could have. Since some beliefs undoubtedly have propositions as their objects, he was led to assert that 'a belief always has a proposition for its object' (1906: 48). Furthermore, no other candidates for the role of 'object of belief' would do, since it is always possible for someone, for example, to believe in, or to believe that there is, a life after death when there is no such life. And how could what does not exist be the object of anything (e.g. 1904: 219; 1912: 193)? Naturally, therefore, at those times when Russell became doubtful about the existence of propositions or even certain of their non-existence, he began to doubt whether belief necessarily had any object and even whether there need be any answer to the question 'What do you believe?' (e.g. 1918: 224).

But it should be stressed that this feeling that there are no such things as propositions and that, therefore, they cannot be the object of beliefs did not lead him to doubt that to believe that p is the same as to believe the proposition that p. What it led him to doubt was whether even the statement expressed by the words 'I believe the proposition p' – and not merely the statement expressed by the words 'I believe that p' – should be analysed as a relation between me and a proposition and even whether the words 'I believe the proposition p' is 'an accurate account of what occurs'. So wedded was Russell to the view that to believe that p is to believe the proposition that p, that in concluding that the words 'p' do not stand for the proposition that p he automatically concluded also that the words 'p' do not stand for what is believed (e.g. 1910: 150–4; 1918: 222–4).

Russell's difficulties over the nature of what is believed or the 'object' of belief spring, I suggest, from a failure to distinguish correctly between two kinds of 'accusative' which can follow verbs like 'believe'. I shall call these the 'object-accusative' and the 'intentional-accusative' and, therefore, sometimes speak, purely for shorthand purposes, of 'what (objectively) is believed' and 'what (intentionally) is believed'. What is believed when one believes a person or a proposition is denoted by an object-accusative, whereas what is believed when one believes that p is denoted by an intentional-accusative. Similarly what is suspected, doubted, feared, diagnosed, advised or believed in when one suspects the butler or his motives, doubts a man or his word, fears one's teacher or his temper, diagnoses a patient, advises a trade union or believes in one's political party is denoted by an object-accusative; whereas what is suspected, doubted, feared, diagnosed, advised or believed in when one suspects foul play, doubts someone's sanity, fears the loss of one's reputation, diagnoses tuberculosis, advises a return to work or believes in fairies is denoted by an intentional-accusative. There are several clear differences between these two kinds of accusatives and consequently between the kinds of thing which are denoted by them.

First, outside of philosophy, it is usually only what is denoted by the object-accusative and not what is denoted by the intentional-accusative which is called the 'object' of what is expressed by the verb. It is the butler, not foul play, that is the object of one's suspicion, a man or his word, not his sanity, that is the object of one's doubt, a teacher or his temper, not the loss of one's reputation, that is the object of one's fear, a man or his story, not that p, which is the object of one's belief.

Second, though some *thing* can be what is suspected, doubted, feared or believed in either of these ways, some *person* can be only the object of one's suspicion, doubt, fear or belief.

Third, the intentional-accusative, but not the object-accusative, has an equivalent nominalisation form, 'that p'. Suspecting foul play, diagnosing tuberculosis and advising a return to work amount to suspecting that there is foul play, diagnosing that there is tuberculosis and advising that there be a return to work; but suspecting the butler, diagnosing a patient and advising a trade union do not amount to suspecting that there is a butler, diagnosing that there is a patient and advising that there be a trade union. Similarly believing in fairies amounts to believing that there are fairies; but believing in one's party does not amount to, even though it implies, believing that there is one's party.

Fourth, the object-accusative, but not the intentional-accusative, must signify something which exists. One can believe or suspect that there is a life after death and believe in fairies or suspect tuberculosis, although it is not the case that there is a life after death or fairies or tuberculosis; but one cannot believe or suspect a person or his story unless he or it exists. Hence, to believe the proposition that p implies that there is the proposition that p, whereas to believe that p does not imply that p.

Fifth, when I believe that there is a life after death, that there is a life after death is my belief, just as when I suspect that there has been foul play and diagnose that my patient has tuberculosis, that there has been foul play is my suspicion and that my patient has tuberculosis is my diagnosis, or just as when I fear the loss of my reputation or advise a return to work, the loss of my reputation is my fear and the return to work is my advice. But when I believe a man or his story, neither he nor his story is my belief, any more than when I suspect the butler, diagnose my patient or advise a trade union is the butler my suspicion, the patient my diagnosis or the trade union my advice.

Sixth, what is disbelieved, mistrusted or viewed with scepticism is, and only is, a person or what he says. One does not disbelieve that the earth is flat and that there is a life after death. To be credulous, is to be too prone to believe people and their stories; it is not to be too prone to believe that p and that q. To be superstitious, on the other hand, is to believe in the supernatural rather than to believe stories about the supernatural.

Seventh, just as suspecting the butler, as contrasted with suspecting foul play, is feeling suspicious of the butler, and advising a trade union, as contrasted with advising a return to work, is giving advice to a trade union, so believing a man or his story as contrasted with believing that p, is putting some trust in him or his story.

Russell's conviction that to believe that p is to believe the proposition that p springs from an assimilation of the kind of accusative denoted by 'that p' to the kind of accusative denoted by 'the proposition that p'. Hence, he thinks of *that p* as being what is believed in the same way as *the proposition that p* is what is believed, namely, as the object of belief. He vehemently rejects the view that what one believes in can be a thing, e.g. Homer, because he thinks that this would imply the nonsensical view that one was related to the non-existent (e.g. 1918: 219–20, cf. 1910: 151). But here he is confusing the harmless non-existence of what is denoted by the intentional-accusative with the contradiction-breeding non-existence of what is denoted by the object-accusative; e.g. the allow-able non-existence of the suspected foul play with the forbidden non-existence of the suspected butler. He thinks that the absence of proposi-tions is as disastrous for the reputation of believing that p as it is for that of believing the proposition that p.

(e) Another reason for Russell's interpretation of believing that p as believing the proposition that p – which also reveals his assimilation of the intentional-accusative to the object-accusative – arises from his assumption that belief is an attitude to what is believed. When what is believed is the object of the belief, e.g. the person or proposition believed, this belief may be an attitude to these, as suspicion may be one's attitude to the butler or fear one's attitude to a teacher. Russell, therefore, assumed that there must be something to which belief is an attitude when it is believed that p. And *proposition* seemed to him to fit this role (1904: 204, 339, 523; 1918: 218; 1919: 309–12; 1921: 243; 1940: 18, 62, 79, 145, 153; 1948: 128). But belief is no more an attitude to what is denoted by the intentional-accusative 'that p' than suspicion is an attitude to foul play, or fear to the loss of one's reputation.

Furthermore, just as Russell's conviction that to believe that p is to believe the proposition that p had led him to hold what he admitted to be the unnatural-sounding view that to desire, expect or remember that p is to desire, expect or remember the proposition that p, so his theory that believing that p is an attitude to a proposition went with the analogous theory that assuming (1904: 339, 343, 522), desiring (1918: 218; 1921: 243), knowing (1904: 217), judging (1904: 509), expecting (1919: 315; 1921: 243) and remembering (1919: 311; 1921: 243, 251) that p are attitudes to propositions. Hence he usually calls all these 'propositional attitudes' (e.g. 1918: 227; 1940: 18, 62, 128, 145, 155).

Once again, whenever Russell became convinced that there are no such things as propositions, he felt forced to abandon his view that belief is an attitude. For how can one have an attitude to what does not exist? But that such an abandonment did not carry with it any realisation that believing that p is not believing the proposition that p is clear from the words in which it is expressed. Russell is still convinced that the words 'I believe (wish) that p' have 'the *form* of relating an object to a proposition' (1918: 227). Incidentally, Russell maintained the view that belief is an attitude even when he abandoned the view, e.g. in 1919, that there is an ego to have such an attitude.

There would, of course, be no inconsistency in holding that belief is an attitude to what (objectively) is believed, e.g. people and propositions – which must exist – and holding that it is not an attitude to what (intentionally) is believed, e.g. that p – which need not exist.

(f) Lying below Russell's attitudinal theory of belief is his more fundamental assumption that all verbs, and *a fortiori* the verb 'believe', signify relations (e.g. 1903: 44; 1910: 150; 1912: 195; cf. 1918: 225). Hence, to believe something must be a way of being related to something. Once again, such a view, whether correct or not, would be a harmless enough analysis of believing a person or a proposition, but when applied to believing that p – or to, for instance, believing in fairies – it has the awkward consequence that, since what is denoted by the intentional-accusative of 'believe' need not be, one would, *per impossibile*, be related to what is not.

The avoidance of this consequence depends on seeing that the supposition that it is what (intentionally) is believed which belief is a relation to – which is the root cause of the confusion – is exactly the same kind of mistake as would be a supposition that suspicion is a relation which one might have to foul play or fear a relation one might have to the loss of one's reputation.

Because Russell did not realise that his mistake was to confuse what (intentionally) is believed with what (objectively) is believed, he still assumed that there must be a relation between the believer and what he (intentionally) believes. He, therefore, sought other ways of finding something to which belief could be a relation. In 1910 and 1912 he made the following suggestion. When Othello wrongly believes that Desdemona loves Cassio, since there is no single object, Desdemona's love for Cassio, for Othello to have the relation of belief to, might it not be that for Othello to believe that Desdemona loves Cassio is for him to have a multiple relation to several objects, namely, Desdemona, Cassio and loving, all together (e.g. 1910: 153 ff.; 1912: 193–8)? In 1918 (pp. 225–7), however, he argued that the verb 'loves', unlike the nouns 'Desdemona' and 'Cassio', could not be the name of an object and, therefore, could not occur as an object term for the relation signified by 'believe'. In 1919 (p. 307) he revealed that he no longer believed in a subject who could have a relation to any object. On most occasions, of course, both before and after this, his solution was to bring in propositions to be that to which belief, whether correct or incorrect, is a relation. It was only during his temporary loss of faith in the existence of propositions in 1918 (p. 222 ff.), that his supposition that what belief is a relation to is what (intentionally) is believed forced him to abandon entirely his relational view of belief.

It might be thought that Russell's frequently stated (e.g. 1904: *passim*; 1919: 304 ff.; 1921: 233 ff.; 1940; 1948; 1959) analysis of belief into three components, namely, the act of belief, the content of belief and the objective of belief, shows his awareness of the distinction between what intentionally and what objectively is believed. This is not so. Russell's distinction between the act and the content of a belief is a distinction between believing, which he took to be an attitude, and what is believed, which he took to be that to which an attitude is directed. His distinction between the content and the objective of a belief – or, as he at other times calls it, the 'objective reference' or the 'verifier' – is a distinction between what is believed and what would make a belief in it true. From 1919 to 1959 he almost invariably supposed that to believe is to have an attitude to what is believed and that what is believed is a proposition. In 1904 when he minimised the role of the content of a belief and equated what is believed with the objective, he still supposed that that is a proposition to which belief is an attitude. In 1906 (p. 48) he suggested, with misgivings, that 'a belief always has a proposition for its object'; such a proposition being a fact when the belief is true, a fiction when it is false. In 1910 and 1912 he tried to analyse belief as a relation to the elements of the objective rather than the objective itself – or perhaps the constituents of the proposition rather than the proposition – e.g. to Desdemona, loving and Cassio rather than to Desdemona's love of Cassio which he asserted we have before our mind when we believe.

Russell's distinction of content and objective is not, therefore, a distinction analogous to that between intentional objects such as that *p*, foul play or the loss of one's reputation and objective objects such as a man's story, the butler or a teacher, but between the intentional object, that *p*, foul play or the loss of one's reputation as something believed in, suspected or feared and the intentional object, that *p*, foul play or the loss of one's reputation as something existing. Hence, having wrongly assimilated what (intentionally) is believed, suspected or feared to what (objectively) is believed, suspected or feared as something towards which one has an attitude of belief, suspicion or fear, he had to find some status for it different from the status of an objective or verifier – which he thought of as a fact, an event, etc. The status accorded to it was that of a proposition, whether in the form of a Meinongian subsistent, the significance of a sentence, a form of words, a set of images or even the state of the believer. He then had to hold that what is believed is not that *p*, but the proposition that *p*, that what is remembered or expected is not what happened in the past or may happen in the future, but the present images of what happened in the past or may happen in the future (e.g. 1921: 233 ff.; 1940: 172; cf. the ambivalent position in 1919: 313–14): a *reductio ad absurdum* which, incidentally, is not unlike that to which elsewhere he was led in the shape of the thesis that what we really see are not things at a distance but something in our own brains. Underlying his theory both of belief and of vision is the fallacious argument that because we allegedly have to introduce a certain mechanism, for example, a propositional image or a brain process, to explain how it is that we believe that p or see X, what we really believe is not that p but this image and what we really see is not X but this brain process. Russell's godfather J. S. Mill had already pointed out the fallacy of this (e.g. *A System of Logic*, vol. I, v, p. 1). Russell's failure to see it was partly due to his assimilation of 'having so-and-so before the mind' – which is an idiomatic variation on 'thinking of so-and-so' – to 'having the image of so-and-so in the mind' (cf. 1910 with 1921).

Had Russell realised that what we believe when we believe that p, like what we suspect when we suspect foul play or what we fear when we fear the loss of our reputation, is quite different from what we believe, suspect or fear when we believe, suspect or fear a person or a thing, he might have realised that, even when we are wrong in our belief, suspicion or fear, it is that p itself that we believe, foul play itself that we suspect, the loss of our reputation itself that we fear, and not some propositional or imaginary simulacra of these existing in our mind and towards which we have an attitude.

He might equally have realised that it is the sun and the stars, not events in our brain, that we see. But that is another story.

(g) A different sort of reason for Russell's identification of the 'content' of a belief, that is, what is believed, with a proposition lies in his contrasting failure to distinguish what is believed, namely, that p, from the belief that p (though contrast 1906: 48–9). This is clear from his frequent assertion that for a belief to be true or false is for what is believed to be true or false (1904: 218, 350, 511, 522; 1919: 304, 314 ff.; 1921: 241; 1948). Once what is believed is assimilated to a belief that is true or false, it is easy to suppose that what is believed is a proposition. Furthermore, Russell's frequent identification of a belief with part of what occurs in the mind of the believer transformed the assimilation of what is believed and the belief into an identification of what is believed with part of what occurs in the mind of the believer (e.g. 1919: 309 ff.; 1921: 233; 1940; 1948). The 'content' in the sense of what is believed became the content in the sense of 'contents' or constituents of the belief (e.g. 1921: 237; cf. 1904: 207, 510). Hence, because we can find from examining a man's mind what his belief is, and hence, what he believes, Russell thought that what he believes 'is something now in his mind' (1921: 233–4). But here Russell is partly a victim of the confusion between the interrogative and the relative 'what', which leads him to argue that because by looking into someone's mind one can discover what he believes – that is, the answer to the question 'What does he believe?' – one thereby discovers in his mind what – that is, the object which – he believes. It would be ludicrous to suppose that, if by looking into a man's mind one could discover that what he suspected was foul play, therefore what one discovered in his mind – perhaps an image of foul play? – was what he suspected. In this ambiguity of 'content' of a belief between what the belief is a belief in and what the belief is composed of there is an interesting parallel to Russell's life-long ambiguity in the 'constituent' of a proposition between what is *mentioned* in the proposition, e.g. people and things, and what is *contained* in the proposition, e.g. concepts, words or images.

Whatever the sources of Russell's identification of a belief and what is believed, it is as mistaken as would be the identification of a suspicion or a fear with what is suspected or feared. A suspicion of foul play or a fear of a loss of reputation is not the same as foul play or a loss of reputation. Suspicion, but not foul play, may be correct or unfounded; while foul play, but not my suspicion of it, may cause me physical injury. Fears, but not a loss of reputation, may be healthy or irrational; while a loss of reputation, but not fear of it, may be due to rumours of which I am unaware. A source of the confusion is that what (intentionally) is believed, suspected or feared may sometimes be called a belief, suspicion or fear in the same way that what is discovered, bequeathed or needed can be called a discovery, bequest or need. But this does not allow the assimilation of the belief, suspicion or fear to what is believed, suspected or feared any more than it allows the assimilation of the discovery, bequest or need of gold to the gold itself.[5]

Department of Philosophy
University of Hull

NOTES

1 *Studies in the Philosophy of Mind*, in the *American Philosophical Quarterly* Monograph Series, 1972.
2 The references are given by date at the end of the chapter.
3 I discuss this in chapter 2, 'Propositions and Sentences', in this book.
4 For example, *The Ways of Paradox* (New York, Random House, 1966: 192); *Word and Object* (Cambridge, Mass, MIT Press, 1960: 213).
5 I am indebted to D. R. Cousin, P. T. Geach, P. H. Gilbert and D. F. Pears for comments on an earlier draft of this chapter.

REFERENCES

1903 *The Principles of Mathematics*, 1st edn (Cambridge University Press, 1903); references here are to the paperback edition, undated.
1904 'Meinong's Theory of Complexes and Assumptions', *Mind*, vol. XIII, 1904; pt I, pp. 204–19; pt II, pp. 336–54; pt III, pp. 509–24.
1905 'On Denoting', *Mind*, vol. XIV (1905: 479–93); references here are to the reprint in *Logic and Knowledge*, R. C. Marsh ed. (London, George Allen & Unwin; New York, Macmillan, 1956).
1906 'On the Nature of Truth', *Proceedings of the Aristotelian Society*, vol. VII (1906–7: 28–49).
1910 'On the Nature of Truth' in *Philosophical Essays* (London, Longmans, Green, 1910); references here are to the revised edition (London, George Allen & Unwin, 1966).

1912   *The Problems of Philosophy* (London, Home University Library, 1912); references here are to the 1936 reprint.

1918   'The Philosophy of Logical Atomism' (1918-19), in *Logic and Knowledge*, R. C. Marsh, ed., op. cit.

1919   'On Propositions: What They Are and How They Mean' (1919), in *Logic and Knowledge*, R. C. Marsh, ed., op. cit.

1921   *The Analysis of Mind* (London, George Allen & Unwin, 1921: ch. XII).

1927   'Truth and Falsehood', in *An Outline of Philosophy* (London, George Allen & Unwin, 1927).

1940   *An Inquiry into Meaning and Truth* (London, George Allen & Unwin, 1940); references here are to the Penguin edn (Harmondsworth, 1962).

1948   *Human Knowledge: Its Scope and Limits* (London, George Allen & Unwin, 1948).

1959   *My Philosophical Development* (London, George Allen & Unwin, 1959).

15

TRUTH, BELIEF AND
MODES OF DESCRIPTION

R. M. Martin

In *An Inquiry into Meaning and Truth*[1] Russell attempts, to some extent at least, to come to terms with the semantic conception of truth. Straight away he accepts the Tarskian hierarchy of language, metalanguage, and so on. 'The arguments for the necessity of a hierarchy of languages are overwhelming', he writes (p. 62), 'and I shall henceforth assume their validity'. Thus, as he notes, 'the words "true" and "false", as applied to the sentences of a given language, always require another language, of higher order, for their adequate definition'. If the semantic definitions of 'true' and 'false' are to be henceforth accepted as fundamental, some of Russell's incisive earlier contentions, in 'On the Nature of Truth' (1910), must be somewhat reconstrued.[2] There, it will be recalled, he wrote that

> broadly speaking, the things that are true or false, in the sense with which we are concerned, are statements, and beliefs or [synonymously] judgments. . . . The truth or falsehood of statements can be defined in terms of the truth or falsehood of beliefs. A statement is true when a person who believes it believes truly, and false when a person who believes it believes falsely.

In view of the semantic notion of truth, however, the situation should now be rather the other way around. The notion of being a true or false belief, or of believing truly or falsely, should somehow be definable in terms of the semantical predicates 'true' and 'false' respectively. The last sentence just quoted from Russell would then obtain as a theorem.

Let '*a*', '*b*', and so on, be syntactical variables for the expressions of the object language and let '*p*' and '*q*', with or without accents or numerical subscripts, be variables for human persons. One might be tempted, by way of reconciling these two approaches, to define

(D1) '*p Blvs-Truly a*' as '(*p Blvs a · Tr a*)',

where '*Tr*' is the semantical truth predicate. This proposal makes statements themselves the objects of belief. It is often thought, however, that extensionality is lost sight of if a definition such as this is adopted. For extensionality presumably requires that

(1) (p) (a) (b) $((Tr\ (a\ tripbar\ b)\ \cdot\ p\ Blvs\ a)\ \supset p\ Blvs\ b)$,

and hence

(2) (p) (a) (b) $((p\ Blvs\text{-}Truly\ a\ \cdot\ Tr\ (a\ tripbar\ b))\ \supset p\ Blvs\text{-}Truly\ b)$,

where '*tripbar*' is the structural-descriptive name of '≡'.[3] According to this last, one would believe truly any statement equivalent to any statement one believes. Thus if one believes truly a single statement, he then believes truly all truths whatsoever. Fortunate person indeed! Of this more in a moment.

In the 1910 paper Russell contended that a judgment cannot have a single object:

> If every judgment [p. 174], whether true or false, consists in a certain relation, called 'judging' or 'believing', to a single object [or 'objective', in Meinong's terminology], which is what we judge or believe, then the distinction of true and false as applied to judgments is derivative from the distinction of true and false as applied to the objects of judgments [as in (D1) above].

The difficulty, so Russell contends, is that there is no non-linguistic entity to be the objective of a *false* judgment.

For true judgments, Russell sees no problem:

> So long as we only consider true judgments [p. 175], the view that they have objectives is plausible: the actual *event* [italics added] which we describe as 'Charles I's death on the scaffold' may be regarded as the objective of the judgment 'Charles I died on the scaffold'. But what is the objective of the judgment 'Charles I died in his bed'? There was no event such as 'Charles I's death in his bed'. To say that there ever was such a thing is merely another way of saying that Charles I died in his bed.

Russell finds it 'difficult to believe that there are such objects', as well he might.

It is interesting to note that in event logic the following principles obtain.[4] Let ' $\langle$ *Ch I, Died* $\rangle$ *e*' express that *e* is an event of Charles I's dying, and let '*e* In (*Ch I's Bed*)' express that *e* took place in his bed. Then clearly:

$$Charles\ I\ died\ in\ his\ bed \equiv (Ee)\ (\langle\ Ch\ I,\ Died\ \rangle\ e\ \cdot\ e\ In\ (Ch\ I's\ Bed)),$$

and hence of course

$$\sim Charles\ I\ died\ in\ his\ bed \equiv\ \sim (Ee)\ (\langle\ Ch\ I,\ Died\ \rangle\ e\ \cdot\ e\ In\ (Ch\ I's\ Bed)).$$

Then the last full sentence quoted from Russell in the paragraph above is also forthcoming as a theorem: 'To say that there ever was such a thing is merely another way of saying that Charles I died in his bed.' Russell thus seems to be on sound grounds in his worry concerning the existence of negative objectives of beliefs or judgments.

It is very interesting that Russell speaks of the plausibility of taking an *event* as the objective of a true judgment rather than a 'fact' or statement. Not too much seriousness is to be attached to this, perhaps, for he does not go on to reflect at all on the inner structure of events, on how they are related to facts, on how they are related to other kinds of individuals, nor on the kind of notation needed to handle them.

The way out of the difficulty of admitting false objectives is, for Russell in 1910, to deny

> that [p. 177], whether we judge truly or whether we judge falsely, there is no one thing that we are judging. When we judge that Charles I died on the scaffold, we have before us, not one object, but several objects, namely, Charles I and dying and the scaffold. . . . These objects are not fictions: they are just as good as the objects of the true judgment.

Thus, in sum (p. 181), 'every judgment is a relation of a mind [person] to several objects, one of which is a relation; the judgment is *true* when the relation which is one of the objects relates the other objects [in the appropriate order], otherwise it is false'.

According to this, we may perhaps let

(3) '*p Blvs Ch I, Died, (Ch I's Bed)*'

express that *p* believes that Charles I died in his bed; and if he, Charles I, actually did so, the 'judgment' is true, otherwise false. But what entity, precisely, is the *judgment* here? Strictly there is none, the form containing as terms only '*p*', '*Ch I*', '*Died*' and '*(Ch I's Bed)*'. A judgment is presumably a statement-as-judged, but even a statement is something over and above its terms taken separately. Strictly Russell has no right here at all to speak of a 'judgment', for there are none provided for in the ontology available. He seems in effect to equate a judgment with a statement, but this will never do. The judgment is perhaps the statement-as-judged, and perhaps could be identified with a couple $\{a, p\}$, where a is a statement judged by p. But Russell nowhere makes this identification.

Even so, the three appropriate arguments, in:

'*p Blvs Ch I, Died, (Ch I's Bed)*'

taken in the order given, are supposed to constitute the 'complex object' of Charles I's dying in his bed, provided he really did so, but not if he did not. If '*Not*' or ' ~ ' were available as a constant on a par with '*Ch I*',

'*Died*' and '(*Ch I's Bed*)', the following form could perhaps be introduced to handle false beliefs:

'*p Blvs Not, Ch I, Died, (Ch I's Bed)*'

on a par with (3). Russell does not mention this alternative. Even in 1910, it would have been too Platonic or realistic to admit '*Not*' as a designating constant on a par with the others.

If form (3) is admitted as the fundamental one, we would be tempted to define

'*p Blvs-Truly Ch I, Died, (Ch I's Bed)*'

as

'(*p Blvs Ch I, Died, (Ch I's Bed)* · (*Ee*) ⟨ *Ch I, Died, Ch I's Bed*) ⟩*e*),

and

'*p Blvs-Falsely Ch I, Died, (Ch I's Bed)*' as '(*p Blvs Ch I, Died, (Ch I's Bed)* · ~ (*Ee*) ⟨ *Ch I, Died, (Ch I's Bed)* ⟩*e*)'.

But this would never do. The form (3) is simply too vague, not providing for the *content* of the belief but only for the *objects*.[5] Form (3) can read merely that *p* believes *of Ch I, of* the relation *Died* and *of (Ch I's Bed)*, without an additional factor giving what it is that is believed of them. It is difficult to see, therefore, how Russell's view can possibly be made to work even for the simple (presumably atomic) sentences he considers. Something very fundamental has been overlooked. Unfortunately, also, Russell tells us nothing as to how molecular sentences are handled, let alone ones containing quantifiers.

To reiterate, Russell seems to think that he has provided for the object judged in instances of true belief of sentences of atomic form. Consider 'A loves B', another of his examples. He gives what he calls 'an exact account of the "correspondence" which constitutes truth' of the judgment 'A loves B'. 'This consists', he writes (p. 183), 'of a relation of the person judging to A and love and B, i.e. to the two terms A and B and the relation "love". . . . The "corresponding" complex object which is required to make our judgment true consists of A related to B [in this order] by the relation which was before us in our judgment'. The critique of the paragraph above is, of course, that Russell does not provide an ontology for this complex object. The object A-related-by-love-to-B is nowhere to be found in his official cosmos, even if A does in fact love B.

If the semantic truth predicate were available, Russell could improve his view by bringing in an appropriate sentence as an additional factor. Thus:

'*p Blvs Ch I, Died, (Ch I's Bed), a*'

could express that p believes the sentence a to hold of *Charles I*, of the relation *Died*, and of (*Ch I's Bed*), where the appropriate words of a designate respectively these entities. The notions *Blvs-Truly* and *Blvs-Falsely* are then readily definable in terms of the semantical truth predicate '*Tr*'. And this form may easily be extended to any finite number of entities as the objects of belief, so that

(4) '*p Blvs* $x_1, \ldots, x_m, F_1, \ldots, F_k, a$'

becomes the general form. There are also alternative forms in which a is taken to be not a sentence but an $(m + k)$-adic predicate, that is, an expression for an $(m + k)$-adic relation.[6]

Bringing in a linguistic factor is, in effect, bringing in Fregean *Art des Gegebenseins*. For example, if the linguistic factor a of (4) is taken as a predicate for an $(m + k)$-adic relation, a good reading of (4) is to the effect that p believes that the predicate a is *true of* $x_1, \ldots, x_m, F_1, \ldots, F_k$ in this order. In other words, p believes that the predicate a applies to these objects, or that the sequence of these objects is taken under the predicate or mode of description a.

Note that bringing in the modes of description need not require the abandonment of extensionality. For the principle here corresponding to (1) need not be assumed. One may well believe that a predicate a is true of given objects without believing that all predicates factually equivalent to a are true of them.

Let us now reflect upon the *Arten des Gegebenseins* further by locating them within the vocabulary of either the speaker, the person whose beliefs are being discussed, or perhaps even the person or person addressed. In other words, let us relativise the modes of description in various ways, in keeping with the desideratum of pressing pragmatic factors as far as we can in the study of language. Let

'*p Assrt a, q*'

express that person p *asserts* the sentence a *to* person q. Sentences as such are not of much interest here, but only sentences as asserted by someone to someone. Sometimes the occasion of assertion is relevant also, but this is forthcoming in terms of acts or events. Thus:

'$\langle p, Assrt, a, q \rangle e$'

expresses that e is an occasion of p's asserting a to q, and concerning e we can go on to say whatever is desired, that it was forceful, or tentative, or whatever.

Consider now

'*BR Blvs Ch I, Died, (Ch I's Bed), F₀*',

where F_0 is the virtual-relation abstract '$\{xRy \ni (x = Ch\ I \cdot R = Died \cdot y = (Ch\ I's\ Bed))\}$' and where '*BR*' is the proper name of a certain person.[7] Suppose person p asserts this to person q. This may be expressed by

(5) '*p Assrt 'BR Blvs Ch I, Died, (Ch I's Bed), F₀', q*'.

To capture the significant circumstance that it is *BR*'s believing that is under discussion by person p, it is assumed here that F_0 is a linguistic item understood by *both BR* and p and is, thus, an item within the vocabulary of both. In general, however, this need not be assumed. Person p may well report *BR*'s beliefs in a vocabulary, or even in a language, unknown to *BR*.

To bring out the importance of this distinction, let us consider a form to the effect that such and such a person asserts to someone that Oedipus believes that he married Jocasta. (To simplify, let us disregard pronouns and tenses throughout.) The form needed to express what is asserted is

(6) '*Oedipus Blvs Jocasta*, '$\{q \ni (q = Jocasta \cdot Oedipus\ Mq)\}$' '
and this is usually regarded as a truth of the Theban saga. It is also true of course that

$Jocasta = (the\ mother\ of\ Oedipus)$,

and thus

(7) '*Oedipus Blvs (the mother of Oedipus)*, '$\{q \ni (q = Jocasta \cdot Oedipus\ Mq)\}$''

is also true, at least as asserted by someone other than Oedipus who knows his plight. Oedipus would presumably not say of himself that he believes of his mother that he married her under the description of her being Jocasta; but someone else might well say so. Thus in sentences concerning belief it is important to know whose vocabulary is being used and whose is being mentioned. Thus, in

(6') '*p Assrt 'Oedipus Blvs Jocasta*, '$\{q \ni (q = Jocasta \cdot Oedipus\ Mq)\}$'', r',

the sentence in quotes is couched in the vocabulary of person p, whereas the one-place abstract '$\{q \ni (q = Jocasta \cdot Oedipus\ Mq)\}$' within that sentence is presumably also in that of Oedipus. Note that p *uses* here the sentence to express his assertion but *mentions* the abstract contained within it, this abstract also being an item within his vocabulary.

Presumably Oedipus did not believe – at the appropriate time – of anyone at all the description that he married her as his mother. Thus:

'$\sim$ *(Ep) (Per p · Oedipus Blvs p, '$\{q$ $\ni$ $(q = (the$ *mother of Oedipus) · Oedipus Mq)$\}$'$)$*',

and hence

(8) '$\sim$ *Oedipus Blvs Jocasta*, '$\{q$ $\ni$ $(q = (the$ *mother of Oedipus) · Oedipus Mq)$\}$*' '

and

(9) '$\sim$ *Oedipus Blvs (the mother of Oedipus)*, '$\{q$ $\ni$ $(q = (the$ *mother of Oedipus) · Oedipus Mq)$\}$*' '

all hold. Here the content of Oedipus's belief is expressed in his own vocabulary, whereas the object of his belief is designated in the vocabulary of the speaker either as '*Jocasta*' or as '*(the mother of Oedipus)*'.

The abstract mentioned in the sentences believed will usually be couched in the vocabulary of the believer, but not necessarily. It might rather be couched only in the vocabulary of the speaker. The abstract must, of course, be a predicate that correctly captures the content of what is believed. One may assert in English that a mouse believes of the cat that he is dangerous, without the mouse's knowing any English at all. But still, the speaker will capture the content of the mouse's belief – provided, of course, that mice may be said to have beliefs at all.

The result of these reflections is that sentence reporting beliefs are not to be regarded as true or false *simpliciter*, but only relative to the speaker or assertor or whatever. Thus, the forms (6), (7), (8) and (9) are neither true nor false without reference to the speaker. An assertion of (6) by Oedipus is presumably true in the Theban saga, but not an assertion of (7), whereas both (6) and (7) are true as asserted by someone other than Oedipus. Likewise an assertion of (8) by Oedipus is false, but of (9) true, whereas assertions by someone else of either are true. Thus, a notation must be sought in which this distinction may be captured.

Throughout this chapter, quotation marks have been used in the usual classical sense for sign designs or shapes, not sign events or inscriptions. But only sign events, it would seem, can be said to be spoken or uttered or asserted in the fundamental sense. Sign events are not entities fixed as such but any entities taken by the user to behave as such. Thus, we may now let the expressional variables range over sign events and let

$$p \ (`\sim`) \ a',$$

for example, express that person p takes sign event a to behave as a tilde. And similarly for concatenates. Thus:

$$p \ (`Oedipus \ Blvs`) \ a'$$

expresses that p takes a to be a sign event of the shape '*Oedipus Blvs*'. And so on.[8]

Not only are the entities asserted to be taken now as sign events, but also the conditions or abstracts giving the content of belief. Thus, the various abstracts in the various formulae above are now likewise to be reconstrued as sign events, not shapes.

Let us consider again (6') above, which is ambiguous, depending upon whether Oedipus's vocabulary is being used for the abstract, or only that of person p (the assertor). To simplify, let p now be the poet Homer and let Γ be the abstract '$\{ q \ni (q = Jocasta \cdot Oedipus\ Mq) \}$'. (6') now becomes

(6″) '$(Ea)\ (Er)\ (Homer\ Assrt\ a,\ r \cdot Homer\ ('(Eb)\ Oedipus\ Blv\ Jocasta,$
     $b \cdot Oedipus\ (\Gamma)\ b \cdot Homer\ (\Gamma)\ b)')a)$'

or

(6‴) '$(Ea)\ (Er)\ (Homer\ Assrt\ a,\ r \cdot Homer\ ('(Eb)\ (Oedipus\ Blv\ Jocasta,$
     $b \cdot Homer\ (\Gamma)\ b)')\ a)$'.

Although (6″) and (6‴) have the same truth-value, the following closely related sentences do not.

(7) '$(Ea)\ (Er)\ (Oedipus\ Assrt\ a,\ r \cdot Oedipus\ ('(Eb)\ (Oedipus\ Blv\ (the$
    $mother\ of\ Oedipus),\ b \cdot Oedipus\ (\Gamma)\ b)')\ a)$'

is false whereas

(7′) '$(Ea)\ (Er)\ (Homer\ Assrt\ a,\ r \cdot Homer\ ('(Eb)\ (Oedipus\ Blv\ (the\ mother\ of$
     $Oedipus),\ b \cdot Oedipus\ (\Gamma)\ b)')a)$'

is true. The various notational distinctions here are, thus, of the utmost importance if truth and falsity for reports of belief sentences are properly to be distinguished.

Note that sentences describing beliefs are not in themselves true or false but only as asserted – or, by appropriate generalisation of the foregoing, by utterance, by apprehension, by remembrance, and so on. Also they are always relativised to the assertor, or utterer, and so on. And, further, reports that p asserts to person r that q believes such and such are themselves meta-metalinguistic sentences. The truth predicate for such reports is also within the meta-metalanguage. Thus:

'$Tr\ Asstn\ \Delta,\ Homer$' may abbreviate '$(Ea)\ (Er)\ (Tr\ a \cdot Homer\ Assrt\ a,$
$\gamma \cdot Homer\ (\ \Delta\ )\ a)$',
where Δ is '$(Eb)\ (Oedipus\ ....\ )$' as in (6″),

and so on.

What holds of belief or judgment would seem to hold of all intentional relations. Precisely how intentional relations differ from non-intentional ones is by no means clear. In fact, part of the criterion of intentionality may perhaps be just this need for a meta-metalinguistic rendition, in which both the assertor and the person whose intentions are under discussion, as well as items in their vocabularies, are explicitly brought into account.

Nothing has been said thus far about the person r addressed. In some cases he also should be considered, for assertions are often explicitly phrased with this in mind. *Tutoiement* in French is a case in point, a logical analysis of which requires mention of the user as well as of the person addressed, together of course with a referential account of pronouns.

A simplification in the foundations of the foregoing is in order. We are not, after all, compelled to handle belief in terms of the forms (4) *et seq*. The objects of belief could be dropped and the content expressed by means of a sentence. Thus:

'p Blvs a'

and

'$\langle p, Blvs, a \rangle e$'

might be taken as the fundamental forms. Instances of (4) would then be definable by requiring that the non-logical words of a in left to right order designate respectively certain objects or virtual classes and relations, and that the abstract of (4) be formed from a in an appropriate way. The foregoing is thus simplified, the various forms (4) *et seq*. being then forthcoming by definition.

It is also interesting to note that, for readers not fond of quotation marks, the various forms above may also be given in disquotational form. Thus, in place of

'p Blvs a',

we may write

'p Blvs that- (. . .)',

where 'a' is taken as the structural or shape description of the sentence '(. . .)'.[9] And similarly for the various defined forms.

Russell regards it as a merit of his theory of 1910, 'that [p. 181] it explains the difference between judgement and perception, and the reason why perception is not liable to error as judgement is'. Perception for Russell is never in error, that is, 'whenever we perceive anything, what we perceive exists, at least so long as we are perceiving it'. In

perception (p. 174) 'the thing perceived is necessarily something different from the act of perceiving it, and the perceiving is a relation between
the person perceiving and the thing perceived'. In accord with this we
might let

'p Perc x'

be the fundamental form. But perception is generally thought to be
intentional and, thus, the *Arten des Gegebenseins* for x here should be
incorporated as an additional factor. Thus:

'p Perc x, a'

may express that person p perceives x under the mode of description or
predicate a. Then

' $\langle p, Perc, x, a \rangle e$'

expresses that e an act of p so perceiving x. And, of course, the e is distinct
from x, from a, from p and from the relation *Perc*. Perceiving is of course
very different from having sensations, or entertaining sense-data, or the
like. To handle this latter – should one wish to – very different forms are
needed.

Some readers might object to the seeming notational complications in
the foregoing material. But this would be a philistine objection. The
simple fact is that the distinction between use and mention, and hence
between language and metalanguage, must be meticulously maintained
in this day of sophisticated methodologies, the arguments in favour of it
being 'overwhelming'. Once this distinction is brought in, then we
simply must for correctness use quotes, quotes within quotes, and so on,
correctly. This makes for some initial discomfort but only until the
notation becomes familiar. Russell lamented in 1910 (p. 185) that

> it is one of the reasons for the slow progress of philosophy that its
> fundamental questions are not, to most people [even professional
> philosophers], the most interesting, and therefore there is a tendency
> to hurry on before the foundations are secure.

Confusion of use and mention in one form or another, with the compen-
satory hypostatisation of abstract entities, accounts in part for the slow
progress in recent years in developing secure foundations for the logic of
belief, and hence for the philosophy of mind.

In other writings, e.g. *The Analysis of Mind* (1921: chs XII, XIII),
Russell speaks of truth and falsehood in terms of such expressions as
'positive facts', 'negative facts', 'meanings', 'propositions', 'objective',
'verifies', 'pointing to the fact', 'pointing away from the fact' – quite a

menagerie really. In terms of these he thinks that (p. 273) 'the purely formal definition of truth and falsehood offers little difficulty'. 'For example', he writes (p. 278), 'if the proposition is "Socrates precedes Plato", the objective which verifies it results from replacing the word "Socrates" by Socrates, the word "Plato" by Plato, and the word "precedes" by the relation of preceding between Socrates and Plato. If the result of this process is a fact, the proposition is true; if not, it is false.' Not much clarity is gained by this, however, and the foundations here seem less secure than in the 1910 paper.

One would have hoped that Russell, having flirted with the semantic concept of truth in *An Inquiry into Meaning and Truth*, would have gone on to explore its connection with the epistemological topics that were his main concern. One would have hoped that his final 'attempt to combine a general outlook akin to Hume's with the methods of modern logic' would have included modern semantics under the latter. One's hopes are disappointed, however, and there is no improvement here over Russell's earlier discussions of the purely technical problem of defining 'true' and 'false'.

Department of Philosophy
Northwestern University
and Boston Center for the
Philosophy of Science

NOTES

1   See p. 62 (London, George Allen & Unwin, 1940).
2   In *Philosophical Essays* (London, Longmans, Green, 1910: 172).
3   On structural descriptions, see my *Truth and Denotation* (University of Chicago Press; London, Routledge & Kegan Paul, 1958: 73 ff.).
4   See H. Reichenbach, *Elements of Symbolic Logic* (New York, Macmillan, 1947: 268), and my *Events, Reference, and Logical Form* (Washington, Catholic University of America Press, 1978).
5   On the distinction between the objects and content of a belief, see my *Belief, Existence, and Meaning* (New York University Press; University of London Press, 1969: 74 ff.).
6   This kind of form has been favoured on occasion also by Quine. See especially his *The Ways of Paradox* (New York, Random House, 1966 : 183); cf. also K. Ajdukiewicz, 'A Method of Eliminating Intensional Sentences and Sentential Formulas', *Atti del XII Congresso Internazionale di Filosofia*, vol. V (Firenze, Sansoni, 1960: 17–24).
7   On virtual classes and relations, see my *Belief, Existence, and Meaning*, (op. cit.: ch. VI).
8   Compare *Events, Reference, and Logical Form*, chs. I, II and III, *passim*, and also my *Semiotic and Linguistic Structure* (Albany, State University of New York Press, 1978).
9   See also my 'On Disquotation and Intentionality' (to appear in *Kant-Studien*, vol. 65 (1974): 111–121).

16

THE CONCERN ABOUT TRUTH[1]

Frederick L. Will

In the Tractatus, *I was unclear about 'logical analysis' and ostensive demonstration* [Erklärung]. *I used to think that there was a direct link* [Verbindung] *between Language and Reality.* (Wittgenstein, comment to Waismann, 1 July, 1932, trans., Toulmin, in A. Janik and S. Toulmin, eds *Wittgenstein's Vienna,* 1973)

The aim of this chapter is not to solve the 'Problem of Truth' but rather to locate, elucidate and render more accessible to philosophical treatment a major philosophical concern to which the phrase 'Problem of Truth' not very aptly refers. One of the consequences of increased understanding of this concern is a realisation that its object is not a problem in any common sense of this term. As with our concerns with poverty or disease, peace or prosperity, the object of this concern is not some definite intellectual or practical puzzle for which a key may be found and a definitive solution effected. This characteristic by no means diminishes the importance of such concerns, while an appreciation of it is valuable in promoting realistic, sustained devotion to them. There is no scarcity of problems to be encountered in dealing intelligently with the philosophical concern about truth, and happily we are by no means without resources for dealing with them. But the first need, and that to which this chapter is directed, is to penetrate some of the obscuring dress in which the concern often appears and discern some of its main features.

(1) The career of the 'Problem' – I will hereafter omit the qualifying quotation marks – has some odd and intriguing features. In their anthology in the theory of knowledge, Nagel and Brandt open the discussion of the topic of truth with the following observation:[2]

Although the pursuit of knowledge is often said to be a 'search for truth', those engaged in it are rarely concerned with the nature of the alleged object of their search. Certainly few investigators in the natural or social sciences have devoted much thought to defining what truth is; and there is no evidence to show that failure to do so has been a handicap in the conduct of scientific inquiry.

Similarly, Pitcher begins the Introduction to his collection of contemporary articles on truth with the observation that although the concept of truth, the meaning of the term 'truth' is a concern of philosophers, 'the great philosophers of history [i.e. the great historical figures] said surprisingly little about this concept: they were far more interested in truths than in truth'.[3]

The divergence remarked by these writers between a concern with truths and a concern with truth itself is interesting and bears investigating. It may be suggested at once that the divergence, though real, by no means signifies that the two concerns are not deeply and importantly related. That it no doubt widely seems otherwise is chiefly due to the fact that in much work on the topic of truth the concern represented in it has been misconceived. In consequence, often the means employed in ministering to the concern have ended up by obscuring and distorting it. This helps to explain the frustration one often experiences in pursuing many recent discussions of the topic, the feeling that somehow, though much energy has been expended, the main issues remain untouched, the main difficulties unscathed, and that after all this diligent effort, one is left singularly empty-handed.

Intense cultivation of this topic dates less than a century ago, as Pitcher notes, and was surely in good part a reaction to the then large-scale hegemony in Western philosophy of the Kantian–Hegelian Idealism. It is not too much to say that the concern about truth which was expressed in the lively controversies over the Coherence, Correspondence and Pragmatic Theories of Truth, was aroused by the accusations of critics of Idealism – among whom Russell was a leader – that the theory of knowledge of this philosophy, however illuminating concerning some aspects of our thought and judgment, was extremely negligent and inadequate concerning the primary question of the truth of that thought and judgment. However limited we are in this thought and judgment, these critics thought it important to emphasise, we do pursue truth, do want, among other things, and not least, this characteristic for our allegations or judgments about how things are. We are not content to realise this aspiration only vicariously in the absolute, and not ready to accept for ourselves, in place of it, an ersatz commodity composed of such ingredients as personal satisfaction, public utility and evolutionary success.

The 'Copernican' revolution in the theory of knowledge effected in the critical philosophy of Kant and his idealistic successors was strikingly effective in discrediting one of the central features of the Cartesian philosophy, which was the notion that knowledge should be conceived in terms of what might be called the paradigm of revelation. Whether the means by which the objects of knowledge revealed themselves was the natural light of reason or experience, the dominant view before Kant in modern philosophy was that there is a source or sources of knowledge by which knowledge of things, including ourselves, is given in some direct, revelatory way. At some fundamental stage in knowledge, if not throughout, we know what we were told by this source, and sometimes this source informs us of the nature of things by 'presenting' to us the things themselves, actually ushering them into the forum of consciousness, conceived to be a milieu so pellucid that in it something needed only *to be*, in order *to be known*. Philosophical wisdom with respect to this source naturally consisted in listening, letting the source speak, not permitting our own impulses to anticipate nature, drown out or garble the information accessible to us in this way.

The effect of the Kantian philosophy, when its implications were eventually worked out and accepted, was to install in place of this theory one in which the necessary condition of knowledge is not the suppression but the employment of what we as knowers, individually and collectively, bring to the knowledge process. Knowledge is something we produce, as an artist or craftsman produces artefacts. These are not delivered to him readymade, if he but assumes an artistic or productive posture; nor does he create or spin them entirely out of himself, like a spider. Recognising that what the artist-craftsman of knowledge brings to the process of forming cognitive products is always a mixture of skill and ignorance, deftness and clumsiness, inspiration and delusion, good and bad materials, one sees also that the new theory of the knowledge process requires a new way of thinking of items of knowledge and of what we do when we evaluate candidates for this position. Gone from the new theory was any place for archetypes, disclosed to a passive knower through the natural light of reason or the deliverances of sense. This seemed to have a revolutionay, subversive bearing upon the question of how we should conceive the character of truth as attributed to our alleged cognitions, as indicated in the following line of reasoning. If there are no archetypes which may be conceived as both independent of our cognitive processes and yet somehow accessible to us for the purpose of conceiving and judging the fidelity of our cognitive products – our propositions, judgments, hypotheses, allegations – then the notion of truth itself as applied to these products must be revised to dispense with such archetypes, either in their old metaphysical dress of 'objects' or 'things', or in the new habiliments of 'facts' or 'states of affairs'.[4] Adherents of the critical philosophy in the main were disposed to affirm the antecedent of this hypothetical pronouncement, dissenters to deny the consequent. And when the dissenters emphasised that we obviously do judge the truth or falsity of our cognitive products in relation to some 'objects' or 'items' accessible to us, the adherents agreed, but urged that in order to make the theory of truth fit our actual practice in pursuit of it, we must conceive the judgmental, relating procedure differently. We must conceive of truth as consisting not in a relation between cognitive products

and things altogether different from them, but in a relation between
these products themselves. (And, of course, in a very different
metaphysic, they likewise conceived of the 'products' differently.)

There are various things to be objected to in reasoning like this. Some
hint of its fragility upon critical impact may be gleaned from considering
that although we cannot now see Abraham Lincoln's face and must
derive what information we have about his facial appearance from such
sources as photographs, portraits and descriptions, it by no means
follows that all the information we now have is information about
photographs, portraits and descriptions, and not about Lincoln himself.
Nevertheless many philosophers who found the general philosophical
conclusion unacceptable sought like Russell to escape from it chiefly by
rejecting the epistemological premises from which it seemed to follow,
rather than the reasoning which made it seem to follow. In this respect
Russell's theory of knowledge was literally reactionary in relation to the
Kantian revolution, and Russell did not mince words in characterising
much of nineteenth-century philosophy carrying out this revolution as
an unfortunate aberration.[5]

The controversy over the Correspondence and Coherence Theories of
Truth (and incidentally over the Pragmatic Theory as well) was thus in
good part a very abstract expression of issues raised in reaction to a
certain kind of theory of knowledge. The strong insistence by many
writers that truth must be conceived in terms of correspondence between
our judgments (beliefs, statements, etc.) and some features of a world
independent of these judgments expressed a conviction that in making
such judgments we are engaged in the project of discerning and portray-
ing the existence and character of things, broadly conceived, in this
world, and that our concern for truth in these judgments is a concern for
accuracy in this discernment, fidelity in the portrayal. The general
theory of knowledge to which objection was being made was one which
seemed to many to be on principle negligent of this concern. Within the
confines of this theory it did not seem possible for one adequately to
understand and construe the concern, so that the effect of the theory was,
at one level, a lack of understanding of it, and, at another, to the extent
that philosophical theory in the matter is translated into action, a
lessening of devotion to it in practice.

The basic reason for the inadequacy charged to the kind of theory of
knowledge in question, both the idealist and pragmatic varieties, was the
emphasis in the theory that universally our knowledge of things, our
judgments, hypotheses, and so on, even our very consciousness of matters of which we are most intimately aware, is always a product of a
complex of determing conditions other than, and extending far beyond,
the states of affairs, objects and events we take ourselves to know. The
judgment that a certain state is realised is never produced by that state
alone. Always it represents a result of the confluence of various determinants, which may or may not include that state, and which, even if

they do include it, must be recognised themselves also to affect our reaction in judgment to and consciousness of that state. All this is illustrated constantly and abundantly in the knowledge of material objects we derive by means of sight and the other modes of sense perception. And the resultant question posed was this: if our cognitive apprehension or consciousness of objects, and our representation of those objects to ourselves and others, is conceived to be effected in a variform type of activity on our part, often spoken of as 'judgment', which is generated and formed by such a complex of influences, how can we determine, and, even more fundamentally, how can we even consistently consider, whether there are objects corresponding to our apprehensions or representations of them? It was this sort of question to which Berkeley long ago was responding, in his own idiom of thought, when he maintained (*Principles*, s. 8) that 'an idea can be like nothing but an idea', and that 'it is impossible for us to conceive a likeness except only between our ideas'. A century later the same basic point was urged by those who argued that a fuller understanding of the main doctrine of the *Critique of Pure Reason* led to the conclusion not only that the alleged question of the relation between phenomena and things-in-themselves could not be answered, but also that the question itself could not survive careful critical examination.

A further important consideration in the evaluation of this doctrine was the increasing realisation that the determinants of judgment were not only more complex than was recognised in the *Critique of Pure Reason*, but also more subject to variation from time to time and from place to place, in different intellectual, social and scientific contexts. The fact that these determinative conditions of our judgments display so much variation and are so liable to change, seemed to render intolerable the conclusion that judgments, so conceived, are the sole vehicles of knowledge. For surely truth, conceived as conformity between judgment and objects, is a primary desideratum in knowledge. How could a theory of knowledge be maintained from which this concern in on principle extruded?

(2) One can be sensitive to the force exerted by reasoning of this kind without succumbing to it. Some appreciation of this force, of the way in which a culminating effect of the reasoning was to render problematic the relation between our judgments, thoughts or beliefs and some system of objects and relations, some 'prior and independent reality' (John Dewey's sometimes deprecatory phrase) with which they might be thought to correspond, is essential for understanding what the objectors to the critical philosophy of knowledge were attempting to elucidate and ensure in their theories and analyses of 'propositions', 'states of affairs' and the 'correspondence relations' between these.[6] Furthermore – and this is essential for understanding the matter – one can understand how this kind of elucidation and analysis was bound to be ineffective, bound to fail to minister to the deep philosophical concern from which it arose.

One point of difficulty only in the vicissitudes of the analysis of correspondence may be attended here. If the judgment or proposition that, say, the cat is on the mat, is true, then there must be some corresponding feature of the world, the present situation in the room, or whatever, some state of affairs, which has this relation with the judgment. Pressed by their critics to specify what this feature is, the correspondence analysts typically and necessarily were driven to appeal to the very form of judgment or statement which was under examination, to employ the form, not necessarily to make a judgment, but to formulate and refer to one in some mode of indirect discourse. What corresponds to the proposition 'The cat is on the mat' and makes it true, if it is true, is the state of affairs that the cat is on the mat, and the same holds correspondingly of the states of affairs to be specified in believing or stating that Desdemona loves Cassio or that Mary is baking pies now. Of course, this is all too easy. In speaking in this way we are saying what we were instructed to say when we learned the formula to the effect that p is true if, and only if, p. What the formula expresses is incontestable, and not negligible. But on the matter at hand it is not helpful, valuable as it may be for some purposes, to have a firm grasp of the relation between the various linguistic expressions or propositions which is codified in this equivalence formula. What makes the proposition true that the number 5 is prime is the state of affairs of the number 5 being prime; and what makes the proposition true that God is three persons in one, if it is true, is presumably just that state of affairs, whatever it is. As a way of proceeding to elucidate the corresponding state of affairs in the case of true propositions, this easy way was thoroughly unsatisfactory. It was very questionable whether the change of linguistic mode was sufficient to specify so rich a set of entities, having just the characteristics desired; and the entities, if specified, seemed to cry for the application of Ockham's Razor. So F. P. Ramsey early, and P. F. Strawson later and in more detail, noting certain parasitic and idle features of philosophical truth theory, proposed a view of our locutions about truth in which the principal function of saying of a certain statement that it is true was not to speak about the relation between the statement and some putative corresponding state, but rather to assume and express towards the statement, on the part of the speaker or any others for whom he presumed to speak, a confirming, endorsing, conceding attitude.[7] And John Austin, though himself convinced of the fundamental rightness of the notion of correspondence for the purpose of elucidating truth language, warned against the tendency of philosophers, to which the Ramsey–Strawson view seemed an extreme and mistaken reaction, to indulge, when speaking of truth, in the linguistic production of dubious entities. Here the twin dangers are, he said, that 'we suppose that there is nothing there but the true statement itself, nothing to which it corresponds, or else we populate the world [and indeed "grossly overpopulate it"] with linguistic *Doppelgänger*'.[8]

Confronted by the challenge to specify what is the state of affairs which makes it true that the cat is on the mat or that Charles I died on the scaffold, what indeed could one do? The dilemma was very much as Austin estimated it: a hard choice between the linguistic conjuration of dubious entities, or a secure theory that afforded relief from the metaphysical extravagance, but at perhaps too high a price. Was there as Austin put it, 'nothing there but the true statement itself, nothing to which it corresponds'? If the project of specifying states of affairs is the consequence of a judgment that there is 'something there'; if success in this project is necessary before one can consistently maintain that ascription of truth to our judgments conveys not just that these are judgments we are led by various considerations and for various purposes to make, but that they do capture and convey how things are; then perhaps our commonsense inclination to think that there is something there is just some form of transcendental illusion. But is that project so closely connected with the theory? Austin himself thought not, and tried to elucidate the matter of statement, fact and the correspondence relation between them in terms of historical acts of stating, historical situations, and demonstrative and descriptive conventions binding specific acts with specific situations.

Much of the criticism which Strawson made of Austin's efforts in this project is persuasive.[9] Strawson argued also that some of the major defects in Austin's account were due to the fact that, setting out to deal with one topic, Austin ended up treating another. The criticism advanced here of attempts generally to elucidate the concern about truth expressed in the Correspondence Theory is similar. In the exercise of identifying judgments or statements, facts or states of affairs, and a correspondence relation between these types of entities, carried on early and late by Russell, Austin and others, the project of dealing with the basic concern from which the theory derived had somehow miscarried. The attempts which regularly led to the introduction of various kinds of dubious entities were well intentioned; behind them lay a legitimate concern. We shall be poorer in our understanding of human knowledge if we permit our proper scepticism of these entities to obscure and cause us to neglect the concern from which they arose.

(3) One may properly react to Russell's early discussion of truth in *The Problems of Philosophy* with doubt that much more is known after the truth or falsehood of Othello's judgment that Desdemona loves Cassio has been explained in terms of the correspondence between the complex composed of Othello, Desdemona, loving and Cassio – namely the judgment itself – and another complex composed of Desdemona, loving and Cassio 'in the same order'. Surely a good bit, perhaps all, of what Russell is saying is that if Othello judges that Desdemona loves Cassio, he judges truly if, and only if, Desdemona loves Cassio. What is said is a philosophical truism. But behind and expressing itself inadequately in

this truism appears to be a deep philosophical concern with entities like Othello's belief or judgment, which are by no means figments of philosophical imagination, and things, circumstances, states or whatever to which they have to be closely related if they are to be beliefs or judgments at all, and further, if they are to be true.

There seems to be more here than an impulse, to which Russell was inclined less than many philosophical writers, to make two linguistic phrases grow where only one grew before. Behind our natural impulse to say with Russell that what makes the judgment about Desdemona true, if it is true, is the complex composed in a certain way of Desdemona, loving and Cassio, i.e. the state of affairs of Desdemona loving Cassio, is an intention to emphasise, as Russell himself indicates, that necessary to the truth of the judgment is the existence in some frame of reference (here Shakespeare's play) of a woman named 'Desdemona' and also an affection, relation, attachment on her part for a man – not a dog, a horse or a variety of sweet wine – named 'Cassio'.

Obviously what is being identified here as the concern about truth is a very old concern, one that has been primary in philosophy throughout its history in the Western world. The view attributed to Thales, the bold speculation that water was the principle or substance of all things, implies at once that when we say that the traveller perished in the desert for lack of water, our way of speaking in some respect does not reflect the actual situation as well as we conceivably might, since surrounded by the sand the traveller, though dying for water to drink, was as surrounded by water in some form as completely as the Ancient Mariner. Similarly Democritus, as reported by Sextus Empiricus, said that 'by convention' there is sweet, there is bitter, and hot, and cold, and similarly colour, 'but in truth there exist atoms in the void'. Among many of the early writers discussing primary and secondary qualities in modern philosophy the concern is even plainer. Descartes, as is well known, held that in judging the piece of wax to be sweet or fragrant, we depart widely from the truth if we conceive the wax to be an independent substance having the very characters of sweetness and fragrance which it arouses as adventitious ideas in us. So Locke recommended that we think of the secondary qualities of matter as powers between which and the sensed qualities of colours, sounds, tastes and so on, there is 'no resemblance . . . at all', the qualities in the bodies being nothing but certain modes of bulk, figure and motion which under certain circumstances produce these sensations in us. And so Hume, in his more pronounced sceptical and phenomenalist moods, urged that in careful thought we would conceive causes or powers themselves as nothing resident in the objects to which in common thought and speech we attribute them, but rather as a propensity or habit in us. And so, in less metaphysical contexts, we find ourselves obliged to say that of course accurately speaking what we call the rise of the sun is not a rise at all, but an apparent rise, due to the rotation of the point from which our observation of the sun is made.

The historical facts just cited are but a minute selection from a long familiar story. What is neither so familiar nor merely factual is the construction put upon the facts here, the assimilation of them with the primary philosophical concern which is represented in the Problem of Truth. If this assimilation is correct, the concern is by no means a new one. And the Problem itself is new or especially prominent in recent philosophy, because it arose as a response to a relatively new, sweeping and powerful challenge to the satisfaction of the concern which seemed to many to derive from a persuasive and dominant theory of knowledge. But in speaking thus of an *old* 'concern' and a *new* 'problem', there is no intention to exploit here the vagueness of principles of individuation applied to philosophical problems, nor to advance a case which derives its plausibility from a special and idiosyncratic distinction between terms. Possibly this way of speaking tends to obscure some important things about the philosophy of truth, for the challenge to the satisfaction of the concern could also fairly be said to have generated a *new* concern. There has been a strong historical tradition of looking at matters in a way that conforms to this latter way of speaking. This is the tradition which sees in philosophy of knowledge from the time of Kant the development of a view which was in a new way 'critical', raising in a newly searching way the capacity of human reason to know reality. Following this way of speaking, the concern about truth merges with the Problem of Truth, and the Problem, that of understanding the nature of truth in the face of a philosophy which in a mystifying way threatened to draw a veil between us and the real world, is one which during most of Western philosophy did not attract the attention of the great figures because the veil had not yet been manufactured.

While adoption of a way of speaking about these matters is not a major concern here, there is a point of doctrine emphasised in one way of speaking which, however one speaks, needs to be insisted upon. This is that the major philosophical question agitated in the controversies over the theory of truth represented a new way of thinking – perhaps it should be thought of as a mutation – about an aspect of knowledge which had previously been the concern of philosophers, though not so perplexing and frustrating a one, because of the prevailing confidence of philosophers outside the sceptical tradition that there were ways of dealing with it. This is not to deny that there were differences of philosophical doctrine concerning the character of these ways. But on the main point the pre-critical tradition in philosophy seems to have been right. There are indeed and have always been ways of dealing with the concern which was dealt with in such an abstract and exacerbated form in the more recently agitated Problem of Truth. The ways are of special but by no means exclusive interest to philosophers. They constitute an *armoire*, a repertory of intellectual skills and methods, of common-sense and theory, which changes as knowledge and methods of investigation change, which did not spring fully equipped from the noble brow of technical philosophy, but which is both an intellectual resource-in-being for that philosophy and a subject of its critical understanding, appraisal and possible emendation.

(4) If the Problem of Truth is understood as an expression of the kind of philosophical concern which has been portrayed here, the fact that few investigators in the natural and social sciences devote much thought to this specific Problem is not odd, just as it is not odd that the great historical figures in philosophy have had little to say about the particular questions which the Problem embraces. The relation of scientists, historians, philosophers, theologians, poets and others to what has been referred to here as the concern about truth, and to the issues met from time to time in attempting to minister to that concern, is an altogether different matter. A scientist busy in the project of discerning and elucidating the conductivity of metals, the features of unsaturated and saturated solutions, or unsaturated or saturated markets, has little occasion in the normal conduct of inquiry (this being one of the things which make it normal) to pause for reflection upon and investigation of the large-scale validity of the composite logical, mathematical, linguistic, experimental-observational, social and historical institution in which he has been indoctrinated and trained and in the disciplined practices of which he is now engaged. But what is normal is not universal. And as some of the historical examples cited testify, there are many occasions in the development of the institutions of knowledge, scientific and otherwise, when the guidance of inquiry, the development of theory and the design of observation and experiment wait upon, demand, just this kind of philosophical investigation. This may be carried out, as in the past, sometimes by persons whom we should naturally call 'scientists', such as Galileo, Gilbert and Newton, and at other times by those whom we more naturally think of as philosophers, such as Descartes, Hobbes and Locke, their work illustrating that, as Émile Meyerson put it, ontology is an integral part of (*fait corps avec*) science itself and cannot be separated from it.[10] All these scientist-philosophers, or philosopher-scientists, were alert to some aspects of the question, not whether truth should be 'defined' as coherence or correspondence or what not, but whether and how the system of thought and judgment in which they and others were operating could be made to respond more sensitively and reflect more accurately the nature of the objects, events, states or whatever it was that seemed to be expressing itself in the phenomena which were at the focus of attention. This same concern was not neglected, but robustly cultivated by the great ancient and modern philosophers: think, for but one example, of the Cave, the Line and the Forms in Plato. What most of these philosophers, Plato again, or Aristotle, or Descartes, or Locke, did not have was the problem of squaring their concern with a complex theory of knowledge and mind, such as was developed in the nineteenth century and seemed radically to subvert it. Thus, Descartes judged that

once clearness and distinctness had been achieved in our ideas, the only substantial reason for doubting the capacity of these ideas to serve as vehicles of knowledge lay in the possibility of the ideas being implanted in us by a malevolent jinni. Even Locke, who disagreed with Descartes concerning the possibility of our developing a science of necessary truths concerning bodies, did not question our capacity to develop 'real' ideas of bodies, that is, ideas which so far as they went, did 'agree with the real existence of things'. He attributed our incapacity to have a science of bodies to our lack of 'adequate' ideas, this term for him conveying the special requirement that the ideas so characterised represent their archetypes 'completely' and 'perfectly'. Thus, in order to have adequate ideas of bodies, he thought, we should need to be able 'to penetrate into the internal fabric and real essence' of them, from which essences, he supposed, their properties would be deducible, just as properties of a triangle are deducible from 'the complex idea of three lines, including a space'.[11]

(5) The comment on Locke makes this perhaps an opportune place to try further to specify what is central in the philosophical concern about truth and distinguish it clearly from what is not. The question about the cat and the mat, or about Desdemona, or about Charles I, is no simple question about what makes it true that the cat is on the mat, and so on. At one level the answer to the cat question is perfectly obvious; it is the cat's being on the mat that makes the judgment true, if it is true. But if, when we talk in this way, we have a nagging feeling that we are somehow begging the question, are somehow winning a point and papering over a difficulty with an easy verbalism, we should take heed. For at a deeper level the question is about the adequacy of the thought and language (let us, for brevity, talk principally of language: not the words, of course, but the practices with the words) which are exemplified in one or another of these judgments or statements. It is a question about the adequacy of this kind of language to capture and represent real features of whatever it is with which it is engaged, the something (or somethings) which apart from our efforts to capture and represent it obviously cannot be captured and represented, must otherwise remain for us a something we know not what.

When we inquire about the truth or falsity, the correspondence with fact, or specific individual judgments, propositions or beliefs, we are already involved in, employing and presuming the adequacy of a complex system of linguistic practices.[12] To ask about truth, about correspondence, *in such a context*, is to suppose that the language is already so well articulated with whatever it is we are dealing with that judgments can be made, propositions formulated, beliefs entertained; it is to suppose that the articulation between language and subject matter is sufficiently well achieved that such specific questions about truth and falsity *can* be asked. When we form the phrases which we employ to pick out or specify individual judgments we normally without further thought suppose that the linguistic machine by means of which, employing these phrases, we refer, describe, represent, and so on, is already in place, in operation and in order. We suppose that with the phrases and the other appurtenances of language we can, for example, mark off some subject, however minute or vast this may be, which can be discriminated by ourselves and others, and with respect to which it is our interest to express ourselves.

We similarly suppose that we can individually signify a great variety of features which we use in discriminating various subjects, be those subjects as concrete as the homely material objects which form the furniture of our lives or as abstract as political constitutions or logistic systems. And with these means we suppose ourselves able to signify to ourselves and others the presence of selected features in discriminated subjects, so that the cherry does not need to be present to us in order for us to appreciate that it is red, nor for us to be able to consider and say that it is white, or even say that white is the colour of cherries.

When we consider the truth or falsity of Othello's judgment about Desdemona, our judgment that the cat is on the mat, we are already operating the machine, could not consider these matters unless we were. And when we ask if one or other judgment was, or is, true, we suppose that the machine is operating well. And because we suppose this, when we ask what makes the judgment that the cat is on the mat true, we naturally say 'That it is on the mat', 'Its being on the mat' or something similar. Of course, if the machine is operating well, *it is* the cat's being on the mat which makes that judgment true, if it is true. But what if the machine is not operating well? What if the question about judgment and fact is not a question to be answered by operating the machine, but rather a question about the machine, about its operation, or more particularly, about the operation of this particular part of it. Then the echo-redundancy which made us somewhat uncomfortable with our answer is of more than stylistic significance. It signifies that in setting out to provide an answer to a question about the well-ordering of some part of the machine we have insensitively used that very part, in effect begged the essential question. So familiar are we with the operation of the machine at this point, so at ease with its employment, that like much language it has become transparent. As with our eyes, we are more apt to become aware of the complex practices of judgment we constantly employ and rely upon when they display malfunction: when we experience the logical analogues of improper focus, blindness with respect to certain features of objects, or the pathological generation of apparent features of objects or apparent objects themselves. There is no fault, of course, in using the judgmental machine unthinkingly to make judgments, just as there is none in using the internal combustion engine for locomotion without constantly dwelling upon the physical and chemical processes developing the energy which make the vehicle move. It is a fault, however, when, in response to a question about some part of the machine, a challenge of its capacity to perform in a certain manner, we use the challenged part of the machine to produce our answer, thus presuming the very capacity on the part of the machine which was challenged in the first place. And when, having done so, we apply our results to the development of a philosophical view of truth, a natural view to take is that the word 'true' and similar words enable us to do what otherwise would be tiresomely repetitive, namely, confirm (agree, concede, etc.) a judgment made, a story told, without making the judgment, telling the story again.

In setting out to answer the kind of questions about our judgmental and linguistic practices which arise out of our concern for truth, while we may not presume the adequacy of just those features of our practice which are in question, we may, and indeed must, presume the adequacy of others. Otherwise there could be no challenge to meet, no question to answer. The avoidance of circularity does not require one to doubt, or try to doubt, all ways of calculating in order to consider fairly the validity of some; and the same goes for proving, measuring, seeing, and so on.

An outstanding feature of that particular historically occasioned expression of philosophical concern which was the Problem of Truth was the extreme, global character which the concern assumed in this form of expression. This alone is sufficient to account for the intractability of the concern when the attempt is made to treat it in this form. Furthermore, when we are released from a preoccupation with this form, we are freer to recognise, what have been before our eyes all along, some of the less hyperbolic, less intellectually paralysing ways in which the concern continues to express itself, as life, knowledge, language and judgment change, and some of the resources with which on occasion we have been able to deal with the concern in successful ways.

(6) References to the practices of ordinary speech are now less imposing than they were a decade or so ago, and for some good reasons. But recognition of the deficiencies, ambiguities and downright contradictions of these practices should not blind us to the excellence of them when regarded, not as a composite of items of philosophic wisdom, secure and irrefragable in detail, but as examples of an epistemic tool, constantly adjusted to its tasks through myriad, diverse applications, and, though glaringly imperfect in many respects, in many others well-ordered, efficient and sensitive beyond comparison with any putative rivals. When we say that the cat is on the mat, we must recognise that what we signify when we use the word 'cat' and, in particular, speak of 'the' cat, when we speak similarly of 'the' mat, and when we signify that there is now this situation of the former being 'on' the latter – we must recognise that what we signify is liable to so much elaboration, revision and rectification, were there occasion for such, that at times we must wonder how we succeeded in doing what we did in saying this, knowing so imperfectly what we were about. Nevertheless the language is apt, is a

model of aptness. For if we are not able securely to discriminate creatures and objects of this kind, and such elemental spatio-physical relations as one body resting upon another, it is hard to imagine in what system of linguistic practice we can take the nouns and relational phrases to fit their objects and hence to be a reliable guide to the kinds of entities, features and composite states incorporating these that partly make up our world.

Various philosophers, speaking sometimes in the material mode about things, and sometimes in the formal mode about our language, have urged, in effect, that whatever metaphysical wisdom we can attain must be a development of the metaphysic already contained in our commonsense language of the portions of the world with which we are intimately concerned: the material objects we deal with, other living things, other creatures and other persons. Some have gone so far as to suggest that the manner of development must be circumscribed so severely that in it nothing can be added to the original story, the end-product being a way of speaking perhaps more precisely and, for certain purposes, more efficiently, of objects, events, features, already included in the original story. While such a view may be appealing to us in moments of philosophical perplexity and frustration, it is surely wrong, and for a variety of reasons, one of which lies close at hand. That is that our commonsense language and metaphysic are not so fixed as this view suggests, and the causes and motives for change do not all come from the kind of specialised examination that philosophers make of them. They change themselves. Within them are forces which prevent them from remaining static, even if we willed and tried to ensure this.

Once a change has been effected and ratified in extended use, it is sometimes hard to recapture the extent of the theoretical, practical and emotional difficulties from which and with which it emerged. Galileo before the Inquisition, and Descartes taking residence in Holland, are but two of the more spectacular reverberations of the emergence of a way of speaking about a familiar feature of our daily lives which has become a fairly secure part of commonsense if not, for pretty plain reasons, a part of common speech. Though we still speak of 'the sky' or 'the heavens', we no longer suppose, as we do with the cat or the mat, that our phrases refer to a definite physical entity, in this case a dome as physically real as, though vastly more extended than, those of St Paul's Cathedral in London or St Peter's in Rome. Similar in some respects, but vastly dissimilar in others, is the gingerly way in which, when we are not doing arithmetic, but thinking philosophically about it, we treat the noun phrase 'the number five' or even the simple noun 'five'. We can readily understand how arithmetical inquiries, emerging from and always conducted against a background of our commonsense language of objects, easily followed a way of speaking which seemed to imply a Platonic view of numerical objects. On the other hand, reflection upon the manifest differences between the number five, the cat, and the mat, must give us pause, which further reflection may or may not transform into full stop.[13] Similarly, when we began to think of the fine structure of matter, we thought of it as composed of 'solid, massy, hard, impenetrable, movable particles' in respect to these properties similar to bodies we are acquainted with, though vastly smaller and 'even so very hard as never to wear and break in pieces'.[14] When thinking thus we naturally supposed each such particle to have at each moment a definite position and motion. And yet there are now strong grounds for regarding our conviction that this must be so as a metaphysical prejudice, to which we were disposed by the linguistic judgmental machine we naturally and necessarily imported into a new area of inquiry. Whatever may hold for molar objects, and however strong may be our derived inclination to attribute both definite position and motion to the election, there may be no good reason to suppose that there must be relational features of the election corresponding to this attribution.[15]

The time is now past when the term 'animal magnetism', applied to a person capable of producing a hypnotic state in another, could be more than an interesting metaphor. This is not because some piercing metaphysical eye enables us to penetrate the real essence of the hypnotist and determine that there is nothing there corresponding to the term. Rather it is because increased information about human mental processes, including phenomena of attention, suggestion and motivation, enables us to understand better what characters we should ascribe to human beings and how increasingly inapt is the ascription deriving from this apparent importation from physics. Much less settled in the same field of inquiry is how to judge the complex attributions of features to human beings which are part of that tradition of modern psychology stemming from Freud. Does the doctrine that the ego represses the id at the bidding of the super-ego express some sober fact? Is it pure mythology? If not, and if the rich personal characters which Freud's use of these terms often connotes are discounted, what are the features and processes in us which these dramatic stories signify, in at least a semi-mythical way, and in what kind of language can they be represented more soberly and accurately?

Some features of our language and thought which have been of special philosophical interest illustrate well what a broad problem we confront sometimes, what extensive considerations are relevant to the consideration of the aptness of the language and thought to its subject, to the question to what extent substance does correspond to subject, characters to predicates, and so on. In modern and recent philosophy much effort has been expended on the language of 'good' and 'bad' employed in both ethical and aesthetic contexts. One vein in the tradition of ethical philosophy, following a mode of treatment exemplified by Hume, urges that our straightforward use of such predicates in the formulation of ethical judgments easily misleads us into thinking that villainy and dishonour represent qualities in the man guilty of treason in the same way as predicates reporting his height, blood pressure or basic rate of metabolism. Logically prior to the question whether 'good' represents a simple property discerned by ethical intuition is the question whether it is a property at all, and if so, what kind: a question, it may be noted, remarkably similar to that posed by the dictum of Democritus concerning 'sweet' and 'bitter' and 'hot' and 'cold'. This, in turn, is a question which one cannot deal with thoroughly without considering in the end what it is to be a property of an object, what are the kinds of difference which distinguish predicates which do represent features, do in this sense correspond to their objects, from those which do not. This is no inquiry to be carried out in abstraction from the uses of our language and the complex institutions, scientific, ethical and otherwise of which these uses are parts. What can be divined from a close consideration of the syntactic forms, or of the obvious, rudimentary features of their semantic application, must be supplemented by and assimilated into a broad philosophical inquiry directed to achieving a comprehensive and coherent view of these institutions, the practices which they embrace, the ends for which these practices are engaged in, and the results which in them are achieved.[16]

The verb 'think' in the indicative mood requires a subject. This was surely a very minor consideration in Descartes's endorsement of the view that mind should be conceived as a thinking *thing*, though some of his arguments seem to take advantage of this syntactic fact. When we say that the speaker thought for a moment before giving his answer, there is an obvious level of examination at which no philosophical theory is necessary in considering whether what we said is true or false. But there is also a deeper level, some appreciation of which is necessary before one can understand what has been identified here as the philosophical concern for truth in its application to this and various other locutions. At this level we are concerned not with this particular instance of judgmental activity, but with the kind of activity of which it is an instance. We are concerned with the linguistic practice, with the distinctions made in such a practice, and with how apt these aspects of practice are to the subjects with which they are employed, how well articulated they are to features of this subject, what they represent, and how they represent them.[17] Again, whether we may construe the language of 'I think' and 'He thinks' as referring to mental substances is not something that can be divined from the grammar, but must be divined concerning the grammar in an extensive examination of, to put it oddly, of course, how adequate this *theory* of 'I think' is, construed as an instance of the philosophy of mind. This requires, as the evaluation of theory typically requires, an examination of the considerations that can be advanced for and against. The wide range of these considerations embraces many familiar and diverse items in the history of the philosophy of mind, derived from such diverse sources as Plato's *Phaedo*, Descartes's *Meditations*, Hume's *Treatise*, and, more recently, the Carus Lectures of C. J.

Ducasse, Russell's *Analysis of Mind*, Ryle's *The Concept of Mind*, Wittgenstein's *Philosophical Investigations* and Sartre's *The Transcendence of the Ego*.

(7) The activities with which we respond to what has been identified here as the concern for truth are many, various and complex. And, it appears, so long as intellectual and practical life continues, they are interminable. They abound in everyday life, in science, history, and *belles-lettres*, in the technical arts and practical disciplines, and so on. Furthermore, what we actively do, in contrast with what gets done in and through us, without conscious activity on our part directed to this end, represents but a portion, and by no means the only important portion, of the total process of response.

As philosophers, scientists and professors of other intellectual disciplines we are especially concerned with what we actively do. In investigating the adequacy of a domain of our language and thought to capture and represent real features of whatever it is with which we are engaged, we are, of course, at the same time investigating, exploring and discriminating these features themselves. And there is no simple decision procedure – indeed, in the common sense of this phrase, there is no decision procedure, simple or complex – for this activity; there is no universal algorithm for metaphysics. When Lavoisier began investigating combustion, part of his resource was a language-in-being involving the term 'phlogiston'. This term was taken to signify a substance intimately involved in combustion, taken so because at the time it appeared that combustion could best be understood as involving a release of this substance from combustibles. We can now see that those who thought in this way were misled by, as it were, a metaphysical shadow; they mistook the shadow of oxygen, a genuine substance, for a substance itself. For this realisation we are indebted to Lavoisier and others, scientists and natural philosophers, who have thus helped us to understand at one and the same time both what kinds of things there are in the world and what is a more adequate language for speaking of them. At the present time we have a language-in-being in which we take ourselves confidently to refer to persons as agents, as distinguished from their bodies or specific organs of these bodies, such as their brains; and we confidently use predicates to ascribe characters to these agents. But how about these subjects and predicates? Are individual persons independent, real entities in exactly the way that our ordinary ways of speaking presume them to be? How will they appear in any scrupulously careful accounting of the contents of the world?

The concern about truth, identifiable in such examples as these, is a concern about the broad constitutive outlines of our knowledge of the world in the various domains in which we presume that we have such knowledge. So, Russell's concern about the circumstances of the death of Charles I, and the disposition of Desdemona's affections, was a concern about the thorough adequacy of the common features of our language and thought in which we pick out objects or persons and attribute to them properties and relations. Confronted by a philosophy which cast suspicion on just these features, for example, individual substances and persons, it was natural for Russell to express his confidence in them by proclaiming in effect that what makes the judgment that Desdemona loves Cassio true, if it is true, *is* the presence (in the world of *Othello*) of a real being, Desdemona, with a real amorous passion for another real being, Cassio. Though natural, this was preaching calculated to appeal only to the converted, to those already equally confident of the metaphysic Russell was espousing. Others, more cognizant of the significance of his performance, were more apt to be impressed by the facility with which the language, interrogated about its own adequacy, could, like an agreeable Epimenides, be made to endorse its own presumptions.

Two different, though not unrelated, questions were being conflated here. One is a broad philosophical question of the general adequacy of the linguistic and thought forms of which this specific judgment is an example, a question about the adequacy of the categories of substance, accident, property and the rest, in comparison with alternatives. The other is a specific, concrete question about correctness of this one individual judgment, exemplifying these categories, in comparison with other similar ones, such as the judgment that Desdemona does not love Cassio, is indifferent to him, positively dislikes him; and so on. To construe an answer to the specific concrete question as an answer to the broad philosophical one is a mistake of the first magnitude. But it is just this which is being done by those who set out to answer the philosophical question of truth in respect to a given judgment by appealing to those suspicious replicas of the judgment itself, namely, corresponding complexes or states of affairs. At the level of use, a question about the correctness of categories used can hardly be responded to except by reaffirming, re-exemplifying the use. What makes my allegation true that a certain named person is related by the directed relation of loving to another named person is that there are two such persons so related. Except for the aspect of reaffirmation or confirmation, which Strawson emphasised, such an affirmation of truth is redundant, and as empty of philosophical substance as he maintained.

(8) In contrast with the variform activity and response in which over the years the concern about truth has been ministered, the Problem of Truth, to which much attention has been given during certain periods of this century, stands, not as a particularly clear response ministering to the concern, but rather as a philosophical response to what appeared to be a strong and sweeping challenge to the concern itself. This challenge arose not from difficulties encountered in activities ministering to the concern, but in a philosophical view which in a fundamental way cast doubt on the efficacy of those activities and thus brought the concern itself into disrepute.

During the periods of controversy over the Problem, the clash of arms over it tended to obscure the actual responses we make to the concern, including the activities we consciously engage in in response to it, and the results achieved in them. Immersion in the literature still has the power to produce the same effect. Against this, the aim of this chapter has been primarily to pierce the obscuring cloud of controversy and expose more clearly the nature of the concern, and, secondarily, to freshen recognition of some of the activities in response to the concern and some of their results. Far from being fundamentally misconceived, the general human enterprise directed to this concern is a healthy, ongoing affair, in the constitution of which there is no guarantee either of invariable success or unremitting failure. What we can expect of it, as of other human enterprises, is a mixture of such outcomes. On the proportions of these we may hope that philosophical understanding will have some favourable effect.

For the questions which arise in the conduct of this enterprise are on many occasions, and not untypically, of a distinctively philosophical character. Broad considerations of method and substance have to be explored and taken into account in trying to provide answers to them. Rival claims have to be adjudicated, each boasting the sanction of some strongly supported, and sometimes deeply entrenched institution or organon of scientific practice. Issues call for resolution which can be resolved only, if at all, when certain cognitive practices are viewed with others, and, sometimes further, are considered in relation to human activities and institutions which are not primarily of a cognitive character. Reference to these is sometimes helpful, as reference to our practices in dealing with the ordinary objects of daily life is helpful, when investigating the capacity of our language to reveal the existence and character of objects beyond us, to understanding what is at stake in the question of whether what we are discriminating are real objects, independent of our discriminations, and similarly whether the characters we attribute to such objects are not artefacts of our own invention, but ones to which differences in the objects do correspond.

The twentieth century of the Christian era did not begin the concern about truth and the responsive activities to it which have been explored here; nor, D.V., will it end them. Philosophers of differing persuasions and temperaments, recognising this concern, may view the relation of their own vocation to those activities in differing ways. Some may recognise in the vocation no requirement of aptitude for or devotion to these activities. But surely, *pace* Marx, part of the vocation is to understand them.

Department of Philosophy
University of Illinois

NOTES

1   I wish to acknowledge gratefully comments on an earlier version of this chapter by Jack W. Meiland, Thomas M. Robertson, Richard M. Rorty, David S. Shwayder and Craig E. Taylor.

2   Ernest Nagel and Richard B. Brandt, *Meaning and Knowledge* (New York, Harcourt, Brace & World, 1965: 121).

3   George Pitcher, ed., *Truth* (Englewood Cliffs, NJ, Prentice-Hall, 1964: 1).

4   'Wondering at how something in experience could be asserted to correspond to something by definition outside experience, which it is, on the basis of epistemological doctrine, the sole means of "knowing", is what originally made me suspicious of the whole epistemological industry' (John Dewey, 'Propositions, Warranted Assertibility, and Truth', *Journal of Philosophy*, vol. 38 (1941), reprinted in part in Nagel and Brandt (op. cit.: 152–60; passage quoted, p. 157).

5   'I respect Descartes, Leibniz, Locke, Berkeley and Hume, all of whom employed the analytic method. I do not believe that Kant or Hegel or Nietzsche or the more modern anti-rationalists have contributed anything that deserves to be remembered.' Also: 'I regard the whole romantic movement, beginning with Rousseau and Kant, and culminating in pragmatism and futurism, as a regrettable aberration. I should take "back to the 18th century" as a battle-cry, if I could entertain any hope that others would rally to it.' (See 'Dr. Schiller's Analysis of *The Analysis of Mind*', *Journal of Philosophy*, vol. XIX (1923: 647, 645).)

6   'Scientific conceptions are not a revelation of prior and independent reality', *The Quest for Certainty* (New York, Minton Bach, 1929: 165); cf. also pp. 185, 195–6. Dewey's exchange on this matter with Arthur E. Murphy in the Schilpp Dewey volume is helpful in revealing that, at least when directly confronting the issue, Dewey wished to have the emphasis in such a pronouncement put on the 'revelation' part rather than the 'prior and independent reality', i.e. to be interpreted as rejecting the view that scientific knowledge is derived by revelation rather than the view that in science we do attain knowledge of such realities. See Dewey, 'Replies', *The Philosophy of John Dewey*, Paul A. Schilpp, ed. (Evanston and Chicago, Northwestern University Press, 1939: 556–9, 563, 565).

7   Ramsey's views date from 1927; see Pitcher (op. cit.: 16–17). Strawson's 'Truth' appeared in *Analysis* in 1949; reprinted in Nagel and Brandt (op. cit.: 160–6).

8   Austin, 'Truth', reprinted from *Proc. Arist. Soc.* suppl. vol. XXIV (1950) in Pitcher (op. cit.: 18–31); and in Nagel and Brandt (op. cit.: 166–76).

9   Strawson, 'Truth', reprinted from *Proc. Arist. Soc.* suppl. vol. XXIV (1950) in Pitcher (op. cit.: 32–53).

10 *Identity and Reality*, trans., K. Loewenberg, 1930; Dover edn (New York, 1962: 384).

11 *Essay Concerning Human Understanding*, bk II, chs XXX–XXXI; bk IV, chs III, XII.

12 As Josiah Royce urged many years ago, a bushman, in contrast with a mathematician, lacks even the capacity to make mistakes about the properties of equations. *The Religious Aspect of Philosophy* (Boston, Houghton, Mifflin, 1885), ch. XI, 'The Possibility of Error'.

13 An exploration of some metaphysical aspects of our language of numbers and properties (cf. below, this section), utilising the resources of recent Anglo-American analytic philosophy, makes up the major portion of David S. Shwayder's *Modes of Referring and the Problem of Universals* (University of California Publications in Philosophy, vol. 35, 1961).

14 Newton, *Optics*, Query 31; see also *Principia*, bk III, 'Rules of Reasoning in Philosophy'.

15 The existential implications of some aspects of the language and methods of physics, and an illuminating contrast between the 'Logic of Idealization' and the 'Logic of Existence Assertions' in physics, is contained in Dudley Shapere's 'Notes toward a Post-Positivistic Interpretation of Science', in *The Legacy of Logical Positivism*, Peter

Achinstein and Stephen F. Barker, eds (Baltimore, Johns Hopkins Press, 1969: 115–60).

16   Compare, for example, Charles L. Stevenson, *Ethics and Language* (New Haven, Yale University Press, 1943); P. H. Nowell-Smith, *Ethics* (Harmondsworth, Penguin Books, 1954); Brand Blandshard, *Reason and Goodness* (London, George Allen & Unwin, 1961); Arthur E. Murphy, *The Theory of Practical Reason* (La Salle, Ill., Open Court, 1964).

17   Similarly one of the key questions posed by Wittgenstein's discussion of sensations in the *Philosophical Investigations* is not whether the writhing, groaning man who says he is in pain is deceiving us, but rather whether we deceive ourselves philosophically when we 'construe the grammar of the expression of sensation on the model of "object and name" ' (pt I, s. 293). Conversely, the principal question facing the Environmental Protection Agency in the case of the industrial plant charged with polluting the air is not the philosophical one of whether colours or odours are to be viewed as properties of material things (though in analogous circumstances, e.g. in a dispute over conformity to aesthetic standards, the corresponding philosophical question may become pertinent).

17

RUSSELL AND THE FORM OF OUTER SENSE

Jay F. Rosenberg

In his 1911 essay 'On the Relations of Universals and Particulars' Russell, not yet securely entrenched in his logical atomism, is attempting to adjudicate between two ontologies. One of these is a 'universals only' or a 'no particulars' ontology (briefly: an *NP ontology*); the other, a 'universals and particulars' ontology (briefly: a *U+P ontology*).

To explain the difference, and to adjudicate it, Russell invites us to a classical thought experiment. He asks us to consider two separated white patches (of, as one says informally, exactly the same size, shape and shade of white) on a black background. An NP ontology and a U+P ontology tell different stories about the patches. An NP ontology, Russell tells us, holds that what exists in one place (where, in our thought experiment, there is a white patch) is *identical* to what exists in the other. It is 'the shade of colour itself'. *Whiteness twice* is what we have – once here, and once there. Do we also have *here* and *there*? Well, thereby hangs a long tale. Let me postpone it for now.

A U+P ontology, on the other hand, holds that what exists in the two places are two numerically different *instances* of the specific shade of white. The shade itself is a universal and a predicate of both the instances, but is not itself in space or time and, *a fortiori*, is neither here nor there. *Whiteness twice instantiated* is what we have, and, as whiteness is a predicate of each of the instances, so each of the instances will have a subject as well. Thus, we will have two particulars as well or, as I shall put it, two different *items*, each of which is white. It is the two items which are, severally, here and there on this account. The universal whiteness is a *tertium quid*, and it, spatio-temporally speaking, is nowhere.

So we have whiteness twice *versus* two white items. How do we choose? According to Russell, we choose by answering a question about the thought experiment. For we have, he says, a datum: we are 'quite certain that the patches are two and not one' (1911: 116). The question asks for an account of this certainty: 'How do we *distinguish* the two white patches as two?' This looks epistemological, but Russell sometimes equates it with a question in the ontological style: 'What *makes* the two white patches two instead of one?' What controls this equation is a principle of phenomenal ontology: no distinction without a difference. Less aphoristically, epistemological distinctions stand in need of an ontological ground. The two white patches are epistemologically diverse. We can 'distinguish them as two'. This diversity stands in need of an ontological ground. There must be something which 'makes them two'. This, Russell believes, yields a verdict in favour of the U+P ontology. But before we look at his answer, let us look at his question.

'How do we distinguish the two patches as two?' The question is a puzzling one. One is tempted to think of it as the question, 'How do we *know* that there are *two* patches?', but to that question there is only one sensible answer, and it yields no ontological verdict. The answer is, 'We counted them', for it is surely by counting that one finds out *how many* of anything there are. Yet in order to count them, must we not *first* distinguish them? Otherwise, how can we be sure that we have counted them all, or not counted one of them several times? So the question of how we distinguish them is apparently not the question of how we know how many there are. But then what *is* the question of how we distinguish them?

At this point, one may well be at a loss as to what to say. When puzzled in this way, it is sometimes useful to return to the text. Perhaps we can get at the sense of the question by seeing how Russell answers it.

Russell's answer has to do with *spatial diversity*. The two patches are in different places. Now Russell eschews what he calls 'absolute space'. What this amounts to is that we must not include *places* in our ontological inventory of the categories of constituents of our phenomenal world. Of course not – places (and times) are not phenomenal entities. A place will be, although Russell does not explicitly put it this way, a logical construction out of what we call 'the contents of a place'. In our thought experiment, we are dealing with *visual space*. We must not suppose, argues Russell, that an individual object of visual perception (e.g. one white patch) is composed of an infinite number of parts which are by their natures imperceptible. Such a supposition, in his words, 'seems incredible' (p. 114). Hence, it is necessary to posit *minimum sensibilia* of finite extent for visual space. A place, then, cannot be taken to be a *point* (for a zero-dimensional white point would be such a by-nature-imperceptible element) nor to be constructed out of *points*. Visual space does not consist of points but of a 'constantly varying number of surfaces or volumes, continually breaking up or joining together according to the fluctuations of attention' (ibid.).[1] A place, then, must be taken to be 'the extent occupied by a single object of perception' (ibid.). More precisely, 'place' may be defined as the space occupied by one undivided object of perception (p. 115). We count places, then, by counting the objects which, as we say informally, occupy them – one place per undivided object of perception.

This characterisation has some immediate corollaries. It follows, for example, that *two* things cannot be simultaneously in the *same* place. One may wonder if this is true. Consider an altered thought experiment in which a red patch and a white patch, of the same shape and size, gradually come together and appear to *coalesce* or *fuse* into a single patch of the same shape and size but which, let us suppose, is uniformly *pink*. Why should we not say here that what has happened is that the white patch and the red patch have come to occupy the same place simultaneously? Russell would speak here of 'substituting a new immediate object [a pink patch] in place of the old one(s)' (p. 114). Is there anything to choose between the two descriptions? In *physical* space the issue can be fairly clearly joined. If the objects were not patches but, say, billiard balls, the resultant pink ball might have the same size and shape as each of the originals but, for example, twice the *mass*. Such a discrepancy would stand in need of explanation, and the hypothesis of simultaneous co-occupation of a volume of space is an economical explanatory hypothesis.

In visual space, however, we have only size, shape and colour to work with. What stands in need of explanation, then, if anything does, is only there being in the visual field a pink patch, and there seems to be little to choose between describing it in Russell's way as the substituting of a new object in place of the old ones and describing it as the simultaneous co-occupation of a region of space by the two original patches. Yet simply putting the matter in this way suggests a ground for choice. For to opt for the hypothesis of simultaneous co-occupation is to suppose that we can mark the pink colour of the single remaining patch as only *apparent*, the result of the simultaneous perception of co-spatial patches *actually* red and *actually* white over a single region of the visual field. It is to presuppose, in other words, that we can make a distinction between real and apparent colour for coloured patches in the visual field. But, since such coloured patches are, *ab initio, phenomenal* objects, that is precisely what we cannot do. To suppose that we can is to abandon entirely *any* principles of counting and individuation for such objects. For what is to determine that what we thought of originally as a patch *actually* red was not *itself* the product of a dozen or a hundred or a thousand co-spatial patches of various hues, saturations and intensities? Any hypothesis other than the unitary one is gratuitous in the case of the red patch and, consequently, any hypothesis other than the unitary one is gratuitous in the case of the pink patch as well. Nor does it help to appeal to the experiential history of the pink patch, for, considered simply as a phenomenal object, this pink patch is not different from any other. If we can say of *this* pink patch that it is a mere appearance resulting from the co-occupation of a region of visual space by patches actually white and red, then we must at least be able sensibly to offer that claim as an *hypothesis* concerning any other pink patch, which may have no experiential history. And this puts us precisely back in the gratuitous situation which we faced a moment ago. I conclude, then, that Russell's definition of 'place' is thus far borne out. If our 'things' be phenomenal objects (e.g. colour patches in visual space), two things *cannot* be in the same place at the same time.

But what about the converse corollary: 'One thing cannot be simultaneously in two places'? This is the maxim which, properly understood, is supposed to do Russell's adjudicatory work for him. In the end, Russell opts for a U+P ontology. His reason, he tells us (p. 121), is that a particular white patch cannot be in two places simultaneously. This is what *makes* the particular patch of white particular. Whiteness, on the other hand, is a universal, and 'if it exists at all, exists wherever there are white things'.

Now this last remark can only be a slip on Russell's part. For if it *were* true that whiteness exists and exists wherever there is a white thing, then we should have, in the situation of the original thought experiment, whiteness to the left of whiteness, contradicting the maxim that a thing cannot be in two places at once. But this is not a U+P ontology. Russell tells us quite clearly that, on a U+P ontology, a universal such as whiteness is not in space or time *at all* (p. 111). *A fortiori*, if whiteness exists, it does not exist wherever there is a white thing for the simple reason that it doesn't make sense of *where* (spatio-temporally) whiteness exists in the first place.

On the face of it, it is hard to see how the maxim 'One thing cannot be simultaneously in two places' can adjudicate between an NP and a U+P ontology. For what are we going to count as a '*thing*'? Well, in one sense, there is a very straightforward answer to this question: A 'thing' is whatever we are presented with; it is a phenomenal object of the sensory mode under discussion. This observation, however, yields no advance on our original question, for the dispute between an NP and a U+P ontology is precisely a dispute about what the phenomenal objects *are*.

We must ask, in other words, *what it is* that we are presented with, when we are presented with the experience canvassed in the original thought experiment. On an NP ontology, what we are presented with is *whiteness twice*. And how many 'things' is that? It is *one* thing, though twice *presented*. On a U+P ontology, by contrast, what we are presented with is *two white items*. Here we have *two* things, each once presented. On an NP ontology, then, one thing *can* be simultaneously (presented) in two places. And perhaps this is not so on a U+P ontology (although some investigation is called for). But what does this show? At best, it shows that the maxim and the NP ontology stand or fall *together*. But for this reason, the maxim cannot adjudicate the question of the ontology. The determination of the truth or falsity of the maxim, it seems, presupposes that we have a count of phenomenal objects, a count of the 'things' presented. And this presupposes, in turn, that we have *already* settled the question of ontology.

Russell's gambit here is to reinterpret the maxim. When presented with the two white patches, we are also and simultaneously presented with an instance of a spatial relation. One patch, for example, is to the left of the other. What Russell takes to be the sense of the maxim is this: 'Every spatial relation implies diversity of its terms' (p. 115). This being so, that the relation *to-the-left-of* is presented in the thought experiment implies that two distinct 'things' are presented (to stand as relata) as well. The maxim thus interpreted entails a determinate count of our phenomenal objects. This count is compatible with a U + P ontology, but incompatible with an NP ontology. And thus is the question supposed to be adjudicated.

But are we really any better off here? One thing we might be tempted to say is that the maxim, thus interpreted, is straightforwardly false. *Spatial coincidence*, after all, is a spatial relation, yet '*X* coincides with *X*' is true for every *X*. So perhaps Russell meant to say that every *irreflexive* spatial relation implies diversity. In any case, he *seems* to recognise a tension here, for his final formulation of the maxim, in his summing up (p.121), is that *certain* spatial relations imply the diversity of their terms.

Yet this line of argument turns out to be fraudulent. What our earlier animadversions on putative cases of fusion or coalescence have, in fact, shown is that *there is no such relation* as spatial coincidence in visual space. That is, there is no groundable use for the notion of *two* phenomenal objects coinciding spatially. But this being so, the judgment that *one* phenomenal object spatially coincides with itself will have no more *content* than the bare claim that the object exists or is presented. Spatial coincidence becomes, like identity, a 'relation' which an object necessarily bears to itself and necessarily can bear only to itself. In fact, in visual space, there is *no* use of 'spatially coincides with' for which we cannot substitute ' = ' without loss or alteration of sense. But then 'spatial coincidence', so-called, simply *is* identity and, thus, not a *spatial* relation at all but a logical 'relation'. (Not so, again, in *physical* space where, as I remarked earlier, 'spatially coincides with' can have non-idle, non-arbitrary application to a *pair* of objects.)

Still, can the maxim thus interpreted adjudicate our ontological question? Of course it can, but only if it is *true*. And is it? Well, that seems to depend again on what we make of our ontology. For suppose the NP account is correct. Then what we are presented with in the thought experiment is one thing twice. Since we are also presented with the relation *to-the-left-of*, we shall have a true instance of 'whiteness to the left of whiteness' and, thus, spatial relatedness without numerical diversity. The maxim, even thus interpreted, and the NP ontology again appear to stand or fall *together*. The maxim was to adjudicate our ontology, but again we apparently cannot assess the truth or falsity of the maxim until we have reached a decision regarding our phenomenal ontology. I conclude, then, that Russell's attempt fails. We cannot ground our ontological decision on the maxim 'A thing cannot be simultaneously in two places', however interpreted, for the determination of the truth or falsity of the maxim, it seems, presupposes an ontological adjudication. On the face of it, Russell's argument is circular. (Russell himself, by the way, had given it up by 1955, but for different reasons. We needn't go into that here, however.)

Yet our investigations of Russell's argument have not been wholly without value, for we do seem to have stumbled across some deep structural connections between spatiality, objectivity and principles of counting. What I should like to do in the remainder of this chapter is to take a fresh start and attempt to tease out these connections in some detail.

Suppose we begin with yet a third thought experiment in which we find a *single* white patch against a uniform black background. Now I speak here, as I have earlier, of a *white patch,* but, interestingly, this phraseology is rarely found in Russell's discussions (although it does occur in op. cit.: 112). Instead, Russell speaks of 'instances of whiteness', once of 'whitenesses' (p. 116) and, most frequently, of 'patches of white'.

'Patch' is a term which needs some discussion. It is, on the face of it, a *dummy sortal* – on a par with 'piece', 'chunk', 'slice', 'pound', 'gallon', and so on – designed to produce a *count* noun from a *mass* noun. Like all such dummy sortals, 'patch' takes an 'of'-phrase modifier. A patch is always a patch *of* something – oil, water, rubber, paint, etc. – in general, a patch of *M*, where '*M*' holds a place for a mass noun, a term signifying a sort of *stuff.* 'White patch', thus, needs completion: white patch of *what*? In physical space, answers are easy enough to come by: white patch of paint, tape, cloth, and so on. But in a phenomenal space (e.g. visual space) such answers are not available. Physical stuffs are *common sensibles* – paint, tape, cloth, and the like can be seen *and* felt *and* tasted *and* smelled – but phenomenal objects in visual space are visual only. There is, then, a grammatical tension here, and it is this tension which gives rise to 'patch of white' from 'white patch'.

But if the role of 'white' in 'patch of white' is adjectival, as ordinary grammar requires, the phrase is still incomplete. In physical space, a white patch of stuff is simply a patch of *white stuff* – white paint, white tape, white cloth, and so on. 'A patch of white' is, thus, still grammatically incomplete – a patch of white *what*? – and we consequently stand yet in need of a mass noun to get our expression into grammatical shape.

What all this suggests is that in Russell's discussion (and others like it) 'white' is itself being *given* a nominal use. Now 'white' *has* a nominal use in English, but only as a *proper* noun equivalent to 'whiteness', the name of a quality:

White(ness) is a colour.

Colour adjectives are peculiar in this regard. Compare, for example,

Circular*ity* is a shape

and

Bitter*ness* is a flavour,

where the nominalising suffix is grammatically mandatory. In 'patch of white', however, 'white' is being used not as this proper noun, but as a *mass* noun, and thus is viewed as picking out a kind of (phenomenal) stuff. On this contrived use, a white patch in visual space is a patch wholly *composed of white*; it is a *piece of white*.

What is most noteworthy about this observation is that 'white' lends itself to this sort of treatment. In this respect, it is very different from, say, such adjectives of *shape* as 'circular', 'square' and 'triangular'. Russell writes (op. cit.: 116) that 'it is perfectly possible for a simple object of perception to have a shape: the shape will be a quality like another [like any other?]'. The suggestion here is that colour and shape will enter *symmetrically* into any ontological account of visual space. A shape will be *just one more* quality. But the data we have so far uncovered belie this suggestion. This is brought out in a particularly striking way by our inability to force adjectives of shape into the role of mass nominatives so congenial to adjectives of colour. While we have no difficulty in characterising the phenomenal object of our thought experiment as a circular patch of white, there appears to be an absolute prohibition against interchanging the two adjectives. 'A white patch of circular' is simply unacceptable. What we need to understand is why this should be so.

Consider again a single – say, square – white patch on a uniform black background. How is *the thing* (the patch) set off from *its environment* (the background)? The patch has a determinate shape and size. It is bounded. It has edges which delineate its shape and size and thereby mark it off from its environment. But what, phenomenally speaking, *is* an edge or boundary? It is *where something differs*. In this thought experiment, it is where the visual field alters from black to white or white to black. I shall say, then, that a *form in* visual space is demarcated by boundaries constituted by differences in the *content of* visual space. For our white patch, then, shape enters as *form* and colour enters as *content*. And there cannot *be* a form unless there is a difference in content, and, *a fortiori*, unless there *are* contents to differ.

It should be noted, by the way, that nothing turns on the selection of visual space as the arena of our thought experiment. Consider, for example, auditory space, and let our thought experiment posit a uniform silence interrupted by a short burst of $A\#$. We find again the same grammatical resistance to interchange of the terms – 'a short burst of $A\#$' is perfectly acceptable, But 'an $A\#$ burst of short' will not do – and the grammar again marks a distinction of form and content. In auditory space, form is *temporal*. Our phenomenal object, however, is still bounded – it has a determinate *duration* – and, again, the boundaries are delineated by a difference in content – silence alters to $A\#$ or $A\#$ to silence. A form in auditory space is, thus, also demarcated by boundaries constituted by differences in content – the content, now, of auditory space. Again, there cannot *be* a form unless there is a difference in content and, *a fortiori*, unless there *are* contents to differ.

This point is precisely one which Berkeley's Philonous scores tellingly against Hylas. Midway through the *First Dialogue*, Hylas has abandoned his crude initial position to arrive at a variety of realism which posits the independent reality of *primary* qualities, while holding that *secondary* qualities are mere appearances, in sensations only.[2] To this, Philonous replies:

> *Phil.* Can you . . . separate the ideas of extension and motion from the ideas of all those qualities which they who make the distinction term 'secondary'?
>
> *Hyl.* What! is it not an easy matter to consider extension and motion by themselves, abstracted from all other sensible qualities? Pray how do the mathematicians treat of them?
>
> *Phil.* I acknowledge, Hylas, it is not difficult to form general propositions and reasonings about those qualities without mentioning any other, and, in this sense, to consider or treat of them abstractedly. But how does it follow that, because I can pronounce the word 'motion' by itself, I can form the idea of it in my mind exclusive of body? . . . Mathematicians treat of quantity without regarding what other sensible qualities it is attended with, as being altogether indifferent to their demonstrations. But when, laying aside the words, they contemplate the bare ideas, I believe you will find they are not the pure abstracted ideas of extension . . . but, for your further satisfaction, try if you can frame the idea of any figure abstracted from . . . other sensible qualities.
>
> *Hyl.* Let me think a little – I do not find that I can.
>
> *Phil.* And can you think it possible that should really exist in nature which implies a repugnancy in its conception?
>
> *Hyl.* By no means.
>
> *Phil.* Since therefore it is impossible even for the mind to disunite the ideas of extension and motion from all other sensible qualities, does it not follow that where the one exist there necessarily the other exist likewise?
>
> *Hyl.* It should seem so. (pp. 34–5)

The thought experiment Philonous asks of Hylas is this: to conceive of a *form* without (a difference in) *content*. And the upshot of the thought experiment is consonant with the results which we have so far collected: form is demarcated by boundaries constituted by a difference of content. Where there is form, then, there must *be* contents to differ.

What should strike us is how neatly the distinction which we have been developing between *form* and *content* maps on to the traditional distinction between *primary* and *secondary* qualities. Now the historical motivations for the distinction between primary and secondary qualities were, in essence, scientific. As Hylas's remarks suggest, what were classified as primary qualities were precisely the parameters treated of by the new mechanics: shape, size, number, motion, rest and 'gravity' (mass).[3] Primary qualities were just those which could be dealt with by 'mathematicians' who 'treat of *quantity*'. The remaining sensible qualities inherited the classification 'secondary', and this rubric was, in turn, supported by the emerging understanding of the physiology of perception. Berkeley's metaphysics, indeed, owes its genesis largely to his 'New Theory of Vision', and, in the *Dialogues*, he makes much of the, then relatively current, realisation that the perceiver is passive in perception – not acting, but rather being acted upon.

What needs some explanation, however, is why the categories of our purely phenomenal investigations – form and content – should thus neatly cohere with a distinction basically motivated by physical and physiological considerations – the distinction between primary and secondary qualities. I think we can begin to get a feel for the grounds of this consilience if we introduce yet another mapping, this time on to a distinction of Kant's.

What I have in mind is the distinction between *extensive* and *intensive* magnitudes, which makes its appearance in Kant's systematic exposition of what he calls the 'synthetic principles of pure understanding'. These he represents as the 'rules for the objective employment' (A161; B200) of the categories. Extensive magnitude belongs with the first group of principles, the Axioms of Intuition: 'Their principle is: All intuitions are extensive magnitudes' (A162; B202); and intensive magnitude with the second group, the Anticipations of Perception: 'In all appearances, the real that is an object of sensation has intensive magnitude, that is, a degree' (B207; cf. A166). Kant characterises an *extensive* magnitude as follows:

> I entitle a magnitude extensive when the representation of the parts makes possible, and therefore necessarily precedes, the representation of the whole. (A162; B203)

Now we may ignore, for our purposes, Kant's talk here of *precedence*, which rests upon his notion of a *successive* synthesis, his taking literally of our occasional informal claim that a line is 'generated' by a moving point or a plane figure by a moving line segment. For what I am up to, the operative term is '*parts*'; an extensive magnitude is a magnitude which something has by virtue of its having *parts*. (For a fuller discussion, see Bennett, *Kant's Analytic*, 1966: 168.) This interpretation contrasts properly with one operative clause of Kant's characterisation of *intensive* magnitude:

> A magnitude which is apprehended only as a unity, and in which multiplicity can be represented only through approximation to negation = 0, I entitle an *intensive* magnitude. (A168; B210)

If we read 'apprehended only as a unity' as 'not possessing parts,' the contrast is clear. What we are to make of 'in which multiplicity can be represented only through approximation to negation $= 0$' remains to be seen, but 'only' here again marks an implicit contrast with those magnitudes to which the notions of 'part' and 'whole' apply. An *extensive* magnitude *can*, presumably, be represented as a *compositum* of a multiplicity of parts whether or not it can also (cf. 'only') be represented as a multiplicity through its approximation to 'negation $= 0$'.

Kant's *examples* of extensive magnitude are uniformly spatio-temporal. It is lines, figures and durations which paradigmatically have extensive magnitude. Intensive magnitudes, in contrast, are exemplified (speaking circularly) by sensations which differ in intensity: a bright as opposed to a dim red, a loud as opposed to a soft sound, a severe as opposed to a mild heat, and so on. Where an increase in extensive magnitude may be viewed as the addition of *more parts* – that is, the added quantum is a *part* of the new totality – a loud sound is not a *compositum* of many soft sounds, nor is a bright red the mereological sum of a multiplicity of dim reds.

The connection with our earlier phenomenal concerns should by now be reasonably clear. An extensive magnitude is a *form*; an intensive magnitude, a *content*. Kant's phrasing of the Anticipations of Perception is revelatory here. He speaks of 'the *real* that is an object of sensation'. What he is thinking of is the *filling up* of a portion of space or time with something ('the real'). 'The real' is the real *in space or time* (see A173; B215) – the real *contents of* a portion of space or time. The question of extensive magnitude is the question of *how much* space or time is filled. The question of intensive magnitude, on the other hand, is the question of *with what* it is filled. The place of these notions in Kant's architectonic now also becomes easier to understand. The Axioms of Intuition (extensive magnitude) correspond within the system to the category of Quantity; the Anticipations of Perception (intensive magnitude), to the category of Quality. 'Intuition' and 'appearance' in Kant map on to our 'phenomenal object'. What Kant is telling us here is that every phenomenal object must have a form and, since a form, a content as well. There must be *so much* of *such-and-such kind of stuff*. This being so, we can understand the earlier consilience with the notions of primary and secondary qualities as well. For primary qualities are precisely those, as we noted earlier, which admit of *quantisation*. Their 'How much?' is a question of extensive magnitude. Secondary qualities, on the other hand, resist quantisation. They cannot be represented – as the mathematics of mechanics demands – as *composita* of parts (points or instants or relations of points and instants) amenable to the mathematics of the calculus. Their 'How much?' can only be the question of intensive magnitude: loud or soft, severe or mild, bright or dim.

We thus have three dichotomies which run, in essence, parallel to one another:

form	*v.*	content	
primary	*v.*	secondary	(qualities)
extensive	*v.*	intensive	(magnitudes)

Kant's 'Axioms of Intuition' are axiomatic and his 'Anticipations of Perception' anticipatory in that, as our earlier investigations show, the mere notion of a phemonenal object, of a *thing* set apart from its (phenomenal) *environment*, itself demands form and content. For the thing to be differentiated from its environment, it must be bounded, thus possess extensive magnitude. And for a thing to be bounded, there must be boundaries. Since a boundary is constituted by a difference in content, there must *be* contents to differ as well, and thus something possessing intensive magnitude.

What is most significant about these developments, however, is that they imply a fundamental ontology for phenomenal space which is neither an NP nor a U+P ontology. Rather, it is what I shall call an ontology of *structured stuffs*. Phenomenal objects, on this view, are neither particulars exemplifying qualia nor presentations of qualia in space. They are rather bits, pieces or chunks of phenomenal stuff, bounded in the appropriate phenomenal space by contrast with a background or environment of differing phenomenal stuff. The appropriate mode of reference to a phenomenal object is thus neither by means of a logical subject-cum-predicate adjective (as on a U+P ontology) nor by means of an abstract singular term (as on an NP ontology), but by means of a dummy sortal plus a mass term.[4] The root notion of *colour*, then, is that of a space-filling phenomenal *stuff*, not that of an abstract (Platonic) individual nor of a multiply-instantiable quality. Colours, in this basic sense, are thus the sorts of entities to which a logic of part and whole – a mereology – *literally* applies.

Although incidental to the main line of our investigations, we are now in a position to make sense of an argument of Sellars's which, since it has attracted considerable attention, is worth digressing to examine. On several occasions,[5] Sellars has insisted that there is an in-principle obstacle to *identifying* sensations with neurophysiological states as conceived by current science. The gist of his claim is that, whereas current science posits a particulate, quantised, 'grainy' universe, the sensible qualia of raw feels must be 'ultimately homogeneous':

> It does not seem plausible to say that for a system of particles to be a pink ice cube is for them to have such and such imperceptible qualities, and to be so related to one another as to make up an approximate cube. *Pink* does not seem to be made up of imperceptible qualities in the way in which being a ladder is made up of being cylindrical (the rungs) rectangular (the frame), wooden, etc. The manifest ice cube presents itself to us as something which is pink through and through, as a pink continuum, all the regions of which, however small, are pink.

It presents itself to us as *ultimately homogeneous*; and an ice cube vari-egated in color is, though not homogeneous in its specific color, 'ultimately homogeneous', in the sense to which I am calling atten-tion, with respect to the generic trait of being colored. (*PSIM*: 26)

In his reply to Cornman (*SSS*), Sellars makes it clear that the principle on which he is here drawing 'belongs, properly speaking, to logic or general ontology, rather than to the philosophy of science' (*SSS*: 411). This principle Sellars calls a 'principle of reducibility', 'to the effect that every (non-relational) property of a system of objects "consists of prop-erties of, and relations between its constituents" ' (*SSS*: 406, quoting *PSIM*: 26). And he goes on to isolate its role in his argument in this way:

> It should be emphasized that the concept of ultimate homogeneity is closely related to the traditional concept of a simple quality. It differs primarily by relating the latter to the logic of whole and part. Applied to my example it says that the pinkness of a whole (the pink ice cube) does not consist in a relationship of non-pink parts. . . . The principle of reducibility to which I made appeal plays a decisive role in the argument. For without it, I cannot conclude from the 'ultimate homogeneity' of color that colored objects do not consist of non-colored constituents (micro-physical particles). Nor could I conclude from the ultimate homogeneity of sense impressions that persons do not consist of particles which severally do not sense. (*SSS*: 407–8)

In terms of our previous discussions, we can now see more clearly what Sellars is up to here. For in the manifest image, as Sellars conceives it, *colour is a content*. As Sellars is thinking of his pink ice cube in the manifest image, it is not correctly characterised as a cubical, pink *piece of ice*. To speak in this way of 'ice' runs together occurrent (sensible) and dispositional (inferred) properties. Saying of a perceived object that it is *ice* attributes to it a complex cluster of causal powers and dispositional properties. It makes reference to what it *does* rather than to what it *is*. But for an account of *visual sensations*, on Sellars's view, we must strip away this conceptual load of inferred causal propensities (the thing's 'nature') and focus only upon what is visually presented in the perceptual experience. And if we do this, what we will find is precisely the ontology of form and content which I have been canvas-sing above. A pink ice cube is, *qua object of visual sensation*, simply a *cube of pink* – and here 'cube' marks a form and 'pink' a content, a bounded piece of phenomenal stuff.

  This being so, we can understand why colours *must* be 'ultimately homogeneous'. For if a cube of pink had, *per impossibile*, parts which were not pink, those 'parts' would, for precisely that reason, belong not to the thing but to its environment. It is just by *consisting of pink* that the *thing* (the cube of pink) is set apart from, marked off from, its visual environment. 'Parts', then, which did not consist of pink logically could not be parts of *that thing*.

It is for this reason that it is beside the point to observe that a *physical* surface which is closely stippled with red and white paint can give, from an appropriate distance, the appearance of being uniformly pink. For what we are concerned about in the treatment of visual sensations is not the physical but the phenomenal object. When, as we say, 'on closer approach' we come to perceive a motley of red and white dots, what we have done is to replace one simple visual sensation by another complex one. At best, we have shown that the physical cause of our original sensation is physically complex. It has physical parts which are not pink. But what we have *not* shown (for it is false) is that our *original sensation* was (phenomenally) complex. Our original sensation was of, say, a square patch of pink. The phenomenal object was *composed of pink* and, thus, what is not pink cannot belong to *that* phenomenal object. To claim that a manifest object as it is visually presented in sensation is ultimately homogeneous, then, is not after all to claim something contentious. It is simply to restate the necessary truth that, since colour is the *content* of visual sensation, a phenomenal object set apart from its visual environment by being of (i.e. *composed* of) a specific colour must be of (i.e. composed of) that colour in all its parts. For putative parts *not* composed of that colour belong necessarily and for just that reason not to that visual object, but to its visual environment.

It is pink in *this* sense – as a phenomenal stuff which is the content of visual sensations – which Sellars is arguing could not *consist of* non-pink parts, however related. And this, we now understand, is, as Sellars claims it is, not a bold defeasible hypothesis, but a necessary consequence of the ontological make-up of phenomenal space as such.

We still have, however, one large and important piece of business left on our agenda. What we have uncovered is an ontology for objects in phenomenal space which is neither an NP nor a U+P ontology, but rather an ontology of structured stuffs. Our everyday ontology of physical objects in physical space, however, is an ontology of *qualified particulars*. This is not quite the same as Russell's U+P ontology, although it is a close relative. On Russell's view, predication is a *relation* between particulars and subsistent qualia. (Compare Bergmann's treatment of exemplification as a *nexus* tying bare particulars to qualia and Strawson's characterising and attributive *ties* between particulars and universals.) On Russell's U+P theory, then, particulars are substrata. They are nothing in themselves (have no natures), but serve as principles of unification for various clusters of quality-instances and grounds of individuation for similar clusters variously presented in space. Predication is a subsistent *tertium quid*, serving to bind such substrata together with the qualia which, speaking informally, they exemplify. On a qualified particulars view, however, particulars are not bare substrata. A round, white, rubber ball is not, as Russell would view it, a bare particular related by predication to roundness, whiteness and elasticity, but rather simply a round, white, elastic particular. Qualia, in our everyday ontology, are not separated and reified, but simply instantiated by a variety of particulars thus variously qualified. There is no need, then, for a *tertium quid* to bind the one to the separate other.[6]

But if the ontology of phenomenal objects is thus radically and categorially different from the ontology of our everyday world, how do we get from one to the other? How can we motivate a transition from *chunks of visual stuff* (colour) to *public* objects instantiating visual qualia *among others*? How can we bridge the gap between a logic of part and whole and a logic of subject and predicate, between mereology and the predicate calculus?

If we allow an ontology encompassing absolute space and time, the problem can be solved. That is the moral of Goodman's *Structure of Appearance*. Admit places and times into your ontology, and you can generate the notion of a *concretum* (a particular) as the mereological sum of a reified quality at a place at a time. But we have already, for good and sufficient reasons, eschewed absolute space and time. Places and times must be 'constructions' out of what we informally refer to as their contents. How, then, are we to proceed?

Well, our earlier observations regarding 'spatial coincidence' give the essential clue here. The notion of a *public*, as opposed to a *phenomenal*, object requires that we be able to make a genuine distinction between, for example, the *actual* (real, objective) colour of the object and its *apparent* (seeming, phenomenal) colour. As I argued above, however, our ability to draw this distinction is correlative to our ability to give a non-vacuous sense to the notion of *spatial coincidence*, that is, to our ability to develop a *full* concept of spatiality which allows for coincidence as well as for separation. But if we limit ourselves to the phenomenal space of a single sensory modality – say, the visual – we cannot do this. Thus, we need to develop the concept of a *common* (public) space in which objects instantiating a variety of qualia belonging to diverse sensory modalities can be presented. And this requires, in turn, that we find a way of *relating* diverse sensory contents in a *single* object, that we arrive, in Kant's terminology, at a *synthesis* of perceptions. And the mention of Kant here reminds us, of course, that this is precisely his conclusion as well.

Following the Axioms of Intuition and the Anticipations of Perception in the Kantian architectonic are the Analogies of Experience:

> The principle of the analogies is: Experience is possible only through the representation of a necessary connection of perceptions. (B218; cf. A177)

Whereas the Axioms and the Anticipations concerned phenomenal objects only ('intuitions' and 'appearances'), the Analogies represent the advance to a common or public empirical object:

Experience is an empirical knowledge, that is, a knowledge which determines an object through perceptions. It is a synthesis of perceptions, not contained in perception but itself containing in one consciousness the synthetic unity of the manifold of perceptions. This synthetic unity constitutes the essential in any knowledge of *objects* of the senses, that is, in experience as distinguished from mere intuition or sensation of the senses. (A177; B218)

The key to this advance, argues Kant, lies in the positing of a *necessary connection* among various perceptions. And this is correct. To see what is meant by it, however, let us return to our second thought experiment, the one involving a putative spatial fusion.

Recall that I there posited a red patch and a white patch of the same shape and size which gradually come together and appear to coalesce or fuse into a single patch of the same shape and size but which is uniformly pink. I argued that, in order to conclude that the red patch and the white patch have, while retaining their identities as separate patches, come to occupy the same spatial position, we should have to be able to mark the pink colour of the resultant single patch as *merely apparent* but that, since the objects in question are *ab initio* phenomenal, there is no way in which we can do this, while relying *only* on what is visually presented to us. What we need to do, then, is to introduce into our story *something else* upon which we can rely. Since this something else cannot be visual, it must belong to some other sensory modality.

Let us, therefore, elaborate our thought experiment by positing a variety of *regularities* correlating phenomena in visual space with phenomena in *auditory* space. To begin with, let us suppose that whenever, and for as long as, a patch of a specific colour is present in the visual field, our auditory experience is characterised by the continuous sounding of a single pure tone. Thus, when our visual field contains a single white patch, let us suppose, our auditory experience consists of a continuous sounding of middle C; when our visual experience is of a single red patch, our auditory experience is of A-above-middle-C; when our visual experience is of a single pink patch, our auditory experience is of D-above-middle-C; and so on. This is the initial stipulation. Now let us complicate it. What will happen when our visual experience is simultaneously of a white and a red patch? Well, let us suppose the obvious: our auditory experience then consists of an A–C *dichord*, the tones middle C and A-above-middle-C sounding simultaneously. Similarly, when our visual experience is of a white patch and a pink patch, we hear a C–D dichord, and so on.

And then one day this happens: a single white patch and a single red patch of the same size and shape gradually come together and appear to coalesce or fuse into a patch of the same size and shape but which is uniformly pink – *and we continue to hear an A–C dichord.*

It is now clear how to elaborate upon this thought experiment. Let us suppose, for example, that *every* pink patch temporally consequent upon (i.e. immediately succeeding) an ostensible fusion of red and white patches is accompanied by such an A–C dichord. Among pink patches which are *not*, within our experience, temporal successors of ostensible red–white fusions, however, we find an anomaly. Such patches, presented *ab initio* as pink, are of *two* sorts: some are accompanied by D-above-middle-C, but others are accompanied by an A–C dichord. Finally, we may suppose that *ab initio* pink patches occasionally undergo ostensible *fission* into pairs of patches, one red and one white – but that it is *only* those patches correlated with an A–C dichord in our auditory experience which appear thus to fission.

If our experience does exhibit such regularities of co-occurrence and succession among visual and auditory objects, I submit, we then have something to dictate a *non-arbitrary* classification of phenomenally pink patches into those exhibiting their *actual* colour and those only *apparently* pink. For we are now free to hold that those pink patches co-occurrent with an A–C dichord are actually spatially coincident pairs of red and white patches. But, as Kant recognised, we can do this *only if we posit a necessary connection between tones and colours*. Most significantly, however, the requisite connection cannot here be correctly phrased as a modalised conditional or biconditional both sides of which make reference to *purely phenomenal* objects. For the terms of our elaborated thought – experiment guarantee that any *such* conditional or biconditional will be false. We will not have, for example,

    Phenomenal pink only if (or: if, and only if) D-above-middle-C

since there are pink presentations correlated with A–C dichords, nor, for example, can we truly assert

    Phenomenal red if (or: if, and only if) A-above-middle-C

since A is heard whenever an A–C dichord is, yet an A–C dichord may be accompanied only by phenomenal pink.

What we must do, then, is to posit tone and colour as being necessarily connected by being aspects or features of something (some single thing) which is *not a phenomenal object*. And precisely here we move from an ontology of structured stuffs to an ontology of qualified particulars, particulars which are *common* sensibles. For the new 'something' which connects tone and colour as its aspects or features will, *a fortiori*, be a coloured *and* sounding something – a public object, instantiating *multiple* contents.

Nor can the *space* in which two such objects may coincide be identified with any phenomenal space – first, because contents specific to two different sensory modalities are involved in such a coincidence and, second, because – as I have already argued – if we *do* limit ourselves to a single phenomenal space (e.g. visual space), there is no way in which we can successfully ground a non-vacuous sense of 'spatial coincidence'. The introduction of public ('outer') objects – qualified particulars – is thus the *same* conceptual move as the introduction of public space, the space of common sensibles, and again the *same* move as the introduction of a concept of *objectivity*, the groundable distinction, for example, between real and apparent colour.

Like any conceptual revision, this introduction of public objects in public space is justified by the explanatory power and economy of the resulting conceptual scheme. Thus, introducing these logically interanimating objective (as opposed to phenomenal) concepts puts us in the position of being able to reintegrate what were phenomenal anomalies into a single unified conceptual framework. That phenomenal pink admits of disparate auditory correlates stands in need of explanation. Our positing of multiply qualified particulars, possibly coincident, in public space and the correlative introduction of a distinction between real and apparent colour provides the requisite explanation. In so doing, we explain as well what was not initially anomalous but what was, in an important sense, arbitrary – such regularities of co-occurrence as those between single patches of phenomenal red and monotone A, phenomenal white and monotone C. The new conceptual framework is thus unitary, coherent, integrative, and explanatorily richer than its phenomenal predecessor. And it is in this way that the new framework of objective particulars *qualifies* as a successor to and replacement for the old.

Kant, we thus see, was exactly on the mark when he pinned the notions of objectivity and the public object in common space to the unitary synthesis of perceptions in time under the relations of duration, succession and coexistence (co-occurrence) (A177; B219). For it is precisely transmodal regularities of duration, succession, and co-occurrence among phenomenal objects which form the indispensable groundwork for the introduction of qualified particulars in public space and the distinction between real (objective) and apparent qualia.

We can understand, too, something of why time is the form of *inner* and space the form of *outer* sense. For phenomenal objects, although in disparate sensory 'spaces', are, already *as phenomenal*, uniformly embedded in a *common* time, as we have seen they must be if the introduction of the conceptual framework of objective particulars is to be possible. The introduction of this framework of public ('outer') objects – variously qualified particulars admitting a groundable distinction of real and apparent qualia – on the other hand, just *is* (as we have also seen) the introduction of the concept of a public space, the space of common sensibles, and the securing of the *full* concept of spatiality which allows for spatial coincidence as well as spatial relatedness in separation. In consequence, whereas a common time is compatible with an 'inner', purely phenomenal, ontology of structured stuffs, a common space entails an 'outer' ontology of objective qualified particulars, instantiating diverse qualia and possibly *appearing* to instantiate diverse others.

I have now bridged the gap between the phenomenal ontology of structured stuffs and the objective, public ontology of qualified particulars in common space, and thereby tied off the remaining loose end of my current discussion, a discussion which has brought me a considerable distance from the essay of Russell's which first engaged our attention. Yet, in the process, I have proposed solutions to two problems which, in one form or another, haunted Russell throughout his philosophical career. The first of these problems was to secure a pluralist ontology of particulars and their qualities; the second, to achieve the 'construction' of physical from phenomenal space. If what I have argued in this chapter is correct, we can now see why – despite his fundamental insights – Russell failed to solve either problem. For, already gripped by the picture of bare substrata and subsistent universals, Russell attempted to secure his ontology of particulars and qualities at the *phenomenal* level where, if I am right, only an ontology of structured stuffs can be supported. And, failing thus to uncover the connection between particularity and objectivity, Russell never made the crucial discovery which leads to the solution of both problems – the discovery that the first problem is the *same* as the second.

This discovery, of course, was originally Kant's. Since it was the stimuli of Bradley's idealism and Moore's 'return to common sense' which, historically, set Russell's problematic and determined the directions of his philosophical thought, he can hardly be faulted for not making it. If he had, he might well have written this century's *Critique of Pure Reason*. What he wrote instead was *Principia Mathematica*, and contemporary philosophy is immeasurably richer because of it. For we already had, after all, Kant's *Critique of Pure Reason*, and it is only a testimony to Russell's greatness to point out that what *he* gave us were the fundamental analytical tools for *doing* something with it.

Department of Philosophy
University of North Carolina
at Chapel Hill

NOTES

1   Compare Kant (*CPR*: A169–70; B211): 'Points and instants are only limits, that is, mere positions which limit space and time. But positions always presuppose the intuitions which they limit or are intended to limit; and out of mere positions, viewed as constituents capable of being given prior to space or time, neither space nor time can be constructed.' The full import of this and other Kantian remarks will return to haunt us later in this chapter. For some development of the point in connection with time, see my *OWUT*. (Abbreviations are of titles given in references at the end of the chapter.)

2   Compare Descartes at the end of the *Second Meditation* on 'the real wax':

The truth of the matter . . . is that this wax was . . . only a body which a little while ago appeared to my senses under these forms and which now makes itself felt under others. But what is it, to speak precisely, that I imagine when I conceive it in this fashion? Let us consider it attentively and, rejecting everything that does not belong to the wax, see what remains. Certainly nothing is left but something extended, flexible, and moveable. (pp. 29–30)

3 Although Berkeley denies that 'gravity' is a *sensible* quality, and this is surely correct.
4 That an ontology of particulars and qualities must have its roots somehow in an ontology of structured stuffs is what Strawson senses dimly in his talk of 'feature-placing sentences' (*I*: 202 ff.). But he attempts to carry off at the level of physical objects what properly belongs to purely phenomenal ontology. Consequently, he can give no more than a hand-waving account of the *conceptual transition* from an ontology of stuffs to an ontology of particulars. The issue is a crucial one, and so I shall try shortly to do better than wave my hands. Interestingly, Bergmann – an arch-purveyor of the sort of thought experiments which we have been examining – *never* discerns an ontology of stuffs as a live option. When he comes to Strawson, in consequence, he completely misses the point. Strawson is accused (*SO*) of proposing an ontology of *facts*.
5 Especially in *PSIM*: 26–31; but see also *SRII*: 356–8; *IAMBP*: 386–8; *P*: 98–105; and *EPM*: 193–4.
6 For a full discussion, see Long (*PTQ*).

REFERENCES

Bennett, Jonathan, *Kant's Analytic (KA)* (London, Cambridge University Press, 1966).
Bergmann, Gustav, 'Strawson's Ontology' *(SO)*, reprinted as pp. 171–92 of *Logic and Reality* (Madison, University of Wisconsin Press, 1964).
Berkeley, George, *Three Dialogues Between Hylas and Philonous* (Indianapolis, Library of Liberal Arts, Bobbs-Merrill, 1954).
Descartes, René, *Meditations on First Philosophy* (Indianapolis, Library of Liberal Arts, Bobbs-Merrill, 1960).
Goodman, Nelson, *The Structure of Appearance* (Cambridge, Mass., Harvard University Press, 1951).
Kant, Immanuel, *Critique of Pure Reason (CPR)*, trans., Norman Kemp Smith (London, Macmillan, 1958).
Long, Douglas, 'Particulars and Their Qualities' *(PTQ)*, *Philosophical Quarterly*, vol. 18, no. 72 (July 1968: 193–206).
Rosenberg, Jay F., 'One Way of Understanding Time' *(OWUT)*, *Philosophia*, vol. 2, no. 4 (October 1972: 283–301).
Russell, Bertrand, 'On the Relations of Universals and Particulars', pp. 103–24 of *Logic and Knowledge*, Robert C. Marsh ed. (London, George Allen & Unwin, 1956).
Sellars, Wilfrid, 'Empiricism and the Philosophy of Mind' *(EPM)*, reprinted as ch. 5, pp. 127–96, of *Science, Perception and Reality* (London, Routledge & Kegan Paul, 1963).
Sellars, Wilfrid, 'The Identity Approach to the Mind–Body Problem' *(IAMBP)*, reprinted as ch. XV, pp. 370–88 of *Philosophical Perspectives* (Springfield, Ill., Charles C. Thomas, 1967).
Sellars, Wilfrid, 'Phenomenalism' *(P)*, reprinted as ch. 3, pp. 60–105 of *Science, Perception and Reality*.
Sellars, Wilfrid, 'Philosophy and the Scientific Image of Man' *(PSIM)*, reprinted as ch. 1, pp. 1–40 of *Science, Perception and Reality*.
Sellars, Wilfrid, 'Science, Sense-Impressions, and Sensa: a reply to Cornman' *(SSS)*, *Review of Metaphysics*, vol. XXIV (March 1971: 391–447).
Sellars, Wilfrid, 'Scientific Realism or Irenic Instrumentalism' *(SRII)*, reprinted as ch. XIV, pp. 337–69 of *Philosophical Perspectives*.
Strawson, P. F., *Individuals (I)* (London, Methuen, 1959).

18

RUSSELL'S THEORY OF PERCEPTION

D. J. O'Connor

(1) The fact that Russell wrote so many philosophical books and papers over so many years makes it very difficult to give an accurate and sequential account either of his philosophy as a whole or of any important part of it. 'As we all know,' wrote Professor Broad, 'Mr Russell produces a different system of philosophy every few years.'[1] Although this was a rhetorical exaggeration, Broad's suggestion was not entirely ungrounded. The variety of opinions and approaches that strike the reader who tries to follow Russell's views in chronological order is at first sight bewildering. In this chapter, I shall try to follow only one group of theories – those about sense perception. But even here, the material is not easy to sort and order so that we can be reasonably confident that we have done Russell justice both in exposition and in criticism. In the years 1912–27 he published five books and a number of papers in which he dealt among other matters with questions of sense perception. And though he returned briefly to the topic in *An Inquiry into Meaning and Truth* (1940) and *Human Knowledge* (1948) he made no substantial changes in his views. He makes this clear in his last writings on philosophy published in 1959.[2]

But although Russell's philosophy is confusing in its variety of surface detail, it is held together by its aims and methods. In his recent study of Russell's philosophy,[3] Professor Ayer lists 'ten main assumptions from which all his characteristic doctrines are derived'. Whether or not Russell's philosophy can plausibly be construed as quite so systematic a structure, is debatable. But it is certain that he did consciously rely upon two methodological principles. The first of these is that philosophical method should be modelled on the methods of science, though philosophers should not pay too much regard to its actual results:[4]

> Much philosophy inspired by science has gone astray through preoccupation with the *results* momentarily supposed to have been achieved. It is not results but *methods* that can be transferred with profit from the sphere of the special sciences to the sphere of philosophy.

This mention of scientific methods might lead us to believe that Russell supposes philosophy to be basically an empirical study which should properly proceed by observation, experiment and the formulation and testing of hypotheses. Nothing was further from his intentions. 'Science' refers here to the formal sciences of logic and mathematics, to the foundations of which he had himself contributed so largely. Indeed, he held that it was a mark of philosophical propositions that while they resembled those of natural science in being *general*, they differed from them in being *a priori* and so were 'such as can neither be proved or disproved by empirical evidence'.[5] And even their generality went beyond that kind which is characteristic of statements of natural science. For science is compartmentalised for convenience, physics dealing with the transformations of energy, biology with living matter, and so on, each science having its peculiar subject matter. Philosophical propositions, on the contrary, were general in the widest sense of the word, so that[6]

> instead of being concerned with the whole of things collectively, [they] are concerned with all things distributively; and not only must they be concerned with all things, but they must be concerned with such properties of all things as do not depend upon the accidental nature of the things that there happen to be, but are true of any possible world, independently of such facts as can only be discovered by our senses.

In consequence of this remarkably austere delineation of its territory, philosophy becomes identical with logic in its modern sense, the discovery and systematisation of those statements which are true in virtue of their form rather than their content, and the analysis and listing of the logical forms of statements and so the logical structure of facts to which statements can apply.

Needless to say, Russell does not live up to this self-imposed austerity. He talks a great deal, especially in *Our Knowledge of the External World*, about scientific method in philosophy but he nowhere uses the formal methods of the logic that he himself developed. There have been philosophers, like Carnap and Professor Goodman, who follow Russell's precepts in this; but he contents himself with pointing the way for others to follow. Nor, indeed, does his treatment of the problem of perception (among others) reach the degree of uninformative abstractness that his recommendations about generality seem to entail. He talks quite happily about brains, nerves, sense organs, patches of colour, and the rest, and links them with the familiarly hypothesised denizens of the physical world, light rays, electrons, and so on. There is indeed, as we shall see, one respect in which his theory of perception does rely on the technicalities of logic. But this is arguably one of its weaker points.

He does, however, keep close to the scientific spirit in the cautious and provisional character of the doctrines that he adopts. Indeed, it is a feature of his philosophical writing, and particularly of his treatment of perception, that he starts each discussion of the topic from the beginning even if he has discussed it thoroughly in previous writings and arrived at conclusions that satisfied him at the time. A characteristic statement of this attitude occurs at the end of his paper on 'Logical Atomism':

> The above summary hypothesis would, of course, need to be amplified and refined in many ways in order to fit in completely with scientific facts. It is not put forward as a finished theory but merely as a suggestion of the kind of thing that may be true.

The second of Russell's methodological principles is his version of Ockham's Razor: 'The supreme maxim in scientific philosophising is this: Wherever possible, logical constructions are to be substituted for inferred entities.'[7] This maxim evinces that 'extreme economy of ontological commitment' which a modern critic of Ockham attributed to Russell's medieval ancestor.[8] As Russell applied this maxim in his writings on perception, it has an unfortunate effect. His theory of perception may be characterised as a causal theory with phenomenalist overtones. These overtones do not harmonise at all well with Russell's main position but they are a consequence of his application of the 'supreme maxim of scientific philosophising' to the problems of perception.

(2) His earliest and simplest account of his views on perception is in *The Problems of Philosophy*. He starts with a question which evidences his unwillingness to give any ontological hostages to fortune: 'Is there any knowledge in the world which is so certain that no reasonable man could doubt it?' From this starting-point, he proceeds by a conventional way into the problem of perception. The physical objects that commonsense accepts uncritically as given to our senses are shown to be properly distinguishable into indubitable *prima facie* appearances and their hypothetical causal bases in the physical world. That the first cannot be literally parts of the second is shown by traditional and well-established arguments: sense data, or what is 'immediately known in sensation' vary with the conditions under which a physical object is observed. Changes of light, perspective or physiological state alter the sense-data, but we know that physical objects are relatively stable substances, independent of being observed by us. Nor can our sense-data be fitted coherently together, either simultaneously or successively, to give entities having the properties of continuity, independence and neutrality that we attribute to the inhabitants of the physical world. 'What reason, then, have we for believing that there are such public neutral objects?'[9]

His answer to this question shows a softening of the rigours of his Cartesian scepticism. We all have a natural unlearned tendency to believe in an external world. And this 'instinctive' hypothesis is corroborated by experience in the main and commends itself on the grounds of simplicity. A continuous, coherent and gap-free physical world is much easier to understand than the intermittent world of phenomena which is all that a strict application of the principle of intellectual economy would allow us. 'Since this belief [in an external world] does not lead to any difficulties, but on the contrary tends to simplify and systematise our account of our experiences, there seems no good reason for rejecting it.'[10] He excuses the fact that 'this conclusion is doubtless less strong than we could wish' on the ground that it is the task of philosophy to display the hierachy of our 'instinctive' beliefs and to reject only those which are inconsistent with the rest.

The next question for one who wishes to espouse a version of the causal theory of perception is: what is the nature of the physical objects that continue to exist independently of my perception of them? To this question, Russell replies, in *The Problems of Philosophy*, that physical science gives us an answer, though one which is admittedly hypothetical and incomplete. Still, it is the best answer that we can get and we have to accept it (though Russell does not argue the point) on much the same grounds as we accept the common sense belief about the world of independent and public physical objects. No doubt the doctrines of physics are not, like our beliefs in the external world, 'instinctive', but they have the same function of simplifying and systematising our account of experience. And they are found to be justified, to a more spectacular degree, by their power of explaining, predicting and controlling experience. But the world that physics reveals to us is sketched in such sparse metrical terms that its presumed similarity to the familiar world of the senses is hard to envisage. Our cognitive materials are found in sense perception. But the cognitive content of physics appears to be alien to those familiar origins, although it is indubitably derived from them.

What, then, is the link between the world of sense and the world of physics? At this point in his argument, Russell introduces a distinction between the 'one public all-embracing physical space' of science in which physical objects (including our brains and sense organs) exist and the innumerable private spaces in which the sense-data of individual observers are ordered. Our individual private spaces are a compound of the various sensory spaces (visual, tactual, kinaesthetic, and the rest) which we learn to co-ordinate into one space. (For example, I learn by experience to stretch out my hand to just the right distance to pick up the object that I identify in my visual field.) But we do not learn about public physical space in this way for we are never directly acquainted with any part of it. On the contrary, we *infer* both its existence and its nature. Its existence is assumed as a matrix in which physical objects are embedded and on the same grounds (innate assumptions pragmatically justified) as the physical objects themselves. Our knowledge of its nature comes in two stages. First, we find that there are certain invariant features of the ways in which our sense-data are ordered, and our experience, corroborated by the experience of others, leads us to assume that these features 'correspond' to those of public physical space. 'Thus we may assume that there is a physical space in which physical objects have spatial relations corresponding to those which the corresponding sense-data have in our private spaces.'[11] It is this system of correspondences, hypothesised by commonsense, which is developed at a second stage into the sophisticated concepts of physics and astronomy.

Two points are worth making here. First, it is noticeable that Russell makes no appeal to the experimental work on space perception carried out by psychologists. It is true that this was not at an advanced stage when he wrote *The Problems of Philosophy*. But, in spite of his respect for science, Russell did not trouble to take account of the evidence of experimental psychology when he returned to the question of private perceptual spaces in his later books. ('Psychology' for Russell tends to mean either psychoanalysis or the cruder forms of behaviourism, neither of which in the event have justified themselves as scientific psychology.) Second, we want to know what he means by 'correspondences' in this context. He does not give any formal definition of 'correspondence', but it is clear from the examples that he offers what he has in mind: 'If one object looks blue and another red, we may reasonably presume that there is some corresponding difference between the physical objects; if two objects both look blue, we may presume a corresponding similarity'.[12]

Russell does not have a great deal to say in *The Problems of Philosophy* about the nature of material objects considered as causes of our sense experience. What he says amounts to the following. We may grant that it is rational to believe in the independent existence of a physical world of which our sense-data are the evidence and, in part, the effect. We do so on the same grounds that lead us to believe in the theories of physics. These grounds are partly pragmatic in so far as physical theory enables us to predict and control some features of the material world. But they are, of course, also logical, even though the logic is what Russell calls 'inductive'. If we ask how belief in physics differs from belief in a causal theory of perception, Russell's answer seems to be that a causal theory of perception is just a rather skeletal abstract of physical theory. We may presume that sensible objects which we perceive as differing in colour, shape or some other modality have physical correlates whose natures we cannot directly know but which may be assumed to differ in ways that correspond systematically to *some* of the differences in our sense-data. And if we ask further about the exact nature of these differences, Russell answers that 'we can know the properties of the relations required to preserve the correspondence with sense data but not the nature of the terms between which the relations hold'.[13]

Physics shows us that matter consists of entities whose only properties, so far as we can know, are position in physical space and powers of movement according to the laws of mechanics. What we are capable of knowing about such things amounts to no more than the spatial and temporal relations of the material entities themselves and the relations which co-ordinate them with those features of our sense experience which they cause. These relational properties are *invariant* features of the physical world and its co-ordination with the world of sense. Such, at least, seems to be the conclusion he wishes us to draw from the analogy he offers:[14]

> If a regiment of men are marching along a road, the *shape* of the regiment will appear different from different points of view, but the men will appear arranged in the same *order* from all points of view. Hence we regard the *order* as true also in physical space, whereas the shape is only supposed to correspond to the physical space so far as is required for the preservation of order.

This one-to-one matching of entities, sensory with physical, and of relations between sensible objects with inferred relations between their hypothesised physical counterparts is what Russell means by 'correspondence'. 'Thus we find that, although the *relations* of physical objects have all sorts of knowable properties derived from their correspondence with the relations of sense data, the physical objects themselves remain unknown in their intrinsic nature, at least so far as can be discovered by means of the senses'.[15] But why may we not go further than this and suppose that physical objects may be more or less like sense-data, even though they cannot (since sense-data are in part determined by the conditions of our sense organs and nervous systems) be exactly like them? (Russell takes this to be the 'most natural' hypothesis.) His reason for rejecting it is that it can be 'shown to be groundless' even though it cannot be refuted. His reason for concluding that it is groundless is that we have good evidence that the detailed content of our visual field (to take one sensory modality) depends on the nature of the light rays that strike the eye. And these are not simply the outcome of the nature of the surfaces from which they are reflected, but are dependent on the nature of the light and of the medium through which the light is transmitted. And we might add, though Russell does not do so here,[16] that the content of our visual field is further conditioned by the structure and working of the particular sense organ and its associated nerves and brain centre as well as by obscure and imperfectly known psychological factors. Thus, the sense-datum itself is the end-product of physical, physiological and psychological factors among which the nature of the physical object is only one among many.

(3) Thus, the theory of perception that Russell presents in *The Problems of Philosophy* is a causal theory; and it is to a causal theory that he returns in *The Analysis of Matter* fifteen years later. In between, he has a lot to say about perception, particularly in *Our Knowledge of the External World* (1914) and *The Analysis of Mind* (1921) as well as in papers, of which the most important were reprinted in *Mysticism and Logic*. But much of what he says in these places is a diversion from his main theme and, moreover,

a diversion which is in some places actually inconsistent with, and in others, irrelevant to his main theory.

These diversions from his main theme result in some of the most characteristic features of his writings on perception. I call them diversions, nevertheless, because they cannot be fitted into the main outlines of his causal theory of perception. They can, moreover, be shown to be open to objection on other grounds. They may be listed as follows: (a) his theory of private and public space and the associated theory of 'perspectives'; (b) his version of neutral monism and an associated acceptance of a form of behaviourism; (c) the replacement of 'sense data' by *'sensibilia'*.

(a) The distinction between public and private spaces was first introduced in *The Problems of Philosophy*, as we have already seen. But it was elaborated in his later writings (starting with the essay on 'The Ultimate Constitutents of Matter', reprinted in *Mysticism and Logic*): 'If, as is generally assumed, position in space is purely relative, it follows that the space of one man's objects and the space of another man's objects have no place in common, that they are in fact different spaces, and not merely different parts of one space.'[17] There are in consequence an indefinitely large number of private three-dimensional spaces in the world: 'There are all those perceived by observers, and presumably also those which are not perceived, merely because no observer is suitably situated for perceiving them.'[18] To avoid the suggestion that these spaces are real only when they are being viewed by someone, Russell introduces the term 'perspective' to stand for 'a private world without assuming a percipient'.[19] So a perspective is any real or potential private space.

These three-dimensional perspectives can be arranged in a three-dimensional series of their own, giving an overall constructed space of six dimensions:[20]

> Since each of the spaces is itself three-dimensional, the whole world of particulars is thus arranged in a six-dimensional space, that is to say, six co-ordinates will be required to assign completely the position of any given particular, namely, three to assign its position in its own space and three more to assign the position of its space among the other spaces.

This talk of dimensions and co-ordinates sounds reassuringly scientific. And Russell's critics have dealt rather indulgently with this curious theory. Professor Ayer, indeed, accuses it of circularity though admitting it to be an 'ingenious theory'.[21] But what does it profit a theory to be ingenious, if it is not even coherent?

In the first place, it is unclear whether this compound six-dimensional space is supposed to be public or private, to follow Russell's own debatable distinction. It appears that it must be a mixture of both, the private spaces being organised in a three-dimensional public space. But if this is so, (i) it is unclear how this six-dimensional hybrid is to be related to the public space of physics, and (ii) it can hardly be the case that 'the whole world of particulars is thus arranged in a six-dimensional space', since particulars are sense-data or at best constructs from sense-data. And sense-data are not public. But second, it is hard to understand what he means by 'six co-ordinates will be required to assign completely the position of any given particular', for co-ordinates are by definition relative to a given arbitrary origin. No doubt I can assign such an origin in a particular (and momentary) private space of my own. But what possible origin could be assigned to fix the position of a given private space among other spaces? Even if this could be done, the first three co-ordinates would be incommensurable with the second three, as the two sets would be measured from different origins. And so they could not, as Russell claims, 'assign completely the position of any given particular' in the way that a co-ordinate set is ordinarily supposed to do. Russell gives no answers to these questions. Indeed, it seems that he is using the prestige of mathematical terms which are inapplicable in this context to hide awkward gaps in his theory.

In any case, there is something very odd about talking about spaces and sense-data as though the first were a kind of receptacle for the second. The investigations of psychologists on the genesis of sense perceptions have shown that visual space, for example, is not something given innately in the way that crude visual sensations are given. It is, on the contrary, something *learned* or, at least, *acquired*, and acquired rather slowly over a period of weeks or months. This has been amply authenticated by the observations of adults blind from birth from congenital cataract who are given their sight by operation.[22] Such examples show, at least, that private space is not necessary for sense perception of the most elementary kind. The only kind of visual private space that is given innately is the two-dimensional expanse of the visual field. The third dimension is added by the learning process.

(b) The second of the diversions which give an irrelevant phenomenalist gloss to his underlying causal theory is Russell's version of the 'neutral monism' derived from the writings of Mach and William James:[23]

> During 1918 my view as to mental events underwent a very important change. I had originally accepted Brentano's view that in sensation there are three elements: act, content and object. I had come to think that the distinction of content and object is unnecessary, but I still thought that sensation is a fundamentally relational occurrence in which a subject is 'aware' of an object.

The next step to abandoning the belief in the knowing subject is justified on grounds similar to those advanced by Hume but expressed in more modern language. We believe in the knowing self, if we do, not because it is ever an object of experience but because it is presupposed by the workings of our languages. But an application of Russell's version of

Ockham's Razor shows that 'nominal entities of this sort' can be effectively replaced by logical constructions out of entities with which we are directly acquainted. A temporally ordered set of states of consciousness can perform any task that the hypothetical bearer of those states can do.

Once we have renounced the concept of the knowing subject, there is no longer any good reason to accept the cognitive status of sensory contents:[24]

> If sensations are occurrences which are not essentially relational, there is not the same need to regard mental and physical occurrences as fundamentally different. It becomes possible to regard both a mind and a piece of matter as logical constructions formed out of material not differing vitally and sometimes actually identical.

The distinction between mind and matter is 'merely one of arrangement'. Grouped as a member of a memory chain, a sensation is part of a mind; 'or it may be grouped with its causal antecedents, in which case it appears as part of the physical world'.[25] Russell is discreetly vague on the mechanics of this 'grouping'. It is a perhaps unintended consequence of this theory either that solipsism is true after all or that sense-data are not private. For if physical objects are constructs from *my* sense-data arranged with their causal antecedents, they cannot be objects in any public physical world. Russell does indeed renounce 'sense-data' in *The Analysis of Mind* (1921), as he reminds us in his last book.[26] But they survive in other guises as 'percepts', 'sensations', 'patches of colour' or even, in *An Inquiry into Meaning and Truth*, 'qualities'.[27]

A switch from a causal theory of perception to a phenomenalist account involves a move from what Professor Ayer calls vertical inference (from observed effect to unseen cause) to horizontal inference (in which we infer inductively the existence of entities of the same type as those we have been observing). To deduce the existence of a physical object corresponding to the appearances of the table is to make a vertical inference. To infer that it will present such and such an appearance if we move a certain distance to the left is to make a horizontal inference. Thus, we find Russell defining a material thing, in *Our Knowledge of the External World* (1914), as 'a certain series of aspects, namely those which would commonly be said to be *of* the thing'.[28] This definition, justified by an explicit appeal to Ockham's Razor, is qualified by adding those necessary conditions required to make it consonant with physical science. The definition finally takes the form: *Things are those series of aspects which obey the laws of physics.* He himself considers the obvious objection to such a definition that sense-data are not the sort of entities that can conform (or fail to conform) to the laws of physics. But he does not satisfactorily answer it.[29]

(c) A third deviation from the causal theory is Russell's introduction of the notion of *sensibilia* to supplement that of sense-data:[30]

I shall give the name of *sensibilia* to those objects which have the same metaphysical status as sense data, without necessarily being data to any mind. Thus the relation of a *sensibilia* to a sense datum is like that of a man to a husband: a man becomes a husband by entering the relation of marriage, and similarly a *sensibile* becomes a sense datum by entering the relation of acquaintance.

This concept is introduced to avoid the unwelcome subjectivity of sense-data. Its introduction is probably unjustified in terms of Russell's own logical method, as Ayer tries to show.[31] But its usefulness disappears with the abandonment of sense-data and the substitution of horizontal for vertical inferences in the search for logical constructions. In any case, a sense-datum cannot be simply a species of the genus *sensibile*. For, as Russell admits, part of the qualities of a sense-datum are dependent upon the workings of individual sense organs, nerves and brain. Thus *sensibilia* have no place either within a causal theory of perception or in a consistent phenomenalism. Their abortive introduction may perhaps be regarded as a belated obeisance to the claims of realist theories of perception, unacknowledged elsewhere in his writings.

It is doubtful, moreover, whether Russell's account of *sensibilia* can be made consistent with the theory of modalities which he puts forward in *The Analysis of Matter*.[32] According to that theory, possibility is a predicate of propositional functions. 'There are sensibilia' should be analysed as 'For *some* values of x, the propositional function "x is sensed" is true' (where 'some' is read, anomalously, as 'some but not all'). But if a particular x_1 is sensed, it is a sense-datum and not just a *sensibile*; and if another x_2 is not sensed, it cannot be a *sensibile* on Russell's account of possibility. For 'possible' is not a predicate applicable to designated individuals. It seems, therefore, that Russell should drop either his account of modalities or his theory of *sensibilia*. In fact, he does not invoke *sensibilia* in later treatments of the problem of perception.

(4) Anyone who proposes a causal account of perception must be prepared to give an account (a) of the nature of the causes that bring about the perceptual effects with which we are familiar, and (b) of the nature of the causal relation which links physical objects and perceptual experience. Russell's theory is no more satisfactory on (a) than on (b). We have seen that the version of the causal theory that he put forward in *The Problems of Philosophy* is not very explicit about what we may infer about physical objects on the evidence of perception alone, except to claim that it is a reasonable hypothesis that sensory fields and their physical counterparts have a common structure based on a 'correspondence' between them. In *The Analysis of Matter*, Russell tries to elucidate this concept of correspondence.

In doing so, he ignores many of the important distinctions that have been elaborated by subsequent writers on perception. For example, he does not pay much attention to Professor Price's important division between the *standing* and the *differential* conditions of a perceptual experience. He concentrates on the differential conditions, those which are required in order that I may have a percept of a particular kind. If at one moment I am looking at a rhinoceros and I then turn to look at a lion, the standing condition (light, diaphanous medium, integrity of sense organs, and so on) remain the same but the percept is different. What can we know about what accounts for this difference?

The inferences on which such knowledge depends rest in Russell's view on two chief postulates. The first of these is induction, and the second 'the assumption of a certain similarity of structure between cause and effect where both are complex'.[33] His account of structure is based on his pioneer work on the logic of relations.[34] The account of structure that he gives in chapter XXIV of *The Analysis of Matter* is substantially that offered nine years earlier in *An Introduction to Mathematical Philosophy*.[35] It can be stated as follows: A given class A can be said to have *the same structure* as another class B, if the following conditions are satisfied: (i) $R_1, \ldots, R_n$ are relations, that is, ordered n-tuples of the elements of A and $S_1, \ldots, S_n$ are relations, that is, ordered n-tuples of the elements of B; (ii) every member of A is in the field of R_i, and every member of B is in the field of S_i (for all i); (iii) there is a one-to-one function T such that A is the domain of T and B is the range of T; (that is, the element of A can be put into a one-to-one correspondence with the elements of B); (iv) for any n-tuple $\langle x_1, \ldots, x_n \rangle$ of members of A such that its components stand in the relation R_j to one another (that is, $R_j \langle x_1, \ldots, x_n \rangle$), the n-tuple $\langle T(x_1), \ldots, T(x_n) \rangle$ of members of B is such that its components stand in the relation S_j (that is, $S_j \langle T(x_1), \ldots, T(x_n) \rangle$).[36]

This definition of 'structure' elucidates what Russell has earlier referred to as 'correspondence':[37]

There has been a great deal of speculation in traditional philosophy which might have been avoided if the importance of structure, and the difficulty of getting behind it, had been realised. For example, it is often said that space and time are subjective, but they have objective counterparts; or that phenomena are subjective, but are caused by things in themselves, which must have differences *inter se* corresponding with the differences in the phenomena to which they give rise. Where such hypotheses are made, it is generally supposed that we can know very little about the objective counterparts. In actual fact, however, if the hypotheses as stated were correct, the objective counterparts would form a world having the same structure as the phenomenal world, and allowing us to infer from phenomena the truth of all propositions that can be stated in abstract terms and are known to be true of phenomena. If the phenomenal world has three dimensions, so must the world behind phenomena; if the phenomenal world is Euclidean, so must the other be; and so on. In short, every proposition having a communicable significance must be true of both worlds or of neither: the only difference must lie in just that essence of individuality which always eludes words and baffles description but which, for that very reason, is irrelevant to science.

The analogies by which Russell elucidates this account of structure are familiar ones – a map and its territory, a gramophone record and the music which it records, and so on. 'Thus it would seem,' he concludes, 'that wherever we infer from perceptions, it is only structure that we can validly infer.'[38] But exactly what can we thus validly infer? After all, scientific reasoning has given us a great deal of information about the nature of the material world. Why does Russell not say: 'Material objects are just as physics shows them to be'? This would give us much more information than he claims for his account of perception. It would not only tell us that the structure, in the sense explained, of the perceptual field has a correspondence with that of the physical world, but would also give us non-structural information like the mass of the electron, the velocity of light, and so on. It would have the disadvantage of failing to distinguish science from philosophy; but on Russell's account there seems to be no very good reason why they require to be distinguished.

He does, indeed, admit that there is one respect in which there is not a perfect structural correspondence between percepts and physical objects. In his first account of structure, he assumes a point-for-point correspondence between ordered differences in the perceptual world and in the physical. But he realises that there is a glaring empirical limitation on this exact correspondence. There are at least two ways in which this limitation can be shown. Russell takes as an instance the case of an event occurring at too great a distance for us to perceive the detail: 'If we are observing a man half a mile away, his appearance is not changed if he frowns, whereas it is changed for a man observing him from a distance of three feet.'[39] But there is a more important point that Russell does not comment on. Our sense organs are not sufficiently accurate instruments to register all the variations in physical stimuli to which they respond. A group of different light waves, of closely similar wavelength, may all be registered in our experience as 'the same colour'; and so on, for all the other physical stimuli which act on our various sense organs. Thus identical, that is, indiscriminable, sense-data may originate from differing stimuli. This means that we may not assume a simple one-one relation linking the world of physical objects and the world of sense. 'But we may substitute a many–one relation, and still obtain something useful.'[40] Moreover:[41]

It is obvious as a matter of logic that, if our correlating relation S is many–one, not one–one, logical inference in the sense in which S goes is just as feasible as before, but logical inference in the opposite sense is more difficult. That is why we assume that differing percepts have differing stimuli, but indistinguishable percepts need not have exactly similar stimuli.

Thus, so far as Russell's philosophical theory of perception goes, the relation between object and percept is what he calls 'semi-similar'. But we know this partly from commonsense inductions, as in the case of the frowning man that he cites, but more importantly from the sciences of physics and physiology.[42] Once again we want to ask where Russell draws the line between philosophy and natural science. Moreover, we naturally want to ask what is the point of formulating an exact and technical definition of 'similarity of structure' in order to elucidate what can be known of the external world from sense experience when the key concept has immediately to be weakened to 'semi-similar' which is nowhere exactly defined. Indeed. an attempt at a parallel definition of 'semi-similar' results in a concept so threadbare as to convey almost no information at all.

And what of (b) above, the nature of the causal relation between the external world and the perceptual field? There are four distinct accounts of the nature of causality to be found in Russell,[43] but only one of these is relevant to his account of perception. This is the notion of a 'causal line' adumbrated first in *Mysticism and Logic* and developed most explicitly in *Human Knowledge*:[44]

> A 'causal line', as I wish to define the term, is a temporal series of events so related that, given some of them, something can be inferred about the others whatever may be happening elsewhere. . . . I should consider the process from speaker to listener in broadcasting one causal line: here the beginning and end are similar in quality as well as in structure, but the intermediate links – sound waves, electromagnetic waves, and physiological processes – have only a resemblance of structure to each other and to the initial and final terms of the series.

In an explanation of this process, he invokes what has usually been regarded as the most eccentric and least defensible of his doctrines – the famous claim that percepts are actually 'in our heads': 'What the physiologist sees when he examines a brain is in the physiologist, not in the brain that he is examining.'[45] Indeed, he claims that[46]

> whoever accepts the causal theory of perception is compelled to conclude that percepts are in our heads, for they come at the end of a causal chain of physical events leading, spatially, from the object to the brain of the percipient. We cannot suppose that, at the end of this process, the last effect suddenly jumps back to the starting-point, like a stretched rope when it snaps.

This rather surprising part of Russell's views on perception seems to have been very dear to him. He did not abandon it even in his last philosophical writings:[47]

> The light from a star travels over intervening space and causes a disturbance in the optic nerve ending in an occurrence in the brain. What I maintain is that the occurrence in the brain *is* a visual sensation.

Later in the same discussion he claims that 'we *can* witness or observe what goes on in our heads, and that we cannot witness or observe anything else at all'.

These assertions seem so outrageously paradoxical that few of Russell's critics seem to have taken them seriously. But the proposal is, after all, just an early and restricted version of the identity theory of mind and body made famous by the contemporary Australian materialists. We do have good evidence from physiology and physics that the nature, structure and position of certain brain events occurring in physical space completely determine the nature, structure and position of the percepts that occur in our sensory fields. And since the literal sense of the relational phrase 'located in' is 'located in physical space', we are justified in saying that percepts are located in our brains (though not, as Russell makes clear,[48] 'a part' of our brains).

Russell admitted, in reply to Professor Nagel's criticism,[49] that his theory involves using the word 'see' in an unusual sense:

> I admit this. The usual sense implies naïve realism, and whoever is not a naïve realist must either eschew the word 'see' or use it in a new sense. Commonsense says: 'I see a brown table.' It will agree to both the statement: 'I see a table' and 'I see something brown'. Since, according to physics, tables have no colour, we must either (a) deny physics, or (b) deny that I see a table, or (c) deny that I see something brown. It is a painful choice; I have chosen (b), but (a) or (c) would lead to at least equal paradoxes.

But in addition to using 'see' in an unusual sense, he also uses 'percept' in a double sense without ever clearly distinguishing the two or justifying the ambiguity. In the first sense, a percept is private to the observer. It is what Russell once called a sense-datum (or a group of such data) and is located only in the sensory field (or what Russell calls the private space) of the percipient. But when he says that 'percepts are in my head' and that 'my head consists of percepts and other similar events',[50] he seems to be using the term to mean 'events that are located in my brain and are therefore physically located in public space'.

If this is so, we must analyse 'I see *X*' in something like the following terms: '(a) I am directly aware of percepts whose necessary and sufficient conditions are certain brain events; (b) these brain events are the final stage of a causal series in whose ancestry some of the events constituting X are a necessary part.' If it be objected that this is a very complex analysis of a simple sentence, the answer must be that on any causal theory of perception the analysis of 'I see X' and similar sentences must be complex. We may perhaps criticise Russell for failing to mark the ambiguity of the term 'percept'. Ockham's Razor resulted here in linguistic as well as conceptual povery. And his doctrinaire abandonment of the term 'sense-datum' is at least partly to blame for the confusion.

But if this interpretation is correct, it removes the air of paradox from the identity theory at the cost of reintroducing a dualism that Russell had always distrusted. And what of the 'proof' that he offers of the identity of percept and brain state? As we saw, it amounts to no more than an appeal to the continuity of the causal process from physical object to percept. The argument is that the final stage of the causal process is identical with the percept; and the percept is an event in the brain. If, indeed, 'percept' is taken in the sense of 'physical event' this conclusion must be accepted. But it is trivial unless Russell can establish the identity of the physical event with what he had earlier called the sense-datum. And this he did not do.

He does not put this version of the identity theory to much use in his writings on perception. But he does suggest in his most elaborate treatment of perceiving in *The Analysis of Matter*[51] that it helps us to get some idea of the nature of the physical world independently of the purely relational knowledge that physics and logic provide us with:

> If there is any intellectual difficulty in supposing that the physical world is quite unlike that of percepts, this is a reason for supposing that there is not this complete unlikeness. And there is a certain ground for such a view, in the fact that percepts are a part of the physical world, and are the only part that we can know without the help of rather elaborate and difficult inferences.

But this suggestion seems to make concessions to realism that are quite inconsistent with arguments against it that he has offered elsewhere.

The outcome of Russell's many attacks on the problems of perception seems to be that physics tells us what the material world is like and physics and physiology tell us how the material world is transmuted into the world of perception. But the peculiarly *philosophical* arguments which he lavishes on the problem, strangely enough, are less persuasive and less conclusive than those of the scientist. If we believed Russell's philosophical arguments about perception, we would know less about the physical world than we do. There is a moral here which Russell himself never draws.

Department of Philosophy
University of Exeter

NOTES

1 *Contemporary British Philosophy*, first series, J. H. Muirhead, ed. (London, George Allen & Unwin, 1924: 79).
2 *My Philosophical Development* (London, George Allen & Unwin, 1959: 18 ff.).
3 *Russell and Moore: the Analytical Heritage* (London, Macmillan, 1971: 12–14).
4 'Scientific Method in Philosophy', in *Mysticism and Logic* (London, George Allen & Unwin, 1963: 105–6).
5 ibid.
6 ibid.
7 *Mysticism and Logic* (London, George Allen & Unwin, 1963: 155).
8 E. A. Moody in *The Encyclopedia of Philosophy*, P. Edwards, ed. (New York, Macmillan), vol. 8, p. 307.
9 *The Problems of Philosophy* (London, Home University Library, 1912: ch. 2, 21).
10 ibid., p. 24.
11 ibid., p. 31.
12 ibid., p. 34.
13 ibid., p. 32.
14 ibid., p. 33.
15 ibid., p. 34.
16 These considerations are taken into account in later writings. See, for example, ch. III of *Our Knowledge of the External World* (London: George Allen & Unwin, 1926).
17 *Mysticism and Logic*, pp. 138–9.
18 ibid.
19 ibid., p. 152.
20 ibid., p. 133.
21 *Russell and Moore: The Analytical Heritage*, p. 60.
22 Gregory, R. L., *Eye and Brain* (London, Weidenfeld & Nicolson, 1966: ch. 11); M. von Senden, trans., P. Heath, *Space and Sight* (London, Methuen, 1960).
23 *My Philosophical Development* (London, Weidenfeld & Nicolson, 1966: 134).
24 ibid., p. 139.
25 ibid.
26 ibid., p. 135.
27 *An Inquiry into Meaning and Truth* (London, George Allen & Unwin, 1940: 98).
28 *Our Knowledge of the External World*, p. 112.
29 ibid., p. 116.
30 *Mysticism and Logic*, p. 143.
31 *Russell and Moore: The Analytical Heritage*, pp. 57–9.
32 *The Analysis of Matter* (London, Kegan Paul, 1927: 170).
33 *The Analysis of Matter*, p. 249.
34 *Principia Mathematica*, 2nd edn, vol. II (Cambridge University Press, 1910–13: 150 ff.).
35 *Introduction to Mathematical Philosophy* (London, George Allen & Unwin; New York: Macmillan, 1919: ch. VI).
36 I am indebted to my colleague Dr G. B. Keene for help with the formulation of this definition in a more explicit form than is to be found in Russell's writings.
37 *Introduction to Mathematical Philosophy*, p. 61. The last sentence of this passage antici- pates Schlick's doctrine (cf. 'Form and Content', *Gesammelte Aufsatze*) that it is structure and not content that can be communicated. Russell comes closer here to a positivist position than he permits himself elsewhere in his writings.
38 *The Analysis of Matter*, p. 254.
39 ibid., p. 225.
40 ibid., p. 254.
41 ibid.

42 Further evidence for this conclusion can be found in the findings of experimental psychology about the so-called 'constancy phenomena'.

43 See Erik Gotlind, *Bertrand Russell's Theories of Causation* (Uppsala, Almqvist & Wicksells Boktryckeri, 1952: ch. V).

44 *Human Knowledge* (London, George Allen & Unwin, 1948: 477).

45 *The Analysis of Matter*, p. 320.

46 ibid.

47 *My Philosophical Development*, p. 25.

48 *The Philosophy of Bertrand Russell*, P. Schilpp, ed. (Evanston, Northwestern University Press, 1944: 705).

49 ibid.

50 *The Analysis of Matter*, p. 382.

51 ibid., p. 164.

19

RUSSELL AND SCHLICK:
A REMARKABLE AGREEMENT ON A
MONISTIC SOLUTION OF THE
MIND–BODY PROBLEM

Herbert Feigl

An important and striking coincidence in the views of two of the greatest philosophers of the first half of the twentieth century has gone practically unnoticed. Moritz Schlick, perhaps best known as the founder and centre of the Vienna Circle of Logical Positivists (*c.* 1924–36) anticipated Bertrand Russell's more recent views on the mind–body problem by at least eleven years. In an article published in 1916 (parts of which had been adumbrated already in an article in 1910),[1] Schlick, stimulated by the views of R. Avenarius, and ultimately referring back to an obscure but highly suggestive brief passage in Kant's *Critique of Pure Reason* (the chapter on Paralogisms of Pure Reason; Rational Psychology), had begun the clarification of the difference between psychological and physical contexts. This he elaborated in his magnificent *Allgemeine Erkenntnislehre* (1918) and explicated even more fully in the 2nd edition (1925) of this truly trail-blazing book. It is likely that Schlick was influenced by the philosophical monism formulated in the second volume of Alois Riehl's *Der Philosophische Kritizismus*.[2] Riehl, in my possibly prejudiced opinion, was the most brilliant and clear-headed among the neo-Kantians. Unfortunately he is all but forgotten nowadays.

Russell, who had still held his well-known neutral monism (strongly related to E. Mach's and William James's epistemologies) and a logically clarified Watsonian behaviourism, displayed a radical change of mind in his *Analysis of Matter* (1927). There he expounded a solution of the mind–matter problem which he elaborated more fully and brilliantly in *Human Knowledge* (1948). By then the philosophical indispensability of a causal theory of perception and a structuralistic view of physical science had become completely clear to Russell.

The crucial point (if we disregard the only very distantly related ancestral metaphysical views of Spinoza and Leibniz) is rather cryptically expressed in no more than half a page in Kant's otherwise so voluminous *Critique of Pure Reason*. To put it in more readily intelligible modern terms, Kant (of course, still within his presupposed metaphysics of the '*Ding an sich*') tells us that the notorious Cartesian problem of the relation of the mental to the physical need not disturb us very deeply. The ultimate reality (*Ding an sich*) to which our physical concepts and theories refer may not be so different in its intrinsic nature from the realities of immediate experience referred to by psychological introspection. (I do not know whether G. T. Fechner's panpsychism was in part stimulated by that exciting passage in Kant.) As far as I can tell, after Schopenhauer's metaphysical views regarding the 'will' as the ultimate reality, it was Riehl (not a panpsychist, though sharply opposed to nineteenth-century German 'crass' materialism) who was the first to formulate in outline but very respectably an approximation of what Russell, I am practically certain independently of the antecedent work of Schlick, presented as his final thoughts on the mind–body problem.

Perhaps the coincidence of Schlick's and Russell's views is not altogether surprising. Both these brilliant thinkers had the great advantage of a thorough early training in the exact sciences; Russell more widely in mathematics and its logical foundations, Schlick more deeply in theoretical physics. But though, of course, Russell excelled as a philosopher of mathematics and was greatly appreciated in this capacity by Schlick, Schlick was (along with C. D. Broad) one of the first philosophers to provide a logical analysis of Einstein's theory of relativity.[3] In addition to their excellent background in mathematics and most of the sciences, both Schlick and Russell were distinguished by their remarkable philosophico-logical acumen. Here Russell was more productive, original and profound than Schlick. Still, Schlick with his (pre-Wittgenstein!) insight into the analytic nature of deductive inference and hence of mathematical proof, and with his philosophical elaboration of the significance of implicit definitions (i.e. 'definitions' by postulates), made significant contributions to the logic of the exact sciences. The much more comprehensive and precise work of R. Carnap and H. Reichenbach may be regarded as the most important *sequelae* to Schlick's informal analyses.

Now in order to expound the Schlick–Russell solution of the mind–body problem,[4] it is important to remove some widespread misunderstandings right at the outset. Neither Schlick nor the *later* Russell were logical behaviourists, let alone materialists. Schlick was not very happy with Carnap's physicalism, although he was (just as was Russell) optimistic about the reduction of *all* scientific truths to those of (a possibly future) basic theoretical physics. What is so frequently *not* understood is that this reductionist position is logically compatible with the recognition of the occurrence of directly experienced ('phenomenal') mental events or processes. Disregarding for the moment the issues of the 'unconscious' (such as in psychoanalytic theories, which Schlick cavalierly ignored but Russell appreciated in his own way), both thinkers in a very definite sense were convinced of Descartes's *cogito*, but neither of '*ergo sum*' as intended by Descartes, nor of course of the Cartesian interactionist dualism or even its two substances. In other words, both Schlick and Russell were fully clear about, and insisted upon, the epistemic primacy of immediate experience, or the 'directly' phenomenally given qualities. Not only did they consider the phenomenal sensory data as the testing-ground of all empirical knowledge claims, they also realised that the occurrence of the (directly *inaccessible*, in the old positivistic, verificationist sense) mental states of other minds is an essential, necessary and cognitive presupposition, but of course not sufficient condition for the meaningfulness of ethical imperatives such as 'Thou shalt not torment other humans – or animals!'

Neither Russell nor Schlick was dogmatic with regard to a doctrine of 'pointillistic' sense-data. Schlick, in fact (and as I recall, Russell, too), sympathised with the gestalt psychologists, especially with Wolfgang Kohler's view according to which the phenomenally given usually presents itself in patterns or configurations. Neither Schlick nor Russell denied the *practical* importance of the outlook and language of commonsense (i.e. what Wilfrid Sellars came to call the 'manifest image' of the world), but both were emphatic on the urgent need for drastic corrections of the direct realism which pervades commonsense knowledge. These corrections are inevitable if the best-established facts and low-level theories of physics, physiology and neurophysiological psychology are taken seriously, even if, in detail, they can be held only 'until further notice'. Neither Schlick (until about 1925 or 1926) nor Russell (certainly after 1927) was in the least worried about the notorious arguments of the Berkeleyan subjective idealists, phenomenalists, positivists and others against a Locke–Helmholtz-type representative realism. The bogeyman of solipsism was met head-on by Russell when he admitted that despite its logical impeccability it could not be sincerely believed by any sane person. I think Russell also realised that by a sort of *reductio ad absurdum* the solipsist could be forced into a retreat to solipsism-of-the-present-moment and thus condemned to permanent silence; and what worse fate could befall a loquacious philosopher? Schlick, who, like the unfortunately almost forgotten Oswald Kulpe[5] (but of course remembered as the leader of the Wurzburg School of psychology) and other German critical realists, mustered in the *Allgemeine Erkenntnislehre* (1918; 1925) impressive arguments against all and sundry 'philosophies of immanence' (as he called the phenomenalistic epistemologies) and defended a metaphysically innocuous 'transcendence', i.e. the assumption of knowable things-in-themselves, namely, those of the world of physics and the biological sciences, including the minds of people other than oneself. Russell presented essentially similar arguments in *Analysis of Matter* and in *Human Knowledge*.

Moreover, both Schlick and Russell, each in his own formulations, insisted on the purely *structural* type of knowledge as the only sort of knowledge we can have of the 'external world' of physics, chemistry, astronomy and biology. The concept of structure was introduced formally in A. N. Whitehead's and B. Russell's *Principia Mathematica* as the 'relation-number' (picturable by a configuration of dots and arrows). The same concept and its profound philosophical significance was informally discussed in Russell's *Introduction to Mathematical Philosophy* as well as in *Human Knowledge*. Just as Schlick drew a fundamental distinction between *Erleben* (direct experience) and *Erkennen* (relational knowledge-proper), so Russell differentiated sharply between acquaintance (and knowledge by acquaintance) on the one hand, and knowledge by description (construction or inference) on the other. This basic distinction enabled both thinkers to propose a monistic solution of the mind–body problem. If a label is wanted, it might be all right to call it the 'twofold knowledge' or the 'twofold access' theory. It is one and the same reality (events, processes) that as far as phenomenal awareness is concerned can be known introspectively, or as probabilistically indicated by behaviour symptoms (e.g. discriminatory, expressive, action-type behaviour), and can be known ultimately, once neurophysiology has sufficiently advanced, by an account of the neural processes in the brain (for fully aware consciousness, probably cortical processes). In recent decades the term 'identity theory' has become widely used.

But it is important to distinguish Schlick's and Russell's views from the much later, deliberately materialistic (though highly sophisticated!) views of such brilliant Australian philosophers as U. T. Place, J. J. C. Smart, D. M. Armstrong, Brian Medlin and Max Deutscher.[6] Much of the Australian identity theory grew out of, but was nevertheless a drastic alteration of, Gilbert Ryle's logical behaviourism formulated in his very influential (though highly questionable) book, *The Concept of Mind* (1949). In the interest of historical fairness, it should be mentioned that some of Ryle's most essential contributions were anticipated by the American philosopher Edgar A. Singer (1911), and independently by Carnap in 1933. At the risk of gross oversimplification, I am inclined to say that the Australian materialism (independent of, though somewhat similar to, that of Roy W. Sellars, the American critical realist) is either eliminative or reductive with regard to the identification of sensations with cerebral events. Perhaps closest to the Schlick–Russell solution, but still distinctly different, is D. M. Armstrong's Central State Materialism. According to him our mental experiences *are* (identical with) those brain states which are 'apt to cause certain behavioural (peripheral) responses'. This is certainly a step in the right direction. But the Australian materialists modelled their identity theory (or theories) on the impressive examples of reduction and identification in the physical sciences. It is quite correct, for example, when a housewife (let us assume she is ignorant of theoretical physics) says 'The soup is hot now', to maintain that she refers to a state of the emulsion, say, of the pea soup, which the experimental physicist might describe as the intensity of heat, measurable in terms of one or another temperature scale by various types of thermometer, using various thermometric substances, e.g. mercury, alcohol or gas. The theoretical physicist then can maintain a contingent (i.e. empirically ascertainable) identity of the temperature of the soup with the mean kinetic energy of the molecules that constitute the emulsion. The first much-discussed example in the philosophical literature was U. T. Place's: 'Lightning is electric discharge' (1956). My own earlier examples, e.g. 'Table salt is NaCl', 'Heat is molecular motion', 'Electric current is "electron gas" in motion', 'Mendelian factors of heredity are genes', have not been so widely noticed or discussed.[7] For the purposes of more meticulous analyses, it has become important to distinguish in such cases the 'is' of identity not only from the obviously and categorially different 'is' of *logical* identity (as is e.g. '2^5 is 64'), but also to differentiate between the 'is' of composition ('Clouds *are* masses of finely distributed tiny water or ice particles'), and the 'is' of elimination ('Caloric is thermal energy') and the 'is' of reduction ('Aethyl alcohol is C_2H_5OH').

Now for an adequate understanding of the (non-materialistic!) Schlick–Russell solution, it might at first seem tempting to say that mental events or states (acts, processes) such as sensations, images, pains, emotions, moods, sentiments, volitions, desires and thoughts are (reductively – or worse, eliminatively) identical with the (speaking dualistically for the sake of easier understanding) 'corresponding' cerebral states, events, processes or dispositions. But this would still be a materialistic view, which, I emphasise once more, was certainly not held by either Schlick or Russell. Both thinkers, perhaps owing to the powerful influence of the idealist tradition in philosophy, and the then more recent impact of Ernst Mach's philosophical and psychobiological outlook, never doubted[8] the ineluctable 'givenness' of immediate experience. As I see it, the affirmation of the 'given', far from being a myth, was for both Schlick and Russell the ultimate testing-ground of all empirical knowledge, including commonsense knowledge claims, the natural and the social-cultural sciences or disciplines. Hence their position was certainly not that of reduction, let alone elimination, of the mental in favour of the physical. Since neither Schlick nor Russell explicated fully and in logical detail what they proposed as their identity view, if indeed it is fair to ascribe an identity view to them, I shall now to the best of my limited ability attempt to make as clear as possible just what these two remarkable thinkers claimed to have shown by logical analysis on behalf of their psychophysical monism.

Perhaps the most important point is to realise that both Schlick and Russell provided an explication of the meaning of 'physical' which, thought not in keeping with the ordinary language and commonsensical use of this term, is in the fullest agreement with what professional physicists at least since Galileo and Newton have meant by the term. 'Thou shalt not make graven images unto thyself' is an excellent piece of advice with regard to the method of understanding physical concepts and theories. It is not denied that pictorial models were and still are heuristically and didactically all but indispensable, and often led and still lead to important discoveries in theoretical physics, chemistry, microbiology, psychoanalytic theory, and so on. But to visualise such things as atoms, electrons or any of the 'zoo' of other subatomic particles, their spins, or the photons, or energy, entropy, the quantum-electrodynamic field, the Hilbert space with its infinite number of dimensions as used in quantum mechanics. can only be misleading. Thus, it makes no sense to ascribe a colour or a temperature to an individual electron. Even though we have beautiful (but oversimplified!) diagrams of Minkowski 4-space of special relativity, it is impossible to visualise adequately what the Lorentz–Einstein transformations mean. Again I grant that it is most helpful in the teaching of relativity theory to make use of the Minkowski pictorial representation. But as already hinted above, the whole point is that our knowledge of the external world achieved with the help of physical concepts and theories is *structural*, in the precise Russellian sense. Schlick, in the same vein, regards our physical knowledge as 'symbolic', and he did not intend anything poetic, mysterious or mystical by putting it that way. All he meant was that any genuine knowledge claim must be capable of formulation by means of words, sentences, mathematical formulae, or the like. Whatever the accompanying imageries (*Begleitvorstellungen* was Carnap's term) amount to, is only of heuristic or didactic significance, but by itself not cognitively significant. If the rules of symbolisation are made explicit – as they can be made explicit – in the syntactical and semantical studies of language (i.e. in the respective metalanguages), these rules will provide us with the meaning of the words (sentences, formulae) that we use in all descriptions of facts or communication thereof. It is, then, merely a terminological matter, as to whether we mean by 'physical' a kind of symbol (or sentence, or formula) or the objects or states of affairs designated by such symbols, sentences or formulae.

At this point a philosopher adhering to one or another of the 'deep' metaphysical traditions might well ask: what do Schlick and Russell believe is the nature of the reality ('Being'!) designated by the symbols and symbolic systems of the sciences (especially theoretical physics, of course)? Schlick and Russell, in full agreement with each other, would (might?) have answered (I paraphrase Russell's more handy English language): Most of the reality of the world is unknown and for physical, i.e. contingent, reasons unknowable by acquaintance. If you want to '*know*' what (for example) an electric current 'really' ('intrinsically') is, you would have to *be* an electric current. But if you want to know what certain cerebral processes (e.g. in the temporal lobe) intrinsically are, we can give you an answer. It may well be musical tones-as-heard; likewise certain processes in the occipital lobe may intrinsically *be* visual sensations such as coloured shapes or configurations.

It is this answer which has led such American critical realists as C. A. Strong and Durant Drake (and in a much more attenuated sense also S. C. Pepper in 1967) to their doctrines of panpsychism. But in this respect both Schlick, some of whose foundations are similar to those of Pepper's 'pan-quality-ism' (a clumsy word, but probably not a nonsensical idea!), and less certainly Russell, are negative. Neither 'pan' ('Does our galaxy have a mental life?'; 'Do atoms?'), nor 'psyche' – it is already extremely unlikely that a unicellular organism like the amoeba possesses anything remotely similar to human consciousness. Russell and Schlick did not accept panpsychism (though they considered analogical reasoning legitimate), because they realised that, if the similarlity with the human case of the external behaviour and the internal neurophysiological processes is extremely tenuous or even entirely absent, then the speculative inferences of the panpsychists are grossly overextended. Nevertheless Schlick (but not Russell) speaks of the 'intrinsic' nature of the world as a 'web of qualities' knowable by acquaintance only if one is the owner of a living functioning brain.

Although I still have tried (e.g. in 1950, 1958, 1963 and 1967) to explicate the mind–body identity roughly along the Fregean line of the identity of reference of a 'label' (for qualities of immediate experience) with the reference of a theoretical concept construed by definite description (of neurophysiology), I am now no longer so confident that this is the best way to understand the basic Schlick–Russell view. Schlick (especially in his London lectures of 1932) was close to saying – if he did not actually put it that way – that the qualities of immediate experience (called 'sentience' by C. A. Strong) are the *content* of the *structures* described in cerebral neurophysiology. Grover Maxwell has attempted to explicate this conception of 'intrinsic' natures or properties in terms of 'first-order properties'. This might suggest the sort of *Aufbau* that Carnap had worked out in his famous book of 1928, i.e. a system of the constitution of empirical concepts, based on a hierarchy of abstractive-contextual ('in use') definitions, patterned in accordance with Russell's (non-ramified) hierarchy of logical types. But I doubt that is what Maxwell intended or that this essentially phenomenalistic reconstruction will render adequately the intent of the Schlick–Russell monism.

The possible dangers of my own reconstruction *à la* Frege (ostensively 'labelling' a referent that is identical with what is described as neurophysiological states) are that this amounts to no more than an extensional identity thesis; this for the simple reason that the meanings of phenomenal (sentience) terms differ categorially from those of physical terms. That is to say that the *salva veritate* condition for translating mental into physical statements (or vice versa) cannot be fulfilled, except for their ranges of application (extension). The traditionalists keep telling me that *this* sort of mental–physical identification is only at best a logically clarified thesis of a double attribute or parallelistic doctrine, reminiscent at least vaguely of Spinoza's 'double-aspect' (historically, rather 'plural-aspects') metaphysics. The question, therefore, keeps arising: why not psychophysiological parallelism or isomorphism (epiphenomenalism not being a plausible theory)? What is the difference that makes an in-principle testable difference between an identity and parallelism? It is fairly obvious that there is no conceivable difference in the usual empiricist sense of 'difference'. At this point many proponents of the identity theory brandish Ockham's Razor (one of Russell's favourite devices in other contexts), i.e. a principle of parsimony or simplicity which is (I think), if properly understood, indeed one of the guiding maxims of scientific theorising. But as I understand the Schlick–Russell solution it does not need any argument from simplicity. To be sure, the resulting simplification (i.e. by only one kind of basic reality, instead of two or more) is just a welcome consequence of the insights gained from neurophysiology on the one hand, and logico-epistemological analysis and clarification on the other.

The attractiveness of the Schlick–Russell solution to the contrary not-withstanding, the identification is (I repeat) admittedly and emphatically a *contingent* one, dependent as it is on empirical findings. Most disturbing among the many criticisms directed *against* an identity theory is Wilfrid Sellars's 'grain argument'. I discuss it briefly in the bibliographical appendix to this chapter. Although the still controversial facts (!) of 'psychic phenomena' (telepathy, precognition, retrocognition, psychokinesis, etc.) may well find an explanation on the basis of a (probably expanded) physical theory, there is no such theory (at least none that is scientifically plausible and testable) in sight; hence *in extremis* the monistic theories might have to be abandoned. In the meantime, it would certainly be in the spirit of Schlick and Russell at least to go through the motions of an open mind in these highly puzzling matters. Both men, typically Victorian in their evolutionistic, reductionistic convictions, completely ignored the endeavours and findings of parapsychology. But, after all, Schlick died in 1936 and Russell did not write anything philosophically new after 1948.

More to the point is the more technical question of the precise and fully adequate explication of the monistic solution in terms of modern logic, involving as it does fundamental considerations regarding the distinctions, and especially the relations between the phenomenal (psychological) spaces and physical space; analogously for phenomenal and physical time. Schlick and Russell are in full agreement on the pivotal importance of the distinction. Russell had repeatedly dealt with the logical construction of physical space–time on the basis of the data in visual, tactual, kinaesthetic space (but hardly the more amorphous proprioceptive spatialities, and whatever little indications there are of auditory, let alone olfactory, spatialities inasmuch as they are aspects of immediate, subjective experience). Russell's analyses, partly utilising A. N. Whitehead's ideas on extensive abstraction, the construction of points on the basis of sets of spatial regions, are too intricate for brief summarisation. Schlick, both in his *Allgemeine Erkenntnislehre* and in later publications, agreed on the purely structural (abstract, non-visualisable) character of physical space-and-time. His ideas in this connection are simpler than those of Russell's and hence probably insufficient. Schlick used the method of coincidences for the construction of points in physical space. He distinguished apparent coincidences, such as that of one's fingertip with a spot on the moon (all in one's visual field), from real coincidences, such as that of one's fingertips of the right hand with those of the left hand; or of the pointer on a measuring instrument with a mark immediately behind the pointer on a scale (as e.g. in ammeters, voltmeters, certain types of photometers, thermometers, or the like). All these cases of objective coincidence are in principle both visual *and* tactual, as well as intersubjective. (As far as I know, Schlick did not discuss the construction of point identities in cases such as in astronomy, where tactual access is excluded; no doubt he would have said that the physical geometry provides methods of triangulation in the case of the not-too-distant stars, and is thus dependent on the assumptions of geometrical optics.) Of course, all this (not only my present brief account) is rather sketchy. The exact reconstruction of the logical relations between physical space and the phenomenal spatialities is an important problem whose solution is indispensable for the final justification of mind—body monism. Schlick and Russell, having provided promising beginnings, might stimulate present-day logicians and philosophers in the search for a more adequate and perspicaciously penetrating analysis.

An important corollary of the mind—body problem is the endlessly disputed free will—determinism issue. Here again we find complete agreement between Russell and Schlick. Their view can be succinctly expressed by quoting the title of R. E. Hobart's epoch making article: 'Free Will as Involving Determinism, and Inconceivable without It' (*Mind*, January 1934). The current fashion of relying on the indeterminism of modern quantum physics as a necessary condition for genuine free will rests on confusions which have long been exposed, if not earlier then certainly by Hume, J. S. Mill, H. Sidgwick, Russell, Schlick, Hobart, A. K. Stout, M. S. Everett, A. J. Ayer, P. H. Nowell-Smith, C. L. Stevenson and many others. The 'nightmare of determinism', a term used by some defenders of a conception of free will that requires indeterminism, seems to me (and I believe Schlick and Russell would concur) to rest on a fallacious identification of ontological with epistemic determinism. Epistemic determinism amounts to the doctrine of strict and complete predictability and retrodictability (*à la* Laplace's demon) of each and every event in the universe, including the mental events (sensations, emotions, desires, volitions, problem solving, artistic and all sorts of inventions, theory-constructions, etc., etc.). The uncanny feeling most of us get when contemplating especially the moral aspects of that 'nightmare' is based on the fallacious identifications of determinism with fatalism and of free choice with absolute chance. Once it is realised that even in an ontologically strictly deterministic universe we can most justifiably, and to a considerable extent, be considered as the *do-ers* of our deeds, as essential links in the causal chains that make up our lives, the problem is dissolved.

In sum, as soon as we realise that the contrary opposite of free choice is compulsion (coercion, constraint) and *not* determinism, and that of course indeterminism is the opposite of determinism (although present-day physics quite consistently assumes deterministic laws, like the conservation laws of energy and momentum, along with the statistical laws of photon-particle interactions, radioactive nuclear disintegration, etc., i.e. for different types of processes), the 'mystery' of the free-will problem disappears. The only thing to remember is that while determinism and indeterminism are generalised scientific or if you will metaphysical conceptions, 'free will' and 'compulsion' ('coercion', 'constraint') have in addition to their objective scientific meaning also an evaluative or normative significance. What a genuinely 'free' person or society 'really is' (or 'ought to be') are such matters that, though the origin of these norms may well be explainable (psychologically, sociologically, anthropologically, historically), their acceptance (our commitment to them) is not entirely justifiable on purely objective, scientific grounds. Once it is clearly seen that epistemic determinism is tantamount to the conjunction of four assumptions, namely, ontological determinism, complete and precise knowledge of the basic laws of nature, complete and precise ascertainability of the initial and boundary conditions of the relevant system – possibly the whole universe (!) – and unlimited capacity for exact mathematical computation of future or past states, it becomes obvious that the epistemic non-inferability of the future or the past need not imply the falsity of ontological determinism. It is one of the other three assumptions that is almost certainly to be rejected as false or extremely implausible. Schlick's main epistemological work, dating back to the years before Max Born's definitively statistical interpretation of Schrödinger's quantum-mechanical wave equations, was, although Schlick later accepted the indeterminism of quantum mechanics, conceived within the frame of classical (ontological) determinism. (This is *my* interpretation of Schlick's views, i.e. the realistic doctrines for which he argued before he was converted to a verificationist positivism by Carnap and Wittgenstein.) Russell, who was quick to grasp the tremendous philosophical significance of quantum mechanics, was a staunch ontological indeterminist. But this did not change his position on the pseudo-problem of free will. Still, I do not think Russell would have opposed such attempts as those of Bohm, Vigier, de Broglie or Einstein to restore physical determinism on a deeper level, e.g. by the introduction of 'hidden variables'. The question whether the indeterminism of quantum mechanics is going to alter significantly the neuro-physiological theories (regarding processes on the microlevel of nerve conduction, synaptic transfers, etc.) is very much under discussion nowadays. But the vitalistic or Cartesian ideas of loopholes in the otherwise largely deterministic neural processes, i.e. conjectures which assume that either some 'emergent' mental occurrence, or a totally non-material 'psychic' event could intervene in the physical brain processes, strike me as scientifically anachronistic, reminiscent of *élan vital*, entelechies, and psychoids as for example speculated about early this century by H. Bergson and H. Driesch.

A very thorny issue, that of Brentano's idea of intentionality, has been dealt with in differing ways by both Schlick and Russell. Much work has followed, especially the development of the contrasting views of Wilfrid Sellars and Roderick Chisholm. I think that Schlick and Russell would have found Sellars's ideas (though sometimes causing the reader some difficulties of understanding) more appealing than those of Chisholm. Once we have the semantical notions of designation, denotation and truth conditions, it becomes possible to explicate the notion of intentionality (reference) semantically, i.e. in a metalanguage which enables us to state what a given word (or symbol) or a given sentence (or formula) in the object language designates (or describes), i.e. the objects or states of affairs that the words or sentences are 'about'. This does not exclude a phenomenological 'side-view' (*à la* Brentano or Husserl) at the intentional relation of our thoughts to their (existent or non-existent) objects. But this in Schlick's, and I believe also in Russell's, view would be a task of descriptive psychology.

Schlick, whose main concern in the mind–body problem has been the problem of *sentience*, though there are interesting chapters in his *Allgemeine Erkenntnislehre* also about *sapience*, never had the (slight?) misgivings to be found occasionally in Russell's writings (I can't find the passage just now that I seem to remember) regarding a complete physicalistic reduction or identification of the *qualities* of direct experience, especially those cherished in moral or aesthetic contexts. It may be readily admitted that a neurophysiological explanation of inventive problem solving or artistic creation will be the most intricate and difficult, and probably the last that the otherwise triumphant progress of physical science will ever (if at all) successfully encompass.

Let me conclude by an admittedly not-very-relevant (philosophically) comparison of the personalities of Russell and Schlick. As all the world knows, Russell was an outspoken, irreligious unbeliever. Schlick was equally humanistically oriented but not as aggressively emphatic about it as was Russell. Schlick was a highly musical person, and as far as I know music meant little to Russell. Schlick's manner of spoken delivery was slow, halting, with only very infrequent touches of humour, irony, let alone the sort of sarcasm in which Russell excelled. Schlick's utopian philosophy of youth is essentially similar to Russell's conception of the meaning of life. But I fear Russell would have found Schlick's famous essay *Vom Sinn des Lebens* a little too sanguine and insipid. Russell was much more fully aware of the evils of our world than the ever-so-optimistic Schlick. I fear that Schlick's rosy outlook on life contributed to the motivation of the indigent, mentally deranged student who assassinated him on the stairway of the University of Vienna in 1936.

Schlick's political views were emphatically pacifist-socialistic in his younger years, but during the last ten years or so of his life he became more individualistic and conservative, perhaps mostly in reaction to the growing Nazi movement. (It was two years after Schlick's death that Hitler and his hordes invaded Vienna.) Russell distinguished himself spectacularly by his work for international understanding and peace, especially during the last thirty years or so of his long life. With regard to their positions in moral philosophy (ethical theory), there were only minor differences in the formulation of the views at which they had arrived quite independently. It is worth remembering that these two profound thinkers – Russell more brilliant in expression, Schlick somewhat more professorial but extremely lucid and free of the notorious Teutonic tenacity – have given us the best philosophical thought of the first half of the twentieth century.

Postscript on A. S. Eddington; and on Structuralism
For readers unfamiliar with or unsympathetic towards philosophical analysis, but with some knowledge of theoretical physics, I recommend warmly the three philosophical books by the late Sir Arthur Eddington, the great British astrophysicist, theoretical physicist and profound thinker: *The Nature of the Physical World* (1928), *New Pathways in Science* (1935) and *The Philosophy of Physical Science* (1939).[9] Eddington acknowledged his deep indebtedness to Russell with regard especially to structuralism and the twofold knowledge situation of the mind–body problem. Eddington's views were almost deliberately misunderstood and, I think, rather maliciously criticised from a positivistic and commonsense point of view by the late British logician (a lady of undeniable merits in her own field) L. Susan Stebbing, in *Philosophy and the Physicists*.[10]

Perhaps a helpful way of understanding the Schlick–Russell–Eddington structuralism is to reflect on the difference of physical from psychological (phenomenal or phenomenological) concept and theory construction. Very briefly: the concepts of the physical sciences are invariant with regard to the difference of the sense modalities (sight, touch, hearing, etc.) which are their ultimate testing-grounds (of confirmation or disconfirmation). For example, although it would be made more difficult and time-consuming for a congenitally blind person to arrive at astronomical or physical knowledge, it is not impossible in principle. The congenitally blind person could be equipped with photoelectric cells which respond to impinging light rays issuing from spectroscopes attached to telescopes (or in biological research, to microscopes), etc. The photoelectric cells could then be connected through amplifiers to loudspeakers or other devices which emit discriminable sounds or change the position of a touchable pointer in front of a Braille scale and thus provide all basically required sensory information to the blind person. If this should appear a bit fantastic at first blush, we should remember that our knowledge regarding the stars or galaxies that emit only ultraviolet or radio waves is just as 'indirect'. So likewise is our knowledge of atomic nuclei, of the spin of subatomic particles, etc., etc. Only the qualities of direct, immediate experience can be recognised and labelled ostensively, i.e. without any detour through the use of special apparatus. All this should make it amply clear that our scientific knowledge of the external world (including, of course, the skin and 'innards' of our own organisms) is always inferential, constructive, hypothetical, abstract-structural; whereas the knowledge of our direct conscious experience is non-inferential, 'by acquaintance' and 'self-evident' (and by contrast invariant in its ostensive links between words and phenomenal items). It is also as minimally dubitable as any knowledge claim can possibly be. Descartes, and with some minor qualifications, Russell, Schlick and C. I. Lewis, were perfectly right on this point. The endless quibbling of the philosophers about 'incorrigibility' can easily be resolved by realising that our empirical knowledge claims simply 'base' the *more* dubitable on the *less* dubitable. Absolute indubitability is, of course, a chimera. But there are practical certainties of our knowledge by acquaintance of the 'given'!

Department of Philosophy
University of Minnesota

NOTES

1 M. Schlick, 'Die Grenze der naturwissenschaftlichen und philosophischen Begriffsbildung', *Vierteljahrsschrift fur Wissenschaftliche Philosophie*, vol. 34, (1910); and 'Idealitat des Raumes, Introjektion and Psychophysiches Problem', ibid., vol. 40 (1916).

2 English translation under the title *Introduction to the Theory of Science and Metaphysics* (London, Kegan Paul, Trench, 1894).

3 M. Schlick, 'Die philosophische Bedeutung des Relativatsprinzips', *Zeitschrift fur Philosophie und Philosophische Kritik*, vol. 159 (1915). Einstein himself widely recommended Schlick's slender book *Raum und Zeit in der Gegenwartigen Physik* (Berlin, Springer, 1917). There is an English translation by M. L. Brose (Oxford University Press, 1920).

4 Schlick called it the 'psychophysical problem', although the relation to the branch of experimental psychology founded by Weber, Fechner and Wundt is removed and almost entirely irrelevant. What *is* relevant is neurophysiological psychology.

5 In *Die Realisierung*, vol. 1, (1912), vols 2 and 3 at later dates. (I cannot locate the name of the German publisher.) An important work; cf. also W. Freytag's books.

6 For references, consult the bibliographies mentioned in the appendix to this chapter. Compare also the fascinating disputes contained in C. F. Presley, ed., *The Identity Theory of Mind* (St Lucia, Australia, University of Queensland Press, 1967). For a general, brief, lucid survey, cf. Keith Campbell's *Body and Mind* (London, Macmillan, 1971).

7 English translation (1959), in A. J. Ayer, *Logical Positivism* (New York, Free Press, 1953); cf. the bibliographies noted in the appendix to this chapter.

8 That is, Russell, after he had abandoned his temporary infatuation with behaviourism.

9   Arthur S. Eddington, *The Nature of the Physical World* (Cambridge University Press, 1928); *New Pathways in Science* (Cambridge University Press, 1935); *The Philosophy of Physical Science* (Cambridge University Press; New York, Macmillan, 1939).
10 L. Susan Stebbing, *Philosophy and the Physicists* (London, Methuen, 1937).

BIBLIOGRAPHICAL APPENDIX

Moritz Schlick and the early Bertrand Russell (*The Problems of Philosophy*, 1912; *Our Knowledge of the External World*, 1914) to begin with diverged considerably in their epistemological views. Schlick, in his *Allgemeine Erkenntnislehre* (Vienna, Springer, 1st edn, 1918; 2nd edn, 1925), which appeared at last in 1974 in the superb English translation by Albert E. Blumberg (Vienna and New York, Springer), criticised Russell's early positivistic, phenomenalistic or 'neutrally-monistic' views ('Critique of the Philosophies of Immanence', in the 2nd edition of 1925 of which Blumberg's is the translation: ch. 26). Naturally, Schlick could not have known of Russell's basic change of epistemological outlook which becomes clear (as far as I can tell) only in Russell's *Analysis of Matter* (1927); and is even more forcefully developed in Russell's *Human Knowledge* (1948), i.e. in his last systematic book in *theoretical* philosophy. (As is well known, he published important contributions to social and political philosophy for many years after 1948.) But there is a beautiful and concise resumé in the chapter 'Mind and Matter' in Russell's *Portraits from Memory* (New York, Simon and Schuster, 1956).

By writing to my former student, Professor Michael Radner, who most kindly spoke to Bertrand Russell's archivist, Mr Kenneth Blackwell, at McMaster University (Hamilton, Ontario, Canada), I must have made reasonably sure that Russell had never read Schlick on the mind–body problem. Schlick's book was not in Russell's private library. I wish here to express my sincerest gratitude for the kind assistance received from Messrs Blackwell and Radner. It is true that Russell had read at least one published essay by Schlick (on 'Meaning and Verification', *Philosophical Review*, 1936) and responded to it in *An Inquiry into Meaning and Truth* (1940: 386 ff.), quite critically. Russell was dissatisfied with Schlick's well-known, but all too exclusive, rather carelessly formulated and Wittgensteinian slogan: 'The meaning of a proposition is the method of its verification.' But this was *after* Schlick had fallen under Wittgenstein's spell, and had almost nothing to do with Schlick's early mind–body monism. Also, partly under the powerful influence of Wittgenstein's later philosophy (Schlick and Wittegenstein kept seeing each other during holidays through the early 1930s), Schlick gave his extremely fascinating three lectures on 'Form and Content' at the University of London, 1932; published posthumously in M. Schlick's *Gesammelte Aufsatze (1926–1936)* (Vienna, Gerold, 1938). The book contains many important essays, some in English, some in German. Friedrich Waismann wrote a most informative, beautiful and emotionally stirring Foreword to this volume. I understand that some or all of these essays, plus some hitherto unpublished papers by Schlick, will appear, in due course, from the D. Reidel Publishing Co., Dordrecht, Holland in the Vienna Circle collection now in preparation. I mention the London lectures because Schlick, partly explicitly in the lectures themselves and partly in personal conversations with me in 1932 and in 1935 –the latter just one year before his tragic and untimely death – indicated that there might be some flaw in his new doctrine of the inexpressibility of content, i.e. of the immediately experienced qualities. It may be remarked that this position has some affinities with the views of such philosophising great scientists as H. Poincaré, A. S. Eddington, H. Weyl, *et al.*, who have at least flirted occasionally with the 'ineffability' of the purely subjective phenomenally mental qualities (in Weyl's case, the 'pure luminous ego').

Schlick, fully aware of thus introducing a '*Ding an sich*' (rather different from that of Kant), and of the dangers of thus relapsing into an agnostic metaphysics, tried to remedy matters by his structuralist view of knowledge and communication. Consistently thought through, this clearly returns Schlick's doctrine to the view so superbly formulated in his *Allgemeine Erkenntnislehre* (both in the 1st and 2nd editions). There he distinguished, more forcefully and lucidly than any philosopher before him, *Erleben* (the mere living through – be it enjoyment or suffering – of mental or direct experience) from *Erkennen* (genuine knowledge, capable of propositional formulation and hence of communication). But since, according to Schlick (and at least the Wittgenstein of the *Tractatus*), whatever a declarative sentence communicates is the logical structure (be it of a truth claim of pure mathematics or one of empirical knowledge), it is indeed possible to formulate 'contents' – i.e. in terms of their *structure*. Naturally, whether we communicate about introspective (phenomenal, phenomenological) psychology, or some natural science, an *ostensive step* that links the symbols (words, formulae, etc.) with the directly experienced data (not necessarily 'sense-data'!) is indispensable. All this presupposes, of course (in opposition to the later Wittgenstein and most of his followers), that we can't even get a public language going, unless we start (logically, not chronologically, let alone child-psychologically) with a *private* language. As the Wittgenstein of the *Tractatus* quite properly realised: 'What the solipsist *means* is quite correct; only it cannot be said, it manifests itself' (it 'shows forth', '*es zeigt sich*').

Schlick's final views regarding the mental-physical problem – perhaps much more independent from Wittgenstein's influence – are very lucidly presented in his essay, 'Über die Beziehung zwischen psychologischen und physikalischen Begriffen', first published in French in *Revue de Synthèse*, vol. 10 (Paris, 1935); the German original is contained in *Gesammelte Aufsatze* (cf. *supra*); and an English translation (by W. Sellars) is contained in H. Feigl and W. Sellars, eds, *Readings in Philosophical Analysis* (New York, Appleton-Century-Crofts, 1949: 293–401). There Schlick returns largely to the solution he presented in 1918 and 1925.

Russell's early attempts to resolve the mind–matter problem(s) – as in *Problems of Philosophy* (1912), *Our Knowledge of the External World* (1914), *Analysis of Mind* (1921) – as well as in some passages of his contributions to the Library of Living Philosophers volume (P. A. Schilpp, ed., *The Philosophy of Bertrand Russell*, Evanston and Chicago, Northwestern University Press, 1944; first paperback edition in 2 vols, Harper Torchbooks, Academy Library, New York, Evanston and London, Harper & Row, 1963), were based on 'neutral monism'. This he developed under the influence of William James (I believe the term 'neutral monism' was coined by H. M. Sheffer, the Harvard logician) and was thus close to the outlook of the American neo-realists, especially E. B. Holt, R. B. Perry, E. McGilvary, *et al*.

It seems very strange that neither Schlick nor Russell paid sufficient attention to the works of the slightly later movement of outstanding American psychophysically monistic critical realists, especially C. A. Strong, Durant Drake and Roy Wood Sellars (who concerned himself a good deal with Russell's views). The exception is George Santayana, whose philosophy (and not only his stylistic elegance) held a certain fascination for both Russell and Schlick. Though Strong and, following him, Drake concluded rather speculatively and precariously with panpsychistic types of metaphysics which neither Russell nor Schlick would ever have found acceptable, their views on the mind–body (or in Sellars, 'mind–brain') problem are in many respects close to those of the later Russell and of Schick. Santayana, as Strong himself told me in 1927, had invented the intriguing title for Strong's first book: *Why the Mind has a Body* (1903) (!). Roy W. Sellars (who died in 1973 at the age of 93) published an informative though rather condensed survey of American realism (both neo- and critical) in his *Reflections on American Philosophy from Within* (South Bend, Ind., Notre Dame University Press, 1969). Although he deals in one chapter with 'Russell's Empiricism', his aversion to the Logical Positivism of the Vienna Circle probably made him overlook Schlick's pre-positivistic theory of knowledge (1918; 1925). In this theory Schlick formulated a very naturalistic, critically-realistic solution of the mind–body problem. This solution was what Sellars was somewhat clumsily groping for (in his 'mind–brain identity' and 'mind-under-the-hat' theories), and it was much more satisfactory from a logical point of view. Somewhat similarly, the late University of California philosopher Stephen C. Pepper, who knew and liked Schlick personally (when Schlick was visiting professor at Berkeley in 1931), was, not surprisingly, so radically opposed to the Wittgensteinian positivism that Schlick represented so emphaticially at that time that he, too, never read the *Allgemeine Erkenntnislehre*. Only a few years before Pepper's death, I pointed out to him that at least the most important aspect of his psycho-neural identity hypothesis (as elaborated, partly explicating and defending my own work), contained in his important book, *Concept and Quality* (La Salle, Ill., Open Court, 1967), had been anticipated by Schlick and by Russell (not to mention the American monistic critical realists, especially Strong, Drake and R. W. Sellars). Perhaps this curious lacuna in Pepper's knowledge was due to his intense preoccupation with his own highly significant work in the theory of values, aesthetics, ethics and his orginal and suggestive approach to metaphysics in the light of root metaphors (cf. his book, *World Hypotheses*, University of California Press, 1942). Pepper was a truly empirically (but *not* positivistically) minded thinker; and while he adopted from Russell the all-important distinction between knowledge by acquaintance and knowledge by description, he does not seem to have read or paid any attention to the later views of Russell on mind–matter monism.

Instead of providing a long list of pertinent references, I am taking the liberty of referring the reader to the two ample bibliographies in my own (slender) book, *The 'Mental' and the 'Physical'* (with postscript) (Minneapolis, University of Minnesota Press, 1967), and to the Selected Bibliography of my article 'Some Crucial Issues of Mind–Body Monism', in the journal *Synthese*, vol. 22 (1971: 295–312).

The following is a partial list of books and articles that have come to my attention since I wrote my *Synthese* paper. Of the items listed in the Selected Bibliography there, I wish to stress the importance of the four published essays by Grover Maxwell, who is currently the most competent and knowledgeable interpreter of Bertrand Russell's work, and who, partly building on Russell's ideas, has developed a thoroughly modern philosophy of science and, since he is not afraid to use the word, a metaphysics very much in keeping with some of Russell's basic intentions. By a curious coincidence, I find an article by Grover

Maxwell's namesake, Nicholas Maxwell, on 'Understanding Sensations', in the *Australasian Journal of Philosophy*, vol. 46, no. 2 (1968: 127–95), also very illuminating. Nicholas Maxwell, though exclusively concerned with the problem of sentience, clarifies successfully what many of us (beginning with Schlick and Russell) have tried to formulate: the essential completeness of a scientific account of human experience in neurophysiological terms, but emphasising the fact that physical science is to be construed as eliminating (in the *one* sense of pure subjectivity) the purely qualitative features of immediate experience. This, I think, is at least a step forward to a solution of the notorious mind–body perplexity regarding the 'homeless qualities', i.e. homeless in a purely physical (physicalistic) world description. Many philosophers and philosophically minded scientists, especially physicists (most recently the brilliant and superbly competent Victor F. Weisskopf in his marvellous book *Physics in the Twentieth Century*, Cambridge, Mass., MIT Press, 1972: 348), tentatively formulate: the physical account of the world is complete – but not all-comprehensive. Of course, it remains a matter of dispute as to whether Niels Bohr's ideas on complementarity can be employed beyond the scope of quantum mechanics, but it seems that Weisskopf deems it plausible. Previously there have been highly suggestive articles by N. Brody and P. Oppenheim (*Journal of Philosophy*, vol. 66 (1969: 97–113), and by G. Globus (*Science*, June 1973), as well as other, partly information-theoretical, cybernetic and system-theoretical articles forthcoming in various periodicals. A very thorough, but perhaps because of its extreme judiciousness somewhat tantalising, book is James W. Cornman's *Materialism and Sensations* (New Haven and London, Yale University Press, 1971). I find his idea of a cross-categorial identity of the mental and the physical quite appealing, and certainly one way of explicating Russell's and Schlick's forms of monism.

The fiercest critics of the Schlick–Russell sort of solution are, of course, the Cartesian interactionist dualists. I shall mention only some prominent thinkers and their publications: A. O. Lovejoy's *The Revolt against Dualism* (1930); C. J. Ducasse's *Nature, Mind and Death* (1951); and more recently and especially Sir Karl Popper's *Objective Knowledge* (Oxford: Clarendon Press, 1972). This latter collection of remarkable essays includes Popper's intriguing though hardly acceptable *tours de force* 'Of Clouds and Clocks', 'Epistemology without a Knowing Subject', 'On the Theory of the Objective Mind', etc. Here one of the most outstanding philosophers of science of our century puts forth extremely stimulating (i.e. thought-provoking and, indeed, highly provocative) views; Schlick and Russell would have decisively disagreed with *these* views of Popper's. Sir John C. Eccles (Nobel Prize winner in Neurophysiology) follows Popper not only with regard to scientific methodology, but also (and here Sherrington's influence also contributed) in his neo-Cartesianism; cf. Eccles's book *Facing Reality* (Heidelberg, Berlin and New York, Springer, 1970). His reasoning is fascinating, but to my mind marred by *non sequiturs*. More irritating, but nevertheless very much worth reading, is the quarrelsome book by Eric P. Polten, *Critique of the Psychophysical Identity Theory* (The Hague and Paris, Mouton, 1973). Polten's background in philosophy of science is essentially Aristotelian, but his views on mind–body are strictly Cartesian. Other (to my mind even more challenging) critical questions regarding identity are contained in P. E. Meehl's brilliant article 'The Compleat Autocerebroscopist', in P. Feyerabend and G. Maxwell, eds, *Mind, Matter and Method* (Minneapolis, University of Minnesota Press, 1966). But see Meehl's qualified defence of 'Psychological Determinism and Human Rationality', in M. Radner and S. Winokur, eds, vol. IV of *Minnesota Studies in the Philosophy of Science*

(1970). Both Schlick and Russell, I feel certain, would have enthusiastically agreed with this masterpiece of philosophical and psychological analysis! Other criticisms of monism that should be taken seriously are presented in 'The Identity Thesis' by Judith Jarvis Thomson, in S. Morgenbesser, P. Suppes and M. White, eds, *Philosophy, Science and Method* (Essays in Honour of Ernest Nagel) (New York, St Martin's Press, 1969). Ernest Nagel, by the way, early on contributed a challenging essay to P. A. Schilpp, ed., *The Philosophy of Bertrand Russell* (Library of Living Philosophers, 1944) under the title 'Russell's Philosophy of Science'. Among other matters Nagel invites Russell's response to questions (raised in the spirit of common sense and common language) regarding Russell's notion of physical objects or events and the mind–matter problem as dealt with in *Analysis of Matter*. In his replies to his critics Russell, I think, answers Nagel's questions very lucidly and adequately, but not without some of the irony and sarcasm we have come to expect of Russell.

One perplexity for mind–body monists (or 'identity theorists') that is not easily overcome has been raised by Wilfred Sellars in his 'The Identity Approach to the Mind-Body Problem', in *Review of Metaphysics*, vol. XVIII, no. 3 (1965); republished in Stuart Hampshire, ed., *Philosophy of Mind* (New York and London, Harper & Row, 1966). Sellars point to the 'grain problem', i.e. the essential difference between, for instance, a homogeneous, continuous patch of colour in one's visual field, or the smooth, continuous tone-as-heard of a trombone, and the neuronal (ultimately molecular-atomic-subatomic) structure of the (dualistically speaking, correlated) corresponding cerebral processes. It is no good claiming that the phenomenal experience has a hidden (latent) structure, and that it is hence illusory. Closely related to this move is the idea of fusion, actually used by such eminent thinkers as Carnap, Pepper and Smart. Fusion makes good sense in psychophysics where we deal with thresholds and just noticeable differences in perception. But unless something like that can also be legitimately assumed for intracerebral processes, such as a scanning by the frontal lobe of events occurring in the occipital, temporal and other sensory centres, or else some confluence of nerve impulses in certain small regions of the cortex or subcortical layers, the difference in the 'graininess' of the phenomenally given and the ('corresponding') neural processes would go against the very notion (Leibniz's) of the indiscernibility of identicals. More thought and work on this thorny issue, it seems to me, is urgently called for. In any case, before we declare with E. Dubois-Reymond the mind-body problem absolutely unsolvable, '*ignoramus et ignorabimus*', it would seem wise to await further developments in neurophysiology (but possibly also in basic theoretical physics, biology, psychology, etc.) *and* to pursue further conceptual clarifications in the logic analysis of the 'mental' and the 'physical'.

20

SELF-ACQUAINTANCE AND THE MEANING OF 'I'

G. N. A. Vesey

(1) *Self-acquaintance*

Hume begins the section of *A Treatise of Human Nature* (1739: bk 1, pt IV, s. vi) on personal identity with the sentence, 'There are some philosophers, who imagine we are every moment intimately conscious of what we call our SELF; that we feel its existence and its continuance in existence; and are certain, beyond the evidence of a demonstration, both of its perfect identity and simplicity'. One of the philosophers he may have had in mind is Joseph Butler. In his dissertation *Of Personal Identity* (1736: s. 2), Butler says that 'by reflecting upon that, which is my self now, and that, which was my self twenty years ago, I discern they are not two, but one and the same self'. This presupposes that a person (i) is now conscious of the self he is now, (ii) is now conscious of the self he was at some time in the past, and (iii) can discern the identity of the self he is now and the self he was at some time in the past. To do the last is presumably, in Hume's words, to feel his self's 'continuance in existence'.

Butler does not argue for, but simply presupposes, that a person is conscious of his self. Bertrand Russell, on the other hand, in *The Problems of Philosophy* (1912: ch.V), gives us an argument:

> The question whether we are acquainted with our bare selves, as opposed to particular thoughts and feelings, is a very difficult one, upon which it would be rash to speak positively. When we try to look into ourselves we always seem to come upon some particular thought or feeling, and not upon the 'I' which has the thought or feeling. Nevertheless there are some reasons for thinking that we are acquainted with the 'I'.

One of the reasons Russell mentions is the following:

> . . . we know the truth 'I am acquainted with this sense-datum'. It is hard to see how we could know this truth, or even understand what is meant by it, unless we were acquainted with something which we call 'I'. . . . Thus, in some sense it would seem we must be acquainted with our Selves as opposed to our particular experiences. But the question

is difficult, and complicated arguments can be adduced on either side. Hence, although acquaintance with ourselves seems *probably* to occur, it is not wise to assert that it undoubtedly does occur.

The argument to which Russell here attaches some weight is: To know the truth, or even the meaning, of a sentence of the form 'I am aware of . . .', the person who utters it must know, by acquaintance, something which he calls 'I'.

Russell does not say what form the 'complicated arguments' about the validity of this argument might take, but the chapter in which it occurs is entitled 'Knowledge by Acquaintance and Knowledge by Description', so it is reasonable to suppose that one thing that was bothering Russell was the possibility that a person who meaningfully uses the word 'I' does so in virtue of knowing something which he calls 'I' not by *acquaintance*, but by *description*.

J. McT. E. McTaggart, in *The Nature of Existence* (1927: vol. II, ch. 36), refers to Russell as having led him 'to accept the view that the self is known to itself by direct perception'. He says that Russell did not work out his position in detail and had ceased to hold the position at all. McTaggart states the argument as follows:

> 'I am aware of equality.' This proposition, whether true or false, has certainly a meaning. And since I know what the proposition means, I must know each constituent of it. I must therefore know 'I'. Whatever is known must be known by acquaintance or by description. If, therefore, 'I' cannot be known by description, it must be known by acquaintance, and I must be aware of it.

What would it be for 'I' to be known by description? McTaggart considers, and dismisses, two possibilities. The first is that to know 'I' by description is to know it not as 'that which is aware of something, or which has a mental state', but as, in Hume's words, 'a bundle or collection of different perceptions'. If we hold this 'bundle' view of the self, he observes,

> we must no longer say that the self perceives, thinks, or loves, or that it has a perception or thought or an emotion. We can only say that the bundle includes a perception, a thought, or an emotion as one of its parts. On this theory, then, when I use the word 'I', I know what 'I' means by description, and it is described as meaning that bundle of mental states of which my use of the word is one member.

McTaggart cannot accept this Humean view because he can discover no relation between mental states which could determine the bundle to which they belong other than one through the self: 'We must say that those states, and those only, which are states of the same self form the bundle of parts of that self.' But this, he says, would be fatal to the attempt to know 'I' by description: 'It would obviously be a vicious circle if I described "I" as being that bundle of states of which my use of the word is a member, and then distinguished that bundle from other groups by describing it as that group of mental states which are states of "I".'

The second possibility McTaggart considers is that two mental states 'belong to the same self when, and only when, the same living body (or what appears as such) stands in a certain relation of causality to both of them'. I think he may have in mind the view advanced by John Stuart Mill in *An Examination of Sir William Hamilton's Philosophy* (1865: ch. 12). Mill analyses material objects into 'permanent groups of possibilities of sensation' and reports finding, among these groups, 'one (my own body) which is not only composed, like the rest, of a mixed multitude of sensations and possibilities, but is also connected, in a peculiar manner, with all my sensations'. The 'peculiar manner' is causal. Mill finds that his body is 'always present as an antecedent condition' of every sensation he has.

McTaggart raises a number of difficulties for this view. The first is that of narrowing down the causal relation so as not to include, as being in the same self, mental states that belong to different selves. The movements of *one* actor's body may cause aesthetic emotions in *many* people. These different people's mental states are caused by the same body, so on the theory in question should be part of the same self. McTaggart comments: 'It might perhaps suffice if we say that the relation between the living body and the mental state must not be mediated by the intervention of any other living body.'[1]

A more serious difficulty is that on the theory in question:

> No man has any reason to say that any two states belong to the same self unless he has a reason to believe them to be caused by the same body. And this means that the vast majority of such statements as 'I was envious yesterday' are absolutely untrustworthy. In the first place, by far the greater number of them have been made by people who have never heard of the doctrine that emotions and judgements are caused by bodily states . . . . In the second place, even those people who have heard of the doctrine, and who accept it, do not, in far the greater number of cases, base their judgements that two states belong to the same self on a previous conviction that they are caused by the same body.

But it is not just that, on the theory, statements like 'I was envious yesterday' become untrustworthy. They become meaningless:

> 'I was envious yesterday' has no meaning for anyone who does not know the meaning of 'I'. Now if 'I' can only be known by description, and the only description which is true of it is 'that group of mental

states, caused by the same living body, of which the envy and my judgement are members', it follows that anyone who does not describe 'I' in that way, will not know what 'I' means, and so will mean nothing when he says 'I was envious yesterday'.

The view McTaggart finds unsatisfactory – that 'I' is known by description – seems to be that to which Russell had become converted when he wrote *The Analysis of Mind* (1921). (I mentioned McTaggart's saying that Russell had ceased to hold his earlier view, that 'I' is known by acquaintance.) But Russell does not distinguish, as McTaggart does, between the Humean 'bundle' view and the view that mental states belong to the same self if they are causally related to the same body. He runs the two views together. He writes (1921: ch. 1):

> It is supposed that thoughts cannot just come and go, but need a person to think them. Now, of course it is true that thoughts can be collected into bundles, so that one bundle is my thoughts, another is your thoughts, and a third is the thoughts of Mr Jones. But I think the person is not an ingredient in the single thought: he is rather consti-tuted by relations of the thoughts to each other and to the body . . . the grammatical forms 'I think', 'you think', and 'Mr Jones thinks', are misleading if regarded as indicating an analysis of a single thought. It would be better to say 'it thinks in me', like 'it rains here'.

Russell refers to Ernst Mach's *Contributions to the Analysis of Sensations* as 'a book of fundamental importance' in connection with the view he is expounding. Mach quotes Lichtenberg:

> We know only the existence of our sensations, percepts, and thoughts. We should say, *It thinks*, just as we say, *It lightens*. It is going too far to say, *cogito*, if we translate *cogito* by *I think*.

Russell agrees with Lichtenberg that we should not say 'I think'. But evidently he thinks 'It thinks' is not enough. There must be something to individuate the thinking in question. So he adds 'in me'. But isn't saying 'in me' smuggling in 'I' by the back door, so to speak? And so re-introducing a possible object of knowledge by acquaintance? So he adds 'like "it rains here" '. One doesn't need to know something by acquaint-ance to use the word 'here' meaningfully. Similarly he seems to be suggesting, one doesn't need to know something by acquaintance to use the expression 'in me' meaningfully.

This raises a lot of questions. Let us consider just two of them. (1) Is it true that the word 'here' is an exception to the rule that knowing the meaning of a word means knowing what is meant by it, that is, knowing something which we call by that word? (2) Supposing that the word 'here' can be used meaningfully without our knowing something which we call 'here', are Russell and McTaggart right in their assumption that the word 'I' is *not* like 'here' in this respect? In other words, are they right in thinking that a person *must* know something he calls 'I', either by acquaintance or by description, to use the word 'I' meaningfully? (If they are *not* right, then we need have no qualms about using the word 'I' in the absence of inward empirical discoveries.)

(2) *The meaning of 'here'*

One use of the word 'here' is the following. My wife, on returning from shopping on Saturday afternoon, calls out 'Where are you?' and I reply 'Here'. She knows, from this, roughly where I am. But how? Did I *say* where I was? No. She heard my voice coming from upstairs, or from the kitchen, or from my workshop. Like most people, she can tell, just by listening, from what direction a sound is coming. She learnt, from my saying 'Here', where I was, although I did not *say* where I was.

I did not *say* where I was and, also, I did not need to *know* where I was. Suppose that in my wife's absence I had been knocked unconscious by a burglar. To give him time to make his getaway he ties me up, blindfolds me, gags me and hides me in a cupboard. I recover consciousness, not knowing where I am. I manage to bite through the gag. When I hear my wife I call out 'I'm here', and she, hearing the sound coming from the cupboard under the stairs, soon releases me. I did not know where I was, but that did not stop me saying 'I'm here'. It would be absurd if my wife were to accuse me of using the word 'here' without meaning, since I did not know where I was. But if I didn't know where I was, what *did* I mean by the word? What meaning could it have had?

Behind this question seems to be the idea that to talk of the 'meaning' of a word is to talk of some *thing* – either some thing in the world, which the word stands for, or some thing in the mind of the person who utters the word and in the mind of the person who hears it. (On the latter view, communication is successful when the things, 'ideas', in the minds of the speaker and hearer correspond. This raises the problem of how one is to tell when they correspond, and the solution to it in terms of a distinction between 'structure' and 'content'.)

But the idea that to talk of the 'meaning' of a word is to talk of some *thing* does not seem to apply to the use we have been considering of the word 'here'. An utterance like 'Here' can have a *use* without there being something that is *meant* by the word uttered, something which the utterer must know, either by acquaintance or by description, for the utterance to have that use. People know where I am, on hearing me say 'Here', not in virtue of knowing what I mean but in virtue of being able to locate sounds. 'Cooee' would have served as well.

But isn't there a difference between 'Cooee' and 'Here'? Someone who calls out 'Cooee' cannot be said to be saying something that is true or false. But isn't someone who says 'Here', in answer to 'Where are you?', speaking the truth? He is where he is, and not somewhere else.

I am inclined to say that 'Here', in answer to 'Where are you?' is true only in so far as it basks in the reflected glory of such genuine truths as 'Here', said as I point into the flower-vase, having been asked 'Where is it?' in the course of a game of hunt-the-thimble. I could be mistaken, or even deliberately telling a falsehood, about the thimble. But how could 'Here', in answer to 'Where are you?', be false? Would it be false if I could actually 'throw my voice' so that it seemed to come from some-where else? If I did this with the intention of deceiving people, would I be telling a lie? I think that people would be justified in rebuking me for deceiving them as to my whereabouts, but that I would no more have actually *lied* than if I had thrown my voice and said 'Cooee'. There can be intentionally deceiving verbal behaviour that does not come under the heading 'telling lies'. (Another example could be my answering the telephone in a high voice so as to make the caller think he is speaking to my sister.) What I mean by 'basks in the reflected glory' is this. When I say 'Here' in answer to 'Where are you?', I *seem* to be *saying* where I am only because there is another use of 'Here', as for example in answer to 'Where's the thimble?', in which I *am saying* where something is.

Why should the first use of 'Here' bask in the reflected glory of the second, granted that the first serves to inform others of my whereabouts only in virtue of their being able to locate sounds? Is it simply a matter of the same word being used, or is there more to it than that?

In pointing into the flower-vase and saying 'Here', I am obviously distinguishing one place from another as the place where the thimble is. If places couldn't be distinguished – by pointing, or naming, or describ-ing, or giving co-ordinates or in some other way – there would be no possibility of the second use of 'Here'. There would be no possibility of the second use of 'Here' in a non-spatial world, or in a spatial world inhabited only by non-spatial beings. This is obvious in the case of the second use of 'Here', because in saying 'Here' one is *saying* where something is. But it is true of the first use, also. For although in saying 'Here', in answer to 'Where are you?', I am not *saying* where I am, nevertheless the hearer *learns* where I am from my saying it. If no one could learn anything from my saying 'Here', in answer to 'Where are you?', there would not be that use of 'Here'. One of the conditions of people learning anything is that they can locate sounds. But there is a more general condition, which the first use of 'Here' shares with the second, namely, the possibility of distinguishing one place from another. If one place could not be distinguished from another there would be nothing for me to seem to be saying in saying 'Here' in answer to 'Where are you?'.

This whole discussion of the meaning of 'here' might be summed up by saying that in so far as 'Here', in reply to 'Where are you?', has a meaning, as distinct from a use, its meaningfulness is parasitic on the meaningfulness of 'Here' in reply to 'Where is it?', the meaningfulness of this being conditional on the possibility of distinguishing places.

(3) *The meaning of 'I'*

Russell said that rather than say 'I think' it would be better to say 'It thinks in me', like 'It rains here'. Evidently he thought that a person can quite properly use the word 'here' without knowing, either by acquaintance or description, some thing which is what the word means, but that the word 'I' is different, and therefore that someone who cannot, however hard he introspects, discover some thing which is what the word means, should not use it.

But is the word 'I' different? Are there not, in fact, striking resemblances between the uses of 'I' and those of 'here'? P. T. Geach (*Mental Acts*, ch. 26) refers to the Cartesian idea 'that introspection can give the word "I" a special sense, which each of us can learn on his own account'. He reminds us, however, that

> The word 'I', spoken by P. T. G., serves to draw people's attention to P. T. G.; and if it is not at once clear who is speaking, there is a genuine question 'Who said that?' or 'Who is "I"?' Now consider Descartes brooding over his *poêle* and saying: 'I'm getting into an awful muddle – but who then is this "I" who is getting into a muddle?' When 'I'm getting into a muddle' is a soliloquy, 'I' certainly does not serve to direct Descartes's attention to Descartes, or to show that it is Descartes, none other, who is getting into a muddle. We are not to argue, though, that since 'I' does not refer to the man René Descartes it has some other, more intangible, thing to refer to. Rather, in this context the word 'I' is idle, superfluous; it is used only because Descartes is habituated to the use of 'I' in expressing his thoughts and feelings to other people.

The use of 'I' in soliloquy may be compared to the use of 'here' in soliloquy. Suppose my wife and I are lost, in cloud , on a mountain. We try to keep in touch by shouting occasionally. 'Where are you?' 'Here'. But we drift apart, and can no longer hear one another. Still lost, I say *to myself*, 'Where am I?' and reply 'Here'. But whereas my wife could have learnt in what direction I was from her had she heard me, there is nothing I can learn from it. It is, as Geach would say, 'idle, superfluous'.

Geach says: 'We are not to argue, though, that since "I" does not refer to the man René Descartes it has some other, more intangible, thing to refer to.' He could have put it more strongly. We are not to argue that 'I' refers to an intangible, invisible, inaudible Cartesian spiritual substance. Can comparison of uses of 'I' with uses of 'here' help us to see why we are not to argue thus?

Instead of uses of 'I', let us consider uses of 'It's me'. (I regard 'It's I' as pedantic.) Suppose I have lost my memory. All I can find in my pockets is a scrap of paper with a telephone number written on it. Perhaps if I ring the number the person who answers will know who I am. I ring the number, and say, 'It's me', hoping for recognition. This case is like the case in which I am lost in cloud and shout out 'Here' to let my wife know where I am. I no more say who I am in this case than I say I'm off to my wife's right in the lost-in-cloud case. I don't know, in both cases. And there is an 'idle', soliloquising use of 'It's me' in this case just as there is an 'idle', soliloquising use of 'Here' in the lost-in-cloud case. I am all set to say, 'It's me', but nobody answers the phone. Emptily I say to myself: 'It's me, whoever I am.'

A use of 'It's me' like that of 'Here' in answer to 'Where is the thimble?' would be the following. Someone asks 'Who is the youngest professor in the faculty?' and I say 'It's me'. As in the case of the whereabouts of the thimble, I could be mistaken, or even deliberately telling a falsehood.

I said that in pointing into the flower-vase and saying 'Here', I am obviously distinguishing one place from another as the place where the thimble is, and that if places couldn't be distinguished – by pointing, or naming, or describing, or giving co-ordinates or in some other way – there would be no possibility of this use of 'Here'. There would be no possibility of it in a non-spatial world, or in a spatial world inhabited only by non-spatial beings.

In saying 'It's me' in answer to 'Who is the youngest professor in the faculty?', am I distinguishing one person from another? The questioner sees who has answered. I could have written 'It's me' on a piece of paper and passed it to him. For him to learn anything from it, he must know who wrote it. Perhaps I simply raise my hand. I don't think it matters whether or not we call this a case of my distinguishing myself from others. The point is that if I could not be distinguished from others in some way, then the utterance 'It's me' would be useless. In other words, the meaningfulness of 'It's me' in reply to 'Who is so-and-so?' is conditional on the possibility of distinguishing people.

We have not yet compared 'It's me', said by the victim of amnesia in hope of recognition, with 'I'm here' in reply to 'Where are you?', in respect of having a meaning as distinct from a use. I said that in so far as 'Here', in reply to 'Where are you?' has a meaning, as distinct from a use, its meaningfulness is parasitic on the meaningfulness of 'Here' in reply to 'Where is it?', the meaningfulness of this being conditional on the possibility of distinguishing places. A parallel remark about 'It's me' would be that in so far as 'It's me', said by the victim of amnesia in hope of recognition, has a meaning, as distinct from a use, its meaningfulness is parasitic on the meaningfulness of 'It's me' in reply to 'Who is the youngest professor?', the meaningfulness of this being conditional on the possibility of distinguishing people. To say this is to deny that 'I' gets its meaning through a speaker knowing, either by acquaintance or by description, something he calls 'I'. It is to deny what Russell and McTaggart assume.

Department of Philosophy
The Open University

NOTE

1 Compare the treatment of the same problem by A. J. Ayer in *The Concept of a Person and Other Essays* (London, Macmillan, 1963: 4th essay).

21

SOME ASPECTS OF KNOWLEDGE (I)

George W. Roberts

(1) In this essay I examine some questions about knowledge of the sorts that preoccupy epistemologists. I mainly examine certain definitions of knowledge and their consequences.

Russell said that logic is the essence of philosophy, and early attempts to utilise the approach his words epitomise often took the form of a search for analytic definitions or logical equivalences, or at least for implication relations. Whether or not the analytic programme conceived in these terms has been shown to be unfulfillable or unilluminating in the most central philosophical areas, Russell's works display a remarkable lack of any satisfactory account of certain notions that appear to underlie such a programme. Russell's treatments of such notions as logical necessity tended to be meagre or patently unacceptable. In this part, I give an example of definitional inquiry with positive results I take to be philosophically illuminating. Among the consequences of this inquiry is an epistemological account of logical necessity that sheds light, *inter alia*, on the nature of philosophical analysis.

The usual current tale about definitions of knowledge is that a well-entrenched traditional definition was first seriously challenged about a dozen years ago, or not many more. Certainly since that time attempts to define knowledge, or various sorts or cases of knowledge, have run rife. Attempts have also been made to show that knowledge, in general at least, is indefinable. Arguments have been given as well to show that what have been taken to be standard conditions of knowledge are not after all necessary. Here I will not attempt to deal directly with much of the extensive literature on these matters or with many of the ramifications of detail that arise from it. When it is necessary for me to give the lie direct to views that have gained some currency in these recent discussions, I usually do so here without ceremony and even without notice.

The traditional definition of knowledge has been held to go something like this:

(T) '*A* knows that *p*' is definable as '(i) *p*, (ii) *A* believes that *p*, and (iii) *A* is justified in believing that *p*'.

This definition has recently been held to be incorrect for a variety of reasons, both for what it has been taken to include and for what it has been taken not to include even by implication.

I am not here concerned to argue with those who propose to omit one or more conditions from this definition, though I am prepared to give them the lie direct. I do, however, give an argument to show that one of the conditions, (iii), is eliminable from a modified version of (T), but only in that it is derivable from the remaining conditions in that version.

In the allegedly traditional definition, condition (iii) has sometimes been treated as equivalent to 'A has reason to believe that p'. 'A has a basis for believing that p' or 'A is entitled to believe that p'. I treat these here as synonymous expressions and I use each of them in a strong sense, to mean respectively 'A is fully justified in believing that p', 'A has sufficient reason to believe that p', 'A has an adequate basis for believing that p' and 'A is fully entitled to believe that p'. I do not, however, use any of these expressions in the strongest possible sense to mean, for instance, that A has the fullest conceivable reason for believing that p. Certainly no condition of this strongest sort is implied in knowledge.

The modifications of the definition (T) put forward of late form a large and various family, but they do form a family. Among the more prominent features in many of its members is the inclusion of causal or modal elements. I believe that some such modification of (T) is definitely needed. What I do here is mainly to explore, first, what I regard as the most adequate modifications of (T) that add only a modal element to its conditions, and second, the modifications of (T) that I regard as correct, which add an additional element besides the modal element.

Here, then, is the first member of the first definition series for knowledge:

(1.1) 'A knows that p' is definable as '(i) p, (ii) A believes that p, (iii) A has reason to believe that p and (iv) it is necessary in the circumstances that each of the conditions (i), (ii), (iii) holds if, and only if, each of the others holds'.

I do not here undertake to say a great deal in initial elucidation of the phrase 'it is necessary in the circumstances' and related expressions. It does not seem to me that a great deal needs to be said in elucidation of such expressions *ab initio*; and this is an important point. Such expressions are in use and are well enough understood in practice; even if a certain generalisation or refinement of the usual uses is called for, it is perhaps advisable to resist the inclinations of those who would call at once for definitions or any other very elaborate explanations at the start. I will say for now only that the circumstances referred to need not be, in whole or even in part, antecedent circumstances.

(2) In the preceding section the first definition of knowledge has been

stated in its first full form. In this section, I argue that the first form is equivalent to a second form of definition:

(1.2)   'A knows that p' is definable as 'It is necessary in the circumstances that (i) p, (ii) A believes that p and (iii) A has reason to believe that p'.

First, I deduce the second form of definition from the first form. From the *definiens* of (1.1) there follows trivially 'p and it is necessary in the circumstances that if p, then A believes that p'. Now I maintain that it follows from this premiss that it is necessary in the circumstances that A believes that p. To effect this deduction, I cite an inference form that serves to elucidate to some extent the notion of necessity in the circumstances, at least as that is here employed:

(I.1) p, it is necessary in the circumstances that if p, then q, and it is not logically necessary that if p, then q; therefore, it is necessary in the circumstances that q.

The inference form (I.1) permits the deduction of 'It is necessary in the circumstances that A believes that p' from the given premiss together with the premiss that it is not logically necessary that if p, then A believes that p. That for no p does p entail that A believes that p is an assertion for which I have argued elsewhere.[1] For the moment, I merely assume this anti-self-intimation or anti-phosphorescence doctrine. No fact entails belief in it by anyone at any time.

The immediate use of this assumption is to permit the deduction of the necessity in the circumstances of A's belief that p from the (1.1) *definiens* of A's knowledge that p. If this assumption is true, it is true as a matter of logical necessity. Consequently, if as I suppose the assumption is true, then it (or strictly an instance of it) is eliminable from the premisses of the given inference; the conjunction of the remaining premisses derived from the (1.1) *definiens* by itself entails the conclusion. I call the principle involved in this argument the eliminability principle.

Once the deduction of 'It is necessary in the circumstances that A believes that p' from the (1.1) *definiens* is accomplished, the further deduction of 'It is necessary in the circumstances that p' and 'It is necessary in the circumstances that A has reason to believe that p' is readily effected. For the (1.1) *definiens* yields immediately that it is necessary in the circumstances that if A believes that p, then p. The previous deduction making use of the anti-phosphorescence principle shows that the (1.1) *definiens* implies that it is necessary in the circumstances that A believes that p. But the following inference form is trivially valid:

(I.2)   It is necessary in the circumstances that if x, then y, and it is necessary in the circumstances that x; therefore, it is necessary in the circumstances that y.

This inference form is patently instantiated in the inference from the given premisses to 'It is necessary in the circumstances that p'. So the first conclusion sought here is reached, and the second conclusion follows *mutatis mutandis*. Furthermore, the inference from the necessity in the circumstances of each of the first three (1.1) *definiens* conditions to the necessity in the circumstances of their conjunction is immediate; so is the converse inference.

Second, I deduce the (1.1) *definiens* from its (1.2) counterpart. For this I employ another inference form:

(I.3) It is necessary in the circumstances that y; therefore, it is necessary in the circumstances that if x, then y.

So given, by a previous deduction from *definiens* (1.2), that it is necessary in the circumstances that p, it follows that it is necessary in the circumstances that if A believes that p, then p. Moreover, it follows from the same premiss by the same form that it is necessary in the circumstances that if A has reason to believe that p, then p. Given, again by a previous deduction from *definiens* (1.2), that it is necessary in the circumstances that A believes that p, it follows by inference form (I.3) that it is necessary in the circumstances that if A believes that p, then p. Moreover, it follows from the same premiss by the same form that it is necessary in the circumstances that if A has reason to believe that p, then p. Given, once more by a previous deduction from *definiens* (1.2), that it is necessary in the circumstances that A has reason to believe that p, it follows by inference form (I.3) that it is necessary in the circumstances that if p, then A has reason to believe that p. It follows from the same premiss by the same form that it is necessary in the circumstances that if A believes that p, then A has reason to believe that p.

These six conclusions in conjunction amount to condition (iv) of *definiens* (1.1). Conditions (i), (ii) and (iii) of *definiens* (1.1) are trivial consequences of the circumstantial necessity of their conjunction in *definiens* (1.2).

So the circumstantial equivalence of the fact, belief and reason conditions in *definiens* (1.1) is implied in the circumstantial necessity of these three conditions, and their circumstantial necessity is implied in the conjunction of the conditions and their circumstantial equivalence.

The third form of the first definition is a by-product of the preceding arguments:

(1.3) 'A knows that p' is definable as '(i) It is necessary in the circumstances that p, (ii) it is necessary in the circumstances that A believes that p and (iii) it is necessary in the circumstances that A has reason to believe that p'.

The second reduction, which establishes the equivalence and indeed the t-equivalence of definitions (1.2) and (1.3), is effected by the following inference forms:

(I.4) It is necessary in the circumstances that x and y; therefore, it is necessary in the circumstances that x and it is necessary in the circumstances that y.

(I.5) It is necessary in the circumstances that x and it is necessary in the circumstances that y; therefore, it is necessary in the circumstances that x and y.

I call the equivalence underlying these forms the conjunction principle for circumstantial necessity. Needless to say the same sort of principle holds true of logical necessity. Such a principle also very evidently holds true of such notions as 'A has reason to believe that p' in the sense in which I use these words here, and less evidently of 'A believes that p'; I am more inclined to make tacit use at times of the more evident of such principles. I take it that all the principles to which I have just alluded are strong equivalences in a particular sense I define in the next section.

(3) The preceding derivations are all of a specially strong type; they turn throughout on what I call 't-implications'. I introduce now a battery of expressions:

(D.1) 'p s-implies q' is defined as 'It is logically necessary that if p, then q'.

(D.2) 'p t-implies q' is defined as 'A believes that p' s-implies 'A believes that q'.

(D.3) 'p r-implies q' is defined as 'A has reason to believe that p' s-implies 'A has reason to believe that q'.

Obviously 'p s-implies q' is just 'p strictly implies q', or 'p implies q' in one very favoured sense in which I use it here. To say this presupposes that 'If p, then q' is equivalent to 'p materially implies q', that is, to 'It is not both the case that p and not-q'.

Russell argued for this equivalence; his conclusion, at least, I accept.[2] However, even if Russell and I are mistaken it will make no difference here. If 'If p, then q' does not mean 'p materially implies q', as Russell and I suppose, then it means 'It is necessary in the circumstances that p materially implies q'. Such forms as 'It is necessary in the circumstances that A believes that if p, then q' will mean the same thing in a strong sense under either interpretation of 'If p, then q'. Such inferences as 'It is necessary in the circumstances that q; therefore, it is necessary in the circumstances that if p, then q, will be valid under either interpretation. So it will appear that the arguments I give remain sound whichever interpretation is true. I do favour Russell's interpretation, though. If 'and' is exempt from claims that it is not a truth-functional connective that may be in part at least because 'It is necessary in the circumstances that p and q' is equivalent to 'It is necessary in the circumstances that p and it is necessary in the circumstances that q.' If, as I imply later, 'A knows that it is necessary in the circumstances that if p, then q' is equivalent to 'A knows that if p, then q', that may help account for the difficulties with regarding 'If p, then q' as 'p materially implies q'.

I should remark on the appropriateness of the terms 't-implies', 's-implies' and 'r-implies'. Plainly 'r-implies' abbreviates 'reason-implies'. The term 't-implies' is appropriate because the implication might have been defined in terms of any merely intentional verb. For instance 'desires', 'imagines' and 'thinks' might have been used rather than 'believes'. At least this is the case unless, for example, 'A imagined that p' is self-contradictory in some cases p in which 'A believes that p' is not self-contradictory. Intentional implications defined in terms of one intentional verb rather than another are, however, equivalent for those cases p in which the two forms are alike self-contradictory or alike not self-contradictory. The 's' in 's-implies' reproduces the 's' in 'intensional implication', which is implication proper, sometimes called entailment.

It appears to be evident that the three sorts of implications defined here can be ordered from stronger to weaker as follows:

$$p \; t\text{-implies} \; q$$
$$p \; s\text{-implies} \; q$$
$$p \; r\text{-implies} \; q.$$

That is, the earlier implications in this series imply the latter. This is certainly not an altogether trivial remark.[3]

The converse implications do not hold. Plainly, 'A believes that the Euclidean postulates $P_1, \ldots, P_5$ are true' does not imply 'A believes that the Pythagorean theorem is true', even though the conjunction of the Euclidean postulates $P_1, \ldots, P_5$ does imply the Pythagorean theorem.[4] Plainly, too, 'It is raining' does not imply 'I know that it is raining', even though 'I have reason to believe that it is raining' does imply 'I have reason to believe that I know that it is raining'. Just as obviously 'I believe that it is raining' does not imply 'I believe that I know that it is raining', even though the implication just mentioned does hold. The example I have just given of an r-implication that is not also an implication or a t-implication is quite significant for what follows, but this is not what I emphasise just now. Of course the t-implications as defined above might be called b-implications, with the 'b' obviously referring to belief. It might, thus, be stressed that the three species of implication defined here correspond to the first three conditions in the definitions of knowledge undergoing examination.

It is worthwhile to mention that all the implications used in derivations so far are t-implications, and that this will continue to be true throughout with the few exceptions noted.

(4) In his *Ethics* (1912) Moore first called attention to certain first-person oddities that could not be construed as self-contradictions.[5] Over the years Moore and his disciples accumulated a number of such oddities, for instance, 'p, but I do not believe that p', 'I believe that p, but not-p', 'p, but I do not know that p', 'p, but I may not believe that p', 'I believe that p, but it may be that not-p'. 'I know that p, but not p' is odd, too, but then it is self-contradictory; its first-person oddity is accompanied by the oddity of the second and third person forms 'You know that p, but not p', 'He (she, it) knows that p, but not p'. 'I know that p, but it may be that not-p' is odd as well, and again accompanied by the oddity of 'You know that p, but it may be that not-p' and 'He (she, it) knows that p, but it may be that not-p'. Likewise 'I am certain that p, but not p' is odd, and so I should say is 'I am certain that p, but it may be that not-p'.

Many attempts have been made to understand the nature of the peculiarly first-person linguistic or logical oddities. 'He believes that p, but not-p' is not at all odd or improper. In a case of straightforward implication the second and third person variants of a first-person oddity are themselves odd. 'He is clothed' implies 'He is not naked', and 'He is clothed but naked' is odd just in the way that 'I am clothed but naked' is odd. In the course of some attempts to understand such oddities it has been said that they correspond to first-person implications. It has been said, for instance, that when I say 'I believe that p' I imply that p even though what I say, namely, that I believe that p, does not imply that p. It has also been said that 'I believe that p' implies that p even though 'He believes that p' does not. It has been said that 'believes that p' implies in the first person that p. It has been said that when I say 'I believe that p' I commit myself to p, or to saying that p. Each of these descriptions has some obvious merits, but I will not here discuss their comparative merits or demerits in any very comprehensive way.

Such oddity relations or first-person implications are not fully fledged implication relations between the things they relate. It is possible, however, that these oddity relations correspond or are equivalent to fully fledged implication relations. An oddity relation between x and y may not be definable as an implication relation between x and y, but it may nevertheless be definable as an implication relation between x' and y', where one or both of x' and y' are not identical or equivalent to x and y, respectively. This is to employ the technique of definition in use, or contextual definition, triumphantly displayed in that paradigm of philosophy, Russell's theory of descriptions.

Remarkably enough the contextual definition of first-person implication in terms of implication proper does not seem to have been attempted until now. Here is my first attempt, which I call the r-interpretation of first-person oddities:

(FP.1) 'It is odd for me to say "p, but not-q" ' is definable as ' "I have reason to believe that p" implies "I have reason not to believe that not-q" '.

(FP.2) 'It is odd for me to say "p, but it may be that not-q" ' is definable as ' "I have reason to believe that p" implies "I have reason to believe that q" '.

It should be emphasised that the occurrences of 'I' and 'me' in these definitions do not render these definitions unsuccessful as eliminations of first-person oddities in favour of implications. This can be brought out by stating corresponding definitions in a non-verbal idiom, as follows:

(FP.3) It is logically necessary that it is odd for one to say that it is the case that p, but not that q if, and only if, one's having reason to believe that p implies one's having reason not to believe that q.

(FP.4) It is logically necessary that it is odd for one to say that it is the case that p, but may not be that q, if, and only if, one's having reason to believe that p implies one's having reason to believe that q.

To set out explicitly the non-verbal formulations corresponding to t-definitions would be more complex. I should note, however, that if first-person oddity is thought to be *prima facie* oddity, then it is not necessarily invariant under substitutions of t-equivalents.

There are several first-person oddity relations to which I must call particular attention for use in arguments here:

(0.1) p, but I do not know that p.
(0.2) p, but I may not know that p.
(0.3) I cannot not believe that p, but not-p.
(0.4) I cannot not believe that p, but it may be that not-p.

The oddity of (0.1) does not entail, but that of (0.2) does entail that for one to say that p is for one to commit oneself to, or to imply, 'I know that p'. The oddity of (0.3) does not entail, but that of (0.4) does entail that for one to say 'I cannot not believe that p', is for one to commit oneself to, or to imply, p. The oddity of (0.1) entails that for one to say that p is for one to commit oneself to not denying 'I know that p'. The oddity of (0.3) entails that for one to say 'I cannot not believe that p' is for one to commit oneself to not denying that p.

Next I must call attention to the following oddities:

(0.5) I cannot not believe that p in the circumstances, but not-p.

(0.6) I cannot not believe that p in the circumstances, but it may be that not-p.

(0.7) It is necessary in the circumstances that I believe that p, but not-p.

(0.8) It is necessary in the circumstances that I believe that p, but it may be that not-p.

Here (0.5) and (0.6) seem to be equivalent to (0.3) and (0.4), respectively. The colloquial 'can' and 'must' seem to me to be very often elliptical for 'can in the circumstances' and 'must in the circumstances', respectively. (0.7) and (0.8) are very straightforwardly equivalent to their respective counterparts (0.5) and (0.6). This is due to the well-recognised equivalence of 'cannot not' with 'must', which implies the equivalence of 'cannot not' sentences to 'necessarily' sentences in which suitable grammatical adjustments are made.

The final oddities to be commented on just now are these:

(0.9)   I am certain that p, but not-p.

(0.10) I am certain that p, but it may be that not-p.

It seems to me quite plausible to suggest that 'I am certain that p' is equivalent to 'I cannot not believe that p'. If this is the case, then (0.9) is equivalent to (0.3), (0.5) and (0.7), while (0.10) is equivalent to (0.4), (0.6) and (0.8).

I might just conclude here by saying that while the oddity of (0.3), (0.5), (0.7) and (0.9) does not show that their respective antecedents commit the speaker to p, those may or may not commit him to something in addition to committing him to not believing that p, namely, to believing 'Probably p'. But this is not a point on which I will much enlarge in this part.

(5) I proceed to give a third reduction of the first definition of knowledge. In this section, I argue that definitions (1.1), (1.2) and (1.3) are equivalent (and indeed t-equivalent) to both of the following:

(1.4) 'A knows that p' is definable as 'It is necessary in the circumstances that (i) p, and (ii) A believes that p'.

(1.5) 'A knows that p' is definable as '(i) It is necessary in the circumstances that p, and (ii) it is necessary in the circumstances that A believes that p'.

The equivalence of definitions (1.4) and (1.5) follows from the conjunction principle for circumstantial necessity.

No doubt what is most striking about this reduction is the absence of any reason condition in the (1.4) and (1.5) *definientia*. I am not saying that no reason condition is implied in a correct *definiens* for knowledge; rather I am saying that a reason condition is implied in conditions that make no mention of reason as such at all. I perform the reduction in the first person. The argument is more immediate stated in this way, and the generalisation of it to valid impersonal form, with 'A' for 'I' in suitable places, is also immediate.

The deductions that establish the third reduction are as follows. First, p r-implies 'I know that p': this can be called the apperception principle. For instance, 'It is raining' r-implies 'I know that it is raining'. By the r-interpretation this sort of r-implication follows from the oddity of (0.2): 'p, but I may not know that p.'

Second, 'I cannot not believe that p in the circumstances' r-implies that p. Under the r-interpretation of the first-person oddity relations this follows from the oddity of (0.4): 'I cannot not believe that p in the circumstances, but it may be that not-p.' Third, 'I cannot not believe that p in the circumstances' implies 'I have reason to believe that p in the circumstances'. The antiphosphorescence principle requires that 'I believe that p' does not imply 'I believe that I believe that p'; facts of belief can no more imply belief in them than other facts can imply belief in themselves. But such immediate facts about oneself as one's existence, one's beliefs and one's momentary sensory states do imply that one has reason to believe in them.

So, for instance, 'I believe that p' implies 'I have reason to believe that I believe that p'. From this it follows by the apperception principle that I have reason to believe that I know that I believe that p. It follows further that I have reason to believe what 'I know that I believe that p' implies. A previous deduction establishes that 'I know that I believe that p' implies 'I cannot not believe that p in the circumstances'. So it follows in turn that I have reason to believe that I cannot not believe that p in the circumstances.

Given that 'I cannot not believe that p in the circumstances' entails 'I have reason to believe that I cannot not believe that p in the circumstances', and that 'I cannot not believe that p in the circumstances' r-implies that p, it follows that 'I cannot not believe that p in the circumstances' implies that I have reason to believe that p. For the r-implication of p by 'I cannot not believe that p in the circumstances' just is the implication of 'I have reason to believe that p' by 'I have reason to believe that I cannot not believe that p in the circumstances'.

The arguments so far show that 'I cannot not believe that p in the circumstances' implies that I have reason to believe that p in the circumstances. It must still be shown that it follows that I cannot not have reason to believe that p in the circumstances. The proof makes use of the following inference form:

(I.6) x implies y; therefore, 'It is necessary in the circumstances that x' implies 'It is necessary in the circumstances that y'.

The principle corresponding to this inference form I call the preservation principle for circumstantial necessity. The reason for this choice of terminology is that the function 'It is necessary in the circumstances that p' preserves implications and so also equivalences. The analogous inference form for logical necessity is also valid:

(I.7) x implies y; therefore, 'It is logically necessary that x' implies 'It is logically necessary that y'.

The underlying principle is called the preservation principle for logical necessity; the function 'It is logically necessary that p' is implication-preserving. Indeed, every necessity operator properly so called is likewise implication-preserving.

The following is an analogous valid inference form:

(I.8) x implies y; therefore, 'A has reason to believe that x' implies 'A has reason to believe that y'.

The underlying principle here I call the preservation principle for reason; each of the functions 'A has reason to believe that p' is implication-preserving, just as the necessity functions are.

The proof here uses an additional principle: 'It is necessary in the circumstances that x' and 'It is necessary in the circumstances that it is necessary in the circumstances that x' are equivalent. This I call the idempotence principle for circumstantial necessity. The analogously stated idempotence principle for logical necessity also holds. Like every other principle I use here, the idempotence principles hold not only as equivalences, but also as t-equivalences.

To proceed, then, with the proof, 'I cannot not believe that p in the circumstances' implies 'I cannot not believe in the circumstances that I cannot not believe in the circumstances that p', by the idempotence principle for circumstantial necessity. Now it follows by the preservation principle for circumstantial necessity that as 'I cannot not believe that p in the circumstances' implies 'I have reason to believe that p in the circumstances', 'I cannot not believe in the circumstances that I cannot not believe that p in the circumstances' implies 'I cannot not have reason to believe that p in the circumstances'. The transitivity of implication yields that 'I cannot not believe that p in the circumstances' implies that 'I cannot not have reason to believe that p in the circumstances'. So condition (iii) in the (1.3) *definiens* is implied in condition (ii) of the (1.5) *definiens*. Conditions (i) and (ii) in the *definientia* are identical. It follows that the *definientia* are equivalent, and as the derivations of each from the other use t-valid inferences the *definientia* (1.1)–(1.5) are all t-equivalent.

(6) In this section, I perform a fourth reduction of the first definition of knowledge. This reduction involves showing that the preceding definitions are equivalent to the following:

(1.6) '*A* knows that *p*' is definable as '(i) It is necessary in the circumstances that *p*, and (ii) *A* believes that it is necessary in the circumstances that *p*'.

The fourth reduction uses one additional assumption. This is that 'It is necessary in the circumstances that *A* believes that *p*' is equivalent to '*A* believes that it is necessary in the circumstances that *p*'. I call this the commutation principle for circumstantial necessity. Needless to say 'It is logically necessary that *A* believes that *p*' is not equivalent to '*A* believes that it is logically necessary that *p*'. In this respect necessity in the circumstances is very different from logical necessity. 'It is necessary in the circumstances that' commutes with '*A* believes that' and with the same form for the other intentional verbs; 'It is logically necessary that' does not.

Given the commutation principle for circumstantial necessity, it follows that condition (ii) of *definiens* (1.5) is equivalent to condition (ii) of *definiens* (1.6). Condition (i) of *definiens* (1.5) is simply identical with condition (i) of *definiens* (1.6). So these two *definientia* are equivalent; the equivalence of the remaining *definientia* in the first series now follows, given the preceding reductions.

Given the idempotence principle for circumstantial necessity, the first definition with the first reduction implies that '*A* knows that *p*' is equivalent to 'It is necessary in the circumstances that *A* knows that *p*'. For the (1.2) *definiens* commences with 'It is necessary in the circumstances', which by the idempotence principle iterates itself as required. The first definition with the fourth reduction implies further that '*A* knows that *p*' is equivalent to '*A* knows that it is necessary in the circumstances that *p*'. Definition (1.6) implies that '*A* knows that it is necessary in the circumstances that *p*' is equivalent to 'It is necessary in the circumstances that it is necessary in the circumstances that *p* and *A* believes that it is necessary in the circumstances that it is necessary in the circumstances that *p*'. By the applicable idempotence principle the first conjunct reduces to 'It is necessary in the circumstances that *p*', which is the first conjunct of the (1.6) *definiens* for '*A* knows that *p*'. The second conjunct reduces to the second conjunct of the (1.6) *definiens* for '*A* knows that *p*'. I do not here merely use the idempotence principle in so far as it states the equivalence of 'It is necessary in the circumstances that *p*' and 'It is necessary in the circumstances that it is necessary in the circumstances that *p*'. I use the idempotence principle in the strong form of a guarantee of *t*-equivalence as well.

From the equivalence of '*A* knows that *p*' and '*A* knows that it is necessary in the circumstances that *p*' it does not follow that '*A* believes that *p*' is equivalent to '*A* believes that it is necessary in the circumstances that *p*'. Nor does it follow that *p* is equivalent to 'It is necessary in the circumstances that *p*'.

(7) As a way of examining this first definition series for knowledge, I turn now to its consequences for an account of knowledge of logically necessary truth. Under the presuppositions of the first and second reductions the following definition of knowledge of a logically necessary truth, l, can readily be derived:

> (L.1) 'A knows that l' is definable as '(i) It is necessary in the circumstances that l, (ii) it is necessary in the circumstances that A believes that l and (iii) it is necessary in the circumstances that A has reason to believe that l'.

Evidently 'It is necessary in the circumstances that l' implies the logical truth l itself. It is also implied in l. A logical necessity implies 'It is logically necessary that l'. Every logical truth implies its own logical necessity, for its logical necessity is itself a logical necessity and so implied in anything at all. 'It is logically necessary that l' implies in turn 'It is necessary in the circumstances that l'.

So the first conjunct of the (L.1) *definiens* is a logical truth eliminable without loss of content to the *definiens*, which leaves the following:

> (L.2) 'A knows that l' is definable as '(i) It is necessary in the circumstances that A believes that l and (ii) it is necessary in the circumstances that A has reason to believe that l'.

Now, however, I deduce 'A has reason to believe that l' from 'A believes that l', without making use of the key assumption of the third reduction. Given that A believes that l, it follows that A exists. But 'A exists' implies 'A has reason to believe that A exists'. Furthermore, 'A exists', which A has reason to believe, implies l, for any logically necessary truth is implied in anything at all. But A has reason to believe whatever is implied in what A has reason to believe, so it follows that A has reason to believe that l.

The completion of this deduction brings matters into this form:

> (L.3) 'A knows that l' is definable as 'It is necessary in the circumstances that A believes that l'.

An alternative derivation of (L.3) is easily provided by the arguments of the third reduction. For by those arguments condition (ii) of *definiens* (L.2), 'It is necessary in the circumstances that A believes that l', implies 'A has reason to believe that l', and so implies 'It is necessary in the circumstances that A has reason to believe that l', which is condition (iii) of the (L.1) *definiens*.

The fourth reduction yields yet a further equivalent formulation here:

> (L.4) 'A knows that l' is definable as 'A believes that it is necessary in the circumstances that l'.

As I have said, a logically necessary truth l is equivalent to 'It is necessary in the circumstances that l'. Indeed l, 'It is logically necessary that l', and 'It is necessary in the circumstances that l' are all three not merely equivalent but t-equivalent. So the fourth reduction yields these additional equivalent formulations:

(L.5) 'A knows that l' is definable as 'A believes that it is logically necessary that l'.

(L.6) 'A knows that l' is definable as 'A believes that l'.

It is the final formulation, (L.6), that is likely to be most startling. Even if the Platonic doctrine that belief and knowledge are mutually exclusive is not accepted, Plato's conviction that knowledge is irreducible to belief is likely to be accepted. Plato did not merely hold that knowledge is not in all cases reducible to belief; patently he held that knowledge is in no case reducible to belief. Yet even those who have some inclination not to be sure that Plato was right about this will be disinclined to accept (L.6), with its consequence that for all logically necessary truths knowledge is just belief. It appears, then, that this consequence of the first definition series is unacceptable. If the reductions are not to be abandoned, the definitions in this series must all be given up. How then, if at all, can the first-series definitions be amended so as to be acceptable?

(8) Perhaps this question can be profitably approached in the following way. Suppose the question is raised 'What is it to know a logically necessary truth axiomatically?' That is, what is it to know such a truth not on the basis of knowledge of any other logically necessary truth, or indeed of any other truth at all? This question can now be transformed into the question 'What, beyond mere belief in it, is required for axiomatic knowledge of a necessary truth?' The matter can look rather perplexing. For such knowledge cannot be based on knowledge of any other necessary truth, either deductively or analogically, nor can it be based on knowledge of non-necessity truths, as for instance in cases of reliance on authority. In either case the knowledge arrived at would not be purely axiomatic knowledge. What is wanted is an account of knowledge of a necessary truth that is taken as a starting-point, not known on the basis of anything else.

If I consider, then, such a question as 'What is it to know that one and one make two?', given that this knowledge is not derivative from knowledge of something else and that it does not consist of mere belief that one and one make two, it seems to me that there is nothing in which such axiomatic knowledge of necessary truth can consist except more of the same sorts of thing that make up the belief in that truth. So, for instance, the sorts of aptitudes and proclivities that constitute or at least manifest the belief that one and one make two, carried to a higher degree, constitute or at least manifest the knowledge that one and one make two. Indeed I am inclined to think that potentialities and dispositions concerning such things as counting and calculating manoeuvres are, in some way at least, interchangeable as between the mere belief and the knowledge that one and one make two.

I sum this up by saying that axiomatic knowledge of necessary truth is just hyperbelief, but I think a further interesting suggestion can be made about the nature of such knowledge. There is evidently a close affinity between A's belief that p and A's belief that he believes that p; indeed, some have held that 'A believes that p' and 'A believes that he believes that p' are equivalent.[6] I deny that these are equivalent; 'I believe that p' cannot imply 'I believe that I believe that p', given the anti-phosphorescence principle that for no x does x imply 'I believe that x'. 'I believe that p' does, however, r-imply 'I believe that I believe that p'; this is merely an instance of the r-implication of 'I believe that x' by x.

It strikes me, though, that matters can be carried further. The relation between A's belief that p and A's belief that he believes that p is similar to the relation between his belief that l and his hyperbelief that l. A's belief that he believes that p seems to me to consist of nothing that could not serve to make up his belief that p, and vice versa. At least this is so in the sense that whatever intrinsically favours 'A believes that p' also intrinsically favours 'A believes that he believes that p' and vice versa. The question 'Does this relation have anything to do with the r-relations?' is natural here. 'I believe that p' r-implies that 'I believe that I believe that p'. However, the converse relation does not hold.

So the relation indicated by the words 'whatever intrinsically favours the one intrinsically favours the other' is not identical with r-implication; at least this relation does not imply r-implication. I christen this relation 'quasi-implication'; 'quasi-equivalence' is to be used in the corresponding way. I cannot here engage in elaborate elucidations of this notion, or deal with the difficulties about it. Perhaps it will be enough here to give this instance. A thing's having horns is intrinsically favourable to its being a cow, even though having horns neither implies nor is implied by being a cow. In particular circumstances having horns may even be conclusive reason to suppose that a thing is not a cow; this is so if, say, there is good inductive reason to suppose that all the cows in the neighbourhood with horns have been slaughtered.

At all events I am claiming that 'A believes that p' and 'A believes that he believes that p' are quasi-equivalent in the defined sense. When A believes that he believes that p, I say 'A metabelieves that p', so I can sum up by saying that belief and metabelief are quasi-equivalent. Obviously the same relation must obtain between 'A believes that he believes that p' and 'A believes that he believes that he believes that p', and so on *ad infinitum*. All such relations are merely instances of the quasi-equivalence of 'A believes that x' and 'A believes that he believes that x'.

I am suggesting, then, that the formula for the relation between hyperbelief, belief and metabelief is just this: hyperbelief is belief plus metabelief. This implies that axiomatic knowledge of a necessary truth l is more than just belief that l, but includes only metabelief that l as an additional component.

If a necessary truth is known as an axiom and not otherwise, the knowledge of it involves, first, its truth, which since it is a necessary truth is an eliminable condition and, second, belief that it is true. (Just as p and 'It is true that p' are equivalent, they are also t-equivalent.) I have argued that A's axiomatic knowledge of l is simply his hyperbelief in l. The question now is whether some necessary truths, but not others, are knowable as axioms, not on the basis of anything else, and so on my account merely by hyperbelief. Elsewhere I have maintained that certain sorts of epistemological status, for instance, the logical possibility of doubt, are equivalence-invariant, that is, that if p and q are logically equivalent, then p and q must alike share or alike lack such sorts of epistemological status. Now I should maintain that logical possibility of being known as an axiom is also equivalence-invariant. The equivalence of all logical necessities, then, implies that not only some, but all necessary truths can conceivably be known as axioms, and so on the present account by mere hyperbelief.

In fact this is not really far from the common opinion on such matters. Everyone allows, or has some inclination to allow, that those remarkable creatures who produce immediately and without conscious calculation the answers to such questions as 'What is the product of 789,567 and 234,987?' know the answers to these questions. Now it is conceivable that such creatures should give their answers without knowing all of the usual axioms for such matters, or knowing them but without those axioms serving in any way as a basis for their answers. I think there would not be much hesitation to allow that in that case these creatures actually know the answers. Even philosophers such as Descartes have allowed that some necessary matters that are known by deduction from other things can also be known in the way necessary axioms are.

Principia Mathematica first made well known the fact that the traditional logical axioms can appear as theorems in a comprehensive deductive system of logic and mathematics. It remains only to allow that such a system might conceivably represent a creature's sole mode of access to knowledge of the traditional axioms, which would then be merely derivative.

So perhaps any necessary truth can be known as an axiom, and perhaps too any necessary truth, even the traditional logical axioms or the elementary truths of arithmetic such as 'One and one make two', can be known not as an axiom, but derivatively.[7]

More can be said to strengthen the view that every necessary truth can be known as an axiom. It can be asked 'If knowledge of an axiom is just hyperbelief, is not knowledge in all other cases the very same thing?' After all, is not the function of a proof to put us in the same state that we are in for its axioms, namely, knowledge? Axioms, it might be said, are simply what is known first. If their being known is their being hyperbelieved, surely this is enough to make any necessary truth known. For surely the prime function of proof here is simply to generate hyperbelief in necessary truths where it was lacking. If that hyperbelief is gained non-derivatively, the result is no less knowledge, and once known non-derivatively any necessary truth can surely serve as an axiom.

Now the thing is to notice the similarity of what might be thought in the case of knowledge of non-necessary truth. As Watling brought out, there is an inclination to allow that a creature who cannot help getting things right knows them, even when the usual sorts of reasons for thinking things to be so are lacking in that creature.[8] As, in effect, Gettier brought out, there is an inclination to allow that those who have the best reasons for their beliefs and are right do not know what they believe if as a matter of fact they could have been wrong.[9]

(9) In an attempt to incorporate these suggestions about knowledge into a new definition series I begin with the following full formulation:

> (2.1) 'A knows that p' is definable as '(i) p, (ii) A believes that p, (iii) A has reason to believe that p, (iv) it is necessary in the circumstances that each of conditions (i), (ii), (iii) holds if, and only if, each of the others holds, (v) it is necessary in the circumstances that A believes that condition (iv) holds and (vi) it is necessary in the circumstances that A has reason to believe that condition (iv) holds'.

In what follows the words 'A believes that A believes that p', for instance, are to be construed as 'A believes that he (she, or it, as appropriate) believes that p'. I indicate this by writing 'A believes that A^* believes that p' in all cases in which some such words are to be taken in this way.

The necessity of distinguishing 'A believes that A believes that p' from 'A believes that A^* believes that p' is illustrated by this Borges-like variation on Shakespeare's *The Tempest*: Ferdinand, who does not believe that he is the King of Naples, believes that he is on an island; he does not believe that the King of Naples is on an island. Ferdinand also believes that he believes that he is on an island, but Ferdinand does not believe that the King of Naples believes that he (Ferdinand) is on an island. Ferdinand is, in fact, the King of Naples; his father is dead, though Ferdinand believes that he is not.

Fortunately some initial simplification of the (2.1) *definiens* is possible without invoking any reduction of the first definition series but the second. Given the definition (2.1), condition (iii) alone yields the conclusion that A has reason to believe that p, A has reason to believe that A^* believes that p, and A has reason to believe that A^* has reason to believe that p.

Condition (iii) of the (2.1) *definiens* is that A has reason to believe that p. By the apperception principle 'A has reason to believe that p' implies 'A has reason to believe that A^* knows that p'. This implies in turn that A has reason to believe what 'A knows that p' implies. Since condition (ii) is implied in the (2.1) *definiens*, the (2.1) definition has the consequence that 'A has reason to believe that p' implies 'A has reason to believe that A^* believes that p'. Given definition (2.1) with its condition (iii), that A has reason to believe that p, the apperception principle also yields the consequence that 'A has reason to believe that p' implies 'A has reason to believe that A^* has reason to believe that p'.

So if the (2.1) definition is correct, then condition (iii) in the *definiens* implies that the two additional conditions (ii^1), 'A has reason to believe that A^* believes that p', and (iii^1), 'A has reason to believe that A^* has reason to believe that p', are satisfied.

Now I make use of the following inference form:

(I.9)   It is necessary in the circumstances that x, and x implies y; therefore, it is necessary in the circumstances that y.

Arguments already given for the (1.1) *definiens* show that conditions (i)–(iv) of the (2.1) *definiens* together yield the consequence (iii.1) 'It is necessary in the circumstances that A has reason to believe that p'. This is just the circumstantial necessity of condition (iii). As condition (iii) implies the additional conditions (ii^1) and (iii^1), and conditions (i)–(iv) together imply condition (iii.1), the inference form (I.9) can be applied to deduce (ii^1.1) 'It is necessary in the circumstances that A has reason to believe that A^* believes that p' and (iii^1.1) 'It is necessary in the circumstances that A has reason to believe that A^* has reason to believe that p'.

It seems to me evident that (ii) 'A believes that p' implies (ii^1) 'A has reason to believe that A^* believes that p'. It also seems to me evident that (iii) 'A has reason to believe that p' implies (iii^1) 'A has reason to believe that A^* has reason to believe that p'. What I have just established is that these evident truths are implied by definition (2.1) in conjunction with the apperception principle. If I had simply taken these implications for granted, I might have argued that conditions (ii) and (iii) in the (2.1) *definiens* suffice by themselves to yield (ii^1) and (iii^1), respectively, and so yield (iii.1), (ii^1.1) and (iii^1.1) in the further argument from the (2.1) *definiens*. In fact, I have argued from no conditions in the (2.1) *definiens* except (i)–(iv); so I might as well have argued from the *definientia* of the first series.

Now a further step is to be made. Premises (iii.1), (ii^1.1) and (iii^1.1), respectively, yield the following:

(iii.1.1)   It is necessary in the circumstances that A has reason to believe that it is necessary in the circumstances that p.

(ii^1.1.1)   It is necessary in the circumstances that A has reason to believe that it is necessary in the circumstances that A^* believes that p.

(iii^1.1.1) It is necessary in the circumstances that A has reason to believe that it is necessary in the circumstances that A^* has reason to believe that p.

These consequences follow by the apperception principle: if A has reason to believe that x, then A has reason to believe that it is necessary in the circumstances that x, for A has reason to believe that A^* knows that x and so has reason to believe what that implies. So, for instance, if A has reason to believe that p, then A has reason to believe that it is necessary in the circumstances that p. The preservation principle for circumstantial necessity then guarantees that it follows that (iii.1) 'It is necessary in the circumstances that A has reason to believe that p' implies (iii.1.1) 'It is necessary in the circumstances that A has reason to believe that it is necessary in the circumstances that p'. (ii^1.1.1) and (iii^1.1.1) are deducible from (ii^1.1) and (iii^1.1), respectively, in the same way, *mutatis mutandis*. It should be noticed that I have here used the apperception principle in an impersonal form, with 'A' for 'I'.

At all events, with the three premisses (iii.1.1), (ii^1.1.1) and (iii^1.1.1) having been derived, a single inference form virtually suffices to complete the deduction of condition (vi) from conditions (i)–(v). Again the deduction relies only on conditions (i)–(iv); condition (v) is not employed. The inference form is:

(I.10)   It is necessary in the circumstances that A has reason to believe that it is necessary in the circumstances that y; therefore, it is necessary in the circumstances that A has reason to believe that it is necessary in the circumstances that if x, then y.

The validity of this inference form follows from the validity of the following inference form:

(I.11)   'A has reason to believe that it is necessary in the circumstances that y; therefore, A has reason to believe that it is necessary in the circumstances that if x, then y.'

The validity of the first inference form follows from the validity of the second inference form by the preservation principle for circumstantial necessity. The validity of the second inference form itself is guaranteed by the validity of this third inference form, in accordance with the preservation principle for reason:

(I.3)   It is necessary in the circumstances that y; therefore, it is necessary in the circumstances that if x, then y.

The third inference form is in turn guaranteed by this fourth inference form:

(I.12) y; therefore, if x, then y.

The preservation principle for circumstantial necessity ensures that the validity of (I.12) implies that of (I.3). (I.3) itself is a valid inference form. In fact, all the inference forms just enumerated are not only valid, but t-valid; condition (vi) in the (2.1) *definiens* is a t-consequence of conditions (i)–(v), and even of conditions (i)–(iv).

The derivation of (vi) follows using at first only the single inference form (I.10), which has now been justified. From the premiss (iii.1.1) 'It is necessary in the circumstances that A has reason to believe that it is necessary in the circumstances that p' it follows, first, that it is necessary in the circumstances that A has reason to believe that it is necessary in the circumstances that if A^* believes that p, then p, and, second, that it is necessary in the circumstances that A has reason to believe that it is necessary in the circumstances that if A^* has reason to believe that p, then p. From the premiss (ii^1.1.1.) 'It is necessary in the circumstances that A has reason to believe that it is necessary in the circumstances that A^* believes that p', it follows, first, that it is necessary in the circumstances that A has reason to believe that it is necessary in the circumstances that if p, then A^* believes that p, and, second, that it is necessary in the circumstances that A has reason to believe that it is necessary in the circumstances that if A^* has reason to believe that p, then A^* believes that p. From the premiss (iii^1.1.1) 'It is necessary in the circumstances that A has reason to believe that it is necessary in the circumstances that A^* has reason to believe that p', it follows, first, that it is necessary in the circumstances that A has reason to believe that it is necessary in the circumstances that if p, then A^* has reason to believe that p and second, that it is necessary in the circumstances that A has reason to believe that it is necessary in the circumstances that if A^* believes that p, then A^* has reason to believe that p. The derivation can be completed using the conjunction principle for circumstantial necessity.

The first three reductions of the first definition series applied to conditions (i)–(iv) in the (2.1) *definiens* yield the following equivalent of (2.1):

(2.2) 'A knows that p' is definable as '(i) It is necessary in the circumstances that p, (ii) it is necessary in the circumstances that A believes that p and (iii) it is necessary in the circumstances that A believes that it is necessary in the circumstances that (a) p if, and only if, A^* believes that p, (b) A believes that p if, and only if, A^* has reason to believe that p and (c) p if, and only if, A^* has reason to believe that p'.

Some further deductions suffice to reduce (2.2) to the following:

(2.3) '*A* knows that *p*' is definable as '(i) It is necessary in the circumstances that *p*, (ii) it is necessary in the circumstances that *A* believes that *p* and (iii) it is necessary in the circumstances that *A* believes that it is necessary in the circumstances that A^* believes that *p*'.

Here is a proof that *definientia* (2.2) and (2.3) are equivalent. First, I show that the (2.3) *definiens* implies the (2.2) *definiens*. The proof here proceeds by an inference form analogous to the inference form (I.10), used to eliminate condition (vi) from the (2.1) *definiens*:

(I.13) It is necessary in the circumstances that *A* believes that it is necessary in the circumstances that *y*; therefore, it is necessary in the circumstances that *A* believes that it is necessary in the circumstances that if *x*, then *y*.

By the preservation principle for circumstantial necessity this inference form is valid if the following inference form is valid:

(I.14) *A* believes that it is necessary in the circumstances that *y*: therefore, *A* believes that it is necessary in the circumstances that if *x*, then *y*.

By the commutation principle for circumstantial necessity this inference form is valid if, and only if, the inference form (I.15) is valid:

(I.15) It is necessary in the circumstances that *A* believes that *y*; therefore, it is necessary in the circumstances that *A* believes that if *x*, then *y*.

Again by the preservation principle for circumstantial necessity the inference form (I.15) is valid if the inference form that follows is valid:

(I.16) *A* believes that *y*; therefore, *A* believes that if *x*, then *y*.

The inference form (I.16) is valid if, and only if, *y* *t*-implies 'If *x*, then *y*'. This *t*-implication appears to hold, at least under suitable conditions.

From condition (ii) in the (2.3) *definiens*, 'It is necessary in the circumstances that *A* believes that *p*', it follows by the idempotence principle for circumstantial necessity that it is necessary in the circumstances that it is necessary in the circumstances that *A* believes that *p*. From this it follows by the commutation principle for circumstantial necessity that it is necessary in the circumstances that *A* believes that it is necessary in the circumstances that *p*. From this as premiss it follows by inference form (I.13), first, that it is necessary in the circumstances that *A* believes that it is necessary in the circumstances that if A^* believes that *p*, then *p* and, second, that it is necessary in the circumstances that A believes that it is necessary in the circumstances that if A^* has reason to believe that p, then p.

From the premiss 'It is necessary in the circumstances that A believes that it is necessary in the circumstances that A^* has reason to believes that p', it follows by inference form (I.13), first that it is necessary in the circumstances that A believes that it is necessary in the circumstances that if A^* believes that p, then A^* has reason to believe that p and, second, that it is necessary in the circumstances that A believes that it is necessary in the circumstances that if p, then A^* has reason to believe that p.

The premiss of the preceding paragraph can itself be deduced from condition (iii) in the (2.3) *definiens*. By the preservation principle for circumstantial necessity 'It is necessary in the circumstances that A believes that it is necessary in the circumstances that A^* has reason to believe that p' is implied in 'It is necessary in the circumstances that A believes that it is necessary in the circumstances that A^* believes that p' if 'A believes that it is necessary in the circumstances that A^* has reason to believe that p' is implied in 'A believes that it is necessary in the circumstances that A^* believes that p'. This last implication just is the t-implication of 'It is necessary in the circumstances that A has reason to believe that p' by 'It is necessary in the circumstances that A believes that p'. It has already been established that 'It is necessary in the circumstances that A believes that p' implies 'A has reason to believe that p'. From this it follows by the preservation principle for circumstantial necessity that 'It is necessary in the circumstances that it is necessary in the circumstances that A believes that p' implies 'It is necessary in the circumstances that A has reason to believe that p'. But the idempotence principle for circumstantial necessity applied to the *implicans* here yields that 'It is necessary in the circumstances that A believes that p' implies 'It is necessary in the circumstances that A has reason to believe that p'. The principles used in this derivation are all t-implications or t-equivalences, so the required t-implication has been established.

From condition (iii) in the (2.3) *definiens*, 'It is necessary in the circumstances that A believes that it is necessary in the circumstances that A^* believes that p', the inference form (I.13) yields, first, that it is necessary in the circumstances that A believes that it is necessary in the circumstances that if p, then A^* believes that p and, second, that it is necessary in the circumstances that A believes that it is necessary in the circumstances that if A has reason to believe that p, then A^* believes that p.

The derivation of the (2.3) *definiens* from the (2.2) *definiens* proceeds as follows. From conditions (i) and (ii) of the (2.2) *definiens* it has now been shown to follow that it is necessary in the circumstances that A believes that p. The presence of subcondition (a) in condition (iii) of that *definiens* makes that condition yield immediately that it is necessary in the circumstances that A believes that it is necessary in the circumstances that if p, then A^* believes that p. I maintain that these premisses imply that it is necessary in the circumstances that A believes that it is necessary in the circumstances that A^* believes that p, which is condition (iii) of *definiens* (2.3). By the preservation principle for circumstantial necessity this implication holds if 'A believes that p and A believes that it is necessary in the circumstances that if p, then A^* believes that p' implies that 'A believes that it is necessary in the circumstances that A^* believes that p'.

This implication holds in turn if 'A believes that p and that it is necessary in the circumstances that if p, then A^* believes that p' implies 'A believes that it is necessary in the circumstances that A^* believes that p'.[10] That the validity of this implication guarantees that of its predecessor follows from the validity of the following inference form:

(I.17) A believes that x and A believes that y; therefore, A believes that x and y.

Such an inference form is valid if, as I have maintained elsewhere, 'A believes that x and A believes that y' is equivalent to 'A believes that x and y'. Indeed, I should maintain that 'A believes that x and y' is t-equivalent to 'A believes that x' and 'A believes that y', and accordingly, that the inference form (I.17) and its converse are t-valid.

The validity of the converse inference form, which follows, is one of the few quite indisputable points of this subject:

(I.18) A believes that x and y; therefore, A believes that x and A believes that y.

The t-validity of this inference form is another matter, but the fact is still sufficiently evident. Moreover, (I.18) is t-valid if the following inference form is valid:

(I.19) 'A believes that p' implies 'A believes that q'; therefore, 'A believes that A believes that p' implies 'A believes that A believes that q'.

The validity of inference form (I.19) is tantamount to that of this inference form:

(I.20) p t-implies q; therefore, 'A believes that p' t-implies 'A believes that q'.

In fact the inference form (I.20) is valid, and the inference form (I.18) is one of the most evident instances of its validity.

At all events, I use as a premiss here the t-implication of 'It is necessary in the circumstances that A believes that p' by 'p and it is necessary in the circumstances that if p, then A believes that p'. This assumption was used in inference form (I.1) to effect the first reduction of the two definition series, but it was used there only in order to establish t-implications or t-equivalences. Here the assumption of this t-implication is used to establish mere implications and equivalences, as well as t-implications and t-equivalences.

Condition (iii) of the (2.3) *definiens* thus follows from the (2.2) *definiens*. Conditions (i) and (ii) in the (2.3) *definiens* are identical with the corresponding conditions in the (2.2) *definiens*. So the *definiens* (2.3) is implied in *definiens* (2.2).

It is easy now to use the commutation principle for circumstantial necessity to derive these two final equivalent formulations of the second definition series:

(2.4) 'A knows that p' is definable as '(i) It is necessary in the circumstances that p, (ii) it is necessary in the circumstances that A believes that p and (iii) it is necessary in the circumstances that A believes that A^* believes that p.

(2.5) 'A knows that p' is definable as '(i) It is necessary in the circumstances that p, (ii) A believes that it is necessary in the circumstances that p and (iii) A believes that A^* believes that it is necessary in the circumstances that p'.

(10) In the light of the second definition series for 'A knows that p', what has become of the matter of knowledge of logically necessary truths? The following definition of knowledge of a logically necessary truth is an immediate consequence of definition (2.3):

(L2.1) 'A knows that l' is definable as '(i) l, (ii) it is necessary in the circumstances that A believes that l and (iii) it is necessary in the circumstances that A believes that it is necessary in the circumstances that A^* believes that l'.

Using the principle that logical truths can be removed or conjoined without alteration of logical content and definition (2.5), the equivalence to (L2.1) of the following definition is derivable:

(L2.2) 'A knows that l' is definable as '(i) A believes that it is necessary in the circumstances that l and (ii) A believes that A^* believes that it is necessary in the circumstances that l'.

the equivalence and indeed t-equivalence of l and 'It is necessary in the circumstances that l' yields this further equivalent definition:

(L2.3) 'A knows that l' is definable as '(i) A believes that l and (ii) A believes that A^* believes that l'.

Given the anti-phosphorescence principle that p does not imply 'A believes that p' for any p at all, it follows that 'A believes that l' does not imply 'A believes that A^* believes that l' for any l. Consequently for no l does 'A knows that l' reduce to 'A believes that l' on the account given by the second definition series. So the paradoxical reduction of knowledge to belief for necessary truths, implied by the first series, has been avoided by the second series.

Can the feature of knowledge of necessary truth indicated by such definitions as (L2.1)–(L2.3) serve to define necessary truth? It might be suggested that necessary truths can be defined as those things that satisfy the following formula:

(F.1) 'A knows that x' is definable as '(i) It is necessary in the circumstances that A believes that x and (ii) it is necessary in the circumstances that A believes that A^* believes that x'.

Equivalently it might be suggested that necessary truths are definable as those things that satisfy the reduced formula that follows:

(F.2) 'A knows that x' is definable as '(i) A believes that it is necessary in the circumstances that x and (ii) A believes that A^* believes that it is necessary in the circumstances that x'.

Again it might be suggested that necessary truths are definable as those things that satisfy this further formula:

(F.3) 'A knows that x' is definable as '(i) A believes that x and (ii) A believes that A^* believes that x'.

If the second definition series is correct, then all logically necessary truths do, indeed, satisfy the formulae (F1)–(F3); but are the things that satisfy these formulae all logically necessary truths? This is plainly false of (F.1). As Descartes emphasised, 'I exist' is implied in 'I believe that I exist', and it is likewise implied in 'I believe that I believe that I exist', so that by the preservation principle for circumstantial necessity 'It is necessary in the circumstances that I exist' is implied in 'It is necessary in the circumstances that I believe that I exist' and in 'It is necessary in the circumstances that I believe that I believe that I exist'. Consequently for 'I exist' condition (i) in the (2.4) *definiens* is implied in condition (ii), or for that matter in condition (iii), which evidently involves that 'I exist' satisfies the formula (F.1). The same argument, *mutatis mutandis*, shows that 'I exist' also satisfies the formula (F.2). But 'I exist' does not satisfy the formula (F.3). Condition (i) of the (2.4) *definiens* applied to 'I exist' is 'It is necessary in the circumstances that I exist'. Neither condition (i) nor condition (ii) of (F.3) applied to 'I exist' implies 'It is necessary in the circumstances that I exist', though both conditions imply 'I exist'. So given the correctness of definition (2.4) 'I know that I exist' is not definable as 'I believe I exist and I believe that I believe that I exist', as required for 'I exist' to satisfy the formula (F.3).

However, there is an epistemological formula that suffices to demarcate logically necessary truth:

> (F.4) '*A* knows that *x*' is definable as '(i) *A* believes that it is logically necessary that *x* and (ii) *A* believes that *A** believes that it is logically necessary that *x*'.

All logically necessary truths satisfy this formula; this follows from their satisfaction of such formulae as (F.1), given the *t*-equivalence of any logically necessary truth *l*, 'It is necessary in the circumstances that *l*', and 'It is logically necessary that *l*'. To believe a logically necessary truth is to believe that it is logically necessary. In this sense no one can grasp a logical necessity without grasp of its logical necessity. Possession of the concept of logical necessity is implied in the grasp and even in the mere understanding of any logical necessity. The modal notion may remain implicit, at least to the extent that it need have no distinct vehicle of expression for one who grasps and even expresses a necessary truth. Yet to recognise that one and one make two is to recognise that it is a matter of necessity that one and one make two. Even to understand, for instance, what it is for Green's theorem to be true is to understand that Green's theorem is, if true, necessarily true. Such recognition or understanding may be very much a matter of recognition or understanding in practice. So, for instance, an excellent grasp of elementary arithmetic does not imply an explicit philosophical appreciation of the logical necessity of arithmetical truths. Still, the explicit philosophical appreciation does merely spell out what is, in a strong sense, already implied in the mathematics; not merely implied, but *t*-implied.

If, however, I maintain that to believe any logical or mathematical truth is to believe that it has a certain general character, so that the concept of logical necessity cannot be lacking to anyone in possession of any logically necessary beliefs, I also maintain that there can be no characterisation of the logically necessary via any definition or equivalence that is non-circular, and that in the strong sense that any correct definition of logical necessity must be such that its *definiens* *t*-implies the possession of the concept of logical necessity. I must explain this last locution. To say that the possession of the concept of *C* is *t*-implied in *p* is to say that '*A* believes that *p*' implies '*A* has the concept of *C*'. It is trivially true that any *t*-equivalent *definiens* for logical necessity must *t*-imply the possession of the concept of logical necessity. I have not merely said that. I have said that any *s*-equivalent *definiens* for logical necessity *t*-implies the possession of that concept.

(11) Yet one more consequence of the second definition series should be

emphasised. In the case of very many contingent matters p, 'I believe that p, but I do not know that p' makes perfect sense, and has no trace of oddity about it *per se*: it is a consequence of 'I believe that p, but I may be wrong', and of 'I believe that p, but it may be that not-p', neither of which is at all odd *per se*. Needless to say, all this is thoroughly in accordance with the definitions of the second series, and for that matter with those of the first. Consider now, however, any logically necessary truth l. Is there any oddity about 'I believe that l, but I do not know that l', or about 'I believe that l, but I may be wrong', or about 'I believe that l, but it may be that not-l'? About this three things can be said for now. First, both 'I believe that l, but I may be wrong' and 'I believe that l, but it may be that not-l' imply 'It may be that not-l'. First of all, 'not-l' is the denial of a necessary truth, and hence an *a priori* absurdity, liable to be revealed as such by reflection; there is, then, at least a latent oddity here. It should be noticed that no such incoherence can lie in wait for 'I believe that p, but I may be wrong' or 'I believe that p, but it may be that not-p' when p is a contingent matter other than the Cartesian favourites implied in 'I believe that p' and 'I believe that not-p' alike.[11]

Second, I have argued that 'I believe that l' implies 'It is necessary in the circumstances that I believe that l' and, equivalently, 'I cannot not believe that l (in the circumstances)'. This fact has revealing consequences. What matters here is not that 'I cannot not believe that l in the circumstances' implies 'I have reason to believe that l'; this leaves matters just where they were. The important thing is the oddity of 'I cannot not believe that p (in the circumstances), but it may be that not-p', from which indeed the implication just mentioned has been derived. This oddity relation itself applied to a necessary truth l yields the oddity of 'I cannot not believe that l (in the circumstances), but it may be that not-l'. Given the t-equivalence of 'I believe that l', 'It is necessary in the circumstances that I believe that l', and 'I cannot not believe that l (in the circumstances)', it follows that the oddity relation is preserved by substituting the first for the third. First-person oddity-relations are not necessarily preserved by substitution of equivalents; but substitution of t-equivalents does preserve them. So I conclude to the oddity of 'I believe that l, but it may be that not-l', and accordingly of 'I believe that l, but I may be wrong'.

Third, 'I believe that l, but I may not know that l' is, by the second definition series, equivalent to 'I believe that l, but it is not the case that all of l, "I believe that l" and "I believe that I believe that l", are true'. This is undoubtedly t-equivalent to 'I believe that l, but it is not the case that l or it is not the case that I believe that I believe that l'. By the eliminability principle this is in turn equivalent to 'I believe that l, but it is not the case that I believe that I believe that l'. This last form is undoubtedly a first-person oddity; it is an instance of the oddity 'x, but it is not the case that I believe that x'. It might then be concluded that 'I believe that p, but I may not know that l' is an oddity given the second series definitions. However, it should be noted that substitution of equivalents, unlike substitution of *t*-equivalents, does not necessarily preserve *prima facie* oddity. If first-person oddity were inconsistent with truth, substitution of equivalents would doubtless preserve such oddity, but oddity and truth are consistent. In the above argument the equivalence generated by the eliminability principle is not a *t*-equivalence.

(12) Next I deal with a sort of difficulty that can be raised for my account of *t*-implication. It might well be asked whether *t*-implication does not reduce to implication if the sorts of inferences I have said are *t*-valid are indeed so. Such a consequence would prove my account of *t*-implication unsound, as it is absurd to say that '*A* believes that *p*' implies '*A* believes *q*' whenever *p* implies *q*. It might be asked how, if at all, such a consequence is to be avoided if I allow the *t*-validity not merely of '*p* and *q*; therefore, *q*', but also that of *modus ponens*. If *modus ponens* is *t*-valid, what inference form is not? Is it at least true that every inference form valid solely in virtue of its truth-functional structure is *t*-valid? If so, is it not implausible even to maintain that every inference drawn by such means is a *t*-valid inference? Surely, it does not follow that I believe every theorem of the truth-functional calculus simply because I believe the axioms of that calculus. It might even be said that if *modus ponens* is・ *t*-valid, then any inference form valid in terms solely of its topic-neutral structure must be *t*-valid. It might, finally, be said that there is no room to discriminate against such inference forms as '*x* is clothed; therefore, *x* is not naked'. If every topic-neutral inference form is *t*-valid, so surely must these be.

Another case of topic-neutral validity in an inference form unaccompanied by *t*-validity is that of the substitution rules for inference so prominent in twentieth-century formal deductive systems. The essential point about such inferences can be made equally well by reference to the following inference form prominent in logic for a very long time:

(I.21) Every *x* is a *y*; *a* is an *x*; therefore, *a* is a *y*.

I take as instances the following:

(I.22) Every positive whole number is the sum of two odd positive whole numbers, and 7 is a positive whole number; therefore, 7 is a sum of two odd positive whole numbers.

(I.23) Every positive whole number is a sum of two odd positive whole numbers, and the product of the solutions of the equations '$2x - 9 = -5$' and '$2x + 5 = 9$' is a positive whole number; therefore, the product of the solutions of the equations '$2x - 9 = -5$' and '$2x + 5 = 9$' is the sum of two odd positive whole numbers.

Both (I.22) and (I.23) are valid, and *t*-valid as well. However, the inferences that follow are also valid by the eliminability principle, since the premisses '7 is a positive whole number' and 'The product of the solutions of the equations "$2x - 9 = -5$" and "$2x + 5 = 9$" is a positive whole number' are logically necessary truths:

(I.24) Every positive whole number is a sum of two odd positive whole numbers; therefore, 7 is a sum of two odd positive whole numbers.

(I.25) Every positive whole number is a sum of two odd positive whole numbers; therefore, the product of the solutions of $2x - 9 = -5$ and $2x + 5 = 9$ is a sum of two odd positive whole numbers.

The inferences (I.24) and (I.25) are valid, but not t-valid. This fact, if not altogether obvious in the case of (I.24), should actually be quite obvious in that of (I.25). I take it, then, that the topic-neutral validity of inference forms does not guarantee their t-validity. There is accordingly no discriminating against such topic-specific inferences as 'x is a quadratic equation; therefore, x is soluble' in maintaining that these, too, are not all t-valid.

In fact, I should maintain that not every truth-functionally valid inference form is t-valid. However, it might be suggested that the only truth-functionally valid forms that are not t-valid are such forms as this:

(I.26) p; therefore, p or q.

It might be suggested, too, that this sort of exception is enough to save this account from unacceptable consequences in the case of deductions in the truth-functional calculus. It is interesting to note, however, that the following inference form may appear to be valid:

(I.27) A believes that p and A comprehends what it is for q to be the case; therefore, A believes that p or q.

Even if (I.27) does not appear to be valid, the following inference form may appear to be valid:

(I.28) A believes that p and A comprehends what it is for p or q to be the case; therefore, A believes that p or q.[12]

'A comprehends what it is for it to be the case that p or q' implies 'A comprehends what it is for it to be the case that q', but even 'A believes that p and A comprehends what it is for it to be the case that q', which implies 'A comprehends what it is for it to be the case that p and A comprehends what it is for it to be the case that q', may not imply 'A comprehends what it is for it to be the case that p or q'. In short, the comprehension of 'p or q' may not follow from the comprehension of p and of q; similarly the comprehension of 'p and q' may not follow from the comprehension of p and of q, in which case the belief that p and q does not follow from the conjunction of the belief that p and the belief that q.[13] Then again these consequences may follow; but 'A is conscious of what it is for it to be the case that p' and 'A is conscious of what it is for it to be the case that q' may not imply 'A is conscious of what it is for it to be the case that p and q' and may not imply 'A is conscious of what it is for it to be the case that p or q'.

So (I.26), while not t-valid, is nevertheless similar to inference forms (I.27) and (I.28), which may appear to be valid. It might now seem that every truth-functionally valid inference form is characterisable in the following way. First, it might be said that every truth-functionally valid inference form can be derived from a series of truth-functionally valid inference forms such that each member of the series is immediately valid. An immediately valid truth-functional inference form is either t-valid or associated with valid inference forms similar to (I.28), such as:

(I.29) A believes that p and A comprehends what it is for it to be the case that $f(q_1, \ldots, q_n)$ (where $f(q_1, \ldots, q_n)$ is a truth function of $q_1, \ldots, q_n$); therefore, $f(q_1, \ldots, q_n)$.

It follows from this account of truth-functional inference that belief in a set of premisses and comprehension of the conclusions that follow truth-functionally from that set implies belief in each of those conclusions. This is clearly an unacceptable result. Furthermore, generalisations of this account of truth-functional inference to all inference yield generalised versions of this unacceptable result. I proceed, therefore, to offer a general account of valid deductive inference that avoids all such difficulties.

That general account of valid deductive inference is statable as follows. First, every immediately valid deductive inference 'p, therefore, c' (with p as the conjunction of its premisses and c as its conclusion) corresponds to a valid inference form such as the following:

(I.30) It occurs to A that p and it occurs to A what it is for it to be the case that c; therefore, A believes that c.

Equivalently, every such valid inference form corresponds to a valid inference form such as this:

(I.31) A is conscious that p and A is conscious of what it is for it to be the case that c; therefore, A believes that c.

Second, every valid deductive inference is obtainable as a series of immediately valid deductive inferences. Valid deductive inferences in accordance with forms such as (I.30) and (I.31) are not exceptions to this generalisation.

So perhaps *modus ponens* is not, after all, a *t*-valid inference form. However, I submit that the following inference form is valid:

(I.32) It occurs to *A* that if *p*, then *q* and that *p*; therefore, *A* believes that *q*.

Equivalently, the following inference form is valid:

(I.33) *A* is conscious that if *p*, then *q* and that *p*; therefore, *A* believes that *q*.

The inference forms corresponding to *modus ponens* for 'occurs to' and 'conscious that' may appear to be valid:

(I.34) It occurs to *A* that if *p*, then *q* and that *p*; therefore, it occurs to *A* that *q*.
(I.35) *A* is conscious that *p* and that if *p*, then *q*; therefore, *A* is conscious that *q*.

But the invalidity of the inference forms (I.34) and (I.35) is suggested by considerations like those that suggest the invalidity of the inference form corresponding to *modus ponens* for 'believes that':

(I.36) *A* believes that *p* and that if *p*, then *q*, therefore, *A* believes that *q*.

The forms that I am suggesting are valid, (I.32) and (I.33), differ from (I.34), (I.35) and (I.36) in that the premisses refer to its occurring to *A* or to *A*'s being conscious that *p* and that if *p*, then *q* while the conclusion states that *A* believes that *q*, not that it occurs to *A* that *q* or that *A* is conscious that *q*. It does not follow from '*A* believes that *x*' that it occurs to *A* that *x* or that *A* is conscious that *x* (at least not in the sense in which 'conscious' is here employed, corresponding to 'It occurs to *A* that *x*'). It does follow from 'It occurs to *A* that *x*' and from '*A* is conscious that *x*' that *A* believes that *x*. It should also be emphasised here that none of these inference forms contains as a distinct premiss 'It occurs to *A* what it is for it to be the case that *q*' or '*A* is conscious of what it is for it to be the case that *q*'. In fact such premisses are superfluous in such inference forms; 'It occurs to *A* what it is for it to be the case that *q*' is implied in 'It occurs to *A* that *p* and that if *p*, then *q*', just as '*A* comprehends what it is for it to be the case that *q*' is implied in '*A* believes that if *p*, then *q* and that *p*', and '*A* is conscious of what it is to be the case that *q*' is implied in '*A* is conscious that if *p*, then *q* and that *q*', just as '*A* comprehends what it is to be the case that *q*' is implied in '*A* believes that if *p*, then *q* and that *p*'.

Finally, it may not hold true on this account that every logical implication corresponds to a valid deductive inference. Whether or not this would show that the account is incorrect, the account at least does not imply that the understood consequences of what is believed must be believed.

It seems to be evident that 'It occurs to *A* that *l*' and 'It occurs to *A* that it is logically necessary that *l*' are not equivalent, even when *l* is a logical truth. But I have maintained that '*A* believes that *l*' and '*A* believes that it is logically necessary that *l*' are equivalent. So I am committed to saying that the equivalence of '*A* believes that *p*' and '*A* believes that *q*' does not imply the equivalence of 'It occurs to *A* that *p*' and 'It occurs to *A* that *q*', though the converse holds. '*A* is conscious that *p*' is like 'It occurs to *A* that *p*' in this respect, though '*A* is conscious that *p* implies *p*' in all cases, while 'It occurs to *A* that *p*' implies *p* only in some cases.

Just when does the entailment of '*A* is conscious that *q*' by '*A* is conscious that *p*' fail, though the entailment of '*A* believes that *q*' by '*A* believes that *p*' holds? When, for that matter, does the latter sort of entailment fail? The rough answer for belief-entailment is: when the belief that *q* involves concepts not involved in the belief that *p*. This answer is undoubtedly rough, if I am right in saying that such things as '*A* believes that *l*' and '*A* believes that it is logically necessary that *l*' are equivalent. The same answer is, however, exactly right for consciousness-entailments. Similar remarks can be made about the differences between belief and consciousness indicated by the validity of conjunctive inference for belief but not consciousness. It begins to be obvious that the concepts distinguishing the logical patterns for belief and knowledge from those for consciousness are some or all of those topic-neutral concepts of special interest to logicians and philosophers. It also begins to be obvious that logic and philosophy make conscious and explicit what is already believed. Whether they perform no functions not closely related to this is a question I pursue no farther at the moment.

Elsewhere I will deal at length with the differences made to the deductions of this part and to the matters raised in the preceding section by the introduction of comprehension conditions and of the *en echelon* account of deduction. For now I record only my persuasion that the equivalences in the definition series can be maintained and that the treatment of those matters is if anything strengthened. The full *r*-interpretation is not needed for the main arguments here; the implication of '*p r*-implies *q*' by the logical oddity of '*p*, but it may not be the case that '*q*' is sufficient without the converse implication. A modified *r*-interpretation will be presented in the second part.*

(13) Some medieval philosophers said that in purely philosophical matters authority is the weakest sort of argument, but I should now like to invoke Russell in support of the anti-phosphorescence principle that has played so crucial a role in these proceedings. Russell did not always

---

* At the time of going to press a second volume of this work is being planned.

advocate the anti-phosphorescence principle; at least what he says in the following passage from *The Problems of Philosophy* (1912) may be inconsistent with it: 'If I am acquainted with a thing which exists, my acquaintance gives me the knowledge that it exists.'[14] However, in *An Inquiry into Meaning and Truth* (1940) Russell gives the anti-phosphorescence principle what is, on the whole, an emphatic endorsement. The passage is stated in terms of knowledge, not belief, but it is plain enough that Russell would have said much the same things of belief as of knowledge here:[15]

> The word 'know' is highly ambiguous. In most senses of the word, 'knowing' an event is a different occurrence from the event which is known; but there is a sense of 'knowing' in which, when you have an experience, there is no difference between the experience and knowing that you have it. It might be maintained that we always know our present experiences; but this cannot be the case if the knowing is something different from the experience. For, if an experience is one thing and knowing it is another, the supposition that we always know an experience when it is happening involves an infinite multiplication of every event. I feel hot; this is one event. I know that I feel hot; this is a second event. And so on *ad infinitum*, which is absurd. We must therefore say either that my present experience is indistinguishable from my knowing it while it is present, or that, as a rule, we do not know our present experiences. On the whole, I prefer to use the word 'know' in a sense which implies that the knowing is different from what is known, and to accept the consequence that, as a rule, we do not know our present experiences.
>
> We are to say, then, that it is one thing to see a puddle, and another to know that I see a puddle.

I do not agree with Russell that the word 'know' is highly ambiguous, nor do I agree with him that 'There is a sense of "knowing" in which, when you have an experience, there is no difference between the experience and knowing that you have it.' Undoubtedly, though, some philosophers do have an inclination to speak in this way, as indeed Russell's remark itself shows, so perhaps there is a 'philosopher's sense' of the word 'knowing'. But to say what Russell does here is to concede too much to the phosphorescence view of knowledge of one's immediate momentary experience. On the whole, however, Russell's views here are healthily anti-phosphorescent. Here is another quotation from the same passage, in which Russell continues his sermon without uneasy glances at the phosphorescence view:[16]

> What must be done with an experience in order that we may know it? Various things are possible. We may use words describing it, we may remember it either in words or in images, or we may merely 'notice' it.

But 'noticing' is a matter of degree, and very hard to define. It seems to consist mainly in isolating from the sensible environment. You may, for instance, in listening to a piece of music, deliberately notice only the part of the cello. You hear the rest, as it said, 'unconsciously' – but this is a word to which it would be hopeless to attempt to attach any definite meaning. In one sense, it may be said that you 'know' a present experience if it rouses in you any emotion, however faint – if it pleases or displeases you, or interests or bores you, or surprises you or is just what you were expecting.

There is an important sense in which you can know anything that is in your present sensible field. If somebody says to you 'are you now seeing yellow?' or 'do you hear a noise?' you can answer with perfect confidence, even if, until you were asked, you were not noticing the yellow or the noise. And often you can be sure that it was already there before your attention was called to it.

It seems, then, that the most immediate knowing of which we have experience involves sensible presence *plus* something more.

There is still too much talk here of different senses of 'know'. But the final sentence expresses what I am principally concerned to take from the passage.

Finally, I should say that the way in which the anti-phosphorescence principle fits in with the other things I have said and arguments I have given here affords them mutual confirmation.

(14) I close this part by indicating a few implications for a wider range of epistemological matters. First, let us consider the implications of a conclusion reached early in this inquiry: p r-implies that A knows that p, so that p r-implies, *inter alia*, that it is necessary in the circumstances that p. This is to say that for anyone to have reason to believe anything at all is for him necessarily to have reason to believe that that thing is necessary in the circumstances. When p is not a matter of logical necessity, then anyone who has reason to believe that p necessarily has reason to believe that p is necessary in the circumstances as a matter of non-logical necessity. Actually this sort of result is available here in a completely general form. The apperceptive principle not only guarantees that p r-implies that it is necessary in the circumstances that p, it also guarantees that p r-implies that it is necessary in the circumstances that A believes that p. For no p is 'A believes that p' a logically necessary truth: this is a corollary of the anti-phosphorescence principle, but it is also evident in itself. So to have reason to believe anything is necessarily to have reason to believe at least one thing to be necessary in the circumstances as a matter of fact, and not as a matter of logical necessity.

Furthermore, the second definition series as well as the first yields the consequence that to know that p is to know that it is necessary in the circumstances that p. To complete the proof of this fact is an easy exercise in applying the strong idempotence principle for circumstantial necessity to condition (iii) in the (I.25) *definiens*. So if either definition series is correct it is inconceivable that a fact should be discovered and then discovered to have no necessitating circumstances. It does not follow that to know that *p* is necessarily to know how *p* is necessitated.

Hume raised certain well-known sceptical doubts about induction and factually necessary connections. Kant's answer to Hume's doubts has often been more or less misunderstood and doubtless lends itself in many ways to such misunderstanding. Nevertheless, Kant's resolution of Hume's problem seems to me to be in at least one essential respect correct. Kant argued that the understanding could not operate without being entitled to apply such notions as that of factually necessary connection. Certainly Kant rejects Hume's picture of us as certain of some matters but without reason for any beliefs about necessary connection. For Kant, Hume's position on necessary connection involves a self-contradiction. To be certain of anything at all, or even to have reason for anything at all, is necessarily to have reason for belief in some factually necessary connection. Yet Kant does not deny – at the very least, he does not consistently deny – Hume's insight that causal connections are not logically necessary connections. Russell was recurrently concerned with such matters at least from *The Problems of Philosophy* (1912) onwards. The famous lecture on 'Logic as the Essence of Philosophy' in *Our Knowledge of the External World* (1914) shows Russell puzzling over status questions about the principles of inductive inference.[17] Such questions are given extended treatment at late as Russell's *Human Knowledge* (1948).[18] These are matters to be discussed in the next part. However, I should say now that I deal with these matters by combining my somewhat Moorean reinterpretation of Kant with Russell's causal analysis of persistence.

Department of Philosophy
Duke University

NOTES

1 In 'Some Questions in Epistemology', *Proceedings of the Aristotelian Society*, vol. LXX (1969–70: 37–60); and in 'Incorrigibility, Behaviourism and Predictionism', *Wisdom: Twelve essays*, Renford Bambrough, ed. (Oxford, Basil Blackwell, 1974: 125–50).

2 Compare Frank J. Leavitt, 'On an Unpublished Remark of Russell's on "If . . . Then" ', *Russell: the Journal of the Bertrand Russell Archives*, no. 6 (Summer 1972).

3 Compare George W. Roberts, 'Some Questions in Epistemology' (op. cit.: 51 ff.).

4 Strictly, I am speaking here of the result of substituting in the appropriate places the statements $P_1, \ldots, P_5$ for the phrase 'the Euclidean postulates $P_1, \ldots, P_5$' and the statement of the Pythagorean theorem for the phrase 'the Pythagorean theorem is true'.

5 G. E. Moore, *Ethics* (London, Williams & Norgate; and New York: Home University, 1912: 125); cf. 'A Reply to My Critics', in *The Philosophy of G. E. Moore*, Schilpp, ed. (Evanston and Chicago, Northwestern University Press, 1942: esp. 541-3); and also G. E. Moore, 'Russell's "Theory of Descriptions" ', in *The Philosophy of Bertrand Russell*, P. A. Schilpp, ed. (Evanston and Chicago: Northwestern University Press, 1944: 177–225); esp. pp. 203–5. Disciples of Moore dealing with this matter are well

represented in Margaret Macdonald, ed., *Philosophy and Analysis* (Oxford, Basil Blackwell, 1954).

6   I use 'he' here for whichever of the 'he', 'she' or 'it' is appropriate.

7   Compare George W. Roberts, 'Incorrigibility, Behaviourism and Predictionism', op. cit.

8   John Watling, 'Inference from the Known to the Unknown', *Proceedings of the Aristotelian Society*, vol. LV (1954–5: 83–108).

9   E. L. Gettier III, 'Is Justified True Belief Knowledge?', *Analysis*, vol. XXIII (1963: 121–3).

10   Throughout I use such forms as '*A* believes that *x* and *y*' and '*A* believes that *x* and that *y*' synonymously. I do not mean to beg the question whether '*A* believes that *x* and *y*' and '*A* believes that *x* and *A* believes that *y*' are equivalent, though I think that this equivalence holds.

11   Compare George W. Roberts, 'Some Questions in Epistemology' and 'Incorrigibility, Behaviourism and Predictionism', op. cit.

12   Needless to say, an identical time-reference is understood in such contexts.

13   I should maintain that even if '*A* believes that *p* and *A* believes that *q*' does not imply '*A* believes that *p* and *q*', it nevertheless follows from 'It is logically possible that *A* believes that *p* and *A* believes that *q*' (with an identical time-reference understood) that it is logically possible that *A* believes that *p* and *q*.

14   Bertrand Russell, *The Problems of Philosophy* (London, Williams & Norgate; and New York, Henry Holt. Home University Library, 1912: 45).

15   Bertrand Russell, *An Inquiry into Meaning and Truth* (London, George Allen & Unwin, 1940: 49–50).

16   ibid., pp. 50–1.

17   Bertrand Russell, *Our Knowledge of the External World* (Chicago, Open Court, 1914: lecture II).

18   Bertrand Russell, *Human Knowledge: Its Scope and Limits* (London, George Allen & Unwin, 1948).

22

RUSSELL'S PHILOSOPHICAL
ACCOUNT OF PROBABILITY[1]

Bas C. van Fraassen

There were two main episodes in Russell's thought about probability and inductive inference. The first occurred around 1930 when he published some short discussions: chapter XXV of his book *Philosophy* (1927), a popular article 'Heads or Tails' in the *Atlantic Monthly* (1930), a review of Ramsey's book in *Mind* (1931), and a shorter review of that same book in the journal *Philosophy* (1932). The outcome of this first brush was a survey of problems, with attention mainly to Keynes and von Mises, and a passing glance at Ramsey's subjectivist alternative.

The second episode began on Russell's return to England in June 1944. In *My Philosophical Development* he reports that he chose non-demonstrative inference as the subject for his annual course at Trinity. The outcome of this work is the theory set forth in parts V and VI of *Human Knowledge: Its Scope and Limits* (1948).

There has been very little discussion of Russell's account of probability and induction; almost all of it can be found in chapter 10 of Kyburg's *Probability and Inductive Logic*. I think this is due in part to the historical placing of Russell's work. In 1927 he could write that someone who had read Keynes's book, Nicod's thesis, and Braithwaite's review of Nicod, would know most of what is known about induction. In the second episode, Russell focused attention in addition on the new work by Reichenbach. But Russell was apparently not acquainted with the concurrent work of Nelson Goodman and Rudolf Carnap. Furthermore, the subjectivist interpretation initiated by de Finetti in 1937 did not become well known in English until Savage's account in 1954, and the propensity interpretation was initiated by Popper in the late 1950s. As a result, Russell's work has remained outside the major context of discussion during the past two decades.

But the neglect is also due to the general conviction that Russell finally found himself on a course into the Sargasso, and that, just possibly, he found himself trying to provide a solution to an unsolvable problem. Since Russell was content to leave the general theory sketchy (quite forgivably so, since he wrote *Human Knowledge* when he was 75), it would be tendentious if not inappropriate to defend Russell against this conviction. I have tried to do something more audacious. I shall follow

Russell's exposition and *problématique*, and then confront that with the propensity theory. Somewhat surprisingly, perhaps, the two approaches are in large agreement, with respect both to the diagnosis and to general features of any candidate for a solution. I shall try to evaluate whether Russell's problems can be solved by a propensity account, without diverging even farther from empiricism than Russell thought necessary.

(1) *Russell's first brush*

The chapter 'The Validity of Inference' in Russell's book *Philosophy* takes the position that general empirical principles and scientific theories are arrived at by inference from known facts. Since Popper's writings on the subject, everyone worries about using the word 'inference' in this context. But we may phrase the view precisely as follows: after considering observed or accepted evidence about the restricted domain of our acquaintance, we go on to accept general principles (consistent with this evidence, but not entailed by it), and there are rational and irrational ways of doing that. The problem is: under what conditions is such a move rational?

Even when this problem is restricted to the consideration of very simple cases, it is extremely difficult to give even a description of what is called rational – let alone an account of why it deserves to be called that. (Note that neither of these already difficult tasks amounts to justifying such inference (or quasi-inference); I do not believe that Russell was at any time minded to produce a 'justification of induction').

Almost everywhere, Russell takes as his paradigm the acceptance of the generalisation 'All A are B', when the evidence entails that some A are B and does not entail that some A are not B. This makes the discussion somewhat vulnerable, because one might hold that there is no rational statistical inference of exactly that form, though perhaps there is of some other form. But the problems explicitly considered by Russell seem to arise equally for inferences to 'Nine out of ten A are B', 'Most A are B' and 'Approximately half of the A are B'. So I do not think Russell's problems disappear if we consider other examples.

As first stage in the development, Russell mentions Mill. Mill's canons for inference of the conclusion 'B is caused by A' are in fact canons for the deduction of this conclusion from the evidence plus a general principle about causality. In a rough and preliminary form the principle might be stated as 'Everything has a cause'. The only real induction occurs in the establishment of this principle, and Mill regards it as itself established inductively, on the basis of our evidence to the effect that many events are known to have causes (in a suitable sense), while none are (were) known not to have causes. So Mill, *pace* Russell, runs into exactly the problem that Russell takes as paradigm.

The next movement is Keynes's. Arguing from basic principles about probability, Keynes demonstrates that the probability of 'All A are B' approaches certainty as more and more A's are examined and all are found to be B, provided certain conditions obtain. The most important such condition is that 'All A are B' should have a finite (non-zero) *prior probability*, that is, probability relative to a body of evidence that contains no, or only irrelevant, information.

So now we have three problems. First, what is probability (and specifically, is it such that Keynes's principles hold)? Second, how would we establish such prior probabilities? Third, is it rational to accept 'All A are B' when our evidence is of the above sort, given this demonstration about the probability tending to certainty?

Russell finds no satisfactory answers to these questions at this point. He notes Keynes's answer to the second question, which is to postulate the *principle of limitation of variety*. This principle says that qualities of objects cohere in groups, so that the number of independent qualities is finite. More precisely, call qualities F and G equivalent if $(x)(Fx \equiv Gx)$ is true. Let the equivalence class $[F]$ of F be the set of all qualities equivalent to F. Then the principle says that there are only finitely many such equivalence classes. This is the strongest form of the postulate; Keynes and Nicod also discussed weaker forms that might suffice. But even from the strong form of the postulate we cannot deduce that 'All A are B' has a non-zero prior probability, unless prior probabilities are assigned by some principle of indifference or equiprobability (of the smallest quality equivalence classes). This may have seemed a matter of course at the time. (Compare also *Human Knowledge*, p. 392, on Keynes's use of a principle of indifference.)

However that may be, Russell explicitly notes his dissatisfaction concerning all three questions above. He is not satisfied with Keynes's interpretation of probability as a logical relation. After a brief description of the frequency interpretation, he says he would prefer this, but does not see how to meet all Keynes's arguments against it. About the second question, he says that the principle of limited variety is in line with current science, but that the principle cannot be justified in that way. Arguing for it by induction, if possible, would make the account circular. Finally, on the third question, Russell says that on Keynes's conception there is an uncomfortable gap between probability (as a logical relation) and fact. Hence it is not clear why it is rational to 'act upon a probability' – for example, to accept the hypothesis 'All A are B' on the basis of probabilities relative to our evidence. Russell conjectures that a frequency interpretation might not suffer from this problem, but has to leave the question open.

(2) *Second brush and the Postulates*
In *Human Knowledge*, Russell begins with an examination of the mathematical theory of probability. He argues that as far as this mathematical theory is concerned, it may be taken to be essentially a theory of finite frequencies, that is, proportions in finite populations. Thus, the axioms are all true if we read

$$P(B/A) = r$$

as being about finite classes B and A, and saying that a fraction r of the A's are B's. That is, writing $\# (X)$ for the number of elements in class X, the above statement may be interpreted as saying

$$\# (B \cap A) = r \# (A),$$

where $B \cap A$ is the common part (intersection) of classes B and A.

It is also possible to show that the theory is true about limits of finite frequencies, when we consider classes as the sum of an expanding series. For example, if one thought that our species will survive forever, and that it will become more and more hairless, one might say that in the total course of human history, almost everyone is bald. This assertion can be accommodated by taking the class A of humans as the sum of the series $\{A(t) = $ the class of humans born before $t\}$ and reconstructing $P(B/A) = 1$ as

the sequence of fractions $P(B/A_t)$ converges to 1 as t increases indefinitely.

This is noted explicitly by Russell, and I do not think we should deny that probability theory can be construed as a theory about finite frequencies, *just because* the theory also considers limits of sequences of such frequencies. But I shall return to this topic below.

Certainly, statements of proportion are of importance in reasoning. An automobile manufacturer who offers a warranty for certain defects during the first year of the car's life had better control the proportion of such defects among the cars manufactured. If we rephrase this by saying that he should take into account the probability of a car's exhibiting such a defect, there is no need to see this as anything but a *façon de parler*. But Russell noted at once that, upon his construal, the theory of probability leaves untouched several major problems.

The first such problem is that of single-case probabilities. Suppose that 95 per cent of all Gemini natives are fickle, what is the probability that Marilyn Monroe was fickle? It is true that she was a Gemini, but she belonged to many other classes as well; for example, her Medium Coeli was in Taurus, and this suggests that, at least as an adult, she was not fickle.

The precise point is this: the probability that single case x is a B, cannot be explicated straightforwardly as a proportion of classes. For the proportion $P(B/\{x\})$ equals either one or zero, and there are cases in which we are not prepared to say that the probability that x is a B equals one or zero. The obvious second attempt is to see '$P(x$ is a $B)$' as short for '$P(B/A)$', where A is some class tacitly specified by the context. The correct A ('problem of the reference class') is usually selected by means of some analogue to a total evidence requirement. That is, if you are asked the probability that Marilyn Monroe was a fickle person, the correct answer is the number P(fickle person/A), where the specification of A takes into account all relevant evidence you have about her. But on this reading, probability in single cases is not a statement of proportion, but a statement about belief and ignorance.

Let me make this charge precise. Of course, if someone asks me what the probability in question was, it is appropriate for me to answer P(fickle person/A), after selecting the class A. Indeed, some case can be made for saying that this is what I should do. But that is very different from offering the above as a *construal* of the single-case probability assertion. As analogous case, suppose someone asks me, what is the probability of Geminis being fickle? Perhaps I do not know what proportion of Geminis are fickle, but I do happen to know or believe that 0·7 of the natives of Airy signs (Gemini, Libra, Aquarius) are fickle. Suppose also that I have no evidence about smaller classes including Gemini natives. Then by the same token as above, one might argue that I should answer the question with '0·7'. But no one would suggest that, even in this context, and in my mouth, the assertion 'The probability of a Gemini native being fickle equals 0·7' is to be construed as 'The proportion of fickle persons in the smallest class including Gemini natives about which I have relevant information, equals 0·7'. Why the difference in construals, when the facts in the two cases, and the reasons for assertion, are so similar?

The second problem which Russell saw concerns inductive inference. Is there any way in which the theory of probability can give a reason for following some statistical acceptance rule for general hypotheses, given non-compelling evidence? Again, Russell turns to the example of someone accepting 'All A are B' on the basis of the evidence that all examined A have been found to be B. At what point, and under what conditions, is it rational to do so?

This may sound very much like a request for a justification of induction. But it is not, or not necessarily. For there is, in fact, a large measure of agreement on acceptance of hypotheses of this sort. Everyone accepts, with unrestricted reference to past, present and future, that fire burns; while many do not accept that all nations and ideological factions commit atrocities when given the chance. The evidence is *prima facie* similar in the two cases. The first task is to delimit the area of general agreement on which 'inferences' of this sort are rational. And this task is prior to the question whether it is justified, in some important way, to call them rational.

Russell showed quite clearly, I think, that the theory of probability can make no essential contribution to this question. Let us take the simplest case, in which we begin by accepting (knowing or believing) that there are only finitely many A. After examining n members of A, and finding all to be B, the question is whether to accept that all A are B. At some point, and under some conditions, we may indeed accept that hypothesis.[2]. One might derive some feeling of security from the fact that, as the number of examined A increases, the proportion of B to examined A must approach the proportion of B to A, *überhaupt*. This is so simply because A is finite. But, in fact, no security derives from this, because the assertion that A is finite never guarantees that the number of examined A is significantly large. On the other hand, if we knew the size of A, and we knew that our sample was comparatively large, we would have no need of induction at all, because we could deduce the proportion of B to A to within an interval determined by the sample size.

There is a definite change here in Russell's outlook. In *Philosophy* he had thought that, on a frequency interpretation, there might not be such an uncomfortable gap between probability and fact. But in *Human Knowledge* he presents the problem of statistical inference as one of the deciding reasons for moving beyond a frequency view. I can illustrate the change in Russell's outlook with a debate between Salmon and Hacking at a conference some twenty years later. Salmon says on page 33 of the Proceedings (ed., Lakatos):

> If we take 'probability' in the frequency sense, we can find some reasons for accepting probable conclusions in preference to improbable ones. In so doing we shall be right more often. Unfortunately, we cannot show that inferences conducted according to any particular rule establish conclusions that are probable in this sense. If we take 'probability' in a non-frequency sense it may be easy to show that inferences which conform to our accepted inductive rules establish their conclusions as probable. Unfortunately, we can find no reason to prefer conclusions which are probable in this sense to those which are improbable.

This is the view with which Russell tentatively ended the discussion in *Philosophy*. By the time of writing *Human Knowledge* (after an examination of the finite frequency interpretation and also von Mises and Reichenbach) he has come to agree with Hacking's retort on page 48 of that future volume:

> Let's consider a modest man who wants to be within 5% of the truth. Call the following fact A: If there is a limiting frequency, there is some trial N such that, if you use the straight rule after N, you will be within 5% of the true value. On Salmon's analysis of long run frequency, A is a fact. It is this fact (or rather, the generalization of it) which he calls inevitable accuracy.
>
> Beside A let me put B: if there is a long run frequency and you use the straight rule after 3 trillion trials, you will be within 5% of the true value. Now B, we must all agree, is no justification for any present human course of action. It will be thousands of years before the

number of individually recorded experimental trials of all sorts put together gets to be 3 trillion. B is no reason at all for any present course of human action. Yet B entails A, and A does not entail B. B is a stronger assertion than A. Since B is no reason for any course of human action, A cannot be either.

Because of these apparent limitations to a frequency view, Russell concluded that there were two kinds of probability, namely, frequency and credibility.

About credibility, Russell tells us very little. He has grave objections to Keynes's view that it is a logical relation. He had long since considered Ramsey's proposals unworkable. He sees no reason why credibility, even if appropriately discussed in terms of degrees, should obey the mathematical probability calculus.

In the paper mentioned above, Hacking could list six arguments for the conclusion that degrees of credibility, or rational belief, or subjective confidence of a rational sort, must obey the probability calculus. But these arguments had for the most part become common currency in the decade following *Human Knowledge*. I do not know how Russell would have reacted to 'Dutch book' arguments. Nor are the arguments listed totally compelling; they have all had their premisses or background assumptions questioned. But nothing hinges on this as far as Russell's discussion is concerned, for he simply does not rule on the question of principles to be obeyed by credibility assertions.

What Russell did instead was to examine a number of *prima facie* cases of non-demonstrative inferences, in an effort to cull from these a set of general underlying principles. In this he felt he had succeeded, and he gives the following Postulates in *Human Knowledge*:

I Of quasi-permanence.
II Of separable causal lines.
III Of spatio-temporal continuity in causal lines ('no action at a distance').
IV Of the common causal origin of similar structures ranged about a centre.
V Of analogy.

Each postulate asserts that something happens often but not necessarily always, and they are meant to justify natural expectations. That is, you may justify some specific expectation (for example, that you will cough again next time you smoke) by appeal to one of these general principles; but the principles themselves are not justifiable.

The exact status of these Postulates is not clear. It is not true that any specific expectation is deducible from them. So the most you can do, in the way of justifying your specific expectations by 'appeal' to a Postulate, is to point out that your expectations are 'in accord with' the pattern described by the Postulate. In what sense this is a justification is not clear. Lytton Strachey's account of Dr Arnold in *Eminent Victorians* uses a simple ironic device: Strachey continually points out that the head-master based his opinions on general principles. Before long, the reader had formed the conviction that the generality of Dr Arnold's principles is their only virtue. Even if it is true that our inferential practices, our normal expectations, are in accord with Russell's Postulates, it does not seem appropriate to speak of justifying the practices by appeal to the principles.

On the other hand, there was no point at which Russell, however loose his language, could be accused of trying to 'justify induction'. If the question is how we shall describe those inferential practices that are called rational, and are current in science and in everyday life, it may be answered appropriately in Russell's way. That is, a good answer to this question may take the following form. People accept hypotheses rationally when they do so in accordance with the following general principles: for example, my expectations about locked-room murder mysteries are rational if they are in accordance with the general principle that walls normally endure through small enough periods of time, and locked doors cannot usually be opened without keys or damage, and so on.

But this does not remove the problems with the specific answer given by Russell. First, his answer does not issue in specific rules of acceptance. Indeed, application of his Postulates waits on account of the conditions under which it is rational to proceed from 'Most A are B' to 'The next A is a B'. Second, there is a lack of clarity about how Russell himself views the Postulates. Sometimes (e.g. *Human Knowledge*, pp. 513 and 515) he speaks as if he has been giving a Transcendental Deduction of principles which are presupposed by scientific inference. That is, as if he has been establishing the *necessity* of the Postulates for scientific inference. There is no doubt but that Russell says this, and if so, he has not given a deduction of necessity to support his claim. But there are also places where he claims only sufficiency (e.g. p. 506). That is, that the truth of the Postulates is sufficient to make scientific inference trustworthy. But neither is this demonstrated; the most Russell does is to give evidence that we believe, or act as if we believe, these general principles.

I shall not continue this discussion of the Postulates, for it is pointless in the absence of Russell's or Russellians' reactions. But I can point to a general conviction Russell had about the general nature of any solution to the problems he had uncovered. This general conviction is evidenced when he says that some propositions involving credibility must be data (that is, believed, or known or accepted without prior evidence; see *Human Knowledge*, p. 399), and also in his insistence that the Postulates are about frequencies. I can best phrase the conviction as follows: in the testing, confirming and accepting of hypotheses, there is an irreducible probabilistic residue. We cannot get to probabilistic assertions, nor test such assertions, with procedures that do not also involve probabilistic assumptions. It was when he had reached this conclusion that Russell disavowed the empiricist theory of knowledge.

To this important conclusion (or, perhaps better, conviction) I shall return later. In the remainder of this chapter, I intend to retrace Russell's steps to some extent, in order to examine an alternative solution to the same problems.

(3) *The finite frequency interpretation*
About the mathematical theory of probability, Russell asserted that we arrive at an adequate interpretation, if (a) we understand its variables as ranging over classes, (b) we take these classes to be finite and (c) we undertand $P(A/B)$ as the fraction or proportion of A in B. This proportion is, of course, the size of the common part $A \cap B$ divided by the size of B. (When B is empty, the formula needs a special dispensation, in some technically convenient fashion.) Let us call this view the finite frequency interpretation.

If this view is correct, one might perhaps go on to say that statistics is essentially a theory of actual proportions among classes of actual things or events. And one might perhaps add that science has need of nothing more; all additions, including infinite sequences and degrees of belief, are either convenient fictions or mnemonics or philosophy's self-created solutions to its self-created problems.

Except for the polemical ending, I shall endorse the preceding paragraph, *rightly understood*. But the qualifications are all, as usual; and I must cry *distinquo!* even to the assertion by Russell reported in the first paragraph of this section.

Let me make Russell's assertion more precise, giving it at once a more contemporary form. The probability calculus has variables $A, B, C, \ldots$; constant K (the universal set); function symbol P; number variables, and the symbols of analysis and set theory. Its axioms are:

I $0 = P(\bar{K}) \leqslant P(A) \leqslant P(K) = 1$.
II $P(\cup \{ A : A \in F \}) = \Sigma \{ P(A) : A \in F \}$, when F is a finite or countable family of mutually disjoint sets.

These axioms are summed up, with brevity if not increased perspicuity, by saying that a probability measure is a normed, real-valued, countably additive function on a Borel field of sets.

A *finite frequency model* will consist of a non-empty finite set K for which we define

$$P(A) = \#(A)/\#(K),$$

where $\#(X)$ is the number of elements in set X. The conditional probability $P(A/B)$ is then defined as $P(A \cap B)/P(B)$, hence equals

$\# (A \cap B) \, / \, \# (B)$ – again with a quick technical dance-step for the case of B empty.

How shall we construe Russell's assertion that attention to finite frequency models alone provides an adequate interpretation for the calculus? In one way that is true: axioms I and II hold for the finite frequency models. The fraction of $A \cup B$ in K, if A and B do not overlap, is clearly the sum of the fractions of A in K and B in K, as axiom II says, for example. But there are many possibilities left open by the axioms that are not excluded by the finite frequency interpretation. For example,

$$P(A) = \sqrt{\tfrac{1}{2}}$$

is logically absurd if construed as an assertion about a finite frequency model.

Russell would not have considered this a serious point. Even in the case of time in physics, he considered it a viable point of view that the rational numbers would do for co-ordinates. But if we add the following

Third axiom $P(A)$ is a rational number,

we are still left with the problem that the probability calculus is incomplete with respect to the finite frequency interpretation. The incompleteness in question is, however, of a sort that was only just beginning to be investigated (notably by Henkin) when Russell was writing *Human Knowledge*. There is a nice adequacy result in the neighbourhood, and this is probably what Russell extrapolated. Let us call PC^* the restricted probability calculus which has axioms I and II, and also the Third axiom, and in which only the Boolean set-theory symbols ($\cap$, $\cup$, $-$) are used. (About numbers, you can use any amount of mathematical symbolry; just what is inside the scope of P must look like formulas of propositional logic, and not be accessible to quantification from outside.) Then we have

A statement of PC^* holds true in all finite frequency models if, and only if, it is a theorem of PC^*.

The proof hinges on my careful pruning of the symbols. Let the statement be ϕ, with class variables $A_1, \ldots, A_n$; and let ϕ be true in a model (not necessarily finite) in which $P(A_1) = r_1/q, \ldots, P(A_n) = r_n/q$. Now make up a new, finite model in which the universal set has size q, and class-variables $A_1, \ldots, A_n$ denote classes of sizes $r_1, \ldots, r_n$, respectively, and any Boolean combination X of classes $A_1, \ldots, A_n$ has size $qP(X)$. Then ϕ also holds true in the new model.

This simple result does not warrant sweeping claims on behalf of finite frequencies. Indeed, there is even some disparity between the truncated PC^* and finite frequencies. This may be seen if we consider infinite families of statements

$$P(A_1) = r_1, P(A_2) = r_2, P(A_3) = r_3, \ldots, P(A_n) = r_n, \ldots.$$

This family is absurd relative to any finite frequency model unless some (indeed, all but finitely many) of the values r_n are identical. In logical jargon, we say *compactness* fails. If we had not insisted on the restriction to Boolean – hence, finite – set operations in PC^*, this example would have yielded the single statement

$$(\forall n) \left(\sum_{i=1}^{n} P(A_i) \neq 1 \right) \& \sum_{i=1}^{\infty} P(A_i) = 1$$

which is absurd relative to any finite frequency model, but consistent with the axioms.

So logical adequacy of the calculus to finitary interpretation is to be expected only if we add

Fourth axiom The range of P is finite,

where the domain of P is the family of sets A such that $P(A)$ is defined. (Note that this still allows K to be infinite. Merely pointing to infinite classes does not upset the finite frequency interpretation.)

Still, as I said earlier, I am willing to endorse the finite frequency view, rightly understood. Part of what I mean by that will have to wait till the end of this chapter: I do not accept the objective presence of probabilities in nature, other than actual relative frequencies. But as to the Third and Fourth axioms, I think a case can be made for saying that they are discarded for mathematical motives. I do *not* identify these motives as *convenience* (on the contrary, inconvenience was preferred to triviality) or as *generality* (that being indistinguishable from irrelevance if the infinite models are denied to be applicable to actual cases). Rather, I believe that there are applications in science where we must consider infinite classes – but that the results needed there are all equivalent to results about infinite families of finite models.

No great philosophical point hinges on this, for the infinite probability models find their place in the mathematical models used in the advanced sciences, and the role of those models must be philosophically explicated *in toto*, not piece by piece. Still, I think the finite frequency view is right in this. In rough historical order, the main impetus for the development of probability theory has come from these applications: games of chance (De Méré's questions to Pascal), combination of observations ('data analysis' in astronomy, e.g. Boscovitch and Laplace), theory of errors (Gauss and Laplace), demography (mortality statistics, life insurance in the eighteenth and nineteenth centuries), applications in biology (for example, Jenkin's famous attack on Darwin in 1867), statistical mechanics (Maxwell, Boltzmann, Gibbs, Poincaré) and quantum mechanics.

Only in the last two cases is there a direct need for infinite models, and almost always one sees the problems approached in terms of denumerable families of finite partitions of the infinite set under consideration. I conjecture that this could always be done.

(4) *The limitations of the frequency view*

Russell had two objections to the view that probability statements are statements of relative frequency. These are still the two main objections today; I shall call them the *single-case problem* and the *inference problem*. The first tends to show that not all probability statements can be construed as relating classes; but the second remains even if we restrict the discussion entirely to statements about classes. After explaining the two problems, I shall display the general features of Russell's diagnosis and solution, and the agreement between this and the propensity view.

The single-case problem is so called because it directs attention to singular probability assertions such as

(1) The probability that the next coin toss yields heads, equals 1/2.

This is to be contrasted with

(2) The probability that a coin toss yields heads equals 1/2,

which the frequentist explicates as

(2*) The ratio of the number (i.e. size of the class) of coin tosses yielding heads to the number of all coin tosses, is 1/2.

If we were to adhere rigidly to this pattern of explication, we would read (1) as

(1*) The ratio of the number of next coin tosses yielding heads to the number of next coin tosses, equals 1/2.

But then (1) is analytically false, because the ratio mentioned in (1*) must equal *one* or *zero*.

We now have three alternatives. The first is to dismiss the problem as academic. The second is to say that (1) is indeed analytically false because the probability mentioned in (1) must equal *one* or *zero*. The third is to attempt a different explication of singular probability statements.

To dismiss the problem as academic is so heroic as to appear Quixotic when we notice, as Kyburg points out, that an exactly similar problem appears about the next 1000 coin tosses. That is, we would like to say that the probability of getting *all* heads in the next 1000 tosses equals $1/2^{1000}$, but the frequency with which we actually get *all* heads on the next

1000 tosses equals either *zero* or *one* (since only one possible sequence of 1000 outcomes is the sequence of the actual next 1000 outcomes).

To say that single-case probabilities must, in fact, equal *one* or *zero* is hardly less heroic. We might justify the assertion by appeal to determinism: objectively, the outcome is thus or so, and Laplace's perfect predictor would know. What, then, causes us to assert (1), or wish to assert (1)? To describe our ignorance, as Laplace would say. This manoeuvre engenders two subobjections, namely:

(a) in addition to frequencies, we need a measure of ignorance;
(b) in the case of indeterministic physical systems, we furthermore need a measure of tendency or propensity.

The frequentist will not capitulate immediately to these demands, of course; if he did, he would outdo dualism by recognising three distinct kinds of probability:

probability$_1$ or credibility   :   measures of ignorance
probability$_2$ or frequency   :   class ratios
probability$_3$ or propensity   :   objective tendencies.

Note that none of these is as yet subjective: my degree of belief is, as the Augustine–Ockham tradition has it, in part a matter of will, while the degree of my ignorance is *prima facie* objective and not subject to my will. Since at the above juncture where ignorance was first mentioned, one might have opted for explaining my wish to assert (1) as a wish to express my degree of belief or willingness to bet, we have furthermore

Probability$_4$ or subjective probability: degrees of belief.

When I said that the second option for the frequentist is hardly less heroic that the first, I had in mind this looming plethora of multiplied distinctions. There certainly are four distinct concepts here, and all may be important; but to belong to a school such as frequentism is, presumably, to have reductionist designs of one sort or other.

Consider then, finally, the third option, that of reinterpreting singular probability statements. This is, perhaps not surprisingly, the course taken by actual frequentists. They explicate (1) as

(1**) The ratio of the number of coin tosses yielding heads to the number of coin tosses which are Φ, equals 1/2,

where Φ is a condition , 'describing the reference class', which depends on the context of the assertion of (1). Reichenbach and Salmon have given different specifications of what this reference class is in given contexts. Both have isolated the speaker's knowledge, beliefs and purposes of inference as the relevant contextual factors. Roughly, Φ should be as follows: the next coin toss should be Φ, the speaker has definite knowledge or beliefs that warrant his assertion of a class ratio for Φ, and there should be no narrower condition Ψ for which both the preceding hold.

As so often in discussions of the correct construal of probability statements, it seems extremely difficult here to disentangle what the statement says from the conditions under which it is reasonable to assert the statement. For example, I am liable to assert

(3) The probability that a Norwegian is Protestant is higher than $1/2$

just because I feel warranted to assert

(4) The probability that a Scandinavian is Protestant is higher than $1/2$

and I have no evidence which suggests that Norwegians are unlike other Scandinavians in this respect. Yet the frequentist construes (3) in the pattern (2)–(2*) and not in the pattern (1)–(1**). Why? What accounts for the asymmetry in explication? If I were to interpret (3) on the pattern of (1)–(1**), the frequentist would accuse me of confusing what the statement says with reasons for asserting what it says. Yet in the single case problem, he wishes to assimilate what these two factors say.

Let us now turn to the second problem, the *inference problem*. This problem concerns the passage from specific data to general hypotheses or theories. Russell considered it in two forms. The first concerns acceptance rules, and he considers the simplest kind of 'straight rule': to infer 'All A are B' when we have evidence to the effect that certain A are B, and no evidence to suggest that some A are not B. That Russell finds this rule wanting is not surprising; it must at least be hedged with qualifications about evidence concerning the randomness and comparative size of the sample, and also probably about the subject and predicate term. But what impressed Russell most in the discussions about this rule is that it showed up the need, within Keynes's approach, for 'initial', 'given' or 'prior' probabilities. Unless the generalisation 'All A are B' has non-zero probability prior to all evidence, no evidence can ever lead us to accept it – again, on Keynes's approach.

A similar conclusion seems to be forced on us in the second point discussed by Russell in this context. This concerns the use, now much more in the limelight than in Russell's day, of Bayes's theorem for evaluating theories in the light of the evidence (see *Human Knowledge*, pp. 427–30). Let H be a general hypothesis or theory, let E be the old evidence and O the new evidence. Then

$$(5)\ \ P(H/E\&O) = \frac{P(H/E) \cdot P(O/H\&E)}{P(O/E)}.$$

As an example, Russell takes Newton's law of gravitation as H, the observation of Neptune in its calculated place as O, and E as the evidence prior to this observation. Since O was the calculated outcome from H and E, we have $P(O/H\&E) = 1$. As values for $P(E/H)$ and $P(O/E)$ Russell suggests (roughly, I gloss over details) 1/36 and 1001/36,000, respectively. Then

$$(6)\ \ P(H/E\&O) = \frac{P(H/E)}{P(O/E)} = \frac{1000}{1001}\ .$$

So if initially both the general law and the specific fact were about as unlikely as double sixes with a die (under given conditions $P(H/E)$ must be greater than or equal to $P(O/E)$), then after the observation, the general law had odds of 1000 to 1 in its favour.

The first problem with this line of argument is that the initial probability $P(H/E)$ needs to be known – or if $P(H/E)$ is defined as $P(H\&E)/P(E)$, then the prior probabilities $P(H\&E)$ and $P(E)$; or if Bayes's theorem is to be used again in the simpler form

$$(7)\ \ P(H/E) = \frac{P(H)\ P(E/H)}{P(E)}\ ,$$

then $P(H)$, $P(E)$ and $P(E/H)$ need to be known. So this method of evaluating, like Keynes's justification of inductive generalisation, requires knowledge of prior probabilities.

The second problem is that many alternative hypotheses are accorded much higher probabilities by the same reasoning. Russell's characteristically ingenious argument goes as follows: let H' be the hypothesis that the law of gravitation holds *until* the time of the observation of Neptune. Again we have $P(O/H'\&E) = 1$. But H' says considerably less than H, hence $P(H'/E) > P(H/E)$. Therefore, applying Bayes's theorem, in form (5) or (6) above, to H', we find

$$P(H'/E\&O) > P(H/E\&O).$$

Inference to the most probable explanatory hypothesis, therefore, leaves us accepting only the correctness of laws prior to the observations. That is – unless, perhaps, we assign a very high prior probability to the persistency of general conditions like that stated by Newton's law of gravitation. Only then is the inductive price of choosing H' over H not exorbitant. But this again introduces a prior probability not compelled by the evidence: a very special one, relating to the 'uniformity of nature'.

The problem that faces the frequency theory at this point is this: to use probability calculations to guide inference, in the sense of acceptance of hypotheses that outstrip the evidence, we need initial probabilities. Can the frequency theory provide them? What would be, or count as, the initial probability of Newton's law of gravitation, for example? There certainly does not seem to be any frequency that might be a candidate for this.

It does not seem that any 'objective probability' (probability$_2$ or probability$_3$ in the above listing of senses) could provide the initial probabilities in question. Even if the planets obey the law of gravity with a certain frequency, or have a certain propensity to obey this law, *that fact* by itself does not give us the assurance, at the start of our process of inference, that the hypothesis does not have probability zero. Inference requires not the existence of prior probabilities, but the knowledge or assumption thereof.

Russell did not reach a very clear evaluation of these problems; to some extent his diagnosis must be inferred from the solution he offers. Let me suggest the following (extrapolated) evaluation. First, the single-case problem throws doubt on the frequency interpretation, though not on the other interpretations. Second, the inference problem purports to throw doubt on both the frequency and the propensity view, but in fact, does not.

The second assertion will sound surprising unless we agree to distinguish 'throws doubt on' from 'suggests limitations to'. There is a feature that 'probability' shares with 'necessity' and which used to cause a good deal of confusion in discussions of modality. This is the feature of occurring *both* in the premisses, and so providing subject matter for logic, *and* in logical statements about inference. The final course followed by logicians was to treat these two sides of the coin as if they had nothing to do with each other, to begin; vindication of this approach eventually included the exhibition of systematic relations between the two. I would suggest that about probability, it is reasonable to begin by separating two tasks: giving a theory of truth conditions for probability statements, and systematising our conceptual apparatus concerning non-demonstrative inference.

There is, it must be noted, a further feature of probability and non-demonstrative inference, that will complicate the task. In deductive logic we have become used to the idea that an adequate theory of truth conditions will yield a theory of correct inference as corollary. The reason is that deductive arguments are supposed to capture exactly this: syntactic transformations preserving truth. But in non-demonstrative inference, where the metause of 'necessity' is replaced by a metause of 'probability', I do not think we can expect such corollaries. The relations between the two sides of the coin are there, I suspect, much more tenuous.

We can distinguish three distinct views which opt for two separate but equal probability concepts: those of Russell, Carnap and Kyburg. Each of these appears to incorporate as mutually irreducible probability$_1$ (objective measure of ignorance, or credibility), probability$_2$ (frequency). Among these, Russell is distinguished from the other two because he insists that there are non-frequency probabilities in the data (or rock-bottom premisses for our current arguments). Here is the crucial passage:

> The concept 'degree of credibility', however, is applicable much more widely than that of mathematical probability; I hold that it applies to every proposition except such as neither are data nor are related to data in any way which is favourable or unfavourable to their acceptance. I hold, in particular, that it applies to propositions that come as near as is possible to merely expressing data. If this view is to be logically tenable, we must hold that the degree of credibility attaching to a proposition is itself sometimes a datum. I think we should also hold that the degree of credibility to be attached to a datum is sometimes a datum, and sometimes (perhaps always) falls short of certainty. We may hold, in such a case, that there is only one datum, namely, a proposition with a degree of credibility attached to it, or we may hold that the datum and its degree of credibility are two separate data. I shall not consider which of these two views should be adopted.
>
> (*Human Knowledge*, p. 399)

This peculiarity, of seeing degrees of credibility themselves among the data, is hard to reconcile with the idea that degrees of credibility are a measure of ignorance. Is Russell here engaged solely in epistemology, and stating that we have sometimes non-inferred knowledge about the extent to which we are ignorant? Or is he asserting that there are in the world irreducible probability facts, which are sometimes known directly? To highlight the puzzling quality of his view, contrast it with the following 'argument' which has been quite influential lately. Carnap was looking for an objective measure of ignorance (or admitted ignorance); but if there is such, it must be calculable from what is actually known (or assumed); but there appears to be no such method of calculation that does not rest on an assignment of prior probabilities without further warrant or justification; therefore, we must switch our attention from his probability$_1$ to probability$_4$ (degrees of belief in the subjective or wilful sense of 'belief'). It is hard to believe that we could construe Russell as cutting the Gordian knot in this argument (*en prévoyant*) by saying: prior probabilities$_1$ are known immediately, as data. A measure of ignorance must be calculable, or not exist at all, it would seem.

(5) *From Russell to propensity*

There would be little charity in pursuing Russell further beyond the bounds of his actual thought. Leaving aside the question of how to sort out the various probability concepts, we find that Russell sees uninferred probabilities at several places: as data playing the role of prior probabilities in even very simple inferences; and as assumptions (the Postulates) which guide our preference for certain general hypotheses over others, in the case of theoretical inference. Let me now sum up the general features of his diagnosis and solution in a very biased way, with an ulterior motive:

(1) Probability statements are always intimately connected with frequency statements (but cannot be everywhere identified with them).
(2) Single-case probability statements are meaningful, and non-trivial, and not explicable in terms of frequencies.
(3) In scientific and ordinary practice there is something other than deduction that is at least analogous to inference: in the light of evidence, decisions are made to accept (provisionally) certain general hypotheses and reject (provisionally) their competitors.
(4) In the testing of hypotheses (general or proportional) there is always a residue of assertions of the sort tested.

The first two points concern frequencies and single cases: single-case probabilities cannot be 'reduced', but are nevertheless intimately connected with frequencies. The third and fourth points concern non-demonstrative inference, and accept the Humean dictum about 'is' and 'ought', and about 'is' and 'is necessary': there is no way in which non-probabilistic facts can by themselves imply probabilities (or singular facts generalities, for that matter). On the consequent Humean dilemma, the non-Humean horn is chosen: if facts do not imply modalities, then there are real, irreducible modalities. That is why Russell said that in *Human Knowledge* he gave up complete empiricism. Finally, Russell tried to give a general formulation of the 'residue' mentioned in (4) in his Postulates.

So far, Russell exegesis. The above four points are also articles of faith for the propensity interpretation. Such views have been presented by Popper, Hacking, Mellor and Giere. Although I have phrased points (3) and (4) above as gingerly as I could, I may have violated a Popperian dictum. To limit the discussion, I shall address myself solely to the latest propensity position, namely, Giere's (see References, below).

The basic subject for a propensity statement is a chance set-up (CSU, for short). You may say, elliptically, that the propensity of this coin to land heads up if tossed equals one-half. But the basic non-elliptic statement is that the set-up consisting of *this* coin and *this* toss mechanism (yourself, *now*) has a propensity of one-half to yield the first outcome in the set {heads, tails}. So a CSU has associated with it an outcome space and an assignment of real numbers in [0,1] to the members (or to subsets) of that outcome space. A CSU is an individual, non-repeatable; attribution of a propensity to a type of CSU is to be construed as the attribution of the same propensity to each member of the class of CSUs that are of this type.

The preceding paragraph outlines the basic ideas of the interpretation. The paradigm for this view is a truly indeterministic system, such as is described in quantum mechanics. For example, a radioactive nucleus will decay. The probability that it will do so within its 'half-life', says the theory, equals 1/2. Assuming that the quantum-theoretical state admits of no (more deterministic) refinement, that is all there is to be known. We have here a single-case probability specified by the theory (under a quite ordinary interpretation, though not under all interpretations), and this is a propensity.

With this paradigm, the theory threatens to have a limited domain: in the case of a macroCSU, all propensities will be near to zero and one. For example, it is certainly not the case that the CSU made up of this tosser and this coin, now, has a propensity of one-half to yield heads-up. But this only means that we must add a measure of ignorance to this measure of objective tendency (as is done with 'mixtures' in applications of quantum mechanics). At this point, the propensity interpretation is not imperialistic; it only insists on there being more to probability than ignorance. (See below for further discussion of this point.)

A strict analogy is drawn between propensities and other theoretical quantities such as mass and force; and this analogy is both ontic and epistemic. The ontic analogy attributes to propensities the status of masses or forces; a CSU has a mass and a centre of mass and a propensity (for each possible outcome). The epistemic analogy concerns both explanation and hypotheses testing. Like mass and force, propensity is introduced to construct a theory that explains certain phenomena. In the case of propensities, the phenomena explained are (regularities in) relative frequencies. The hypothesis that, say, a certain (kind of) CSU has certain propensities is open to verification, falsification or confirmation in the same limited sense as a hypothesis that it has a certain mass or charge. That is, relative to a theory and some auxiliary assumptions, one might be able to determine the quantities exactly by experiment; but, *überhaupt*, the theoretical quantities are as far beyond experimental inspection as sainthood.

Since Duhem we have been acutely conscious of the role played by auxiliary hypotheses assumed in the course of experimental testing. The evidence that confronts a propensity hypothesis is evidence about relative frequencies. But the interpretation or utilisation of this evidence may need to involve assumptions of a more theoretical nature. Giere gives this example:

> Suppose one wishes to test a hypothesis concerning the half-life of a radioactive nucleus Z. The standard procedure, as any physics text reveals, is to obtain a large number, say 10^{18}, of such nuclei and to count the relative numbers decaying within specified time intervals. This procedure, however, assumes that each nucleus in the sample has the same half-life, whatever its value. Thus the test assumes the truth of some propensity statements, though of course not the truth of the hypothesis being tested. (Giere, 1971, p. 19)

In this respect, however, propensity hypotheses are different neither from theoretical hypotheses in general, nor from probability hypotheses in general. (The usual example of a residue of probabilistic assumption in a statistical test is that of a certain sampling procedure being random or unbiased.)

Finally, Giere sees the introduction of propensities as violating a strict or Humean empiricism, in just the way that Russell saw his introduction of ineliminable probability data. This is just to say that a propensity statement is not equivalent, in any acceptable sense of equivalence, to a relative frequency statement. To say that the relative frequency of A to B equals r is to make a statement about the actual course and content of world history. Such a statement cannot entail, nor is entailed by, the statement that a certain class of CSUs have each a certain propensity to produce an outcome which is B if A. Consider again the half-life of nucleus Z; the nucleus could, in fact, decay at any time whatsoever without falsifying or verifying a statement about its half-life. The same is true about any actual collection of 10^{18} such nuclei, even if we assume the theory that attributes to each the same half-life, and even though it is extremely probable that half of this collection will have decayed during its half-life.

There is here, indeed, a typical Humean dilemma. The empiricist asserts that 'is' implies neither 'ought' nor 'is necessary' – and not only the empiricist. To remain an empiricist at this point is to choose one horn of the consequent dilemma, namely, to refuse to grant objective status to modal statements (deontic or alethic). To embrace the other horn is to grant the modal statements an equally objective status, and adjust one's world-view, ontology, ethics and epistemology to follow suit. Just so, there is no entailment between purely factual statements and purely probabilistic statements except (as also with 'ought' and 'necessary') in some special cases. Probabilities are also modalities. Propensities and irreducible probabilities beckon from the second horn of Hume's dilemma.

(6) Problems about propensities

In this section, I shall raise four problems about propensities. I think that they can all be answered, roughly within the context of Giere's version – though the solutions I suggest may not all be acceptable to any specific propensity theorist. Discussion of the Humean dilemma sketched in the preceding section, I shall leave aside until the next section.

The first problem is this: how should propensities be supplemented to yield an account of all (important!) probabilistic discourse? This is an especially pressing problem, because most ordinary statistical discussions will concern macrosystems which are very nearly deterministic. Hence the propensities involved are very nearly one or zero. But in the case of Toronto's weather tomorrow, or our friend Winston's lung cancer expectancy, we find ourselves with macrosystems and probabilities that are not nearly one or zero.

The problem is somewhat ameliorated by the fact, discussed above, that so much ordinary probabilistic discourse can be construed as asserting actual relative frequencies. The chance that a Swiss is Protestant is no more nor less than the proportion of Protestants to Swiss. I think we must resist the temptation to translate this as the propensity of a specific random sampling device to pick a Protestant from among the Swiss, unless that device is a strictly indeterministic system manufactured by a microphysicist.

But Toronto's weather tomorrow and Winston's lung cancer expectancy are about specific macrosystems, about which we have a great deal of ignorance. Here the propensity theorist must apparently make a choice between using probability$_1$ (objective measure of ignorance) or probability$_4$ (subjective degree of belief, betting ratio). The interpretations of probability developed by Kyburg and de Finetti, respectively, recommend themselves. The propensity interpretation *as such* says nothing on the question. However, the analogy between propensity hypotheses and the theoretical hypotheses of physics have suggested to Giere an approach that may eliminate reliance on someone else's explication of probability$_1$ or probability$_4$. This is the approach of introducing fictional propensities, of giving an indeterministic theory about a deterministic process (of which a number of relevant parameters are left out of consideration), and then viewing that theory instrumentalistically. Here are Giere's words:

> Due to the operation of many uncontrollable variables, series of trials of such mechanisms are often experimentally indistinguishable from series that would be generated by a sequence of genuinely indeterministic individual trials. This empirical fact justifies our using probability theory in such cases, and even makes it natural to apply probability language to individual trials. But it must be realized that this is only a convenient way of talking and that the implied physical probabilities really do not exist. (Giere, 1971, p. 22)

In just this way, the classical kinetic theory of gases might be used in engineering thermodynamics, because its results (are believed to) approximate to actual phenomena – but no one believes that the classical molecules exist.

This proposal of Giere is radical, and constitutes an independent explication of probability$_1$, in terms of propensities. Consider the statement

(1) The probability that the next coin toss yields heads equals one-half.

This is explicated as the context-dependent assertion

(1g) For present purposes, this coin-tossing CSU may be viewed as a CSU with propensity one-half for the heads-up outcome.

If this is conjoined with the further assertion that this is so for a large class of similar CSUs, we have an empirical hypothesis; indeed, in its epistemic relation to relative frequency evidence, this hypothesis is no different from

(1g*) This coin-tossing CSU *is* a CSU with propensity one-half for the heads-up outcome.

There is a difference between (1g) and (1g*), namely, that the former is true and the latter false, but this difference is not one that affects their relation to evidence which is purely about relative frequencies in coin-tossing trials. With this move, Giere may have eliminated the need for probability concepts that are essentially independent of propensities.

The second problem I wish to discuss is: what is a CSU? A CSU is an individual, not a type; it is unrepeatable; examples are coin-tossing devices and radioactive nuclei. The preceding sentence sums up the intuitive data for an explication, but the data are conflicting. An experiment, or process, taken as an individual rather than a type, is unrepeatable. To 'repeat an experiment' is to produce or conduct several individuals belonging to the same type. But a device or a nucleus is not an event or process, it is a physical object. Propensities may, as far as grammar and usage are concerned, be attributed to either objects or processes. Men seem to have a non-negligible propensity for killing their fellows with flame-throwers; the My Lai situation was conducive to violence; the process of defoliation has a definite tendency to decimate the animal population as well.

Rather than spin out a discussion of usage, which can in any case only give inclining reasons for the grammar of a new theoretical term, I shall at once present my explication. A CSU is a physical system, which involves generally several other physical systems (continuants); which is subject to a specified process; whose existence is coterminous with that process; and whose possible final states are classified (exhaustively and disjointly) into its set of possible outcomes ('outcome space').

To specify a CSU is to identify the physical continuants involved in it; the conditions under which the process begins; the conditions under which it ends; the outcome space; the conditions under which the process is correctly said to have one outcome or other. Example: my next tossing of this coin. This CSU involves me and this coin, it begins when I next give the coin an upward motion that removes it from my hand; it ends as soon as the coin has landed thereafter; the outcome space is {*heads*, *tails*}; the process has outcome *heads* if the coin lands with heads up, and has outcome *tails* if the coin lands with tails up.

Of course, I and the coin each exist before and after the process in question, but the CSU exists only as long as the process is going on. In just the same way a committee exists during only a part of the existence of its members, and a committee is the sort of system whose dynamics are presumably studied by sociologists. A planetary system might similarly cease to exist before its members, or a molecule before its component atoms.

It is also important that two different committees might, accidentally, have the same members. In the case of a CSU, we might have two experiments being conducted simultaneously, by an inextricably complex battery of instruments, on the same object. Here we would have two CSUs, involving the same continuants with either the same characteristic process or two coterminous characteristic processes, but certainly two different outcome spaces.

Ontologists might have much to say about such individuals as these, and their ontic status or lack thereof. Consider, for instance, the two CSUs involving the same toss of the same die, but with outcome spaces $\{1, 2, 3, 4, 5, 6\}$ and $\{even, odd\}$, respectively. I shall not worry about questions of ontology in this respect. Two distinct experiments are here performed on the same object; propensities must, cannot but, be attributed with reference to possible outcomes. If there are important relations between these two CSUs and the respective propensities, we need a theory to spell them out. The theory should have room for both lawlike and (quasi-) logical relations among propensities, and then both for simply related CSUs as in the above example, and not so simple ones as in the Einstein–Podolski–Rosen correlations in quantum mechanics.

This brings me to the third problem: must propensities follow (some analogue to) the probability calculus? Patrick Suppes saw it as a possibility trivialising fact about the propensity interpretation (earlier versions) that soundness for the probability calculus is automatic. (Other interpretations construct complicated models, and prove that the probability calculus axioms hold, with greater or lesser difficulty.) Giere, on the other hand, entertains the idea that propensities violate the probability calculus. He refers to the non-classical probabilities which have been studied in connection with quantum logic. Using an extension of classical probability theory, Popper proved that the propositions or events to which his conditional probabilities are assigned must form a Boolean algebra. This cannot be proved if only the usual axioms are assumed, although there are results in that direction (so to speak); still, in the usual treatment, probability measures are defined as having a Boolean (sigma-) algebra for domain. Therefore, when quantum logic replaced Boolean algebras by orthocomplemented, orthomodular lattices, similar measures on those lattices began to be studied. They are referred to as non-classical probabilities.

To highlight the difference, consider the probability theorem

(T) $P(A \cup B) = P(A) + P(B) - P(A \cap B)$.

This follows from the usual additivity axiom for probabilities

(A) $P(X \cup Y) = P(X) + P(Y)$ if $X \cap Y = \wedge$

via the laws of Boolean algebra

(L1) $A \cup B = (A \cap \bar{B}) \cup (A \cap B) \cup (\bar{A} \cap B)$
(L2) $A = (A \cap \bar{B}) \cup (A \cap B)$
(L3) $B = (A \cap B) \cup (\bar{A} \cap B)$.

But in quantum logic, none of (L1)–(L3) hold in general. And so (T) does not hold either, even for a function P for which (A) holds.

It would take a long discussion to do justice to this topic. But I shall quickly sketch the view according to which there really are no non-classical probabilities at all, that all the probabilities to be found in quantum theory are ordinary. Quantum theory provides us, in its basic axioms, with a family of probability measures $P^m{}_\alpha$, one for each state α and each observable (= physical quantity) m. A statement like

$$P^m{}_\alpha ([1/2, 3/4]) = 0.9$$

says that the probability of having an outcome that falls within the interval $[1/2, 3/4]$, if a measurement of quantity m is made on a system in state α, equals 0.9. The function $P^m{}_\alpha$ is an ordinary probability measure.

Now, consider a special family of propositions, let me call it F, whose members are all those propositions of form

(m,E): if an m-measurement is made, the outcome will be in set E,

where E is a set in the domain of the probability measures $P^m{}_\alpha$. Notice that F is a family of *conditional* propositions. We can certainly define a function

$$P_\alpha : P_\alpha (m,E) = P^m{}_\alpha (E)$$

on the family F. What P_α *assigns* are the ordinary probability values $P^m{}_\alpha (E)$. In *that* sense P_α is an assignment of probabilities. But the family F is not a Boolean algebra. This is a general fact about conditionals; we cannot, in general, find a conditional $P \rightarrow Q$ such that

$$(A \rightarrow B) \text{ v } (C \rightarrow D) = P \rightarrow Q$$

must hold, at least, not if $\rightarrow$ is an interesting conditional connective.

Therefore, the domain of P_α is not the domain of an ordinary probability measure. So, of course, P_α itself is not a probability measure. It is just an artificial construct from probability measures. And that does not imply for a moment that the values it assigns do not follow suit to the classical probability axioms.[3]

We are back, then, with the original question: must propensities follow the ordinary probability laws? The above discussion forces us to consider this, for the conceivability of violations has been raised. Must we just choose to lay down one postulate or another? It seems to me there is a better alternative, namely, to construct models in which phenomena and propensities both find their place. At the end we shall still have to accept a postulate – that the evidence can always be shown to fit one of these models – but there will be more coherence to the account, and it will be less abstract, than if we merely cite historic precedent. An attempt along these lines has been made by Kyburg, using a possible world semantics.[4] From this point of view, propensity discourse can be translated into discourse about distributions in different possible worlds.

Finally, then, the fourth problem. Theoretical quantities are introduced to explain the phenomena. Mechanical phenomena could not be explained as long as physicists followed Descartes in eschewing mass and force, occult though those quantities seemed at the time. Presumably, propensities are introduced for the same reason. A theory attributing propensities may explain where determinism-plus-ignorance theories fail. The problem I want to confront is this: given contemporary accounts of explanation, can propensities really be said to explain?

The question requires a quick discussion of 'explanation'. As Duhem has detailed, there used to be a time when explanation was distinguished from description in the following way. To explain the phenomena is to show why they must be as they are; to describe them (scientifically) is to produce a single, unified, coherent account of how they are. With this distinction in mind, Cardinal Bellarmini urged Galileo to claim for Copernicus's astronomy only the virtues of a simpler and more convenient description. Galileo, not having learned from the nominalists who preceded him, seems to have accepted the distinction but denied the request. Had he known today's accounts of explanation, he would have had no need of such heroism. Duhem concluded that science can only offer description of a superior sort, and not explanation. But now we all agree that this superior sort of description may correctly be called 'explanation', just because it is what science gives us.

Still, there have been some important changes in the concept of explanation. The view advanced in the 1940s was this: the phenomena O are explained by a theory T, if we can exhibit antecedent, independent facts F such that T and F logically imply O. This is a nomological-deductive explanation. There is also an inductive-statistical explanation: if T and F together make it highly probable that

O. This is to be read as a conditional probability assertion: $P(O/T \& F)$ is high.

After many skirmishes, a new view has emerged. On the deductive side, we recall from Duhem that in the typical case the 'facts' F will include many assumptions or postulates, called 'auxiliary hypotheses'. Hence Putnam argued that a scientific explanation, even in the paradigm case of celestial mechanics, consists in the demonstration that there are *possible* assumptions A which, together with known facts E, and the theory (T), logically imply O. This is a drastic revision, for it turns an explanation into a *consistency proof*, instead of a deduction. The revision did perhaps not sound so drastic, just because on the level of deductive logic, assertions about consistency are intertranslatable with assertions about implication.[5]

The same point had been made much more clearly and dramatically by Morton Beckner in *The Biological Way of Thought* in connection with evolution theory. Beckner argues convincingly, in effect, that explanations by evolutionists are typically semantic consistency proofs:

> My own view is that evolution theory consists of a family of related models; that most evolutionary explanations are based upon assumptions that, in the individual case, are not highly confirmed; but that the various models in the theory provide evidential support for their neighbors. (p. 160)

> Selectionists have devoted a great deal of effort to the construction of models that are aimed at demonstrating that some observed or suspected phenomena are possible, that is, that they are compatible with the established or confirmed biological hypotheses, in particular, the hypotheses of genetics. We have already mentioned some examples, namely, the model-explanations of the origin of the chordates, the evolution of dominance, the evolution of genetic isolating mechanisms, and the occurrence of hypertelic or otherwise dysteleological trends. These models all state roughly that if conditions were (or are) so and so, then, the laws of genetics being what they are, the phenomena in question must occur. The assumptions may not be known to be true, but they are known to be not impossible. (p. 165)

Unfortunately, this philosophical book on biology did not have as much impact on the discussion of explanation as it should have had.

On the side of statistical explanation, the developments have been more dramatic, presumably because nothing analogous to the intertranslatability of assertions about consistency and about implication is possible. Because of many examples, we have found ourselves forced to agree that an explanation of O may not only fail to give O a high probability, but may even decrease its probability. In a series of articles by Salmon, Jeffrey and Greene (see Salmon, 1971), the following view

has emerged: this is called the *statistical relevance* or SR model of explanation. On this view, an explanation is any assembly of facts statistically
relevant to the explanandum *O*. This sounds very bare (it is the probabilistic analogue of a consistency proof, and establishes very little). The
view is made more interesting by adding attempts to measure the
explanatory power of a theory; to give an explanation of the SR sort is at
least to give *more information* (in the quantitative, information theory
sense) which is in addition *relevant to* the explanandum (the relevance
being statistical relevance: *A* is relevant to *B* exactly if $P(B/A) \neq P(B)$).

Do propensities explain? The phenomena in question must be relative
frequencies. There can be no entailment: a propensity does not *entail* any
relative frequency, not even in the limit or 'long run'. Consistency, on the
other hand, is trivial. Are propensities statistically relevant to relative
frequencies? Yes; given a propensity of one-half for heads up, Rosen-
crantz and Guildenstern should be very surprised. But note what happens here: the assertion of statistical relevance has the form

P (the relative frequency/the propensity) $\neq P$(the relative frequency).

What is this *P*? It is a probability, but presumably not a propensity. In
other words, the very purpose for which propensities are introduced,
cannot be stated without the introduction of another probability – presumably a measure of ignorance or a degree of belief or a logical confirmation function.

At this point in our discussion, the need for non-propensity probabilities is perhaps not surprising. But we also saw that Giere avoided
the introduction of such probabilities by a certain form of instrumentalism in one case. It does not seem to me that such a manoeuvre could be
executed here. As I have said before, probabilities, like necessities, seem
to have two distinct roles: to figure in the content of scientific hypotheses,
and also to figure in metadiscourse relating such hypotheses to each
other and to evidence. Of course, necessity has no basic or primitive
status in such metadiscourse, and it may be that probability does not
either. But, at the least, the propensity view seems to have need of an
auxiliary account of probabilistic metadiscourse.

As I said at the outset, none of the above problems seems to me
crippling to the propensity interpretation. In each case I have sketched a
response that might be acceptable to propensity advocates. The main
task before them, as I see it, is the construction of the models called for by
problem three. Possibly the explication of what a CSU is, in response to
problem two, can be the beginning stage for this main task.

(7) *Empiricist retrospect*
As I have related, Russell held that probabilities cannot entirely be
explicated in terms of frequencies, and that there must be probabilities
among our basic data or assumptions. These basic probabilities he

sought to sum up in the Postulates. At least when he first introduced the notion of basic probabilities not reducible to frequencies, he seems to have had in mind some epistemic kind of probability – very likely what I called probability$_2$ or measure of ignorance. But because some of his basic probabilities are single-case probabilities, and because his Postulates largely concern tendencies in nature or at least the 'external world', it is also not impossible to class Russell with the propensity theorists.

In this closing section, I wish to look at Russell's dismayed realisation that he seemed to be leaving empiricism behind. As I have posed the problem, Hume's empiricism presents us with a dilemma: from 'is' we can infer neither 'ought' nor 'necessary' nor 'probable'; therefore, we must either accept the modalities as independently objective, or deny them altogether.

In my opinion, the dilemma is illusory. I agree with the preliminary thesis about inference; I also appreciate the important and quite possibly indispensable role that modal concepts play in our thought. Yet a philosopher need only do justice to the facts, and from this it does not follow that he must reify the concepts. The picture of a physical theory, whether deterministic or probabilistic, to which I subscribe, is a very modal picture (see van Fraassen, 1970; 1972). In this picture, a scientific theory delimits the possibilities, and (if it is a non-relativistic theory) describes the temporal development of the possible. This is done, explicitly or implicitly, by means of mathematical models. The basic scientific assertion, the assertion of a scientific hypothesis, has the form: *the actual will fit one of these models*. Modal language is the pictorial language describing the models, whether that language is the language of physical necessity or of physical probability.

If this is so, the ontological locus of modality is our consciousness, and not the world we describe. The traditional realist objection to this view is that we cannot – even in principle – have a conceptual scheme or language totally devoid of modality. As Kant already pointed out about the judgment that a thing is heavy: such a judgment goes beyond the certain and immediate data, yet such a judgment is so basic that all our data for rational inquiry take such a form. But if that is so, if we cannot even in principle find an epistemic rock-bottom, the very distinction between fact and modality proves illusory.

I should like to know how that last inference follows! Suppose that indeed natural language and human thought can never be de-mythologised, that there is never a point – or never an interesting point – where we can say: this is a judgment which has in it nothing dubitable, theoretical or hypothetical. Does it follow from this that there is no objective distinction between what is fact and what is counterfactual? How does it follow? In my view, it is indeed impossible to demythologise our thought and language totally, while nevertheless any given myth or modal assertion or physical theory could be replaced by an alternative. The above realist argument establishes only, if it is a sound argument, that what is in common to all the languages or conceptual schemes that would be successful (survival adaptive?) in our world, is either nothing or so little as not to matter. But this does not show that any of the alternative equally adequate schemes is in some covert or metaphysical way more 'correct' or 'true' than its rivals.

We are now well inside a major debate in philosophy of science, between scientific realism and its opposition. I shall not go further on this occasion. Just as I ended the last section with a task for the propensity theorists, however, I shall end this section with a further task. In the case of a deterministic theory, to show that the phenomena fit is nothing more nor less than a consistency proof: the phenomena have a structure that the theory allows. But in the case of a probabilistic theory, there are obvious degrees of fit. If a coin lands heads-up 1000 times in a row, we can still consistently assert that the probability for heads, on any trial, is one-half. However, the phenomena fit this hypothesis less well than they do the alternative hypothesis that the coin is biased. If the propensity theorist takes seriously the task, outlined in the preceding section, of constructing propensity/possible frequency models for the phenomena, he must then secondly adapt the usual discussions of goodness of fit into an auxiliary theory about the relation between his models and the actual phenomena.

But on Hume's dilemma I reiterate that to assert a theory is to assert that the actual, whatever it be, shall fit (to a significant degree) the possibilities delimited by that theory. And I perceive no valid inference from this type of assertion to any form of realism with respect to possibilities or propensities.

Department of Philosophy
University of Toronto

NOTES

1   The research for this paper was supported by Canada Council grant S73–0849. I wish to thank Professor R. Giere for much helpful discussion and correspondence about probabilities, and also Professors N. Cartwright, I. Hacking, W. Harper, C. A. Hooker and H. E. Kyburg, Jr.

2   I think that the crucial thorn in the problem's side is this 'under some conditions'. These conditions will generally have little to do with frequencies of examined instances. If some do not accept the aforementioned hypothesis about atrocities, it is presumably because they feel that humans can improve human practice, if they want to. This conviction may also have something to do with frequencies, but is not a function of the relative frequencies in the classes mentioned in the evidence for the hypothesis.

3   These remarks are not dismissive; the functions P are important. Nor is this subject closed. I have written on various aspects of probabilities in quantum mechanics in the References (1972; 1973; 1974), and also in forthcoming work on the Einstein–Podolski–Rosen paradox and (jointly with Professor C. A. Hooker) on Bohr's views on quantum-mechanical assertions.

4   In comments on J. H. Fetzer, 'The Statistician's Dilemma', at the American Philosophical Association, Eastern Division, December 1972.

5   At a symposium at the University of Illinois at Urbana, March 1969. The proceedings
have been published: F. Suppe, ed., *The Structure of Scientific Theories* (Urbana, University of Illinois Press, 1974).

The same volume has my comments, 'Putnam on Corroboration', but I did not, at
that time, perceive clearly the drastic revisions necessary to the older account of
scientific explanation due to Hempel and Oppenheim.

REFERENCES

Beckner, M., *The Biological Way of Thought* (New York, Columbia University Press, 1959).
van Fraassen, B. C., 'On the Extension of Beth's Semantics of Physical Theories', *Philosophy of Science*, vol. 37 (1970: 325–34).
van Fraassen, B. C., 'Probabilities and the Problem of Individuation', in S. Luckenbach,
ed., *Probabilities, Problems and Paradoxes* (Encino, Calif., Dickenson, 1972).
van Fraassen, B. C., 'A Formal Approach to Philosophy of Science', in R. Colodny, ed.,
Paradigms and Paradoxes (University of Pittsburgh Press, 1972: 303–6).
van Fraassen, B. C., 'Semantic Analysis of Quantum Logic', in C. A. Hooker, ed.,
Contemporary Research in the Foundations and Philosophy of Quantum Theory (Dordrecht, D.
Reidel, 1973: 80–113).
van Fraassen, B. C., 'Formal Representation of Physical Quantities', *Boston Studies in the
Philosophy of Science*, vol. XIII (Dordrecht, D. Reidel, 1974).
Giere, R., 'Objective Single Case Probabilities and the Foundations of Statistics', pre-
sented at the Fourth International Congress on Logic, Methodology and Philosophy of
Science, Bucharest, 1971.
Giere, R., 'Empirical Probability, Objective Statistical Methods, and Scientific Inquiry',
presented at the University of Western Ontario Conference on the Foundations of
Statistics and Probability, May 1974.
Giere, R., 'A Matter of Chance' (review of D. H. Mellor, *The Matter of Chance*), forthcoming.
Keynes, J. M., *Treatise on Probability* (London, Macmillan, 1921).
Kyburg, H. E., Jr, *Probability and Inductive Logic* (New York, Macmillan, 1970).
Lakatos, I., ed., *The Problem of Inductive Logic* (Amsterdam, North-Holland, 1968).
Popper, K., 'The Propensity Interpretation of the Calculus of Probability and the Quan-
tum Theory', S. Körner, ed., *The Colston Papers*, vol. 9 (1957: 65–70).
Russell, B., *Philosophy* (New York, W. W. Norton, 1927).
Russell, B., 'Heads or Tails', *Atlantic Monthly*, vol. 146 (1930: 163–70).
Russell, B., Review of F. P. Ramsey, *The Foundations of Mathematics and Other Logical Essays,
Mind*. n.s., vol. XL (1931: 476–82).
Russell, B., Review of F. P. Ramsey, *The Foundations of Mathematics and Other Logical Essays,
Philosophy*, vol. 7 (1932: 84–6).
Russell, B., *Human Knowledge: Its Scope and Limits* (London, George Allen & Unwin, 1948).
Russell, B., *My Philosophical Development* (London, George Allen & Unwin, 1959).
Salmon W. C., *Statistical Explanation and Statistical Relevance* (with contributions by R. C.
Jeffrey and J. G. Greene) (University of Pittsburgh Press, 1971).
Savage, L. J., *The Foundations of Statistics* (New York, John Wiley, 1954).

23

FOUNDATIONS

Renford Bambrough

> *There was a most ingenious Architect who had contrived a new Method for building Houses, by beginning at the Roof, and working downwards to the Foundation; which he justified to me by the like Practice of those two prudent Insects the Bee and the Spider.* (Swift, *A Voyage to Laputa*, Nonesuch edn, p. 176)

Cohen and Nagel say that '*the systematic basis* for the discoveries of Galileo concerning falling bodies was laid *after* his work was formulated by him' (M. Cohen and E. Nagel, *An Introduction to Logic and Scientific Method*, p. 278).

There is virtue in those italics. Without them, many a jaded reader of philosophy would fail to notice the absurdity of laying the foundations after building the roof and the walls (presumably in that order). The metaphor and its misuse are both worn so smooth that even the italics will not save everybody from missing the wild paradox that is trapped in the cliché.

Works whose titles explicitly use the image of foundations or of groundwork range over many centuries, many countries, and most fields of philosophy. There are regular inspections of the foundations of mathematics, ethics and empirical knowledge by teams of surveyors who have little in common but the partiality of their understanding of their own imagery. The closely related metaphor of beginnings or origins (*archai, principia*, starting-points, principles) adds dozens more, and most of the philosophers who have left both metaphors out of their titles have nevertheless been guided consciously or unconsciously by the pictures from which they originate and to which they give rise.

So there is no special reason, apart perhaps from their italics, for picking on Cohen and Nagel. I want to discuss some assumptions that they have made only in the most distinguished company, including that of Plato and Aristotle, Descartes and Russell.

Professor, P. T. Geach shows himself properly inimical to such assumptions when (in his 1965 British Academy lecture, 'Some Problems about Time') he says that predicates in which dates are mentioned are 'a long way *above* the most fundamental level of temporal discourse'.

This time the italics are mine; they are there to mark the welcome rarity of a philosopher's foundations that are *below* what rests on them. Geach goes on:

> Our ability to keep track of the date and the time of day depends on a set of enormously complicated natural phenomena; such phenomena, serving 'for signs and for seasons and for days and for years', might easily not have been available. We can easily imagine rational beings, living on a cloud-bound planet like Venus, who had no ready means of keeping dates or telling the time, and were too well endowed by Nature with the necessities and amenities of life to feel any need to contrive such means. Clearly, such creatures might still speak of one thing's happening at the same time as another, or after another, and might have past, present and future tenses in their language. This is grass-roots temporal discourse; it is perverse to try to analyse it by means of the vastly more complex notions that are involved in saying 'in 1901' or 'at time t.[1]

Grass roots make a soothing change from buildings hanging upside down with philosophical bats in their belfries. Geach's eyes are still turned in the right direction when he goes on to point out that ordinary simultaneity propositions cannot be analysed in terms of what happens at some time:

> On the contrary, telling the time depends on knowing some of these primitive simultaneity propositions to be true. Telling the time by an ordinary clock involves observing that the long hand points (say) to the 12 and the short hand *at the same time* points to the 6; clearly we do not need another clock to verify that it *is* at the same time. A physicist may protest that he simply cannot understand 'at the same time' except via elaborate stipulations about observing instruments: his protest may be dismissed out of hand, for he could not describe the set-up of any apparatus except by certain conditions having to be fulfilled *together*, i.e. simultaneously, by the parts of the apparatus.

A cruder instance of the same type of confusion is provided by the physiologist who offers the results of his researches as grounds for the philosophical conclusion that we never see things as they really are.

If we now return to Cohen and Nagel we find that their next sentence, after their remark about Galileo, is *all* printed in italics: *'The order of nature, and the order of logical dependence, are not the same as the order of our discoveries'*. This is emphatic enough, but not very clear. We are certainly concerned here with questions of priority and order – in fact, with priorities among priorities and the ordering of types of order – but Cohen and Nagel do not make clear what concepts of order they have in mind, or even how many types of order they mean to be distinguished by their emphatic sentence. Are the order of nature and the order of logical dependence two orders, or one order under two names? Is the order of our discoveries merely chronological and accidental, or is it envisaged as necessarily differing from the order of nature and /or the order of logical dependence in such a way that even if Galileo had had the advantage of reading Cohen and Nagel, and had otherwise been better qualified and equipped, he still could not possibly have laid down his foundations until his castle was high in the air?

It is usual for philosophers and logicians not to be very clear about these questions. In some discussions of the foundations of mathematics, for example, the exhilarating impression is given that until Russell comes down the mountainside bearing Peano's axioms, the snow still fresh on his boots, it would be rash to be confident that seven 7s are 49.

Russell himself, at least sometimes, is clearer about the relation between his work on foundations and our ordinary arithmetical knowledge, even if he is also, at least sometimes, unclear about the relation between philosophical or epistemological work in general and our ordinary knowledge in general. In several places he draws a distinction between logical priority and epistemological priority, and though his references to it are brief and undeveloped they form useful points of departure for a fuller examination of the distinctions and connections between logic and epistemology that have to be understood before we can either safely use or legitimately dispense with the traditional metaphor of the foundations of knowledge.

In the opening pages of *Introduction to Mathematical Philosophy* Russell speaks of the two opposite directions in which mathematics may be pursued by one who starts from its most familiar portions. One road leads to the complexities of higher mathematics, the other to greater logical simplicity. In following this second road we are engaged in mathematical philosophy rather than in mathematics: 'instead of asking what can be defined and deduced from what is assumed to begin with, we ask instead what more general ideas and principles can be found, in terms of which what was our starting point can be defined or deduced.' In the same passage he uses an analogy with telescopes and microscopes: 'we need two sorts of instruments for the enlargement of our logical powers, one to take us forward to the higher mathematics, the other to take us backward to the logical foundations of the things that we are inclined to take for granted in mathematics.'

The use of the imagery here is closer to that of Geach than to that of Cohen and Nagel. It would be little better than a pun to notice that *higher* mathematics is represented as being *above* its logical foundations. What is more important is the distinction that Russell draws between foundations and *starting-points*. The *archai* and *principia* of some older philosophers were required to be both the starting-points that their names would imply and also the logical foundations of our knowledge. The nature and importance of the distinction may be seen more clearly in a more extensive quotation from 'Logical Atomism' (*Contemporary British Philosophy*, 1st series; reprinted in *Logic and Knowledge*):

> When pure mathematics is organised as a deductive system – i.e. as the set of all those propositions that can be deduced from an assigned set of premises – it becomes obvious that, if we are to believe in the truth of pure mathematics, it cannot be solely because we believe in the truth of the set of premises. Some of the premises are much less obvious than some of their consequences, and are believed chiefly because of their consequences. This will be found to be always the case when a science is arranged as a deductive system. It is not the logically simplest propositions of the system that are the most obvious, or that provide the chief part of our reasons for believing in the system. With the empirical sciences this is evident. Electro-dynamics, for example, can be concentrated into Maxwell's equations, but these equations are believed because of the observed truth of certain of their logical consequences. Exactly the same thing happens in the pure realm of logic; the logically first principles of logic – at least some of them – are to be believed, not on their own account, but on account of their consequences. The epistemological question: 'Why should I believe this set of propositions?' is quite different from the logical question: 'What is the smallest and logically simplest group of propositions from which this set of propositions can be deduced?' Our reasons for believing logic and pure mathematics are, in part, only inductive and probable, in spite of the fact that, in their *logical* order, the propositions of logic and pure mathematics follow from the premises of logic by pure deduction. I think this point important, since errors are liable to arise from assimilating the logical to the epistemological order, and also, conversely, from assimilating the epistemological to the logical order. (*Logic and Knowledge,* pp. 325–6)

There are other places where Russell makes a similar distinction between logic and epistemology but then goes on to compromise it by giving to the logical foundations a role comparable to that given to them by many of his predecessors and therefore quite distinct from the one assigned to them in the passages I have quoted. In one such place (*An Inquiry into Meaning and Truth,* p. 16) he commends the method of Cartesian doubt in terms that recall the traditional picture of the search for logical foundations as the process of establishing or justifying what he had earlier recognised to stand in no need of such a justification. In another ('The Philosophy of Logical Atomism', *Logic and Knowledge,* pp. 179–81) he adds to a stronger endorsement of the Cartesian method some hints of a more than Cartesian scepticism to which the method and the metaphor of foundations will naturally lead any philosopher who takes them seriously and follows them logically. In the last words of his 1950 paper on logical positivism, which are also the last words of *Logic and Knowledge,* Russell makes his scepticism all but explicit:

> There is one matter of great philosophic importance in which a careful analysis of scientific inference and logical syntax leads – if I am not mistaken – to a conclusion which is unwelcome to me and (I believe) to almost all logical positivists. This conclusion is, that uncompromising empiricism is untenable. From a finite number of observations no general proposition can be inferred to be even probable unless we postulate some general principle of inference which cannot be established empirically. So far, there is agreement among logical positivists. But as to what is to be done in consequence there is no agreement. Some hold that truth does not consist in conformity with fact, but only in coherence with other propositions already accepted for some undefined reason. Others, like Reichenbach, favour a posit which is a mere act of will and is admitted to be not intellectually justified. Yet others make attempts – to my mind futile – to dispense with general propositions. For my part, I assume that science is broadly speaking true, and arrive at the necessary postulates by analysis. But against the thorough-going sceptic I can advance no argument except that I do not believe him to be sincere. (ibid.: 381–2)

An accusation of insincerity is not an argument, and so Russell does not seem to be in a much better position than those who frankly speak of posits made by act of will; and they in turn are more closely related than they recognise to intuitionists who also hold that reasoning must start with premises or principles for which no reasons can be given.

The idea that it is necessary to find a bedrock and the idea that it is possible to find a bedrock are the two main ingredients of intuitionism. The sceptic combines the idea that a bedrock is necessary with the idea that a bedrock is impossible.

It is neither necessary nor possible to find a bedrock.

Resistance to the customary misuses of these metaphors has been sporadic but sometimes penetrating and pungent. Some of the most explicit and sustained opposition has come from C. S. Peirce. His remark that 'no universal principle can in its universality be comprised in a special case or can be requisite for the validity of any ordinary inference' (*Values in a Universe of Chance,* ed., P. Wiener, p. 164) is a clear sign that his epistemological arrows point upwards to the top of the blackboard, in the opposite direction to the arrows of logic. Elsewhere, and especially when rejecting the Cartesian assumptions that Russell commends, he shows a clear recognition of the wider epistemological importance of the recurrent disputes between those who seek a bedrock and those whose starting-point is the common understanding:

> Philosophers of very diverse stripes propose that philosophy shall take

its start from one or another state of mind in which no man, least of all a beginner in philosophy, actually is. One proposes that you shall begin by doubting everything, and says that there is only one thing that you cannot doubt, as if doubting were 'as easy as lying'. Another proposes that we should begin by observing 'the first impressions of sense', forgetting that our very percepts are the results of cognitive elaboration. But in truth, there is but one state of mind from which you can 'set out' – namely, the very state of mind in which you actually find yourself at the time you do 'set out' – a state in which you are laden with an immense mass of cognition already formed, of which you cannot divest yourself even if you would; and who knows whether, if you could, you would not have made all knowledge impossible to yourself? Do you call it *doubting* to write down on a piece of paper that you doubt? If so, doubt has nothing to do with any serious business. (*Philosophical Writings of Peirce,* ed., J. Buchler, p. 256)

Peirce tells another part of the same story in some remarks about surprise and expectation that would be most surprising and unexpected if they were taken by themselves and disconnected from the detail of his examination of reason, truth and knowledge. He reasons, he says, not for the sake of delight in reasoning, but solely to avoid disappointment and surprise. The whole motive of reasoning is to avoid surprise (ibid.: 125). The purpose of an explanatory hypothesis is 'to lead to the avoidance of all surprise and to the establishment of a habit of positive expectation that shall not be disappointed' (ibid.: 267).

These remarks serve to illustrate their own point, since they are at first sight surprising but turn out on reflection to be such that their falsehood would be even more surprising than their truth. By the same token they illustrate Aristotle's remark in the second chapter of the first book of the *Metaphysics* that while we begin by being surprised that, e.g. the diagonal of a square is incommensurable with the side, the man who understands the matter is one who would now be surprised if it were not so. Peirce's paradox can be converted by way of Aristotle's comment into the platitude that the man who knows and understands most is least often surprised.

Moore's defences of common sense and Hume's argument against miracles make use of principles that are implicit in Peirce's remarks (though it happens that Peirce is severely critical in other places of some aspects of Hume's account).

Moore sometimes states and repeatedly uses the principle that the antecedent certainty of a proposition may be such as to amount to a conclusive reason for supposing that some argument against the proposition has a false premiss or an invalid step, even if we do not know which premiss or step is invalid or false or cannot show that it is invalid or false. And a similar comparison of degrees of antecedent certainty is involved in Hume's contention that a miracle story may rationally be accepted as true only if it is supported by such testimony that given that testimony the falsehood of the miracle story would be a greater miracle than its truth.

There is a widespread idea, which is plausible in itself and which has been given currency by some of the little books on How to Think Clearly, that it is always wrong to conclude that an argument is fallacious or that a conclusion is false unless and until one is in a position to point out what is wrong with the argument or to identify the mistake that has been made in arriving at the false conclusion. But it is easily shown that Hume and Peirce and Moore were right to be opposed in principle and practice to any such assumption.

I may tease a child by purporting to prove to him that all cats have three tails:

Any cat has one more tail than no cat.
No cat has two tails.
Therefore any cat has three tails.

It may take an exceptional child to see and to show *what* is wrong with this argument, but every child sees at once that there must be *something* wrong with it. The conclusion is certainly false, and therefore there must be something wrong with at least one of the premisses or with the step from the premisses to the conclusion.

The accounts department of a campus bookstore once sent me, at the end of a month in which I had bought half a dozen books and a few items of stationery, a bill for more than twenty-two thousand dollars. If I had followed the advice of the little books I should have checked the arithmetic, and looked up the invoices and the prices marked in the books, before 'jumping to the conclusion' that there had been some mistake. But, of course, I knew at once that there had been some mistake, though I still do not know exactly what mistake had been made.

A philosopher who declines to take Zeno's paradoxes as a proof of the impossibility of motion but who has no diagnosis to offer of the defects in Zeno's arguments is proceeding in the same sensible and rational manner as the average child in the case of the cat paradox. For the function of reasoning is to effect economies of surprise, and one should always believe the less surprising of two alternative hypotheses. The hypothesis that is initially more surprising may be right, but it will be shown to be right and we shall be given reason for believing it only when we are given such evidence that on that evidence it is no longer more surprising.

We may at first be astonished by the account that Copernicus gives of the motions of the sun and the planets, but we accept it as soon as he is able to show us that the consequences of insisting on the Ptolemaic alternative have become *intolerably* surprising. He is able to show us that it is he and not Ptolemy who 'saves the appearances', and hence that if we are not prepared to pay his price we shall sooner or later have to pay a higher price in the same coin.

The conclusion that all innovations must justify themselves by reference to the *status quo* does not have the conservative implications that might be feared or hoped for. It involves a recognition that every new idea must be defended by evidence or argument, but this is quite compatible with the recognition that any old idea may at any time need to be defended by evidence or argument. And to point out that a new idea can be rationally defended only by being related to old ideas is not to set any limit on the content or on the degree of surprisingness of the ideas that we may on pain of irrationality be called upon to incorporate in our common stock of knowledge and understanding. The limitation it does impose is a purely formal one that offers no greater obstacle to the Einsteins and Freuds of the future than it did to those of the past.

The fact that when I set out on a journey I must start from where I now am does not by itself impose any limits on my means of transport, route or destination. Even Cook and Livingstone and Scott had to start their expeditions at their own front doors.

Whether the space I am exploring is physical or logical or moral or psychological, it is true that there must always be somewhere that is the place that I must start from, but it is not true that there must be somewhere that is always the place that I must start from.

If I am to disagree with you there must be some things on which I agree with you, but there are no things that are *the* things on which I must agree with you if I am to disagree with you.

There can be no battle without a battlefield, and a battlefield is common ground. But there are no fields that are always and only battlefields.

Even if all knowledge needs foundations there are no foundations that all knowledge needs.

St. John's College
University of Cambridge

NOTES

1   In P. F. Strawson, ed., *Studies in the Philosophy of Thought and Action* (London, Oxford University Press, 1968: 184–5).

24

RUSSELL'S ETHICS

W. I. Matson

Spinoza is the noblest and most lovable of the great philosophers. Intellectually, some others have surpassed him, but ethically he is supreme. As a natural consequence, he was considered, during his lifetime and for a century after his death, a man of appalling wickedness. (*A History of Western Philosophy*, New York, Simon & Schuster, 1945: 569; a passage written with the fervour of fellow feeling, soon after the CCNY affair)

The first I heard of Bertrand Russell was in the 1930s when half a page, with portrait, was devoted to vituperating him in the Hearst Sunday paper. I can't remember the particular occasion; I think he was just being denounced on general principles as an enemy of the people, an atheist and immoralist. He was quoted as having described his outlook as like that of Lucretius – an opening which the author exploited in this way: 'All we know of Lucretius comes from Bishop Eusebius, who in his *Chronology* notes for the year 55 BC: "T. Lucretius Caro died. Having been driven mad by a love potion, in intervals of sanity he wrote some poems which were edited by Quintus Cicero." ' That's the kind of man Russell is (the furious scholar continued): an admirer of sexual psychopaths.

With youthful perversity I was led to find out more about Russell, and Lucretius too, whose poems, I discovered, were still extant in our public library. So I took up philosophy because William Randolph Hearst hated Bertrand Russell. There must be many of my generation who, whether or not as a result of these protreptic discourses, got their first enthusiasm for philosophy from some encounter with Russell's work. Not mathematics, philosophy; and not epistemology, ethics; for what first aroused our interests and passions were the same books and essays that shocked Hearst, those coolly sensible, humorous, and humane disquisitions on what kind of life is worth living for a human being.

Man has been called a rational animal, yet to look at the human condition rationally is often thought an inhuman thing to do. Most people cannot examine life; some, like Dr Johnson, can but do not want to; of the few who are willing and able, most, like Plato, Marx and Freud, throw away received opinions only to set up new orthodoxies often more constricting than the old, thus justifying Dr Johnson. It was the rare merit of Russell, as of Voltaire, to have looked at the way of the world with a gaze childlike in its directness yet deeply penetrating and to have asked of what he saw: Does this help or hinder a man in his effort to live a life worth living by a rational animal? If not, why do we have it, and could we not have something better?

Life does not get examined even by its appointed examiners unless some shock sets them off. With Russell it was the First World War. No wonder. He was not a pacifist, but he saw that there was not enough at stake on either side to justify the slaughter, and that a negotiated settlement, on almost any terms, would be better than its continuance. This empirical approach, whereby what it would be best to do is decided not in accordance with rigid and mechanical deduction from abstract principles, but by attention to the particular circumstances of the case at hand, is the rule from which he never deviated. In the seventeenth century he would have been called a trimmer; in the twentieth he was an act utilitarian.[1]

Like Aristotle's, Spinoza's and John Stuart Mill's, Russell's idea of the happiness that ought to be the aim of conduct is not titillation but the untrammelled development and exercise of innate powers: vitality. Vital activity manifests itself more as what we do on impulse than in accordance with plans and schemes, Russell believed. In his early ethico-political treatise *Principles of Social Reconstruction*, impulse, hymned as the very 'expression of life', generated some curiously sophisticated varieties, such as an impulse towards art and science, and even one 'to avoid the hostility of public opinion'. He recognised that not all impulses are splendid, nor all premeditated actions mean, and the tone of *HSEP* is more cautious. Nevertheless Russell always saw happiness as roughly measurable by the scope afforded to spontaneity, and the occupational malady of civilised life as the subordination of impulse to purpose that it necessarily imposed.

The means–end distinction has great importance in Russell's ethical thinking, defining the place of reason in conduct and clarifying the difference between purpose and impulse. Reason, we are told, is concerned only with 'the choice of the right means to an end that you wish to achieve. It has nothing whatever to do with the choice of ends' (*HSEP*: 8), which are the bailiwick of the emotions. The picture is familiar. There are the things you want – the objects of your impulses and feelings, and there are the means you may adopt to get them, your planned actions. The latter are the domain of reason, the finding out of how things are and of the logical relations that may hold between statements. Whether such and such a course of action is likely to obtain what you want, is something on which reason may deliver a verdict. But whether you want it or not is simply a matter for feeling – you just *do*, or don't, have this emotional attitude towards the thing. It is not reasonable, nor unreasonable, to like or dislike anything for its own sake. 'There is no such thing as an irrational aim except in the sense of one that is impossible of realization' (*HSEP*: 11). When we call something good or bad, we are not making a statement that is true or false, we are making an exclamation, expressing a wish, or commanding or suggesting.

Some philosophers in this century have been content with this emotive ethical theory descended from Hutcheson through Hume. Russell, however, was dissatisfied, at least part of the time, and strove through his life to work out a version that would not lead to the consequence, which he confessed to *feeling* was profoundly wrong, that reason has nothing to choose between the ends pursued by Adolf Hitler, on the one hand, and Dag Hammarskjöld, on the other. Much of his last and most important ethical work, *HSEP*, is concerned with the problem of avoiding having to say that no ethical judgment is liable to criticism on grounds of truth – that condemnation of Nero boils down to 'Nero? Oh fie!' (*HSEP*: 26).

His way out was to hold that although ethical judgments are based on feelings, still the feelings of mankind are sufficiently in agreement to allow for the possibility of ethical generalisations valid for all animals like us. He summed up his efforts in four 'propositions and definitions' which, he claimed, 'provide a coherent body of ethical propositions, which are true (or false) in the same sense as if they were propositions of science':

(1) Surveying the acts which arouse emotions of approval or disapproval, we find that, as a general rule, the acts which are approved of are those believed likely to have, on the balance, effects of certain kinds, while opposite effects are expected from acts that are disapproved of.

(2) Effects that lead to approval are defined as 'good', and those leading to disapproval as 'bad'.

(3) An act of which, on the available evidence, the effects are likely to be better than those of any other act that is possible in the circumstances, is defined as 'right'; any other act is 'wrong'. What we 'ought' to do is, by definition, the act which is right.

(4) It is right to feel approval of a right act and disapproval of a wrong act. (*HSEP*: 115 ff.)

If ethics is to be founded on 'the fundamental data of feelings and emotions' (*HSEP*: 25), this is a more plausible version than some others. It does not base goodness and badness directly on the feelings that we allegedly report when we assign the words 'good' and 'bad' to things. Rather Russell says that we have 'emotions of approval' (whatever those might be) for reasons that boil down to beliefs about the likely consequences of the acts approved. If the Aztec approves of human sacrifice and cannibalism, that is because he believes them important for securing a bumper crop of maize. We may disagree with his belief, but we do not disagree with his contention that a bumper maize crop is a good thing – or at any rate that feeding the surviving people is good. The relevant agreement would still exist even if we happen not to desire the continued supply of maize to Aztecs. For what the Aztec thinks is a good thing is enough maize for his group; we likewise value food for *our* herd. This is not a logical truth – the Aztec, or we, could desire the starvation of our respective groups without violating any logical laws – but Russell thinks it unlikely, in fact, that we would. He is saying that, as a general rule, human beings disagree only about means, not about ends. And disagreement about means is not really moral disagreement, for the question whether a certain act is likely to have a certain effect is a factual one, resolvable in principle by scientific methods. We could grow maize with and without the assistance of human sacrifice, and by statistical analysis of the yields conclude whether the means proposed was, in fact, efficacious.

Again the means–ends distinction is made to bear the whole philosophical load. This is a heavy burden. Except for the acts of God, everything we have to contend with is the effect of a human action, and anything at all may be approved or disapproved. So you may approve, and I disapprove, the same act, just because we both believe (correctly, let us assume) that it is likely to have the effect of diminishing the population of X's. As this kind of disagreement is frequent, this kind of effect cannot be what Russell has in mind as falling within the scope of the generalisation (1), which affirms general agreement of the 'emotional' reactions to agreed facts. And the reason is easy to see. Disagreement at this level doesn't count, for we have not yet reached the realm of ends. Why do you approve of diminishing the population of X's, while I disapprove? Because you think that something ultimately desirable, let us say the ecological balance, will thereby be furthered. But perhaps I agree with this estimation of the facts, and still disapprove: perhaps because I think it's better to upset the ecology, which within broad limits can take care of itself, rather than cause widespread and acute suffering here and now. So we have to go on to a still higher plateau, where you want the ecology let alone in order to produce a better world (or at any rate not a worse one), and I likewise want a better, or non-worse, world. Here we agree, but it is a sterile kind of agreement. What, indeed, would it be like to wish for a worse world – worse for everyone and everything, and for oneself as well? We have reached the end, to find there only a tautology. Thus, it was not quite right of Russell to claim that the ethical propositions advocated were 'true (or false) in the same sense as if they were propositions of science', at least not if one holds, as Russell did, that the most general propositions of science are non-tautological.

One should not make too much of objections like these to the four-proposition ethics, however. For that was not really the ethical system that Russell advocated, even though he sincerely believed he did.

Russell thought along these lines: Ethics ought to be objective. Objectivity means being scientific. Being scientific means generalising by induction from particular data. Now, the data of ethics are not the sense-data out of which science is constructed; but they are another species of the genus consciousness, namely, feelings or emotions. Ethical propositions, therefore, are generalisations from those feelings in which mankind agree, as science is generalisations from the percepts that command agreement.

We need not here consider whether this is a satisfactory conception of the structure of science, for the analogy with ethics does not hold. An 'objective' system based on feelings as data would be, as we have seen, either false or trivial. And even if it were neither, it would still not be ethics, but rather a compendious statement of what people feel – sociology or psychology, without normative import, despite the 'definitions' in the second and third propositions. This is not to say that you can't derive 'ought' from 'is' – but you can't do it this way. You might just as well come right out and say something like

What ought to be approved is what enhances vitality.

If you are an optimist, you may also say

What is approved = What ought to be approved.

Russell certainly believed the first of these. Equally certainly he did not believe the second. But there is also the Kantian element: Russell wrote of 'that respect for the human being as such, out of which all true morality must spring' (*Marriage and Morals*, New York, 1929: 153), and however little formal attention this non-utilitarian principle got, it is never far beneath the surface in all his particular disquisitions.

Thus, Russell's real ethics was at least in part Aristotelian-cum-Kantian – somewhat ironically in view of the rough treatment he gave those philosophers in his *History* and elsewhere. That this was his real 'system' can be seen, for example, in his consistent and emphatic opposition to Marxism, an opposition for which the four-proposition ethic provides no grounds; on the contrary, the two almost conflate themselves. Russell detested Marxism because it is a philosophy stemming from and perpetuating hatred,[2] manipulating human beings and suppressing their spontaneity and individuality more thoroughly than any other.

No one in his century had a mind freer of cant than Russell's. Such freedom had its price, as he often found to his rue. He could not solace himself among the intellectual herd when buffeted by Hearst & Co. If Russell had lived only to the age recommended by the Psalmist, he would have died in poverty, far from home and virtually friendless. Happily, he survived to attain high honours and moderate wealth. But he would not have been pleased to see, as I did, his portrait stuck on the wall in the place of honour between Mao Tse-Tung and Che Guevara in a den of student revolutionaries. It is a nice question whether it is better to be praised for the wrong reasons than not to be praised at all. But an undoctrinaire apostle of common sense seldom has another choice.

Department of Philosophy
University of California
at Berkeley

NOTES

1 An act of which, on the available evidence, the effects are likely to be better than those of any other act that is possible in the circumstances, is defined as 'right' (*Human Society in Ethics and Politics (HSEP)*, London, George Allen & Unwin, 1954: 116). This is vastly different from rule utilitarianism, *alias* the domino theory, which got us into the Vietnam War.
2 Even more perhaps from envy, an emotion whose importance in human affairs Russell aristocratically underestimated.

25

RUSSELL'S JUDGMENT ON BOLSHEVISM

Antony Flew

(1) In 1920 Russell visited the USSR in the company, although not strictly as a member, of a British Labour Party delegation. In the same year he published *The Practice and Theory of Bolshevism*, his assessment of the régime established by what was later to take the name of the Communist Party of the Soviet Union (Bolsheviks). In his Prefatory Note for the 2nd edition, written in October 1948, Russell was able to say: 'If I were writing now, some things would be differently said, but in all major respects I adhere to the view of Russian Communism which I took in 1920, and its subsequent development has been not unlike what I expected.'[1]

The gist of Russell's assessment can be given in a few sentences: 'Regarded as a splendid attempt . . . Bolshevism deserves the gratitude and admiration of all the progressive part of mankind . . . if Bolshevism falls, it will have contributed a legend and a heroic attempt without which ultimate success might never have come.'[2] But:[3]

Western Socialists who have visited Russia have seen fit to suppress the harsher features of the present régime. . . . Even those Socialists who are not Bolsheviks for their own country have mostly done very little to help men in appraising the merits or demerits of Bolshevik methods. By this lack of courage they have exposed Western Socialism to the danger of becoming Bolshevik through ignorance of the price that has to be paid and of the uncertainty as to whether the desired goal will be reached in the end. I believe that the West is capable of adopting less painful and more certain methods of reaching Socialism than those which have seemed necessary in Russia. And I believe that while some forms of Socialism are immeasurably better than capitalism, others are even worse. Among those that are worse I reckon the form which is being achieved in Russia, not only in itself, but as a more insuperable barrier to further progress.

When, still later, he looked back upon the reception given to his own exercise in courage, and in dissenting integrity, Russell wrote:[4]

The end of the war was not the end of my isolation, but, on the contrary, the prelude to an even more complete isolation (except from close personal friends) which was due to my failure to applaud the new revolutionary government of Russia. When the Russian Revolution first broke out I welcomed it as did almost everybody else, including the British Embassy in Petrograd (as it then was). . . . But in 1920 I went to Russia. . . . I thought the régime already hateful and certain to become more so. I found the source of evil in a contempt for liberty and democracy which was a natural outcome of fanaticism. It was thought by Radicals in those days that one ought to support the Russian Revolution whatever it might be doing, since it was opposed by reactionaries, and criticism of it played into their hands. I felt the force of this argument. . . . But in the end I decided in favour of what seemed to me to be the truth. I stated publicly that I thought the Bolshevik régime abominable, and I have never seen any reason to change this opinion. . . . Most people still hated me for having opposed the war, and the minority, who did not hate me on this ground, denounced me for not praising the Bolsheviks.

Russell must, I think, have penned this retrospect without refreshing his memories of what he published in 1920. For here in *Portraits from Memory* he goes on:[5]

My visit to Russia in 1920 was a turning-point in my life. During the time that I was there I felt a gradually increasing horror which became an almost intolerable oppression. The country seemed to me one vast prison in which the jailers were cruel bigots. When I found my friends applauding these men as liberators and regarding the régime that they were creating as a paradise, I wondered in a bewildered manner whether it was my friends or I that were mad.

Whereas Russell earlier had been prepared to match for the Bolsheviks of 1917, the tribute paid by Marx to the Communards of 1871, who 'stormed heaven', Russell now is no longer reflecting that 'if Bolshevism falls, it will have contributed a legend and a heroic attempt without which ultimate success might never have come'.

Again, the Russell of 1956 is harsher than the Russell of 1920 in his appreciation of the Bolshevik leaders. Thus, to the more Chomsky Russell of 1920, characteristically:[6]

It seems evident, from the attitude of the capitalist world to Soviet Russia, of the Entente to the Central Empires, and of England to Ireland and India, that there is no depth of cruelty, perfidy or brutality from which the present holders of power will shrink when they feel themselves threatened. . . . The present holders of power are evil men, and the present manner of life is doomed.

It is, on the other hand, 'essential . . . that melodrama should no longer determine our views of the Bolsheviks: they are neither angels to be worshipped nor devils to be exterminated, but merely bold and able men attempting with great skill an almost impossible task'.[7]

When in 1920 Russell reports his personal contacts with some of these Bolshevik leaders, they are not dismissed in the wholesale fashion – Ought we not to say 'melodramatic'? – deemed proper with the damned 'present holders of power' at points further West. Of Trotsky Russell said:[8]

> I thought, perhaps wrongly, that his vanity was even greater than his love of power. . . . But I had no means of estimating the strength of his Communist conviction, which may be very sincere and profound.

Nor was Lenin then presented as a monster of wickedness:[9]

> He laughs a great deal; at first his laugh seems merely friendly and jolly, but gradually I came to feel it rather grim. He is dictatorial, calm, incapable of fear, extraordinarily devoid of self-seeking, an embodied theory.

The nearest the 1920 book comes to saying that Lenin was not only bigoted but also cruel is the statement that he 'laughed over the exchange the peasant is compelled to make, of food for paper . . .'. And whereas, presumably, Lenin was, in fact, amused that peasants were being in this sophisticated and collectivist way robbed, Russell added as his own explanation then: 'the worthlessness of Russian paper struck him as comic'.[10] It was, so far as I know, only in 1950 that Russell published in book form his second specimen of Lenin's Bolshevik humour:[11]

> my most vivid impressions were of bigotry and Mongolian cruelty . . . he explained with glee how he had incited the poorer peasants against the richer ones 'and they soon hanged them from the nearest tree – ha ha ha!' His guffaw at the thought of those massacred made my blood run cold.

These differences between what actually was said in the book of 1920, and what books of 1950 or 1956 say or suggest was said, are, however, relatively unimportant. Certainly nothing which, in fact, was said in the former is either inconsistent with, or should lead us to be surprised by, such drastic and quite un-Chomsky later remarks as: 'I have no doubt that the Soviet government is even worse than Hitler's, and it will be a misfortune if it survives';[12] and 'For a long time after the Russian Revolution, it was customary to say, "No doubt the new régime has its faults, but at any rate it is better than that which it has superseded". This was a complete delusion.'[13]

The first of these remarks was made in 1941. It could, by anyone prepared to be condemned for 'professional anti-communism', or dismissed as a 'Cold War warrior',[14] be provided with some precision and backing by appealing to comparisons between the proportions of the peoples concerned who have been deliberately exiled, imprisoned, dispossessed, executed or starved to death.[15] Russell himself supports the second remark by pointing to material in the lives of Trotsky and other revolutionaries. This 'reveals a degree of political and intellectual freedom to which there is nothing comparable in present-day Russia'.[16]

What ought both to surprise and to distress us, and what are hard if not impossible to reconcile with any of Russell's earlier verdicts on Bolshevism, are some of the statements and actions of his latest years. Certainly Russell remained to the end eager to act on behalf of individual victims of persecution – irrespective of whether their victimisation was or was not approved by the local Communist parties. Certainly (like a few of those parties themselves), he condemned the 1968 reconquest of Czechoslovakia, and (like rather fewer of them) he never backslid from his condemnation. Nevertheless Russell's pronouncements upon the Cuban missile crises, or the Vietnam war, or many other issues of the period, can scarcely be said to have been formed or informed by any of the insights acquired from that first visit to the USSR.

It is, for instance, one thing to maintain that the USA was misguided, or even that it was morally at fault, to intervene militarily on behalf of the governments of South Vietnam, first against the local Vietcong, and then later also against the invaders from the north. But it was, surely, quite another to send to Hanoi, as Russell did on 11 June 1966, a message which concluded:[17]

I extend my warm regards and full solidarity for President Ho Chi Minh and for the people of Vietnam. I convey my great wish that the day may not be far off when a united and liberated Vietnam will celebrate its victory in a free Saigon.

Happily the present chapter is not immediately or primarily concerned with such questions; neither with questions of consistency or inconsistency throughout a very long lifetime; nor with questions of the relative or absolute badness of different régimes. I want instead to consider some matters of what might be called, in a rather broad sense, political theory. These still – perhaps increasingly – urgent issues arise from things either said, or significantly not said, by Russell in *The Practice and Theory of Bolshevism*. Even where I disagree with Russell's conclusions, or otherwise fault him, everything I say springs from the same fundamental shared conviction:[18]

I think there are lessons to be learnt which must be learnt if the world is ever to achieve what is desired by those in the West who have sympathy with the original aims of the Bolsheviks. I do not think these lessons can be learnt except by facing frankly and fully whatever elements of failure there are in Russia. I think these elements of failure are . . . attributable . . . to an impatient philosophy, which aims at creating a new world without sufficient preparation in the opinions and feelings of ordinary men and women.

(2) Although Russell does say here that the main trouble is a bad philosophy, the word 'philosophy' seems to be being employed only in the sort of sense in which a playboy might employ it to proclaim: 'My philosophy is, the more sex the better.' Certainly, there is nothing in the whole book to falsify S. N. Hampshire's contention: 'Unlike his predecessors and peers in public philosophy – Plato, Aristotle, Spinoza, Locke, Hume, Hegel – Russell did not apply to politics the analytical methods which he called for in the theory of knowledge'.[19]

Such philosophical alertness and acumen could have been most usefully directed to the key idea, or key ideas, of socialism. It is not. Russell begins: 'By far the most important aspect of the Russian Revolution is as an attempt to realize Socialism. I believe that Socialism is necessary to the world. . . .'[20] On the following page he tells us two things. First, 'the method by which Moscow aims at establishing Socialism is a pioneer method, rough and dangerous, too heroic to count the cost of the opposition it arouses', and 'I do not believe that by this method a stable or desirable form of Socialism can be established'. Second, 'although I do not believe that Socialism can be realized immediately by the spread of Bolshevism, I do believe that, if Bolshevism falls, it will have contributed a legend and a heroic attempt without which ultimate success might never have come'.[21]

(a) Although these two claims are not, exactly as they stand, contradictory, it does nevertheless appear that Russell wants to maintain: both, at the top of the page, that Bolshevik methods can produce socialism – albeit not a stable or desirable variety; and, at the bottom of the page, that they cannot produce any kind of socialism at all – whether stable or unstable, desirable or undesirable. Clearly, what we need is some distinction between two senses of 'socialism'. In one the realisation of socialism must necessarily involve the realisation of (at least a large part of) Russell's ideals. In the other Russell could consistently say (as we have already seen that he elsewhere does say), 'that while some forms of Socialism are immeasurably better than capitalism, others are even worse'.

Once this first need is appreciated, it becomes, to any politically literate Englishman, obvious that we must start, even if we do not finish, by specifying both senses of 'socialism' partly or wholly in terms of some version of clause IV of the Constitution of the British Labour Party. This is the clause by which that party has since 1918 been committed as its ultimate aim to transferring into some form of public or communal ownership all the means of production, distribution and exchange. It is this clause – now slightly, but only slightly, revised – which has for as long as I can remember been printed as the only statement of aims on every membership card. (It was there when I joined in 1946; still there when I resigned in the early 1950s; and, in its revised form, still there when at long last in 1973 my wife too resigned!)

That something like this clause IV must be at least part of the essence of socialism may not seem equally obvious to citizens of the USA. For there it is usual – especially among those opposed to them – to describe publicly financed welfare measures, which are by no means necessarily connected with any public ownership of the economy, as socialistic – or even as rank socialism. Yet the difference which is thus obscured may be believed to be – and I myself believe is – extremely important. In Britain, for instance, a Conservative so totally opposed to nationalisation, and so dedicated to economic liberalism, as Mr Enoch Powell, does not feel bound for that reason to oppose in principle a publicly financed National Health Service. On the contrary: Mr Powell himself was, and remains, proud to have served as a Minister of Health, in very active charge of the development of that service. Once we appreciate the distinction just made, it becomes clear that his position is not in this respect inconsistent.

The usage common in the USA is, therefore, unfortunate. Failure to appreciate the difference which it obscures must have played at least some small part in strengthening opposition to Medicare programmes: programmes which surely are – if a non-citizen may be permitted to express an opinion upon a purely domestic matter – in some form or other that country's most urgent welfare need. This failure tends to associate such programmes with Britain's notoriously abysmal economic performance. It is, however, though perhaps surprising, true that many British Conservatives would argue that the main reason why the once famous British 'Welfare State' has recently in many respects fallen behind its opposite numbers in North-West Europe is that the social democratic parties there have nothing like the same hostility to private enterprise, to profits and to free markets as is shown by the more doctrinaire British Labour Party. Both in and out of office, but through the trade unions always in power, that corrosive hostility tends, we maintain, to choke the goose which might have laid so many more of the golden eggs of welfare.

Be all that as it may. What, tendentiously, I have asserted to be obvious to any politically literate Englishman, is what is relevant to present purposes. Russell was always incorrigibly English, and he had by 1920 been for several years a member of the Labour Party. For the Bolsheviks, too, clause IV is logically essential to socialism. Lenin and his colleagues displayed their commitment to this total socialism immediately after completing their coup in October. They proceeded forthwith to decree nationalisation, without compensation, for all industrial plant, banks and railways.

The first sense which Russell needs – and by no means only Russell – is one in which the realisation of socialism must involve both the full implementation of some version of clause IV and something else – perhaps a lot else – as well. The second sense which Russell needs – and, for the foreseeable future, everyone else too – is one in which that implementation must by itself constitute the consummation wished by some so persistently, if not perhaps devoutly. In the former, enriched, sense there might reasonably be dispute as to whether the Bolsheviks already had in 1920 achieved socialism, or in due course would; although a precondition of its reasonableness is to stipulate what the something else is to be.

In the latter, the basic clause IV sense, the only room for disagreement is about agriculture. For by 1920 the Bolsheviks had only redistributed that small proportion of the land which was not by 1917 already in the hands of the peasants.[22] Russell asked Lenin, 'what to reply to critics who say that in the country' the Bolsheviks have 'merely created peasant proprietorship, not Communism: he replied that that is not quite the truth, but he did not say what the truth is'.[23] There is no indication that this was even part of Russell's reason for doubting whether they had established, or could hope to establish, socialism. But the point certainly was pressed with that aim by the doyen of orthodox Marxism, Karl Kautsky, in a work written in the August of 1918.[24]

(b) It is common nowadays – much too common – to find people dedicated to basic socialism (clause IV) who try to dismiss embarrassing evidence about conditions in countries which are in this sense undeniably socialist as irrelevant: 'that is not truly socialism, or true socialism', they say; but only, perhaps, 'state capitalism'. Provided that some appropriate usage is stipulated, both for the term 'socialism' in the second sense suggested (*true* socialism), and for the paradoxical expression 'state capitalism'; and provided that that usage is in fact followed, with scrupulous consistency: then maybe no harm is done – except that others may still be confused through failing to grasp exactly what is going on.

These seemingly modest provisos are, however, much less easy to meet than one might in innocence have hoped; and much less often met. I have, for instance, twice in the last few months seen in the British quality press reports, one about Egypt and the other about Iraq, in which arrangements which are in the basic sense unquestionably socialist were described, with no explanation given, not as socialist but as 'state capitalist'.[25] Russell himself in discussing the Russian Bolsheviks speaks not of state capitalism, but of 'state socialism'. He too fails to make explicit what other and contrasting sort of socialism it is supposed that there might be, and which he cherishes as his own ideal: '. . . the successors of Peter the Great . . . are preparing to develop the natural resources of their country by the methods of State Socialism, for which, in Russia, there is much to be said.'[26]

Although Russell is, as we have seen, here confused in his treatment of socialism, he does both here and elsewhere give useful clues as to how he would have wanted to enrich the basic idea. The first, and more manifest, way is by somehow building into the enriched concept some stipulation about equality in distribution. The second way, which is in this book much less manifest, is by inserting a similar demand for democracy as a third essential.

(i) The concern for equality is revealed first in a rather oblique fashion. Russell, who was surely one of those who believe that justice requires levelling, wrote in the original Preface: 'If a more just economic system were only attainable by closing men's minds against free inquiry, and plunging them back into the intellectual prison of the middle ages, I should consider the price too high.'[27] Later the same concern for justice as levelling comes out in his characteristic and lamentably neglected emphases upon the importance, both of the desire for power, and of making its distribution more even. Thus, Russell estimates what is 'likely to happen in Russia: the establishment of a bureaucratic aristocracy, concentrating authority in its own hands'.[28] He then glosses this estimate:[29]

Marxians never sufficiently recognize that the love of power is quite as strong a motive, and quite as great a source of injustice, as love of money; yet this must be obvious to any unbiased student of politics. It is also obvious that the method of violent revolution leading to a minority dictatorship is one peculiarly calculated to create habits of despotism which would survive the crisis by which they were generated.

Later there is a set-piece statement:[30]

What are the chief evils of the present system? I do not think that mere inequality of wealth, in itself, is a very grave evil. If everybody had enough, the fact that some have more than enough would be unimportant. With a very moderate improvement in methods of production, it would be easy to ensure that everybody should have enough, even under capitalism. . . . The graver evils of the capitalist system all arise from its uneven distribution of power.

It is tempting to digress into a consideration of the implications of the essential relativity of the notion of poverty. But our next business is to call in evidence one further passage, this time from a much later work:[31]

Only democracy and free publicity prevent the holders of power from establishing a servile state, with luxury for the few and overworked poverty for the many. That is what is being done by the Soviet government wherever it is in secure control.

Now, what can we develop from these hints? The answer is that we can develop, but here only sketch, a double-barrelled argument for a practically important conclusion. The conclusion is that for anyone for whom even in part 'Socialism is about equality', a commitment to socialism must also be a commitment to democracy. The first, and philosophically uninteresting, reason is suggested by the last of the passages from Russell just quoted. This reason is empirical but general. Systems in which power is concentrated, and in which criticism of the high and the mighty is drastically inhibited, have, as compared with systems in which power is more diffused, and in which criticism is more free, a much greater inherent tendency towards the erection and retention of inordinate privilege. For – as Marxists must be the first to agree – those who are excluded from privileges are those most likely to attack the system which sanctions such privileges; while these same unprivileged persons can and will make their opposition effective only and precisely in so far as they are able to know what is going on, and have some power to alter things. Systems in which power derives (not from the barrel of a gun but) from electorates possess a built-in bias towards fiercely progressive taxation and other widely popular forms of levelling.

This is not the place to deploy at length, with abundant supporting illustrations, a case for what are anyway obvious, empirical truths. Suffice it merely to draw attention to the nature and importance of this argument; and to notice that in 1920 Russell 'talked to an obviously hungry working man in Moscow, who pointed to the Kremlin and remarked: "In there they have enough to eat" '.[32] This incident will remind those who lived through the Second World War of the far crueller contrasts reported then by Western representatives attending the state banquets inside.[33] The carnal details were not, of course, printed in the Soviet press or described on the Soviet radio. But it would in any case have been in the last degree imprudent, as well as futile, for the successors of Russell's working man to have demanded the imposition of more 'equality of sacrifice'.

The second and theoretically interesting reason why, if socialism is to be even in part about equality, a commitment to socialism must also be a commitment to democracy, is of a different kind. While the first depends on an appeal to fundamental contingent facts, about how the universe actually is (but conceivably might not have been); the second involves an analysis of concepts, and urges that one part of this possible ideal of socialism (enriched) appears to require the other also. This is not, I think, an instance of entailment. At least at the present level of abstraction, our notions of egalitarianism, and of democracy, are too polymorphous and too indeterminate for that. It is, rather, a matter of what can and cannot be maintained without an intolerable degree of arbitrariness.

It is scarcely possible to formulate a substantial egalitarian principle which is both presentably general and yet narrow enough to exclude politics. But if that egalitarian principle does require one man, or, I trust, one person one vote, then it must by the same token also require that the casting of these votes has some relevance and significance. This condition is not met if there are no alternatives for the elector to make a choice between; or if, in whatever sense the choice is made, that choice in fact determines nothing. Suppose that the elector is presented with a single official list and no other. Or suppose that, although there are alternatives on offer, it will nevertheless make no difference at all to anything whoever wins the election. Then there is a vast gulf, an enormous and flagrant inequality: between any and all of the ordinary run-of-the-mill electors and those fortunate and privileged few who make the actual decisions.

Such élitist and authoritarian offences, offences against both egalitarianism and democracy, are in the world today so common as to constitute the *de facto* norm, both within the 'socialist bloc', and outside.[34] But for us here one in particular is the pre-eminently appropriate illustration. Immediately after the October coup the elections for a Constituent Assembly were held, more or less as previously arranged by the provisional government:[35]

> According to Lenin's own figures, the Bolsheviks got just over 9 million votes, the Socialist Revolutionaries nearly 21 million, and liberal groups over $4\frac{1}{2}$ million. When that Constituent Assembly, for which all Russia's revolutionaries and liberals had worked for nearly a century, met in January 1918, it was simply dissolved by force.

The inequality between any and all of the vast mass of ordinary electors and the decisive handful on Lenin's Central Committee is here immeasurably more flagrant than the most extreme inequalities of mere wealth or income, without political power.

(ii) The concern for democracy appears in the present book as a concern about the best or only means rather than as a concern for one constitutive element in an (enriched) socialist ideal. Thus, as we saw in the second paragraph of our section (1), Russell writes in the original Preface: 'I believe that the West is capable of adopting less painful and more certain methods of reaching Socialism than those which have seemed necessary in Russia'. Later he once or twice notices that methods first adopted and justified as means must have their effects upon the agents themselves, and will consequently in part determine the actual outcome. He observes, for instance:[36]

> The Bolshevik theory is that a small minority are to seize power, and are to hold it until Communism is accepted practically universally. . . . But power is sweet, and few men surrender it voluntarily. It is especially sweet to those who have the habit of it, and the habit becomes most ingrained in those who have governed by bayonets.

Again, in contending that 'Self-government in industry is . . . the road by which England can best approach Socialism', Russell remarks 'that the practice of self-government is the only effective method of political education'.[37]

In all this it is accepted that the disagreements between communist parties and social democratic parties of the old pre-Leninist type are disagreements only about possible or most desirable routes for reaching exactly the same desired destination, socialism. But this frame of reference fits only in so far as the word 'socialism' is construed in its most basic sense (clause IV). It is quite another story when such basic socialism becomes, either itself a means to some different end, or only one element in an enriched socialist ideal. In this changed perspective a common commitment only to the implementation of clause IV should no longer be seen as a natural or even as a possible basis for a political alliance. For differences between the ends to which basic socialism is desired as a means, or differences over the further ends encapsulated in the new and enriched concept of socialism, may quite reasonably render the individuals or the parties sharing the clause IV commitment still practically irreconcilable. When – as today in France and Chile – communist parties press for a united or popular front to be supported by all socialists, it is wise to ponder the Chinese proverb: 'Those who are going in opposite directions do not make plans together.'

With the passing years the inappropriateness of the framework accepted by Russell in 1920, and by so many others since, ought to have become increasingly obvious. It has, indeed, also become progressively more inappropriate. For those processes of self-change through action and inaction, which at the end of the previous paragraph we noticed Russell noticing, have of course continued to operate on all the people and all the organisations concerned. The man who created 'a party of a new type', used it to seize power in a coup, then retained and extended that power by chicanery and terror, must thereby have transformed himself. That party too must have been, and was, at the same time both wittingly and otherwise transforming itself similarly. The actually operative ideals both of persons and of institutions may be, and almost always are, changed both by their circumstances and by their own practice. What were once our means or our ends thus change places, or cease to be either.[38]

Allow that the young Lenin did share the ideals, though not the opinions, of the Russell of 1920. Still it must be in the last degree unlikely that after living the life he did live the operative ideals of the Lenin of 1920 were substantially those of the Lenin of, say, 1905. The same must apply even more, with appropriate alterations, to institutions. For, with the effluxion of time, a continuing institution will be manned by successors. And the people who devote themselves to outlaw parties without for the foreseeable future any prospects of power, will be of another sort from the people who join when there can be more or less immediate hopes of place and privilege.

It is the opinion of the Russell of 1920 that democracy is the only, or the best, means to the end of socialism, or of a desirable form of socialism. In earlier works there are strong hints of some more than contingent connection between the two. Thus a quarter of a century before, in his study of *German Social Democracy*, he had picked out as 'two essential items', objectives which he believed that 'the Party could not abandon without political suicide . . . *Political Democracy* and *Economic Collectivism*'.[39] Although he went on in the following sentence to speak of 'carrying the ideals of political democracy into the economic sphere', his point then was institutional rather than conceptual. But there is in *Roads to Freedom* a definite suggestion of a strictly conceptual link:[40]

> I think we shall come nearest to the essence of Socialism by defining it as the advocacy of the communal ownership of land and capital. Communal ownership may mean ownership by a democratic state, but cannot be held to include ownership by any state which is not democratic.

The conceptual point which needs to be developed and underlined most emphatically, is this. Someone can significantly be said to share in the ownership of something only and precisely in so far as that person has, even if he or she chooses not to use, a right to a part-share in the disposition of those assets of which he or she is being described as being the part-owner. Most of what is, in fact, called public ownership, or even common ownership, would, therefore, be more correctly characterised as state ownership. People may of course benefit, just as they may suffer, as a result of the exploitation of such state-owned assets. But being in this way a beneficiary no more makes you in any non-Pickwickian sense an owner than being, correspondingly, a victim makes you an owner. Ownership is about rights to control.

To say that something is state-owned is not to say that all the citizens of the state in question must, simply in virtue of their citizenship, possess some rights to share, however indirectly, in the disposition of that state-owned asset. It is to say only that the state itself possesses all such rights. Assets may, therefore, be state-owned in some country which no one at all would wish to call democratic; and where, consequently, these assets, precisely because they are owned by the state, are in no way subject to the control of the citizens as such. On the other hand, following Russell, I stipulatively so define 'communal ownership' that every member of the community in question must as such have a right to a share in the disposition of any assets so owned. Given this stipulative definition of 'communal ownership', something may be: either state-owned, but not communally owned: or communally owned, but not state-owned: or both state-owned and communally owned.

Now suppose that the word 'socialism' is itself defined in terms not of state-ownership but of communal ownership. Then it will follow that whatever is to be said to be thus owned must be subject to the control of those who are to be asserted to be its communal owners. It is from this that it surely follows, in turn, that socialism, construed as a commitment to communal ownership, necessarily involves a measure of democracy; I claim that Russell grasped this, if only momentarily, in *Roads to Freedom*.

Please recognise both how much, and how little, this involves. Since the premiss is vague, the conclusion has to be equally vague. For example: in this interpretation, the socialist is as such committed to democracy only in the operation of socialist enterprises. We have to describe as socialist any set-up in which all or most economic undertakings are communally owned. We should have to say this just the same even in a case where the state machinery was not subject to any democratic control. On the other hand, once we have given the word 'socialist' this meaning, it becomes false and scandalous for us to characterise as socialist a country in which clause IV is law, and all the means of production, distribution and exchange are owned by the state; but where the state machinery is in the hands of an electorally irremovable Leninist élite, ensuring that every legal organisation acts as a 'transmission belt' implementing whatevery policies the central directorate may from time to time privately determine. In the real world: Yugoslavia appears to approach most nearly to the first of these two extremes; while the second possibility is as near as makes little matter fully realised in all the official card-carrying members of the 'socialist bloc', and perhaps now in some few other countries as well.

(c) It would be a great gain for clear thinking, and indirectly for the beleaguered cause of liberal democracy also, if this distinction between state ownership and communal ownership were everywhere understood, and if everyone always employed a vocabulary which brought out the issues clearly and correctly. We have already, at the beginning of the previous sub-subsection (2)(b)(ii), looked at one potentially catastrophic confusion encouraged by the fact that the basic clause IV sense of 'socialism' is indeterminate in respect of this distinction. Another such confusion can be approached by meditating upon a passage quoted once before:[41]

> And I believe that while some forms of Socialism are immeasurably better than capitalism, others are even worse. Among those that are worse I reckon the form which is being achieved in Russia, not only in itself, but as a more insuperable barrier to further progress.

Concentrate upon that final clause; and, in terms of our distinction between basic and enriched senses of the ambiguous word 'socialism', think of what Russell is saying. Following but improving on Russell, we may hold that the point is that it would be far more difficult, and it would take far longer, to establish enriched socialism in the USSR, than it would in many countries where very little of the economy is as yet basically socialist. Indeed – though now myself no socialist in either sense – I would be prepared, given a suitable occasion, to argue that the prospects for such an enriched socialism were in Russia generally better before the October Revolution than they have since become. But the point which I have to make here is of another kind altogether. This point is – whether or not even the more modest Russellian thesis is true – that it must be unsound in principle to infer: from the premiss that basic socialism is a theoretically necessary condition of enriched socialism; the conclusion that to achieve basic socialism is necessarily to take a step, even a giant step, towards enriched socialism.

This unsound inference is enormously tempting. It is, nevertheless, unsound. It is unsound because it equivocates between two totally different interpretations of the key expression 'necessary condition'. In the premiss this is construed as being equivalent to 'logically necessary condition'. In this interpretation, the premiss is certainly true. It is certainly true because basic socialism (clause IV), which is indeterminate as between state ownership and communal ownership, is part of what is meant by the word 'socialism', taken in any enriched sense. But the proposed conclusion of the argument is not in this way merely verbal. It is rather, that any country where clause IV is law is in practice farther along the road to socialism, in some enriched and essentially democratic construction of that word. The argument is, therefore, as invalid as its conclusion is, in Russell's view and mine, false.

I labour the point about the invalidity of this and other arguments to that false conclusion, because these arguments and this conclusion still possess continuing baleful appeal – despite all the experience of Bolshevism accumulated since 1917. Never a day passes but we have forced upon our attention instances of their influence upon the hearts and minds and conduct of many who claim, and think themselves sincere in claiming, to be socialists in some enriched sense essentially involving democracy and civil liberties.

For example, in the week during which I was actually writing the present chapter, Prime Minister Whitlam of Australia committed his country to supporting – among other things – any United Nations move to oust 'colonialist Portugal' from her African territories. Suppose, perhaps too charitably, we allow this to be neither a politically disingenuous gesture – designed to enable rich, white, Australia to pass as a country of 'the Third World' – nor yet the expression of ignorance of the comparable realities of 'the Second World' – ignorance which would disgrace the chairman of a rural district council. Then how else are we to explain Premier Whitlam's failure to include in his robust repudiation of all colonial subjection the case of reconquered Tibet, or those of any of the non-Russian peoples within the empire of what the new mandarins now so aptly call 'the new Tsars'? How else, save as an expression of the indulgence thought to be due to those whom the premier still cannot help seeing as his fellow socialists?[42]

(3) At the beginning of section (2), I quoted Hampshire: 'Russell did not apply to politics the analytical methods which he called for in the theory of knowledge.' The whole section then displayed both the need, and Russell's failure, to apply such methods to the crucial concept, or concepts, of socialism. His treatment of Bolshevism as a religion constitutes another, and more subtle, example of the same thing. Again it is one which continues to be relevant to the problems of our later generation.

Decades before the Kremlin found it convenient to become the Protector of the Arabs, Russell discerned the similarities between Bolshevism and Islam: 'Bolshevism combines the characteristics of the French Revolution with those of the rise of Islam'[43] and 'Marx has taught that Communism is fatally predestined to come about; this . . . produces a state of mind not unlike that of the early successors of Mahomet.[44] So Russell concludes: 'Mahommedanism and Bolshevism are practical, social, unspiritual, concerned to win the empire of this world. . . . What Mahommedanism did for the Arabs, Bolshevism may do for the Russians.'[45]

From this religious aspect of Bolshevism Russell, as we should expect, differs fundamentally:[46]

> This habit, of militant certainty about objectively doubtful matters, is one from which, since the Renaissance, the world has been gradually emerging, into that temper of constructive and fruitful scepticism which constitutes the scientific outlook. I believe the scientific outlook to be immeasurably important to the human race.

It is immediately after this, and as his reason, that Russell expresses a judgment quoted earlier: 'If a more just economic system were only attainable by closing men's minds against free inquiry, and plunging them back into the intellectual prison of the middle ages, I should consider the price too high.'

Certainly I do not wish to dissent from anything quoted in the previous two paragraphs – so far as it goes. But what we have to notice is that Russell is conspicuously not relating his academic to his social values. There is here no Popperian suggestion that the exploratory and undogmatic approach which is required in the investigation of nature, is even more urgently needed in the development and vindication of social policies: 'A policy is a hypothesis which has to be tested against reality and corrected in the light of experience.'[47] Because the subject matter of social policies is people; because what happens to people matters more than anything else; and because every social policy is bound to have at least some unintended consequences: the protagonists of such policies ought always to be willing to learn from experience, and to revise or to withdraw such policies in the light of that experience.

It is not necessary to develop here what should now be the familiar Popperian argument: 'Rationality, logic, and a scientific approach all point to a society which is "open" and pluralistic, within which incompatible views are expressed and conflicting aims pursued . . . and above all a society in which the government's policies are changed in the light of criticism.'[48] But it is worth indicating that and how questions about willingness not merely to permit but to encourage independent investigation of the actual effects of policies, and to take account of criticism based upon such investigation, are connected with questions about the nature and sincerity of the aims professed by protagonists of these policies.

The crux, and it is a crux with innumerable and important practical implications, is this. Suppose that you propose a certain policy. Suppose, too, that you offer as your reasons for wanting this policy to be implemented, that it will have such and such effects; which effects you hold to be good. And suppose next that you are uninterested in the question what effects it actually does have; that you even attempt to inhibit free inquiry in this area; or that you resolutely refuse to adapt the favoured policy to take account of the results of whatever investigations may in fact be made. Then the moral which we have to draw must surely be that you either always were, or have since become, indifferent to the objectives to which you originally referred. The policy now appeals to you, it seems, or perhaps really it always has appealed to you: either as something in itself desirable, rather than as a means to further ends; or else, though still as a means, as a means to ends different from those proclaimed when the policy was first proposed.

Let us make the case a little more concrete. If, and in so far as, for you the implementation of socialism (clause IV) is a means to various other supposed or actual goods; then, and to that extent, you will be concerned to monitor the actual operation of whatever socialist policies are adopted. You will be so concerned – or you will be so concerned in so far as you are rational – both in order to know how far your ends are in fact being achieved, and still more to ensure that the policies adopted as means to these ends shall be revised or abandoned in so far as they prove to be ineffective or counterproductive. This just is what it is to be a rational man treating something as a means to some end outside itself.

Now, by way of contrast, suppose someone equally rational, who also maintains that socialism (clause IV) is for him not an end in itself but the means to the same putative goods. But suppose that this other person is uninterested in the findings of inquiry; or even tries to prevent any such inquiry; and when relevant results are available still resolutely refuses to think of revising his socialist policies – much less abandoning them. Then, surely, we have no option but to infer that, for him, either the true ends lie elsewhere, or else the policies themselves are the ends. (Or, of course, and as always, a bit of both. But to specify such complications every time would make the arguments, for no sufficient reason, unreadably complex.)

The application of all this to our understanding of the actual aims and commitments of contemporary Bolshevism is, or ought to be, obvious.[49] So let us conclude the present section with a quotation from the much-abused but little-read Karl Kautsky. He makes it clear, both that for him socialism (clause IV) is a means, and that he appreciates what this involves:[50]

> If . . . we place the Socialist way of production as the goal, it is because in the technical and economic conditions which prevail today Socialistic production appears to be the sole means of attaining our object. Should it be proved to us that we are wrong in so doing, and that somehow the emancipation of the proletariat and of mankind could be achieved solely on the basis of private property . . . then we would throw Socialism overboard, without in the least giving up our object, and even in the interests of this object.

(4) At only one point in *The Practice and Theory of Bolshevism* is the reader reminded that the author was at the time of writing the most distinguished living British philosopher. This is when Russell says: 'Far closer than any actual historical parallel is the parallel of Plato's Republic.'[51] But even here Russell does not proceed to make any kind of philosophical comparison. He says only: 'The Communist Party corresponds to the guardians; the soldiers have about the same status in both; there is in Russia an attempt to deal with family life more or less as Plato suggested.' What is missing is any review of the differences and similarities between the doctrines offered in justification, as well as a thorough comparison of actual Bolshevik institutions with those proposed by Plato.[52]

For us the most relevant comparison is between the foundations of authority in the two cases. Where Plato urged the necessity of discovering and breeding golden natures, which must then also be appropriately trained; the Communist parties put all their emphasis upon the environment and the possibilities of environmental manipulation. (Stalin's support for Lysenko's onslaught on genetics and geneticists was no ephemeral fluke, any more than is the recent neo-Lysenkoist hostility to the notion of IQ and the practice of IQ testing.) Again, where communist ideology is, in Marxist terms, materialist, Plato's account of the nature and status of the forms is, in terms of the same Marxist antithesis, a paradigm case of idealism. What the guardian order and the Communist parties have in common is a claim to absolute power and authority, based upon their peculiar knowledge of the true ideology.

Through their knowledge of the forms the guardians become uniquely qualified to prescribe for everyone what is good, and hence what ought to be. It is precisely and only on the grounds that they and they alone possess this knowledge that the Socrates of *The Republic* contends that philosophers – true philosophers – should be kings. The guardians are, by both vocation and training, truly philosophers. For the word 'philosopher' is persuasively defined as 'one who knows the forms'. So all manner of things will be well if, but only if, all power is rendered up to these true philosophers. Communists are, in the first instance, concerned only for the proletariat. It is through and only through their own Marxist-Leninist understanding and leadership that the interests of the proletariat can and will triumph. And ultimately, by this triumph, a society will be produced which satisfies the interests and fulfils the needs of all.

Notice now how this shared claim to absolute authority is one which refers, and must refer, to needs or interests, rather than to actual wants. For while there may be room for an expert to tell me what is in my interests, or what it is that I need for some purpose, or even what I ought to do; there can be no room at all for experts knowing better than I do myself what it is that I actually and consciously want. This is why Plato is forever using – and most grossly abusing[53] – medical analogies. My doctor can tell me, thanks to his professional knowledge, what treatment I need if I am to satisfy my want to get well. But the doctor has no such special competence – nor is any required – to determine whether or not I do, in fact, want to get well. There can be occasions when in fact I do not; and then – in so far as the doctor is serving me as my professional adviser – he will leave me alone.

Much more to the present purpose, this is why the contemporary communist concept of democracy stresses interests and needs rather than wants. A free election might reveal that most of them want us communists out. But, even supposing that we were in some unguarded moment to concede that this is in fact so, still we could quite consistently maintain – and would – that our power serves their interests, and meets their needs. Thus, it was in just such a moment of truth that Janos Kadar, addressing the Hungarian National Assembly on 11 May 1957, the year after the friendly neighbourhood Soviet tanks has installed him in office, said:[54]

> The task of the leaders is not to put into effect the wishes and will of the masses. . . . The task of the leaders is to accomplish the interests of the masses. Why do I differentiate between the will and the interests of the masses? In the recent past we have encountered the phenomenon of certain categories of workers acting against their interests.

This point about the contemporary communist concept of democracy is the more worth making, since it is so often obscured by various politically motivated attempts to make out that the communist régimes and the communist parties are democratic in quite a different sense. It is sometimes suggested that the word 'democracy' is beyond redemption. I once heard the late Professor J. L. Austin say as much in a lecture.[55] But this is far too defeatist. All that is required to give the word a harmless and necessary life – or lives – is that we should first make, and always thereafter insist upon, certain distinctions.

Suppose we put on one side as irrelevant that established sense in which it refers to social equality and equality of opportunity. It is in this sense that people talk of the need to democratise the British Foreign Service; meaning that its officials should be drawn from a wider range of schools, and that missions abroad should have more comprehensive and less socially exclusive contacts.

Then there is one fundamental distinction to make. This is the distinction, already suggested: between a sense which refers to the people's needs or interests, and a sense which refers to their actual wishes. In the latter sense a set-up is democratic precisely and only to the extent that those above can be voted out by those below. Whether the wishes thus expressed happen to coincide with their interests or their needs is, as far as the question of democracy is concerned, neither here nor there. Given these two basic senses of the word 'democracy' – which we will have to call 'Eastern' and 'Western', respectively, until someone invents a better pair of labels – then we may if we wish proceed to introduce or to distinguish further, enriched, senses.

What we must not do, once we have allowed that there are these two fundamentally different senses of the word 'democracy', is to think of these as two different forms of democracy. There may indeed be, and surely are, different forms of both democracy (Western) and democracy (Eastern). But, exactly in so far as the word 'democracy' is indeed ambiguous, the different forms of the former and the different forms of the latter cannot together constitute a collection of the varieties within one and the same univocal species, democracy. (I have to report that I recently heard an able and active philosopher employ this shameful sophism. He wanted to reconcile his claim to be a socialist, in a sense which he says essentially involves (Western) democracy, with his practice of describing – and systematically favouring – the countries of the 'socialist bloc' as socialist.)

Earlier in the present section I allowed that 'there may be room for an expert to tell me what is in my interests, or what it is that I need for some purpose, or even what I ought to do'. I now conclude the section by quoting from a leading Radical philosopher a few sentences referring to the third of these possible kinds of expertise. He is referring to 'the claim that fundamental value judgements are not truth-claims but have a non-cognitive logical status'. Having elsewhere contended that this claim is false,[56]

> ... I want to argue that such an account of normative or value judgments indirectly supports and reinforces pluralism and bour-

geois individualism. . . . If someone accepts and takes this conception of valuation to heart, he is very likely to accept democratic
pluralism as the most adequate political model. . . . What is reasonable to do . . . is simply, where possible, to give people whatever it is
they want, when doing that is compatible with others having their
wants treated in the same way. . . . On such an account, it is thought
to be a kind of cultural imperialism . . . to tell people what they should
want or to say that certain wants are irrational.

Cognitivism about value is, thus, commended as the basis for telling
people what they should want, and working to ensure that willy-nilly
that, and only that, is what they shall have.

(5) At the beginning of the previous section, I noticed that *The Practice
and Theory of Bolshevism* does almost nothing to remind the reader 'that the
author must have been at the time of writing the most distinguished
living British philosopher'. Perhaps even more remarkable, the nearest
we get to a hint that he was also the author of *German Social Democracy* is
his comment that in the USSR 'The police play, altogether, a much
greater part in daily life than they do in other countries – much greater
than they did, for example, in Prussia twenty-five years ago, when there
was a vigorous campaign against Socialism'.[57]

It was most unfortunate that Russell thus made no attempt to relate
his Russian experience to what he had learnt a quarter of a century
earlier, both about German social democracy as an institution, and
about Marx's materialist conception of history as then interpreted. Such
knowledge was then even rarer among British observers than it is now.
Had Russell used it, he could have achieved deeper perspective and
richer understanding. As it is, he compounds this first neglect by failing – like so many others since – to distinguish the February revolution
against the Tsarist autocracy, from the Bolshevik coup against the
provisional government of Kerensky in October. He speaks indiscrimi-
nately of 'the Russian Revolution' and of 'the October Revolution'.

Even much later, in *Portraits from Memory*, he is capable of writing, as we
saw earlier: 'When the Russian Revolution first broke out I welcomed it
as did almost everyone else, including the British Embassy.'[58] Although
he is talking about the Bolsheviks, he does not notice that even a British
embassy could scarcely have welcomed a coup by a party committed to
abandoning, among others, its British allies. Russell thus did his bit to
encourage, even if he did not himself actually share, one deplor-
able – and deplorably common – popular misconception: that the Bolsheviks executed a revolution against the Tsarist government; and that
what they did may be justified by reference to the, always grotesquely
exaggerated, demerits of that régime.

A good way to see what Russell might have seen, had he deployed all
the resources available to him, is to look at Karl Kautsky's *The Dictatorship of the Proletariat*. This was written, and first published, in German

in the summer of 1918. Kautsky in his youth had known both Marx and Engels. He virtually founded, and for thirty-five years edited, *Die Neue Zeit*, the theoretical organ of German social democracy. He at least had been the almost universally recognised doyen of Marxist orthodoxy. Up till the outbreak of the First World War Lenin himself always spoke of him with great respect, trying to show that his own position squared with Marxism as interpreted by Kautsky. In particular Lenin had approved of Kautsky's stand against the revisionism of Bernstein. Both Kautsky and Bernstein, it must be emphasised, stood for the realisation of socialism through democracy. Kautsky's anti-revisionism consisted in his suggestion that in face of the resistance of the German ruling classes neither democracy nor socialism could be attained peacefully.

The gist of what Kautsky said in 1918 was, in effect, that 'Marxism-Leninism' is a self-contradictory expression: first, because democracy was essential to the ideals and practice of traditional German social democracy; and, second, because a successful proletarian revolution in the Russia of 1917 must constitute a decisive falsification of that very conception of history in the name of which it was made. It is significant that Lenin's counterblast, *The Proletarian Revolution and the Renegade Kautsky*, was, even by Lenin's standards, egregiously vituperative.[59]

(a) In presenting the first count of his indictment Kautsky appeals both to the traditions of social democracy as an institution and to the writings of Marx. The appeals to Marx will strike those who have also read Lenin as agreeably scholarly, with none of that religious temper which so distressed Russell. Kautsky said of Marx:[60]

The dictatorship of the proletariat was for him a condition which necessarily arose in a real democracy, because of the overwhelming numbers of the proletariat. Marx must not, therefore, be cited by those who support dictatorship in preference to democracy. Of course, this does not prove it to be wrong.

But Kautsky's main, substantive point comes immediately after the sentences quoted already at the end of section (3), above. It is, surely, if 'liberation' is to be the name of the game, a knockout:[61]

Socialism and democracy are therefore not distinguished by the one being a means and the other the end. Both are means to the same end. The distinction between them must be sought elsewhere. Socialism as a means to the emancipation of the proletariat, without democracy, is unthinkable.

It is at this point that we ought to recall: first, when Lenin first put forward his proposals for a party of a new type; second, how he then justified these proposals; and, third, against what sort of régime the

October revolution was made. These proposals – what later came to be known, half-truly, as the principles of democratic centralism – were first put forward in such pamphlets as *What is to be Done?* (1902), *A Letter to a Comrade on our Organization Tasks* (1902) and *One Step Forward, Two Steps Back* (1904).[62] They were at that time justified as necessary for effective struggle in the conditions of Tsarist repression; and Lenin himself contrasted these conspiratorial necessities with the openness and democracy enviably possible in the happier conditions of German social democracy.[63] Yet Lenin in 1917 used the instrument forged in and for the struggle against Tsarism in order to execute a coup against a régime which was moving towards representative democracy. And he used it in conditions in which openness and free assembly were in Russia possible as never before – or since.

It was, therefore, wrong for Russell, while rightly deploring 'that truly terrible degree of centralization which now exists in Russia', to add, charitably, that 'The Russians have been forced to centralize'.[64] Lenin and the Bolsheviks were not forced by intolerable oppression to revolt in October. Lenin saw an opportunity to seize power, and he took it. Nor was he compelled to refuse to share that power with other parties; or to dissolve the Constituent Assembly by force; and so on; and on and on. He was compelled, that is, only in so far as the desire to have and to hold such absolute power is itself allowed to be the compulsion.

In part, Russell dissents from those 'apologists of Bolshevism' who 'excuse its harshness on the ground that it has been produced by the necessity of fighting the Entente and its mercenaries'. He then says: 'A great part of the despotism which characterizes the Bolsheviks belongs to the essence of their social philosophy'.[65] Yet he also lapses into the typically British illusion that foreigners are only what we make them: 'If we continue to antagonize the Bolsheviks, I do not see what force exists that can prevent them from acquiring the whole of Asia within ten years'.[66] What Russell never discerns is how the despotic social philosophy is rooted in the Leninist party.

For this insight we have to go not to Russell, nor to Kautsky, but to Rosa Luxemburg. In a pamphlet first published in 1904, she said of *One Step Forward, Two Steps Back*:[67]

> The viewpoint presented with incomparable vigour and logic in this book, is that of pitiless centralism. . . . Lenin's thesis is that the party Central Committee should have the privilege of naming all the local committees of the party. . . . It should have the right to rule without appeal on such questions as the dissolution and reconstitution of local organizations. This way the Central Committee could determine, to suit itself, the composition of the highest party organs as well as the party congress.

She concluded: 'What is today only a phantom haunting Lenin's imagination may become reality tomorrow.'[68] To understand Bolshevism it is essential to come to terms with this reality.

(b) Kautsky's second point was about neither ideals nor institutions, but Marxist theory. The Russia of 1917 did not satisfy the conditions for a successful proletarian revolution: capitalism, and consequently the proletariat, were insufficently developed. This was the universal Marxist, and Bolshevik, assessment until Lenin returned to Russia on 3 April 1917; and, to everyone's astonishment, presented his April theses. Then and later Lenin's own achievements in turning the course of history themselves constitute a further decisive falsification of Marxism. For neither Marxism, nor indeed any other similar theory, can possibly allow so enormous a role to such an accidental factor as the presence or absence and particular qualities of one individual. But this is not Kautsky's thesis.[69] His point was simply that the materialist conception of history could not compass a proletarian revolution at that time and in that place.

Kautsky quoted Marx: '. . . even when a society has got on the right track for the discovery of the natural laws of its movement – it can neither clear by bold leaps, nor remove by legal enactments, the obstacles offered by the successive phases of its normal development.'[70] The expropriators cannot be expropriated, before they have produced their own despoilers. Capitalism cannot be buried, before it has given birth to its grave diggers.

Department of Philosophy
University of Reading

NOTES

1   My references to *TPTB* will all be to this 2nd edition (London, George Allen & Unwin, 1949). The text differs from that of the 1st edition in only two respects:
    On the one hand, I have omitted a chapter of which I was not the author; on the other hand, I have found it necessary, in order to conform to modern usage, to alter the word 'Communism' to 'Socialism' in many places. In 1920, there was not yet the sharp distinction between the two words that now exists, and a wrong impression would be made but for this change. (p. 5)

2   *TPTB*, pp. 7–9.

3   ibid., pp. 20–1.

4   *Portraits from Memory* (London, George Allen & Unwin, 1956: 13); hereafter *PFM*. For reasons of the same sort as those given by Russell for altering 'the word "Communism" to "Socialism" ' I have promoted his original 'radicals' to 'Radicals'.

5   *PFM*, pp. 13–14.

6   *TPTB*, p. 10.

7   ibid., p. 76.

8   ibid., p. 38.

9   ibid., p. 33.

10 ibid., p. 35.

11 *Unpopular Essays* (London: George Allen & Unwin, 1950: 219); hereafter *UE*.

12 In a letter to Gilbert Murray, dated 18 January 1941, printed in *The Autobiography of Bertrand Russell*, vol. II (London, George Allen & Unwin, 1968: 248–9).

13 *PFM*, pp. 203–4. Anyone surprised or distressed either here or elsewhere by my hostile

references to Noam Chomsky ought to look again, in a perhaps cooler hour, at his *American Power and the New Mandarins* (New York, Pantheon and Vintage, hardcover and paperback, respectively, 1969); maybe with the help of my 'New Left Isolationism', *Humanist* (Buffalo) (September–October 1971: 38–40).

Chomsky is, for instance, capable of writing, in a throwaway aside on p. 12: 'the people of Vietnam (the Communists, that is)'. Chomsky, thus, by implication dismisses all Vietnamese anti-communists – including many hundreds of thousands of Roman Catholic refugees from communist religious persecution – as not really people, nor deserving of consideration as such. Irrespective of our assessments of American involvement in Vietnam, we ought to be able to see that this is – despite all professions to the contrary, both from Chomsky, and from his fans – an expression of a concern which is motivated more by political venom than by impartial morality.

Its pretensions to be humanist are equally to be rejected. We humanists – if not, apparently, these new Radicals – recognise even our religious and political opponents as human beings. It is a sad index of the disarray into which the Vietnam war threw so much American liberal opinion that Chomsky's political outbursts used, I am told, to get standing ovations from university audiences.

14   I have myself met these two phrases most recently on the back cover of H. E. Salisbury's edition of A. D. Sakharov's *Progress, Coexistence and Intellectual Freedom* (Harmondsworth, Penguin, 1969), and in Kai Nielsen's 'In Defence of Radicalism', in *Question 7* (London, Pemberton, 1974), respectively. Their attraction to those who use them – whether committed Radicals or mere trendies – lies precisely in the imprecision of the offence. No one thus sneeringly dismissed can know against what charge he has to try to defend himself – other than that of membership in a despised, detested and untrendy out-group.

15   For some data on the less well publicised side of such comparisons see, for instance, Robert Conquest *The Great Terror* (London, Macmillan, 1968: esp. 19–26 and 525–35). Compare also the same author's *The Nation Killers* (London, Macmillan, 1970).

16   *PFM*, p. 204. For some quantitative material see, for instance, Robert Conquest *Lenin* (London, Fontana, 1972: 126–9).

17   For plenty more of this sort of stuff see: on Cuba and the USSR, his *Unarmed Victory* (Harmondsworth, Penguin, 1963); and, on Vietnam, his *War Crimes in Vietnam* (London, George Allen & Unwin, 1967).

18   *TPTB*, p. 8.

19   In 'Russell, Radicalism, and Reason', a review of the third volume of the *Autobiography* for *The New York Review of Books*, reprinted in V. Held, K. Nielsen, and C. Parsons, eds, *Philosophy and Political Action* (New York, Oxford University Press, 1972: 262).

20   *TPTB*, p. 7.

21   ibid., p. 8.

22   In a parenthetic comment upon the agrarian policies of Prime Minister Stolypin under Nicholas II, Conquest writes: '(And in fact by 1917 the peasants already owned more than three-quarters of the land. The gain in arable land to the peasantry of all the confiscations and reforms of the Revolution was about 16 per cent)' (*Lenin*: 61–2).

23   *TPTB*, p. 36.

24   This is available in English as *The Dictatorship of the Proletariat*, J. H. Kautsky, ed. (Ann Arbor, Michigan University Press, 1964); see ch. IX (a), 'Agriculture'. As a glimpse of the world we have lost, notice that it simply does not occur to Kautsky that the peasants might be forced into collective farms; as at the end of a decade they were.

Karl Kautsky, as we shall be seeing later, insisted that democracy was essential to traditional Marxist social democracy; as it quite certainly is, for instance, to the non-Marxist and largely non-socialist (clause IV) contemporary social democracy of Chancellor Willi Brandt.

25   The first, reprinted from the *Guardian*, I saw in the *Calgary Herald*, 27 March 1973, while the second was in the *Financial Times*, 24 July 1973.

26   *TPTB*, p. 69.

27   ibid., p. 9.

28 ibid., p. 92. It is a pity but again, I am afraid, characteristic that the final clause of the sentence reads: 'and creating a régime just as oppressive and cruel as that of capitalism'. To anyone who has really taken the measure of what Russell was later to call 'the vast horror of Russian Communism' (*PFM*: 11), such a comparison between its evils and all the relatively minor evils of the advanced capitalist countries must now sound silly, and – to borrow a favourite boo-word of our Leninising student milit-ants – hysterical. But, since anything I say on such matters will, in the quarters where it needs to be said, be dismissed as the unfashionable carping of an avowed enemy of socialism, I appeal for support to a well-known media figure, who has fought elections for the Labour Party, and intends to continue without repentance in the same course. So see Bryan Magee, *The New Radicalism* (London, Secker & Warburg, 1962: 102–10, 142–3, and *passim*).

29 *TPTB*, pp. 92–3.

30 ibid., p. 109.

31 *UE*, p. 59.

32 *TPTB*, p. 117.

33 They may also remember the surprise and shock of those British and American servicemen who met high-ranking Soviet officers in 1945, and discovered that the factors by which pay of a Soviet marshal differed from the pay of a Soviet private were significantly greater that the comparable factors in their own services. They also discovered that, of course, Soviet income taxes are much less punitively progressive than those sustained by the electorates of democratic countries.

I cannot now put my hand on a suitably authoritative source in the case of the USSR. But many may be even more startled to learn that much the same applied in China. Edgar Snow's *Red China Today*, a source very sympathetic indeed to the régime, says that in that country in 1962 – giving rough equivalents in US dollars – 'privates started at $2·50; corporals got $4 . . . marshals of the army, $360–$400' (p. 285). Incidentally, Snow is another who employs, without explanation of how its referent is supposed to differ from socialism, the expression 'state capitalism' (pp. 194–5).

34 Those who are sincerely devoted to either or both of these ideals may obtain some trifle of consolation from recognising that the shams themselves constitute good evidence of the popularity of the real thing. They are the hypocritical tribute which élitist and authoritarian vice pays to egalitarian and democratic virtue. There would be no point in staging the shams if no one had any desire for the genuine article. See 'What Socrates should have said to Thrasymachus', in C. L. Carter, ed., *Skepticism and Moral Principles* (Evanston, New University Press, 1973).

35 R. Conquest, *Lenin*, p. 92.

36 *TPTB*, p. 106.

37 ibid., pp. 127 and 129.

38 A most sinister and relevant example is provided by some sentences from a document, 'The Falsifiers of Scientific Communism', issued early in 1972 by the Institute of Marxism–Leninism in Moscow. These sentences suggest that, whereas Lenin first created his 'party of a new type' as an instrument to bring about socialism, the present central directors of such parties are now more inclined to see socialism (clause IV) as itself the means to secure irremovable and absolute dominion for their parties: 'Having once acquired political power, the working class implements the liquidation of the private ownership of the means of production. . . . As a result, under Socialism, there remains no ground for the existence of any opposition parties counterbalancing the Communist Party.' The whole document was published originally in the Moscow journal *Kommunist*, no. 3 (1972: 101–15). But this crucial passage is most easily found in *The Economist* (London) 17 June 1972: 23).

39 (London, George Allen & Unwin, 1896: 165); emphasis his.

40 (London, George Allen & Unwin, 1918: 23).

41 *TPTB*, p. 21.

42 See the files of any good newspaper for the week beginning 13 August 1973. Magee gives many examples of similar thinking in the British Labour Party (op. cit.: e.g.

11–12, 89–90, 99–100, and 107–8). There is perhaps an element of speculation in my interpretation of the distant mental processes of Mr Whitlam. The same could not be said of the case of the position of my former colleague Kai Nielsen, examined in pt II of my 'In Defence of Reformism', *Question 7* (London, Pemberton, 1974).

Notice, too, Jean-François Revel's *Without Marx or Jesus* (London, Paladin, 1972). The author of this admirably non-conformist work needs all the distinctions developed in the present section (2), yet appears to be unable himself to make any of them. See, if you doubt it, my review in the *New Humanist* (London) for August 1973.

43 *TPTB*, p. 7.
44 ibid., p. 27.
45 ibid., p. 74.
46 ibid., p. 9.
47 Bryan Magee, *Popper* (London, Fontana, 1973: 75). This excellent short work perhaps provides a better introduction than any of Popper's own more elaborate books to Popper's social ideas, especially to the connections between these social ideas, on the one hand, and the Popperian rationale for science, on the other. Russell himself had come much closer to this kind of integration of the practical-political with the theoretical-scientific by 1950 (cf. *UE*: 27–32).
48 Magee (op. cit.: 79).
49 See, however, n. 38 above; and consider the maybe false assumption which seems to have guided the leadership of the countries participating in the 1968 invasion of Czechoslovakia. They and their spokesmen throughout the world insisted, and still do insist, that the liberal reforms initiated by Alexander Dubcek and his associates were as near as makes no matter certain to result in the overthrow of socialism – unless checked in the nick of time by the tanks of normalisation!
50 Kautsky (op. cit.: 5). Of course, I am not suggesting that Kautsky was any sort of premature Popperian. For one thing, and it is only one thing, any sort of commitment to total socialism (clause IV) would presumably be seen by Popper as involving at least a hankering after 'Utopian social engineering'. Magee, wishing for his own reasons to make out that the Labour Party is not in this sense socialist, notwithstanding that as of now it quite obviously is, generates a gratuitous problem of understanding why Popper, who admittedly 'is no longer a socialist', fails, as Magee puts it, 'to accept in matters of practical politics, the radical consequences of his own ideas' (*Popper*: 84).
51 *TPTB*, pp. 28–9.
52 For an essay on these lines, see R. H. S. Crossman's *Plato Today* (London, George Allen & Unwin, rev. 2nd edn, 1959: ch. VIII). This is the same Crossman who was a leading Labour Party politician. The first edition was published in 1937, while Crossman was still a philosophy don at Oxford. It was a landmark in Platonic studies, treating 'the founder of the Academy not as the first academic but as a politician manqué' (p.7).
53 See, on Plato's psychiatric imperialism, my *Crime or Disease?* (London and New York, Macmillan; and Barnes and Noble, 1973: pt I).
54 Reported in *East Europe* (July 1957: 56). I owe this reference to Sidney Hook's *Political Power and Personal Freedom* (New York, Collier, 1962: 147). It would be mean not to share my own favourite, from a speech by the late Abdul Kharume, first Vice-President of Tanzania: 'Our Government is democratic because it makes its decisions in the interests of and for the benefit of the people. I wonder why men who are unemployed are surprised and resentful at the Government . . . sending them back to the land for their own advantage.' This was reported in the Dar-es-Salaam press on 8 July 1967. Mr Kharume, who has since been assassinated, was, as his Afro-Shirazi Party in Zanzibar still is, strongly influenced by advisers from the German Democratic Republic.
55 'There are, however, a few notoriously useless words – "democracy", for instance' (*Sense and Sensibilia*, Oxford, Clarendon Press, 1962: 127).
56 Kai Nielsen, 'Is Empiricism an Ideology?', *Metaphilosophy* (October 1972: 269, 270, and 271).

Since Nielsen proceeds to appeal to Marcuse, it is both fair and relevant to say that Marcuse makes it about as plain as he ever makes anything that his revolution requires 'the dictatorship of an élite over the people'. It is, indeed, for Marcuse a main grievance against the 'late capitalist' order that the despised majority not merely does not want, but has no interest in, the Marcusian revolution:

> By the same token, those minorities which strive for a change in the whole itself will . . . be left free to deliberate and discuss, to speak and to assemble . . . and will be left harmless and helpless in the face of the overwhelming majority. . . . The majority is firmly grounded in the increasing satisfaction of *needs*, and technological and mental co-ordination, which testify to the general helplessness of radical groups in a well-functioning social system. (H. Marcuse, B. Moore and R. Wolff, *A Critique of Pure Tolerance*, London, Cape, 1969: 107–8, 134; emphasis added).

For an examination of the appeal of Marxist ideas to impatient and authoritarian intellectuals, see L. S. Feuer, *Marx and the Intellectuals* (Garden City, NY., Doubleday Anchor, 1969).

57   *TPTB*, p. 58.

58   *PFM*, p. 13.

59   There are many editions in many languages; mine is volume 21 in the Little Lenin Library (New York, International Publishers, 1934). Trotsky's *Terrorism and Communism* was a contribution to the same controversy. This, too, is available in English edited by M. Shachtman (Ann Arbor, University of Michigan Press, 1961). Kautsky returned to the charge, several times.

60   Kautsky (op. cit.: 45).

61   ibid., p. 5.

62   The relevant volumes of Lenin's *Collected Works* are V–VII (Moscow, Foreign Languages Publishing House, 1961). My references to *What is to be Done?* are to the edition by S. V. Utechin (London, Panther, 1970).

63   *What is to be Done?*, pp. 163 ff., on the justification; and pp.185–6, on the happier conditions. Notice that at this stage Lenin was not, apparently, inclined to claim that such conspiratorial organisation is democratic; but rather that democratic organisation, however desirable, was not in the unfortunate conditions of Tsarist Russia practically possible.

64   *TPTB*, p. 128.

65   ibid., p. 22.

66   ibid., p. 70.

67   *Leninism or Marxism?* available in English, edited by B. D. Wolfe, bound up in one volume with *The Russian Revolution* (Ann Arbor; University of Michigan Press, 1961: 84–5).

68   ibid., p. 102.

69   It is, however, persuasively developed by Sidney Hook in ch. X of *The Hero in History* (New York, Humanities Press, 1943).

70   Preface to the 1st edition of *Capital*, quoted Kautsky (op. cit.: 98).

26

SOLIPSISTIC POLITICS:
RUSSELL'S EMPIRICIST LIBERALISM

Benjamin R. Barber

*In our day, as in the time of Locke, empiricist Liberalism is
the only philosophy that can be adopted by a man who . . .
demands some scientific evidence for his beliefs, and . . .
desires human happiness more than the prevalence of this or
that party or creed.* 'Philosophy and Politics', *Unpopular
Essays*)

Among the multiple products of Bertrand Russell's panoptic intelli-
gence, his writings on politics have been rather slighted. Admirers of his
analytic lucidity are content to celebrate his mathematical philosophy
and some of his later work in the philosophy of science and philosophy of
mind, while those stunned by his persona and touched by his moral
courage dwell on his life – his practical engagement in the great issues of
suffrage, pacifism, nuclear disarmament and world peace. Consequently, his political thought, falling somewhere between pure theory
and vigorous praxis, is often treated as a function of his journalism. The
political books, in this view, are a kind of tribute exacted by his political
principles, popular 'potboilers' (Russell's own term) to pay the bills that
academic emoluments might have met had he kept his politics to himself
and lived passively as a distinguished academic logician. A. J. Ayer,
thus, pays Russell's political thought little heed, passing over it entirely
in his *Russell and Moore* and just grazing it in the 'Moral Philosophy'
chapter in his *Modern Masters* account.

Nor can it be said that Russell's political writings evince the systematic continuity and relative immunity to time and topicality that might
attract permanent attention. The early works assail Bolshevism with a
spirit of ardent individualism, principled pacifism and a hint of anarchism. Later, power and authority emerge as dominant concepts, while the
quest for liberty seems overshadowed by the quest for peace – almost at
any cost. Each book thus seems to speak its own language, develop its
own inflections, create its own context depending on the relevant issues
of the day and the pertinent subject at hand. Each is to some degree a
livre d'occasion, although Russell's lively independence assures that the

livre is always a good deal less fashionable than the *occasion*. Finally, Russell's political theory may seem even to the sympathetic observer to be superficial, journalistic, inconsistent, eclectic and unoriginal – too often the hostage of Russell's practical engagements, too seldom addressed to the great discourse that defines the history of mankind's political thought.

Yet such a judgment would undervalue Russell's political writing egregiously. To begin with, charges of inconsistency and lack of continuity seem quite beside the point. The leaps that carried Russell from pacifism to humanistic patriotism, from visions of mutualist utopia to reluctant advocacy of American or Russian world hegemony in the name of survival were no more staggering and certainly (as I hope to show here) no less explicable than the leaps that carried him from early Platonism to scientific empiricism and, after a glancing encounter with mysticism, to radical empiricism, to scepticism and beyond.[1] A man who lives nearly 100 years, if his mind does not predecease his body, had better change his views several times – in politics and in metaphysics. There is nothing like a timely death to lend rigour and consistency to a life's work. Russell had to contend with staying alive, and by the time he was 90 consistency must have seemed to him less like the hobgoblin of little minds than the hallmark of a short life.

Moreover, although he was amply self-critical about many of his books, he took his political writing entirely seriously. He regarded the thesis of *Power* as being of great importance and was disappointed that, despite its popularity, it was not always treated with the seriousness he thought it deserved;[2] he testified repeatedly to the continuity of theory and praxis in his own life, observing in his contrived 'obituary' that Russell's 'principles were curious, but, such as they were, they governed his actions'.[3]

The continuity between his political theory and his philosophy was no less striking, which brings me to the intentions of this chapter. Perhaps the most unfortunate consequence of the neglect shown Russell's political thought has been the failure to perceive and understand the vital connection between his radical empiricism and his persistent liberalism. Russell was one of the last of that long line of British philosophers whose work epitomised the most dynamic and fruitful liaison of the modern era: the alliance of empiricism and liberalism. Perhaps he was even the last of the line, 'the last survivor of a dead epoch' as he mischievously suggests.[4] If we count Hobbes as a dubious forefather and trace the lineage from Locke and Berkeley down through Hume and Mill, then Russell is indeed the last empiricist liberal, the last to try to wring from the justificatory enterprise arguments that both describe the world and prescribe human conduct in the social setting, the last to try to render the metaphysics of sense experience consistent with the politics of liberty secured by power, the last to try to answer the question 'What can Man do?' by asking the question 'What can Man know?'

I want to argue that when we take Russell's self-appellation 'empiricist liberal' seriously, we provide a context for apprehending his political thought that both clarifies its essential liberalism and throws into sharp relief its relationship to the polarised premises of the empiricist metaphysic. I believe that many of the strengths and not a few of the deficiencies of liberal thought derive from the close kinship that ties the empirical and liberal traditions together in British philosophy and politics; and that Russell's political ideas are made comprehensible in their almost schizophrenic treatment of liberty and power when they are examined in the context of the interface between these traditions.

That Russell is a liberal requires elaboration rather than demonstration. He often depicted himself as a 'British Whig, with a British love of compromise and moderation',[5] though moderation was not, as I will argue, well served by his liberalism. In describing early liberalism in the *History of Western Philosophy*, he might almost be describing himself: 'early liberalism', he contends, 'was optimistic, energetic and philosophic . . . it appeared likely . . . to bring great benefits to mankind . . . it was opposed to everything medieval, both in philosophy and politics . . . the distinctive character of the whole movement [was] . . . individualism'.[6] The liberal political programme was in its major thrust Russell's political programme, its dilemmas were his dilemmas. Jean-Jacques Rousseau, in preparing to suggest a postliberal or transliberal resolution, nevertheless posed the dilemma in paradigmatic liberal terms: 'the problem', he states in *The Social Contract*, 'is to find a form of association which will defend and protect with the whole common force the person and goods of each associate, and in which each, while uniting himself with all, may still obey himself alone, and remain as free as before'.[7] This is the liberal programme, to accommodate conflict and ameliorate competition without surrendering individuality, to employ power in the service of liberty, to contain the aggressiveness that issues out of man's individuality without destroying the liberty that is individuality's chief virtue. In an early letter written during his visit to the nascent Soviet state, Russell perceives the liberal dilemma in movingly personal terms:[8]

I know that for collective action the individual must be turned into a machine . . . yet it is the individual soul that I love . . . its loneliness, its hopes and fears, its quick impulses and sudden advances. It is such a long journey from this to armies and officials; and yet it is only by making this journey that one can avoid a useless sentimentalism.

In *The Practice and Theory of Bolshevism*, he puts it with less agony but greater simplicity: 'Government and the law, in their very essence, consist of restrictions on freedom, and freedom is the greatest of political goals.'[9] Yet he is also clear (later, in *Power*) that 'there must be power, either that of governments or that of anarchical adventurers. There must even be naked power, so long as there are rebels against government, or even ordinary criminals'.[10] There must, in brief, be liberty – that is the end, the aim, the object of politics. Yet there must be power – for that is the essence, the substance, the *sine qua non* of politics. The natural issue of liberty, uncontained, is anarchism; the natural issue of power, uncontained, is dominion. The liberal dilemma is simply how to preserve liberty without falling into anarchy, how to use power without falling into dominion. 'Every community is faced with two dangers, anarchy and despotism . . . [both] are alike disastrous.'[11] Liberty denies power, but what, then, will deny anarchy? Power thwarts anarchy, but what, then, will thwart dominion?

Locke, chiding Hobbes for investing the Sovereign Leviathan with unlimited powers, warns of the injuries that Lions (sovereign states) may do to 'pole-cats and foxes' who are so foolish as to entrust their safety from one another's claws to the Lion's sovereign teeth. For while the Lion may save them from each other, who will save them from the Lion?[12] Anarchy or despotism – this polarity seems built into liberal theory, giving it its characteristic instability, its restlessness, its ambivalence towards both liberty (a virtue fraught with vice) and power (a vice that may serve virtue).

It might appear that power can, in liberal thought, never have any other end than the security of the individual and the guarantee of his liberty. 'It is the individual,' Russell is certain, 'in whom all that is good must be realized, and the free growth of the individual must be the supreme end of a political system which is to refashion the world.'[13] Yet the individual persons in whose name power is always exercised often seek power as an end in itself. They are closer to beasts than to gods; they are 'pole-cats and foxes', contentious and quarrelsome even in Locke's somewhat civilised gloss on Hobbesian man. Russell's conception, infused with Freudian irrationalism, is little different. Politics issue out of the needs of passion-impelled individuals, who are distinguishable from the beasts not by the transcending but only by the boundlessness of their desires. Whereas animal desires are specific and satiable, human desires are 'essentially boundless and incapable of complete satisfaction',[14] giving rise to adverse conditions that make politics both necessary and possible. From mankind's 'infinite desires', from its endless lust for power which, in a 'Titanic combination of nobility and impiety', drives it to attempt to 'be God', comes 'competition, the need of compromise and government, the impulse to rebellion . . . [and] the need of morality to restrain anarchic self-assertion'.[15]

The individual creature who lurks behind liberal political formulas is an awesome animal, evoking our approbation as he excites our fears. He is a 'wild beast' whose 'primitive lusts and egoisms' must be curbed,[16] but whose saving individuality must be cherished and protected. Contemplating the beast can lead a liberal to 'abandon political thinking as a bad job, and to conclude that the strong and ruthless must always exploit the weaker and kindlier'[17] – can lead him, in other words, to acknowledge dominion as man's natural fate. A part of Russell remained in permanent revolt against the ugliness of the portrait of man drawn by his Freudian realism. During the First World War and again in the 1930s he had to grapple with a paralysing despair that, as it suffused him with melancholia, nearly immobilised him. In a bitter letter, written during the height of Britain's war hysteria in 1917, he wrote: 'I hate the world and almost all the people in it . . . I hate the planet and the human race – I am ashamed to belong to such a species – And what is the good of me in that mood?'[18] Yet for a 'vigorous and temperamentally hopeful person',[19] for, in other words, a liberal, man the beast cannot entirely eclipse man the individual. Indeed, it is precisely the hope of liberal politics that the individual can be rescued from the beast, that through the skilful utilisation of man's capacity for power his lust for power can be contained. Government, for Russell, as for his liberal predecessors, is an artifice of necessity occasioned by the collision of power-seeking men with one another, with – it might almost be said – their own natures. It is calculated to secure natural individuality by restraining individualism (anarchy). It is thus always prudential, a manipulative instrument in the service of minimalist objectives like security, justice (narrowly construed) and conservation, rather than a creative vehicle for achieving progress or promoting welfare or uncovering a public weal.[20]

Consequently, Russell's liberalism tends to be only incidentally egalitarian – interested in justice but indifferent to democracy *per se*. Nineteenth-century aristocrat that he was, he had little patience with the masses. He shared completely John Stuart Mill's distrust of the 'few wise and many foolish individuals called the public',[21] warning in his essay 'The Need for Political Scepticism', that 'an honest politician will not be tolerated by a democracy unless he is very stupid . . . because only a very stupid man can honestly share the prejudices of more than half the nation'.[22] His cynicism is even more extravagant in *Power*, where he notes that 'the most successful democratic politicians are those who succeed in abolishing democracy and becoming dictators'.[23] If power is always perilous, popular power unchecked by wisdom, prudence or limits on its exercise is positively devastating. Majoritarianism has never held any inherent appeal for ambivalence-ridden liberal advocates of power (in its place) like Mill, de Tocqueville, Ortega y Gasset or Walter Lippmann. It should not, then, be surprising to find that it held no appeal for Russell, whose natural inclination towards contemplation conjoined with his liberal focus on individuality tainted his professed egalitarianism from the outset. Dispositional élitism linked with radical individualism is hardly a formula likely to precipitate democracy. Keeping his tongue out of his cheek. Russell reminded readers in *In Praise of Idleness* that the leisure class, whatever economic oppressions and political tyrannies it may have fostered,[24] contributed nearly the whole of what we call civilization. It cultivated the arts and discovered the sciences; it wrote the books, invented the philosophies and refined social relations . . . without the leisure class, man never would have emerged from barbarism.

The few, it would seem, save the many from themselves, and thus preserve the best in mankind from the worst. Individuality is threatened by the plurality of individuals, necessitating the forms of power and control; but power, exercised plurally (i.e. democratically), continues to threaten individuality and the excellence upon which civilisation depends. Thus, individualism is, in the typical liberal fashion, pitted against itself, adumbrating the tension between quality and equality that has characterised all liberal-democratic régimes.

Self-contradiction is also built into the liberal idea of power: the beast who is father to the individual needs to be both tamed (controlled by power) and preserved (insulated from power). Politics is human zoo-keeping of a particularly delicate nature where too many cages, though they keep the animals from one another, destroy their natural character, while too few, though uninhibiting to be sure, unleash the beasts upon one another. Power in its liberal manifestation is thus the means by which it curbs itself as an end, the device arising out of desire that permits desire to be limited; it coerces in order to free, and so serves man's individuality by subduing man's will.

These contradictions and ambiguities can be found everywhere in Russell's liberalism. To some degree, his entire political career – the whole of his political thought – is devoted to a largely unsuccessful search for answers to the Confucian riddle from Lao-tzu that serves as the epigraph to his early *Roads to Freedom*: 'Production without possession, action without self-assertion, development without domination . . .' And, one might add, excellence without inequality, individuality without anarchy, and power without dominion; how to use power to emancipate man from the yoke of nature's scarcity and from his own insatiable desires (of which scarcity is but nature's reflection) and yet prevent his enslavement to the instruments of his liberation? How to preserve freedom by curtailing it? Where to find a lion bold enough to contain the strife of pole-cats yet mild enough to trust? These are dilemmas that arise at every step in the development of Russell's liberal thought and which, I believe, are endemic to the liberal way of thinking about politics. I am suggesting, then, that Russell is a liberal not simply because he is an individualist and an instrumentalist who sees in politics a necessary but dangerous instrument of prudential power, but because for him the road to freedom is always paved with power, and thus its own worst impediment; he is a liberal because he can find no middle ground between anarchy and despotism, for all his temperamental moderation; he is a liberal because democracy strikes him as being more necessary than desirable; he is a liberal because power draws him with an awesomeness than horrifies him, defines man's nature with a decisiveness that appals him, captures the purposes of human life with a finality that fills him with despair. His life is a struggle with, for and about power: the need to express, to do, to change, to manipulate, to cause, to overcome and to liberate. 'Power over people's minds,' he writes, in the second volume of the *Autobiography*, 'is the main personal desire of my life.'[25] The goal may be liberty, but power, finally, is what politics is all about – in the political world of the liberal.

The argument I am pursuing requires, however, a good deal more than merely depicting the dilemmas of liberalism as they manifest themselves in Russell's political thought. I have suggested that the form taken by liberalism may reflect the shape of empiricism, and if this is so then there ought to be a significant relationship between the liberal dichotomisation of liberty and power and elements in the empiricist metaphysic.

Empiricism was in part a response to and a concomitant of the disappointment with rationalism, with naturalism and with revelation that attended the emergence of modern science. Revelation was mired in superstition and authoritarianism; naturalism had been too generous with its favours, giving sustenance to far too many divergent normative systems under the indeterminate name of 'descriptive nature'; reason, as an active faculty seeking out the forms of external reality, was declared unfit either to inspire discovery or to certify knowledge. Sense experience, on the other hand, although it narrowed our notions of what was to qualify as knowledge, extended our epistemological confidence in the status of what could be known. The observational method engineered by the early empiricists penetrated the world by withdrawing from it, enlarged the realm of intersubjective communication by restricting the realm of communicative discourse. Reason was appropriately devalued, reduced to an instrument of ratiocination without the power to apprehend, to posit or to evaluate.

Russell was, in these somewhat overstated terms, a complete empiricist. In *Human Knowledge*, he writes, 'individual percepts are the basis of all our knowledge, and no method exists by which we can begin with data which are public to many observers'.[26] Although he was increasingly sceptical, over his lifetime, about the ontological status of the external world, he was certain even in his more confident moments that its existence depended on 'unobservable entities' that could only be inferred (at best) from percepts.

The pertinent question is, then: what sorts of common patterns are to be found (if any) in Russell's empiricism and in his dilemma-strewn liberalism? I am not solely concerned here with the well-discussed parallels of such metaphorically linked pairs as logical atomism and individualism, mechanistic reductionism and the state of nature, or physical mechanics and psychological hedonism (see Hobbes), albeit these do illuminate vital features of the relationship between liberalism and empiricism and impinge on my argument at several points. I want rather to get at those features of empiricism that may help to illuminate and perhaps even account for the central polarity between liberty and power (anarchy and dominion) that I have depicted as the chief dilemma of liberalism. I believe I can demonstrate with some force that empiricism is itself characterised by a deep psychological (and perhaps logical) ambivalence towards certainty and mankind's capacity to know the world that mirrors to some degree the dichotomic elements in the liberal dilemma; and that Russell's empiricism was particularly inclined to this ambivalence in ways that help to illuminate the ambiguity of his attitudes towards liberty and power. For the purposes of this chapter, I will be satisfied if I can suggest certain striking parallels in the conceptual structures of empiricism and liberalism. Whether these parallels reflect a causal interplay between the two, either historically or psychologically, is beyond the resources of my argument. None the less, if the argument as advanced here can be sustained, there may be good reason to entertain some form of causal interaction, at least as a provocative hypothesis.

The ambivalence towards uncertainty that I have claimed is endemic to empiricism issues directly and, I believe, unavoidably, out of its methodological solipsism – its preoccupation with subjective sense-data as the necessarily privatistic starting-point for all knowledge. For solipsism is psychologically disposed towards both passivity and aggression. It proclaims its humility ('All knowledge is subjective') in the language of hubris ('Subjective knowledge is *all* the knowledge there is'). I believe that in the interplay of humility and hubris in the empiricist metaphysic lie vital clues to the interplay of liberty and power in liberal political thought; and I suspect that Russell's outlook will reveal a common pattern in the two forms of interplay.

Solipsism's inclination towards humility appears to be a psychological reflection of certain logical features in its philosophical structure. Sensory experience is, to begin with, very much a trap: it not only closes persons off from the 'real world' that percepts can only project inferentially, but also denies them direct access to the experiential content of other persons' percepts. In Russell's description of Locke's empiricism:[27]

we cannot know of the existence of other people, or of the physical world, for these, if they exist, are not merely ideas in my mind. Each one of us, accordingly, must, so far as knowledge is concerned, be shut up in himself, and cut off from all contact with the outer world.

We can know what others experience only as mediated by our own experience, which is to say we can never really *know* what others experience. This paradox belongs to Russell as well as to Locke. Ultimately it compels him to conclude, in the closing paragraph of *Human Knowledge*, that 'all human knowledge is uncertain, inexact, and partial. To this doctrine we have not found any limitation whatsoever.'[28] This bleak conclusion, rendered inevitable by methodological solipsism's lack of ontological confidence in the self, is radically discomfiting in its implications. It leads Russell eventually to adopt a position 'not unlike that of Berkeley', but far more depressing because it is 'without his God and his Anglican complacency'.[29] Humility is eventually converted into desperation, as depression becomes dismay. 'Solipsism', he recalls in the *Autobiography*, in a passage redolent of Carl Becker:[30]

> oppressed me [during the early 1930s] . . . it seemed that what we had thought of as laws of nature were only linguistic conventions, and that physics was not really concerned with an external world. I do not mean that I quite believed this, but that it became a haunting nightmare.

Russell summed up the nightmare in a 'pessimistic meditation' written at Telegraph House during this period. Its almost nihilistic tone is worth citing at length:[31]

> The revolutions of nebulae, the birth and death of stars, are no more than convenient fictions in the trivial work of linking together my own sensations, and perhaps those of other men not much better than myself. No dungeon was ever constructed so dark and narrow as that in which the shadow physics of our time imprisons us, for every prisoner has believed that outside his walls a free world existed; but now the prison has become the whole universe. There is darkness without, and when I die there will be darkness within. There is no splendour, no vastness, anywhere; only triviality for a moment, and then nothing.
> Why live in such a world? Why even die?

Yet if solipsism issued in scepticism and promoted a dark, despairing passivity, if it was finally a 'dead end' (as Russell suggested in the *History of Western Philosophy*)[32] terminating in nihilism, it was also capable of nourishing assertiveness. In denying our capacity ever to know directly the external world other than through the subjective senses, it brought the self, the subjective perceptor, into new prominence – not, as happened with idealism, as a metaphysical surrogate for the world, but as a methodological avenue leading back into the world. In this, it promised that modesty might have its rewards, that epistemological humility might actually facilitate scientific conquest. Abjuring the epistemologies of revelation and rational naturalism had, after all, had as its aim the enhancement of certainty, not the cultivation of scepticism. Traditional epistemology, for all its bold claims, had finally stood in the way of mastery over nature. As Russell noted late in his philosophical career, 'it is not by prayer and humility that you cause things to go as you wish, but by acquiring a knowledge of natural laws . . . the power to be acquired in this way is very much greater than the power that men formerly sought to achieve by theological means'.[33] If methodological solipsism provoked a certain scepticism, more often it seemed to generate hubris. At the time he wrote *The Problems of Philosophy* (1912), Russell was still confident enough of the existence of the external world to warn against the dangers of assertive solipsism in the most dramatic terms:[34]

> Greatness of the soul is not fostered by those philosophies which assimilate the universe to Man . . . there is a widespread philosophical tendency towards the view which tells us that Man is the measure of all things, that truth is man-made, that space and time and the world of universals are properties of the mind, and that, if there be anything not created by the mind, it is unknowable and of no account to us. This view is . . . untrue [and] has the effect of robbing philosophic contemplation of all that gives it value, since it fetters contemplation to Self.

While Russell was clearly concerned in this passage with forms of subjectivist idealism, his strictures apply with equal force to subjectivist empiricism; for empiricism affects to know the world by reducing it to a measure of the self even narrower than idealism's *a priori* ideas, namely, sensations or percepts. Indeed, the solipsism that he assails in *The Problems of Philosophy* is the solipsism to which he falls prey in the 1930s. And although science is probably better understood as a continuation of common sense than as a continuation of philosophy,[35] the roots of its modern successes are to be discovered at least in part in the power of solipsistic empiricism, with its disposition towards mastering the world by assimilating it to criteria precipitated by the atomic, sensory self. Its boldness arose not simply out of faith in induction or, as Popper claims, the decisive potency of falsification, but out of its preoccupation with sense observations, with percepts as basic data, with a reading of the world taken in the first instance through the senses or instrumental (technological) extensions of the senses. It was, in sum, not induction but observation, not verification (or falsification) but sense perception, not the positing of objectivity but a surrender to subjectivity that made possible the rise of an aggressive, manipulative science.

If methodological solipsism is as disposed, as an attitude, to certainty as to scepticism, as disposed, practically, to mastery as to abdication, then although 'the external world may be an illusion . . . [and] order, unity and continuity . . . human inventions just as truly as are catalogues and encyclopedias' (solipsism as scepticism), nevertheless, 'human inventions can, within limits, be made to prevail in our human world' (solipsism as mastery).[36]

Empiricism's ambivalence – the paradox of solipsism – thus comes full circle. Man exerts ever-greater control, thanks to empiricism, over a world which, thanks to empiricism, disappears before his inquiring eyes.

The cosmos is mastered by techniques arising out of the premiss that it cannot be shown to exist, and the more effectively it is mastered the less warrant there is for believing it does exist. So that we finally arrive at the ultimate irony of Hiroshima where forces known to us only as abstractions, resting on a physics that wrests from philosophers the last vestiges of a belief in the existence of an orderly external world, none the less manage to lay waste a city, decide a world war, and revolutionise the course of human history – threatening, as it were, to reunite us in mundane practice with the nothingness to which our scepticism commits us in metaphysical theory. Russell, his life fairly swimming in such ironies, thus feels compelled by modern physics both to abandon all philosophical certitude about the world *and* to plunge nobly into the world to save it from the practical consequences of the self-same physics that has inspired his doubts.

In one of those frequent jeremiads with which he tempered his natural optimism, he went so far as to suggest that solipsism was a form of insanity.[37] Russell's primary target was idealism, but there is also a sense in which solipsistic empiricism seems to move towards insanity at both ends of its ambivalence: towards the insanity of nihilism as it moves towards scepticism (where 'the lunatic who believes he is a poached egg is to be condemned solely on the ground that he is in a minority'),[38] towards the insanity of annihilation as it moves towards mastery (where 'unless power can be tamed . . . all must die').[39] The two extremes converge somewhere in the realm of nothingness, nihilism insisting there is nothing as annihilation guarantees that there will be nothing. The empirical approach has, of course, resisted these extremes; it aspires to a common sensical moderation that can secure it against the excesses to which it is logically disposed. Yet the empiricist metaphysic that has nourished both scepticism and science appears inherently unstable, forever on the verge of lunacy, seemingly unable to accommodate notions that are life-affirming but non-imperial, that are modest yet immune to nihilism. Indeed, methodological solipsism has been as incapable of moderation in resisting the twin lunacies of nihilism and annihilation as liberal political theory has in resisting anarchy or despotism. And that is precisely the point of this comparative exercise: for it is here that the metaphysic of empiricism and the political theory of liberalism exhibit certain decisive parallels suggesting that significant interface hinted a earlier.

To put it more provocatively, what they seem to share is a common insanity – the more tellingly ironic in the light of their common claim to reasonable moderation – defined by an incapacity to occupy the middle ground, to elude the seductiveness of logical extremes, to adduce epistemological or political constructs appropriate to the middling realities of the common human condition. In both cases, methodological solipsism gives to the subjective self a paramountcy that leads either to the total denial of an external, law-governed world, or to its assimilation and conquest – nihilism or annihilation in the metaphysic and its philosophical-scientific precipitates, anarchy or despotism in the politics. It might even be said that the quest for certainty, the attempt to buy verifiability by surrendering intelligibility, the substitution of epistemology for ontology, the entire enterprise of trying to overcome the world by knowing it in some limited but certain way, *is* in its political expression the quest for power, for order, for security and for dominion; and that, by the same token, the flight into scepticism, into particularism, into subjectivity, *is* in its political expression the flight into anarchism, radical individualism and a nearly misanthropic self-sufficiency.

Confronted with the world as 'whirl', the sensory self in whom the empiricist reposes total epistemological confidence can only deny it by deeming it unknowable and, thus, without ontological status, or overcome it by conjuring science from patterns arising out of percepts. What it apparently cannot do is to live in and with the world in noetic eqilibrium, able to apprehend without dominating, able to doubt without negating. Confronted with other humans, the atomistic, self-sufficient self in whom the liberal reposes an equivalent political confidence can only deny them by asserting its own solitary freedom, or overcome them by obtaining total dominion over them. What it cannot do is to live in and with fellow humans in social equilibrium, able to maintain autonomy without surrendering mutuality, able to secure order without risking despotism. Indeed, it would sometimes seem that what distinguishes liberalism is that where other approaches to the political have been concerned to show how men do, or ought to, live together with one another in just polities, the liberal has tried to show that they can live only alone (the state of nature) or under sovereign dominion – in splendid libertarian isolation (suggested by such liberal constructs as 'privacy', 'natural rights' and 'freedom' itself), or in chains (suggested by terms such as 'sovereignty', 'power' and 'sanction').

Just as scepticism and mastery are natural tendencies in an epistemology rooted in individual sense perception, so anarchy and despotism are natural tendencies in a political philosophy rooted in individual hedonism and private interest. Solipsistic imperialism reflects the same consciousness, the same climate of opinion, the same unstable attitude towards certainty, whether it expresses itself in the sovereign artifices of empirical science or the sovereign artifices of the liberal state; and solipsistic scepticism reflects the same doubts, the same particularistic subjectivity, whether it is recommending epistemological humility or dictating liberty, privacy and tolerance. In this sense, to describe Russell as an empiricist liberal may even verge on redundance; in this sense, his liberalism and his empiricism become inseparable facets of a single approach to the human condition; in this sense, the dilemmas of knowledge expressed by Russell the philosopher converge with the dilemmas of politics expressed by Russell the political theorist.

Having said this much, I must add that I can hardly conceive of a more provocative or controversial way to treat Russell's political thought: it is at once too neat and too perverse, too all-encompassing and too idiosyncratic. Yet, I want to suggest, what may seem incautious as interpretation turns out to be Russell's own mode of expression. For in describing the politics of liberty and the politics of power, Russell himself liquidates the conventional barriers that keep politics and epistemology apart even more decisively than I have done above. It may be useful, then, before trying to measure the consequences of these dilemmas and posit certain alternatives, to devote some space to a more careful and textually illuminating treatment of Russell's own understanding of the relationship between power politics and freedom politics and the empiricist epistemology.

The relationship between power and manipulative science is a theme throughout Russell's work, but is perhaps most clearly stated in *The Scientific Outlook*, where Russell advances the blunt claim that 'scientific thought . . . is essentially power thought';[40] this is so because 'the fundamental impulse to which [scientific thought] appeals is the love of power . . . the desire to be the cause of as many and as large effects as possible'.[41] The equation is simple enough: power is the production of intended effects (as defined in *Power*), while science is the art of understanding how to produce effects. Science is thus a critical mode in the exercise of power. Perhaps even more significantly, it lends to the 'natural' human quest for power a 'new ruthlessness' born of 'intoxication' with its modern technological possibilities.[42]

Science, regarded as knowledge in the service of mastery over nature, hence becomes a direct extension of man's aggressive nature, defined (in Russell's Freudian-Hobbesian imagery) by insatiable and boundless desires and an interminable quest for 'power after power that ceaseth only in death'. It seems to me noteworthy that Russell, despite the changing contexts and evolving concerns of many different books, managed to make power the central element in every definition of human nature he proferred over a period of half of a century. In *Roads to Freedom* he cites 'competitiveness, love of power and envy' as the defining traits of humanity;[43] in *The Practice and Theory of Bolshevism*, 'acquisitiveness, vanity, rivalry, and love of power' are the 'basic instincts';[44] in *Marriage and Morals*, 'power, sex, and parenthood' are decisive; and of these, 'power begins first and ends last';[45] and in *Power*, not surprisingly, it is the impulse to power and to glory that rank first. Power and envy, power and vanity, power and sex, power and glory – but always power, always the unquenchable thirst to drink from the fountains of the gods. Power not only provided the key to human nature, it defined the character of social relations. 'The laws of social dynamics are only capable of being stated in terms of power in its various forms', he wrote in an early section of *Power*, hoping to combat the authority of economists, lawyers and idealists who were foolish enough to think that utilities, legal institutions or ideas could somehow sufficiently convey the essence of politics.[46] Indeed, to Russell the book on power constituted a significant attempt to convince social scientists that 'power, rather than wealth, should be the basic concept in social theory', a claim he had first started making decades earlier in *The Practice and Theory of Bolshevism*.[47]

There was, of course, in all of this a typical liberal ambiguity. Power might, in one sense, be an undesirable perversion of man's nature, and science, in consequence, a catalyst of unsavoury transmutations. Yet it was also a necessary feature of man's condition and a defining aspect of the political process and, thus, could hardly be regarded as entirely perverse or wholly undesirable – particularly in the absence of some such preliberal or illiberal notion as original sin. Power was, after all, an object in Russell's own life, though presumably only as a means. The attempt to distinguish between power as a means and as an end is at the core of the liberal ambivalence about power. Hobbes had commenced, innocently enough, with an apparently instrumental definition stipulating that power was merely 'a present means to obtain some future good', but eventually went on to imply far darker forces, suggesting mankind was destined to 'a perpetual and restless desire of power after power, that ceaseth only in death'.[48] Power as a prudential facilitator confronted power as a kind of deontological lust with no other end than its own sprawling perpetuation: neither Hobbes nor his liberal successors seemed able quite to reconcile the two. Russell is at pains to distinguish 'power desired as a means and power desired as an end in itself', but never seems altogether certain which of the two is endemic to human nature. He would prefer it to be the former, but his own portrait of human psychology, human history and human politics can only persuade us that it is the latter. In *The Practice and Theory of Bolshevism* he acknowledged that power was being used as a means to desirable ends by the young Soviet state, but feared the means might too easily become the ends. The intelligent utilisation of concentrated power was indisputably vital if the sort of socialist organisation 'essential to the progress and happiness of mankind' was to be obtained;[49] yet the transition held 'appalling dangers', for it risked unleashing the 'wild beast' and giving a 'free rein to the primitive lusts and egoisms which civilization to some degree curbs.[50] Power as a means was energised by the lust for power as an end, and thus could never be conjured into use in the service of civilisation without fear of awakening the beast that civilisation aspired to tame. In *The Semblance of Peace*, Yeats wrote:

> Civilization is hoped together, brought
> Under a rule, under the semblance of peace,
> By manifold illusion.

What was illusory, if Russell's account of human nature is to be our guide, is the hope that the beastly in man (power) can somehow subdue the beast – that power can be its own remedy. Not that Russell ever had a great deal of confidence in the forces indwelling in the human heart. Drawn to darkly impassioned writers like Lawrence and Conrad, he had continually to resist the seductions of an anguished morbidity about man's fate. Too often, his anatomy of the human soul portrayed eyes glinting with avarice and envy, a will yearning for power, and a heart shrouded in darkness.[51] The perennial optimist in Russell was forever averting his eyes, but despair always remained at the periphery of his field of vision. In his blacker moods, science seemed to him not only to enhance power, but to threaten a world of perverse insanities. In *The Scientific Outlook*, he left readers with a dismal prophecy anticipating the very worst:[52]

> Gradually the world will grow more dark and more terrible. Strange perversions of instinct will first lurk in dark corners and then gradually overwhelm men in high places. Sadistic pleasures will not suffer the moral condemnation that will be meted out to the softer joys . . . in the end such a system will break down either in an orgy of bloodshed or in the rediscovery of love.

Moreover, the only consolation likely to be available in the grim age to come is chemical mesmerisers that will induce the population to 'bear whatever its scientific masters may decide to be for its good'. 'All these', Russell concludes, 'are possibilities in a world governed by knowledge without love, and power without delight'.[53] Even in the period of *Marriage and Morals*, he could 'foresee the time when all who care for the freedom of the human spirit will have to rebel against a scientific tyranny',[54] and by the time he wrote *The Scientific Outlook* this prospect had become a 'real danger'. For although 'the impulse towards scientific construction is admirable when it does not thwart any of the major impulses that give value to human life . . . [when] it is allowed to forbid all outlet to everything but itself it becomes a form of cruel tyranny'.[55]

For all its dangers, however, there is no eluding power: to act in the world, to treat effectively with the human condition, is to use power, to rely on science as a means to other human ends. The love of power is, after all, a part of normal human nature, and neither can nor ought to be wholly shunned. Prudently used, power can not only remake the world, but remake mankind as well. The beastly is ultimately capable of doing more than taming the beast: it may extirpate it. Here, Russell the neo-Freudian pessimist faces Russell the liberal optimist, the advocate of man's perfectibility. Beastly though it may be, human nature is not for Russell 'a fixed datum, but a product of circumstances, education and opportunity operating upon a highly malleable native disposition'.[56] Without a notion of malleability, human nature would represent an incurable disease rather than a compound of malignant and benign potentialities. Without it, Russell's own political involvements would have been absurd, and the idea purveyed implicitly in late writings like *Unarmed Victory* and *Common Sense and Nuclear Warfare* that individuals can make a difference in an international process that is for the most part regarded as exclusively power-responsive would have been unthinkable. However rooted in desire, lust and compulsion human affairs might be, Russell had to conclude, along with liberal predecessors like J. S. Mill, that moral suasion, rational argument and liberal education could have an effect upon them. Science, used for ends other than itself, was once again the model. If the world was governed by necessity and a set of fixed laws extending even to man's own nature, man none the less was capable of rising above necessity and directing his own evolution by acquiring knowledge. To cite a passage alluded to earlier, 'it is not by prayer and humility that you cause things to go as you wish, but by acquiring a knowledge of natural laws'.[57]

The essence of this form of power remains manipulation, but manipulation for ends other than power itself. It is rather power used to secure liberty, power used to overcome necessity, power used to civilise man, power used to move man away from power towards perfection. It is not man insisting he *is* God, as pure solipsism suggests, but man aspiring to *become* that which is godly in him.

This less nefarious form of prudentialism cannot, however, entirely escape solipsism. When it is contrasted with classical thought in its focus on contemplation and its wariness of the sense world of unfounded opinion (*doxa*), or with Christian thought pointed towards the other-worldly and distrustful of human pride and its propelling hubris, even a restrained instrumentalism with humanistic goals appears arrogant. Liberal politics may employ power only to curb it, may manipulate human nature only to rescue the best in it from the worst, may command men only to liberate them, but it still refuses to leave the world alone; it still confronts human imagination and human understanding as tools designed to conquer the world. Whether expressed in prudential or deontological language, the modes of thought that have pervaded scientific understanding and political action in the post-Renaissance world have been action, assertion, aggression, manipulation, conquest and mastery – the active self seeking to gratify itself while satisfying the claims of other self-gratifiers, the active mind overcoming the senselessness of a sense-mediated world by erecting a manipulative science on precisely those percepts that have rendered the world senseless. These are the parallel products of solipsistic empiricism's assertive side.

Solipsism, as I have argued, has another side as well. Radical empiricism promotes the self as sense perceptor, but it also denies the external world – the objective world of other. Hubris issues naturally out of the promotion of self, but scepticism tends to follow a thoughtful contemplation of the denial of the world. Scepticism and doubt, introduced into the political realm, offer alternatives to power and manipulation, and give to liberalism its defining libertarian colour. John Stuart

Mill states the political consequences of sceptical fallibilism in this way:[58]

> that mankind are not infallible; that their truths, for the most part, are only half-truths; that unity of opinion, unless resulting from the fullest and freest comparison of opposite opinions, is not desirable, and diversity not an evil, but a good, until mankind are much more capable than at present of recognizing all sides of the truth, are principles applicable to men's mode of action, not less than to their opinions.

If we can never know with certainty, we have no right to compel with authority; if reason is incapable of apprehending truth, then politics cannot legislate truth by fiat; if there is no philosophical warrant for maintaining that there *is* a world, there can surely be none for dogmatic assertions about what the world is or ought to be like. The fatal admission 'I could be wrong' entails the principle 'the enforcement of right is unjustified'. If, as Hume says, 'moral distinctions are not the offspring of reason', then reasonable men will be tolerant, pluralistic and open-minded – distrustful of governments that speak in the name of right, sympathetic with minimalist constructions of political authority. In Russell's own words, the quasi-sceptical confession that 'almost all knowledge . . . is in some degree doubtful . . . [has] in the sphere of practical politics . . . important consequences' that include tolerance, an unwillingness to inflict present pain in the name of future good, a bias against violent coercion in the settlement of disputes, and other similar liberal values.[59]

The contention that empiricism in its fallibilist manifestations is linked with liberalism in its minimalist inclinations is not an unfamiliar one. Karl Popper, whose understanding of empiricism is radically fallibilist, transforms scepticism into a foundation for the politics of the open society. One bite from the apple of knowledge may nourish pride and corrupt the species, but eating the fruit whole, Popper seems to say, has the opposite effect: for full knowledge reveals only its own limits, while reason exposes its own bankruptcy, leaving us finally only certain that we must forever live with uncertainty.[60] The only fit habitat for a race confronting in perpetuity the reality of its meagre noetic capacities is an open society where neither dogma nor authority is permitted to legislate what reason shows can never be known. Russell notes pointedly that Locke, 'who first developed in detail the empiricist theory of knowledge, preached also religious toleration, representative institutions, and the limitations of governmental power by the system of checks and balances'.[61] 'Order without authority,' he concludes, 'can be taken as the motto both of science and Liberalism.' Minimalist politics justified only to the extent that they serve liberty and private interest, representative institutions that permit numbers to adjudicate what reason cannot determine, and sufficient tolerance, diversity and constitutionalism to hem in public authority and safeguard the individual upon whom the system is erected: these are the only political measures warranted by a temperate scepticism whose goal is order without authority.

It must, of course, be said that Russell never wavers in thinking that scepticism is politically viable only when informed by temperateness. In a passage that captures fully his sense of the correspondence between epistemology and politics, he writes:[62]

> the temper that is required to make a success of democracy is, in the practical life, exactly what the scientific temper is in the intellectual life; it is a half-way house between scepticism and dogmatism. Truth, it holds, is neither completely obtainable, nor completely unattainable; it is attainable only to a certain degree, and that only with difficulty.

Yet, as I have tried to argue, liberal politics no more lends itself to temperateness than methodological solipsism lends itself to noetic equilibrium. However attractive a median point may be, there is no logical stopping-place between dogma and scepticism once knowledge has been reduced to private sensory experience and politics has been reduced to the science of power in paradoxical pursuit of liberty (and the science of liberty in paradoxical pursuit of power). Russell himself had no easy time holding the middle ground. In his youth he was drawn to anarchism, in his senatorial years he acquiesced increasingly in the necessity of power – even naked power – in the quest for an orderly international system that could guarantee human survival.[63] When Robert Paul Wolff concluded in his essay on violence that 'philosophical anarchism is true' because 'there is not, and there could not be, a state that has a right to command and whose subjects have a binding obligation to obey,' he is doing no more than carrying scepticism to its logical political extreme (although he is not, as I have argued elsewhere, carrying it to its politically logical end).[64]

Scepticism is infectious, as Hume well understood: those who deploy it to undermine an adversary authority soon find that it destroys their own advocacy as well. The aim is to curb authority, but the result is the annihilation of all legitimacy and thus of even minimal order. Every minimalist notion of politics that views mutuality as a form of evil but necessary submission is inclined to anarchy; every instrumentalist notion of politics that conceives power as a means to security, and government as the only barrier between man and his defining bestiality, is inclined to despotism. A theory that insists on both notions is hopelessly schizophrenic – torn between incompatible strategies aimed simultaneously at libertarian independence and a power-forged orderliness. It is the liberal heritage out of which Marx and Lenin come that accounts for their conflicted approach to power and liberty; and what is true for Marx is more decisively true for liberals like Mill and Russell.

Russell's liberal schizophrenia leaves out the very moderation to which he aspires; it makes impossible that half-way house which he rightly sees as indispensable to liberal-democratic politics. Finally, Russell's liberalism omits politics itself, understood as a collaborative activity manifesting man's social inclinations and serving the common ends of justice and the public weal. For all its humanistic rhetoric, and despite the considerable success of the institutions whose experience it reflects, it has left modern man with a legacy of discontent. Its predisposition towards anarchy has manifested itself in practice as anomie; its preoccupation with asocial liberty has precipitated an estrangement that has alienated men both from their fellows and from the public identity as citizens; its refusal to develop public norms in the face of metaphysical uncertainty has left man as a social being without standards, vulnerable alike to meaninglessness and authoritarianism defenceless in the face of heteronomy, contingency and mere accident; its fascination with power both as a means and as an expression of the species' defining self-assertiveness has run the twin risks of megalomania and subservience. Without norms, without a legitimate notion of public justice, how can power have any other issue than dominion? Without a concept of mutuality, without common goals, how can liberty produce anything but misanthropy, envy, greed and war? Scepticism and mastery, liberty and power, can create passive, solitary loners or secure slaves (though some think themselves masters), innocent misanthropes or craven followers in pursuit of craven masters.[65] But they cannot create citizens, and without citizens there can be no politics, no middle ground, no treating with reality as a temperate mundanity that eschews both dogma and scepticism, both anarchy and dominion. If men are to be regarded as something more than beasts and something less than gods, there is no room for empiricist liberalism's ambivalent polarities. Politics demands a different mode of thought.

Russell is more sensitive to this line of argument than his liberalism might suggest. Like Hume, who recognised that scepticism can be thought but not lived, Russell regarded it as 'logically impeccable' but 'psychologically impossible'. 'Knowing and feeling,' he writes in *The Scientific Outlook*, 'are equally essential ingredients both in the life of the individual and that of the community.'[66] As John Stuart Mill had once been drawn to Coleridge, so Russell was drawn to Conrad and to Lawrence. Part of him remained in permanent rebellion against the austere logic of scepticism, compliantly yielding to the seduction of passions he could none the less not quite trust. Love of power and the irrational quest for dominion were, after all, affective expressions of the passionate soul no less than compassion or friendship. 'If social life,' he warns in *Power*, 'is to satisfy social desires, it must be based upon some philosophy not derived from love of power'[67] – no easily filled prescription for Russell, since materialism, idealism and pragmatism all appeared to him to be power philosophies. The problem is how to generate a politics of love, of community and of justice that is immune to both anarchy and dominion – a politics that will neither permit power to overwhelm liberty nor permit liberty to undermine mutuality. While Russell aspires to a solution, the dichotomies springing from his empiricist perspective make it difficult for him to conceptualise the issue in any but polar terms; which, naturally, aggravates the problem still further. His dilemma is evident in *The Scientific Outlook*, where he writes:[68]

> it is only in so far as we renounce the world as its lovers that we can conquer it as technicians. But this division of the soul is fatal to what is best in man. As soon as the failure of science as metaphysic is realized, the power conferred by science as technique is only obtainable by something analogous to the worship of Satan, that is to say, the renunciation of love.

To live in the world, Russell seems to say, is to master it; but we pay for our mastery with our souls. To love in the world is to leave the world alone; but we pay for our abstinence with frustration and impotence. He can offer only the choice between an impotent if reverent passivity – an unproductive anarchy that will not sustain life – or an aggressive manipulativeness that in the pursuit of efficient productivity and secure order abjures love.

I believe, to the degree these dilemmas are not endemic to the human condition, that their resistance to resolution arises in part out of the liberal belief in the unity of epistemology and politics. The very continuity that implicates his political theory and his philosophical empiricism in common dilemmas dooms Russell to an unsatisfactory politics. To insist, as liberals have always done, that the criteria by which we elucidate standards of knowledge must somehow correspond with criteria by which we fashion a common life, is a particularly pernicious kind of folly. To think that the attitudes with which we approach nature must somehow reflect on the attitudes with which we approach the civic polity promotes an extremism of the mind incompatible with the social requirements of common living. Thinking about what we know and how we know it and thinking about politics are both *thinking*, to be sure: but political thinking makes special demands that suggest it may be a unique activity. The trouble, then, with empiricist liberalism is precisely its redundancy, its incapacity to distinguish between epistemology as a descriptive activity that makes a science of self-consciousness, and politics as a prescriptive activity of citizens in search of common purposes – a science of 'other-consciousness' as it were.

Russell's genius lent to everything he wrote about politics a wisdom that argument cannot deny; his moral courage invested his activity with a nobility that is irreproachable. Yet I cannot help but feel that the conundrums in which his liberalism inevitably involved him and the polarities forced on him by his empiricism closed him off from the political alternatives towards which his soul instinctively leaned.[69] He aspired to a transcending humanity, but his liberal psychology insisted men were beasts or gods, but not mere humans. He hoped for a politics of love, but could anticipate only a politics of anarchy or a politics of dominion or some weak, unstable compound of the two. He wanted to forge new solutions but could raise only traditional problems in the inflexible language of traditional rational-sceptical philosophy. Finally, his philosophy confounded his genius.

In the preface to the final volume of his *Autobiography* he wondered morosely whether his last words would be

> The bright day is done
> And we are for the dark,

or, as he sometimes 'allowed himself to hope',

> The world's great age begins anew,
> The golden years return.

He longed for golden years, and prophesised darkness, unable from the uncompromising perspective of empiricist liberalism to comprehend that men live in a twilight where the human soul burns too ardently ever quite to be extinguished by shadows, but too languidly to overcome the restless night that awaits us all.

Department of Political Science
Rutgers University

NOTES

1   C. D. Broad complained that Russell 'produces a different system of philosophy every few years'. Cited by A. J. Ayer, *Russell and Moore: the Analytic Heritage* (London, Macmillan, 1971: 9).
2   *The Autobiography of Bertrand Russell,* vol. II (London, George Allen & Unwin, 1968: 193).
3   *Unpopular Essays* (London, Unwin Books, 1968: 158).
4   ibid.
5   *Sceptical Essays* (London, Unwin Books, 1960: 9).
6   *The History of Western Philosophy,* rev. edn (London, George Allen & Unwin, 1961: 578).
7   Jean-Jacques Rousseau, *The Social Contract,* bk I, ch. 6; Hobbes, Locke and Mill also understand the problem as one of surrendering some of man's freedom in order to guarantee the rest.
8   *The Autobiography,* vol. II, p. 105.
9   *The Practice and Theory of Bolshevism* (London, Unwin Books, 1962: 82).
10 *Power: A New Social Analysis* (London, George Allen & Unwin, 1938: 106).
11 ibid., p. 211.
12 John Locke, *The Second Treatise of Civil Government,* ch. 7, section 93.

13 *Roads to Freedom: Socialism, Anarchism and Syndicalism* (London, Unwin Books, 1966: 97).
14 *Power*, p. 7.
15 ibid., p. 9.
16 *Roads to Freedom*, p. 73.
17 ibid., p. 79.
18 In a letter to Colette, *Autobiography*, vol. II, p. 77. His moroseness reappears in *The Scientific Outlook*, where he wrote: 'When I consider [the human race's] atomic bombs, their researches into bacteriological warfare, their meannesses, cruelties and oppressions, I find them, considered as the crowning gem of the creation, somewhat lacking in lustre' (London, George Allen and Unwin, 2nd edn, 1949: 127).
19 *The Practice and Theory of Bolshevism*, p. 79.
20 See *Authority and the Individual: the Reith Lectures for 1948–49* (London, Unwin Books, 1964: 67).
21 John Stuart Mill, *On Liberty* (Everyman edn: 83).
22 *Sceptical Essays*, p. 99.
23 *Power*, p. 47.
24 *In Praise of Idleness* (London, Unwin Books, 1960: 19). Russell seems here to be more the English aristocrat than the Freudian critic of civilisation and its discontents.
25 In a letter to Lucy Donnelly, *Autobiography*, vol. II, p. 59.
26 *Human Knowledge: Its Scope and Limits* (London, George Allen & Unwin, 1948: 22).
27 *History of Western Philosophy*, p. 591.
28 *Human Knowledge*, p. 527.
29 *Autobiography*, vol. II, p. 160. In reaching this sober diagnosis he notes:
   the best years of my life were given to the Principles of Mathematics, in the hope of finding somewhere some certain knowledge. The whole of this effort, in spite of three big volumes, ended inwardly in doubt and bewilderment.
30 ibid., p. 158.
31 ibid., pp. 158–9. Moody disconsolateness seemed widespread in the 1930s. Carl Becker, thus, wrote in the same period, 'Man is but a foundling in the cosmos, abandoned by the forces that created him', in *The Heavenly City of Eighteenth Century Philosophers* (New Haven, Yale University Press, 1932: 15) – a book in which some of Russell's more dismal portraits of man and nature are approvingly cited.
32 *History of Western Philosophy*, p. 634.
33 *Autobiography*, vol. III, p. 29.
34 *The Problems of Philosophy* (London, Oxford Paperbacks, 1959: 92–3).
35 Karl Popper's notion of science as problem solving and W. V. Quine's belief that science 'is a continuation of common sense, and it continues the common-sense expedient of swelling ontology to simplify theory' exemplify the typical view; see Quine, 'Two Dogmas of Empiricism', *The Philosophical Review*, vol. 60, no. 1 (January 1951: 42).
36 *The Scientific Outlook*, pp. 101–2.
37 'The success of insanity, in literature, in philosophy, and in politics, is one of the peculiarities of our age, and the successful form of insanity proceeds almost entirely from impulses towards power' (*Power*: 270).
38 *History of Western Philosophy*, p. 646.
39 *Power*, p. 39.
40 *The Scientific Outlook*, p. 167.
41 ibid., p. 179.
42 ibid., p. 167.
43 *Roads to Freedom*, p. 109.
44 *The Practice and Theory of Bolshevism*, p. 64.
45 *Marriage and Morals* (London, Unwin Books, 1961: 149).
46 *Power*, p. 13.
47 *The Practice and Theory of Bolshevism*, p. 63.
48 The first definition is found in *Leviathan*, pt I, ch 10; the second, in pt I, ch. 11. To C. B. Macpherson, the transition is crucial to the transformation of mechanistic into market

arguments in Hobbes; see *The Political Theory of Possessive Individualism: Hobbes to Locke* (London, Oxford University Press, 1962: 35 ff.).

49 *The Practice and Theory of Bolshevism*, p. 83.

50 ibid., p. 72.

51 Russell seems to have found in Conrad's view of man's soul a picture that mirrored his own. In the first volume of his *Autobiography*, he writes of their very first meeting,

> we talked with continually increasing intimacy. We seemed to sink through layer after layer of what was superficial, till gradually both reached the central fire. It was an experience unlike any other that I have known. We looked into each other's eyes, half appalled and half intoxicated to find ourselves in such a region. The emotion was as intense as passionate love, and at the same time all-embracing. (vol. I, p. 323)

52 *The Scientific Outlook*, p. 267. Anxiety about the potential of science for tyranny has, of course, been commonplace among anti-utopians like Orwell, and critics of positivist social science like A. R. Louch, who has written 'totalitarianism is too weak a word and too inefficient an instrument to describe the perfect scientific society'. *Explanation and Human Action* (Berkeley, Calif., University of California Press, 1969: 239). But it is far less common among empiricist advocates of science who tend, like Karl Popper, to equate science and the open society.

53 *The Scientific Outlook*, p. 268.

54 *Marriage and Morals*, p. 136.

55 *The Scientific Outlook*, p. 269.

56 *Roads to Freedom*, p. 109.

57 *Autobiography*, vol. III, p. 29.

58 *On Liberty*, p. 114.

59 'Philosophy and Politics', in *Unpopular Essays* (London, Unwin Books, 1968: 23). The same kind of argument is advanced by Russell in *Power*, where he writes 'a diffused liberal sentiment, tinged with scepticism, makes social co-operation much less difficult, and liberty correspondingly more possible' (p. 308).

60 Popper writes:

> There is no return to a harmonious state of nature. If we turn back, then we must go the whole way – we must return to the beasts . . . but if we wish to remain human, then there is only one way, the way into the open society. We must go on into the unknown, the uncertain and insecure. (K. R. Popper, *The Open Society and Its Enemies* (London, Routledge & Kegan Paul, 1957; rev. edn, vol. I, *The Spell of Plato*, pp. 200–1).

61 *Unpopular Essays*, p. 22.

62 *Power*, pp. 312–13.

63 Underlying an apparent vacillation in his later years in his attitudes towards the Soviet Union (which seemed to be the object of his fears in the late 1940s) and the United States (which received his opprobrium in the late 1950s and 1960s) was a constancy of principle: the need for world hegemony by *some* power to secure world peace, whether under the auspices of the Soviet Union, the United States or some international body. See *Common Sense and Nuclear Warfare* (London, George Allen & Unwin, 1959); and *Has Man a Future?* (London, George Allen & Unwin, 1961).

64 Robert Paul Wolff, 'On Violence', *Journal of Philosophy*, vol. LXVI, no. 19 (1969: 607). My objections to Wolff, which are reflected in the final part of this essay, can be found in my *Superman and Common Men: Freedom, Anarchy and the Revolution* (New York: Praeger, 1971: 34–5 and *passim*).

65 In *Power*, Russell thus suggests that political men tend to fall into two discrete classes – leaders and followers – neither of which, I would argue, encompasses citizens (*Power*: ch. 2).

66   *The Scientific Outlook*, p. 278.
67   *Power*, p. 273.
68   *The Scientific Outlook*, p. 273.
69   It was a sad irony that Russell was least able to understand those political philosophers who sought a way out of the liberal dilemma. He was viciously unkind to Rousseau and wholly unsympathetic to Kant: yet these two spent their lives attempting to elucidate a politics of mutuality separate from self-interest, and a notion of justice separate from both power and utility. Was it the reflection of his own instincts that made him so anxious?

INDEX